# COMPUTER TESTING SUPPLEMENT
## FOR
## AIRLINE TRANSPORT PILOT
## AND
## AIRCRAFT DISPATCHER

## 2005

U.S. DEPARTMENT OF TRANSPORTATION
### FEDERAL AVIATION ADMINISTRATION
Flight Standards Service

# PREFACE

This computer testing supplement is designed by the Flight Standards Service of the Federal Aviation Administration (FAA) for use by computer testing designees (CTDs) and testing centers in the administration of airman knowledge tests in the following knowledge areas:

Airline Transport Pilot (FAR 121) Airplane (ATP)
Airline Transport Pilot (FAR 135) Airplane (ATA)
Airline Transport Pilot (FAR 135) Added Rating—Airplane (ARA)
Airline Transport Pilot (FAR 135) Helicopter (ATH)
Airline Transport Pilot (FAR 135) Added Rating—Helicopter (ARH)
Aircraft Dispatcher

FAA-CT-8080-7C supercedes FAA-CT-8080-7B dated 1998.

Comments regarding this supplement should be sent to:

U.S. Department of Transportation
Federal Aviation Administration
Flight Standards Service
Airman Testing Standards Branch, AFS-630
P.O. Box 25082
Oklahoma City, OK 73125

## CONTENTS

## APPENDIX 1

# APPENDIX 2

# CONTENTS—Continued

# CONTENTS—Continued

# CONTENTS—Continued

# CONTENTS—Continued

# CONTENTS—Continued

# ADDENDUM A

# ADDENDUM B

## CONTENTS—Continued

## ADDENDUM C

# CONTENTS—Continued

# CONTENTS—Continued

# APPENDIX 1

94118
# GENERAL INFO

## ABBREVIATIONS

ADF . . . . . . . . . . . . . . . Automatic Direction Finder
ALS . . . . . . . . . . . . . . . Approach Light System
ALSF . . . . . . . . . . . . . . Approach Light System with Sequenced Flashing Lights
APP CON . . . . . . . . . . . Approach Control
ARR . . . . . . . . . . . . . . . Arrival
ASR/PAR . . . . . . . . . . . Published Radar Minimums at this Airport
ATIS . . . . . . . . . . . . . . . Automatic Terminal Information Service
AWOS . . . . . . . . . . . . . Automated Weather Observing System
AZ . . . . . . . . . . . . . . . . . Azimuth
BC . . . . . . . . . . . . . . . . . Back Course
C . . . . . . . . . . . . . . . . . . Circling
CAT . . . . . . . . . . . . . . . Category
CCW . . . . . . . . . . . . . . Counter Clockwise
Chan . . . . . . . . . . . . . . Channel
CLNC DEL . . . . . . . . . . Clearance Delivery
CTAF . . . . . . . . . . . . . . Common Traffic Advisory Frequency
CW . . . . . . . . . . . . . . . . Clockwise
DH . . . . . . . . . . . . . . . . Decision Heights
DME . . . . . . . . . . . . . . . Distance Measuring Equipment
DR . . . . . . . . . . . . . . . . Dead Reckoning
ELEV . . . . . . . . . . . . . . Elevation
FAF . . . . . . . . . . . . . . . Final Approach Fix
FM . . . . . . . . . . . . . . . . Fan Marker
GPI . . . . . . . . . . . . . . . . Ground Point of Interception
GPS . . . . . . . . . . . . . . . Global Positioning System
GS . . . . . . . . . . . . . . . . . Glide Slope
HAA . . . . . . . . . . . . . . . Height Above Airport
HAL . . . . . . . . . . . . . . . Height Above Landing
HAT . . . . . . . . . . . . . . . Height Above Touchdown
HIRL . . . . . . . . . . . . . . High Intensity Runway Lights
IAF . . . . . . . . . . . . . . . . Initial Approach Fix
ICAO . . . . . . . . . . . . . . International Civil Aviation Organization
IM . . . . . . . . . . . . . . . . . Inner Marker
Intcp . . . . . . . . . . . . . . Intercept
INT . . . . . . . . . . . . . . . . Intersection
LDA . . . . . . . . . . . . . . . Localizer Type Directional Aid
Ldg . . . . . . . . . . . . . . . . Landing
LDIN . . . . . . . . . . . . . . Lead in Light System
LIRL . . . . . . . . . . . . . . . Low Intensity Runway Lights
LOC . . . . . . . . . . . . . . . Localizer
LR . . . . . . . . . . . . . . . . . Lead Radial. Provides at least 2 NM (Copter 1 NM) of lead to assist in turning onto the intermediate/final course
MALS . . . . . . . . . . . . . . Medium Intensity Approach Light System
MALSR . . . . . . . . . . . . . Medium Intensity Approach Light Systems with RAIL
MAP . . . . . . . . . . . . . . . Missed Approach Point
MDA . . . . . . . . . . . . . . . Minimum Descent Altitude
MIRL . . . . . . . . . . . . . . Medium Intensity Runway Lights
MLS . . . . . . . . . . . . . . . Microwave Landing System
MM . . . . . . . . . . . . . . . . Middle Marker
NA . . . . . . . . . . . . . . . . Not Authorized
NDB . . . . . . . . . . . . . . . Non-directional Radio Beacon
NM . . . . . . . . . . . . . . . . Nautical Miles
NoPT . . . . . . . . . . . . . . No Procedure Turn Required (Procedure Turn shall not be executed without ATC clearance)
ODALS . . . . . . . . . . . . . Omnidirectional Approach Light System
OM . . . . . . . . . . . . . . . . Outer Marker
R . . . . . . . . . . . . . . . . . . Radial
RA . . . . . . . . . . . . . . . . Radio Altimeter setting height
Radar Required . . . . . . . Radar vectoring required for this approach
RAIL . . . . . . . . . . . . . . . Runway Alignment Indicator Lights
RBn . . . . . . . . . . . . . . . Radio Beacon
RCLS . . . . . . . . . . . . . . Runway Centerline Light System
REIL . . . . . . . . . . . . . . . Runway End Identifier Lights
RNAV . . . . . . . . . . . . . . Area Navigation
RPI . . . . . . . . . . . . . . . . Runway Point of Intercept(ion)
RRL . . . . . . . . . . . . . . . Runway Remaining Lights
Runway Touchdown Zone . . . . . First 3000' of Runway
Rwy . . . . . . . . . . . . . . . Runway
RVR . . . . . . . . . . . . . . . Runway Visual Range
S . . . . . . . . . . . . . . . . . . Straight-in
SALS . . . . . . . . . . . . . . Short Approach Light System
SSALR . . . . . . . . . . . . . Simplified Short Approach Light System with RAIL
SDF . . . . . . . . . . . . . . . Simplified Directional Facility
TA . . . . . . . . . . . . . . . . Transition Altitude
TAC . . . . . . . . . . . . . . . TACAN
TCH . . . . . . . . . . . . . . . Threshold Crossing Height (height in feet Above Ground Level)
TDZ . . . . . . . . . . . . . . . Touchdown Zone
TDZE . . . . . . . . . . . . . . Touchdown Zone Elevation
TDZ/CL . . . . . . . . . . . . Touchdown Zone and Runway Centerline Lighting
TDZL . . . . . . . . . . . . . . Touchdown Zone Lights
TLv . . . . . . . . . . . . . . . . Transition Level
VASI . . . . . . . . . . . . . . . Visual Approach Slope Indicator
VDP . . . . . . . . . . . . . . . Visual Descent Point
WPT . . . . . . . . . . . . . . . Waypoint (RNAV)
X . . . . . . . . . . . . . . . . . . Radar Only Frequency

## PILOT CONTROLLED AIRPORT LIGHTING SYSTEMS

Available pilot controlled lighting (PCL) systems are indicated as follows:
1. Approach lighting systems that bear a system identification are symbolized using negative symbology, e.g.,
2. Approach lighting systems that do not bear a system identification are indicated with a negative " " beside the name.

A star (*) indicates non-standard PCL, consult Directory/Supplement, e.g.,

To activate lights use frequency indicated in the communication section of the chart with a  or the appropriate lighting system identification e.g., UNICOM 122.8

| KEY MIKE | FUNCTION |
| --- | --- |
| 7 times within 5 seconds | Highest intensity available |
| 5 times within 5 seconds | Medium or lower intensity (Lower REIL or REIL-off) |
| 3 times within 5 seconds | Lowest intensity available (Lower REIL or REIL-off) |

LEGEND 1.—General Information and Abbreviations.

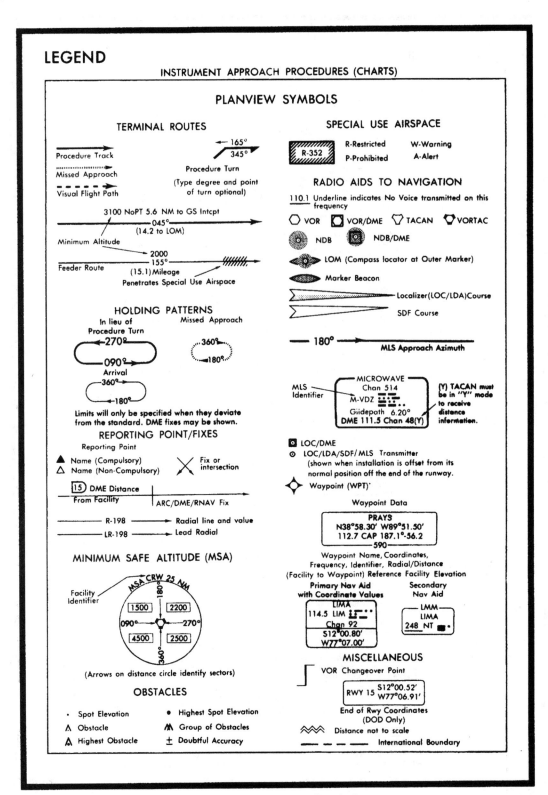

LEGEND 2.—Planview Symbols.

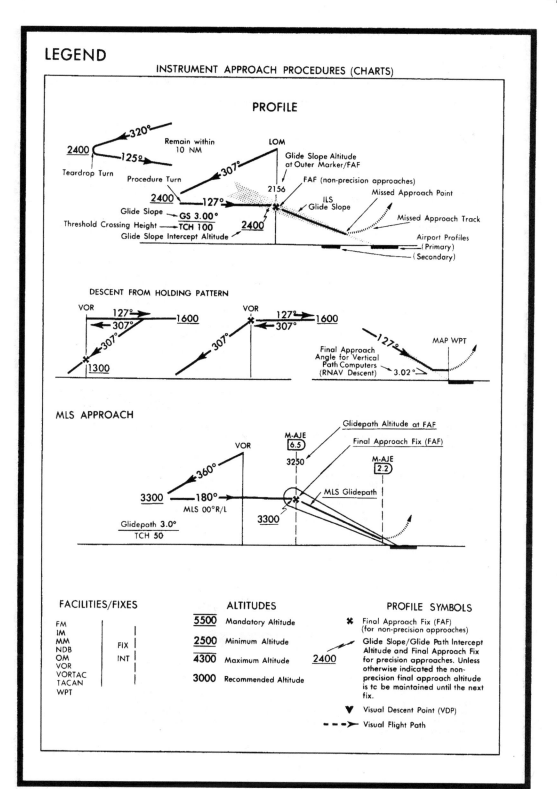

LEGEND 3.—Profile.

94286
# LEGEND

## INSTRUMENT APPROACH PROCEDURES (CHARTS)

### AIRPORT DIAGRAM/AIRPORT SKETCH

**Runways**

| Hard Surface | Other Than Hard Surface | Stopways, Taxiways, Parking Areas | Displaced Threshold |
|---|---|---|---|

| Closed Runway | Closed Taxiway | Under Construction | Metal Surface | Runway Centerline Lighting |
|---|---|---|---|---|

**ARRESTING GEAR:** Specific arresting gear systems; e.g., BAK-12, MA-1A etc., shown on airport diagrams, not applicable to Civil Pilots. Military Pilots Refer to Appropriate DOD Publications.

uni-directional    bi-directional    Jet Barrier

**REFERENCE FEATURES**

Buildings . . . . . . . . . . . . . . . . . . . . . . . . . . . . ■

Tanks . . . . . . . . . . . . . . . . . . . . . . . . . . . . . . ●

Obstruction . . . . . . . . . . . . . . . . . . . . . . . . . ∧

Airport Beacon # . . . . . . . . . . . . . . . . . . . . . ☆

Runway
Radar Reflectors . . . . . . . . . . . . . . . . . . . . . . ⧗

Control Tower # . . . . . . . . . . . . . . . . . . . . . . . ▪

\#  When Control Tower and Rotating Beacon are co-located, Beacon symbol will be used and further identified as TWR.

Runway length depicted is the physical length of the runway (end-to-end, including displaced thresholds if any) but excluding areas designated as overruns or stopways. Where a displaced threshold is shown and/or part of the runway is otherwise not available for landing, an annotation is added to indicate the landing length of the runway; e.g., RWY 13 ldg 5000'.

Runway Weight Bearing Capacity is shown as a codified expression. Refer to the appropriate Supplement/Directory for applicable codes, e.g., RWY 14-32
   S75, T185, ST175, TT325

**Helicopter Alighting Areas**  Ⓗ ⊞ Ⓗ ⚠ ⊞

Negative Symbols used to identify Copter Procedures

landing point . . . . . . . . . . . Ⓗ ⊞ Ⓗ ⚠ ⊞

Runway TDZ elevation . . . . . . . TDZE 123
                              ◄─0.3% DOWN
Runway Slope . . . . . . . . . . . . . . 0.8% UP ─►
      (shown when runway slope exceeds 0.3%)
NOTE:
Runway Slope measured to midpoint on runways 8000 feet or longer.

▣ U.S. Navy Optical Landing System (OLS) "OLS" location is shown because of its height of approximately 7 feet and proximity to edge of runway may create an obstruction for some types of aircraft.

Approach light symbols are shown in the Flight Information Handbook.

Airport diagram scales are variable.

True/magnetic North orientation may vary from diagram to diagram.

Coordinate values are shown in 1 or ½ minute increments. They are further broken down into 6 second ticks, within each 1 minute increment.

Positional accuracy within ±600 feet unless otherwise noted on the chart.

NOTE:
All new and revised airport diagrams are shown referenced to the World Geodetic System (W G S) (noted on appropriate diagram), and may not be compatible with local coordinates published in FLIP. (Foreign Only)

Runway Slope · FIELD ELEV 174 · Rwy 2 ldg 8000'
BAK-12 · 0.7% UP ─► · 20 · 9000 X 200 · ◄─023.2°─ · 1000 X 200 · Runway Identification
Runway End Elevation ─ ELEV 164 · Runway Dimensions (in feet) · Runway Heading (Magnetic) · Overrun/Stopway Dimensions (in feet)

### SCOPE

Airport diagrams are specifically designed to assist in the movement of ground traffic at locations with complex runway/taxiway configurations and provide information for updating Computer Based Navigation Systems (I.E., INS, GPS) aboard aircraft. Airport diagrams are not intended to be used for approach and landing or departure operations. For revisions to Airport Diagrams: Consult FAA Order 7910.4B.

LEGEND 4.—Airport Diagram/Airport Sketch.

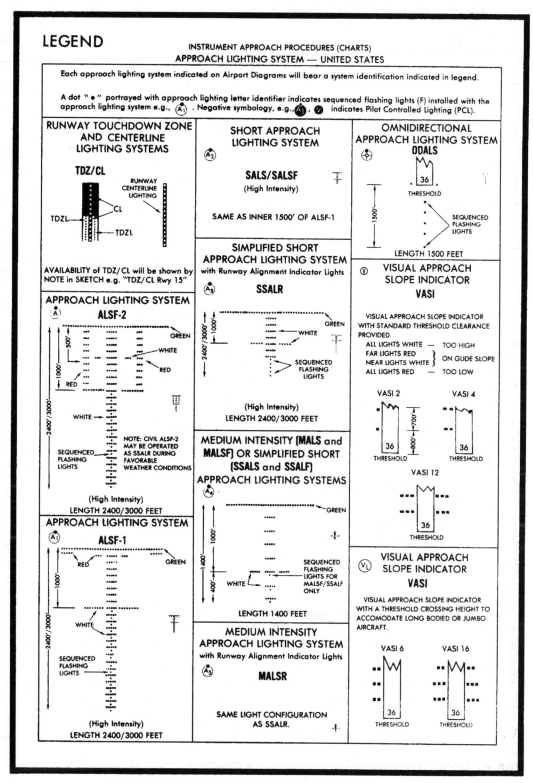

LEGEND 5.—Approach Lighting System—United States.

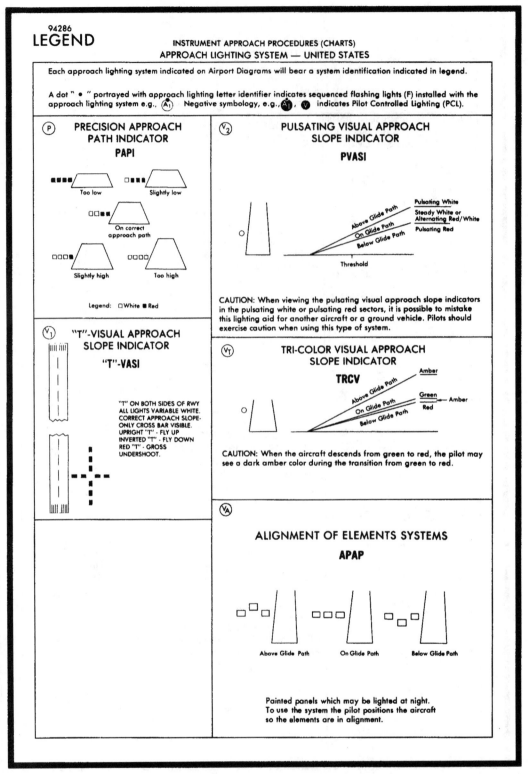

LEGEND 6.—Approach Lighting System—United States.

# TERMS/LANDING MINIMA DATA

## IFR LANDING MINIMA

Landing minima are established for six aircraft approach categories (ABCDE and COPTER). In the absence of COPTER MINIMA, helicopters may use the CAT A minimums of other procedures. The standard format for portrayal of landing minima is as follows:

### AIRCRAFT APPROACH CATEGORIES

Speeds are based on 1.3 times the stall speed in the landing configuration of maximum gross landing weight. An aircraft shall fit in only one category. If it is necessary to maneuver at speeds in excess of the upper limit of a speed range for a category, the minimums for the next higher category should be used. For example, an aircraft which falls in Category A, but is circling to land at a speed in excess of 91 knots, should use the approach Category B minimums when circling to land. See following category limits:

### MANEUVERING TABLE

| Approach Category | A | B | C | D | E |
|---|---|---|---|---|---|
| Speed (Knots) | 0-90 | 91-120 | 121-140 | 141-165 | Abv 165 |

### RVR/Meteorological Visibility Comparable Values

The following table shall be used for converting RVR to meteorological visibility when RVR is not reported for the runway of intended operation. Adjustment of landing minima may be required — see Inoperative Components Table.

| RVR (feet) | Visibility (statute miles) | RVR (feet) | Visibility (statute miles) |
|---|---|---|---|
| 1600 | ¼ | 4000 | ¾ |
| 2000 | ⅜ | 4500 | ⅞ |
| 2400 | ½ | 5000 | 1 |
| 3200 | ⅝ | 6000 | 1¼ |

### LANDING MINIMA FORMAT

In this example airport elevation is 1179, and runway touchdown zone elevation is 1152.

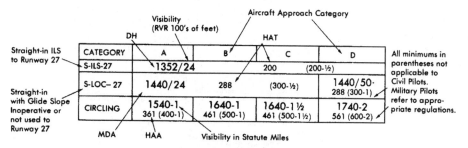

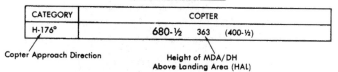

Copter Approach Direction     Height of MDA/DH Above Landing Area (HAL)

No circling minimums are provided

LEGEND 7.—IFR Landing Minima.

# TERMS/LANDING MINIMA DATA
91262

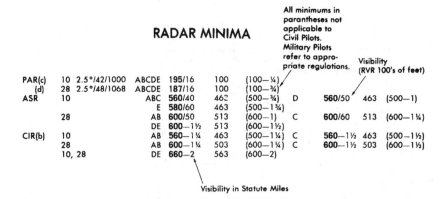

### RADAR MINIMA

All minimums in parantheses not applicable to Civil Pilots. Military Pilots refer to appropriate regulations.

Visibility (RVR 100's of feet)

| | | | | | | | | | |
|---|---|---|---|---|---|---|---|---|---|
| PAR(c) | 10 | 2.5°/42/1000 | ABCDE | **195/16** | 100 | (100—¼) | | | |
| (d) | 28 | 2.5°/48/1068 | ABCDE | **187/16** | 100 | (100—¾) | | | |
| ASR | 10 | | ABC | **560/40** | 462 | (500—¾) | D | 560/50 | 463 | (500—1) |
| | | | E | **580/60** | 463 | (500—1¾) | | | |
| | 28 | | AB | **600/50** | 513 | (600—1) | C | 600/60 | 513 | (600—1¼) |
| | | | DE | **600—1½** | 513 | (600—1½) | | | |
| CIR(b) | 10 | | AB | **560—1¼** | 463 | (500—1¼) | C | 560—1½ | 463 | (500—1½) |
| | 28 | | AB | **600—1¼** | 503 | (600—1¼) | C | 600—1½ | 503 | (600—1½) |
| | 10, 28 | | DE | **660—2** | 563 | (600—2) | | | |

Visibility in Statute Miles

Radar Minima:

1. Minima shown are the lowest permitted by established criteria. Pilots should consult applicable directives for their category of aircraft.
2. The circling MDA and weather minima to be used are those for the runway to which the final approach is flown - not the landing runway. In the above RADAR MINIMA example, a category C aircraft flying a radar approach to runway 10, circling to land on runway 28, must use an MDA of 560 feet with weather minima of 500-1½.

△ Alternate Minimums not standard. Civil users refer to tabulation. USA/USN/USAF pilots refer to appropriate regulations.

△ NA Alternate minimums are Not Authorized due to unmonitored facility or absence of weather reporting service.

▼ Take-off Minimums not standard and/or Departure Procedures are published. Refer to tabulation.

## EXPLANATION OF TERMS

The United States Standard for Terminal Instrument Procedures (TERPS) is the approved criteria for formulating instrument approach procedures.

LEGEND 8.—Radar Minima.

# INSTRUMENT APPROACH PROCEDURE CHARTS
## RATE OF DESCENT TABLE
### (ft. per min.)

A rate of descent table is provided for use in planning and executing precision descents under known or approximate ground speed conditions. It will be especially useful for approaches when the localizer only is used for course guidance. A best speed, power, attitude combination can be programmed which will result in a stable glide rate and attitude favorable for executing a landing if minimums exist upon breakout. Care should always be exercised so that the minimum descent altitude and missed approach point are not exceeded.

| ANGLE OF DESCENT (degrees and tenths) | GROUND SPEED (knots) | | | | | | | | | | |
|---|---|---|---|---|---|---|---|---|---|---|---|
| | 30 | 45 | 60 | 75 | 90 | 105 | 120 | 135 | 150 | 165 | 180 |
| 2.0 | 105 | 160 | 210 | 265 | 320 | 370 | 425 | 475 | 530 | 585 | 635 |
| 2.5 | 130 | 200 | 265 | 330 | 395 | 465 | 530 | 595 | 665 | 730 | 795 |
| 3.0 | 160 | 240 | 320 | 395 | 480 | 555 | 635 | 715 | 795 | 875 | 955 |
| 3.5 | 185 | 280 | 370 | 465 | 555 | 650 | 740 | 835 | 925 | 1020 | 1110 |
| 4.0 | 210 | 315 | 425 | 530 | 635 | 740 | 845 | 955 | 1060 | 1165 | 1270 |
| 4.5 | 240 | 355 | 475 | 595 | 715 | 835 | 955 | 1075 | 1190 | 1310 | 1430 |
| 5.0 | 265 | 395 | 530 | 660 | 795 | 925 | 1060 | 1190 | 1325 | 1455 | 1590 |
| 5.5 | 290 | 435 | 580 | 730 | 875 | 1020 | 1165 | 1310 | 1455 | 1600 | 1745 |
| 6.0 | 315 | 475 | 635 | 795 | 955 | 1110 | 1270 | 1430 | 1590 | 1745 | 1905 |
| 6.5 | 345 | 515 | 690 | 860 | 1030 | 1205 | 1375 | 1550 | 1720 | 1890 | 2065 |
| 7.0 | 370 | 555 | 740 | 925 | 1110 | 1295 | 1480 | 1665 | 1850 | 2035 | 2220 |
| 7.5 | 395 | 595 | 795 | 990 | 1190 | 1390 | 1585 | 1785 | 1985 | 2180 | 2380 |
| 8.0 | 425 | 635 | 845 | 1055 | 1270 | 1480 | 1690 | 1905 | 2115 | 2325 | 2540 |
| 8.5 | 450 | 675 | 900 | 1120 | 1345 | 1570 | 1795 | 2020 | 2245 | 2470 | 2695 |
| 9.0 | 475 | 715 | 950 | 1190 | 1425 | 1665 | 1900 | 2140 | 2375 | 2615 | 2855 |
| 9.5 | 500 | 750 | 1005 | 1255 | 1505 | 1755 | 2005 | 2255 | 2510 | 2760 | 3010 |
| 10.0 | 530 | 790 | 1055 | 1320 | 1585 | 1845 | 2110 | 2375 | 2640 | 2900 | 3165 |
| 10.5 | 555 | 830 | 1105 | 1385 | 1660 | 1940 | 2215 | 2490 | 2770 | 3045 | 3320 |
| 11.0 | 580 | 870 | 1160 | 1450 | 1740 | 2030 | 2320 | 2610 | 2900 | 3190 | 3480 |
| 11.5 | 605 | 910 | 1210 | 1515 | 1820 | 2120 | 2425 | 2725 | 3030 | 3335 | 3635 |
| 12.0 | 630 | 945 | 1260 | 1575 | 1890 | 2205 | 2520 | 2835 | 3150 | 3465 | 3780 |

LEGEND 9.—Rate-of-Descent Table.

## INSTRUMENT TAKEOFF PROCEDURE CHARTS

### RATE OF CLIMB TABLE

(ft. per min.)

A rate of climb table is provided for use in planning and executing
takeoff procedures under known or approximate ground speed conditions.

| REQUIRED CLIMB RATE (ft. per NM) | GROUND SPEED (KNOTS) | | | | | | |
|---|---|---|---|---|---|---|---|
| | 30 | 60 | 80 | 90 | 100 | 120 | 140 |
| 200 | 100 | 200 | 267 | 300 | 333 | 400 | 467 |
| 250 | 125 | 250 | 333 | 375 | 417 | 500 | 583 |
| 300 | 150 | 300 | 400 | 450 | 500 | 600 | 700 |
| 350 | 175 | 350 | 467 | 525 | 583 | 700 | 816 |
| 400 | 200 | 400 | 533 | 600 | 667 | 800 | 933 |
| 450 | 225 | 450 | 600 | 675 | 750 | 900 | 1050 |
| 500 | 250 | 500 | 667 | 750 | 833 | 1000 | 1167 |
| 550 | 275 | 550 | 733 | 825 | 917 | 1100 | 1283 |
| 600 | 300 | 600 | 800 | 900 | 1000 | 1200 | 1400 |
| 650 | 325 | 650 | 867 | 975 | 1083 | 1300 | 1516 |
| 700 | 350 | 700 | 933 | 1050 | 1167 | 1400 | 1633 |

| REQUIRED CLIMB RATE (ft. per NM) | GROUND SPEED (KNOTS) | | | | | |
|---|---|---|---|---|---|---|
| | 150 | 180 | 210 | 240 | 270 | 300 |
| 200 | 500 | 600 | 700 | 800 | 900 | 1000 |
| 250 | 625 | 750 | 875 | 1000 | 1125 | 1250 |
| 300 | 750 | 900 | 1050 | 1200 | 1350 | 1500 |
| 350 | 875 | 1050 | 1225 | 1400 | 1575 | 1750 |
| 400 | 1000 | 1200 | 1400 | 1600 | 1700 | 2000 |
| 450 | 1125 | 1350 | 1575 | 1800 | 2025 | 2250 |
| 500 | 1250 | 1500 | 1750 | 2000 | 2250 | 2500 |
| 550 | 1375 | 1650 | 1925 | 2200 | 2475 | 2750 |
| 600 | 1500 | 1800 | 2100 | 2400 | 2700 | 3000 |
| 650 | 1625 | 1950 | 2275 | 2600 | 2925 | 3250 |
| 700 | 1750 | 2100 | 2450 | 2800 | 3150 | 3500 |

LEGEND 10.—Rate-of-Climb Table.

# INOPERATIVE COMPONENTS OR VISUAL AIDS TABLE

Landing minimums published on instrument approach procedure charts are based upon full operation of all components and visual aids associated with the particular instrument approach chart being used. Higher minimums are required with inoperative components or visual aids as indicated below. If more than one component is inoperative, each minimum is raised to the highest minimum required by any single component that is inoperative. ILS glide slope inoperative minimums are published on instrument approach charts as localizer minimums. This table may be amended by notes on the approach chart. Such notes apply only to the particular approach category(ies) as stated. See legend page for description of components indicated below.

(1) ILS, MLS, and PAR

| Inoperative Component or Aid | Approach Category | Increase Visibility |
|---|---|---|
| ALSF 1 & 2, MALSR, & SSALR | ABCD | 1/4 mile |

(2) ILS with visibility minimum of 1,800 RVR.

| | | |
|---|---|---|
| ALSF 1 & 2, MALSR, &SSALR | ABCD | To 4000 RVR |
| TDZI RCLS | ABCD | To 2400 RVR |
| RVR | ABCD | To 1/2 mile |

(3) VOR, VOR/DME, VORTAC, VOR (TAC), VOR/DME (TAC), LOC, LOC/DME, LDA, LDA/DME, SDF, SDF/DME, RNAV, and ASR

| Inoperative Visual Aid | Approach Category | Increase Visibility |
|---|---|---|
| ALSF 1 & 2, MALSR, & SSALR | ABCD | 1/2 mile |
| SSALS, MALS, & ODALS | ABC | 1/4 mile |

(4) NDB

| | | |
|---|---|---|
| ALSF 1 & 2, MALSR & SSALR | C | 1/2 mile |
| | ABD | 1/4 mile |
| MALS, SSALS, ODALS | ABC | 1/4 mile |

LEGEND 11.—Inoperative Components or Visual Aids Table.

# DIRECTORY LEGEND

## ABBREVIATIONS

The following abbreviations are those commonly used within this directory. Other abbreviations may be found in the Legend and are not duplicated below:

| | | | |
|---|---|---|---|
| AAS | airport advisory service | ldg | landing |
| acft | aircraft | med | medium |
| apch | approach | NFCT | non-federal control tower |
| arpt | airport | ngt | night |
| avbl | available | NSTD | nonstandard |
| bcn | beacon | ntc | notice |
| blo | below | opr | operate |
| byd | beyond | ops | operates operation |
| clsd | closed | ovrn | overrun |
| ctc | contact | p-line | power line |
| dalgt | daylight | PPR | prior permission required |
| dsplc | displace | req | request |
| dsplcd | displaced | rqr | requires |
| durn | duration | rgt tfc | right traffic |
| emerg | emergency | rwy | runway |
| extd | extend, extended | svc | service |
| fld | field | tmpry | temporary, temporarily |
| FSS | Flight Service Station | tkf | takeoff |
| ints | intensity | tfc | traffic |
| lgtd | lighted | thld | threshold |
| lgts | lights | twr | tower |

Legend 12.—Abbreviations.

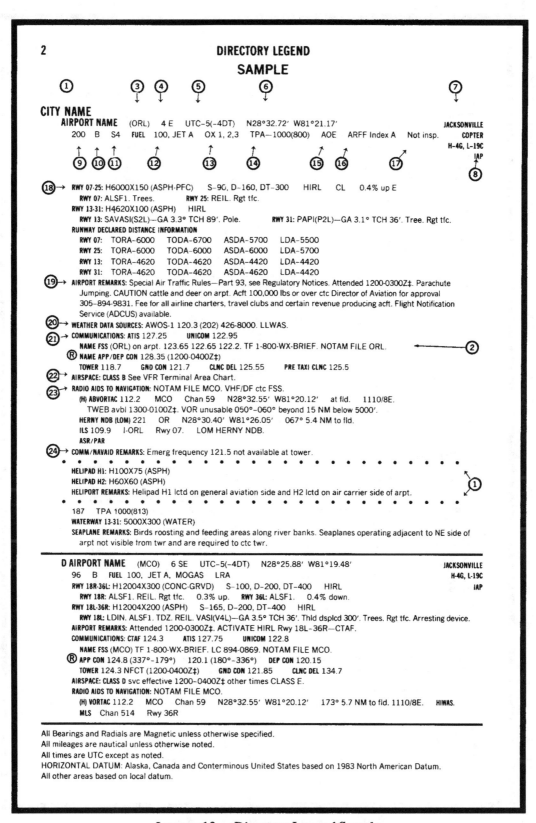

LEGEND 13.—Directory Legend Sample.

### LEGEND

This Directory is an alphabetical listing of data on record with the FAA on all airports that are open to the public, associated terminal control facilities, air route traffic control centers and radio aids to navigation within the conterminous United States, Puerto Rico and the Virgin Islands. Airports are listed alphabetically by associated city name and cross referenced by airport name. Facilities associated with an airport, but with a different name, are listed individually under their own name, as well as under the airport with which they are associated.

The listing of an airport in this directory merely indicates the airport operator's willingness to accommodate transient aircraft, and does not represent that the facility conforms with any Federal or local standards, or that it has been approved for use on the part of the general public.

The information on obstructions is taken from reports submitted to the FAA. It has not been verified in all cases. Pilots are cautioned that objects not indicated in this tabulation (or on charts) may exist which can create a hazard to flight operation.

Detailed specifics concerning services and facilities tabulated within this directory are contained in Airman's Information Manual, Basic Flight Information and ATC Procedures.

The legend items that follow explain in detail the contents of this Directory and are keyed to the circled numbers on the sample on the preceding page.

### ① CITY/AIRPORT NAME

Airports and facilities in this directory are listed alphabetically by associated city and state. Where the city name is different from the airport name the city name will appear on the line above the airport name. Airports with the same associated city name will be listed alphabetically by airport name and will be separated by a dashed rule line. All others will be separated by a solid rule line. (Designated Helipads and Seaplane Landing Areas (Water) associated with a land airport will be separated by a dotted line.)

### ② NOTAM SERVICE

All public use landing areas are provided NOTAM "D" (distant dissemination) and NOTAM "L" (local dissemination) service. Airport NOTAM file identifier is shown following the associated FSS data for individual airports, e.g. "NOTAM FILE IAD". See AIM, Basic Flight Information and ATC Procedures for detailed description of NOTAM's.

### ③ LOCATION IDENTIFIER

A three or four character code assigned to airports. These identifiers are used by ATC in lieu of the airport name in flight plans, flight strips and other written records and computer operations.

### ④ AIRPORT LOCATION

Airport location is expressed as distance and direction from the center of the associated city in nautical miles and cardinal points, i.e., 4 NE.

### ⑤ TIME CONVERSION

Hours of operation of all facilities are expressed in Coordinated Universal Time (UTC) and shown as "Z" time. The directory indicates the number of hours to be subtracted from UTC to obtain local standard time and local daylight saving time UTC–5(–4DT). The symbol ‡ indicates that during periods of Daylight Saving Time effective hours will be one hour earlier than shown. In those areas where daylight saving time is not observed that (–4DT) and ‡ will not be shown. All states observe daylight savings time except Arizona and that portion of Indiana in the Eastern Time Zone and Puerto Rico and the Virgin Islands.

### ⑥ GEOGRAPHIC POSITION OF AIRPORT

Positions are shown in degrees, minutes and hundredths of a minute.

### ⑦ CHARTS

The Sectional Chart and Low and High Altitude Enroute Chart and panel on which the airport or facility is located. Helicopter Chart locations will be indicated as, i.e., COPTER.

### ⑧ INSTRUMENT APPROACH PROCEDURES

IAP indicates an airport for which a prescribed (Public Use) FAA Instrument Approach Procedure has been published.

### ⑨ ELEVATION

Elevation is given in feet above mean sea level and is the highest point on the landing surface. When elevation is sea level it will be indicated as (00). When elevation is below sea level a minus (–) sign will precede the figure.

### ⑩ ROTATING LIGHT BEACON

B indicates rotating beacon is available. Rotating beacons operate dusk to dawn unless otherwise indicated in AIRPORT REMARKS.

### ⑪ SERVICING

S1: Minor airframe repairs.
S2: Minor airframe and minor powerplant repairs.

S3: Major airframe and minor powerplant repairs.
S4: Major airframe and major powerplant repairs.

LEGEND 14.—Directory Legend.

# 4  DIRECTORY LEGEND

## ⑫ FUEL

| CODE | FUEL |
|------|------|
| 80 | Grade 80 gasoline (Red) |
| 100 | Grade 100 gasoline (Green) |
| 100LL | 100LL gasoline (low lead) (Blue) |
| 115 | Grade 115 gasoline |
| A | Jet A—Kerosene freeze point–40° C. |
| A1 | Jet A-1—Kerosene freeze point–50°C. |
| A1+ | Jet A-1—Kerosene with icing inhibitor, freeze point–50° C. |

| CODE | FUEL |
|------|------|
| B | Jet B—Wide-cut turbine fuel, freeze point–50° C. |
| B+ | Jet B—Wide-cut turbine fuel with icing inhibitor, freeze point–50° C. |
| MOGAS | Automobile gasoline which is to be used as aircraft fuel. |

NOTE: Automobile Gasoline. Certain automobile gasoline may be used in specific aircraft engines if a FAA supplemental type cetificate has been obtained. Automobile gasoline which is to be used in aircraft engines will be identified as "MOGAS", however, the grade/type and other octane rating will not be published.

Data shown on fuel availability represents the most recent information the publisher has been able to acquire. Because of a variety of factors, the fuel listed may not always be obtainable by transient civil pilots. Confirmation of availability of fuel should be made directly with fuel dispensers at locations where refueling is planned.

## ⑬ OXYGEN

OX 1  High Pressure
OX 2  Low Pressure
OX 3  High Pressure—Replacement Bottles
OX 4  Low Pressure—Replacement Bottles

## ⑭ TRAFFIC PATTERN ALTITUDE

Traffic Pattern Altitude (TPA)—The first figure shown is TPA above mean sea level. The second figure in parentheses is TPA above airport elevation.

## ⑮ AIRPORT OF ENTRY, LANDING RIGHTS, AND CUSTOMS USER FEE AIRPORTS

U.S. CUSTOMS USER FEE AIRPORT—Private Aircraft operators are frequently required to pay the costs associated with customs processing.

AOE—Airport of Entry—A customs Airport of Entry where permission from U.S. Customs is not required, however, at least one hour advance notice of arrival must be furnished.

LRA—Landing Rights Airport—Application for permission to land must be submitted in advance to U.S. Customs. At least one hour advance notice of arrival must be furnished.

NOTE: Advance notice of arrival at both an AOE and LRA airport may be included in the flight plan when filed in Canada or Mexico, where Flight Notification Service (ADCUS) is available the airport remark will indicate this service. This notice will also be treated as an application for permission to land in the case of an LRA. Although advance notice of arrival may be relayed to Customs through Mexico, Canadian, and U.S. Communications facilities by flight plan, the aircraft operator is solely responsible for insuring that Customs receives the notification. (See Customs, Immigration and Naturalization, Public Health and Agriculture Department requirements in the International Flight Information Manual for further details.)

## ⑯ CERTIFICATED AIRPORT (FAR 139)

Airports serving Department of Transportation certified carriers and certified under FAR, Part 139, are indicated by the ARFF index; i.e., ARFF Index A, which relates to the availability of crash, fire, rescue equipment.

### FAR-PART 139 CERTIFICATED AIRPORTS
INDICES AND AIRCRAFT RESCUE AND FIRE FIGHTING EQUIPMENT REQUIREMENTS

| Airport Index | Required No. Vehicles | Aircraft Length | Scheduled Departures | Agent + Water for Foam |
|---------------|----------------------|-----------------|---------------------|------------------------|
| A | 1 | <90' | ≥1 | 500#DC or HALON 1211 or 450#DC + 100 gal $H_2O$ |
| B | 1 or 2 | ≥90', <126' | ≥5 | Index A + 1500 gal $H_2O$ |
|   |   | ≥126', <159' | <5 | |
| C | 2 or 3 | ≥126', <159' | ≥5 | Index A + 3000 gal $H_2O$ |
|   |   | ≥159', <200' | <5 | |
| D | 3 | ≥159', <200' | ≥5 | Index A + 4000 gal $H_2O$ |
|   |   | >200' | <5 | |
| E | 3 | ≥200' | ≥5 | Index A + 6000 gal $H_2O$ |

> Greater Than; < Less Than; ≥ Equal or Greater Than; ≤ Equal or Less Than; $H_2O$–Water; DC–Dry Chemical.

LEGEND 15.—Directory Legend.

15

# DIRECTORY LEGEND

NOTE: The listing of ARFF index does not necessarily assure coverage for non-air carrier operations or at other than prescribed times for air carrier. ARFF Index Ltd.—indicates ARFF coverage may or may not be available, for information contact airport manager prior to flight.

## ⑰ FAA INSPECTION

All airports not inspected by FAA will be identified by the note: Not insp. This indicates that the airport information has been provided by the owner or operator of the field.

## ⑱ RUNWAY DATA

Runway information is shown on two lines. That information common to the entire runway is shown on the first line while information concerning the runway ends are shown on the second or following line. Lengthy information will be placed in the Airport Remarks.

Runway direction, surface, length, width, weight bearing capacity, lighting, gradient and appropriate remarks are shown for each runway. Direction, length, width, lighting and remarks are shown for sealanes. The full dimensions of helipads are shown, i.e., 50X150.

### RUNWAY SURFACE AND LENGTH

Runway lengths prefixed by the letter "H" indicate that the runways are hard surfaced (concrete, asphalt). If the runway length is not prefixed, the surface is sod, clay, etc. The runway surface composition is indicated in parentheses after runway length as follows:

| | | |
|---|---|---|
| (AFSC)—Aggregate friction seal coat | (GRVD)—Grooved | (RFSC)—Rubberized friction seal coat |
| (ASPH)—Asphalt | (GRVL)—Gravel, or cinders | (TURF)—Turf |
| (CONC)—Concrete | (PFC)—Porous friction courses | (TRTD)—Treated |
| (DIRT)—Dirt | (PSP)—Pierced steel plank | (WC)—Wire combed |

### RUNWAY WEIGHT BEARING CAPACITY

Runway strength data shown in this publication is derived from available information and is a realistic estimate of capability at an average level of activity. It is not intended as a maximum allowable weight or as an operating limitation. Many airport pavements are capable of supporting limited operations with gross weights of 25-50% in excess of the published figures. Permissible operating weights, insofar as runway strengths are concerned, are a matter of agreement between the owner and user. When desiring to operate into any airport at weights in excess of those published in the publication, users should contact the airport management for permission. Add 000 to figure following S, D, DT, DDT, AUW, etc., for gross weight capacity:

S—Single-wheel type landing gear. (DC-3), (C-47), (F-15), etc.

D—Dual-wheel type landing gear. (DC-6), etc.

T—Twin-wheel type landing gear. (DC-6), (C-9A), etc.

ST—Single-tandem type landing gear. (C-130).

SBTT—Single-belly twin tandem landing gear (KC-10).

DT—Dual-tandem type landing gear, (707), etc.

TT—Twin-tandem type (includes quadricycle) landing gear (707), (B-52), (C-135), etc.

TRT—Triple-tandem landing gear, (C-17).

DDT—Double dual-tandem landing gear. (E4A/747).

TDT—Twin delta-tandem landing gear. (C-5, Concorde).

AUW—All up weight. Maximum weight bearing capacity for any aircraft irrespective of landing gear configuration.

SWL—Single Wheel Loading. (This includes information submitted in terms of Equivalent Single Wheel Loading (ESWL) and Single Isolated Wheel Loading). SWL figures are shown in thousands of pounds with the last three figures being omitted.

PSI—Pounds per square inch. PSI is the actual figure expressing maximum pounds per square inch runway will support, e.g., (SWL 000/PSI 535).

Quadricycle and dual-tandem are considered virtually equal for runway weight bearing consideration, as are single-tandem and dual-wheel.

Omission of weight bearing capacity indicates information unknown.

### RUNWAY LIGHTING

Lights are in operation sunset to sunrise. Lighting available by prior arrangement only or operating part of the night only and/or pilot controlled and with specific operating hours are indicated under airport remarks. Since obstructions are usually lighted, obstruction lighting is not included in this code. Unlighted obstructions on or surrounding an airport will be noted in airport remarks. Runway lights nonstandard (NSTD) are systems for which the light fixtures are not FAA approved L-800 series: color, intensity, or spacing does not meet FAA standards. Nonstandard runway lights, VASI, or any other system not listed below will be shown in airport remarks.

Temporary, emergency or limited runway edge lighting such as flares, smudge pots, lanterns or portable runway lights will also be shown in airport remarks.

Types of lighting are shown with the runway or runway end they serve.

| | |
|---|---|
| NSTD—Light system fails to meet FAA standards. | TDZ—Touchdown Zone Lights |
| LIRL—Low Intensity Runway Lights | ODALS—Omni Directional Approach Lighting System. |
| MIRL—Medium Intensity Runway Lights | AF OVRN—Air Force Overrun 1000' Standard |
| HIRL—High Intensity Runway Lights | Approach Lighting System. |
| RAIL—Runway Alignment Indicator Lights | LDIN—Lead-In Lighting System. |
| REIL—Runway End Identifier Lights | MALS—Medium Intensity Approach Lighting System. |
| CL—Centerline Lights | MALSF—Medium Intensity Approach Lighting System with Sequenced Flashing Lights. |

LEGEND 16.—Directory Legend.

## 6           DIRECTORY LEGEND

MALSR—Medium Intensity Approach Lighting System with Runway Alignment Indicator Lights.

SALS—Short Approach Lighting System.

SALSF—Short Approach Lighting System with Sequenced Flashing Lights.

SSALS—Simplified Short Approach Lighting System.

SSALF—Simplified Short Approach Lighting System with Sequenced Flashing Lights.

SSALR—Simplified Short Approach Lighting System with Runway Alignment Indicator Lights.

ALSAF--High Intensity Approach Lighting System with Sequenced Flashing Lights

ALSF1—High Intensity Approach Lighting System with Sequenced Flashing Lights, Category I, Configuration.

ALSF2—High Intensity Approach Lighting System with Sequenced Flashing Lights, Category II, Configuration.

VASI—Visual Approach Slope Indicator System.

NOTE: Civil ALSF-2 may be operated as SSALR during favorable weather conditions.

### VISUAL GLIDESLOPE INDICATORS

APAP—A system of panels, which may or may not be lighted, used for alignment of approach path.

| PNIL | APAP on left side of runway |
| PNIR | APAP on right side of runway |

PAPI—Precision Approach Path Indicator

| P2L | 2-identical light units placed on left side of runway |
| P2R | 2-identical light units placed on right side of runway |
| P4L | 4-identical light units placed on left side of runway |
| P4R | 4-identical light units placed on right side of runway |

PVASI—Pulsating/steady burning visual approach slope indicator, normally a single light unit projecting two colors.

| PSIL- | PVASI on left side of runway |
| PSIR- | PVASI on right side of runway |

SAVASI—Simplified Abbreviated Visual Approach Slope Indicator

| S2L | 2-box SAVASI on left side of runway |
| S2R | 2-box SAVASI on right side of runway |

TRCV—Tri-color visual approach slope indicator, normally a single light unit projecting three colors.

| TRIL | TRCV on left side of runway |
| TRIR | TRCV on right side of runway |

VASI—Visual Approach Slope Indicator

| V2L | 2-box VASI on left side of runway |
| V2R | 2-box VASI on right side of runway |
| V4L | 4-box VASI on left side of runway |
| V4R | 4-box VASI on right side of runway |
| V6L | 6-box VASI on left side of runway |
| V6R | 6-box VASI on right side of runway |
| V12 | 12-box VASI on both sides of runway |
| V16 | 16-box VASI on both sides of runway |

NOTE: Approach slope angle and threshold crossing height will be shown when available; i.e., –GA 3.5° TCH 37'.

### PILOT CONTROL OF AIRPORT LIGHTING

| Key Mike | Function |
| --- | --- |
| 7 times within 5 seconds | Highest intensity available |
| 5 times within 5 seconds | Medium or lower intensity (Lower REIL or REIL-Off) |
| 3 times within 5 seconds | Lowest intensity available (Lower REIL or REIL-Off) |

Available systems will be indicated in the Airport Remarks, as follows:

ACTIVATE MALSR Rwy 07, HIRL Rwy 07–25–122.8 (or CTAF).

or

ACTIVATE MIRL Rwy 18–36–122.8 (or CTAF).

or

ACTIVATE VASI and REIL, Rwy 07–122.8 (or CTAF).

Where the airport is not served by an instrument approach procedure and/or has an independent type system of different specification installed by the airport sponsor, descriptions of the type lights, method of control, and operating frequency will be explained in clear text. See AIM, "Basic Flight Information and ATC Procedures," for detailed description of pilot control of airport lighting.

### RUNWAY SLOPE

Runway slope will be shown only when it is 0.3 percent or more. On runways less than 8000 feet: When available the direction of the slope upward will be indicated, ie., 0.3% up NW. On runways 8000 feet or greater: When available the slope will be shown on the runway end line, ie., RWY 13: 0.3% up., RWY 21: Pole. Rgt tfc. 0.4% down.

### RUNWAY END DATA

Lighting systems such as VASI, MALSR, REIL; obstructions; displaced thresholds will be shown on the specific runway end. "Rgt tfc"—Right traffic indicates right turns should be made on landing and takeoff for specified runway end.

LEGEND 17.—Directory Legend Visual Glide Slope Indicators.

## DIRECTORY LEGEND

7

### RUNWAY DECLARED DISTANCE INFORMATION

TORA—Take-off Run Available
TODA—Take-off Distance Available
ASDA—Accelerate-Stop Distance Available
LDA—Landing Distance Available

### ⑲ AIRPORT REMARKS

Landing Fee indicates landing charges for private or non-revenue producing aircraft, in addition, fees may be charged for planes that remain over a couple of hours and buy no services, or at major airline terminals for all aircraft.
Remarks—Data is confined to operational items affecting the status and usability of the airport.
Parachute Jumping.—See "PARACHUTE" tabulation for details.
Unless otherwise stated, remarks including runway ends refer to the runway's approach end.

### ⑳ WEATHER DATA SOURCES

ASOS—Automated Surface Observing System. Reports the same as an AWOS-3 plus precipitation identification and intensity, and freezing rain occurrence (future enhancement).
AWOS—Automated Weather Observing System

AWOS-A—reports altimeter setting.
AWOS-1—reports altimeter setting, wind data and usually temperature, dewpoint and density altitude.
AWOS-2—reports the same as AWOS-1 plus visibility.
AWOS-3—reports the same as AWOS-1 plus visibility and cloud/ceiling data.
See AIM, Basic Flight Information and ATC Procedures for detailed description of AWOS.

HIWAS—See RADIO AIDS TO NAVIGATION
LAWRS—Limited Aviation Weather Reporting Station where observers report cloud height, weather, obstructions to vision, temperature and dewpoint (in most cases), surface wind, altimeter and pertinent remarks.
LLWAS—indicates a Low Level Wind Shear Alert System consisting of a center field and several field perimeter anemometers.
SAWRS—identifies airports that have a Supplemental Aviation Weather Reporting Station available to pilots for current weather information.

SWSL—Supplemental Weather Service Location providing current local weather information via radio and telephone.

### ㉑ COMMUNICATIONS

Communications will be listed in sequence in the order shown below:
Common Traffic Advisory Frequency (CTAF), Automatic Terminal Information Service (ATIS) and Aeronautical Advisory Stations (UNICOM) along with their frequency is shown, where available, on the line following the heading "COMMUNICATIONS." When the CTAF and UNICOM is the same frequency, the frequency will be shown as CTAF/UNICOM freq.
Flight Service Station (FSS) information. The associated FSS will be shown followed by the identifier and information concerning availability of telephone service, e.g., Direct Line (DL), Local Call (LC-384-2341), Toll free call, dial (TF 800-852-7036 or TF 1-800-227-7160), Long Distance (LD 202-426-8800 or LD 1-202-555-1212) etc. The airport NOTAM file identifier will be shown as "NOTAM FILE IAD." Where the FSS is located on the field it will be indicated as "on arpt" following the identifier. Frequencies available will follow. The FSS telephone number will follow along with any significant operational information. FSS's whose name is not the same as the airport on which located will also be listed in the normal alphabetical name listing for the state in which located. Remote Communications Outlet (RCO) providing service to the airport followed by the frequency and name of the Controlling FSS.
FSS's provide information on airport conditions, radio aids and other facilities, and process flight plans. Local Airport Advisory Service is provided on the CTAF by FSS's located at non-tower airports or airports where the tower is not in operation.
(See AIM, Par. 157/158 Traffic Advisory Practices at airports where a tower is not in operation or AC 90 - 42C.)
Aviation weather briefing service is provided by FSS specialists. Flight and weather briefing services are also available by calling the telephone numbers listed.
Remote Communications Outlet (RCO)—An unmanned air/ground communications facility, remotely controlled and providing UHF or VHF communications capability to extend the service range of an FSS.
Civil Communications Frequencies—Civil communications frequencies used in the FSS air/ground system are now operated simplex on 122.0, 122.2, 122.3, 122.4, 122.6, 123.6; emergency 121.5; plus receive-only on 122.05, 122.1, 122.15, and 123.6.
   a. 122.0 is assigned as the Enroute Flight Advisory Service channel at selected FSS's.
   b. 122.2 is assigned to most FSS's as a common enroute simplex service.
   c. 123.6 is assigned as the airport advisory channel at non-tower FSS locations, however, it is still in commission at some FSS's collocated with towers to provide part time Local Airport Advisory Service.
   d. 122.1 is the primary receive-only frequency at VOR's. 122.05, 122.15 and 123.6 are assigned at selected VOR's meeting certain criteria.
   e. Some FSS's are assigned 50 kHz channels for simplex operation in the 122-123 MHz band (e.g. 122.35). Pilots using the FSS A/G system should refer to this directory or appropriate charts to determine frequencies available at the FSS or remoted facility through which they wish to communicate.
Part time FSS hours of operation are shown in remarks under facility name.

Emergency frequency 121.5 is available at all Flight Service Stations, Towers, Approach Control and RADAR facilities, unless indicated as not available.
Frequencies published followed by the letter "T" or "R", indicate that the facility will only transmit or receive respectively on that frequency. All radio aids to navigation frequencies are transmit only.

LEGEND 18.—Directory Legend.

## 8        DIRECTORY LEGEND

### TERMINAL SERVICES

CTAF—A program designed to get all vehicles and aircraft at uncontrolled airports on a common frequency.

ATIS—A continuous broadcast of recorded non-control information in selected areas of high activity.

UNICOM—A non-government air/ground radio communications facility utilized to provide general airport advisory service.

APP CON —Approach Control. The symbol Ⓡ indicates radar approach control.

TOWER—Control tower

GND CON—Ground Control

DEP CON—Departure Control. The symbol Ⓡ indicates radar departure control.

CLNC DEL—Clearance Delivery.

PRE TAXI CLNC—Pre taxi clearance

VFR ADVSY SVC—VFR Advisory Service. Service provided by Non-Radar Approach Control.

    Advisory Service for VFR aircraft (upon a workload basis) ctc APP CON.

TOWER, APP CON and DEP CON RADIO CALL will be the same as the airport name unless indicated otherwise.

### ㉒ AIRSPACE

CLASS C—CLASS C service provided

CLASS B—Radar Sequencing and Separation Service for all aircraft in CLASS B airspace

TRSA—Radar Sequencing and Separation Service for participating VFR Aircraft within a Terminal Radar Service Area

### ㉓ RADIO AIDS TO NAVIGATION

The Airport Facility Directory lists by facility name all Radio Aids to Navigation, except Military TACANS, that appear on National Ocean Service Visual or IFR Aeronautical Charts and those upon which the FAA has approved an Instrument Approach Procedure. All VOR, VORTAC ILS and MLS equipment in the National Airspace System has an automatic monitoring and shutdown feature in the event of malfunction. Unmonitored, as used in this publication for any navigational aid, means that FSS or tower personnel cannot observe the malfunction or shutdown signal. The NAVAID NOTAM file identifier will be shown as "NOTAM FILE IAD" and will be listed on the Radio Aids to Navigation line. When two or more NAVAIDS are listed and the NOTAM file identifier is different than shown on the Radio Aids to Navigation line, then it will be shown with the NAVAID listing. NOTAM file identifiers for ILS's and their components (e.g., NDB (LOM) are the same as the identifiers for the associated airports and are not repeated. Hazardous Inflight Weather Advisory Service (HIWAS) will be shown where this service is broadcast over selected VOR's.

NAVAID information is tabulated as indicated in the following sample:

VOR unusable 020°-060° beyond 26 NM below 3500'

Restriction within the normal altitude/range of the navigational aid (See primary alphabetical listing for restrictions on VORTAC and VOR/DME).

    Note: Those DME channel numbers with a (Y) suffix require TACAN to be placed in the "Y" mode to receive distance information.

HIWAS—Hazardous Inflight Weather Advisory Service is a continuous broadcast of inflight weather advisories including summarized SIGMETs, convective SIGMETs, AIRMETs and urgent PIREPs. HIWAS is presently broadcast over selected VOR's and will be implemented throughout the conterminous U.S.

ASR/PAR—Indicates that Surveillance (ASR) or Precision (PAR) radar instrument approach minimums are published in U.S. Government Instrument Approach Procedures.

### RADIO CLASS DESIGNATIONS

#### VOR/DME/TACAN Standard Service Volume (SSV) Classifications

| SSV Class | Altitudes | Distance (NM) |
|---|---|---|
| (T) Terminal | 1000' to 12,000' | 25 |
| (L) Low Altitude | 1000' to 18,000' | 40 |
| (H) High Altitude | 1000' to 14,500' | 40 |
|  | 14,500' to 18,000' | 100 |
|  | 18,000' to 45,000' | 130 |
|  | 45,000' to 60,000' | 100 |

NOTE: Additionally, (H) facilities provide (L) and (T) service volume and (L) facilities provide (T) service. Altitudes are with respect to the station's site elevation. Coverage is not available in a cone of airspace directly above the facility.

LEGEND 19.—Directory Legend.

## DIRECTORY LEGEND
9

The term VOR is, operationally, a general term covering the VHF omnidirectional bearing type of facility without regard to the fact that the power, the frequency protected service volume, the equipment configuration, and operational requirements may vary between facilities at different locations.

| | |
|---|---|
| AB | Automatic Weather Broadcast |
| DF | Direction Finding Service. |
| DME | UHF standard (TACAN compatible) distance measuring equipment. |
| DME(Y) | UHF standard (TACAN compatible) distance measuring equipment that require TACAN to be placed in the "Y" mode to receive DME. |
| H | Non-directional radio beacon (homing), power 50 watts to less than 2,000 watts (50 NM at all altitudes). |
| HH | Non-directional radio beacon (homing), power 2,000 watts or more (75 NM at all altitudes). |
| H-SAB | Non-directional radio beacons providing automatic transcribed weather service. |
| ILS | Instrument Landing System (voice, where available, on localizer channel). |
| ISMLS | Interim Standard Microwave Landing System. |
| LDA | Localizer Directional Aid. |
| LMM | Compass locator station when installed at middle marker site (15 NM at all altitudes). |
| LOM | Compass locator station when installed at outer marker site (15 NM at all altitudes). |
| MH | Non-directional radio beacon (homing) power less than 50 watts (25 NM at all altitudes). |
| MLS | Microwave Landing System |
| S | Simultaneous range homing signal and/or voice. |
| SABH | Non-directional radio beacon not authorized for IFR or ATC. Provides automatic weather broadcasts. |
| SDF | Simplified Direction Facility. |
| TACAN | UHF navigational facility-omnidirectional course and distance information. |
| VOR | VHF navigational facility-omnidirectional course only. |
| VOR/DME | Collocated VOR navigational facility and UHF standard distance measuring equipment. |
| VORTAC | Collocated VOR and TACAN navigational facilities. |
| W | Without voice on radio facility frequency. |
| Z | VHF station location marker at a LF radio facility. |

### FREQUENCY PAIRING PLAN AND MLS CHANNELING

| MLS CHANNEL | VHF FREQUENCY | TACAN CHANNEL | MLS CHANNEL | VHF FREQUENCY | TACAN CHANNEL | MLS CHANNEL | VHF FREQUENCY | TACAN CHANNEL |
|---|---|---|---|---|---|---|---|---|
| 500 | 108.10 | 18X | 568 | 109.45 | 31Y | 634 | 114.05 | 87Y |
| 502 | 108.30 | 20X | 570 | 109.55 | 32Y | 636 | 114.15 | 88Y |
| 504 | 108.50 | 22X | 572 | 109.65 | 33Y | 638 | 114.25 | 89Y |
| 506 | 108.70 | 24X | 574 | 109.75 | 34Y | 640 | 114.35 | 90Y |
| 508 | 108.90 | 26X | 576 | 109.85 | 35Y | 642 | 114.45 | 91Y |
| 510 | 109.10 | 28X | 578 | 109.95 | 36Y | 644 | 114.55 | 92Y |
| 512 | 109.30 | 30X | 580 | 110.05 | 37Y | 646 | 114.65 | 93Y |
| 514 | 109.50 | 32X | 582 | 110.15 | 38Y | 648 | 114.75 | 94Y |
| 516 | 109.70 | 34X | 584 | 110.25 | 39Y | 650 | 114.85 | 95Y |
| 518 | 109.90 | 36X | 586 | 110.35 | 40Y | 652 | 114.95 | 96Y |
| 520 | 110.10 | 38X | 588 | 110.45 | 41Y | 654 | 115.05 | 97Y |
| 522 | 110.30 | 40X | 590 | 110.55 | 42Y | 656 | 115.15 | 98Y |
| 524 | 110.50 | 42X | 592 | 110.65 | 43Y | 658 | 115.25 | 99Y |
| 526 | 110.70 | 44X | 594 | 110.75 | 44Y | 660 | 115.35 | 100Y |
| 528 | 110.90 | 46X | 596 | 110.85 | 45Y | 662 | 115.45 | 101Y |
| 530 | 111.10 | 48X | 598 | 110.95 | 46Y | 664 | 115.55 | 102Y |
| 532 | 111.30 | 50X | 600 | 111.05 | 47Y | 666 | 115.65 | 103Y |
| 534 | 111.50 | 52X | 602 | 111.15 | 48Y | 668 | 115.75 | 104Y |
| 536 | 111.70 | 54X | 604 | 111.25 | 49Y | 670 | 115.85 | 105Y |
| 538 | 111.90 | 56X | 606 | 111.35 | 50Y | 672 | 115.95 | 106Y |
| 540 | 108.05 | 17Y | 608 | 111.45 | 51Y | 674 | 116.05 | 107Y |
| 542 | 108.15 | 18Y | 610 | 111.55 | 52Y | 676 | 116.15 | 108Y |
| 544 | 108.25 | 19Y | 612 | 111.65 | 53Y | 678 | 116.25 | 109Y |
| 546 | 108.35 | 20Y | 614 | 111.75 | 54Y | 680 | 116.35 | 110Y |
| 548 | 108.45 | 21Y | 616 | 111.85 | 55Y | 682 | 116.45 | 111Y |
| 550 | 108.55 | 22Y | 618 | 111.95 | 56Y | 684 | 116.55 | 112Y |
| 552 | 108.65 | 23Y | 620 | 113.35 | 80Y | 686 | 116.65 | 113Y |
| 554 | 108.75 | 24Y | 622 | 113.45 | 81Y | 688 | 116.75 | 114Y |
| 556 | 108.85 | 25Y | 624 | 113.55 | 82Y | 690 | 116.85 | 115Y |
| 558 | 108.95 | 26Y | 626 | 113.65 | 83Y | 692 | 116.95 | 116Y |
| 560 | 109.05 | 27Y | 628 | 113.75 | 84Y | 694 | 117.05 | 117Y |
| 562 | 109.15 | 28Y | 630 | 113.85 | 85Y | 696 | 117.15 | 118Y |
| 564 | 109.25 | 29Y | 632 | 113.95 | 86Y | 698 | 117.25 | 119Y |
| 566 | 109.35 | 30Y | | | | | | |

Legend 20.—Frequency Pairing Plan and MLS Channeling.

# DIRECTORY LEGEND
## FREQUENCY PAIRING PLAN AND MLS CHANNELING

The following is a list of paired VOR/ILS VHF frequencies with TACAN channels and MLS channels.

| TACAN CHANNEL | VHF FREQUENCY | MLS CHANNEL | TACAN CHANNEL | VHF FREQUENCY | MLS CHANNEL | TACAN CHANNEL | VHF FREQUENCY | MLS CHANNEL |
|---|---|---|---|---|---|---|---|---|
| 17X | 108.00 | - | 50Y | 111.35 | 606 | 94X | 114.70 | - |
| 17Y | 108.05 | 540 | 51X | 111.40 | - | 94Y | 114.75 | 648 |
| 18X | 108.10 | 500 | 51Y | 111.45 | 608 | 95X | 114.80 | - |
| 18Y | 108.15 | 542 | 52X | 111.50 | 534 | 95Y | 114.85 | 650 |
| 19X | 108.20 | - | 52Y | 111.55 | 610 | 96X | 114.90 | - |
| 19Y | 108.25 | 544 | 53X | 111.60 | - | 96Y | 114.95 | 652 |
| 20X | 108.30 | 502 | 53Y | 111.65 | 612 | 97X | 115.00 | - |
| 20Y | 108.35 | 546 | 54X | 111.70 | 536 | 97Y | 115.05 | 654 |
| 21X | 108.40 | - | 54Y | 111.75 | 614 | 98X | 115.10 | - |
| 21Y | 108.45 | 548 | 55X | 111.80 | - | 98Y | 115.15 | 656 |
| 22X | 108.50 | 504 | 55Y | 111.85 | 616 | 99X | 115.20 | - |
| 22Y | 108.55 | 550 | 56X | 111.90 | 538 | 99Y | 115.25 | 658 |
| 23X | 108.60 | - | 56Y | 111.95 | 618 | 100X | 115.30 | -660 |
| 23Y | 108.65 | 552 | 57X | 112.00 | - | 100Y | 115.35 | - |
| 24X | 108.70 | 506 | 57Y | 112.05 | - | 101X | 115.40 | 662 |
| 24Y | 108.75 | 554 | 58X | 112.10 | - | 101Y | 115.45 | - |
| 25X | 108.80 | - | 58Y | 112.15 | - | 102X | 115.50 | 664 |
| 25Y | 108.85 | 556 | 59X | 112.20 | - | 102Y | 115.55 | - |
| 26X | 108.90 | 508 | 59Y | 112.25 | - | 103X | 115.60 | 666 |
| 26Y | 108.95 | 558 | 70X | 112.30 | - | 103Y | 115.65 | - |
| 27X | 109.00 | - | 70Y | 112.35 | - | 104X | 115.70 | 668 |
| 27Y | 109.05 | 560 | 71X | 112.40 | - | 104Y | 115.75 | - |
| 28X | 109.10 | 510 | 71Y | 112.45 | - | 105X | 115.80 | 670 |
| 28Y | 109.15 | 562 | 72X | 112.50 | - | 105Y | 115.85 | - |
| 29X | 109.20 | - | 72Y | 112.55 | - | 106X | 115.90 | 672 |
| 29Y | 109.25 | 564 | 73X | 112.60 | - | 106Y | 115.95 | - |
| 30X | 109.30 | 512 | 73Y | 112.65 | - | 107X | 116.00 | 674 |
| 30Y | 109.35 | 566 | 74X | 112.70 | - | 107Y | 116.05 | - |
| 31X | 109.40 | - | 74Y | 112.75 | - | 108X | 116.10 | 676 |
| 31Y | 109.45 | 568 | 75X | 112.80 | - | 108Y | 116.15 | - |
| 32X | 109.50 | 514 | 75Y | 112.85 | - | 109X | 116.20 | 678 |
| 32Y | 109.55 | 570 | 76X | 112.90 | - | 109Y | 116.25 | - |
| 33X | 109.60 | - | 76Y | 112.95 | - | 110X | 116.30 | 680 |
| 33Y | 109.65 | 572 | 77X | 113.00 | - | 110Y | 116.35 | - |
| 34X | 109.70 | 516 | 77Y | 113.05 | - | 111X | 116.40 | 682 |
| 34Y | 109.75 | 574 | 78X | 113.10 | - | 111Y | 116.45 | - |
| 35X | 109.80 | - | 78Y | 113.15 | - | 112X | 116.50 | 684 |
| 35Y | 109.85 | 576 | 79X | 113.20 | - | 112Y | 116.55 | - |
| 36X | 109.90 | 518 | 79Y | 113.25 | - | 113X | 116.60 | 686 |
| 36Y | 109.95 | 578 | 80X | 113.30 | - | 113Y | 116.65 | - |
| 37X | 110.00 | - | 80Y | 113.35 | 620 | 114X | 116.70 | 688 |
| 37Y | 110.05 | 580 | 81X | 113.40 | - | 114Y | 116.75 | - |
| 38X | 110.10 | 520 | 81Y | 113.45 | 622 | 115X | 116.80 | 690 |
| 38Y | 110.15 | 582 | 82X | 113.50 | - | 115Y | 116.85 | - |
| 39X | 110.20 | - | 82Y | 113.55 | 624 | 116X | 116.90 | 692 |
| 39Y | 110.25 | 584 | 83X | 113.60 | - | 116Y | 116.95 | - |
| 40X | 110.30 | 522 | 83Y | 113.65 | 626 | 117X | 117.00 | 694 |
| 40Y | 110.35 | 586 | 84X | 113.70 | - | 117Y | 117.05 | - |
| 41X | 110.40 | - | 84Y | 113.75 | 628 | 118X | 117.10 | 696 |
| 41Y | 110.45 | 588 | 85X | 113.80 | - | 118Y | 117.15 | - |
| 42X | 110.50 | 524 | 85Y | 113.85 | 630 | 119X | 117.20 | 698 |
| 42Y | 110.55 | 590 | 86X | 113.90 | - | 119Y | 117.25 | - |
| 43X | 110.60 | - | 86Y | 113.95 | 632 | 120X | 117.30 | - |
| 43Y | 110.65 | 592 | 87X | 114.00 | - | 120Y | 117.35 | - |
| 44X | 110.70 | 526 | 87Y | 114.05 | 634 | 121X | 117.40 | - |
| 44Y | 110.75 | 594 | 88X | 114.10 | - | 121Y | 117.45 | - |
| 45X | 110.80 | - | 88Y | 114.15 | 636 | 122X | 117.50 | - |
| 45Y | 110.85 | 596 | 89X | 114.20 | - | 122Y | 117.55 | - |
| 46X | 110.90 | 528 | 89Y | 114.25 | 638 | 123X | 117.60 | - |
| 46Y | 110.95 | 598 | 90X | 114.30 | - | 123Y | 117.65 | - |
| 47X | 111.00 | - | 90Y | 114.35 | 640 | 124X | 117.70 | - |
| 47Y | 111.05 | 600 | 91X | 114.40 | - | 124Y | 117.75 | - |
| 48X | 111.10 | 530 | 91Y | 114.45 | 642 | 125X | 117.80 | - |
| 48Y | 111.15 | 602 | 92X | 114.50 | - | 125Y | 117.85 | - |
| 49X | 111.20 | - | 92Y | 114.55 | 644 | 126X | 117.90 | - |
| 49Y | 111.25 | 604 | 93X | 114.60 | - | 126Y | 117.95 | |
| 50X | 111.30 | 532 | 93Y | 114.65 | 646 | | | |

(23) COMM/NAVAID REMARKS:
Pertinent remarks concerning communications and NAVAIDS.

LEGEND 21.—Frequency Pairing Plan and MLS Channeling.

**Appendix 1**

## AIRPORT LORAN TD
## CORRECTION TABLE

The following LORAN - C time difference (TD) table contains the TD correction values for each airport with a published LORAN RNAV instrument approach procedure. This TD correction value must be entered into the LORAN airborne receiver prior to beginning the approach. TD values from this table should be transferred to the TD correction box shown in the plan view of the LORAN RNAV approach for the destination airport.

Pilots are advised to check LORAN (LRN) NOTAM's to obtain the status of the LORAN chain or group repetition interval (GRI) and NOTAM's for the LORAN monitor location identifier (MLID) at their destination and alternate airport.

| CITY | ST | NAME | LID | MLID | GRI | TRI | V | W | X | Y | Z |
|---|---|---|---|---|---|---|---|---|---|---|---|
| BURLINGTON | VT | BURLINGTON INTL | BTV | .BTV | 9960 | MWX | | 10.0 | 09.8 | | |
| COLUMBUS | OH | OHIO STATE UNIV. | OSU | OSU | 9960 | MYZ | | | | 08.6 | 11.6 |
| NEW ORLEANS | LA | LAKEFRONT | NEW | NEW | 7980 | MWX | | 11.5 | 11.2 | | |
| ORLANDO | FL | ORLANDO EXEC. | ORL | ORL | 7980 | MYZ | | | | 11.3 | 11.7 |
| PORTLAND | OR | PORTLAND INTL. | PDX | PDX | 9940 | MWX | | 11.7 | 09.4 | | |
| VENICE | LA | CHEVRON | 8LA5 | NEW | 7980 | MWX | | 11.5 | 11.2 | | |

LEGEND 22.—Airport Loran TD Correction Table.

22

# EXCERPT FROM CFR 49 PART 175

## PART 175—CARRIAGE BY AIRCRAFT

### Subpart A—General Information and Regulations

### Subpart B—Loading, Unloading and Handling

### Subpart C—Specific Regulations Applicable According to Classification of Material

LEGEND 23.—Excerpt from CFR 49 Part 175.

# EXCERPT FROM CFR 49 PART 175

Sec.

175.640 Special requirements for other regulated materials.

175.700 Special requirements for radioactive materials.

175.710 Special requirements for fissile Class III radioactive materials.

AUTHORITY: 49 U.S.C. 1803, 1804, 1808; 49 CFR 1.53(e), unless otherwise noted.

SOURCE: Amdt. 175-1, 41 FR 16106, Apr. 15, 1976, unless otherwise noted.

NOTE: Nomenclature changes to Part 175 appear at 43 FR 48645, Oct. 19, 1978 (Amdt. 175-6).

## Subpart A—General Information and Regulations

### § 175.1 Purpose and scope.

This part prescribes requirements, in addition to those contained in Parts 171, 172 and 173 of this subchapter, to be observed by aircraft operators with respect to the transportation of hazardous materials aboard (including attached to or suspended from) civil aircraft.

### § 175.3 Unacceptable hazardous materials shipments.

A shipment of hazardous materials that is not prepared for shipment in accordance with Parts 172 and 173 of this subchapter may not be accepted for transportation or transported aboard an aircraft.

### § 175.5 Applicability.

This part contains regulations pertaining to the acceptance of hazardous materials for transportation, and the loading and transportation of hazardous materials, in any civil aircraft in the United States and in civil aircraft of United States registry anywhere in air commerce, except aircraft of United States registry under lease to and operated solely by foreign nationals outside the United States.

### § 175.10 Exceptions.

(a) This subchapter does not apply to—

(1) Aviation fuel and oil in tanks that are in compliance with the installation provisions of 14 CFR, Chapter 1.

(2) Aircraft parts, equipment, and supplies (other than fuel) carried by an aircraft operator if authorized or required aboard his aircraft for their operation including:

(i) Fire extinguishers;

(ii) Cylinders containing compressed gases;

(iii) Aerosol dispensers;

(iv) Distilled spirits;

(v) Hydraulic accumulators;

(vi) Non-spillable batteries;

(vii) First-aid kits;

(viii) Signaling devices;

(ix) Tires; and

(x) Items of replacement therefor, except that batteries, aerosol dispensers, and signaling devices must be packed in strong outside containers, and tires must be deflated to a pressure not greater than 100 p.s.i.g.

(3) Hazardous materials loaded and carried in hoppers or tanks of aircraft certificated for use in aerial seeding, dusting, spraying, fertilizing, crop improvement, or pest control, to be dispensed during such an operation.

(4) Medicinal and toilet articles carried by a crewmember or passenger in his baggage (including carry-on baggage) when:

(i) The total capacity of all the containers used by a crewmember or passenger does not exceed 75 ounces (net weight ounces and fluid ounces);

(ii) The capacity of each container other than an aerosol container does not exceed 16 fluid ounces or 1 pound of material.

(5) Small-arms ammunition for personal use carried by a crewmember or passenger in his baggage (excluding carry-on baggage) if securely packed in fiber, wood, or metal boxes.

(6) Prior to May 3, 1981, radioactive materials which meet the requirements of § 173.391(a), (b), or (c) of this subchapter in effect on May 3, 1979.

(7) Oxygen, or any hazardous material used for the generation of oxygen, carried for medical use by a passenger in accordance with 14 CFR 121.574 or 135.114.

(8) Human beings and animals with an implanted medical device, such as a heart pacemaker, that contains radioactive material or with radio-pharmaceuticals that have been injected or ingested.

LEGEND 24.—Excerpt from CFR 49 Part 175.

# EXCERPT FROM CFR 49 PART 175

(9) Smoke grenades, flares, or similar devices carried only for use during a sport parachute jumping activity.

(10) Personal smoking materials intended for use by any individual when carried on his person except lighters with flammable liquid reservoirs and containers containing lighter fluid for use in refilling lighters.

(11) Smoke grenades, flares, and pyrotechnic devices affixed to aircraft carrying no person other than a required flight crewmember during any flight conducted at and as a part of a scheduled air show or exhibition of aeronautical skill. The affixed installation accommodating the smoke grenades, flares, or pyrotechnic devices on the aircraft must be approved by the FAA for its intended use.

(12) Hazardous materials which are loaded and carried on or in cargo-only aircraft and which are to be dispensed or expended during flight for weather control, forest preservation and protection, or avalanche control purposes when the following requirements are met:

(i) Operations may not be conducted over densely populated areas, in a congested airway, or near any airport where air carrier passenger operations are conducted.

(ii) Each operator shall prepare and keep current a manual containing operational guidelines and handling procedures, for the use and guidance of flight, maintenance, and ground personnel concerned in the dispensing or expending of hazardous materials. The manual must be approved by the FAA District Office having jurisdiction over the operator's certificate, if any, or the FAA Regional Office in the region where the operator is located. Each operation must be conducted in accordance with the manual.

(iii) No person other than a required flight crewmember, FAA inspector, or person necessary for handling or dispensing the hazardous material may be carried on the aircraft.

(iv) The operator of the aircraft must have advance permission from the owner of any airport to be used for the dispensing or expending operation.

(v) When dynamite and blasting caps are carried for avalanche control flights, the explosives must be handled, and, at all times be, under the control of a blaster who is licensed under a state or local authority identified in writing to the FAA district office having jurisdiction over the operator's certificate, if any, or the FAA regional office in the region where the operator is located.

(49 U.S.C. 1803, 1804, 1806, 1808; 49 CFR 1.53 and App. A to Part 1)

[Amdt. 175-1, 41 FR 16106, Apr. 15, 1976, as amended by Amdt. 175-1A, 41 FR 40686, Sept. 20, 1976]

NOTE: For amendments to § 175.10 see the List of CFR Sections Affected appearing in the Finding Aids section of this volume.

## § 175.20  Compliance.

Unless the regulations in this subchapter specifically provide that another person must perform a duty, each operator shall comply with all the regulations in Parts 102, 171, 172, and 175 of this subchapter and shall thoroughly instruct his employees in relation thereto. (See 14 CFR 121.135, 121.401, 121.433a, 135.27 and 135.140.)

## § 175.30  Accepting shipments.

(a) No person may accept a hazardous material for transportation aboard an aircraft unless the hazardous material is—

(1) Authorized, and is within the quantity limitations specified for carriage aboard aircraft according to § 172.101 of this subchapter;

(2) Described and certified on a shipping paper prepared in duplicate in accordance with Subpart C of Part 172 of this subchapter. The originating aircraft operator must retain one copy of each shipping paper for 90 days;

(3) Labeled and marked, or placarded (when required), in accordance with Subparts D, E and F of Part 172 of this subchapter; and

(4) Labeled with a "CARGO AIRCRAFT ONLY" label (see § 172.448 of this subchapter) if the material as presented is not permitted aboard passenger-carrying aircraft.

(b) Except as provided in paragraph (c) of this section, no person may carry any hazardous material aboard an aircraft unless, prior to placing the material aboard the aircraft, the operator of the aircraft has inspected the package, or the outside container pre-

LEGEND 25.—Excerpt from CFR 49 Part 175.

# EXCERPT FROM CFR 49 PART 175

pared in accordance with § 173.25 of this subchapter which contains the material, and has determined that—it has no holes, leakage, or other indication that its integrity has been compromised, and for radioactive materials that the package seal has not been broken.

(c) The requirements of paragraph (b) of this section do not apply to ORM-D materials packed in a freight container and offered for transportation by one consignor.

[Amdt. 175-1, 41 FR 16106, Apr. 15, 1976, as amended by Amdt. 175-1A, 41 FR 40686, Sept. 20, 1976; Amdt. 175-1B, 41 FR 57072, Dec. 30, 1976]

### § 175.33  Notification of pilot-in-command.

When materials subject to the provisions of this subchapter are carried in an aircraft, the operator of the aircraft shall give the pilot-in-command the following information in writing before takeoff:

(a) The information required by §§ 172-202 and 172.203 of this subchapter;

(b) The location of the hazardous material in the aircraft; and

(c) The results of the inspection required by § 175.30(b).

[Amdt. 175-1A, 41 FR 40686, Sept. 20, 1976]

### § 175.35  Shipping papers aboard aircraft.

(a) A copy of the shipping papers required by § 175.30(a)(2) must accompany the shipment it covers during transportation aboard an aircraft.

(b) The documents required by paragraph (a) of this section and § 175.33 may be combined into one document if it is given to the pilot-in-command before departure of the aircraft.

### § 175.40  Keeping and replacement of labels.

(a) Aircraft operators who engage in the transportation of hazardous materials must keep an adequate supply of the labels specified in Subpart E of Part 172 of this subchapter, on hand at each location where shipments are loaded aboard aircraft.

(b) Lost or detached labels for packages of hazardous materials must be replaced in accordance with the information provided on the shipping papers.

### § 175.45  Reporting hazardous materials incidents.

(a) Each operator that transports hazardous materials shall report to the nearest Air Carrier District Office (ACDO), Flight Standards District Office (FSDO), General Aviation District Office (GADO) or other FAA facility, except that in place of reporting to the nearest of those facilities a certificate holder under 14 CFR Part 121, 127, or 135 may report to the FAA District Office holding the carrier's operating certificate and charged with overall inspection of its operations, by telephone at the earliest practicable moment after each incident that occurs during the course of transportation (including loading, unloading or temporary storage) in which as a direct result of any hazardous material—

(1) A person is killed;

(2) A person receives injuries requiring his or her hospitalization;

(3) Estimated carrier or other property damage, or both, exceeds $50,000;

(4) Fire, breakage, or spillage or suspected radioactive contamination occurs involving shipment of radioactive materials (see § 175.700(b));

(5) Fire, breakage, spillage, or suspected contamination occurs involving shipment of etiologic agents. In addition to the report required by paragraph (a) of this section, a report on an incident involving etiologic agents should be telephoned directly to the Director, Center for Disease Control, U.S. Public Health, Atlanta, Georgia, area code 404-633-5313; or

(6) A situation exists of such a nature that, in the judgment of the carrier, it should be reported to the Department even though it does not meet the criteria of paragraph (b)(1), (2), or (3) of this section, e.g., a continuing danger to life exists at the scene of the incident.

(7) If the operator conforms to the provisions of this section, the carrier requirements of § 171.15 except § 171.15(c) of this subchapter shall be deemed to have been satisfied.

(b) The following information shall be furnished in each report:

LEGEND 26.—Excerpt from CFR 49 Part 175.

# EXCERPT FROM CFR 49 PART 175

**Chapter I—Research and Special Programs Administration**  § 175.85

(1) Name of reporting person;

(2) Name and address of carrier represented by reporter;

(3) Phone number where reporter can be contacted;

(4) Date, time, and location of incident;

(5) The extent of the injuries, if any; and

(6) Classification, name and quantity of hazardous material involvement and whether a continuing danger to life exists at the scene.

(c) Each operator who transports hazardous materials shall report in writing, in duplicate, on DOT Form F 5800.1 within 15 days of the date of discovery, each incident that occurs during the course of transportation (including loading, unloading, or temporary storage) in which, as a direct result to hazardous materials, any of the circumstances set forth in paragraph (a) of this section occurs or there has been an unintentional release of hazardous materials from a package. Each operator making a report under this section shall send that report to the Materials Transportation Bureau, Office of Hazardous Materials Regulation, Department of Transportation, Washington, D.C. 20590, with a separate copy to the FAA facility indicated in paragraph (a) of this section.

[Amdt. 175-1, 41 FR 16106, Apr. 15, 1976, as amended by Amdt. 175-1A, 41 FR 40686, Sept. 20, 1976]

## Subpart B—Loading, Unloading and Handling

**§ 175.75  Quantity limitations aboard aircraft.**

(a) Except as provided in § 175.85(b), no person may carry on an aircraft—

(1) A hazardous material except as permitted in Part 172 of this subchapter;

(2) More than 50 pounds net weight of hazardous material (and in addition thereto, 150 pounds net weight of nonflammable compressed gas) permitted to be carried aboard passenger-carrying aircraft—

(i) In an inaccessible cargo compartment,

(ii) In any freight container within an accessible cargo compartment, or

(iii) In any accessible cargo compartment in a cargo-only aircraft in a manner that makes it inaccessible unless in a freight container;

(3) Packages containing radioactive materials when their combined transport indices exceed 50.

(b) No limitation applies to the number of packages of ORM material aboard an aircraft.

[Amdt. 175-1A, 41 FR 40686, Sept. 20, 1976]

**§ 175.78  Stowage compatibility of cargo.**

(a) No person may stow a package of a corrosive material on an aircraft next to or in a position that will allow contact with a package of flammable solids, oxidizing materials, or organic peroxides.

(b) No person may stow a package labeled BLASTING AGENT on an aircraft next to, or in a position that will allow contact with a package of special fireworks or railway torpedoes.

[Amdt. 175-1, 41 FR 16106, Apr. 15, 1976, as amended by Amdt. 175-8, 44 FR 31184, May 31, 1979]

**§ 175.79  Orientation of cargo.**

(a) A package containing hazardous materials marked "THIS SIDE UP", "THIS END UP", or with arrows to indicate the proper orientation of the package, must be stored, loaded abroad an aircraft in accordance with such markings, and secured in a manner that will prevent any movement which would change the orientation of the package.

(b) A package containing liquid hazardous materials not marked as indicated in paragraph (a) of this section must be stored and loaded with closures up.

**§ 175.85  Cargo location.**

(a) No person may carry a hazardous material subject to the requirements of this subchapter in the cabin of a passenger-carrying aircraft.

(b) Each person carrying materials acceptable only for cargo-only aircraft shall carry those materials in a location accessible to a crewmember during flight. However, when materials acceptable for cargo-only or pas-

LEGEND 27.—Excerpt from CFR 49 Part 175.

# EXCERPT FROM CFR 49 PART 175

senger carrying aircraft are carried on a small, single pilot, cargo-only aircraft being used where other means of transportation are impracticable or not available, they may be carried without quantity limitation as specified in § 175.75 in a location that is not accessible to the pilot subject to the following conditions.

(1) No person other than the pilot, an FAA inspector, the shipper or consignee of the material or a representative of the shipper or consignee so designated in writing, or a person necessary for handling the material may be carried on the aircraft.

(2) The pilot must be provided with written instructions on characteristics and proper handling of the material.

(3) Whenever a change of pilots occurs while the material is on board, the new pilot must be briefed under a hand-to-hand signature service provided by the operator of the aircraft.

(c) No person may load magnetized material (which might cause an erroneous magnetic compass reading) on an aircraft, in the vicinity of a magnetic compass, or compass master unit, that is a part of the instrument equipment of the aircraft, in a manner that affects its operation. If this requirement cannot be met, a special aircraft swing and compass calibration may be made. No person loading magnetized materials may obscure the warning labels.

(d) No person may carry materials subject to the requirements of this subchapter in an aircraft unless they are suitably safeguarded to prevent their becoming a hazard by shifting. For packages bearing "RADIOACTIVE YELLOW-II" or "RADIOACTIVE YELLOW-III" labels, such safeguarding must prevent movement that would permit the package to be closer to a space that is occupied by a person or an animal than is permitted by § 175.700.

(e) No person may carry a material subject to the requirements of this subchapter that is acceptable for carriage in a passenger-carrying aircraft (other than magnetized materials) unless it is located in the aircraft in a place that is inaccessible to persons other than crew-members.

[Amdt. 175-1, 41 FR 16106, Apr. 15, 1976, as amended by Amdt. 175-1A, 41 FR 40686, Sept. 20, 1976]

## § 175.90  Damaged shipments.

Except as provided for in § 175.700, the operator of an aircraft shall remove from the aircraft any package subject to this subchapter that appears to be damaged or leaking. No person shall place or transport a package that is damaged or appears to be damaged or leaking aboard an aircraft subject to this Part.

[Amdt. 175-1, 41 FR 16106, Apr. 15, 1976, as amended by Amdt 175-1A, 41 FR 40686, Sept. 20, 1976]

## Subpart C—Specific Regulations Applicable According to Classification of Material

### § 175.305  Self-propelled vehicles.

(a) Self-propelled vehicles are exempt from the drainage requirements of § 173.120 of this subchapter when carried in aircraft designed or modified for vehicle ferry operations and when all of the following conditions are met:

(1) Authorization for this type operation has been given by the appropriate authority in the government of the country in which the aircraft is registered;

(2) Each vehicle is secured in an upright position;

(3) Each fuel tank is filled in a manner and only to a degree that will preclude spillage of fuel during loading, unloading, and transportation; and

(4) Ventilation rates to be maintained in the vehicle storage compartment have been approved by the appropriate authority in the government of the country in which the aircraft is registered.

### § 175.310  Transportation of flammable liquid fuel in small, passenger-carrying aircraft.

A small aircraft or helicopter operated entirely within the State of Alaska or into a remote area elsewhere in the United States may carry, in other than scheduled passenger operations, not more than 20 gallons of flammable liquid fuel, if—

LEGEND 28.—Excerpt from CFR 49 Part 175.

# EXCERPT FROM CFR 49 PART 175

**Chapter I—Research and Special Programs Administration** § 175.320

(a) Transportation by air is the only practical means of providing suitable fuel;

(b) The flight is necessary to meet the needs of a passenger;

(c) The fuel is carried in metal containers that are either—

(1) DOT Specification 2A containers of not more than 5 gallons capacity, each packed inside a DOT Specification 12B fiberboard box or each packed inside a DOT Specification 15A, 15B, 15C, 16A, 19A or 19B wooden box, or in the case of a small aircraft in Alaska, each packed inside a wooden box of at least one-half inch thickness;

(2) Airtight, leakproof, inside containers of not more than 10 gallons capacity and of at least 28-gauge metal, each packed inside a DOT Specification 15A, 15B, 15C, 16A, 19A, or 19B wooden box or, in the case of a small aircraft in Alaska, each packed inside a wooden box of at least one-half inch thickness;

(3) DOT Specification 17E containers of not more than 5 gallons capacity; or

(4) Fuel tanks attached to flammable liquid fuel powered equipment under the following conditions:

(i) Each piece of equipment is secured in an upright position;

(ii) Each fuel tank is filled in a manner that will preclude spillage of fuel during loading, unloading, and transportation; and

(iii) Ventilation rates which are maintained in the compartment in which the equipment is carried have been approved by the FAA district office responsible for inspection and surveillance of the aircraft on which the equipment is carried.

(d) In the case of a helicopter, the fuel is carried on external cargo racks;

(e) The area or compartment in which the fuel is loaded is ventilated so as to prevent the accumulation of fumes;

(f) Before each flight, the pilot-in-command—

(1) Informs each passenger of the location of the fuel and the hazards involved; and

(2) Prohibits smoking, lighting matches, the carrying of any lighted cigar, pipe, cigarette or flame, and the use of anything that might cause an open flame or spark, while loading or unloading or in flight; and

(g) Fuel is transferred to the fuel tanks only while the aircraft is on the surface.

[Amdt. 175-1, 41 FR 16106, Apr. 15, 1976, as amended by Amdt. 175-1A, 41 FR 40686, Sept. 20, 1976]

§ 175.320 Cargo-only aircraft; only means of transportation.

(a) Notwithstanding § 172.101, when means of transportation other than air are impracticable or not available, hazardous materials listed in the following table may be carried on a cargo-only aircraft subject to the conditions stated in the table and in paragraph (b) of this section and, when appropriate, paragraph (c) of this section:

| Material description | Class | Conditions |
|---|---|---|
| Electric blasting caps (more than 1,000). | Class A explosives | Permitted only when no other cargo is aboard the aircraft. However, if the electric blasting caps are packed in an IME 22 container (see 49 CFR 171.7(d)(9)), they may be transported in the same aircraft with materials that are not classed as hazardous materials. |
| Electric blasting caps (1,000 or less). | Class C explosives | Permitted only when no other cargo is aboard the aircraft. However, if the electric blasting caps are packed in a DOT MC 201 container (49 CFR 178.318) or an IME 22 container (see 49 CFR 171.7(d)(9)), they may be transported in the same aircraft with materials other than class A or class B explosives. |
| Gasoline | Flammable liquid | Permitted in metal drums having rated capacities of 55 gal. or less. May not be transported in the same aircraft with materials classed as class A, B, or C explosives, blasting agents, corrosive materials or oxidizing materials. Permitted in installed tanks each having a capacity of more than 110 gal. Subject to the conditions specified in para. (c) of this section. |

LEGEND 29.—Excerpt from CFR 49 Part 175.

# EXCERPT FROM CFR 49 PART 175

**§ 175.320**                                    **Title 49—Transportation**

| Material description | Class | Conditions |
|---|---|---|
| High explosives | Class A explosives | Limited to explosives to be used for blasting. Permitted only when no other cargo is aboard the aircraft or when being transported in the same aircraft with an authorized shipment of any 1 or more of the following materials to be used for blasting:<br>Ammonium nitrate-fuel oil mixtures Blasting agent, n.o.s.<br>Cordeau detonant fuse.<br>Propellant explosive (solid) class B (water gels only).<br>Propellant explosive (liquid) class B (water gels only). |
| Oil n.o.s.; petroleum oil or petroleum oil, n.o.s. | Flammable liquid | Permitted in metal drums having rated capacities of 55 gal. or less. May not be transported in the same aircraft with materials classed as class A, B, or C explosives, blasting agents, corrosive materials, or oxidizing materials. Permitted in installed tanks each having a capacity of more than 110 gal. subject to the conditions specified in para. (c) of this section. |
| Combustible liquid, n.o.s. | Combustible liquid | Permitted in installed tanks each having a capacity of more than 110 gal subject to the conditions specified in par. (c) of this section. |

(b) The following conditions apply to the carriage of hazardous materials performed under the authority of this section:

(1) No person other than a required flight crewmember, an FAA inspector, the shipper or consignee of the material or a representative of the shipper or consignee so designated in writing, or a person necessary for handling the material may be carried on the aircraft.

(2) The operator of the aircraft must have advance permission from the owner or operator of each manned airport where the material is to be loaded or unloaded or where the aircraft is to land while the material is on board. When the destination is changed after departure because of weather or other unforeseen circumstances, permission from the owner or operator of the alternate airport should be obtained as soon as practicable before landing.

(3) At any airport where the airport owner or operator or authorized representative thereof has designated a location for loading or unloading the material concerned, the material may not be loaded or unloaded at any other location.

(4) If the material concerned can create destructive forces or have lethal or injurious effects over an appreciable area as a result of an accident involving the aircraft or the material, the loading and unloading of the aircraft and its operation in takeoff, en route, and in landing must be conducted at a safe distance from heavily populated areas and from any place of human abode or assembly.

(5) If the aircraft is being operated by a holder of a certificate issued under 14 CFR Part 121, Part 127, or Part 135, operations must be conducted in accordance with conditions and limitations specified in the certificate holder's operations specifications or operations manual accepted by the FAA. If the aircraft is being operated under 14 CFR Part 91, operations must be conducted in accordance with an operations plan accepted and acknowledged in writing by the operator's FAA District Office.

(6) Each pilot of the aircraft must be provided written instructions stating the conditions and limitations of the operation being conducted and the name of the airport official[s] granting the advance permission required by the first sentence of paragraph (b)(2) of this section.

(7) The aircraft and the loading arrangement to be used must be approved for safe carriage of the particular materials concerned by the FAA District Office holding the operator's certificate and charged with overall inspection of its operations, or the appropriate FAA District Office serving the place where the material is to be loaded.

LEGEND 30.—Excerpt from CFR 49 Part 175.

# EXCERPT FROM CFR 49 PART 175

**Chapter I—Research and Special Programs Administration** § 175.700

(8) When Class A explosives are carried under the authority of this section, the operator of the aircraft shall obtain route approval from the FAA inspector in the operator's FAA District Office.

(9) During loading and unloading, no person may smoke, carry a lighted cigarette, cigar, or pipe, or operate any device capable of causing an open flame or spark within 50 feet of the aircraft.

(c) The following additional conditions apply to the carriage of flammable liquids and combustible liquids in tanks each having a capacity of more than 110 gallons under the authority of this section:

(1) The tanks and their associated piping and equipment and the installation thereof must have been approved for the material to be transported by the appropriate FAA Regional Office.

(2) In the case of an aircraft being operated by a certificate holder, the operator shall list the aircraft and the approval information in its operating specifications. If the aircraft is being operated by other than a certificate holder, a copy of the FAA Regional Office approval required by this section must be carried on the aircraft.

(3) The crew of the aircraft must be thoroughly briefed on the operation of the particular bulk tank system being used.

(4) During loading and unloading and thereafter until any remaining fumes within the aircraft are dissipated:

(i) Only those electrically operated bulk tank shutoff valves that have been approved under a supplemental type certificate may be electrically operated.

(ii) No engine or electrical equipment, avionic equipment, or auxiliary power units may be operated, except position lights in the steady position and equipment required by approved loading or unloading procedures, as set forth in the operator's operations manual, or for operators that are not certificate holders, as set forth in a written statement.

(iii) No person may fill a container, other than an approved bulk tank, with a flammable or combustible liquid or discharge a flammable or combustible liquid from a container, other than an approved bulk tank, while that container is inside or within 50 feet of the aircraft.

(iv) When filling an approved bulk tank by hose from inside the aircraft, the doors and hatches must be fully open to insure proper ventilation.

(v) Static ground wires must be connected between the storage tank or fueler and the aircraft, and between the aircraft and a positive ground device.

[Amdt. 175-1, 41 FR 16106, Apr. 15, 1976, as amended by Amdt. 175-1A, 41 FR 40686, Sept. 20, 1976]

Note: For amendments to § 175.320 see the List of CFR Sections Affected appearing in the Finding Aids section of this volume.

§ 175.630 **Special requirements for poisons.**

(a) No person may transport a package bearing a POISON label aboard an aircraft in the same cargo compartment with material which is marked as or known to be food stuff, feed, or any other edible material intended for consumption by humans or animals.

(b) No person may operate an aircraft that has been used to transport any package bearing a POISON label unless, upon removal of such package, the area in the aircraft in which it was carried is visually inspected for evidence of leakage, spillage, or other contamination. All contamination discovered must be either isolated or removed from the aircraft. The operation of an aircraft contaminated with such poisons is considered to be the carriage of poisonous materials under paragraph (a) of this section.

§ 175.640 **Special requirements for other regulated materials.**

Asbestos must be loaded, handled, and unloaded, and any asbestos contamination of aircraft removed, in a manner that will minimize occupational exposure to airborne asbestos particles released incident to transportation. (See § 173.1090 of this subchapter.)

[Amdt. 175-7, 43 FR 56668, Dec. 4, 1978]

§ 175.700 **Special requirements for radioactive materials.**

(a) No person may place any package of radioactive materials bearing

LEGEND 31.—Excerpt from CFR 49 Part 175.

# EXCERPT FROM CFR 49 PART 175

§ 175.700                                                    **Title 49—Transportation**

"RADIOACTIVE YELLOW-II" or "RADIOACTIVE YELLOW-III" labels in an aircraft closer than the distances shown in the following table to a space (or dividing partition between spaces) which may be continuously occupied by people, or shipments of animals, or closer than the distances shown in the following table to any package containing undeveloped film (if so marked). If more than one of these packages is present, the distance shall be computed from the following table on the basis of the total transport index numbers shown on labels of the individual packages in the aircraft:

| Total transport index | Minimum separation distances in feet to the nearest undeveloped film for various times of transit | | | | | Minimum distance in feet to area of persons, or minimum distance in feet from dividing partition of cargo compartment |
|---|---|---|---|---|---|---|
| | Up to 2 hr | 2–4 hr | 4–8 hr | 8–12 hr | Over 12 hr | |
| None | 0 | 0 | 0 | 0 | 0 | 0 |
| 0.1 to 1.0 | 1 | 2 | 3 | 4 | 5 | 1 |
| 1.1 to 5.0 | 3 | 4 | 6 | 8 | 11 | 2 |
| 5.1 to 10.0 | 4 | 6 | 9 | 11 | 15 | 3 |
| 10.1 to 20.0 | 5 | 8 | 12 | 16 | 22 | 4 |
| 20.1 to 30.0 | 7 | 10 | 15 | 20 | 29 | 5 |
| 30.1 to 40.0 | 8 | 11 | 17 | 22 | 33 | 6 |
| 40.1 to 50.0 | 9 | 12 | 19 | 24 | 36 | 7 |

(b) In addition to the reporting requirements of § 175.45, the carrier must also notify the shipper at the earliest practicable moment following any incident in which there has been breakage, spillage, or suspected radioactive contamination involving radioactive materials shipments. Aircraft in which radioactive materials have been spilled may not be again placed in service or routinely occupied until the radiation does rate at any accessible surface is less than 0.5 millirem per hour and there is no significant removable radioactive surface contamination (see § 173.397 of this subchapter). In these instances, the package or materials should be segregated as far as practicable from personnel contact. If radiological advice or assistance is needed, the U.S. Energy Research and Development Administration should also be notified. In case of obvious leakage, or if it appears likely that the inside container may have been damaged, care should be taken to avoid inhalation, ingestion, or contact with the radioactive materials. Any loose radioactive materials should be left in a segregated area pending disposal instructions from qualified persons.

(c) No person may carry aboard a passenger-carrying aircraft any package of radioactive material which contains a large quantity (large radioactive source) of radioactivity (as defined in § 173.389(b) of this subchapter), except as specifically approved by the Director, Office of Hazardous Materials Regulation, Materials Transportation Bureau, Department of Transportation.

(d) Except as provided in this paragraph, no person may carry aboard a passenger-carrying aircraft any radioactive material other than a radioactive material intended for use in, or incident to, research or medical diagnosis or treatment. Prior to May 3, 1981, this prohibition does not apply to materials which meet the requirements of § 173.391(a), (b), or (c) of this subchapter in effect on May 3, 1979.

(49 U.S.C. 1803, 1804, 1806, 1808; 49 CFR 1.53 and App. A to Part 1)

[Amdt. 175–1, 41 FR 16106, Apr. 15, 1976, as amended by Amdt. 175–4, 42 FR 22367, May 3, 1977]

NOTE: For amendments to § 175.700 see the List of CFR Sections Affected appearing in the Finding Aids section of this volume.

LEGEND 32.—Excerpt from CFR 49 Part 175.

# EXCERPT FROM CFR 49 PART 175

## Chapter I—Research and Special Programs Administration          § 175.710

§ 175.710 Special requirements for fissile Class III radioactive materials.

(a) No person may carry aboard any aircraft any package of fissile Class III radioactive material (as defined in § 173.389(a)(3) of this subchapter), except as follows:

(1) On a cargo-only aircraft which has been assigned for the sole use of the consignor for the specific shipment of fissile radioactive material. Instructions for such sole use must be provided for in special arrangements between the consignor and carrier, with instructions to that effect issued with shipping papers; or

(2) On any aircraft on which there is no other package of radioactive materials required to bear one of the RADIOACTIVE labels described in §§ 172.436, 172.438, and 172.440 of this subchapter. Specific arrangements must be effected between the shipper and carriers, with instructions to that effect issued with the shipping papers; or

(3) In accordance with any other procedure specifically approved by the Director, Office of Hazardous Materials Regulation, Materials Transportation Bureau.

[Amdt. 175-1, 41 FR 16106, Apr. 15, 1976, as amended by Amdt. 175-6, 43 FR 48645, Oct. 19, 1978]

LEGEND 33.—Excerpt from CFR 49 Part 175.

## EXCERPT FROM CFR 49 PART 172
### Chapter 1—Research and Special Programs Administration    §172.101

## §172.101 Hazardous Materials Table (cont'd)

| (1) | (2) Hazardous materials descriptions and proper shipping names | (3) Hazard class | (4) Label(s) required (if not excepted) | (5) Packaging | | (6) Maximum net quantity in one package | | (7) Water shipments | | |
|---|---|---|---|---|---|---|---|---|---|---|
| | | | | (a) Exceptions | (b) Specific requirements | (a) Passenger carrying aircraft or railcar | (b) Cargo only aircraft | (a) Cargo vessel | (b) Passenger vessel | (c) Other requirements |
| | Accumulator, pressurized (pneumatic or hydraulic), containing nonflammable gas | Nonflammable gas | Nonflammable gas | 173.306 | | No limit | No limit | 1,2 | 1,2 | |
| | Acetal | Flammable liquid | Flammable liquid | 173.118 | 173.119 | 1 quart | 10 gallons | 1,3 | 4 | |
| | Acetaldehyde (ethyl aldehyde) | Flammable liquid | Flammable liquid | None | 173.119 | Forbidden | 10 gallons | 1,3 | 5 | |
| A | Acetaldehyde ammonia | ORM-A | None | 173.505 | 173.510 | No limit | No limit | | | |
| □ | Acetic acid (aqueous solution) | Corrosive material | Corrosive | 173.244 | 173.245 | 1 quart | 10 gallons | 1,2 | 1,2 | Stow separate from nitric acid or oxidizing materials. |
| | Acetic acid, glacial | Corrosive material | Corrosive | 173.244 | 173.245 | 1 quart | 10 gallons | 1,2 | 1,2 | Stow separate from nitric acid or oxidizing materials. Segregation same as for flammable liquids |
| | Acetic anhydride | Corrosive material | Corrosive | 173.244 | 173.245 | 1 quart | 1 gallon | 1,2 | 1,2 | |
| | Acetone | Flammable liquid | Flammable liquid | 173.118 | 173.119 | 1 quart | 10 gallons | 1,3 | 4 | Shade from radiant heat. Stow away from corrosive materials. |
| | Acetone cyanohydrin | Poison B | Poison | None | 173.346 | Forbidden | 55 gallons | 1 | 5 | |
| | Acetone oil | Flammable liquid | Flammable liquid | 173.118 | 173.119 | 1 quart | 10 gallons | 1,2 | 1 | |
| | Acetonitrile | Flammable liquid | Flammable liquid | 173.118 | 173.119 | 1 quart | 10 gallons | 1 | 4 | Shade from radiant heat. |
| | Acetyl benzoyl peroxide, solid | Forbidden | | | | | | | | |
| | Acetyl benzoyl peroxide solution, not over 40% peroxide | Organic peroxide | Organic peroxide | None | 173.222 | Forbidden | 1 quart | 1,2 | 1 | |
| | Acetyl bromide | Corrosive material | Corrosive | 173.244 | 173.247 | 1 quart | 1 gallon | 1 | 1 | Keep dry. Glass carboys not permitted on passenger vessels. |

LEGEND 34.—Hazardous Materials Table (CFR 49 Part 172).

## EXCERPT FROM CFR 49 PART 172

§172.101                                        Title 49—Transportation

## §172.101 Hazardous Materials Table (cont'd)

| (1) CY/W/A | (2) Hazardous materials descriptions and proper shipping names | (3) Hazard class | (4) Label(s) required (if not excepted) | (5) Packaging (a) Exceptions | (5) Packaging (b) Specific requirements | (6) Maximum net quantity in one package (a) Passenger carrying aircraft or railcar | (6) (b) Cargo only aircraft | (7) Water shipments (a) Cargo vessel | (7) (b) Passenger vessel | (7) (c) Other requirements |
|---|---|---|---|---|---|---|---|---|---|---|
| | Acetyl chloride | Flammable liquid | Flammable liquid | 173.244 | 173.247 | 1 quart | 1 gallon | 1 | 1 | Stow away from alcohols. Keep cool and dry. Separate longitudinally by an intervening complete compartment or hold from explosives. |
| | Acetylene | Flammable gas | Flammable gas | None | 173.303 | Forbidden | 300 pounds | 1 | 1 | Shade from radiant heat. |
| A | Acetylene tetrabromide | ORM-A | None | 173.505 | 173.510 | 10 gallons | 55 gallons | | | |
| | Acetyl iodide | Corrosive material | Corrosive | 173.244 | 173.247 | 1 quart | 1 gallon | 1 | 1 | Keep dry. Glass carboys not permitted on passenger vessels. |
| | Acetyl peroxide solution, not over 25% peroxide | Organic peroxide | Organic peroxide | 173.153 | 173.222 | Forbidden | 1 quart | i,2 | 1 | |
| | Acid butyl phosphate | Corrosive material | Corrosive | 173.244 | 173.245 | 1 quart | 5 gallons | 1,2 | 1,2 | Glass carboys in hampers not permitted under deck. |
| ▢ | Acid carboy empty. See Carboy, empty Acid, liquid, n.o.s. | | | | | | | | | |
| ▢ | Acid, sludge | Corrosive material | Corrosive | 173.244 | 173.245 | 1 quart | 5 pints | 1 | 4 | Keep cool. |
| | Acrolein, inhibited | Flammable liquid | Flammable liquid and Poison | None | 173.248 | Forbidden | 1 quart | 1,2 | 1 | Keep cool. Stow away from living quarters. |
| | Acrylic acid | Corrosive material | Corrosive | 173.244 | 173.122 | Forbidden | 1 quart | 1,2 | 5 | Keep cool. Stow away from living quarters. |
| | Acrylonitrile | Flammable liquid | Flammable liquid and Poison | 173.244 | 173.245 | 1 quart | 5 pints | 1 | 1 | Keep cool. |
| | | | | None | 173.119 | Forbidden | 1 quart | 1,2 | 5 | Keep cool. |

LEGEND 35.—Hazardous Materials Table (CFR 49 Part 172) (Cont'd).

EXCERPT FROM CFR 49 PART 172

§172.101  Title 49—Transportation

## §172.101 Hazardous Materials Table (cont'd)

| (1) | (2) Hazardous materials descriptions and proper shipping names | (3) Hazard class | (4) Label(s) required (if not excepted) | (5) Packaging | | (6) Maximum net quantity in one package | | (7) Water shipments | | |
|---|---|---|---|---|---|---|---|---|---|---|
| D/W/A | | | | (a) Exceptions | (b) Specific requirements | (a) Passenger carrying aircraft or railcar | (b) Cargo only aircraft | (a) Cargo vessel | (b) Passenger vessel | (c) Other requirements |
| | Alkyl aluminum halides. See Pyrophoric liquid, n.o.s. | | | | | | | | | |
| A | Allethrin | ORM-A | None | 173.505 | 173.510 | No limit | No limit | | | |
| | Allyl alcohol | Flammable liquid | Flammable liquid and Poison | 173.118 | 173.119 | 1 quart | 10 gallons | 1,2 | 1 | |
| | Allyl bromide | Flammable liquid | Flammable liquid | 173.118 | 173.119 | Forbidden | 10 gallons | 1,2 | 1 | |
| | Allyl chloride | Flammable liquid | Flammable liquid | None | 173.119 | Forbidden | 10 gallons | 1,3 | 5 | |
| | Allyl chlorocarbonate | Flammable liquid | Flammable liquid | None | 173.288 | Forbidden | 5 pints | 1 | 5 | Keep dry. Separate longitudinally by an intervening complete hold or compartment from explosives. Segregation same as for corrosive materials. |
| | Allyl chloroformate. See Allyl chlorocarbonate. | | | | | | | | | |
| | Allyl trichlorosilane | Corrosive material | Corrosive | None | 173.280 | Forbidden | 10 gallons | 1 | 1 | Keep dry. |
| | Aluminum alkyls. See Pyrophoric liquid n.o.s. | | | | | | | | | |
| | Aluminum bromide, anhydrous | Corrosive material | Corrosive | 173.244 | 173.245b | 25 pounds | 100 pounds | 1,2 | 1,2 | Keep dry. |
| | Aluminum dross, wet or hot. See Sec. 173.173 | | | | | | | | | |
| | Aluminum hydride | Flammable solid | Flammable solid and Dangerous when wet | None | 173.206 | Forbidden | 25 pounds | 1,2 | 5 | Segregation same as for flammable solid labeled Dangerous When Wet. |

LEGEND 36.—Hazardous Materials Table (CFR 49 Part 172) (Cont'd).

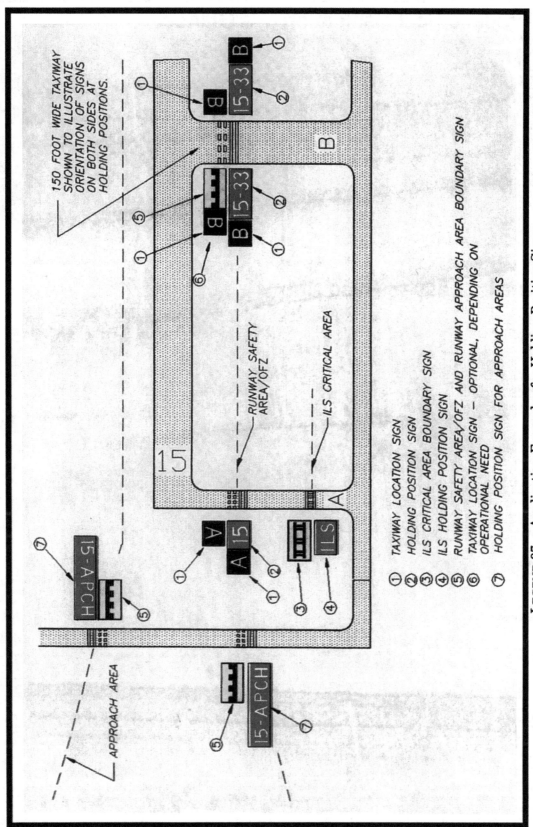

LEGEND 37.—Application Examples for Holding Position Signs.

① TAXIWAY LOCATION SIGN
② HOLDING POSITION SIGN
③ ILS CRITICAL AREA BOUNDARY SIGN
④ ILS HOLDING POSITION SIGN
⑤ RUNWAY SAFETY AREA/OFZ AND RUNWAY APPROACH AREA BOUNDARY SIGN
⑥ TAXIWAY LOCATION SIGN – OPTIONAL, DEPENDING ON OPERATIONAL NEED
⑦ HOLDING POSITION SIGN FOR APPROACH AREAS

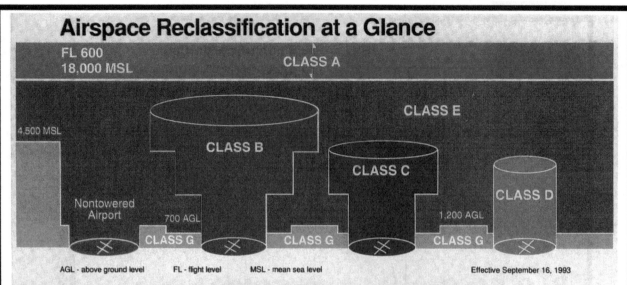

# Airspace Reclassification at a Glance

**FL 600 / 18,000 MSL** — CLASS A

4,500 MSL — CLASS B — CLASS E — CLASS C — CLASS D

Nontowered Airport — 700 AGL — CLASS G — CLASS G — 1,200 AGL — CLASS G

AGL - above ground level    FL - flight level    MSL - mean sea level    Effective September 16, 1993

# And an Easy-to-Read Chart

| Airspace Features | Class A | Class B | Class C | Class D | Class E | Class G |
|---|---|---|---|---|---|---|
| Former Airspace Equivalent | Positive Control Area (PCA) | Terminal Control Area (TCA) | Airport Radar Service Area (ARSA) | Airport Traffic Area (ATA) and Control Zone (CZ) | General Controlled Airspace | Uncontrolled Airspace |
| Operations Permitted | IFR | IFR and VFR | IFR and VFR | IFR and VFR | IFR and VFR | IFR and VFR |
| Entry Requirements | ATC clearance | ATC clearance | ATC clearance for IFR. All require radio contact. | ATC clearance for IFR. All require radio contact. | ATC clearance for IFR. All IFR require radio contact. | None |
| Minimum Pilot Qualifications | Instrument Rating | Private or student certificate | Student certificate | Student certificate | Student certificate | Student certificate |
| Two-way Radio Communications | Yes | Yes | Yes | Yes | Yes for IFR | No |
| VFR Minimum Visibility | N/A | 3 statute miles | 3 statute miles | 3 statute miles | [1]3 statute miles | [2]1 statute mile |
| VFR Minimum Distance from Clouds | N/A | Clear of clouds | 500' below, 1,000' above, and 2,000' horizontal | 500' below, 1,000' above, and 2,000' horizontal | [1]500' below, 1,000' above, and 2,000' horizontal | Clear of clouds |
| Aircraft Separation | All | All | IFR, SVFR, and runway operations | IFR, SVFR, and runway operations | IFR and SVFR | None |
| Conflict Resolution | N/A | N/A | Between IFR and VFR ops | No | No | No |
| Traffic Advisories | N/A | N/A | Yes | Workload permitting | Workload permitting | Workload permitting |
| Safety Advisories | Yes | Yes | Yes | Yes | Yes. | Yes |
| Differs from ICAO | No | [3]Yes | [3,4]Yes | [4]Yes for VFR | No | [5]Yes for VFR |
| Changes the Existing Rule | No | [6]Yes for VFR | No | [7,8,9]Yes | No | No |

[1] Different visibility minima and distance from cloud requirements exist for operations above 10,000 feet MSL

[2] Different visibility minima and distance from cloud requirements exist for night operations above 10,000 feet MSL, and operations below 1,200 feet AGL

[3] ICAO does not have speed restrictions in this class - U.S. will retain the 250 KIAS rule

[4] ICAO requires an ATC clearance for VFR

[5] ICAO requires 3 statute miles visibility

[6] Reduces the cloud clearance distance from standard to clear of clouds

[7] Generally, the upper limits of the Control Zone have been lowered from 14,500 MSL to 2,500 feet AGL

[8] Generally, the upper limits of the Airport Traffic Area has been lowered from 2,999 feet AGL to 2,500 feet AGL

[9] The requirement for two-way communications for Airport Traffic Areas has been retained

LEGEND 38.—Airspace Reclassification.

94062
# GENERAL INFO

## GENERAL INFORMATION

This publication includes Instrument Approach Procedures (IAPs), Standard Instrument Departures (SIDs), Standard Terminal Arrivals (STARs) and Profile Descent Procedures for use by both civil and military aviation and is issued every 56 days.

### STANDARD TERMINAL ARRIVAL AND STANDARD INSTRUMENT DEPARTURES

The use of the associated codified STAR/SID and transition identifiers are requested of users when filing flight plans via teletype and are required for users filing flight plans via computer interface. It must be noted that when filing a STAR/SID with a transition, the first three coded characters of the STAR and the last three coded characters of the SID are replaced by the transition code. Examples: ACTON SIX ARRIVAL, file (AQN.AQN6); ACTON SIX ARRIVAL EDNAS TRANSITION, file (EDNAS.AQN6). FREEHOLD THREE DEPARTURE, file (FREH3. RBV), FREEHOLD THREE DEPARTURE, ELWOOD CITY TRANSITION, file (FREH3.EWC).

### PROFILE DESCENT PROCEDURAL NOTE

A profile descent is an uninterrupted descent (except where level flight is required for speed adjustment, e.g., 250 knots at 10,000 feet MSL) from cruising altitude/level to interception of a glide slope or to a minimum altitude specified for the initial or intermediate approach segment of a non-precision instrument approach. The profile descent normally terminates at the approach gate or where the glide slope or other appropriate minimum altitude is intercepted.

Profile descent clearances are subject to traffic conditions and may be altered by ATC if necessary. Acceptance, by the pilot, of a profile descent clearance; i.e., "cleared for Runway 28 profile descent," requires the pilot to adhere to all depicted procedures on the profile descent chart.

After a profile descent has been issued and accepted:

(1) Any subsequent ATC revision of altitude or route cancels the remaining portion of the charted profile descent procedure. ATC will then assign necessary altitude, route, and speed clearances.

(2) Any subsequent revision of depicted speed restriction voids all charted speed restrictions. Charted route and altitude restrictions are not affected by revision to depicted speed restrictions. If the pilot cannot comply with charted route and/or altitude restrictions because of revised speed, he is expected to so advise ATC.

THE PROFILE DESCENT CLEARANCES DOES NOT CONSTITUTE CLEARANCE TO FLY AN INSTRUMENT APPROACH PROCEDURE (IAP). The last "maintain altitude" specified in the PROFILE DESCENT procedure constitutes that the last ATC assigned altitude and the pilot must maintain such altitude until he is cleared for an approach unless another altitude is assigned by ATC.

PILOTS SHOULD REVIEW RUNWAY PROFILE DESCENT CHARTS BEFORE FLIGHT INTO AIRPORTS WITH CHARTED PROCEDURES.

### MISCELLANEOUS

★  Indicates control tower or ATIS operates non-continuously.
#  Indicates control tower temporarily closed UFN.
Distances in nautical miles (except visibility in statute miles and Runway Visual Range in hundreds of feet). Runway Dimensions in feet. Elevations in feet. Mean Sea Level (MSL). Ceilings in feet above airport elevation. Radials/bearings/headings/courses are magnetic. Horizontal Datum: Unless otherwise noted on the chart, all coordinates are referenced to North American Datum 1983 (NAD 83), which for charting purposes is considered equivalent to World Geodetic System 1984 (WGS84).

LEGEND 39.—General Information on SIDs, STARs, and PROFILE DESCENTS.

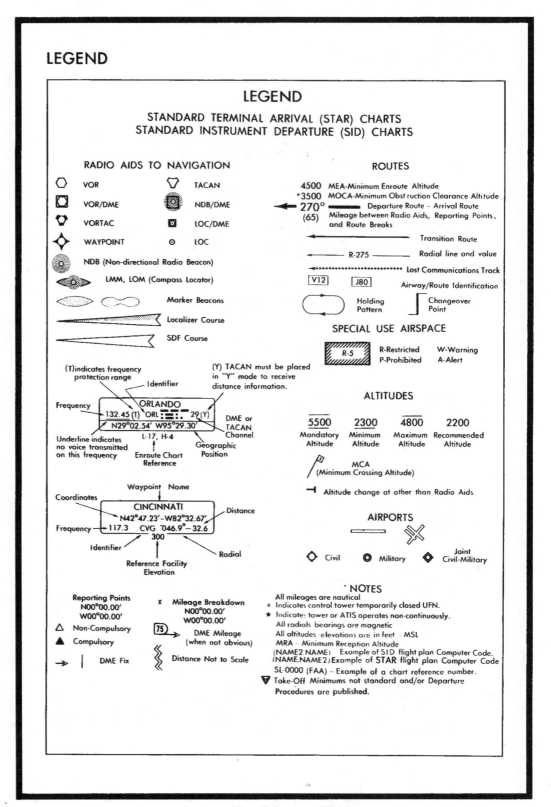

LEGEND 40.—SIDs and STARs.

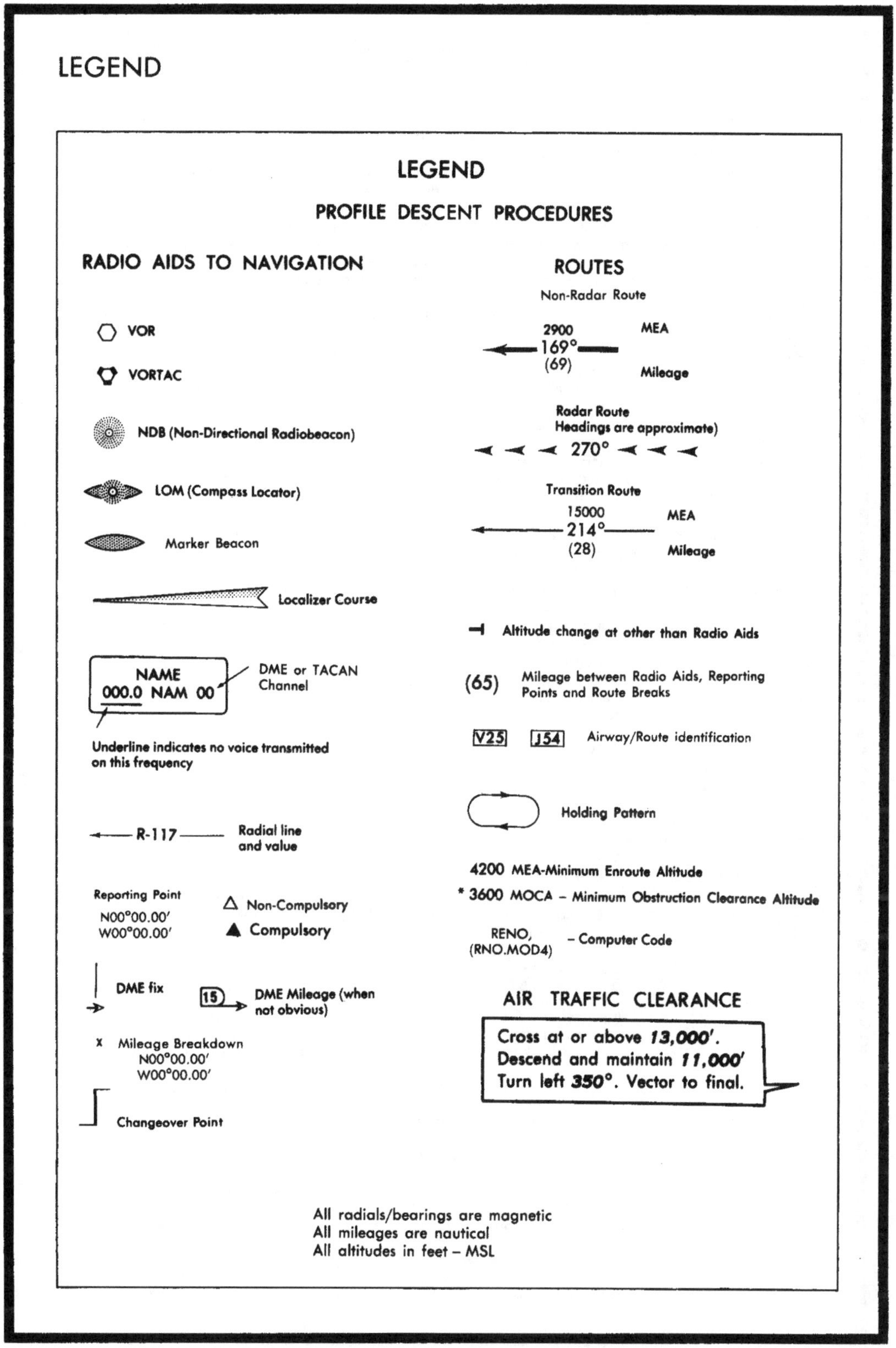

# LEGEND

## LEGEND

### PROFILE DESCENT PROCEDURES

#### RADIO AIDS TO NAVIGATION

⬡ VOR

⬠ VORTAC

⊙ NDB (Non-Directional Radiobeacon)

◈ LOM (Compass Locator)

◆ Marker Beacon

◁ Localizer Course

```
┌─────────────────┐
│     NAME        │  DME or TACAN
│  000.0 NAM 00   │  Channel
└─────────────────┘
```

Underline indicates no voice transmitted
on this frequency

◄── R-117 ── Radial line
and value

Reporting Point
N00°00.00'
W00°00.00'

△ Non-Compulsory
▲ Compulsory

DME fix

15 DME Mileage (when
not obvious)

x Mileage Breakdown
N00°00.00'
W00°00.00'

Changeover Point

#### ROUTES

Non-Radar Route

2900 ── MEA
◄── 169° ──
(69) ── Mileage

Radar Route
Headings are approximate)
◄ ◄ ◄ 270° ◄ ◄ ◄

Transition Route
15000 ── MEA
◄── 214° ──
(28) ── Mileage

⊣ Altitude change at other than Radio Aids

(65) Mileage between Radio Aids, Reporting
Points and Route Breaks

V25  J54  Airway/Route identification

⬭ Holding Pattern

4200 MEA-Minimum Enroute Altitude

* 3600 MOCA – Minimum Obstruction Clearance Altitude

RENO,
(RNO.MOD4) – Computer Code

#### AIR TRAFFIC CLEARANCE

Cross at or above **13,000'**.
Descend and maintain **11,000'**
Turn left **350°**. Vector to final.

All radials/bearings are magnetic
All mileages are nautical
All altitudes in feet – MSL

LEGEND 41.—Profile Descent Procedures.

332        TOWER ENROUTE CONTROL
## (TEC)

Within the national airspace system it is possible for a pilot to fly IFR from one point to another without leaving approach control airspace. This is referred to as "tower enroute" which allows flight beneath the enroute structure. The tower enroute concept has been expanded (where practical) by reallocating airspace vertically/geographically to allow flight planning between city pairs while remaining within approach control airspace. Pilots are encouraged to solicit tower enroute information from FSS's and to use the route descriptions provided in this directory when filing flight plans. Other airways which appear to be more direct between two points may take the aircraft out of approach control airspace thereby resulting in additional delays or other complications. All published TEC routes are designed to avoid enroute airspace and the majority are within radar coverage. Additional routes and other changes will appear in forthcoming editions as necessary. The acronym "TEC" should be included in the remarks section of the flight plan. This will advise ATC that the pilot intends to remain within approach control airspace for the entire flight. The following items should be noted before using the graphics and route descriptions:

    1. The graphic is not to be used for navigation nor detailed flight planning. Not all city pairs are depicted. It is intended to show general geographic areas connected by tower enroute control. Pilots should refer to route descriptions for specific flight planning.

    2. The route description contains four columns of information; i.e., the approach control area (listed alphabetically) within which the departure airport is located (check appropriate flight information publications), the specific route (airway, radial, etc.), the highest altitude allowed for the route, and the destination airport (listed alphabetically).

    3. The word "DIRECT" will appear as the route when radar vectors will be used or no airway exists. Also, this indicates that a Standard Instrument Departure (SID) or Standard Terminal Arrival Route (STAR) may be applied by ATC.

    4. When a NAVAID or intersection identifier appears with no airway immediately preceding or following the identifier, the routing is understood to be DIRECT to or from that point unless otherwise cleared by ATC.

    5. Routes beginning or ending with an airway indicate that the airway essentially overflies the airport or radar vectors will be applied.

    6. Where more than one route is listed to the same destination, the pilot may select which route is desired. Unless otherwise stated, all routes may be flown in either direction.

    7. Routes are effective only during each respective terminal facility's normal operating hours. Pilots are cautioned to check NOTAMS to ensure appropriate terminal facilities will be operating for the planned flight time.

    8. All identifiers used for NAVAIDS, airports, and intersections are official identifiers.

    9. Altitudes are listed in thousands of feet. ATC may require altitude changes to maintain flight within approach control airspace. ATC will provide radar monitoring and, if necessary, course guidance if the highest altitude assigned by ATC is below the Minimum Enroute Altitude (MEA).

    10. Although all airports are not listed under the destination column, IFR flight may be planned to satellite airports in proximity to major airports via the same routing.

    11. Flight plans should be filed with a Flight Service Station (FSS).

### TOWER ENROUTE CONTROL CITY PAIRS

(1) Single Engine only.
(2) Props less than 210 KT IAS.
(3) Props less than 250 KT IAS.
(4) Jets and Props greater than 210 KT IAS.
Boston—NO SATS = BED/LWM/BVY/AYE/FIT/B09/6B6/2B2
           SO SATS = BOS/OWD/NZW/1B9/3B2

| Approach Control Area (Including Satellites) | Route | Highest Altitude | Destination |
|---|---|---|---|
| Albany | V14 V428 V29 | 6000 | Binghamton |
| | V130 | 7000 | Bradley |
| | V14 | 10,000 | Buffalo |
| | V14 V428 | 8000 | Elmira |
| | V14 V428 | 8000 | Ithaca |
| | V2 | 10,000 | Rochester |
| | V14 BEEPS | 10,000 | Rochester |
| | V2 | 10,000 | Utica/Rome |
| Allentown | FJC V149 LHY | 8000 | Albany |
| | ETX LHY | 8000 | Albany |
| | FJC ARD V276 DIXIE V229 | 5000 (only) | Atlantic City |
| | V93 LRP | 8000 | Baltimore |
| | ETX V162 DUMMR V93 LRP | 6000 | Baltimore |
| | V39 LRP | 8000 (only) | Baltimore |
| | FJC BWZ | 5000 (only) | Caldwell, NJ |
| | (2) ETX V30 SBJ | 5000 (only) | Farmingdale, NY |
| | (2) FJC V6 SBJ | 5000 (only) | Farmingdale, NY |
| | ETX V162 HAR | 8000 | Harrisburg |
| | ETX ETX004 WEISS | 4000 (only) | Hazleton |
| | ETX V39 | 4000 | Lancaster |
| | (2) ETX V30 SBJ | 5000 (only) | Newark |

LEGEND 42.—Tower Enroute Control (NE).

## TOWER ENROUTE CONTROL 343

| Approach Control Area (Including Satellites) | Route | Highest Altitude | Destination |
|---|---|---|---|
| New York /Kennedy | SAX V249 SBJ V30 ETX (Non jet/Non turboprop) | 8000 | Allentown |
| | DIXIE V229 ACY (Props only) | 6000 | Atlantic City |
| | DIXIE V1 HOWIE (Jets only) | 8000 | Atlantic City |
| | DIXIE V1 V308 OTT (Props only) | 6000 | Andrews AFB |
| | DIXIE V16 ENO V268 SWANN (Props only) | 6000 | Baltimore |
| | COL | 2000 | Belmar |
| | BDR MAD V475 V188 TMU | 9000 | Block Island |
| | BDR V229 HFD V3 WOONS | 9000 | Boston |
| | BDR V229 HFD HFD053 DREEM | 9000 | Boston (North) |
| | BDR BDR014 JUDDS V419 BRISS | 9000 | Bradley |
| | BDR BDR014 JUDDS V419 BRISS (Jets only) | 10000 | Bradley |
| | BDR | 3000 | Bridgeport |
| | SAX V249 SBJ V30 ETX V162 HAR (Non jet/Non turboprop) | 8000 | Capital City |
| | DIXIE V1 LEEAH V268 BAL BAL291 KROLL AML (Non-pressurized aircraft only) | 6000 | Dulles |
| | BDR MAD MAD126 MONDI | 9000 | Groton |
| | R/V CCC 232 CCC HTO | 3000 | Hampton |
| | BDR V229 HFD | 9000 | Hartford |
| | BDR V229 HFD V167 PVD V151 GAILS | 9000 | Hyannis |
| | R/V ILS 6 LOC (Text Info) | 3000 | Islip |
| | R/V CCC232 CCC | 3000 | Islip |
| | Direct | 2000 | LaGuardia |
| | SAX V249 SBJ V30 ETX V162 V93 LRP (Props only) | 8000 | Lancaster |
| | DIXIE V16 CYN | 6000 | McGuire |
| | BDR MAD V475 V188 TMU V374 MVY | 9000 | Martha's Vineyard |
| | BDR MAD | 3000 | Meriden Markham |
| | DIXIE V16 VCN (Props only) | 6000 | Millville |
| | BDR MAD V475 V188 TMU V374 MVY | 9000 | Nantucket |
| | COL V232 SBJ | 3000 | Newark |
| | BDR MAD V475 V188 TMU V374 MINNK | 9000 | New Bedford |
| | DIXIE V1 (Props only) | 6000 | Norfolk |
| | DIXIE V276 ARD | 4000 | N. Philadelphia |
| | DIXIE V16 CYN V312 OOD (Props only) | 6000 | Philadelphia |
| | DIXIE V16 CYN V312 OOD (Jets only) | 8000 | Philadelphia |
| | BDR MAD V475 V188 TMU (210 kts +) | 9000 | Providence |
| | BDR MAD V475 V188 TMU | 9000 | Quonset |
| | SAX V249 SBJ V30 ETX V39 FLOAT (Non jet/Non turboprop only) | 8000 | Reading |
| | DIXIE V16 (Props only) | 6000 | Richmond |
| | DIXIE V1 (Props only) | 6000 | Salisbury |
| | DIXIE V1 V308 OTT (Props only) | 6000 | Washington |
| | DPK V483 CMK | 2000 | Westchester Co |
| | BDR MAD V475 V188 TMU | 9000 | Westerly |
| | DIXIE V229 PANZE V44 SIE (Props only) | 6000 | Wildwood |
| | DIXIE V1 HOWIE (Jets only) | 8000 | Wildwood |
| | BDR MAD V1 GRAYM | 9000 | Worcester |
| New York/ LaGuardia | SAX V249 SBJ V30 ETX | 8000 | Allentown |
| | DIXIE V229 ACY (Props only) | 6000 | Atlantic City |
| | DIXIE V1 HOWIE (Jets only) | 8000 | Atlantic City |
| | ABBYS V403 GLOMO V408 V93 BAL (Props only) | 7000 | Andrews AFB |
| | ABBYS V403 BELAY V378 BAL (Props only) | 7000 | Baltimore |
| | JFK COL | 6000 | Belmar |
| | BDR MAD V475 V188 TMU | 9000 | Block Island |
| | BDR V229 HFD V3 WOONS | 9000 | Boston |
| | BDR V229 HFD HFD053 DREEM | 9000 | Boston (North) |
| | BDR BDR014 JUDDS V419 BRISS (Props only) | 9000 | Bradley |
| | BDR BDR014 JUDDS V419 BRISS (Jets only) | 10000 | Bradley |
| | BDR 248 CCC285 PUGGS V229 BDR | 5000 | Bridgeport |
| | R/V BDR248 BDR. . .(Helicopter Route) | 5000 | Bridgeport (Points NE) |
| | SAX V249 SBJ V30 ETX V162 HAR | 8000 | Capital City |
| | SAX V249 SBJ V30 ETX V162 V93 V143 ROBRT AML (Props only) | 8000 | Dulles |

LEGEND 42A—Tower Enroute Control Continued.

# TOWER ENROUTE CONTROL

| Approach Control Area (Including Satellites) | | Route | Highest Altitude | Destination |
|---|---|---|---|---|
| | .......... | ABBYS V403 GLOMO V408 V93 BAL (Props only) | 7000 | Washington |
| | .......... | DIXIE V229 PANZE V44 SIE (Props only) | 6000 | Wildwood |
| | .......... | DIXIE V1 HOWIE (Jets only) | 8000 | Wildwood |
| | .......... | CMK V3 HFD V1 GRAYM | 9000 | Worcester |
| Norfolk | .......... | CCV CCV345 PXT175 PXT | 5000 | Patuxent River |
| | .......... | HPW V260 RIC (West-bound only) | 9000 | Richmond |
| | .......... | CCV V1 SBY | 5000 | Salisbury |
| | .......... | CCV V139 SWL (Northeast-bound only) | 5000 | Snow Hill |
| | .......... | HCM HCM330 SVILL | 7000 | Washington |
| Patuxent | .......... | SWL V139 | 5000 | Atlantic City |
| | .......... | PXT V16 V44 | 5000 | Atlantic City |
| | .......... | SBY V1 V44 | 5000 | Atlantic City |
| | .......... | SBY332 BAL130 | 4000 | Baltimore |
| | .......... | PXT V93 | 5000 | Baltimore |
| | .......... | SBY V29 ENO | 5000 | Dover AFB |
| | .......... | PXT V16 ENO | 5000 | Dover AFB |
| | .......... | PXT V16 | 5000 | Dover AFB |
| | .......... | SBY VI ATR | 5000 | Dover AFB |
| | .......... | PXT V213 V286 FLUKY | 6000 | Dulles |
| | .......... | COLIN V33 HCM | 6000 | Newport News |
| | .......... | SBY V1 CCV | 6000 | Norfolk |
| | .......... | SWL V139 CCV | 6000 | Norfolk |
| | .......... | WHINO V33 V286 STEIN | 5000 | Norfolk |
| | .......... | PXT V213 ENO V29 DQO | 5000 | Philadelphia |
| | .......... | SBY V29 DQO | 5000 | Philadelphia |
| | .......... | PXT V16 | 6000 | Richmond |
| | .......... | SBY V1 JAMIE HCM | 6000 | Richmond |
| | .......... | COLIN V33 HCM | 6000 | Richmond |
| | .......... | PXT V31 OTT (No Overflight of D.C. Area) | 4000 | Washington |
| | .......... | SBY CHURK OTT (No Overflight of D.C. Area) | 4000 | Washington |
| Pease | .......... | RAYMY LWM | 8000 | Boston |
| | .......... | EXALT V139 V141 GAILS | 10000 | Hyannis |
| | .......... | V106 GDM V14 ORW V16 CCC | 10000 | Islip |
| | .......... | V106 GDM V14 ORW V16 DPK | 10000 | Kennedy |
| | .......... | EXALT V139 BURDY | 10000 | Providence |
| Philadelphia | .......... | RV FJC180 FJC | 4000 | Allentown |
| | .......... | OOD VCN V184 ACY | 3000 | Atlantic City |
| | .......... | MXE V378 BAL | 6000 | Baltimore |
| | .......... | DQO V166 V378 BAL | 6000 | Baltimore |
| | .......... | OOD V157 ENO | 4000 | Dover AFB |
| | .......... | DQO V29 ENO | 4000 | Dover AFB |
| | .......... | MXE V408 ROBRT AML | 8000 | Dulles |
| | .......... | MXE V184 MXE283027 V469 HAR | 6000 | Harrisburg |
| | .......... | PNE PNE090 ARD126 V16 DIXIE (Direct) (Single Engine only) | 5000 | Kennedy |
| | .......... | PNE PNE090 ARD126 V16 V276 ZIGGI (Direct) (No Single Engine) | 5000 | Kennedy |
| | .......... | RBV V123 PROUD | 7000 | LaGuardia |
| | .......... | MXE MXE295 HABER LRP137 LRP | 4000 | Lancaster |
| | .......... | ARD V214 METRO (Non Turbojets only) | 5000 | Newark |
| | .......... | RBV V213 WARRD (Turbojets only) | 7000 | Newark |
| | .......... | MXE MXE334 HUMEL | 4000 | Reading |
| | .......... | ARD V214 METRO | 5000 | Teterboro |
| | .......... | MXE V408 VINNY V93 BAL | 8000 | Washington |
| | .......... | DQO V166 V93 BAL | 8000 | Washington |
| | .......... | RV FJC180 FJC BWZ SAX V39 BREZY | 5000 | Westchester Co. |
| | .......... | RV FJC180 FJC V149 RITTY | 5000 | Wilkes Barre/Scranton |
| Pittsburgh | .......... | BSV (Westbound only) | 8000 | Akron-Canton |
| | .......... | V37 (Southbound only) | 8000 | Clarksburg |
| | .......... | EWC V37 (Northbound only) | 8000 | Erie |

LEGEND 42B.—Tower Enroute Control Continued.

# TOWER ENROUTE CONTROL

## (TEC)

Within the national airspace system it is possible for a pilot to fly IFR from one point to another without leaving approach control airspace. This is referred to as "Tower Enroute" which allows flight beneath the enroute structure. The tower enroute concept has been expanded (where practical) by reallocating airspace vertically/geographically to allow flight planning between city pairs while remaining within approach control airspace. Pilots are encouraged to use the TEC route descriptions provided in the Southwest U.S. Airport/Facility Directory when filing flight plans. Other airways which appear to be more direct between two points may take the aircraft out of approach control airspace thereby resulting in additional delays or other complications. All published TEC routes are designed to avoid enroute airspace and the majority are within radar coverage. The following items should be noted before using the graphics and route descriptions.

1. The graphic is not to be used for navigation nor detailed flight planning. Not all city pairs are depicted. It is intended to show geographic areas connected by tower enroute control. Pilots should refer to route descriptions for specific flight planning.

2. The route description contains four colums of information after approach control area listed in the heading, where the departure airport is located; i.e., the airport/airports of intended landing using FAA three letter/letter-two number identifiers, the coded route number (this should be used when filing the flight plan and will be used by ATC in lieu of reading out the full route description), the specific route (airway, radial, etc.), the altitude allowed for type of aircraft and the routes.

3. The word "DIRECT" will appear as the route when radar vectors will be used or no airway exists. Also this indicates that a Standard Instrument Departure (SID) or Standard Terminal Arrival (STAR) may be applied by ATC.

4. When a NAVAID or intersection identifier appears with no airway immediately preceding or following the identifier, the routing is understood to be DIRECT to or from that point unless otherwise cleared by ATC or radials are listed (See item 5).

5. Routes beginning and ending with an airway indicate that the airway essentially overflies the airport or radar vectors will be applied.

6. Where more than one route is listed to the same destination, ensure you file correct route for type of aircraft which are denoted after the route in the altitude column using J,M,P, or Q. These are listed after item 10 under Aircraft Classification.

7. Although all airports are not listed under the destination column, IFR flight may be planned to satellite airports in the proximity to major airports via the same routing.

8. Los Angeles International Airport (LAX) and four other airports (ONT–SAN–TOA–SNA) have two options due to winds and these affect the traffic flows and runways in use. To indicate the difference the following symbols are used after the airport: Runway Number, W for west indicating normal conditions, E for East and N for North indicating other than normal operation. If nothing follows the airport use this route on either West, East or North plan. Other destinations have different arrivals due to LAX being East and they have the notation "(LAXE)." Torrance Airport is also unique in that the airport is split between Los Angeles and Coast TRACON, for Runway 11 departures use Coast TRACON routings and for Runway 29 departures use LAX TRACON routings.

9. When filing flight plans, the coded route identifier i.e. SANJ2, VTUJ4, POMJ3 may be used in lieu of the route of flight.

10. Aircraft types i.e. J, M, P, and Q are listed at the beginning of the altitude and should be used with the route of flight filed. (See Aircraft Classification below). The altitudes shown are to be used for the route. This allows for separation of various arrival routes, departure routes, and overflights to, from, and over all airports in the Southern California area.

## LEGENDS

### AIRCRAFT CLASSIFICATION

(J) = Jet powered
(M) = Turbo Props/Special (cruise speed 190 knots or greater)
(P) = Non-jet (cruise speed 190 knots or greater)
(Q) = Non-jet (cruise speed 189 knots or less)

LEGEND 43.—Tower Enroute Control (SW).

**236**  TOWER ENROUTE CONTROL

**BURBANK TRACON**
**FROM:** BUR VNY WHP

| TO: | ROUTE ID | ROUTE | ALTITUDE |
|---|---|---|---|
| FUL LGB SLI TOA (RWY 29) | BURJ1 | V186 V394 SLI | MPQ50 |
| LAX | BURJ2 | V186 PURMS | JMPQ40 |
| LAX (LAXE) | BURJ3 | VNY SMO | JM50PQ40 |
| TOA (RWY 11) | BURJ4 | VNY VNY095 DARTS SMO | JMPQ40 |
| SMO | BURJ5 | V186 DARTS | JMPQ30 |
| CCB CNO EMT HMT L12 L65 L66 L67 F70 ONT POC RAL RIR RIV SBD | BURJ6 | V186 PDZ | JM70PQ50 |
| CRQ NFG NKX L39 L32 | BURJ7 | V186 V363 V23 OCN | JM70PQ50 |
| MYF NRS NZY SAN SDM SEE | BURJ8 | V186 V363 V23 MZB | PQ50 |
| MYF NRS NZY SAN SDM SEE | BURJ9 | V186 POM164 V208 MZB320 MZB | JM70 |
| OXR CMA | BURJ10 | VNY | JMPQ40 |
| SBA | BURJ11 | FIM V186 V27 KWANG | JMPQ60 |
| SNA | BURJ12 | V186 V363 V8 SLI | JMPQ50 |
| SAN (SANE) | BURJ13 | V186 V363 V23 V165 SARGS | PQ50 |
| SAN (SANE) | BURJ14 | V186 POM164 V25 V165 SARGS | JM70 |
| NZJ NTK | BURJ15 | V186 V363 V23 DAMPS | JM70PQ50 |
| AVX | BURJ16 | V186 V363 KRAUZ SXC | JM70PQ50 |
| HHR | BURJ17 | V186 ELMOO | JMPQ40 |
| LGB | BURJ18 | V186 V363 V23 SLI | J70 |

**COAST TRACON**
**FROM:** FUL LGB SLI SNA TOA (RWY 11) NTK NZJ

| TO: | ROUTE ID | ROUTE | ALTITUDE |
|---|---|---|---|
| BUR VNY WHP | CSTJ1 | SLI V23 LAX LAX316 SILEX | JM60PQ40 |
| BUR VNY WHP (LAXE) | CSTJ2 | SLI SLI333 V186 VNY | JM50PQ40 |
| CMA OXR (LAXE) | CSTJ3 | SLI SLI333 V186 FIM | JM50PQ40 |
| LAX | CSTJ4 | SLI | JM70PQ40 |
| LAX (LAXE) | CSTJ5 | SLI V8 TANDY | JM50PQ40 |
| SMO | CSTJ6 | SLI V23 LAX LAX046 ELMOO | JM70PQ40 |
| SMO (LAXE) | CSTJ7 | SLI SLI333 V186 DARTS | JM50PQ40 |
| CCB EMT POC CNO HMT L12 L65 L66 L67 F70 ONT RAL RIR RIV SBD | CSTJ8 | SLI V8 V363 POM | JMPQ50 |
| CNO HMT L12 L65 L66 L67 F70 ONT RAL RIR RIV SBD | CSTJ9 | SLI V8 PDZ (SNA RWY 19 ONLY) | JM60 |
| CRQ L39 NFG NKX L32 | CSTJ10 | SLI V8 PDZ | JMPQ50 |
| CRQ L39 NFG NKX L32 | CSTJ12 | V25 V208 OCN | JM70 |
| MYF NRS NZY SAN SDM SEE | CSTJ14 | V25 V208 MZB320 MZB | J110M90 |
| OXR CMA | CSTJ15 | SLI V23 LAX VNY | M50PQ40 |
| OXR CMA | CSTJ16 | SXC SXC295 VTU160 VTU | J80 |
| SBA | CSTJ17 | SLI V23 LAX VTU KWANG | PQ40 |
| SBA (LAXE) | CSTJ18 | SLI SLI333 V186 V27 KWANG | M50PQ40 |
| SBA | CSTJ19 | SXC SXC295 VTU160 VTU KWANG | JM80 |
| SAN (SANE) | CSTJ21 | V25 V165 SARGS | J110M90 |
| HHR | CSTJ26 | SLI SLI340 WELLZ LOC | JM70PQ40 |

**FROM:** SNA NTK NZJ and when SNAN FUL LGB SLI TOA RWY 11

| TO: | ROUTE ID | ROUTE | ALTITUDE |
|---|---|---|---|
| CRQ L39 NFG NKX L32 | CSTJ11 | V23 OCN | PQ50 |
| MYF NRS NZY SAN SDM SEE | CSTJ13 | V23 MZB | PQ50 |
| SAN (SANE) | CSTJ20 | V23 V165 SARGS | PQ50 |

**FROM:** AVX (DEPARTURES ONLY)

| TO: | ROUTE ID | ROUTE | ALTITUDE |
|---|---|---|---|
| CRQ L39 NFG NKX L32 | CSTJ22 | SXC V208 OCN | JMPQ50 |
| MYF NRS NZY SAN SDM SEE | CSTJ23 | SXC V208 MZB320 MZB | J110M90 |
| MYF NRS NZY SAN SDM SEE (SANE ) | CSTJ24 | SXC V208 OCN V165 SARGS | PQ50 |
| MYF NRS NZY SAN SDM SEE | CSTJ25 | SXC V208 OCN V23 MZB | PQ50 |

LEGEND 43A.—Tower Enroute Control Continued.

# APPENDIX 2

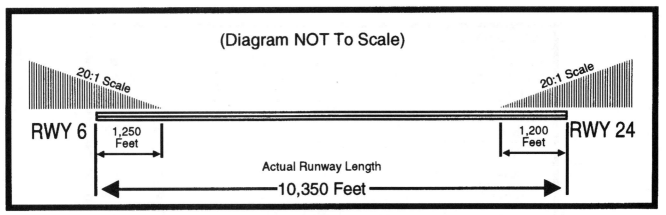

FIGURE 1.—Runway Diagram.

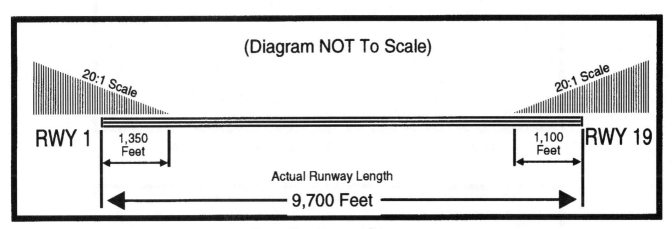

FIGURE 2.—Runway Diagram.

| LOADING CONDITIONS | BE-1 | BE-2 | BE-3 | BE-4 | BE-5 |
|---|---|---|---|---|---|
| CREW | 360 | 340 | 350 | 340 | 360 |
| PASSENGERS ROW 1 | 350 | 300 | 120 | - | - |
| ROW 2 | 260 | 250 | 340 | 370 | - |
| ROW 3 | 200 | 190 | 350 | 400 | 170 |
| ROW 4 | 340 | 170 | 300 | 290 | 200 |
| ROW 5 | 120 | 190 | 170 | 200 | 290 |
| ROW 6 | 400 | 340 | - | 170 | 400 |
| ROW 7 | 120 | 190 | - | 210 | 370 |
| ROW 8 | 250 | - | - | 190 | 340 |
| ROW 9 | - | - | - | 420 | 430 |
| BAGGAGE NOSE | 60 | - | 80 | - | 100 |
| FWD CABIN | 250 | 100 | 120 | - | 200 |
| AFT (FWD SEC) | 500 | 200 | 250 | 800 | - |
| AFT (AFT SEC) | - | 600 | 500 | - | - |
| FUEL GAL | 370 | 390 | 400 | 290 | 340 |
| TYPE | JET B | JET A | JET B | JET A | JET B |
| TEMP | +5 ˚C | +15 ˚C | -15 ˚C | +10 ˚C | +25 ˚C |

FIGURE 3.—Beech 1900 – Loading Passenger Configuration.

| LOADING CONDITIONS | BE-6 | BE-7 | BE-8 | BE-9 | BE-10 |
|---|---|---|---|---|---|
| CREW | 360 | 340 | 350 | 370 | 420 |
| CARGO SECTION A | 500 | - | 600 | 600 | 350 |
| B | 500 | 400 | 200 | 600 | 450 |
| C | 550 | 450 | 400 | 600 | 450 |
| D | 550 | 600 | 400 | 600 | 550 |
| E | 600 | 600 | 200 | 550 | 550 |
| F | 600 | 600 | 200 | 350 | 600 |
| G | 450 | 500 | 200 | 250 | 600 |
| H | - | - | 200 | 250 | - |
| J | 350 | - | 300 | 150 | - |
| K | - | - | 250 | 200 | - |
| L | - | - | 100 | 100 | - |
| FUEL GAL | 340 | 370 | 390 | 290 | 400 |
| TYPE | JET B | JET B | JET A | JET A | JET B |
| TEMP | +25 ˚C | +5 ˚C | +15 ˚C | +10 ˚C | -15 ˚C |
| BASIC OPERATING WEIGHT - 9,005 POUNDS, 25,934 MOM/100 | | | | | |

FIGURE 4.—Beech 1900 – Loading Cargo Configuration.

| OPERATING CONDITIONS | BE-11 | BE-12 | BE-13 | BE-14 | BE-15 |
|---|---|---|---|---|---|
| BASIC EMPTY WT | | | | | |
|    WEIGHT | 9,225 | 9,100 | 9,000 | 8,910 | 9,150 |
|    MOM/100 | 25,820 | 24,990 | 24,710 | 24,570 | 25,240 |
| CREW WEIGHT | 340 | 380 | 360 | 400 | 370 |
| PASS AND BAG | | | | | |
|    WEIGHT | 4,200 | 4,530 | 4,630 | 4,690 | 4,500 |
|    MOM/100 | 15,025 | 16,480 | 16,743 | 13,724 | 13,561 |
| FUEL (6.8 LB/GAL) | | | | | |
|    RAMP LOAD-GAL | 360 | 320 | 340 | 310 | 410 |
|    USED START AND TAXI | 20 | 20 | 10 | 20 | 30 |
|    REMAIN AT LDG | 100 | 160 | 140 | 100 | 120 |

FIGURE 5.—Beech 1900 – Loading Limitations.

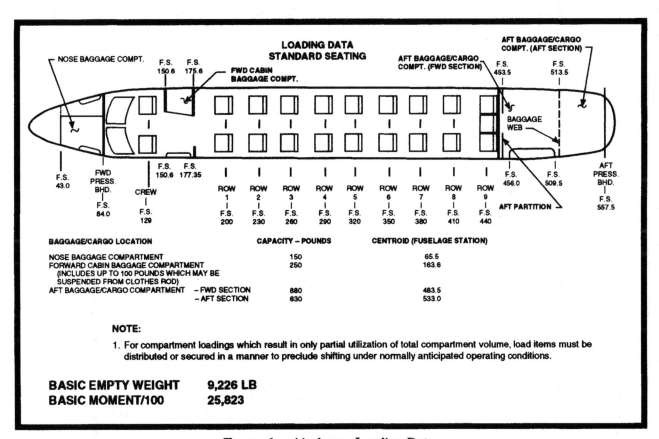

FIGURE 6.—Airplane – Loading Data.

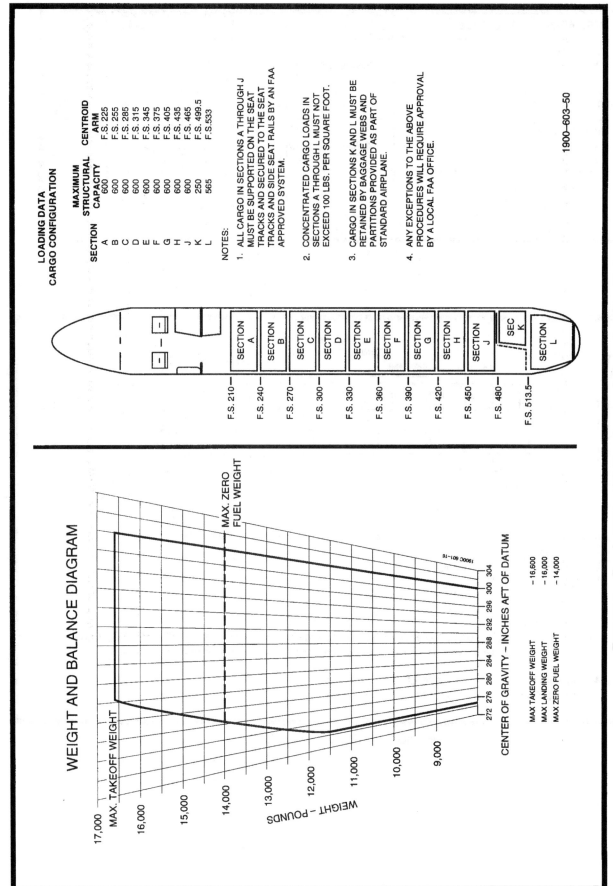

FIGURE 7.—Beech 1900 – CG Envelope and Cargo Loading Data.

4

# USEFUL LOAD WEIGHTS AND MOMENTS

## BAGGAGE

| WEIGHT | NOSE BAGGAGE COMPART-MENT F.S. 65.5 | FORWARD CABIN BAGGAGE COMPART-MENT F.S. 163.6 | AFT BAGGAGE/ CARGO COMPART-MENT (FORWARD SECTION) F.S. 483.5 | AFT BAGGAGE/ CARGO COMPART-MENT (AFT SECTION) F.S. 533.0 |
|---|---|---|---|---|
| | | MOMENT/100 | | |
| 10 | 7 | 16 | 48 | 53 |
| 20 | 13 | 33 | 97 | 107 |
| 30 | 20 | 49 | 145 | 160 |
| 40 | 26 | 65 | 193 | 213 |
| 50 | 33 | 82 | 242 | 266 |
| 60 | 39 | 98 | 290 | 320 |
| 70 | 46 | 115 | 338 | 373 |
| 80 | 52 | 131 | 387 | 426 |
| 90 | 59 | 147 | 435 | 480 |
| 100 | 66 | 164 | 484 | 533 |
| 150 | 98 | 245 | 725 | 800 |
| 200 | | 327 | 967 | 1066 |
| 250 | | 409 | 1209 | 1332 |
| 300 | | | 1450 | 1599 |
| 350 | | | 1692 | 1866 |
| 400 | | | 1934 | 2132 |
| 450 | | | 2176 | 2398 |
| 500 | | | 2418 | 2665 |
| 550 | | | 2659 | 2932 |
| 600 | | | 2901 | 3198 |
| 630 | | | 3046 | 3358 |
| 650 | | | 3143 | |
| 700 | | | 3384 | |
| 750 | | | 3626 | |
| 800 | | | 3868 | |
| 850 | | | 4110 | |
| 880 | | | 4255 | |

FIGURE 8.—Airplane – Weights and Moments – Baggage.

## USEFUL LOAD WEIGHTS AND MOMENTS

## OCCUPANTS

| WEIGHT | CREW F.S. 129 | CABIN SEATS | | | | | | | | |
|---|---|---|---|---|---|---|---|---|---|---|
| | | F.S. 200 | F.S. 230 | F.S. 260 | F.S. 290 | F.S. 320 | F.S. 350 | F.S. 380 | F.S. 410 | F.S. 440 |
| | MOMENT/100 | | | | | | | | | |
| 80 | 103 | 160 | 184 | 208 | 232 | 256 | 280 | 304 | 328 | 352 |
| 90 | 116 | 180 | 207 | 234 | 261 | 288 | 315 | 342 | 369 | 396 |
| 100 | 129 | 200 | 230 | 260 | 290 | 320 | 350 | 380 | 410 | 440 |
| 110 | 142 | 220 | 253 | 286 | 319 | 352 | 385 | 418 | 451 | 484 |
| 120 | 155 | 240 | 276 | 312 | 348 | 384 | 420 | 456 | 492 | 528 |
| 130 | 168 | 260 | 299 | 338 | 377 | 416 | 455 | 494 | 533 | 572 |
| 140 | 181 | 280 | 322 | 364 | 406 | 448 | 490 | 532 | 574 | 616 |
| 150 | 194 | 300 | 345 | 390 | 435 | 480 | 525 | 570 | 615 | 660 |
| 160 | 206 | 320 | 368 | 416 | 464 | 512 | 560 | 608 | 656 | 704 |
| 170 | 219 | 340 | 391 | 442 | 493 | 544 | 595 | 646 | 697 | 748 |
| 180 | 232 | 360 | 414 | 468 | 522 | 576 | 630 | 684 | 738 | 792 |
| 190 | 245 | 380 | 437 | 494 | 551 | 608 | 665 | 722 | 779 | 836 |
| 200 | 258 | 400 | 460 | 520 | 580 | 640 | 700 | 760 | 820 | 880 |
| 210 | 271 | 420 | 483 | 546 | 609 | 672 | 735 | 798 | 861 | 924 |
| 220 | 284 | 440 | 506 | 572 | 638 | 704 | 770 | 836 | 902 | 968 |
| 230 | 297 | 460 | 529 | 598 | 667 | 736 | 805 | 874 | 943 | 1012 |
| 240 | 310 | 480 | 552 | 624 | 696 | 768 | 840 | 912 | 984 | 1056 |
| 250 | 323 | 500 | 575 | 650 | 725 | 800 | 875 | 950 | 1025 | 1100 |

Note: Weights reflected in above table represent weight per seat.

FIGURE 9.—Beech 1900 – Weights and Moments – Occupants.

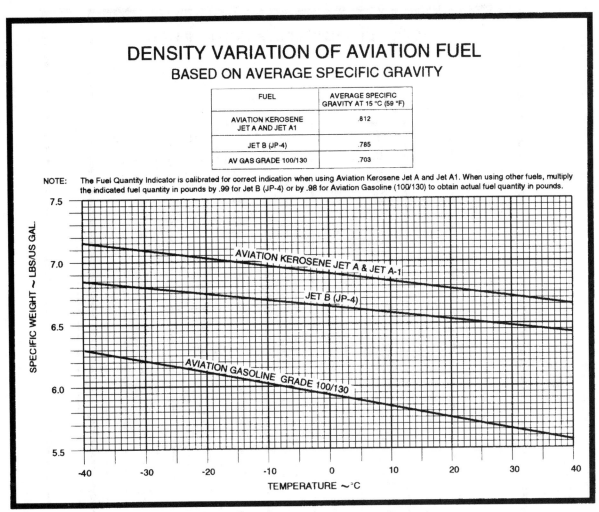

FIGURE 10.—Density Variation of Aviation Fuel.

## USEFUL LOAD WEIGHTS AND MOMENTS

### USABLE FUEL

| GALLONS | 6.5 LB/GAL | | 6.6 LB/GAL | | 6.7 LB/GAL | | 6.8 LB/GAL | |
|---|---|---|---|---|---|---|---|---|
| | WEIGHT | MOMENT 100 | WEIGHT | MOMENT 100 | WEIGHT | MOMENT 100 | WEIGHT | MOMENT 100 |
| 10 | 65 | 197 | 66 | 200 | 67 | 203 | 68 | 206 |
| 20 | 130 | 394 | 132 | 401 | 134 | 407 | 136 | 413 |
| 30 | 195 | 592 | 198 | 601 | 201 | 610 | 204 | 619 |
| 40 | 260 | 789 | 264 | 802 | 268 | 814 | 272 | 826 |
| 50 | 325 | 987 | 330 | 1002 | 335 | 1018 | 340 | 1033 |
| 60 | 390 | 1185 | 396 | 1203 | 402 | 1222 | 408 | 1240 |
| 70 | 455 | 1383 | 462 | 1404 | 469 | 1426 | 476 | 1447 |
| 80 | 520 | 1581 | 528 | 1605 | 536 | 1630 | 544 | 1654 |
| 90 | 585 | 1779 | 594 | 1806 | 603 | 1834 | 612 | 1861 |
| 100 | 650 | 1977 | 660 | 2007 | 670 | 2038 | 680 | 2068 |
| 110 | 715 | 2175 | 726 | 2208 | 737 | 2242 | 748 | 2275 |
| 120 | 780 | 2372 | 792 | 2409 | 804 | 2445 | 816 | 2482 |
| 130 | 845 | 2569 | 858 | 2608 | 871 | 2648 | 884 | 2687 |
| 140 | 910 | 2765 | 924 | 2808 | 938 | 2850 | 952 | 2893 |
| 150 | 975 | 2962 | 990 | 3007 | 1005 | 3053 | 1020 | 3099 |
| 160 | 1040 | 3157 | 1056 | 3205 | 1072 | 3254 | 1088 | 3303 |
| 170 | 1105 | 3351 | 1122 | 3403 | 1139 | 3454 | 1156 | 3506 |
| 180 | 1170 | 3545 | 1188 | 3600 | 1206 | 3654 | 1224 | 3709 |
| 190 | 1235 | 3739 | 1254 | 3797 | 1273 | 3854 | 1292 | 3912 |
| 200 | 1300 | 3932 | 1320 | 3992 | 1340 | 4053 | 1360 | 4113 |
| 210 | 1365 | 4124 | 1386 | 4187 | 1407 | 4250 | 1428 | 4314 |
| 220 | 1430 | 4315 | 1452 | 4382 | 1474 | 4448 | 1496 | 4514 |
| 230 | 1495 | 4507 | 1518 | 4576 | 1541 | 4646 | 1564 | 4715 |
| 240 | 1560 | 4698 | 1584 | 4770 | 1608 | 4843 | 1632 | 4915 |
| 250 | 1625 | 4889 | 1650 | 4964 | 1675 | 5040 | 1700 | 5115 |
| 260 | 1690 | 5080 | 1716 | 5158 | 1742 | 5236 | 1768 | 5315 |
| 270 | 1755 | 5271 | 1782 | 5352 | 1809 | 5433 | 1836 | 5514 |
| 280 | 1820 | 5462 | 1848 | 5546 | 1876 | 5630 | 1904 | 5714 |
| 290 | 1885 | 5651 | 1914 | 5738 | 1943 | 5825 | 1972 | 5912 |
| 300 | 1950 | 5842 | 1980 | 5932 | 2010 | 6022 | 2040 | 6112 |
| 310 | 2015 | 6032 | 2046 | 6125 | 2077 | 6218 | 2108 | 6311 |
| 320 | 2080 | 6225 | 2112 | 6321 | 2144 | 6416 | 2176 | 6512 |
| 330 | 2145 | 6417 | 2178 | 6516 | 2211 | 6615 | 2244 | 6713 |
| 340 | 2210 | 6610 | 2244 | 6711 | 2278 | 6813 | 2312 | 6915 |
| 350 | 2275 | 6802 | 2310 | 6907 | 2345 | 7011 | 2380 | 7116 |
| 360 | 2340 | 6995 | 2376 | 7103 | 2412 | 7210 | 2448 | 7318 |
| 370 | 2405 | 7188 | 2442 | 7299 | 2479 | 7409 | 2516 | 7520 |
| 380 | 2470 | 7381 | 2508 | 7495 | 2546 | 7609 | 2584 | 7722 |
| 390 | 2535 | 7575 | 2574 | 7691 | 2613 | 7808 | 2652 | 7924 |
| 400 | 2600 | 7768 | 2640 | 7888 | 2680 | 8007 | 2720 | 8127 |
| 410 | 2665 | 7962 | 2706 | 8085 | 2747 | 8207 | 2788 | 8330 |
| 420 | 2730 | 8156 | 2772 | 8282 | 2814 | 8407 | 2856 | 8532 |
| 425 | 2763 | 8259 | 2805 | 8386 | 2848 | 8513 | 2890 | 8640 |

FIGURE 11.—Beech 1900 – Weights and Moments – Usable Fuel.

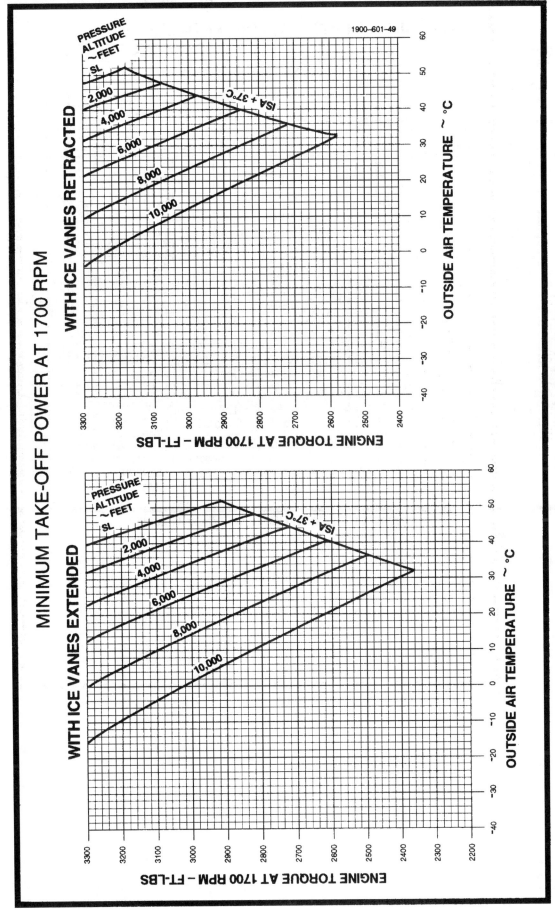

FIGURE 12.—Minimum Takeoff Power at 1700 RPM.

# TAKE-OFF DISTANCE – FLAPS TAKEOFF

ASSOCIATED CONDITIONS:
POWER ...................... TAKE-OFF POWER SET
                           BEFORE BRAKE RELEASE
LANDING GEAR ......... RETRACT AFTER LIFT-OFF
RUNWAY ................... PAVED, LEVEL, DRY SURFACE

NOTE:  FOR OPERATION WITH ICE VANES EXTENDED
       ADD 5 °C TO THE ACTUAL OAT BEFORE
       ENTERING GRAPH.

| WEIGHT ~ POUNDS | TAKE-OFF SPEED ~ KNOTS | |
| --- | --- | --- |
| | $V_1$ | $V_2$ |
| 16,600 | 108 | 115 |
| 16,000 | 107 | 114 |
| 14,000 | 102 | 112 |
| 12,000 | 102 | 112 |
| 10,000 | 102 | 112 |

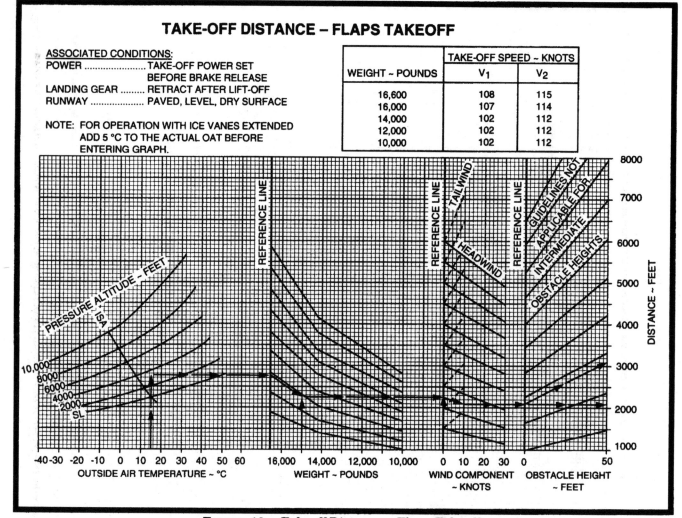

FIGURE 13.—Takeoff Distance – Flaps Takeoff.

# ACCELERATE–STOP — FLAPS TAKEOFF

ASSOCIATED CONDITIONS:

POWER ............................. 1. TAKE-OFF POWER SET
                                        BEFORE BRAKE RELEASE
                                   2. BOTH ENGINES IDLE AT $V_1$ SPEED
AUTOFEATHER ................. ARMED
BRAKING ........................... MAXIMUM
RUNWAY ............................ PAVED, LEVEL, DRY SURFACE

NOTE:  FOR OPERATION WITH ICE VANES EXTENDED,
           ADD 3 °C TO THE ACTUAL OAT BEFORE
           ENTERING GRAPH.

| WEIGHT ~ POUNDS | $V_1$ ~ KNOTS |
|---|---|
| 16,600 | 108 |
| 16,000 | 107 |
| 14,000 | 102 |
| 12,000 | 102 |
| 10,000 | 102 |

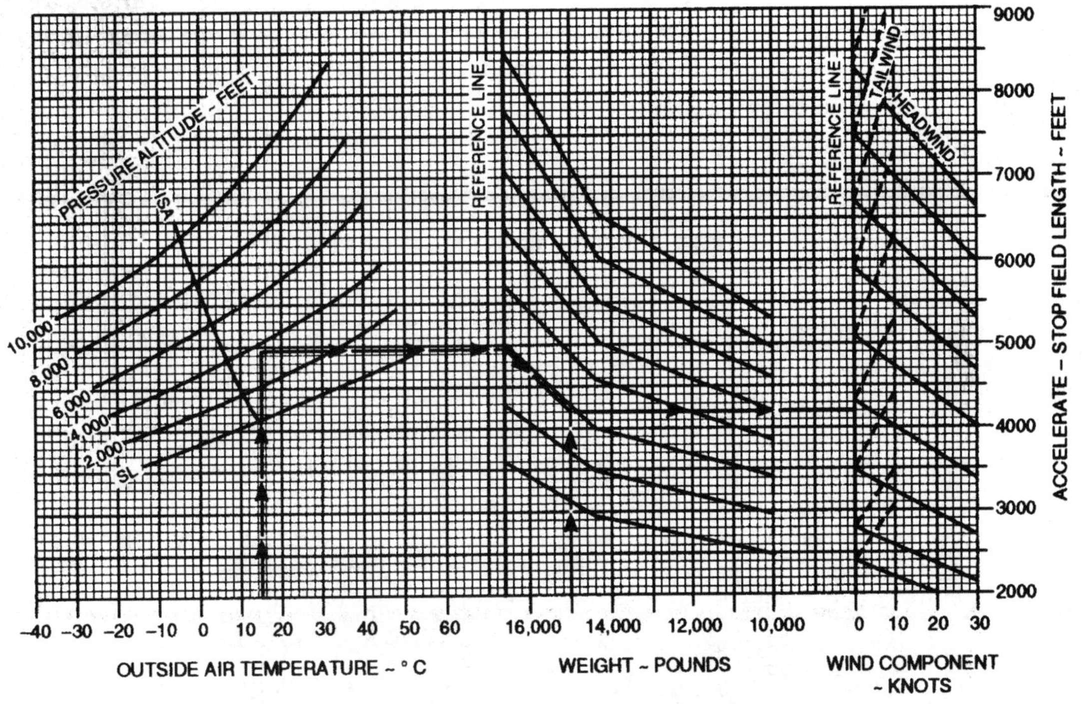

FIGURE 14.—Accelerate-Stop – Flaps Takeoff.

| OPERATING CONDITIONS | BE-21 | BE-22 | BE-23 | BE-24 | BE-25 |
|---|---|---|---|---|---|
| OAT AT TAKEOFF | +10 °C | 0 °C | +20 °C | +25 °C | −10 °C |
| OAT AT CRUISE | −20 °C | −25 °C | ISA | 0 °C | −40 °C |
| AIRPORT PRESS ALTITUDE | 2,000 | 1,000 | 3,000 | 4,000 | 5,000 |
| CRUISE ALTITUDE | 16,000 | 18,000 | 20,000 | 14,000 | 22,000 |
| INITIAL CLIMB WEIGHT | 16,600 | 14,000 | 15,000 | 16,000 | 14,000 |
| ICE VANES | RETRACT | EXTEND | RETRACT | RETRACT | EXTEND |

FIGURE 15.— Beech 1900 – Climb.

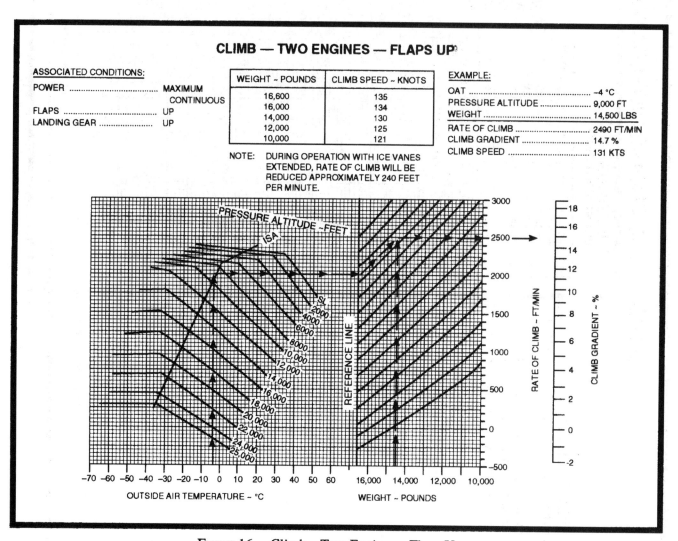

FIGURE 16.—Climb – Two Engines – Flaps Up.

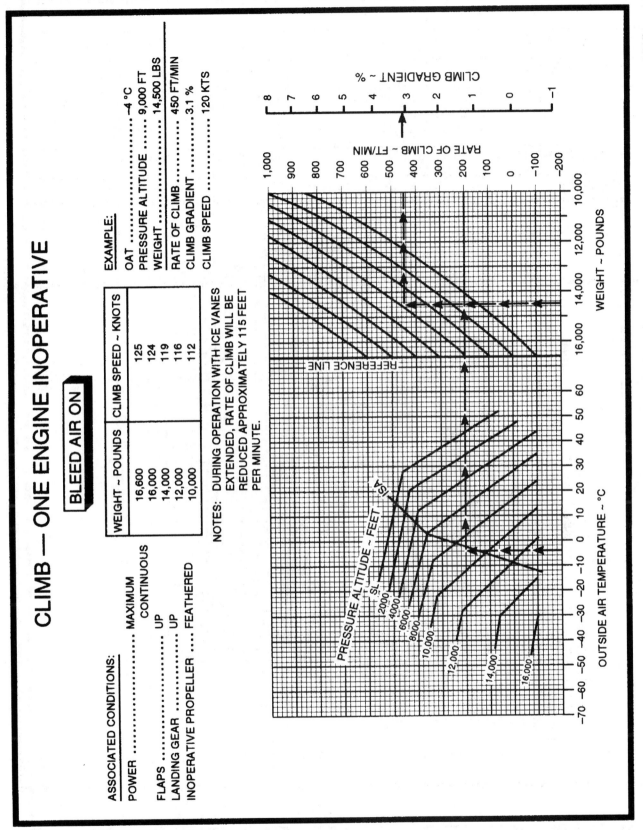

FIGURE 17.—Climb – One Engine Inoperative.

13

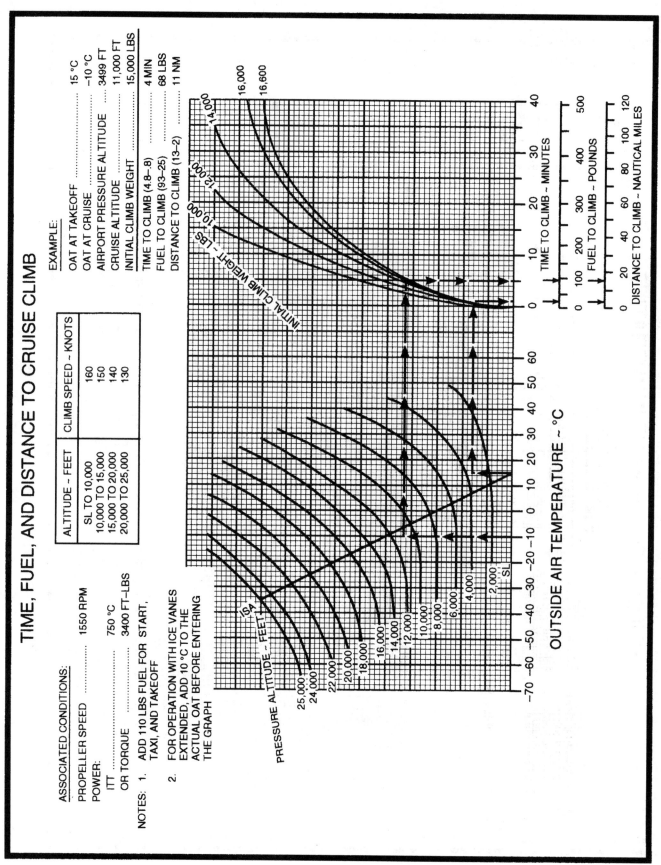

FIGURE 18.—Time, Fuel, and Distance to Cruise Climb.

| OPERATING CONDITIONS | BE-26 | BE-27 | BE-28 | BE-29 | BE-30 |
|---|---|---|---|---|---|
| OAT AT MEA | −8 °C | +30 °C | +5 °C | +18 °C | +22 °C |
| WEIGHT | 15,500 | 16,600 | 16,000 | 16,300 | 14,500 |
| ROUTE SEGMENT MEA | 6,000 | 5,500 | 9,000 | 7,000 | 9,500 |
| BLEED AIR | ON | ON | OFF | ON | OFF |

FIGURE 19.—Beech 1900 – Service Ceiling.

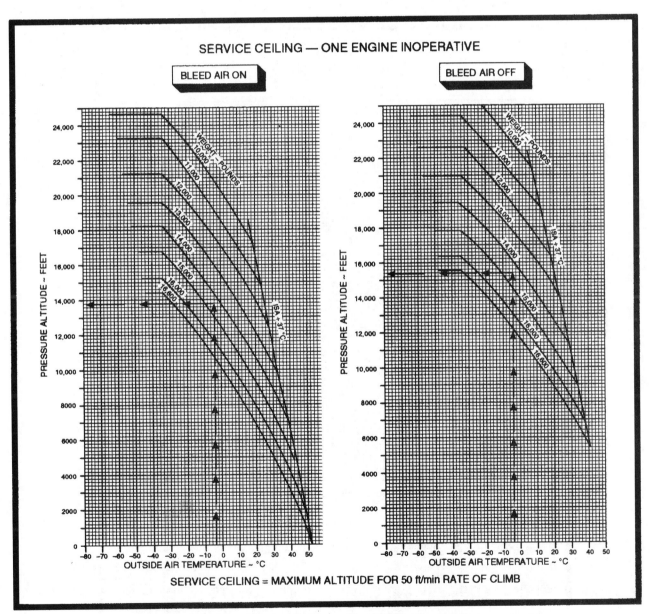

FIGURE 20.—Service Ceiling – One Engine Inoperative.

| OPERATING CONDITIONS | BE-31 | BE-32 | BE-33 | BE-34 | BE-35 |
|---|---|---|---|---|---|
| WEIGHT | 15,000 | 14,000 | 13,000 | 16,000 | 11,000 |
| PRESSURE ALTITUDE | 22,000 | 17,000 | 20,000 | 23,000 | 14,000 |
| TEMPERATURE (OAT) | –19 °C | –19 °C | –35 °C | –31 °C | –3 °C |
| TRUE COURSE | 110 | 270 | 185 | 020 | 305 |
| WIND | 180/30 | 020/35 | 135/45 | 340/25 | 040/50 |
| CRUISE DISTANCE | 280 | 320 | 400 | 230 | 300 |

FIGURE 21.—Beech 1900 – Cruise.

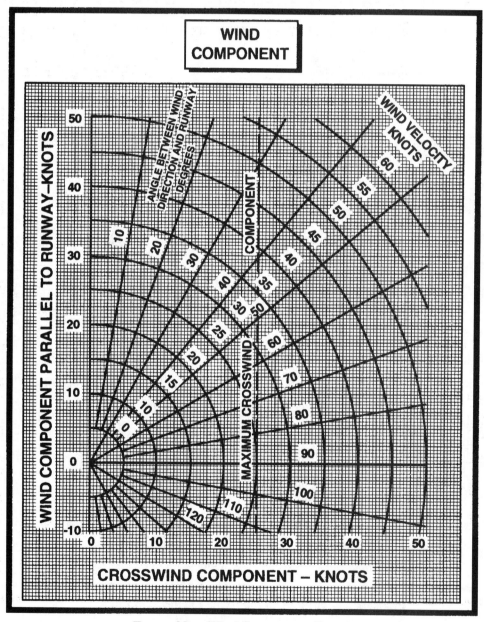

FIGURE 22.—Wind Component Chart.

# RECOMMENDED CRUISE POWER

## 1550 RPM

## ISA +10 °C

| PRESSURE ALTITUDE | IOAT | OAT | 16,000 POUNDS | | | | | 14,000 POUNDS | | | | | 12,000 POUNDS | | | | | 10,000 POUNDS | | | | |
|---|---|---|---|---|---|---|---|---|---|---|---|---|---|---|---|---|---|---|---|---|---|---|
| | | | TORQUE PER ENG | FUEL FLOW PER ENG | TOTAL FUEL FLOW | IAS | TAS | TORQUE PER ENG | FUEL FLOW PER ENG | TOTAL FUEL FLOW | IAS | TAS | TORQUE PER ENG | FUEL FLOW PER ENG | TOTAL FUEL FLOW | IAS | TAS | TORQUE PER ENG | FUEL FLOW PER ENG | TOTAL FUEL FLOW | IAS | TAS |
| FEET | °C | °C | FT-LBS | LBS/HR | LBS/HR | KTS | KTS | FT-LBS | LBS/HR | LBS/HR | KTS | KTS | FT-LBS | LBS/HR | LBS/HR | KTS | KTS | FT-LBS | LBS/HR | LBS/HR | KTS | KTS |
| SL | 30 | 25 | 3294 | 577 | 1154 | 232 | 239 | 3301 | 577 | 1154 | 235 | 241 | 3307 | 577 | 1154 | 237 | 243 | 3312 | 577 | 1154 | 238 | 245 |
| 2000 | 26 | 21 | 3191 | 551 | 1102 | 227 | 240 | 3198 | 551 | 1102 | 230 | 243 | 3204 | 552 | 1104 | 232 | 245 | 3209 | 552 | 1104 | 233 | 247 |
| 4000 | 22 | 17 | 3092 | 527 | 1054 | 222 | 242 | 3100 | 528 | 1056 | 224 | 244 | 3106 | 528 | 1056 | 227 | 247 | 3111 | 528 | 1056 | 228 | 249 |
| 6000 | 19 | 13 | 2992 | 504 | 1008 | 216 | 243 | 3000 | 505 | 1010 | 219 | 246 | 3006 | 505 | 1010 | 222 | 249 | 3012 | 505 | 1010 | 224 | 251 |
| 8000 | 15 | 9 | 2886 | 481 | 962 | 211 | 244 | 2896 | 482 | 964 | 214 | 247 | 2903 | 482 | 964 | 216 | 250 | 2909 | 482 | 964 | 219 | 253 |
| 10,000 | 11 | 5 | 2778 | 458 | 916 | 205 | 244 | 2789 | 458 | 916 | 208 | 248 | 2797 | 459 | 918 | 211 | 252 | 2804 | 459 | 918 | 213 | 254 |
| 12,000 | 7 | 1 | 2636 | 432 | 864 | 198 | 243 | 2648 | 433 | 866 | 202 | 248 | 2657 | 433 | 866 | 205 | 252 | 2664 | 434 | 868 | 207 | 255 |
| 14,000 | 3 | -3 | 2495 | 408 | 816 | 190 | 241 | 2508 | 409 | 818 | 195 | 247 | 2518 | 409 | 818 | 198 | 251 | 2525 | 409 | 818 | 201 | 255 |
| 16,000 | -1 | -7 | 2352 | 384 | 768 | 182 | 239 | 2367 | 385 | 770 | 188 | 246 | 2378 | 385 | 770 | 192 | 251 | 2386 | 386 | 772 | 195 | 255 |
| 18,000 | -6 | -11 | 2208 | 361 | 722 | 174 | 235 | 2226 | 362 | 724 | 180 | 243 | 2239 | 363 | 726 | 185 | 250 | 2248 | 363 | 726 | 188 | 254 |
| 20,000 | -10 | -15 | 2063 | 338 | 676 | 164 | 229 | 2085 | 340 | 680 | 172 | 240 | 2100 | 341 | 682 | 177 | 248 | 2111 | 341 | 682 | 181 | 253 |
| 22,000 | -14 | -19 | 1911 | 316 | 632 | 153 | 221 | 1939 | 317 | 634 | 163 | 235 | 1957 | 319 | 638 | 169 | 245 | 1969 | 319 | 638 | 174 | 252 |
| 24,000 | -19 | -23 | 1749 | 292 | 584 | 137 | 206 | 1790 | 295 | 590 | 152 | 229 | 1812 | 297 | 594 | 161 | 241 | 1827 | 298 | 596 | 167 | 249 |
| 25,000 | -21 | -25 | 1649 | 279 | 558 | 122 | 187 | 1714 | 284 | 568 | 147 | 224 | 1739 | 286 | 572 | 156 | 238 | 1756 | 287 | 574 | 163 | 248 |

FIGURE 23.—Recommended Cruise Power – ISA + 10 °C.

# RECOMMENDED CRUISE POWER

## 1550 RPM

### ISA

| PRESSURE ALTITUDE FEET | IOAT °C | OAT °C | 16,000 POUNDS TORQUE PER ENG FT-LBS | FUEL FLOW PER ENG LBS/HR | TOTAL FUEL FLOW LBS/HR | IAS KTS | TAS KTS | 14,000 POUNDS TORQUE PER ENG FT-LBS | FUEL FLOW PER ENG LBS/HR | TOTAL FUEL FLOW LBS/HR | IAS KTS | TAS KTS | 12,000 POUNDS TORQUE PER ENG FT-LBS | FUEL FLOW PER ENG LBS/HR | TOTAL FUEL FLOW LBS/HR | IAS KTS | TAS KTS | 10,000 POUNDS TORQUE PER ENG FT-LBS | FUEL FLOW PER ENG LBS/HR | TOTAL FUEL FLOW LBS/HR | IAS KTS | TAS KTS |
|---|---|---|---|---|---|---|---|---|---|---|---|---|---|---|---|---|---|---|---|---|---|---|
| SL | 20 | 15 | 3400 | 586 | 1172 | 237 | 239 | 3400 | 585 | 1170 | 239 | 241 | 3400 | 585 | 1170 | 241 | 243 | 3400 | 585 | 1170 | 242 | 244 |
| 2000 | 17 | 11 | 3400 | 573 | 1146 | 234 | 244 | 3400 | 573 | 1146 | 236 | 246 | 3400 | 572 | 1144 | 238 | 248 | 3400 | 572 | 1144 | 240 | 249 |
| 4000 | 13 | 7 | 3400 | 560 | 1120 | 232 | 248 | 3400 | 559 | 1118 | 234 | 250 | 3400 | 559 | 1118 | 236 | 252 | 3400 | 559 | 1118 | 237 | 254 |
| 6000 | 9 | 3 | 3397 | 548 | 1096 | 229 | 252 | 3400 | 548 | 1096 | 231 | 255 | 3400 | 547 | 1094 | 233 | 257 | 3400 | 547 | 1094 | 235 | 259 |
| 8000 | 5 | -1 | 3253 | 521 | 1042 | 223 | 253 | 3260 | 522 | 1044 | 225 | 256 | 3265 | 522 | 1044 | 228 | 258 | 3270 | 522 | 1044 | 229 | 260 |
| 10,000 | 1 | -5 | 3092 | 494 | 988 | 216 | 252 | 3100 | 494 | 988 | 219 | 256 | 3107 | 495 | 990 | 221 | 258 | 3112 | 495 | 990 | 223 | 261 |
| 12,000 | -3 | -9 | 2929 | 466 | 932 | 208 | 251 | 2937 | 467 | 934 | 212 | 255 | 2945 | 467 | 934 | 214 | 258 | 2950 | 467 | 934 | 217 | 261 |
| 14,000 | -7 | -13 | 2772 | 440 | 880 | 201 | 250 | 2781 | 441 | 882 | 205 | 255 | 2789 | 441 | 882 | 208 | 258 | 2795 | 442 | 884 | 210 | 261 |
| 16,000 | -11 | -17 | 2606 | 414 | 828 | 193 | 248 | 2618 | 414 | 828 | 197 | 253 | 2626 | 415 | 830 | 201 | 258 | 2633 | 415 | 830 | 203 | 261 |
| 18,000 | -15 | -21 | 2435 | 288 | 776 | 184 | 244 | 2449 | 389 | 778 | 189 | 251 | 2459 | 389 | 778 | 193 | 256 | 2467 | 390 | 780 | 196 | 260 |
| 20,000 | -19 | -25 | 2263 | 363 | 726 | 175 | 239 | 2282 | 364 | 728 | 181 | 248 | 2294 | 365 | 730 | 186 | 254 | 2302 | 365 | 730 | 189 | 259 |
| 22,000 | -24 | -29 | 2094 | 338 | 676 | 164 | 233 | 2118 | 340 | 680 | 172 | 244 | 2133 | 341 | 682 | 178 | 251 | 2144 | 342 | 684 | 182 | 257 |
| 24,000 | -28 | -33 | 1931 | 315 | 630 | 152 | 223 | 1960 | 317 | 634 | 163 | 238 | 1979 | 318 | 636 | 169 | 248 | 1991 | 319 | 638 | 174 | 255 |
| 25,000 | -30 | -35 | 1846 | 303 | 606 | 145 | 216 | 1880 | 305 | 610 | 157 | 235 | 1901 | 307 | 614 | 165 | 246 | 1915 | 308 | 616 | 170 | 253 |

FIGURE 24.—Recommended Cruise Power – ISA.

# RECOMMENDED CRUISE POWER

## 1550 RPM

## ISA -10 °C

| WEIGHT | | | 16,000 POUNDS | | | | | 14,000 POUNDS | | | | | 12,000 POUNDS | | | | | 10,000 POUNDS | | | | |
|---|---|---|---|---|---|---|---|---|---|---|---|---|---|---|---|---|---|---|---|---|---|---|
| PRESSURE ALTITUDE | IOAT | OAT | TORQUE PER ENG | FUEL FLOW PER ENG | TOTAL FUEL FLOW | IAS | TAS | TORQUE PER ENG | FUEL FLOW PER ENG | TOTAL FUEL FLOW | IAS | TAS | TORQUE PER ENG | FUEL FLOW PER ENG | TOTAL FUEL FLOW | IAS | TAS | TORQUE PER ENG | FUEL FLOW PER ENG | TOTAL FUEL FLOW | IAS | TAS |
| FEET | °C | °C | FT-LBS | LBS/HR | LBS/HR | KTS | KTS | FT-LBS | LBS/HR | LBS/HR | KTS | KTS | FT-LBS | LBS/HR | LBS/HR | KTS | KTS | FT-LBS | LBS/HR | LBS/HR | KTS | KTS |
| SL | 10 | 5 | 3400 | 582 | 1164 | 238 | 237 | 3400 | 582 | 1164 | 240 | 239 | 3400 | 581 | 1162 | 242 | 240 | 3400 | 581 | 1162 | 243 | 242 |
| 2000 | 6 | 1 | 3400 | 569 | 1138 | 236 | 241 | 3400 | 569 | 1138 | 238 | 243 | 3400 | 568 | 1136 | 240 | 245 | 3400 | 568 | 1136 | 241 | 246 |
| 4000 | 3 | -3 | 3400 | 558 | 1116 | 233 | 245 | 3400 | 557 | 1114 | 236 | 248 | 3400 | 557 | 1114 | 237 | 249 | 3400 | 557 | 1114 | 239 | 251 |
| 6000 | -1 | -7 | 3400 | 548 | 1096 | 231 | 250 | 3400 | 547 | 1094 | 233 | 252 | 3400 | 547 | 1094 | 235 | 254 | 3400 | 546 | 1092 | 236 | 256 |
| 8000 | -5 | -11 | 3400 | 538 | 1076 | 228 | 254 | 3400 | 538 | 1076 | 231 | 257 | 3400 | 538 | 1076 | 232 | 259 | 3400 | 537 | 1074 | 234 | 261 |
| 10,000 | -9 | -15 | 3400 | 530 | 1060 | 226 | 259 | 3400 | 530 | 1060 | 228 | 262 | 3400 | 530 | 1060 | 230 | 264 | 3400 | 529 | 1058 | 232 | 266 |
| 12,000 | -13 | -19 | 3200 | 499 | 998 | 218 | 258 | 3208 | 500 | 1000 | 221 | 261 | 3215 | 500 | 1000 | 223 | 264 | 3220 | 501 | 1002 | 225 | 266 |
| 14,000 | -17 | -23 | 3010 | 470 | 940 | 210 | 256 | 3019 | 471 | 942 | 213 | 260 | 3026 | 471 | 942 | 216 | 263 | 3032 | 472 | 944 | 218 | 266 |
| 16,000 | -21 | -27 | 2823 | 442 | 884 | 202 | 254 | 2833 | 442 | 884 | 205 | 258 | 2841 | 443 | 886 | 209 | 262 | 2848 | 443 | 886 | 211 | 265 |
| 18,000 | -25 | -31 | 2641 | 414 | 828 | 193 | 251 | 2652 | 415 | 830 | 198 | 256 | 2661 | 416 | 832 | 201 | 261 | 2668 | 416 | 832 | 204 | 264 |
| 20,000 | -29 | -35 | 2456 | 387 | 774 | 184 | 247 | 2471 | 388 | 776 | 189 | 254 | 2481 | 389 | 778 | 193 | 259 | 2489 | 390 | 780 | 196 | 263 |
| 22,000 | -33 | -39 | 2277 | 361 | 722 | 174 | 242 | 2296 | 363 | 726 | 181 | 250 | 2308 | 363 | 726 | 185 | 256 | 2318 | 364 | 728 | 189 | 261 |
| 24,000 | -37 | -43 | 2105 | 336 | 672 | 163 | 234 | 2128 | 338 | 676 | 172 | 246 | 2144 | 339 | 678 | 177 | 254 | 2155 | 340 | 680 | 181 | 260 |
| 25,000 | -40 | -45 | 2017 | 324 | 648 | 157 | 230 | 2044 | 326 | 652 | 167 | 243 | 2061 | 327 | 654 | 173 | 252 | 2073 | 328 | 656 | 177 | 258 |

FIGURE 25.—Recommended Cruise Power – ISA –10 °C.

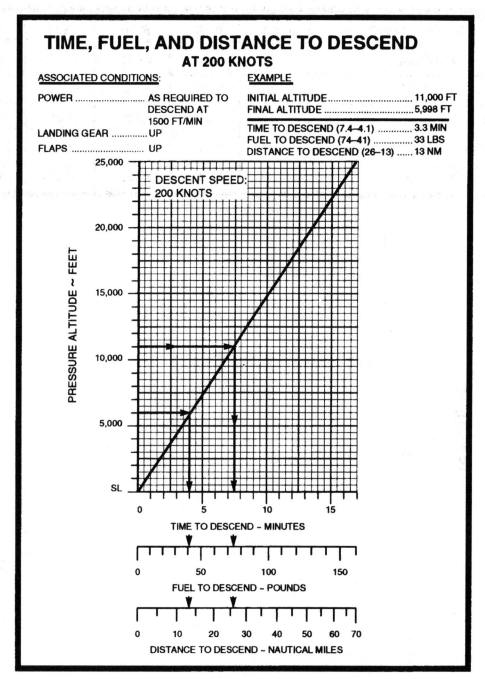

FIGURE 26.—Time, Fuel, and Distance to Descend.

| OPERATING CONDITIONS | B–36 | B–37 | B–38 | B–39 | B–40 |
|---|---|---|---|---|---|
| PRESSURE ALTITUDE | SL | 1,000 | 2,000 | 4,000 | 5,000 |
| TEMPERATURE (OAT) | +30 °C | +16 °C | 0 °C | +20 °C | ISA |
| WEIGHT | 16,000 | 14,500 | 13,500 | 15,000 | 12,500 |
| WIND COMPONENT (KTS) | 20 HW | 10 TW | 15 HW | 5 TW | 25 HW |
| RUNWAY LENGTH (FT) | 4,000 | 4,500 | 3,800 | 5,000 | 4,000 |

FIGURE 27.—Beech 1900 – Landing.

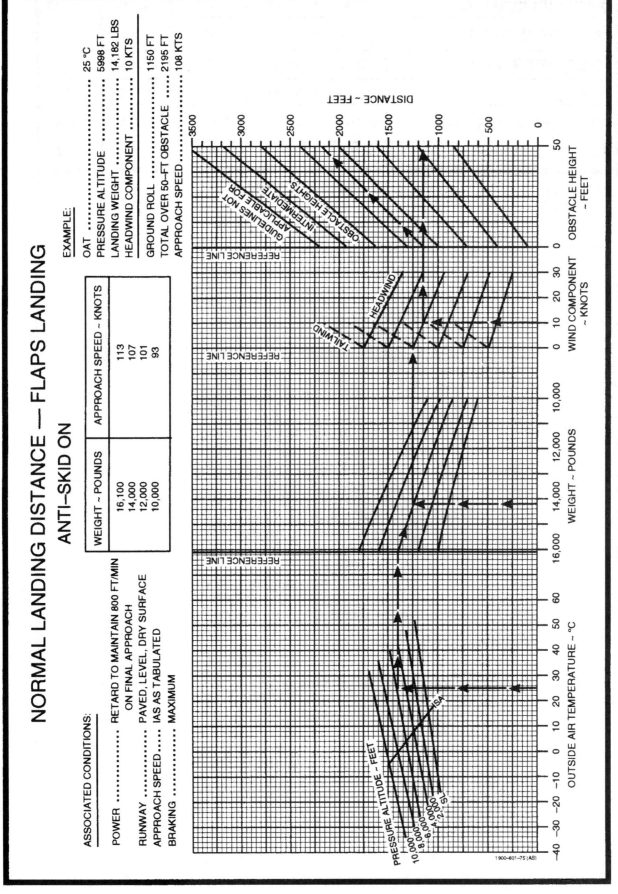

FIGURE 28.—Normal Landing Distance – Flaps Landing.

| OPERATING CONDITIONS | BL-1 | BL-2 | BL-3 | BL-4 | BL-5 |
|---|---|---|---|---|---|
| CREW WEIGHT | 340 | 400 | 360 | 380 | 370 |
| PASSENGER WT<br>ROW 1 | 700 | 620 | — | 180 | 680 |
| ROW 2 | 830 | 700 | 750 | 800 | 950 |
| ROW 3 | 800 | 680 | 810 | 720 | 850 |
| ROW 4 | — | 400 | 650 | 200 | 500 |
| BAGGAGE<br>CENTER | 500 | 550 | 300 | 200 | 450 |
| LEFT AND RIGHT | 200 | 250 | — | 100 | — |
| FUEL<br>GALLONS | 300 | 250 | 360 | 400 | 260 |
| TYPE | JET A | JET B | JET A | JET B | JET A |

FIGURE 29.—Bell 214 ST – Loading.

| LOADING CONDITIONS | BL-6 | BL-7 | BL-8 | BL-9 | BL-10 |
|---|---|---|---|---|---|
| BASIC WEIGHT | 10,225 | 9,450 | 9,000 | 9,510 | 9,375 |
| BASIC MOM/100 | 25562.5 | 23236.0 | 22020.5 | 23499.9 | 23296.8 |
| CREW WEIGHT | 340 | 380 | 410 | 360 | 400 |
| PASSENGER WEIGHT | 3,280 | 2,880 | 3,150 | 2,040 | 2,400 |
| PASSENGER MOM/100 | 6722.5 | 5418.6 | 6425.8 | 4732.2 | 4560.7 |
| BAGGAGE (CENTER) | 700 | 600 | 300 | 550 | 650 |
| FUEL LOAD (6.8 LB/GAL) | 435 | 290 | 220 | 435 | 380 |
| TRIP FUEL BURN (GAL) | 355 | 190 | 190 | 325 | 330 |
| LATERAL CG IS ON LONGITUDINAL AXIS | | | | | |

FIGURE 30.—Bell 214 ST – Weight Shift and Limits.

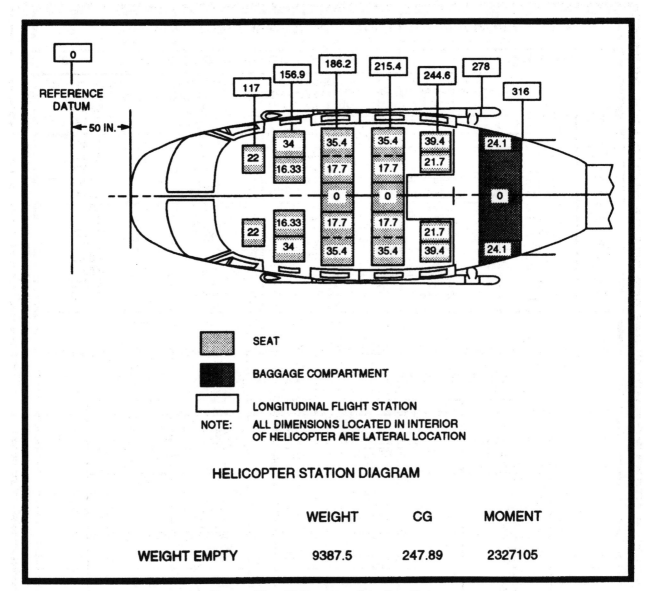

FIGURE 31.—Helicopter – Loading Data.

## CREW AND PASSENGER TABLE OF MOMENTS (IN-LB)

| WEIGHT LBS | CREW SEATS F.S. 117 | AIRLINE PASSENGEER SEATS | | | |
|---|---|---|---|---|---|
| | | FIRST ROW (FOUR PASSENGER) SEATS F.S. 156.9 | SECOND ROW (FIVE PASSENGER) SEATS F.S. 186.2 | THIRD ROW (FIVE PASSENGER) SEATS F.S. 215.4 | FOURTH ROW (FOUR PASSENGER) SEATS F.S. 244.6 |
| 100 | 11700 | 15690 | 18620 | 21540 | 24460 |
| 110 | 12870 | 17259 | 20482 | 23694 | 26906 |
| 120 | 14040 | 18828 | 22344 | 25848 | 29352 |
| 130 | 15210 | 20397 | 24206 | 28002 | 31798 |
| 140 | 16380 | 21966 | 26068 | 30156 | 34244 |
| 150 | 17550 | 23535 | 27930 | 32310 | 36690 |
| 160 | 18720 | 25104 | 29792 | 34464 | 39136 |
| 170 | 19890 | 26673 | 31654 | 36618 | 41582 |
| 180 | 21060 | 28242 | 33516 | 38772 | 44028 |
| 190 | 22230 | 29811 | 35378 | 40926 | 46474 |
| 200 | 23400 | 31380 | 37240 | 43080 | 48920 |
| 210 | 24570 | 32949 | 39102 | 45234 | 51366 |
| 220 | 25740 | 34518 | 40964 | 47388 | 53812 |

## BAGGAGE COMPARTMENT LOADING TABLE (IN-LB ÷ 100)

| BAGGAGE WEIGHT LBS | LEFT AND RIGHT BAGGAGE COMPARTMENT STA. 278.0 TO 316.0 F.S. 295.2 | CENTER BAGGAGE COMPARTMENT STA. 278.0 TO 316.0 F.S. 297.0 |
|---|---|---|
| 50 | 147.6 | 148.5 |
| 100 | 295.2 | 297.0 |
| 150 | 442.8 | 445.5 |
| 200 | 590.4 | 594.0 |
| 250 | 738.0 | 742.5 |
| 300 | 885.6 | 891.0 |
| 350 | 1033.2 | 1039.5 |
| 400 | 1180.8 | 1188.0 |
| 450 | 1328.4 | 1336.5 |
| 500 | 1476.0 | 1485.0 |
| 530 | 1564.6 | 1574.1 |
| 550 | | 1633.5 |
| 600 | | 1782.0 |
| 650 | | 1930.5 |
| 700 | | 2079.0 |
| 740 | | 2197.8 |

FIGURE 32.—Helicopter – Weights and Moments – Crew, Passengers, and Baggage.

## USABLE FUEL LOADING TABLE (ENGLISH)

### JET A, JET A-1, JP-5 (6.8 LBS/GAL)

| U.S. GAL | WEIGHT LBS | C.G. | MOMENT IN. LB. ÷ 100 | U.S. GAL | WEIGHT LBS | C.G. | MOMENT IN. LB. ÷ 100 |
|---|---|---|---|---|---|---|---|
| 10 | 68 | 244.3 | 166 | 220 | 1496 | 246.9 | 3694 |
| 20 | 136 | 244.3 | 332 | 230 | 1564 | 244.3 | 3820 |
| 30 | 204 | 244.4 | 499 | 240 | 1632 | 241.8 | 3947 |
| **37.1 | 252 | 244.4 | 616 | 250 | 1700 | 239.6 | 4073 |
| 40 | 272 | 242.8 | 660 | 260 | 1768 | 237.6 | 4200 |
| 50 | 340 | 237.8 | 808 | 270 | 1836 | 235.6 | 4326 |
| 60 | 408 | 234.5 | 957 | 280 | 1904 | 233.9 | 4453 |
| 70 | 476 | 232.1 | 1105 | 290 | 1972 | 232.2 | 4579 |
| 80 | 544 | 230.9 | 1256 | **291.4 | 1982 | 232.0 | 4597 |
| 90 | 612 | 229.2 | 1403 | 300 | 2040 | 233.1 | 4754 |
| *99.7 | 678 | 228.2 | 1546 | 310 | 2108 | 234.0 | 4934 |
| *109.2 | 743 | 228.2 | 1695 | 320 | 2176 | 235.1 | 5115 |
| 110 | 748 | 228.5 | 1709 | 330 | 2244 | 236.0 | 5296 |
| 120 | 816 | 231.7 | 1890 | 340 | 2312 | 236.9 | 5477 |
| 130 | 884 | 234.4 | 2072 | 350 | 2380 | 237.7 | 5658 |
| 140 | 952 | 236.7 | 2253 | 360 | 2448 | 238.5 | 5839 |
| 150 | 1020 | 238.6 | 2434 | 370 | 2516 | 239.3 | 6021 |
| 160 | 1088 | 240.4 | 2615 | 380 | 2584 | 240.0 | 6202 |
| 170 | 1156 | 242.0 | 2798 | 390 | 2652 | 240.7 | 6383 |
| 180 | 1224 | 243.3 | 2978 | 400 | 2720 | 241.3 | 6564 |
| 190 | 1292 | 244.5 | 3159 | 410 | 2788 | 241.9 | 6745 |
| 200 | 1360 | 245.6 | 3340 | 420 | 2856 | 242.5 | 6927 |
| 210 | 1428 | 246.6 | 3521 | 430 | 2924 | 243.1 | 7108 |
| *218.4 | 1484 | 247.3 | 3673 | 435.0 | 2958 | 243.4 | 7199 |

### JET B, JP-4 (6.5 LBS/GAL)

| U.S. GAL | WEIGHT LBS | C.G. | MOMENT IN. LB. ÷ 100 | U.S. GAL | WEIGHT LBS | C.G. | MOMENT IN. LB. ÷ 100 |
|---|---|---|---|---|---|---|---|
| 10 | 65 | 244.3 | 159 | 220 | 1430 | 246.9 | 3531 |
| 20 | 130 | 244.3 | 318 | 230 | 1495 | 244.3 | 3652 |
| 30 | 195 | 244.5 | 477 | 240 | 1560 | 241.8 | 3772 |
| **37.1 | 241 | 244.4 | 589 | 250 | 1625 | 239.6 | 3894 |
| 40 | 260 | 242.8 | 631 | 260 | 1690 | 237.6 | 4015 |
| 50 | 325 | 237.8 | 773 | 270 | 1755 | 235.6 | 4135 |
| 60 | 390 | 234.5 | 915 | 280 | 1820 | 233.9 | 4257 |
| 70 | 455 | 232.1 | 1056 | 290 | 1885 | 232.2 | 4377 |
| 80 | 520 | 230.9 | 1201 | **291.4 | 1894 | 232.0 | 4394 |
| 90 | 585 | 229.2 | 1341 | 300 | 1950 | 233.1 | 4545 |
| *99.7 | 648 | 228.2 | 1479 | 310 | 2015 | 234.0 | 4715 |
| *109.2 | 710 | 228.2 | 1620 | 320 | 2080 | 235.1 | 4890 |
| 110 | 715 | 228.5 | 1634 | 330 | 2145 | 236.0 | 5062 |
| 120 | 780 | 231.7 | 1807 | 340 | 2210 | 236.9 | 5235 |
| 130 | 845 | 234.4 | 1981 | 350 | 2275 | 237.7 | 5408 |
| 140 | 910 | 236.7 | 2154 | 360 | 2340 | 238.5 | 5581 |
| 150 | 975 | 238.6 | 2326 | 370 | 2405 | 239.3 | 5755 |
| 160 | 1040 | 240.4 | 2500 | 380 | 2470 | 240.5 | 5928 |
| 170 | 1105 | 242.0 | 2674 | 390 | 2535 | 240.7 | 6102 |
| 180 | 1170 | 243.3 | 2847 | 400 | 2600 | 241.3 | 6274 |
| 190 | 1235 | 244.5 | 3020 | 410 | 2665 | 241.9 | 6447 |
| 200 | 1300 | 245.6 | 3193 | 420 | 2730 | 242.5 | 6620 |
| 210 | 1365 | 246.6 | 3366 | 430 | 2795 | 243.1 | 6795 |
| *218.4 | 1420 | 247.3 | 3512 | 435 | 2827.5 | 243.4 | 6882 |

* Extreme limits of fuel C.G.
** Point of C.G. direction change.

Weights given are nominal weights at 15 °C.

FIGURE 33.—Helicopter – Weights and Moments – Usable Fuel.

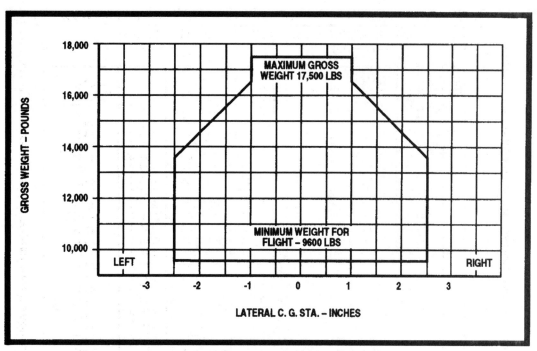

FIGURE 34.—Helicopter – Lateral CG Envelope.

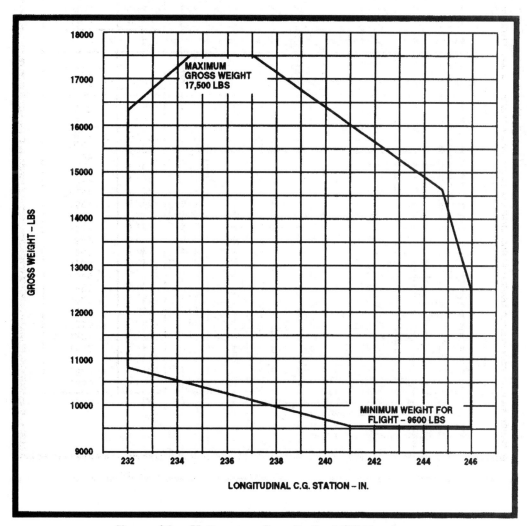

FIGURE 35.—Helicopter – Longitudinal CG Envelope.

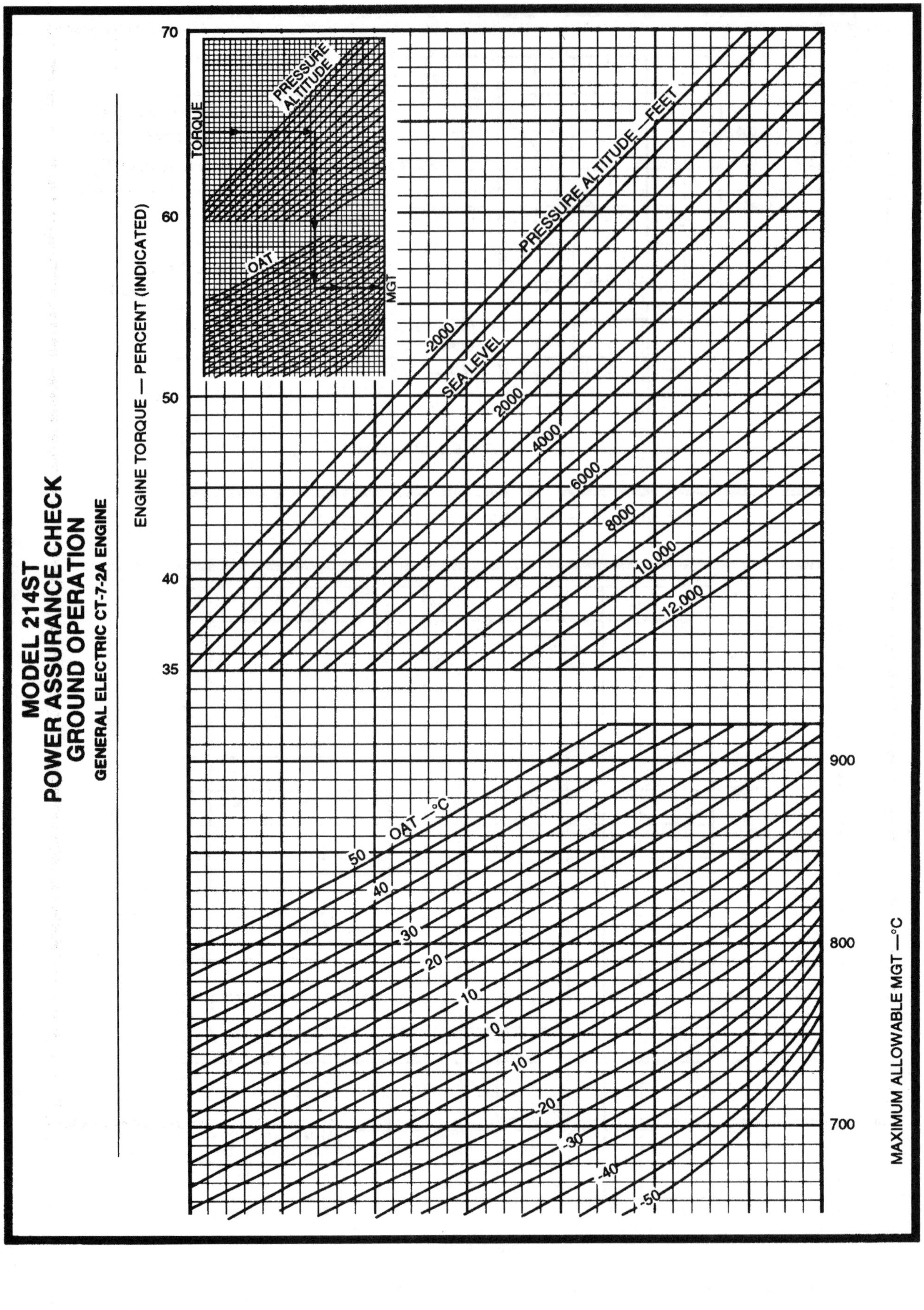

MODEL 214ST
POWER ASSURANCE CHECK
GROUND OPERATION
GENERAL ELECTRIC CT-7-2A ENGINE

FIGURE 36.—Bell 214 – Power Assurance Check.

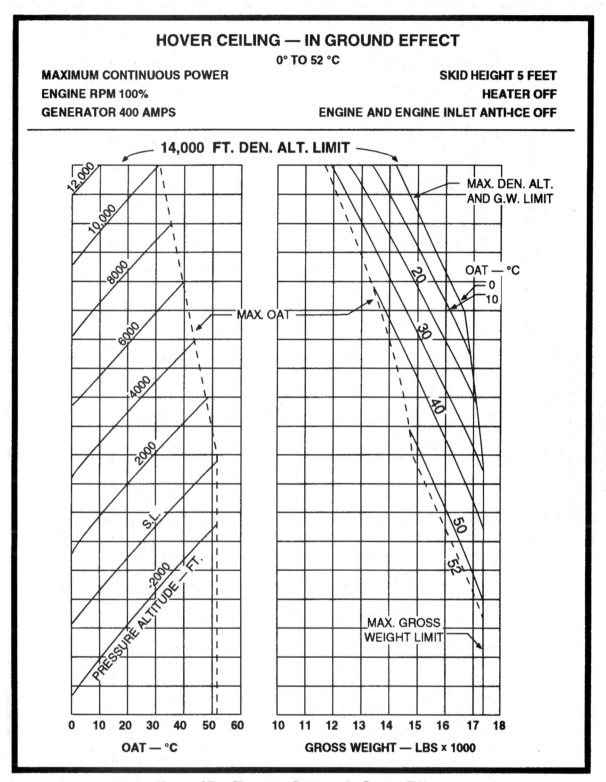

FIGURE 37.——Hovering Ceiling – In Ground Effect.

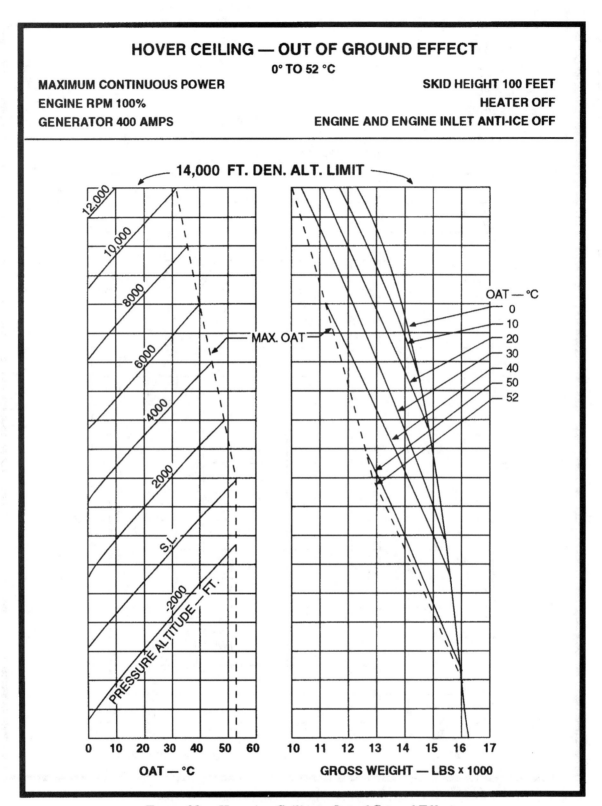

FIGURE 38.—Hovering Ceiling – Out of Ground Effect.

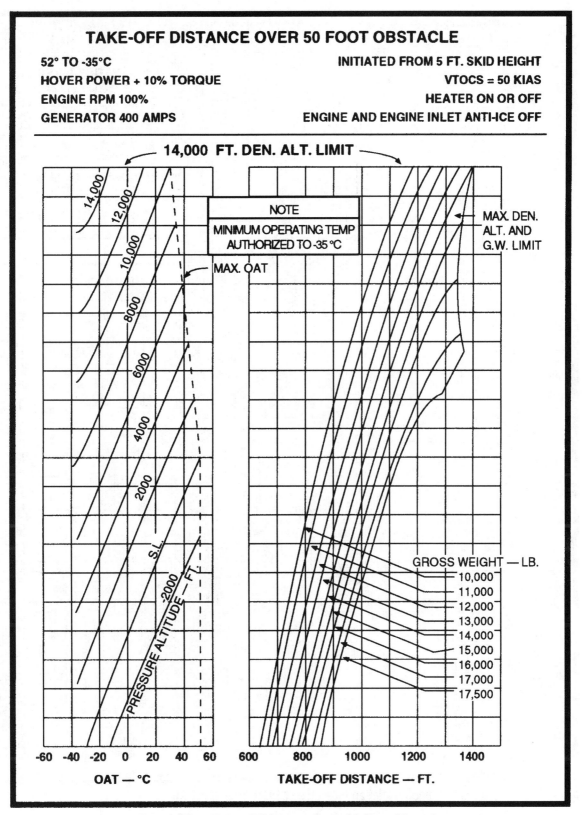

FIGURE 39.—Takeoff Distance Over 50-Foot Obstacle.

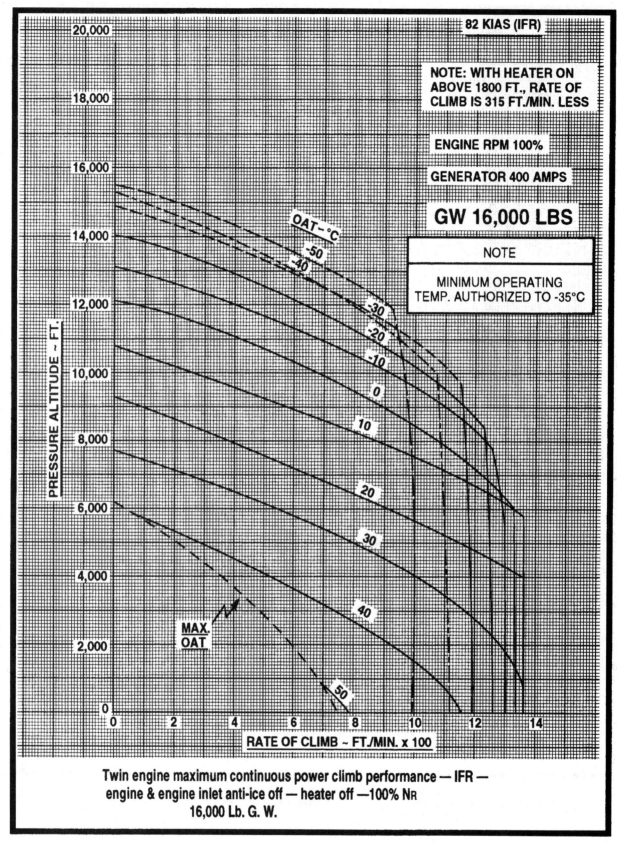

FIGURE 40.—Twin-Engine Climb Performance.

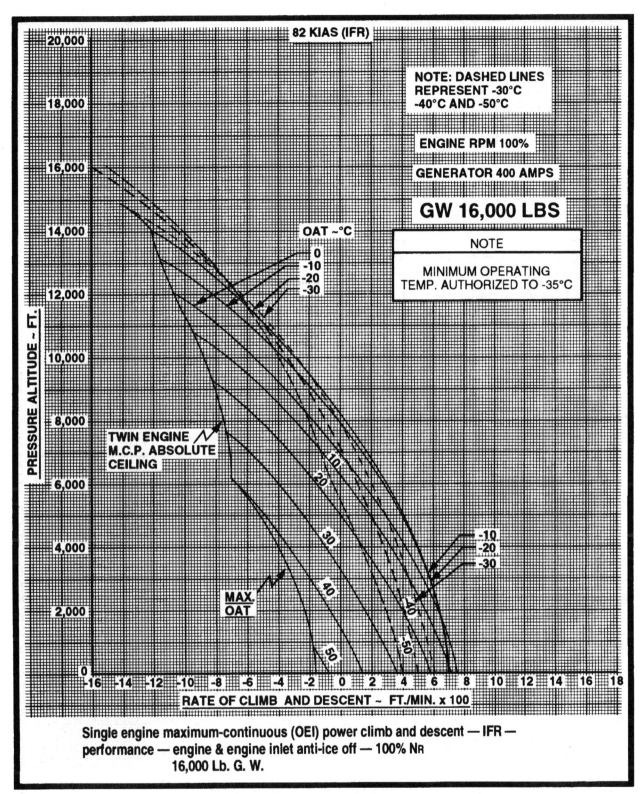

FIGURE 41.—Single-Engine Climb Performance.

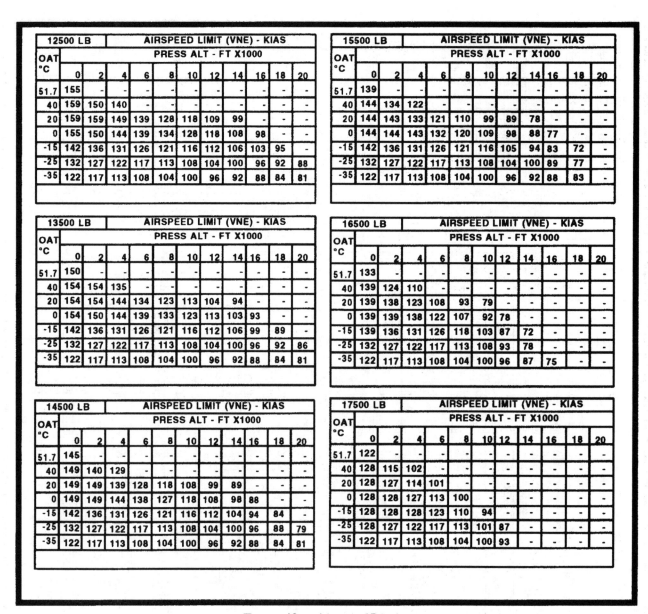

FIGURE 42.—Airspeed Limit.

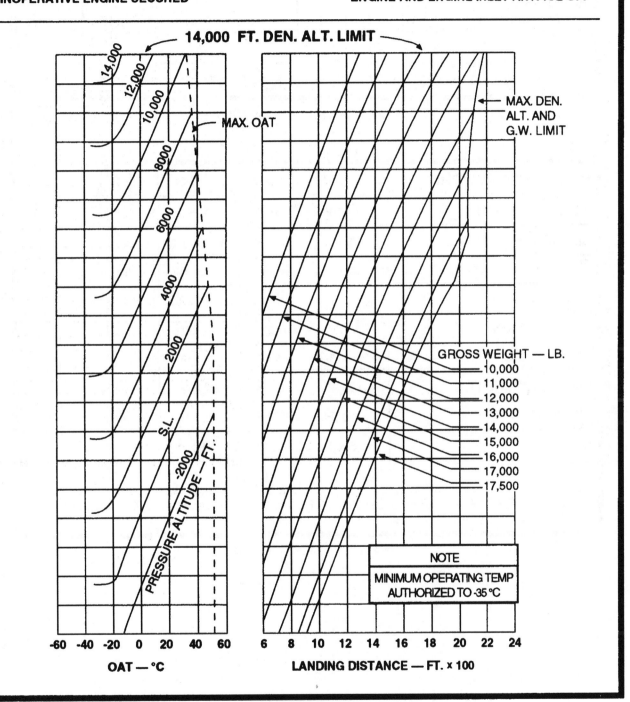

FIGURE 43.—Single-Engine Landing Distance Over 50-Foot Obstacle.

| LOADING CONDITIONS | WS-1 | WS-2 | WS-3 | WS-4 | WS-5 |
|---|---|---|---|---|---|
| LOADED WEIGHT | 90,000 | 85,000 | 84,500 | 81,700 | 88,300 |
| LOADED CG (% MAC) | 22.5% | 28.4% | 19.8% | 30.3% | 25.5% |
| WEIGHT CHANGE (POUNDS) | 2,500 | 1,800 | 3,000 | 2,100 | 3,300 |
| FWD COMPT CENTROID – STA 352.1 AND –227.9 INDEX ARM AFT COMPT CENTROID – STA 724.9 AND +144.9 INDEX ARM MAC – 141.5 INCHES, LEMAC – STA 549.13, AND –30.87 INDEX ARM | | | | | |

FIGURE 44.—DC-9 – Weight Shift.

| OPERATING CONDITIONS | A-1 | A-2 | A-3 | A-4 | A-5 |
|---|---|---|---|---|---|
| FIELD ELEVATION | 2,500 | 600 | 4,200 | 5,100 | 2,100 |
| ALTIMETER SETTING | 29.40" | 30.50" | 1020mb | 29.35" | 1035mb |
| AMBIENT TEMPERATURE | +10 °F | +80 °F | 0 °C | +30 °F | +20 °C |
| WEIGHT (X1000) | 75 | 85 | 90 | 80 | 65 |
| FLAP POSITION | 20° | 20° | 20° | 20° | 20° |
| RUNWAY SLOPE % | +1% | –1.5% | 0 | +1.5% | –2% |
| WIND COMPONENT | 10 HW | 10 TW | 15 HW | 5 TW | 20 HW |
| ICE PROTECTION | BOTH | NONE | BOTH | ENGINE | NONE |
| CG STATION | 590.2 | — | 580.3 | — | 594.4 |
| CG INDEX ARM | — | –3.1 | — | +5.9 | — |
| INDEX ARM REF – STA 580.0, LEMAC – STA 549.13, AND –30.87 INDEX, MAC 141.5 CG % MAC = STAB TRIM SETTING | | | | | |

FIGURE 45.—DC-9 – Takeoff.

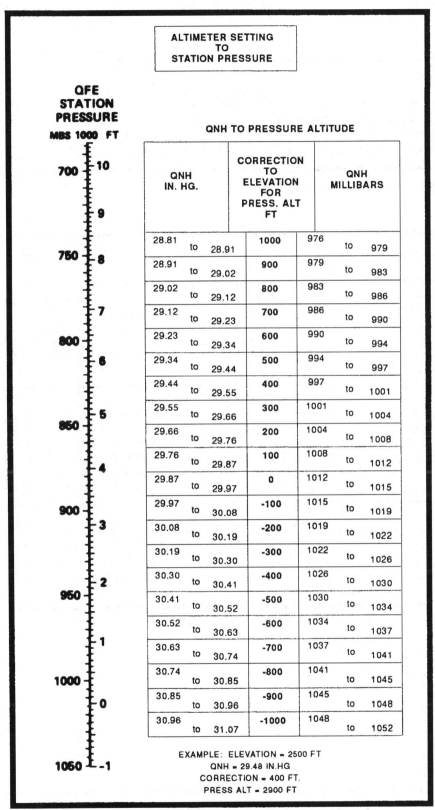

FIGURE 46.—Altimeter Setting to Pressure Altitude.

# MODEL DC–9
# TAKEOFF SPEEDS
### JT8D–1 ENGINES

## TAKEOFF SPEED – 20 ° FLAPS
### EITHER NO ICE PROTECTION OR ENGINE ICE PROTECTION ONLY

| TAKEOFF WEIGHT (1000 LB) | 60 | 65 | 70 | 75 | 80 | 85 | 90 | 95 |
|---|---|---|---|---|---|---|---|---|
| $V_1$ (KNOTS, IAS) | 104.0 | 110.0 | 115.0 | 120.5 | 125.0 | 129.5 | 133.5 | 136.0 |
| $V_R$ (KNOTS, IAS) | 106.5 | 112.5 | 118.0 | 123.5 | 129.0 | 134.0 | 139.0 | 143.5 |
| $V_2$ (KNOTS, IAS) | 117.0 | 121.5 | 126.5 | 130.5 | 135.0 | 139.0 | 143.0 | 147.0 |

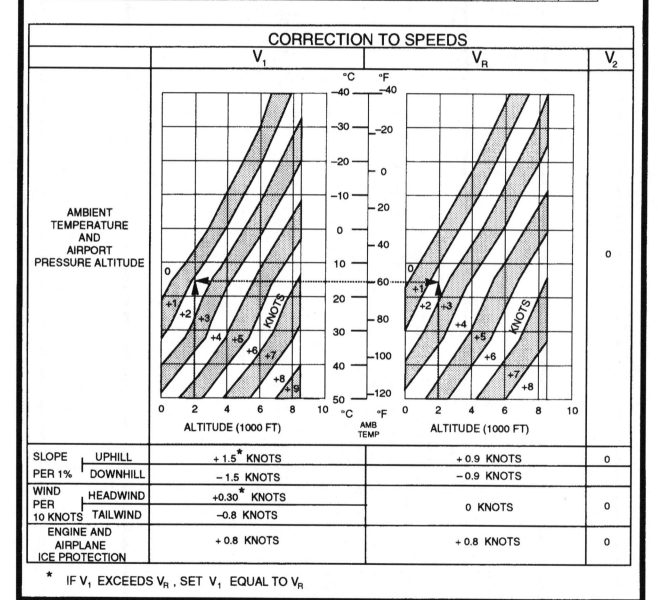

## CORRECTION TO SPEEDS

| | | $V_1$ | $V_R$ | $V_2$ |
|---|---|---|---|---|
| SLOPE PER 1% | UPHILL | + 1.5* KNOTS | + 0.9 KNOTS | 0 |
| | DOWNHILL | – 1.5 KNOTS | – 0.9 KNOTS | |
| WIND PER 10 KNOTS | HEADWIND | +0.30* KNOTS | 0 KNOTS | 0 |
| | TAILWIND | –0.8 KNOTS | | |
| ENGINE AND AIRPLANE ICE PROTECTION | | + 0.8 KNOTS | + 0.8 KNOTS | 0 |

\* IF $V_1$ EXCEEDS $V_R$, SET $V_1$ EQUAL TO $V_R$

FIGURE 47.—DC-9 – Takeoff Speeds.

| OPERATING CONDITIONS | W-1 | W-2 | W-3 | W-4 | W-5 |
|---|---|---|---|---|---|
| CLIMB SCHEDULE | LR | HS | LR | HS | HS |
| INITIAL WEIGHT (X1000) | 84 | 86 | 78 | 88 | 92 |
| CRUISE PRESS ALTITUDE | 34,000 | 28,000 | 32,000 | 22,000 | 24,000 |
| ISA TEMPERATURE | ISA | ISA | ISA | ISA | ISA |
| AVG WIND COMP (KTS) | 20 HW | 30 HW | 10 TW | 20 TW | 40 HW |

FIGURE 48.—DC-9 – En Route Climb.

## TIME, FUEL, AND DISTANCE TO CLIMB
## JT8D-1 ENGINES - NORMAL BLEED
## DC-9 SERIES 10 - HIGH SPEED CLIMB SCHEDULE
## CLIMB AT 320 KNOTS IAS TO 23500 FT ALTITUDE THEN CLIMB AT M .74

### INITIAL WEIGHT = 86000. POUNDS

| PRES. ALT. FEET | TIME MIN. | FUEL BURNED LB. | DIST. N. MI. |
|---|---|---|---|
| 0. | 0. | 0. | 0. |
| 2000. | 0.5 | 133. | 2.8 |
| 4000. | 1.1 | 267. | 5.9 |
| 6000. | 1.7 | 403. | 9.3 |
| 8000. | 2.3 | 541. | 13.0 |
| 10000. | 3.0 | 684. | 17.2 |
| 12000. | 3.8 | 830. | 21.3 |
| 14000. | 4.6 | 982. | 27.0 |
| 16000. | 5.5 | 1141. | 32.9 |
| 18000. | 6.4 | 1309. | 39.6 |
| 20000. | 7.6 | 1489. | 47.4 |
| 22000. | 8.8 | 1684. | 56.6 |
| 23500. | 9.9 | 1845. | 64.7 |
| 23500. | 9.9 | 1845. | 64.7 |
| 24000. | 10.2 | 1886. | 66.8 |
| 26000. | 11.4 | 2052. | 75.9 |
| 28000. | 12.8 | 2225. | 85.8 |
| 30000. | 14.3 | 2410. | 97.1 |
| 32000. | 16.2 | 2613. | 110.3 |
| 34000. | 18.4 | 2844. | 126.3 |
| 36000. | 21.4 | 3136. | 147.8 |

### INITIAL WEIGHT = 90000. POUNDS

| PRES. ALT. FEET | TIME MIN. | FUEL BURNED LB. | DIST. N. MI. |
|---|---|---|---|
| 0. | 0. | 0. | 0. |
| 2000. | 0.6 | 140. | 3.0 |
| 4000. | 1.1 | 282. | 6.3 |
| 6000. | 1.8 | 426. | 9.8 |
| 8000. | 2.5 | 573. | 13.8 |
| 10000. | 3.2 | 724. | 18.2 |
| 12000. | 4.0 | 879. | 23.1 |
| 14000. | 4.8 | 1041. | 28.6 |
| 16000. | 5.8 | 1211. | 34.9 |
| 18000. | 6.9 | 1390. | 42.1 |
| 20000. | 8.0 | 1583. | 50.4 |
| 22000. | 9.4 | 1793. | 60.3 |
| 23500. | 10.6 | 1968. | 69.1 |
| 23500. | 10.6 | 1968. | 69.1 |
| 24000. | 10.9 | 2013. | 71.5 |
| 26000. | 12.3 | 2196. | 81.5 |
| 28000. | 13.8 | 2389. | 92.6 |
| 30000. | 15.5 | 2598. | 105.4 |
| 32000. | 17.6 | 2833. | 120.6 |
| 34000. | 20.3 | 3110. | 139.8 |
| 36000. | 24.3 | 3494. | 168.0 |

### INITIAL WEIGHT = 88000. POUNDS

| PRES. ALT. FEET | TIME MIN. | FUEL BURNED LB. | DIST. N. MI. |
|---|---|---|---|
| 0. | 0. | 0. | 0. |
| 2000. | 0.5 | 136. | 2.9 |
| 4000. | 1.1 | 274. | 6.1 |
| 6000. | 1.7 | 414. | 9.6 |
| 8000. | 2.4 | 557. | 13.4 |
| 10000. | 3.1 | 703. | 17.7 |
| 12000. | 3.9 | 855. | 22.5 |
| 14000. | 4.7 | 1012. | 27.8 |
| 16000. | 5.6 | 1176. | 33.9 |
| 18000. | 6.6 | 1349. | 40.8 |
| 20000. | 7.8 | 1535. | 48.9 |
| 22000. | 9.1 | 1738. | 58.4 |
| 23500. | 10.3 | 1906. | 66.9 |
| 23500. | 10.3 | 1906. | 66.9 |
| 24000. | 10.6 | 1949. | 69.1 |
| 26000. | 11.9 | 2123. | 78.6 |
| 28000. | 13.3 | 2306. | 89.1 |
| 30000. | 14.9 | 2502. | 101.2 |
| 32000. | 16.9 | 2720. | 115.3 |
| 34000. | 19.3 | 2973. | 132.8 |
| 36000. | 22.7 | 3304. | 157.2 |

### INITIAL WEIGHT = 92000. POUNDS

| PRES. ALT. FEET | TIME MIN. | FUEL BURNED LB. | DIST. N. MI. |
|---|---|---|---|
| 0. | 0. | 0. | 0. |
| 2000. | 0.6 | 144. | 3.1 |
| 4000. | 1.2 | 290. | 6.4 |
| 6000. | 1.8 | 438. | 10.1 |
| 8000. | 2.5 | 589. | 14.2 |
| 10000. | 3.3 | 744. | 18.7 |
| 12000. | 4.1 | 905. | 23.8 |
| 14000. | 5.0 | 1072. | 29.5 |
| 16000. | 6.0 | 1247. | 36.0 |
| 18000. | 7.1 | 1432. | 43.4 |
| 20000. | 8.3 | 1631. | 52.0 |
| 22000. | 9.7 | 1850. | 62.3 |
| 23500. | 11.0 | 2032. | 71.5 |
| 23500. | 11.0 | 2032. | 71.5 |
| 24000. | 11.3 | 2079. | 73.9 |
| 26000. | 12.7 | 2272. | 84.4 |
| 28000. | 14.3 | 2476. | 96.2 |
| 30000. | 16.2 | 2693. | 109.8 |
| 32000. | 18.4 | 2951. | 126.2 |
| 34000. | 21.4 | 3258. | 147.4 |
| 36000. | 26.1 | 3713. | 181.0 |

FIGURE 49.—High-Speed Climb Schedule.

## TIME, FUEL, AND DISTANCE TO CLIMB
## JT8D-1 ENGINES - NORMAL BLEED
## DC-9 SERIES 10 - LONG RANGE CLIMB SCHEDULE
## CLIMB AT 290 KNOTS IAS TO 26860 FT ALTITUDE THEN CLIMB AT M .72

| INITIAL WEIGHT = 78000. POUNDS | | | | INITIAL WEIGHT = 82000. POUNDS | | | |
|---|---|---|---|---|---|---|---|
| PRES. ALT. FEET | TIME MIN. | FUEL BURNED LB. | DIST. N. MI. | PRES. ALT. FEET | TIME MIN. | FUEL BURNED LB. | DIST. N. MI. |
| 0. | 0. | 0. | 0. | 0. | 0. | 0. | 0. |
| 2000. | 0.5 | 113. | 2.2 | 2000. | 0.5 | 120. | 2.4 |
| 4000. | 0.9 | 227. | 4.6 | 4000. | 1.0 | 241. | 4.9 |
| 6000. | 1.5 | 342. | 7.3 | 6000. | 1.5 | 363. | 7.7 |
| 8000. | 2.0 | 457. | 10.2 | 8000. | 2.1 | 486. | 10.8 |
| 10000. | 2.6 | 574. | 13.3 | 10000. | 2.7 | 610. | 14.2 |
| 12000. | 3.2 | 693. | 16.8 | 12000. | 3.4 | 737. | 17.9 |
| 14000. | 3.9 | 815. | 20.7 | 14000. | 4.1 | 868. | 22.1 |
| 16000. | 4.6 | 941. | 25.0 | 16000. | 4.9 | 1002. | 26.7 |
| 18000. | 5.4 | 1070. | 29.9 | 18000. | 5.7 | 1141. | 31.9 |
| 20000. | 6.3 | 1205. | 35.4 | 20000. | 6.7 | 1286. | 37.9 |
| 22000. | 7.2 | 1347. | 41.7 | 22000. | 7.7 | 1439. | 44.6 |
| 24000. | 8.3 | 1498. | 49.0 | 24000. | 8.9 | 1602. | 52.5 |
| 26000. | 9.5 | 1661. | 57.6 | 26000. | 10.2 | 1780. | 61.9 |
| 26860. | 10.1 | 1736. | 61.8 | 26860. | 10.9 | 1863. | 66.5 |
| 26860. | 10.1 | 1736. | 61.8 | 26860. | 10.9 | 1863. | 66.5 |
| 28000. | 10.7 | 1813. | 66.2 | 28000. | 11.6 | 1948. | 71.4 |
| 30000. | 11.9 | 1953. | 74.6 | 30000. | 12.9 | 2104. | 80.8 |
| 32000. | 13.3 | 2102. | 84.2 | 32000. | 14.4 | 2274. | 91.7 |
| 34000. | 14.9 | 2267. | 95.4 | 34000. | 16.3 | 2464. | 104.6 |
| 36000. | 16.9 | 2456. | 109.2 | 36000. | 18.7 | 2693. | 121.3 |

| INITIAL WEIGHT = 80000. POUNDS | | | | INITIAL WEIGHT = 84000. POUNDS | | | |
|---|---|---|---|---|---|---|---|
| 0. | 0. | 0. | 0. | 0. | 0. | 0. | 0. |
| 2000. | 0.5 | 117. | 2.3 | 2000. | 0.5 | 124. | 2.4 |
| 4000. | 1.0 | 234. | 4.8 | 4000. | 1.0 | 248. | 5.1 |
| 6000. | 1.5 | 352. | 7.5 | 6000. | 1.6 | 374. | 8.0 |
| 8000. | 2.1 | 471. | 10.5 | 8000. | 2.2 | 500. | 11.1 |
| 10000. | 2.7 | 592. | 13.7 | 10000. | 2.8 | 629. | 14.6 |
| 12000. | 3.3 | 715. | 17.4 | 12000. | 3.5 | 760. | 18.5 |
| 14000. | 4.0 | 841. | 21.4 | 14000. | 4.2 | 894. | 22.8 |
| 16000. | 4.7 | 971. | 25.9 | 16000. | 5.1 | 1033. | 27.6 |
| 18000. | 5.6 | 1105. | 30.9 | 18000. | 5.9 | 1177. | 33.0 |
| 20000. | 6.5 | 1245. | 36.6 | 20000. | 6.9 | 1327. | 39.1 |
| 22000. | 7.5 | 1392. | 43.2 | 22000. | 8.0 | 1486. | 46.2 |
| 24000. | 8.6 | 1549. | 50.7 | 24000. | 9.2 | 1656. | 54.4 |
| 26000. | 9.9 | 1719. | 59.7 | 26000. | 10.6 | 1841. | 64.1 |
| 26860. | 10.5 | 1798. | 64.1 | 26860. | 11.3 | 1928. | 69.0 |
| 26860. | 10.5 | 1798. | 64.1 | 26860. | 11.3 | 1928. | 69.0 |
| 28000. | 11.1 | 1879. | 68.7 | 28000. | 12.0 | 2018. | 74.1 |
| 30000. | 12.4 | 2027. | 77.7 | 30000. | 13.4 | 2183. | 84.1 |
| 32000. | 13.8 | 2186. | 87.8 | 32000. | 15.0 | 2364. | 95.7 |
| 34000. | 15.6 | 2362. | 99.8 | 34000. | 17.1 | 2570. | 109.7 |
| 36000. | 17.7 | 2570. | 114.9 | 36000. | 19.7 | 2826. | 128.3 |

FIGURE 50.—Long-Range Climb Schedule.

| OPERATING CONDITIONS | L-1 | L-2 | L-3 | L-4 | L-5 |
|---|---|---|---|---|---|
| WEIGHT (START TO ALT) | 85,000 | 70,000 | 86,000 | 76,000 | 82,000 |
| DISTANCE (NAM) | 110 | 190 | 330 | 50 | 240 |
| WIND COMPONENT (KTS) | 15 HW | 40 TW | 50 HW | 20 TW | 45 HW |
| HOLDING TIME AT ALT (MIN) | 15 | 15 | 15 | 15 | 15 |

FIGURE 51.—DC-9 – Alternate Planning.

## ALTERNATE PLANNING CHART

| DIST. - NAM | 20 | 30 | 40 | 50 | 60 | 70 | 80 | 90 | 100 | 110 | 120 | 130 | 140 |
|---|---|---|---|---|---|---|---|---|---|---|---|---|---|
| OPTM. ALT. | 2000 | 3000 | 4000 | 5000 | 6000 | 7000 | 8000 | 9000 | 10000 | 11000 | 12000 | 13000 | 14000 |
| TIME: | :16 | :17 | :19 | :20 | :22 | :23 | :25 | :26 | :28 | :29 | :30 | :32 | :33 |
| FUEL | 2500 | 2600 | 2700 | 2800 | 2900 | 3000 | 3100 | 3200 | 3300 | 3400 | 3500 | 3600 | 3700 |
| TAS | 275 | 280 | 283 | 286 | 289 | 292 | 296 | 300 | 303 | 306 | 309 | 312 | 315 |

| DIST. NAM | 150 | 160 | 170 | 180 | 190 | 200 | 210 | 220 | 230 | 240 | 250 | 260 | 270 |
|---|---|---|---|---|---|---|---|---|---|---|---|---|---|
| OPTM. ALT. | 15000 | 16000 | 17000 | 18000 | 19000 | 20000 | 21000 | 22000 | 23000 | 24000 | 25000 | 26000 | 27000 |
| TIME: | :35 | :36 | :38 | :39 | :40 | :42 | :43 | :45 | :46 | :48 | :49 | :50 | :52 |
| FUEL | 3800 | 3900 | 4000 | 4100 | 4200 | 4300 | 4400 | 4500 | 4600 | 4700 | 4800 | 4900 | 5000 |
| TAS | 319 | 323 | 326 | 330 | 334 | 338 | 341 | 345 | 349 | 353 | 357 | 361 | 365 |

| DIST. - NAM | 280 | 290 | 300 | 310 | 320 | 330 | 340 | 350 | 360 | 370 | 380 | 390 | 400 |
|---|---|---|---|---|---|---|---|---|---|---|---|---|---|
| OPTM. ALT. | 27000 | 28000 | 28000 | 29000 | 29000 | 30000 | 30000 | 31000 | 31000 | 31000 | 31000 | 31000 | 31000 |
| TIME: | :53 | :55 | :56 | :58 | :59 | 1:00 | 1:02 | 1:03 | 1:04 | 1:05 | 1:07 | 1:08 | 1:10 |
| FUEL | 5150 | 5250 | 5350 | 5450 | 5600 | 5700 | 5800 | 5900 | 6050 | 6150 | 6250 | 6350 | 6500 |
| TAS | 368 | 372 | 376 | 380 | 385 | 388 | 392 | 397 | 397 | 397 | 397 | 397 | 397 |

**NOTES:**

1. Fuel includes 1/2 climb distance en route credit, fuel to cruise remaining distance at LRC schedule, 15 minutes holding at alternate, and 800 lbs. for descent.

2. Time includes 1/2 climb distance credit, time to cruise distance shown at LRC schedule and 8 minutes for descent. 15 minutes holding is not included in time.

FIGURE 52.—DC-9 – Alternate Planning Chart.

| OPERATING CONDITIONS | R-1 | R-2 | R-3 | R-4 | R-5 |
|---|---|---|---|---|---|
| FIELD ELEVATION | 100 | 4,000 | 950 | 2,000 | 50 |
| ALTIMETER SETTING | 29.50" | 1032 mb | 29.40" | 1017 mb | 30.15" |
| TEMPERATURE (OAT) | +50 °F | −15 °C | +59 °F | 0 °C | +95 °F |
| WEIGHT (X1000) | 90 | 110 | 100 | 85 | 95 |
| FLAP POSITION | 15° | 5° | 5° | 1° | 1° |
| WIND COMPONENT (KTS) | 5 HW | 5 TW | 20 HW | 10 TW | 7 HW |
| RUNWAY SLOPE % | 1% UP | 1% DN | 1% UP | 2% DN | 1.5% UP |
| AIR CONDITIONING | ON | ON | OFF | ON | OFF |
| ENGINE ANTI-ICE | OFF | ON | OFF | ON | OFF |
| CG STATION | 635.7 | 643.8 | 665.2 | 657.2 | 638.4 |
| LEMAC STA 625.0, MAC 134.0 | | | | | |

FIGURE 53.—B-737 – Takeoff.

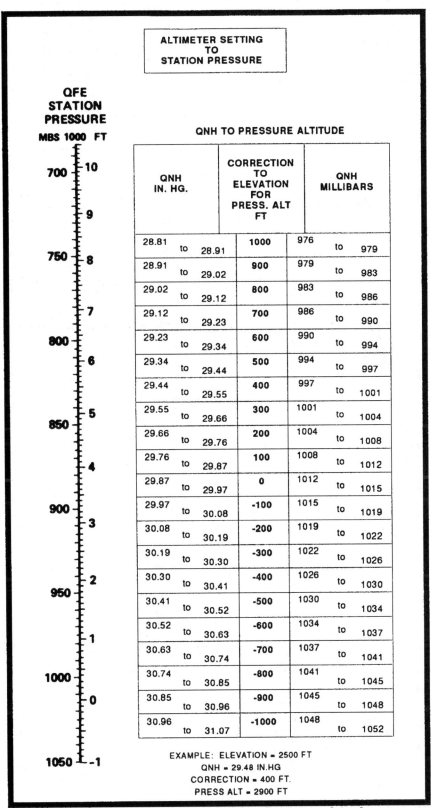

**ALTIMETER SETTING TO STATION PRESSURE**

QFE
STATION
PRESSURE

MBS 1000 FT

QNH TO PRESSURE ALTITUDE

| QNH IN. HG. | | CORRECTION TO ELEVATION FOR PRESS. ALT FT | QNH MILLIBARS | |
|---|---|---|---|---|
| 28.81 | to 28.91 | 1000 | 976 | to 979 |
| 28.91 | to 29.02 | 900 | 979 | to 983 |
| 29.02 | to 29.12 | 800 | 983 | to 986 |
| 29.12 | to 29.23 | 700 | 986 | to 990 |
| 29.23 | to 29.34 | 600 | 990 | to 994 |
| 29.34 | to 29.44 | 500 | 994 | to 997 |
| 29.44 | to 29.55 | 400 | 997 | to 1001 |
| 29.55 | to 29.66 | 300 | 1001 | to 1004 |
| 29.66 | to 29.76 | 200 | 1004 | to 1008 |
| 29.76 | to 29.87 | 100 | 1008 | to 1012 |
| 29.87 | to 29.97 | 0 | 1012 | to 1015 |
| 29.97 | to 30.08 | -100 | 1015 | to 1019 |
| 30.08 | to 30.19 | -200 | 1019 | to 1022 |
| 30.19 | to 30.30 | -300 | 1022 | to 1026 |
| 30.30 | to 30.41 | -400 | 1026 | to 1030 |
| 30.41 | to 30.52 | -500 | 1030 | to 1034 |
| 30.52 | to 30.63 | -600 | 1034 | to 1037 |
| 30.63 | to 30.74 | -700 | 1037 | to 1041 |
| 30.74 | to 30.85 | -800 | 1041 | to 1045 |
| 30.85 | to 30.96 | -900 | 1045 | to 1048 |
| 30.96 | to 31.07 | -1000 | 1048 | to 1052 |

EXAMPLE: ELEVATION = 2500 FT
QNH = 29.48 IN.HG
CORRECTION = 400 FT.
PRESS ALT = 2900 FT

FIGURE 54.—Altimeter Setting to Pressure Altitude.

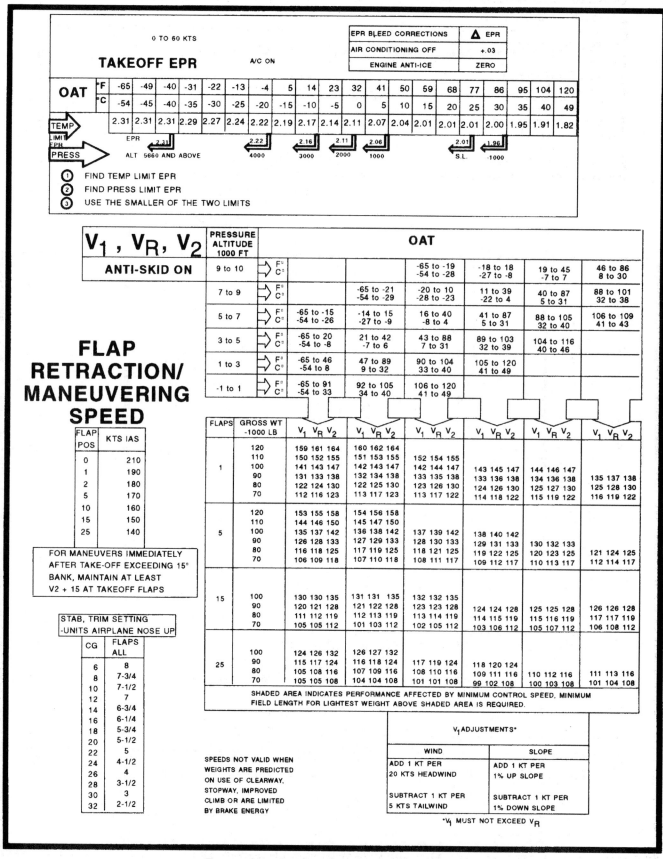

FIGURE 55.—B-737 – Takeoff Performance.

| OPERATING CONDITIONS | V-1 | V-2 | V-3 | V-4 | V-5 |
|---|---|---|---|---|---|
| BRK REL WEIGHT (X1000) | 110 | 95 | 85 | 105 | 75 |
| CRUISE PRESS ALT | 33,000 | 27,000 | 35,000 | 22,000 | 31,000 |
| AIRPORT ELEVATION | 2,000 | 3,000 | 2,000 | 4,000 | 2,000 |
| ISA TEMPERATURE | +10° | ISA | ISA | +10° | +10° |
| AVG WIND COMP (KTS) | 20 HW | 20 TW | 30 HW | 10 TW | 40 HW |

FIGURE 56.—B-737 – En Route Climb.

## EN ROUTE CLIMB 280/.70 ISA

| PRESSURE ALTITUDE -FT | UNITS MIN/LB NM/KNOTS | BRAKE RELEASE WEIGHT - LB | | | | | | | | | | |
|---|---|---|---|---|---|---|---|---|---|---|---|---|
| | | 120000 | 115000 | 110000 | 105000 | 100000 | 95000 | 90000 | 85000 | 80000 | 75000 | 65000 |
| 37000 | TIME/FUEL DIST./TAS | | 41/5700 251/387 | 32/4700 192/384 | 27/4100 162/382 | 24/3700 140/380 | 21/3400 124/379 | 19/3100 111/378 | 17/2800 100/377 | 16/2500 90/376 | 14/2300 82/375 | 12/1900 67/374 |
| 36000 | TIME/FUEL DIST./TAS | 41/ 5900 246/386 | 33/4900 194/383 | 28/4300 164/381 | 25/3900 143/379 | 22/3500 127/378 | 20/3200 114/377 | 18/2900 103/376 | 16/2700 93/375 | 15/2500 84/374 | 14/2300 77/374 | 11/1900 63/373 |
| 35000 | TIME/FUEL DIST./TAS | 33/5100 197/382 | 29/4500 168/380 | 25/4100 147/378 | 23/3700 131/377 | 21/3400 117/376 | 19/3100 106/375 | 17/2800 96/374 | 16/2600 87/373 | 14/2400 80/373 | 13/2200 73/372 | 11/1800 60/371 |
| 34000 | TIME/FUEL DIST./TAS | 29/4700 171/379 | 26/4300 150/377 | 23/3900 134/376 | 21/3500 120/375 | 19/3200 109/374 | 18/3000 99/373 | 16/2700 90/372 | 15/2500 82/372 | 14/2300 75/371 | 12/2100 69/371 | 10/1800 57/370 |
| 33000 | TIME/FUEL DIST./TAS | 27/4400 153/376 | 24/4000 137/375 | 22/3700 123/374 | 20/3400 112/373 | 18/3100 102/372 | 17/2900 93/371 | 15/2700 85/370 | 14/2500 78/370 | 13/2300 71/369 | 12/2100 65/369 | 10/1700 54/368 |
| 32000 | TIME/FUEL DIST./TAS | 25/4200 139/374 | 23/3900 126/372 | 21/3600 114/371 | 19/3300 104/370 | 17/3000 95/370 | 16/2800 87/369 | 15/2600 80/368 | 14/2400 74/368 | 12/2200 67/367 | 11/2000 62/367 | 10/1700 51/366 |
| 31000 | TIME/FUEL DIST./TAS | 23/4000 128/371 | 21/3700 117/370 | 19/3400 107/369 | 18/3200 98/368 | 16/2900 90/367 | 15/2700 82/367 | 14/2500 76/366 | 13/2300 70/366 | 12/2100 64/365 | 11/2000 59/365 | 9/1700 49/364 |
| 30000 | TIME/FUEL DIST./TAS | 22/3900 119/368 | 20/3600 109/367 | 18/3300 100/366 | 17/3100 92/365 | 16/2800 84/365 | 15/2600 78/364 | 13/2400 72/364 | 12/2300 66/363 | 11/2100 61/363 | 11/1900 56/363 | 9/1600 47/362 |
| 29000 | TIME/FUEL DIST./TAS | 21/3700 111/365 | 19/3400 102/364 | 18/3200 93/363 | 16/3000 86/363 | 15/2700 79/362 | 14/2500 73/362 | 13/2400 68/361 | 12/2200 62/361 | 11/2000 57/361 | 10/1900 53/360 | 9/1600 44/360 |
| 28000 | TIME/FUEL DIST./TAS | 19/3600 103/362 | 18/3300 95/361 | 17/3100 88/360 | 15/2900 81/360 | 14/2700 75/359 | 13/2500 69/359 | 12/2300 64/359 | 11/2100 59/358 | 11/2000 54/358 | 10/1800 50/358 | 8/1500 42/357 |
| 27000 | TIME/FUEL DIST./TAS | 19/3400 96/358 | 17/3200 89/358 | 16/3000 82/357 | 15/2800 76/357 | 14/2600 71/356 | 13/2400 65/356 | 12/2200 60/356 | 11/2100 56/356 | 10/1900 52/355 | 9/1800 47/355 | 8/1500 40/355 |
| 26000 | TIME/FUEL DIST./TAS | 17/3300 88/354 | 16/3000 82/354 | 15/2800 76/353 | 14/2600 70/353 | 13/2500 65/352 | 12/2300 60/352 | 11/2100 56/352 | 10/2000 52/352 | 10/1800 48/351 | 9/1700 44/351 | 7/1400 37/351 |
| 25000 | TIME/FUEL DIST./TAS | 16/3100 81/350 | 15/2900 75/350 | 14/2700 70/349 | 13/2500 65/349 | 12/2400 60/349 | 11/2200 56/348 | 11/2000 52/348 | 10/1900 48/348 | 9/1800 45/348 | 8/1600 41/348 | 7/1400 35/347 |
| 24000 | TIME/FUEL DIST./TAS | 15/3000 75/346 | 14/2800 69/346 | 13/2600 65/345 | 12/2400 60/345 | 12/2300 56/345 | 11/2100 52/345 | 10/2000 48/345 | 9/1800 45/344 | 9/1700 41/344 | 8/1600 38/344 | 7/1300 32/344 |
| 23000 | TIME/FUEL DIST./TAS | 14/2800 69/342 | 13/2700 64/342 | 13/2500 60/342 | 12/2300 56/342 | 11/2200 52/342 | 10/2000 48/341 | 9/1900 45/341 | 9/1800 41/341 | 8/1600 38/341 | 8/1500 35/341 | 6/1300 30/341 |
| 22000 | TIME/FUEL DIST./TAS | 14/2700 63/339 | 13/2500 59/339 | 12/2400 55/338 | 11/2200 51/338 | 10/2100 48/338 | 10/1900 45/338 | 9/1800 41/338 | 8/1700 38/338 | 8/1600 36/338 | 7/1400 33/338 | 6/1200 28/337 |
| 6000 | TIME/FUEL DIST./TAS | 4/1000 9/295 | 4/1000 9/295 | 4/900 8/295 | 4/800 8/295 | 3/800 7/295 | 3/700 7/295 | 3/700 6/295 | 3/700 6/295 | 3/600 5/295 | 2/600 5/295 | 2/500 4/295 |
| 1500 | TIME/FUEL | 2/600 | 2/600 | 2/500 | 2/500 | 2/500 | 2/400 | 2/400 | 2/400 | 1/400 | 1/300 | 1/300 |

| FUEL ADJUSTMENT FOR HIGH ELEVATION AIRPORTS | AIRPORT ELEVATION | 2000 | 4000 | 6000 | 8000 | 10000 | 12000 |
|---|---|---|---|---|---|---|---|
| EFFECT ON TIME AND DISTANCE IS NEGLIGIBLE | FUEL ADJUSTMENT | -100 | -200 | -400 | -500 | -600 | -700 |

FIGURE 57.—En Route Climb 280/.70 ISA.

# EN ROUTE CLIMB 280/.70 ISA +10 ˚C

| PRESSURE ALTITUDE -FT | UNITS MIM/LB NM/KNOTS | BRAKE RELEASE WEIGHT - LB | | | | | | | | | | |
|---|---|---|---|---|---|---|---|---|---|---|---|---|
| | | 120000 | 115000 | 110000 | 105000 | 100000 | 95000 | 90000 | 85000 | 80000 | 75000 | 65000 |
| 37000 | TIME/FUEL DIST./TAS | | | 42/5700 263/395 | 34/4700 206/391 | 29/4100 174/389 | 25/3700 151/388 | 23/3300 133/386 | 20/3000 119/385 | 18/2700 107/384 | 16/2500 96/384 | 13/2100 78/382 |
| 36000 | TIME/FUEL DIST./TAS | | 43/5900 266/394 | 35/5000 211/391 | 30/4400 179/389 | 26/3900 156/387 | 23/3500 138/385 | 21/3200 123/384 | 19/2900 111/383 | 17/2700 100/383 | 16/2400 90/382 | 13/2000 74/381 |
| 35000 | TIME/FUEL DIST./TAS | 45/6200 275/394 | 36/5300 219/390 | 31/4600 186/388 | 27/4100 162/386 | 24/3700 143/385 | 22/3400 128/384 | 20/3100 115/383 | 10/2800 104/382 | 16/2600 94/381 | 15/2400 85/380 | 12/2000 70/379 |
| 34000 | TIME/FUEL DIST./TAS | 38/5600 228/390 | 32/4900 193/387 | 28/4400 168/386 | 25/3900 149/384 | 23/3600 133/383 | 21/3300 120/382 | 19/3000 108/381 | 17/2700 98/380 | 16/2600 89/379 | 14/2300 81/379 | 12/1900 67/378 |
| 33000 | TIME/FUEL DIST./TAS | 34/5100 200/387 | 30/4600 174/385 | 26/4100 154/383 | 24/3800 138/382 | 22/3400 124/381 | 20/3100 113/380 | 18/2900 102/379 | 16/2600 93/378 | 15/2400 85/378 | 14/2200 77/377 | 11/1900 64/376 |
| 32000 | TIME/FUEL DIST./TAS | 31/4800 180/384 | 28/4400 160/382 | 25/4000 143/381 | 23/3600 129/379 | 21/3300 116/378 | 19/3000 106/378 | 17/2800 96/377 | 16/2600 88/376 | 14/2400 80/376 | 13/2200 73/375 | 11/1800 61/374 |
| 31000 | TIME/FUEL DIST./TAS | 29/4600 165/381 | 26/4200 147/379 | 23/3800 133/378 | 21/3500 120/377 | 20/3200 109/376 | 18/2900 100/375 | 16/2700 91/375 | 15/2500 83/374 | 14/2300 76/374 | 13/2100 70/373 | 11/1800 58/372 |
| 30000 | TIME/FUEL DIST./TAS | 27/4400 152/378 | 24/4000 137/376 | 22/3700 124/375 | 20/3400 113/374 | 19/3100 103/374 | 17/2900 94/373 | 16/2600 86/372 | 14/2400 79/372 | 13/2200 72/371 | 12/2100 66/371 | 10/1700 55/370 |
| 29000 | TIME/FUEL DIST./TAS | 25/4200 141/375 | 23/3800 128/374 | 21/3500 116/373 | 19/3200 106/372 | 18/3000 97/371 | 16/2800 89/370 | 15/2600 82/370 | 14/2400 75/369 | 13/2200 69/369 | 12/2000 63/369 | 10/1700 52/368 |
| 28000 | TIME/FUEL DIST./TAS | 24/4000 131/371 | 22/3700 119/370 | 20/3400 109/369 | 18/3100 100/369 | 17/2900 91/368 | 16/2700 84/368 | 14/2500 77/367 | 13/2300 71/367 | 12/2100 65/366 | 11/1900 60/366 | 9/1600 50/365 |
| 27000 | TIME/FUEL DIST./TAS | 22/3800 121/368 | 21/3500 111/367 | 19/3300 102/366 | 18/3000 93/366 | 16/2800 86/365 | 15/2600 79/364 | 14/2400 73/364 | 13/2200 67/364 | 12/2000 61/363 | 11/1900 56/363 | 9/1600 47/363 |
| 26000 | TIME/FUEL DIST./TAS | 21/3600 110/363 | 19/3400 101/362 | 18/3100 93/362 | 16/2900 86/361 | 15/2700 79/361 | 14/2500 73/360 | 13/2300 67/360 | 12/2100 62/360 | 11/2000 57/359 | 10/1800 52/359 | 9/1500 44/359 |
| 25000 | TIME/FUEL DIST./TAS | 19/3400 101/358 | 18/3200 93/358 | 17/3000 85/357 | 15/2800 79/357 | 14/2600 73/357 | 13/2400 67/356 | 12/2200 62/356 | 11/2000 57/356 | 10/1900 53/356 | 10/1700 48/355 | 8/1500 41/355 |
| 24000 | TIME/FUEL DIST./TAS | 18/3300 92/354 | 17/3000 85/354 | 16/2800 78/353 | 15/2600 72/353 | 13/2400 67/353 | 12/2300 62/352 | 12/2100 57/352 | 11/1900 53/352 | 10/1800 49/352 | 9/1700 45/352 | 8/1400 38/351 |
| 23000 | TIME/FUEL DIST./TAS | 17/3100 84/350 | 16/2900 78/350 | 15/2900 72/350 | 14/2500 67/349 | 13/2300 62/349 | 12/2200 57/349 | 11/2000 53/349 | 10/1900 49/348 | 9/1700 45/348 | 9/1600 42/348 | 7/1300 35/348 |
| 22000 | TIME/FUEL DIST./TAS | 16/3000 77/346 | 15/2800 71/346 | 14/2600 66/346 | 13/2400 61/346 | 12/2200 57/345 | 11/2100 53/345 | 10/1900 49/345 | 10/1800 45/345 | 9/1700 42/345 | 8/1500 38/345 | 7/1300 32/344 |
| 6000 | TIME/FUEL DIST./TAS | 5/1100 10/301 | 4/1000 10/301 | 4/900 9/301 | 4/900 9/301 | 4/800 8/301 | 3/800 8/301 | 3/700 7/301 | 3/700 7/301 | 3/600 6/301 | 3/600 6/301 | 2/500 5/301 |
| 1500 | TIME/FUEL | 3/600 | 2/600 | 2/500 | 2/500 | 2/500 | 2/500 | 2/400 | 2/400 | 2/400 | 1/300 | 1/300 |

| FUEL ADJUSTMENT FOR HIGH ELEVATION AIRPORTS | AIRPORT ELEVATION | 2000 | 4000 | 6000 | 8000 | 10000 | 12000 |
|---|---|---|---|---|---|---|---|
| EFFECT ON TIME AND DISTANCE IS NEGLIGIBLE | FUEL ADJUSTMENT | -100 | -300 | -400 | -500 | -600 | -800 |

FIGURE 58.—En Route Climb 280/.70 ISA +10 °C.

| OPERATING CONDITIONS | T-1 | T-2 | T-3 | T-4 | T-5 |
|---|---|---|---|---|---|
| TOTAL AIR TEMP (TAT) | +10 °C | 0 °C | –15 °C | –30 °C | +15 °C |
| ALTITUDE | 10,000 | 5,000 | 25,000 | 35,000 | 18,000 |
| ENGINE ANTI-ICE | ON | ON | ON | ON | OFF |
| WING ANTI-ICE | OFF | 2 ON | 2 ON | 1 ON | OFF |
| AIR CONDITIONING | ON | OFF | ON | ON | OFF |

FIGURE 59.—B-737 – Climb and Cruise Power.

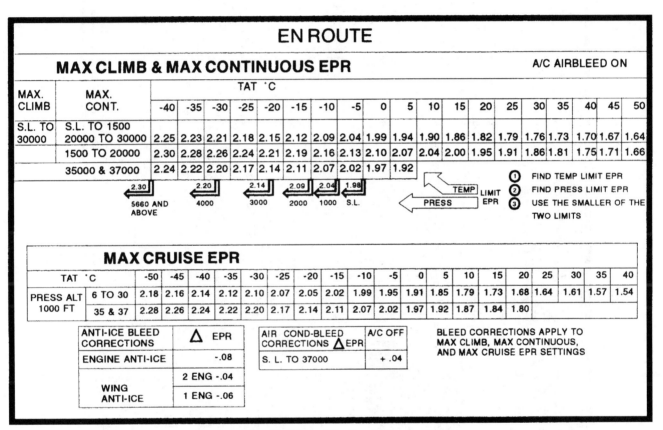

FIGURE 60.—B-737 – Climb and Cruise Power.

| OPERATING CONDITIONS | X-1 | X-2 | X-3 | X-4 | X-5 |
|---|---|---|---|---|---|
| DISTANCE (NM) | 2,000 | 2,400 | 1,800 | 2,800 | 1,200 |
| WIND COMPONENT (KTS) | 50 TW | 50 HW | 20 HW | 50 TW | 30 HW |
| CRUISE PRESS ALTITUDE | 27,000 | 35,000 | 20,000 | 29,000 | 37,000 |
| ISA TEMPERATURE | +10° | ISA | +20° | −10° | +10° |
| LANDING WEIGHT (X1000) | 70 | 75 | 75 | 65 | 90 |

FIGURE 61.—Flight Planning at .78 Mach Cruise.

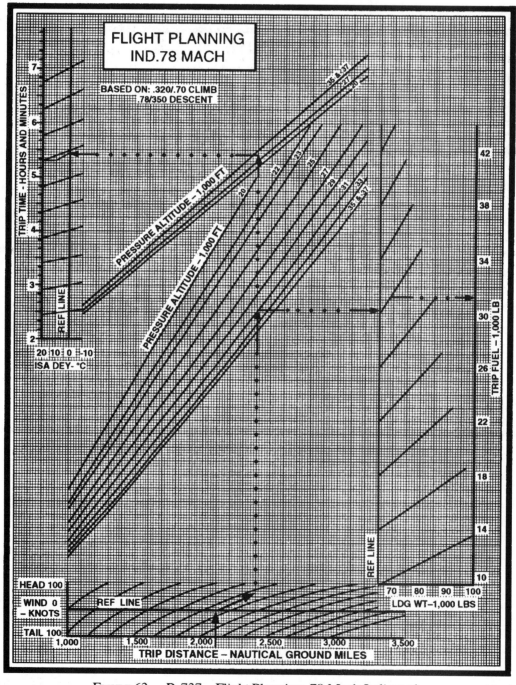

FIGURE 62.—B-737 – Flight Planning .78 Mach Indicated.

| OPERATING CONDITIONS | Q–1 | Q–2 | Q–3 | Q–4 | Q–5 |
|---|---|---|---|---|---|
| WEIGHT (X1000) | 110 | 70 | 90 | 80 | 100 |
| PRESSURE ALTITUDE | 30,000 | 25,000 | 35,000 | 20,000 | 10,000 |
| TOTAL AIR TEMP (TAT) | –8 °C | –23 °C | –16 °C | +4 °C | –6 °C |

FIGURE 63.—B-737– Turbulent Air RPM.

## TURBULENT AIR PENETRATION

| TARGET SPEED IAS/MACH | PRESS ALT -1000 FT | GROSS WEIGHT - 1000 LB | | | | | ISA TAT -°C | % N₁ ADJUSTMENT PER 10 °C VARIATION FROM TABLE TAT COLDER - WARMER + |
|---|---|---|---|---|---|---|---|---|
| | | 70 | 80 | 90 | 100 | 110 | | |
| | | APPROXIMATE POWER SETTING -%N1 RPM | | | | | | |
| 280/.70 | 35 | 77.1 | 79.0 | 81.0 | 83.4 | | -36 | 1.6 |
| | 30 | 77.2 | 78.2 | 79.4 | 81.1 | 82.4 | -23 | 1.6 |
| | 25 | 76.7 | 77.5 | 78.3 | 79.2 | 80.1 | -13 | 1.5 |
| | 20 | 74.7 | 75.4 | 76.1 | 77.0 | 77.9 | -6 | 1.4 |
| | 15 | 72.7 | 73.5 | 74.2 | 74.8 | 75.7 | 1 | 1.2 |
| | 10 | 70.5 | 71.3 | 72.1 | 72.9 | 73.9 | 9 | 1.3 |

FIGURE 64.—B-737 – Turbulent Air Penetration.

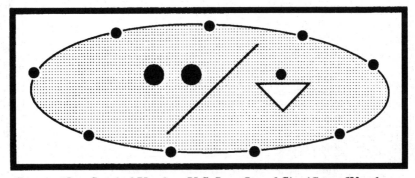

FIGURE 65.—Symbol Used on U.S. Low Level Significant Weather Prog Chart.

| OPERATING CONDITIONS | Z-1 | Z-2 | Z-3 | Z-4 | Z-5 |
|---|---|---|---|---|---|
| DISTANCE (NM) | 340 | 650 | 900 | 290 | 400 |
| AVG WIND COMP (KTS) | 25 TW | 45 HW | 35 TW | 25 HW | 60 HW |

FIGURE 66.—Flight Planning at .74 Mach Cruise.

## ABBREVIATED FLIGHT PLANNING
### .280/.70 CLIMB
### .74/320/340 DESCENT
### 250 KTS CRUISE BELOW 10000 FT.
### 320 KTS CRUISE 10000 THRU 23000 FT.
### .74 MACH CRUISE 24000 FT. AND ABOVE

| DIST. N. MI. | REC. ALT. | TAS KTS | AIR TIME MINS. | FUEL LBS. |
|---|---|---|---|---|
| 50 | 6000-7000 | 279 | 16 | 1800 |
| 60 | 6000-7000 | 279 | 18 | 1950 |
| | | | | |
| 260 | 26000-27000 | 447 | 44 | 4600 |
| 270 | 26000-27000 | 447 | 45 | 4750 |
| 280 | 27000-28000 | 445 | 47 | 4850 |
| 290 | 28000-29000 | 443 | 48 | 4950 |
| 300 | 28000-29000 | 443 | 49 | 5100 |
| 310 | 28000-29000 | 443 | 51 | 5200 |
| 320 | 29000-31000 | 441 | 52 | 5300 |
| 330 | 29000-31000 | 441 | 53 | 5400 |
| 340 | 31000-33000 | 438 | 55 | 5550 |
| 350 | 31000-33000 | 438 | 56 | 5650 |
| 400 | 33000-35000 | 433 | 62 | 6250 |
| 450 | 33000-35000 | 433 | 69 | 6850 |
| 500 | 33000-35000 | 433 | 76 | 7500 |
| 550 | 33000-35000 | 433 | 82 | 8100 |
| 600 | 33000-35000 | 433 | 89 | 8700 |
| 650 | 33000-35000 | 433 | 96 | 9300 |
| 700 | 33000-35000 | 433 | 102 | 9900 |
| 750 | 33000-35000 | 433 | 109 | 10500 |
| 800 | 33000-35000 | 433 | 115 | 11100 |
| 850 | 33000-35000 | 433 | 122 | 11700 |
| 900 | 33000-35000 | 433 | 129 | 12300 |
| 950 | 33000-35000 | 433 | 135 | 12900 |
| 1000 | 33000-35000 | 433 | 142 | 13500 |

### TIME AND FUEL CORRECTION FOR WIND
△ TIME = TIME X WIND COMPONENT ÷ TAS
△ FUEL = FUEL X WIND COMPONENT ÷ TAS

EXAMPLE: DIST. = 250
STILL AIR TIME = 43 MIN.
STILL AIR FUEL = 4500 LBS.
WIND COMPONENT = 20 KTS.

△ TIME = 43 X 20 ÷ 449 = MIN.
△ FUEL = 4500 X 20 = 449 = 200 LBS.
ADD △ TIME AND △ FUEL FOR THE HEADWIND; SUBTRACT FOR TAILWIND

FIGURE 67.—Abbreviated Flight Planning.

| OPERATING CONDITIONS | O-1 | O-2 | O-3 | O-4 | O-5 |
|---|---|---|---|---|---|
| ALTITUDE | 31,000 | 23,000 | 17,000 | 8,000 | 4,000 |
| WEIGHT (X1000) | 102 | 93 | 104 | 113 | 109 |
| ENGINES OPERATING | 2 | 2 | 2 | 2 | 2 |
| HOLDING TIME (MIN) | 20 | 40 | 35 | 15 | 25 |

FIGURE 68.—B-737 – Holding.

**HOLDING**

EPR
IAS    KNOTS
FF PER ENGINE    LB/HR

| FLIGHT LEVEL | GROSS WEIGHT   1000 LB | | | | | | | | | | |
|---|---|---|---|---|---|---|---|---|---|---|---|
| | 115 | 110 | 105 | 100 | 95 | 90 | 85 | 80 | 75 | 70 | 65 |
| 350 | 2.13 | 2.07 | 2.01 | 1.95 | 1.90 | 1.85 | 1.80 | 1.76 | 1.71 | 1.67 | 1.64 |
| | 234 | 228 | 223 | 217 | 211 | 210 | 210 | 210 | 210 | 210 | 210 |
| | 2830 | 2810 | 2630 | 2460 | 2290 | 2180 | 2070 | 1960 | 1870 | 1780 | 1700 |
| 300 | 1.86 | 1.82 | 1.79 | 1.75 | 1.71 | 1.67 | 1.64 | 1.60 | 1.57 | 1.54 | 1.51 |
| | 231 | 226 | 220 | 215 | 210 | 210 | 210 | 210 | 210 | 210 | 210 |
| | 2740 | 2600 | 2470 | 2370 | 2250 | 2140 | 2050 | 1960 | 1880 | 1790 | 1720 |
| 250 | 1.69 | 1.66 | 1.63 | 1.60 | 1.57 | 1.54 | 1.51 | 1.48 | 1.45 | 1.43 | 1.41 |
| | 229 | 224 | 218 | 213 | 210 | 210 | 210 | 210 | 210 | 210 | 210 |
| | 2710 | 2610 | 2490 | 2370 | 2260 | 2180 | 2080 | 1980 | 1920 | 1840 | 1780 |
| 200 | 1.56 | 1.53 | 1.50 | 1.48 | 1.45 | 1.43 | 1.40 | 1.38 | 1.36 | 1.34 | 1.32 |
| | 227 | 222 | 217 | 211 | 210 | 210 | 210 | 210 | 210 | 210 | 210 |
| | 2716 | 2590 | 2490 | 2390 | 2310 | 2230 | 2130 | 2060 | 2000 | 1920 | 1860 |
| 150 | 1.45 | 1.43 | 1.40 | 1.38 | 1.36 | 1.34 | 1.32 | 1.31 | 1.29 | 1.27 | 1.26 |
| | 226 | 221 | 216 | 210 | 210 | 210 | 210 | 210 | 210 | 210 | 210 |
| | 2790 | 2680 | 2570 | 2470 | 2380 | 2290 | 2220 | 2140 | 2070 | 2000 | 1990 |
| 100 | 1.36 | 1.34 | 1.33 | 1.31 | 1.29 | 1.28 | 1.26 | 1.25 | 1.24 | 1.22 | 1.21 |
| | 225 | 220 | 215 | 210 | 210 | 210 | 210 | 210 | 210 | 210 | 210 |
| | 2860 | 2780 | 2670 | 2560 | 2470 | 2390 | 2310 | 2240 | 2170 | 2100 | 2030 |
| 050 | 1.29 | 1.28 | 1.27 | 1.25 | 1.24 | 1.23 | 1.21 | 1.20 | 1.19 | 1.18 | 1.17 |
| | 224 | 219 | 214 | 210 | 210 | 210 | 210 | 210 | 210 | 210 | 210 |
| | 2960 | 2870 | 2770 | 2670 | 2580 | 2500 | 2420 | 2350 | 2290 | 2230 | 2150 |
| 015 | 1.25 | 1.24 | 1.23 | 1.22 | 1.21 | 1.20 | 1.19 | 1.18 | 1.17 | 1.16 | 1.15 |
| | 224 | 219 | 214 | 210 | 210 | 210 | 210 | 210 | 210 | 210 | 210 |
| | 3050 | 2950 | 2850 | 2790 | 2670 | 2590 | 2510 | 2430 | 2370 | 2300 | 2240 |

FIGURE 69.—B-737 – Holding Performance Chart.

| INITIAL FUEL WEIGHT 1000 LB | ENDING FUEL WEIGHT - 1000 LB | | | | | | | | | | | | | | | |
|---|---|---|---|---|---|---|---|---|---|---|---|---|---|---|---|---|
| | 10 | 14 | 18 | 22 | 26 | 30 | 34 | 38 | 42 | 46 | 50 | 54 | 58 | 62 | 64 | 70 |
| 70 | 28 | 27 | 25 | 23 | 22 | 20 | 18 | 17 | 15 | 13 | 12 | 10 | 8 | 5 | 3 | 0 |
| 66 | 26 | 25 | 23 | 21 | 20 | 18 | 16 | 15 | 13 | 12 | 10 | 8 | 5 | 3 | 0 | |
| 62 | 23 | 23 | 20 | 18 | 17 | 15 | 13 | 11 | 10 | 8 | 7 | 5 | 3 | 0 | | |
| 58 | 21 | 20 | 18 | 16 | 15 | 13 | 11 | 10 | 8 | 6 | 5 | 3 | 0 | | | |
| 54 | 18 | 16 | 15 | 13 | 12 | 10 | 8 | 7 | 5 | 3 | 2 | 0 | | | | |
| 50 | 16 | 15 | 13 | 12 | 10 | 8 | 7 | 5 | 3 | 2 | 0 | | | | | |
| 46 | 15 | 13 | 12 | 10 | 8 | 7 | 5 | 3 | 2 | 0 | | | | | | |
| 42 | 13 | 12 | 10 | 8 | 7 | 5 | 3 | 2 | 0 | | FUEL DUMP TIME | | | | | |
| 38 | 12 | 10 | 8 | 7 | 5 | 3 | 2 | 0 | | | | | | | | |
| 34 | 10 | 8 | 7 | 5 | 3 | 2 | 0 | | | | | | | | | |
| 30 | 8 | 7 | 5 | 3 | 2 | 0 | | | | | | | | | | |
| 26 | 7 | 5 | 3 | 2 | 0 | | | | | | | | | | | |
| 22 | 5 | 3 | 2 | 0 | | | | | | | | | | | | |
| 18 | 3 | 2 | 0 | | | | FUEL JETTISON TIME-MINUTES | | | | | | | | | |
| 14 | 2 | 0 | | | | | | | | | | | | | | |
| 10 | 0 | | | | | | | | | | | | | | | |

FIGURE 70.—Fuel Dump Time.

| OPERATING CONDITIONS | D–1 | D–2 | D–3 | D–4 | D–5 |
|---|---|---|---|---|---|
| WT AT ENG FAIL (X1000) | 100 | 110 | 90 | 80 | 120 |
| ENGINE ANTI-ICE | ON | OFF | ON | ON | ON |
| WING ANTI-ICE | OFF | OFF | ON | ON | OFF |
| ISA TEMPERATURE | ISA | +10° | –10° | –10° | +20° |
| AIR CONDITIONING | OFF | OFF | OFF | OFF | OFF |

FIGURE 71. —B-737– Drift-Down.

# 1 ENGINE INOP

**ENGINE A/I  OFF**

| GROSS WEIGHT  1000 LB | | OPTIMUM DRIFTDOWN SPEED KIAS | ISA DEV °C | | | |
|---|---|---|---|---|---|---|
| AT ENGINE FAILURE | AT LEVEL OFF (APPROX) | | -10 | 0 | 10 | 20 |
| | | | APPROX GROSS LEVEL OFF PRESS ALT FT | | | |
| 80 | 77 | 184 | 27900 | 26800 | 25400 | 22800 |
| 90 | 86 | 195 | 25000 | 23800 | 21700 | 20000 |
| 100 | 96 | 206 | 22000 | 20500 | 20000 | 18500 |
| 110 | 105 | 216 | 20000 | 19100 | 17500 | 15400 |
| 120 | 114 | 224 | 18200 | 16600 | 14700 | 12200 |

**ENGINE A/I  ON**

| GROSS WEIGHT  1000 LB | | OPTIMUM DRIFTDOWN SPEED KIAS | ISA DEV °C | | | |
|---|---|---|---|---|---|---|
| AT ENGINE FAILURE | AT LEVEL OFF (APPROX) | | -10 | 0 | 10 | 20 |
| | | | APPROX GROSS LEVEL OFF PRESS ALT FT | | | |
| 80 | 77 | 184 | 25500 | 24600 | 22800 | 20000 |
| 90 | 86 | 195 | 23000 | 21400 | 20000 | 19400 |
| 100 | 96 | 206 | 20000 | 19400 | 18700 | 15600 |
| 110 | 105 | 216 | 18100 | 16600 | 14700 | 12200 |
| 120 | 114 | 224 | 15500 | 13800 | 11800 | 8800 |

**ENGINE AND WING A/I  ON**

| GROSS WEIGHT  1000 LB | | OPTIMUM DRIFTDOWN SPEED KIAS | ISA DEV °C | | | |
|---|---|---|---|---|---|---|
| AT ENGINE FAILURE | AT LEVEL OFF (APPROX) | | -10 | 0 | 10 | 20 |
| | | | APPROX GROSS LEVEL OFF PRESS ALT FT | | | |
| 80 | 77 | 184 | 24400 | 23400 | 21400 | 20000 |
| 90 | 86 | 195 | 21600 | 20100 | 19800 | 18000 |
| 100 | 96 | 206 | 19600 | 18000 | 16400 | 14200 |
| 110 | 105 | 216 | 16800 | 15100 | 13300 | 10700 |
| 120 | 114 | 224 | 14000 | 12200 | 10300 | 7200 |

**NOTE:**

**WHEN ENGINE BLEED FOR AIR CONDITIONING IS OFF BELOW 17,000 FT., INCREASE LEVEL-OFF ALTITUDE BY 800 FT.**

FIGURE 72.—Drift-Down Performance Chart.

| OPERATING CONDITIONS | L-1 | L-2 | L-3 | L-4 | L-5 |
|---|---|---|---|---|---|
| TEMPERATURE | +15 °C TAT | +27 °F OAT | –8 °C OAT | –10 °C TAT | +55 °F OAT |
| PRESSURE ALTITUDE | 500 | 3,100 | 2,500 | 2,100 | 1,200 |
| AIR CONDITIONING | OFF | ON | ON | ON | ON |
| WING ANTI-ICE | OFF | 2 ON | 1 ON | 2 ON | OFF |
| WEIGHT (X1000) | 100 | 95 | 90 | 105 | 85 |
| FLAP SETTING | 30° | 25° | 15° | 40° | 30° |
| RUNWAY ASSIGNED | 35 | 04 | 27 | 34 | 09 |
| SURFACE WIND | 300/20 | 350/15 | 310/20 | 030/10 | 130/15 |

FIGURE 73.—B-737 – Landing.

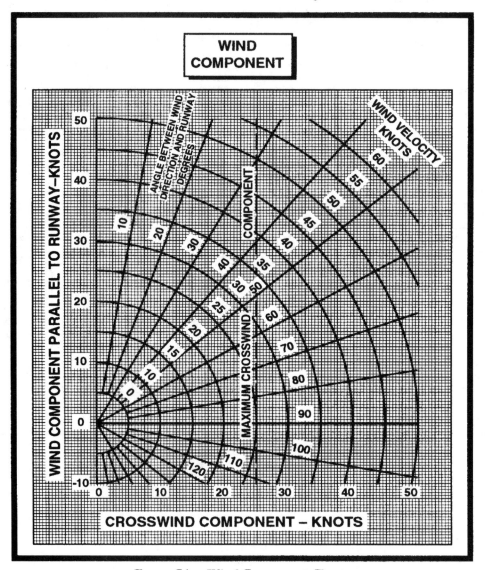

FIGURE 74.—Wind Component Chart.

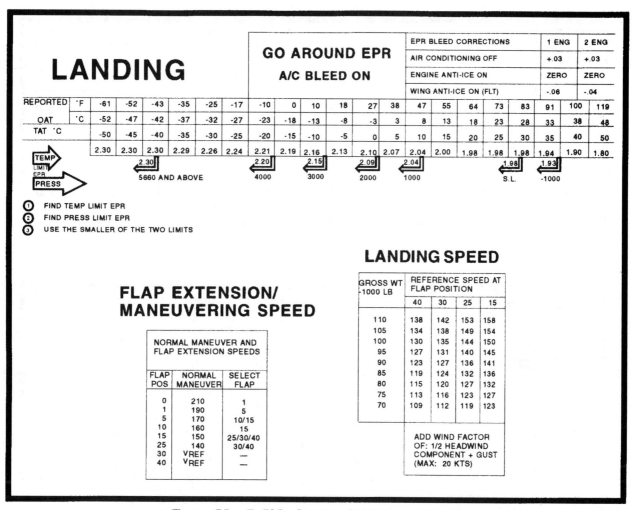

FIGURE 75.—B-737 – Landing Performance Chart.

| LOADING CONDITIONS | WT-1 | WT-2 | WT-3 | WT-4 | WT-5 |
|---|---|---|---|---|---|
| PASSENGERS | | | | | |
|     FORWARD COMPT | 18 | 23 | 12 | 28 | 26 |
|     AFT COMPT | 95 | 112 | 75 | 122 | 103 |
| CARGO | | | | | |
|     FORWARD HOLD | 1,500 | 2,500 | 3,500 | 850 | 1,400 |
|     AFT HOLD | 2,500 | 3,500 | 4,200 | 1,500 | 2,200 |
| FUEL | | | | | |
|     TANKS 1 AND 3 (EACH) | 10,500 | 11,000 | FULL | 10,000 | 11,500 |
|     TANK 2 | 28,000 | 27,000 | 24,250 | 26,200 | 25,200 |

FIGURE 76.—B-727 – Loading.

| LOADING CONDITIONS | WT-6 | WT-7 | WT-8 | WT-9 | WT-10 |
|---|---|---|---|---|---|
| PASSENGERS | | | | | |
|     FORWARD COMPT | 10 | 27 | 6 | 29 | 21 |
|     AFT COMPT | 132 | 83 | 98 | 133 | 127 |
| CARGO | | | | | |
|     FORWARD HOLD | 5,000 | 4,500 | 1,300 | 975 | 2,300 |
|     AFT HOLD | 6,000 | 5,500 | 3,300 | 1,250 | 2,400 |
| FUEL | | | | | |
|     TANKS 1 AND 3 (EACH) | 9,500 | 9,000 | FULL | 11,000 | 10,500 |
|     TANK 2 | 21,700 | 19,800 | 12,000 | 29,300 | 22,700 |

FIGURE 77.—B-727 – Loading.

| LOADING CONDITIONS | WT-11 | WT-12 | WT-13 | WT-14 | WT-15 |
|---|---|---|---|---|---|
| PASSENGERS | | | | | |
|     FORWARD COMPT | 11 | 28 | 22 | 17 | 3 |
|     AFT COMPT | 99 | 105 | 76 | 124 | 130 |
| CARGO | | | | | |
|     FORWARD HOLD | 3,100 | 4,200 | 1,600 | 3,800 | 1,800 |
|     AFT HOLD | 5,500 | 4,400 | 5,700 | 4,800 | 3,800 |
| FUEL | | | | | |
|     TANKS 1 AND 3 (EACH) | 8,500 | 11,500 | 12,000 | 11,000 | 10,500 |
|     TANK 2 | 19,600 | 27,800 | 29,100 | 25,400 | 21,900 |

FIGURE 78.—B-727 – Loading.

## AIRPLANE DATUM CONSTANTS

MAC . . . . . . . . . . . . . . . . . . . . . . . . . . . . . . . . . . . . . . . . . . . . . . . . . . . . . . . . . . 180.9 inches
L.E. of MAC . . . . . . . . . . . . . . . . . . . . . . . . . . . . . . . . . . . . . . . . . . . . . . . . . . 860.5 inches
Basic Operating Index . . . . . . . . . . . . . . . . . . . . . . . . . . . . . . . . . . . . . . . . . . $\frac{92,837.0}{1,000}$

## OPERATING LIMITATIONS

Maximum Takeoff Slope . . . . . . . . . . . . . . . . . . . . . . . . . . . . . . . . . . . . . . . . . ±2%
Maximum Takeoff / Landing Crosswind Component . . . . . . . . . . . . . . . . . . . 32 knots
Maximum Takeoff / Landing Tailwind Component . . . . . . . . . . . . . . . . . . . . . 12 knots

## WEIGHT LIMITATIONS

Basic Operating Weight . . . . . . . . . . . . . . . . . . . . . . . . . . . . . . . . . . . . . . . . . 105,500 pounds
Maximum Zero Fuel Weight . . . . . . . . . . . . . . . . . . . . . . . . . . . . . . . . . . . . . 138,500 pounds
Maximum Taxi Weight . . . . . . . . . . . . . . . . . . . . . . . . . . . . . . . . . . . . . . . . . 185,700 pounds
Maximum Takeoff Weight (Brake Release) . . . . . . . . . . . . . . . . . . . . . . . . . . 184,700 pounds
Maximum In-flight Weight (Flaps 30) . . . . . . . . . . . . . . . . . . . . . . . . . . . . . . 155,500 pounds
                  (Flaps 40) . . . . . . . . . . . . . . . . . . . . . . . . . . . . . . 144,000 pounds
Maximum Landing Weight (Flaps 30) . . . . . . . . . . . . . . . . . . . . . . . . . . . . . . 155,000 pounds
                  (Flaps 40) . . . . . . . . . . . . . . . . . . . . . . . . . . . . . . 143,000 pounds

FIGURE 79.—B-727 – Table of Weights and Limits.

## PASSENGER LOADING TABLE

| Number of Pass. | Weight Lbs. | Moment 1000 |
|---|---|---|
| **Forward Compartment Centroid-582.0** | | |
| 5 | 850 | 495 |
| 10 | 1,700 | 989 |
| 15 | 2,550 | 1,484 |
| 20 | 3,400 | 1,979 |
| 25 | 4,250 | 2,473 |
| 29 | 4,930 | 2,869 |
| **AFT Compartment Centroid-1028.0** | | |
| 10 | 1,700 | 1,748 |
| 20 | 3,400 | 3,495 |
| 30 | 5,100 | 5,243 |
| 40 | 6,800 | 6,990 |
| 50 | 8,500 | 8,738 |
| 60 | 10,200 | 10,486 |
| 70 | 11,900 | 12,233 |
| 80 | 13,600 | 13,980 |
| 90 | 15,300 | 15,728 |
| 100 | 17,000 | 17,476 |
| 110 | 18,700 | 19,223 |
| 120 | 20,400 | 20,971 |
| 133 | 22,610 | 23,243 |

## CARGO LOADING TABLE

| | Moment 1000 | |
|---|---|---|
| | Forward Hold | Aft Hold |
| Weight Lbs. | Arm 680.0 | Arm 1166.0 |
| 6,000 | | 6,966 |
| 5,000 | 3,400 | 5,830 |
| 4,000 | 2,720 | 4,664 |
| 3,000 | 2,040 | 3,498 |
| 2,000 | 1,360 | 2,332 |
| 1,000 | 680 | 1,166 |
| 900 | 612 | 1,049 |
| 800 | 544 | 933 |
| 700 | 476 | 816 |
| 600 | 408 | 700 |
| 500 | 340 | 583 |
| 400 | 272 | 466 |
| 300 | 204 | 350 |
| 200 | 136 | 233 |
| 100 | 68 | 117 |

NOTE: These computations are to be used for testing purposes only.

## FUEL LOADING TABLE

| TANKS 1 & 3 (EACH) | | | TANKS 2 (3 CELL) | | | | | |
|---|---|---|---|---|---|---|---|---|
| Weight Lbs. | Arm | Moment 1000 | Weight Lbs. | Arm | Moment 1000 | Weight Lbs. | Arm | Moment 1000 |
| 8,500 | 992.1 | 8,433 | 8,500 | 917.5 | 7,799 | 22,500 | 914.5 | 20,576 |
| 9,000 | 993.0 | 8,937 | 9,000 | 917.2 | 8,255 | 23,000 | 914.5 | 21,034 |
| 9,500 | 993.9 | 9,442 | 9,500 | 917.0 | 8,711 | 23,500 | 914.4 | 21,488 |
| 10,000 | 994.7 | 9,947 | 10,000 | 916.8 | 9,168 | 24,000 | 914.3 | 21,943 |
| 10,500 | 995.4 | 10,451 | 10,500 | 916.6 | 9,624 | 24,500 | 914.3 | 22,400 |
| 11,000 | 996.1 | 10,957 | 11,000 | 916.5 | 10,082 | 25,000 | 914.2 | 22,855 |
| 11,500 | 996.8 | 11,463 | 11,500 | 916.3 | 10,537 | 25,500 | 914.2 | 23,312 |
| 12,000 | 997.5 | 11,970 | 12,000 | 916.1 | 10,993 | 26,000 | 914.1 | 23,767 |
| | | | | | | 26,500 | 914.1 | 24,244 |
| **FULL CAPACITY** | | | **\*\*(See note at lower left)** | | | 27,000 | 914.0 | 24,678 |
| | | | 18,500 | 915.1 | 16,929 | 27,500 | 913.9 | 25,132 |
| \*\*Note: Computations for Tank 2 weights for 12,500 lbs. to 18,000 lbs. have been purposely omitted. | | | 19,000 | 915.0 | 17,385 | 28,000 | 913.9 | 25,589 |
| | | | 19,500 | 914.9 | 17,841 | 28,500 | 913.8 | 26,043 |
| | | | 20,000 | 914.9 | 18,298 | 29,000 | 913.7 | 26,497 |
| | | | 20,500 | 914.8 | 18,753 | 29,500 | 913.7 | 26,954 |
| | | | 21,000 | 914.7 | 19,209 | 30,000 | 913.6 | 27,408 |
| | | | 21,500 | 914.6 | 19,664 | **FULL CAPACITY** | | |
| | | | 22,000 | 914.6 | 20,121 | | | |

FIGURE 80.—Loading Tables.

| OPERATING CONDITIONS | G-1 | G-2 | G-3 | G-4 | G-5 |
|---|---|---|---|---|---|
| FIELD ELEVATION FT | 1,050 | 2,000 | 4,350 | 3,050 | 2,150 |
| ALTIMETER SETTING | 29.36" | 1016 mb | 30.10" | 1010 mb | 29.54" |
| TEMPERATURE | +23 °F | +10 °C | +68 °F | –5 °C | +5 °F |
| AIR COND ENGS 1 AND 3 | OFF | ON | ON | ON | ON |
| ANTI-ICE ENG 2 | ON | OFF | OFF | ON | ON |
| GROSS WEIGHT (X1000) | 140 | 190 | 180 | 160 | 120 |
| 6TH STAGE BLEED | OFF | ON | ON | OFF | OFF |
| FLAP POSITION | 15° | 5° | 25° | 15° | 5° |
| CG STATION | 911.2 | 882.2 | 914.8 | 932.9 | 925.6 |
| LEMAC – STA 860.5, MAC 180.9" | | | | | |

FIGURE 81.—B-727 – Takeoff.

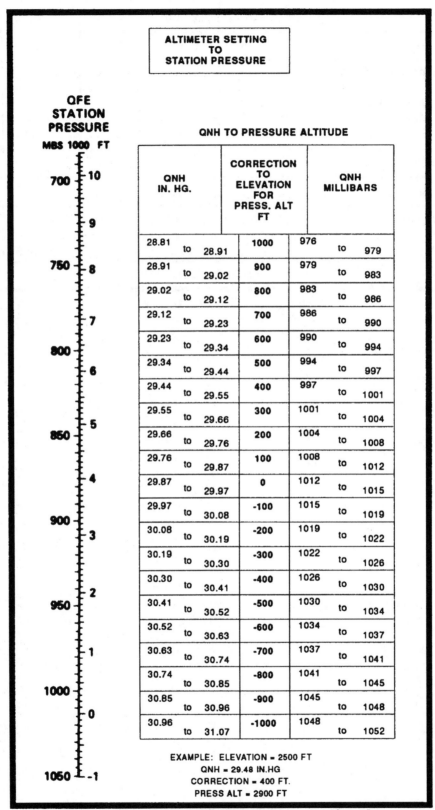

FIGURE 82.—Altimeter Setting to Pressure Altitude.

## TAKEOFF EPR, SPEEDS
## AND
## STAB TRIM SETTING

### MAX TAKEOFF EPR

ENG 1 & 3  AIRBLEED ON
ENG 2  NO AIRBLEED

0 - 60 KNOTS

| PRESS ALT FT | OAT °F / °C | 67 TO -9 / -55 TO -23 | -4 / -20 | 5 / -15 | 14 / -10 | 23 / -5 | 32 / 0 | 41 / 5 | 50 / 10 | 59 / 15 | 68 / 20 | 77 / 25 | 86 / 30 | 95 / 35 | 104 / 40 | 113 / 45 | 120 / 49 |
|---|---|---|---|---|---|---|---|---|---|---|---|---|---|---|---|---|---|
| -1000 | 1 & 3 | 2.04 | 2.04 | 2.04 | 2.04 | 2.04 | 2.04 | 2.04 | 2.04 | 2.04 | 2.04 | 2.04 | 2.03 | 1.99 | 1.94 | 1.91 | |
| | 2 | 2.06 | 2.06 | 2.06 | 2.06 | 2.06 | 2.06 | 2.06 | 2.06 | 2.06 | 2.06 | 2.06 | 2.05 | 2.00 | 1.96 | 1.92 | |
| S.L. | 1 & 3 | 2.10 | 2.10 | 2.10 | 2.10 | 2.10 | 2.10 | 2.10 | 2.10 | 2.10 | 2.10 | 2.08 | 2.03 | 1.99 | 1.94 | 1.91 | |
| | 2 | 2.11 | 2.11 | 2.11 | 2.11 | 2.11 | 2.11 | 2.11 | 2.11 | 2.11 | 2.11 | 2.10 | 2.05 | 2.00 | 1.96 | 1.92 | |
| 1000 | 1 & 3 | 2.15 | 2.15 | 2.15 | 2.15 | 2.15 | 2.15 | 2.15 | 2.13 | 2.12 | 2.11 | 2.08 | 2.03 | 1.99 | 1.94 | 1.91 | |
| | 2 | 2.16 | 2.16 | 2.16 | 2.16 | 2.16 | 2.16 | 2.16 | 2.15 | 2.13 | 2.13 | 2.12 | 2.10 | 2.05 | 2.00 | 1.96 | 1.92 |
| 2000 | 1 & 3 | 2.21 | 2.21 | 2.21 | 2.21 | 2.21 | 2.20 | 2.17 | 2.14 | 2.14 | 2.14 | 2.11 | 2.08 | 2.03 | 1.99 | 1.94 | 1.91 |
| | 2 | 2.22 | 2.22 | 2.22 | 2.22 | 2.22 | 2.21 | 2.18 | 2.16 | 2.16 | 2.15 | 2.12 | 2.10 | 2.05 | 2.00 | 1.96 | 1.92 |
| 3000 | 1 & 3 | 2.26 | 2.26 | 2.26 | 2.25 | 2.23 | 2.20 | 2.17 | 2.14 | 2.14 | 2.14 | 2.11 | 2.08 | 2.03 | 1.99 | 1.94 | 1.91 |
| | 2 | 2.28 | 2.28 | 2.28 | 2.27 | 2.24 | 2.21 | 2.18 | 2.16 | 2.16 | 2.15 | 2.12 | 2.10 | 2.05 | 2.00 | 1.96 | 1.92 |
| 3856 & ABOVE | 1 & 3 | 2.29 | 2.29 | 2.27 | 2.25 | 2.23 | 2.20 | 2.17 | 2.14 | 2.14 | 2.14 | 2.11 | 2.08 | 2.03 | 1.99 | 1.94 | 1.91 |
| | 2 | 2.32 | 2.31 | 2.29 | 2.27 | 2.24 | 2.21 | 2.18 | 2.16 | 2.16 | 2.15 | 2.12 | 2.10 | 2.05 | 2.00 | 1.96 | 1.92 |

| EPR BLEED CORRECTIONS | ENG 1 & 3 | ENG 2 |
|---|---|---|
| AIR CONDITIONING | OFF +.04 | - |
| ENGINE ANTI-ICE ON | - | -.03 |

REDUCE ENG 2 EPR BY .05 WITH 6TH
STAGE BLEED ON (IF INSTALLED) FOR 10 °C
(50 °F) OAT & WARMER

$V_1$ , $V_R$ , $V_2$
ANTI-SKID OPERATIVE

### STAB TRIM SETTING

| CG | FLAPS 5 | FLAPS 15 / 20 | FLAPS 25 |
|---|---|---|---|
| | UNITS AIRPLANE NOSE UP | | |
| 10 | 6 3/4 | 7 1/2 | 8 1/4 |
| 12 | 6 1/2 | 7 1/4 | 8 |
| 14 | 6 1/4 | 7 | 7 3/4 |
| 16 | 6 | 6 3/4 | 7 1/2 |
| 18 | 5 3/4 | 6 1/2 | 7 |
| 20 | 5 1/2 | 6 | 6 1/2 |
| 22 | 5 | 5 3/4 | 6 1/4 |
| 24 | 4 3/4 | 5 1/4 | 5 3/4 |
| 26 | 4 1/2 | 4 3/4 | 5 1/4 |
| 28 | 4 | 4 1/2 | 4 3/4 |
| 30 | 3 3/4 | 4 | 4 1/4 |
| 32 | 3 1/2 | 3 3/4 | 4 |
| 34 | 3 1/4 | 3 1/4 | 3 1/2 |
| 36 | 2 3/4 | 3 | 3 |
| 38 | 2 1/2 | 2 1/2 | 2 1/2 |
| 40 | 2 1/2 | 2 1/2 | 2 1/2 |
| 42 | 2 1/2 | 2 1/2 | 2 1/2 |

### FLAP RETRACTION/ MANEUVERING SPEEDS

| GROSS WEIGHT LB | FLAP POSITION 15 | 5 | 2 | 0 |
|---|---|---|---|---|
| 154500 & BELOW | 150 | 160 | 190 | 200 |
| 154501 TO 176000 | 160 | 170 | 200 | 210 |
| 176001 TO 191000 | 170 | 180 | 210 | 220 |
| ABOVE 191000 | 180 | 190 | 225 | 235 |

FOR MANEUVERS IMMEDIATELY AFTER
TAKEOFF EXCEEDING 15° BANK MAINTAIN
AT LEAST $V_2$ +10 AT TAKEOFF FLAPS

| PRESSURE ALT - 1000 FT | | OAT | | | |
|---|---|---|---|---|---|
| 9 TO 11 | °F / °C | (ABOVE CERTIFIED ALTITUDE) | | -65 TO 25 / -54 TO -4 | 26 TO 87 / -3 TO 31 |
| 7 TO 9 | °F / °C | | -65 TO 9 / -54 TO -13 | 10 TO 75 / -12 TO 24 | 76 TO 104 / 25 TO 40 |
| 5 TO 7 | °F / °C | -65 TO -10 / -54 TO -23 | -8 TO 42 / -22 TO 5 | 43 TO 97 / 6 TO 36 | 98 TO 111 / 37 TO 44 |
| 3 TO 5 | °F / °C | -65 TO 32 / -54 TO 0 | 33 TO 90 / 1 TO 32 | 91 TO 113 / 33 TO 45 | 114 TO 120 / 46 TO 49 |
| 1 TO 3 | °F / °C | -65 TO 83 / -54 TO 28 | 84 TO 106 / 29 TO 41 | 107 TO 120 / 42 TO 49 | |
| -1 TO 1 | °F / °C | -65 TO 99 / -54 TO 37 | 100 TO 120 / 38 TO 49 | | |

| FLAPS | GROSS WEIGHT 1000 LB | $V_1 = V_R$ | $V_2$ | $V_1 = V_R$ | $V_2$ | $V_1 = V_R$ | $V_2$ | $V_1 = V_R$ | $V_2$ |
|---|---|---|---|---|---|---|---|---|---|
| 5 | 210 | 165 | 175 | 166 | 175 | | | | |
| | 200 | 160 | 171 | 162 | 171 | | | | |
| | 190 | 155 | 167 | 157 | 167 | 158 | 167 | | |
| | 180 | 150 | 163 | 152 | 163 | 154 | 163 | | |
| | 170 | 144 | 159 | 147 | 159 | 149 | 159 | 150 | 158 |
| | 160 | 140 | 154 | 141 | 153 | 143 | 153 | 145 | 153 |
| | 150 | 135 | 149 | 136 | 149 | 138 | 149 | 140 | 148 |
| | 140 | 129 | 145 | 130 | 145 | 132 | 144 | 134 | 144 |
| | 130 | 124 | 140 | 125 | 139 | 126 | 138 | 128 | 138 |
| | 120 | 119 | 135 | 120 | 134 | 120 | 134 | 121 | 133 |
| 15 | 210 | 156 | 166 | 157 | 166 | | | | |
| | 200 | 151 | 162 | 153 | 162 | | | | |
| | 190 | 146 | 158 | 148 | 158 | 149 | 158 | | |
| | 180 | 141 | 154 | 143 | 154 | 145 | 154 | | |
| | 170 | 136 | 150 | 138 | 150 | 140 | 150 | 141 | 149 |
| | 160 | 132 | 146 | 133 | 145 | 135 | 145 | 137 | 145 |
| | 150 | 127 | 141 | 128 | 141 | 130 | 141 | 132 | 140 |
| | 140 | 122 | 137 | 123 | 137 | 124 | 136 | 126 | 136 |
| | 130 | 117 | 133 | 118 | 132 | 118 | 131 | 120 | 131 |
| | 120 | 112 | 128 | 113 | 127 | 113 | 127 | 115 | 126 |
| 20 | 210 | 151 | 161 | 152 | 161 | | | | |
| | 200 | 146 | 157 | 148 | 157 | | | | |
| | 190 | 141 | 153 | 143 | 153 | 144 | 153 | | |
| | 180 | 136 | 150 | 138 | 150 | 140 | 149 | | |
| | 170 | 132 | 146 | 133 | 146 | 135 | 145 | 136 | 145 |
| | 160 | 128 | 142 | 129 | 141 | 131 | 141 | 133 | 141 |
| | 150 | 123 | 137 | 124 | 137 | 126 | 136 | 128 | 136 |
| | 140 | 118 | 133 | 119 | 133 | 120 | 132 | 122 | 132 |
| | 130 | 113 | 129 | 114 | 129 | 114 | 127 | 116 | 127 |
| | 120 | 109 | 124 | 109 | 123 | 109 | 123 | 111 | 122 |
| 25 | 210 | 146 | 157 | 147 | 157 | | | | |
| | 200 | 141 | 153 | 143 | 153 | | | | |
| | 190 | 137 | 149 | 138 | 149 | 139 | 149 | | |
| | 180 | 132 | 145 | 134 | 145 | 136 | 145 | | |
| | 170 | 127 | 141 | 129 | 141 | 131 | 141 | 132 | 140 |
| | 160 | 123 | 137 | 124 | 137 | 126 | 137 | 128 | 136 |
| | 150 | 119 | 133 | 120 | 133 | 122 | 133 | 124 | 132 |
| | 140 | 114 | 129 | 115 | 129 | 116 | 128 | 118 | 128 |
| | 130 | 109 | 125 | 110 | 124 | 110 | 124 | 112 | 123 |
| | 120 | 105 | 120 | 106 | 120 | 106 | 119 | 108 | 118 |

FIGURE 83.—Takeoff Performance.

| OPERATING CONDITIONS | H-1 | H-2 | H-3 | H-4 | H-5 |
|---|---|---|---|---|---|
| ALTITUDE | 24,000 | 17,000 | 8,000 | 18,000 | 22,000 |
| WEIGHT (X1000) | 195 | 185 | 155 | 135 | 175 |
| ENGINES OPERATING | 3 | 3 | 3 | 3 | 3 |
| HOLDING TIME (MIN) | 15 | 30 | 45 | 25 | 35 |

FIGURE 84.—B-727 – Holding.

| EPR<br>IAS - KTS<br>FF PER ENG - LB/HR | **HOLDING** | | | | | | | **B-727** | |
|---|---|---|---|---|---|---|---|---|---|
| PRESSURE ALTITUDE FT | GROSS WEIGHT - 1000 LB | | | | | | | | |
| | 200 | 190 | 180 | 170 | 160 | 150 | 140 | 130 | 120 |
| 25000 | 1.85<br>268<br>3600 | 1.81<br>261<br>3400 | 1.77<br>253<br>3210 | 1.73<br>246<br>3030 | 1.69<br>238<br>2860 | 1.64<br>230<br>2680 | 1.60<br>222<br>2510 | 1.55<br>213<br>2340 | 1.51<br>205<br>2180 |
| 20000 | 1.69<br>265<br>3630 | 1.66<br>258<br>3450 | 1.62<br>251<br>3280 | 1.59<br>244<br>3110 | 1.55<br>236<br>2940 | 1.51<br>228<br>2770 | 1.48<br>220<br>2600 | 1.44<br>212<br>2440 | 1.40<br>204<br>2270 |
| 15000 | 1.56<br>263<br>3670 | 1.53<br>256<br>3500 | 1.50<br>249<br>3340 | 1.47<br>242<br>3170 | 1.44<br>235<br>3000 | 1.41<br>227<br>2850 | 1.38<br>219<br>2680 | 1.35<br>211<br>2520 | 1.32<br>203<br>2350 |
| 10000 | 1.45<br>262<br>3800 | 1.43<br>255<br>3640 | 1.40<br>248<br>3460 | 1.38<br>241<br>3310 | 1.35<br>234<br>3140 | 1.33<br>226<br>2970 | 1.30<br>218<br>2810 | 1.28<br>210<br>2640 | 1.25<br>202<br>2480 |
| 5000 | 1.36<br>260<br>3890 | 1.34<br>254<br>3720 | 1.32<br>247<br>3550 | 1.30<br>240<br>3380 | 1.28<br>233<br>3220 | 1.26<br>225<br>3060 | 1.24<br>218<br>2890 | 1.22<br>210<br>2730 | 1.20<br>201<br>2560 |

FIGURE 85.—B-727 – Holding Performance Chart.

| OPERATING CONDITIONS | S–1 | S–2 | S–3 | S–4 | S–5 |
|---|---|---|---|---|---|
| FLIGHT LEVEL | 370 | 350 | 410 | 390 | 330 |
| LANDING WEIGHT (X1000) | 130 | 150 | 135 | 155 | 125 |
| DESCENT TYPE | .80M/ 250 | .80M/ 280/250 | .80M/ 320/250 | .80M/ 350/250 | .80M/ 320/250 |

FIGURE 86.—Descent Performance.

## .80M/250 KIAS

| FLIGHT LEVEL | TIME MIN | FUEL LB | DISTANCE NAM AT LANDING WEIGHTS | | |
|---|---|---|---|---|---|
| | | | 120,000 LB | 140,000 LB | 160,000 LB |
| 410 | 27 | 1610 | 133 | 137 | 138 |
| 390 | 27 | 1600 | 130 | 134 | 136 |
| 370 | 26 | 1570 | 123 | 128 | 129 |
| 350 | 25 | 1540 | 116 | 120 | 122 |
| 330 | 24 | 1510 | 110 | 113 | 115 |
| 310 | 23 | 1480 | 103 | 107 | 108 |
| 290 | 22 | 1450 | 97 | 100 | 101 |
| 270 | 21 | 1420 | 90 | 93 | 95 |
| 250 | 20 | 1390 | 84 | 87 | 88 |
| 230 | 19 | 1360 | 78 | 80 | 81 |
| 210 | 18 | 1320 | 72 | 74 | 75 |
| 190 | 17 | 1280 | 66 | 68 | 68 |
| 170 | 16 | 1240 | 60 | 62 | 62 |
| 150 | 14 | 1190 | 54 | 56 | 56 |
| 100 | 11 | 1050 | 39 | 40 | 40 |
| 050 | 8 | 870 | 24 | 24 | 24 |
| 015 | 5 | 700 | 12 | 12 | 12 |

## .80M/280/250 KIAS

| FLIGHT LEVEL | TIME MIN | FUEL LB | DISTANCE NAM AT LANDING WEIGHTS | | |
|---|---|---|---|---|---|
| | | | 120,000 LB | 140,000 LB | 160,000 LB |
| 410 | 25 | 1550 | 123 | 129 | 132 |
| 390 | 24 | 1540 | 121 | 127 | 130 |
| 370 | 24 | 1520 | 115 | 121 | 125 |
| 350 | 23 | 1500 | 111 | 117 | 120 |
| 330 | 23 | 1480 | 106 | 111 | 115 |
| 310 | 22 | 1450 | 100 | 105 | 108 |
| 290 | 21 | 1430 | 94 | 99 | 102 |
| 270 | 20 | 1400 | 88 | 93 | 95 |
| 250 | 19 | 1370 | 83 | 87 | 89 |
| 230 | 18 | 1350 | 77 | 81 | 83 |
| 210 | 17 | 1310 | 72 | 75 | 76 |
| 190 | 16 | 1280 | 66 | 69 | 70 |
| 170 | 15 | 1240 | 61 | 63 | 64 |
| 150 | 14 | 1200 | 55 | 57 | 58 |
| 100 | 12 | 1080 | 42 | 42 | 42 |
| 050 | 8 | 870 | 24 | 24 | 24 |
| 015 | 5 | 700 | 12 | 12 | 12 |

## .80M/320/250 KIAS

| FLIGHT LEVEL | TIME MIN | FUEL LB | DISTANCE NAM AT LANDING WEIGHTS | | |
|---|---|---|---|---|---|
| | | | 120,000 LB | 140,000 LB | 160,000 LB |
| 410 | 22 | 1490 | 113 | 120 | 123 |
| 390 | 22 | 1480 | 111 | 117 | 121 |
| 370 | 21 | 1460 | 105 | 112 | 116 |
| 350 | 21 | 1440 | 101 | 107 | 111 |
| 330 | 20 | 1420 | 96 | 103 | 107 |
| 310 | 20 | 1400 | 92 | 98 | 102 |
| 290 | 19 | 1390 | 89 | 94 | 98 |
| 270 | 19 | 1370 | 85 | 90 | 94 |
| 250 | 18 | 1350 | 80 | 85 | 88 |
| 230 | 17 | 1330 | 75 | 79 | 82 |
| 210 | 17 | 1300 | 71 | 74 | 77 |
| 190 | 16 | 1270 | 66 | 69 | 71 |
| 170 | 15 | 1240 | 61 | 64 | 65 |
| 150 | 14 | 1210 | 56 | 59 | 60 |
| 100 | 12 | 1110 | 45 | 46 | 46 |
| 050 | 8 | 870 | 24 | 24 | 24 |
| 015 | 5 | 700 | 12 | 12 | 12 |

## .80M/350/250 KIAS

| FLIGHT LEVEL | TIME MIN | FUEL LB | DISTANCE NAM AT LANDING WEIGHTS | | |
|---|---|---|---|---|---|
| | | | 120,000 LB | 140,000 LB | 160,000 LB |
| 410 | 21 | 1440 | 106 | 112 | 116 |
| 390 | 21 | 1430 | 103 | 110 | 114 |
| 370 | 20 | 1420 | 99 | 106 | 110 |
| 350 | 20 | 1400 | 95 | 101 | 106 |
| 330 | 19 | 1390 | 91 | 98 | 102 |
| 310 | 19 | 1380 | 88 | 94 | 98 |
| 290 | 18 | 1360 | 85 | 90 | 95 |
| 270 | 18 | 1350 | 82 | 87 | 91 |
| 250 | 17 | 1330 | 78 | 83 | 87 |
| 230 | 17 | 1310 | 74 | 78 | 81 |
| 210 | 16 | 1290 | 70 | 74 | 76 |
| 190 | 16 | 1270 | 65 | 69 | 71 |
| 170 | 15 | 1240 | 61 | 64 | 66 |
| 150 | 14 | 1210 | 57 | 60 | 61 |
| 100 | 13 | 1130 | 47 | 48 | 49 |
| 050 | 8 | 870 | 24 | 24 | 24 |
| 015 | 5 | 700 | 12 | 12 | 12 |

NOTE: FUEL FOR A STRAIGHT-IN APPROACH IS INCLUDED

FIGURE 87.—Descent Performance Chart.

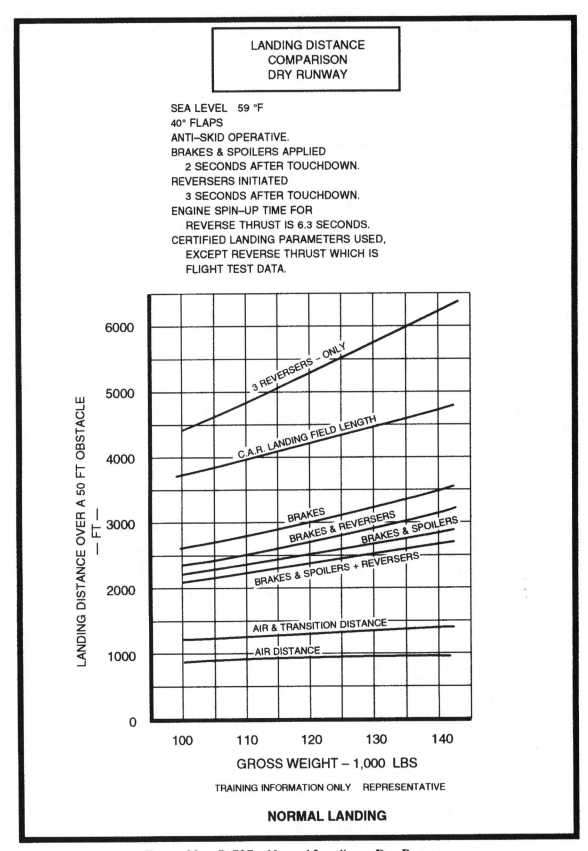

FIGURE 88.—B-727 – Normal Landing – Dry Runway.

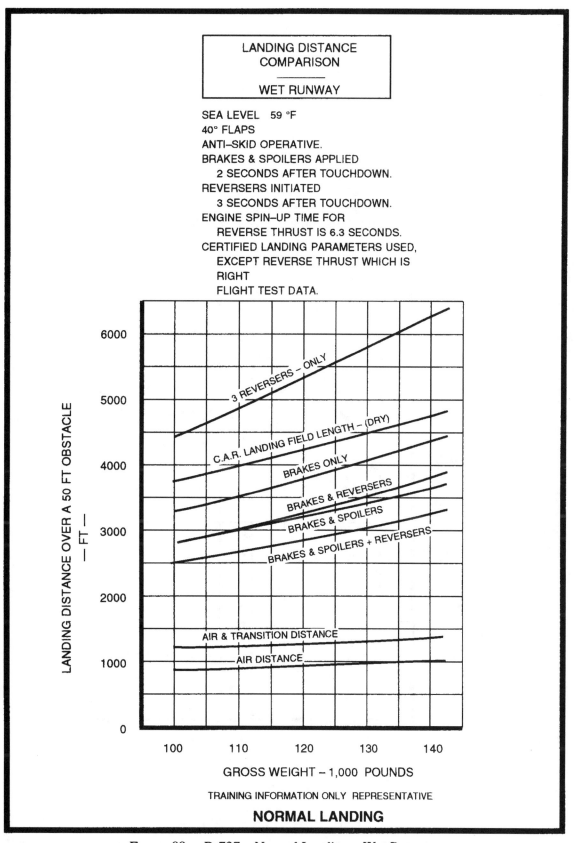

FIGURE 89.—B-727 – Normal Landing – Wet Runway.

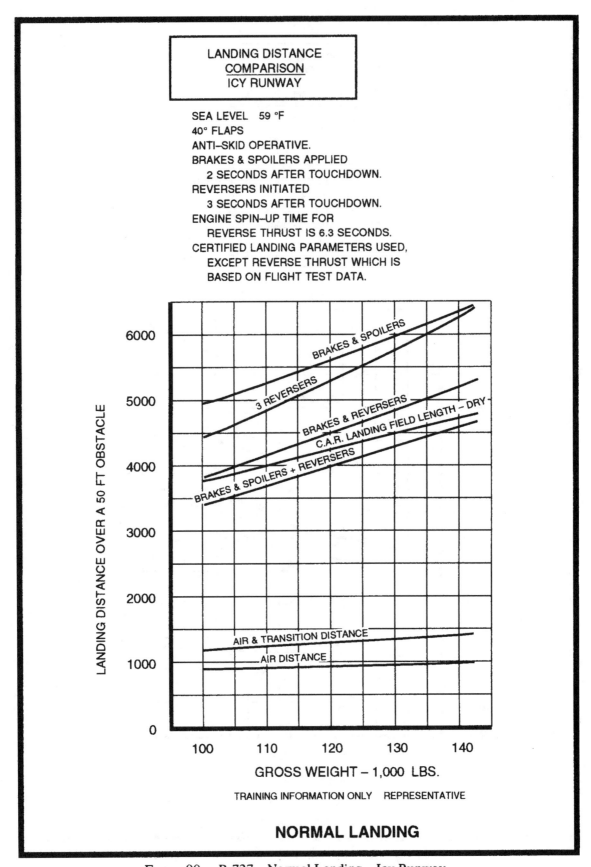

FIGURE 90.—B-727 – Normal Landing – Icy Runway.

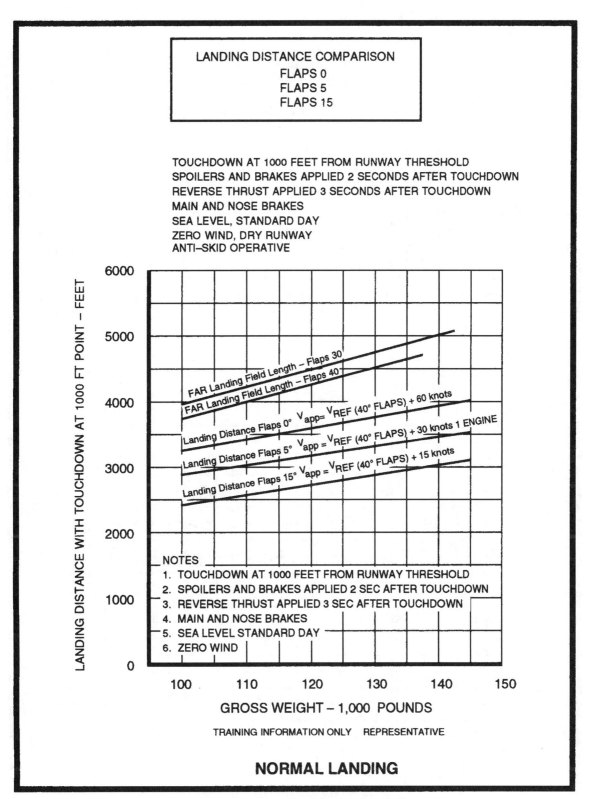

FIGURE 91.—B-727 – Normal Landing Distance Comparison.

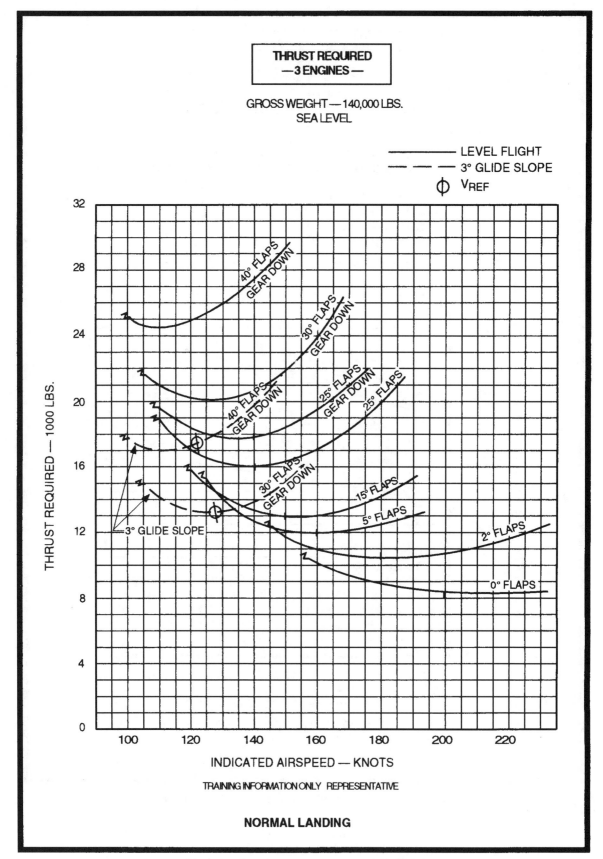

FIGURE 92.—B-727 – Landing Thrust – 140,000 Pounds.

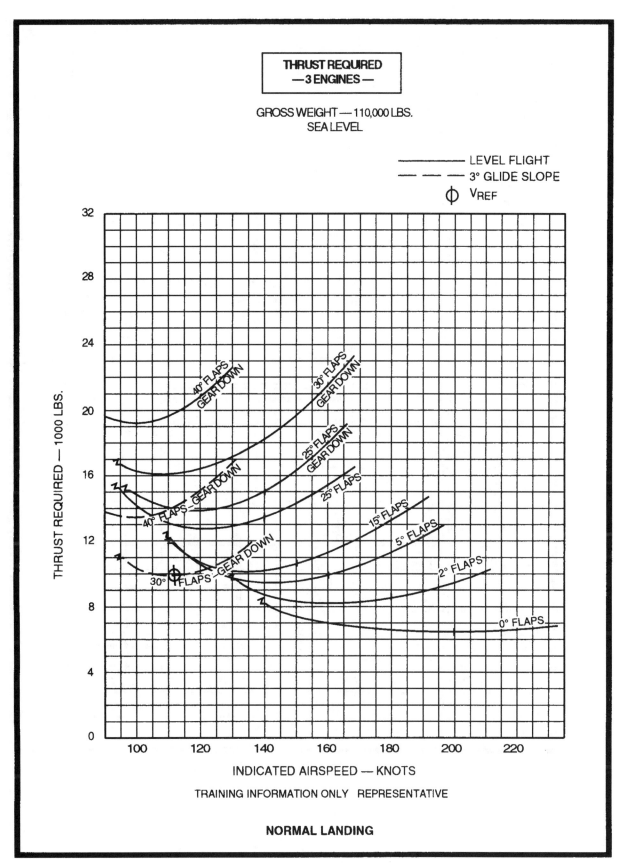

FIGURE 93.—B-727 – Landing Thrust – 110,000 Pounds.

Form Approved: OMB No. 2120-0034

| U.S. DEPARTMENT OF TRANSPORTATION FEDERAL AVIATION ADMINISTRATION **FLIGHT PLAN** | (FAA USE ONLY) | ☐ PILOT BRIEFING | ☐ VNR | TIME STARTED | SPECIALIST INITIALS |
| --- | --- | --- | --- | --- | --- |
| | | ☐ STOPOVER | | | |

| 1. TYPE | 2. AIRCRAFT IDENTIFICATION | 3. AIRCRAFT TYPE/ SPECIAL EQUIPMENT | 4. TRUE AIRSPEED | 5. DEPARTURE POINT | 6. DEPARTURE TIME | | 7. CRUISING ALTITUDE |
| --- | --- | --- | --- | --- | --- | --- | --- |
| VFR | | | | | PROPOSED (Z) | ACTUAL (Z) | |
| X  IFR | N60JB | C208/R | 160 | MDW Chicago Midway | | | FL190 |
| DVFR | | | KTS | | | | |

**8. ROUTE OF FLIGHT**

Midway Four Dep. GIJ, J554 CRL, J586 YXU, J547 BUF

| 9. DESTINATION (Name of airport and city) BUF Greater Buffalo Int'l. Buffalo | 10. EST. TIME ENROUTE | | 11. REMARKS   L/O = Level off.   PPH = Pounds Per Hour  L/O R-270/19 GIJ  Variation: GIJ 1W, CRL 3W, YXU 6W, BUF 8W. |
| --- | --- | --- | --- |
| | HOURS | MINUTES | |

| 12. FUEL ON BOARD | | 13. ALTERNATE AIRPORT(S) | 14. PILOT'S NAME, ADDRESS & TELEPHONE NUMBER & AIRCRAFT HOME BASE | 15. NUMBER ABOARD |
| --- | --- | --- | --- | --- |
| HOURS | MINUTES | ROC Rochester | | 2 |
| 3 | 20 | | 17. DESTINATION CONTACT/TELEPHONE (OPTIONAL) | |

| 16. COLOR OF AIRCRAFT Brown/Tan | CIVIL AIRCRAFT PILOTS. FAR Part 91 requires you file an IFR flight plan to operate under instrument flight rules in controlled airspace. Failure to file could result in a civil penalty not to exceed $1,000 for each violation (Section 901 of the Federal Aviation Act of 1958, as amended). Filing of a VFR flight plan is recommended as a good operating practice. See also Part 99 for requirements concerning DVFR flight plans. |
| --- | --- |

FAA Form 7233-1 (8-82)   CLOSE VFR FLIGHT PLAN WITH _____ FSS ON ARRIVAL

---

# FLIGHT LOG

| CHECK POINTS | | ROUTE | | WIND | SPEED-KTS | | DIST | TIME | | FUEL | |
| --- | --- | --- | --- | --- | --- | --- | --- | --- | --- | --- | --- |
| FROM | TO | ALTITUDE | COURSE | TEMP | TAS | GS | NM | LEG | TOT | LEG | TOT |
| MDW | L/O GIJ R-270/19 | MDW 4 Climb | | | | | 49 | | :19:00 | | 327* |
| R-270/19 GIJ | GIJ | Direct FL190 | | 230/51 ISA | | | | | | | |
| GIJ | CRL | J554 FL190 | | | | | | | | | |
| CRL | YXU | J586 FL190 | | 240/59 ISA | | | | | | | |
| YXU | BUF R-282/30 | J547 FL190 | | 250/62 ISA | | | | | | | |
| BUF R-282/30 | BUF | Descent & Approach | | | | | 30 | :14:00 | | 121.5 | |
| BUF | ROC | V2 7000 | | | 150 | | 44 | :20:00 | | | |

| OTHER DATA: * Includes Taxi Fuel NOTE:  Use 610 PPH Total Fuel Flow From L/O To Start Of Descent. Use 710 PPH Total Fuel Flow For Reserve And Alternate Requirements. A Missed Approach Requires 81# of Fuel. | TIME and FUEL: As required by FARs. | | |
| --- | --- | --- | --- |
| | TIME | FUEL (LB) | |
| | | | EN ROUTE |
| | | | RESERVE |
| | | | ALTERNATE |
| | | | TOTAL |

FIGURE 94.—Flight Plan/Flight Log.

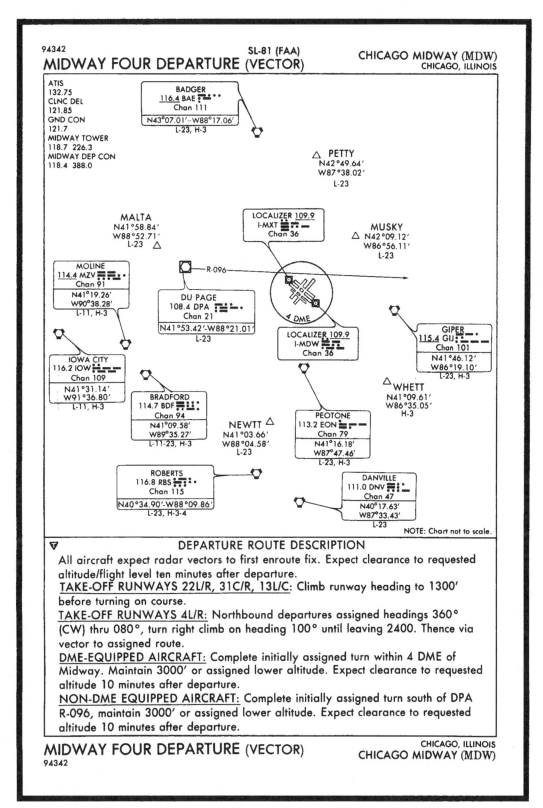

94342              SL-81 (FAA)             CHICAGO MIDWAY (MDW)

# MIDWAY FOUR DEPARTURE (VECTOR)
CHICAGO, ILLINOIS

ATIS 132.75
CLNC DEL 121.85
GND CON 121.7
MIDWAY TOWER 118.7 226.3
MIDWAY DEP CON 118.4 388.0

**BADGER**
116.4 BAE
Chan 111
N43°07.01'−W88°17.06'
L-23, H-3

△ **PETTY**
N42°49.64'
W87°38.02'
L-23

**MALTA**
N41°58.84'
W88°52.71'
L-23 △

**LOCALIZER** 109.9
I-MXT
Chan 36

**MUSKY**
△ N42°09.12'
W86°56.11'
L-23

**MOLINE**
114.4 MZV
Chan 91
N41°19.26'
W90°38.28'
L-11, H-3

R-096

**DU PAGE**
108.4 DPA
Chan 21
N41°53.42'−W88°21.01'
L-23

4 DME

**LOCALIZER** 109.9
I-MDW
Chan 36

**GIPER**
115.4 GIJ
Chan 101
N41°46.12'
W86°19.10'
L-23, H-3

**IOWA CITY**
116.2 IOW
Chan 109
N41°31.14'
W91°36.80'
L-11, H-3

**BRADFORD**
114.7 BDF
Chan 94
N41°09.58'
W89°35.27'
L-11-23, H-3

**NEWTT** △
N41°03.66'
W88°04.58'
L-23

△ **WHETT**
N41°09.61'
W86°35.05'
H-3

**PEOTONE**
113.2 EON
Chan 79
N41°16.18'
W87°47.46'
L-23, H-3

**ROBERTS**
116.8 RBS
Chan 115
N40°34.90'−W88°09.86'
L-23, H-3-4

**DANVILLE**
111.0 DNV
Chan 47
N40°17.63'
W87°33.43'
L-23

NOTE: Chart not to scale.

## DEPARTURE ROUTE DESCRIPTION

All aircraft expect radar vectors to first enroute fix. Expect clearance to requested altitude/flight level ten minutes after departure.

<u>TAKE-OFF RUNWAYS 22L/R, 31C/R, 13L/C:</u> Climb runway heading to 1300' before turning on course.

<u>TAKE-OFF RUNWAYS 4L/R:</u> Northbound departures assigned headings 360° (CW) thru 080°, turn right climb on heading 100° until leaving 2400. Thence via vector to assigned route.

<u>DME-EQUIPPED AIRCRAFT:</u> Complete initially assigned turn within 4 DME of Midway. Maintain 3000' or assigned lower altitude. Expect clearance to requested altitude 10 minutes after departure.

<u>NON-DME EQUIPPED AIRCRAFT:</u> Complete initially assigned turn south of DPA R-096, maintain 3000' or assigned lower altitude. Expect clearance to requested altitude 10 minutes after departure.

**MIDWAY FOUR DEPARTURE** (VECTOR)
94342

CHICAGO, ILLINOIS
CHICAGO MIDWAY (MDW)

FIGURE 95.—Midway Four Departure (Vector).

THIS PAGE INTENTIONALLY LEFT BLANK

ILLINOIS

## CHAMPAIGN (URBANA)
**UNIVERSITY OF ILLINOIS-WILLARD** (CMI)  5 SW  UTC–6(–5DT)
N40°02.36′ W88°16.68′
754   B   S4   FUEL 100LL, JET A1 +   OX 1   ARFF Index A
RWY 14R-32L: H8100X150 (CONC-GRVD)   S-100, D-180, DT-260   HIRL
  RWY 14R: VASI(V4L)—GA 3.0° TCH 31′.    RWY 32L: MALSR. VASI(V4L)—GA 3.0° TCH 54′.
RWY 04L-22R: H6500X150 (CONC-GRVD)   S-100, D-180, DT-260   MIRL
  RWY 04L: VASI(V4L)—GA 3.0° TCH 45′.    RWY 22R: VASI(V4L)—GA 3.0° TCH 41′. Tree.
RWY 18-36: H5299X150 (CONC)   S-40, D-50, DT-90   MIRL
  RWY 36: VASI(V4L)—GA 3.0° TCH 40′. Tree.
AIRPORT REMARKS: Attended continuously. Rwy 18-36 CLOSED 0600-1200Z‡ indefinitely. PPR for unscheduled air
carrier operations with more than 30 passenger seats between 0400-1200Z‡, call arpt manager 217-244-8604.
Rwy 04R-22L and Rwy 14L-32R VFR day only, restricted to authorized Flight Schools only. When twr clsd HIRL
Rwy 14R-32L preset low ints, to increase ints and ACTIVATE MIRL Rwys 04L-22R MALSR Rwy 32L—CTAF.
Itinerant parking on southeast ramp only. Taxiway D not available for air carrier ops with more than 30
passenger seats. NOTE: See Land and Hold Short Operations Section.
COMMUNICATIONS: CTAF 120.4   ATIS 124.85   UNICOM 122.95
ST LOUIS FSS (STL) TF 1–800–WX–BRIEF. NOTAM FILE CMI.
CHAMPAIGN RCO 122.1R 110.0T (KANKAKEE FSS)
CHAMPAIGN (URBANA) RCO 122.45 (ST LOUIS FSS)
Ⓡ CHAMPAIGN APP/DEP CON 132.85 (134°-312°) 121.35 (313°-133°) 118.25 (1200-0600Z‡)
CHICAGO CENTER APP/DEP CON 121.35 (0600-1200Z‡)
CHAMPAIGN TOWER 120.4 (1200-0600Z‡)   GND CON 121.8   CLNC DEL 128.75
AIRSPACE: CLASS C svc 1200-0600Z‡ ctc APP CON other times CLASS G.
RADIO AIDS TO NAVIGATION: NOTAM FILE CMI.
CHAMPAIGN (L) VORTAC 110.0   CMI   Chan 37   N40°02.07′ W88°16.56′   at fld. 750/3E.
VEALS NDB (LOM) 407   CM   N39°57.97′ W88°10.95′   315°6.2 NM to fld.
ILS 109.1   I-CMI   Rwy 32L.   LOM VEALS NDB. ILS unmonitored when twr clsd.
ASR

## CHICAGO
**CHICAGO MIDWAY** (MDW)  9SW  UTC–6(–5DT)   N41°47.16′ W87°45.15′
620   B   S4   FUEL 100LL, JET A1 +   OX 2, 4   AOE   ARFF Index C
RWY 13C-31C: H6522X150 (CONC-GRVD)   S-95, D-165, DT-250   HIRL
  RWY 13C: ALSF1. PAPI (P4L)—GA 3.0° TCH 47′. Thld dsplcd 462′. Pole.
  RWY 31C: LDIN. REIL. VASI(V4L)—GA 3.0° TCH 52′. Thld dsplcd 696′. Tree.
RWY 04R-22L: H6446X150 (CONC-ASPH-GRVD)   S-95, D-165, DT-250   HIRL
  RWY 04R: REIL. VASI(V4R)—GA 3.4° TCH 64. Thld dsplcd 518′. Building.
  RWY 22L: REIL. VASI(V4R)—GA 3.0° TCH 53′. Thld dsplcd 634′. Pole.
RWY 04L-22R: H5509X150 (ASPH)   S-30, D-40   MIRL
  RWY 04L: VASI(V4R). Thld dsplcd 758′. Tree.    RWY 22R: VASI(V4L). Building.
RWY 13L-31R: H5412X150 (ASPH)   S-30, D-40   MIRL
  RWY 13L: Thld dsplcd 753′. Tree.    RWY 31R: Pole.
Rwy 13R-31L: H3859X60 (CONC)   S-12.5   MIRL
  RWY 13R: Pole.    RWY 31L: Tree.
AIRPORT REMARKS: Attended continuously. Landing fee. Arpt CLOSED to solo student training. Birds on and in vicinity
of arpt. Noise abatement procedures: All departures are requested to expedite climb through 1500 ft MSL
0400-1200Z‡. Rwys 13L-31R and 04R-22R not avbl for air carrier ops with more than 30 passenger seats. Rwy
13C PAPI and RVR out of svc indefinitely. Flight Notification Service (ADCUS) available.
WEATHER DATA SOURCES: LAWRS.
COMMUNICATIONS: ATIS 132.75   UNICOM 122.95
KANKAKEE FSS (IKK) TF 1–800–WX–BRIEF. NOTAM FILE MDW.
Ⓡ APP/DEP CON 118.4 126.05
MIDWAY TOWER 118.7 135.2 (helicopter ops)   GND CON 121.7   CLNC DEL 121.85   PRE TAXI CLNC 121.85
AIRSPACE: CLASS C svc continuous ctc MIDWAY RADAR 119.45
RADIO AIDS TO NAVIGATION: NOTAM FILE IKK.
CHICAGO HEIGHTS (L) VORTAC 114.2   CGT   Chan 89   N41°30.60′ W87°34.29′   332° 18.5 NM to fld. 630/2E.
ERMIN NDB (MHW/LOM) 332   HK   N41°43.14′ W87°50.19′   044° 5.5 NM to fld. NOTAM FILE MDW.
KEDZI NDB (MHW/LOM) 248   MX   N41°44.49′ W87°41.38′   315° 3.9 NM to fld. NOTAM FILE MDW.
ILS/DME 109.9   I-MDW   Chan 36   Rwy 13C.
ILS 111.5   I-HKH   Rwy 04R.   LOM ERMIN NDB.
ILS/DME 109.9   I-MXT   Chan 36   Rwy 31C.   LOM KEDZI NDB.
MLS   Chan 660   Rwy 22L.   MLS unusable 246°-262° byd 10NM blo 3500′; unusable clockwise byd 262°;
elevation unusable clockwise beyond 226° blo 2.0°; elevation unusable counterclockwise byd 222° blo 2.0°.
Disregard guidance signals found clockwise byd 314°. Disregard guidance signals found counterclockwise byd
184°.

FIGURE 95A.—Excerpt (MDW).

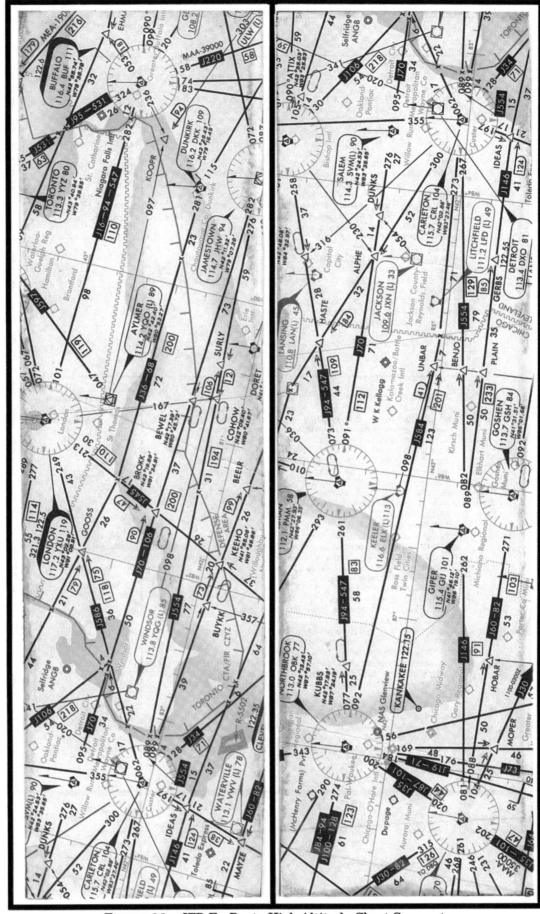

FIGURE 96.—IFR En Route High Altitude Chart Segment.

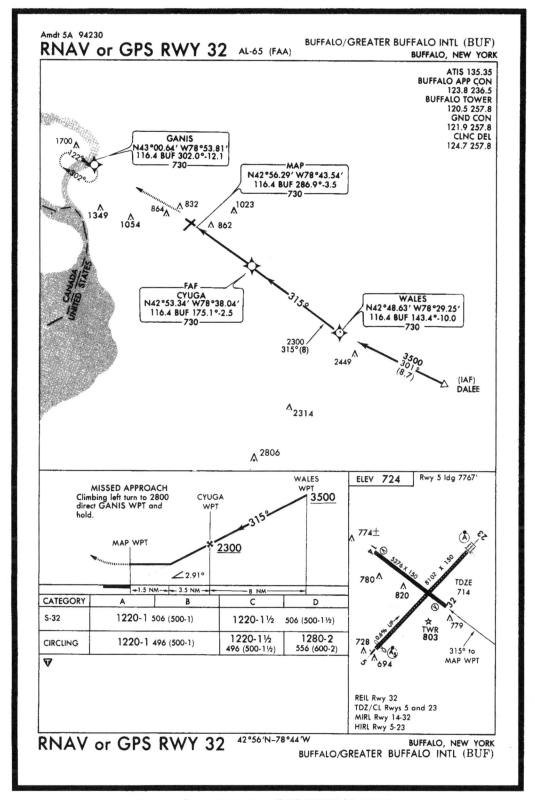

FIGURE 97.—RNAV or GPS RWY 32 (BUF).

THIS PAGE INTENTIONALLY LEFT BLANK

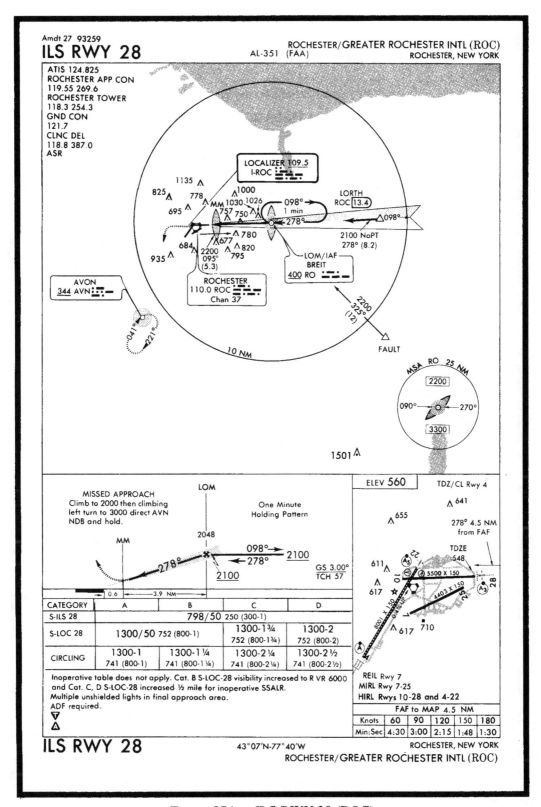

FIGURE 97A.—ILS RWY 28 (ROC).

**ALTERNATE MINS**

INSTRUMENT APPROACH PROCEDURE CHARTS

 IFR ALTERNATE MINIMUMS

(NOT APPLICABLE TO USA/USN/USAF)

Standard alternate minimums for non precision approaches are 800-2 (NDB, VOR, LOC, TACAN, LDA, VORTAC, VOR/DME or ASR); for precision approaches 600-2 (ILS or PAR). Airports within this geographical area that require alternate minimums other than standard or alternate minimums with restrictions are listed below. NA - means alternate minimums are not authorized due to unmonitored facility or absence of weather reporting service. Civil pilots see FAR 91. USA/USN/USAF pilots refer to appropriate regulations.

NAME          ALTERNATE MINIMUMS

**ALBANY, NY**
ALBANY COUNTY ............................ ILS Rwy 1[1]
ILS Rwy 19[1]
VOR/DME or GPS Rwy 1[1]
VOR Rwy 1[2]
VOR or GPS Rwy 19[1]
VOR or GPS Rwy 28[1]
[1]Category D, 800-2½.
[2]Category C, 800-2¼; Category D, 800-2½.

**ALLENTOWN, PA**
LEHIGH VALLEY INTL ..................... ILS Rwy 13
ILS, Categories A,B,C, 700-2; Category D, 700-2¼. LOC, Category D, 800-2¼.

**ALTOONA, PA**
ALTOONA-BLAIR COUNTY ............ ILS Rwy 20[1]
VOR or GPS-A[2]
[1]Categories A,B,C, 900-2½, Category D, 1100-3.
[2]Category D, 1100-3.

**BRADFORD, PA**
BRADFORD REGIONAL ....... VOR/DME Rwy 14
NA when BFD FSS closed.

**CORTLAND, NY**
CORTLAND COUNTY-
CHASE FIELD ........................... VOR or GPS-A
Categories A,B, 1100-2,Categories C,D, 1100-3.

**DUBOIS, PA**
DUBOIS-JEFFERSON COUNTY ..... ILS Rwy 25
LOC, NA.

NAME          ALTERNATE MINIMUMS

**ELMIRA, NY**
ELMIRA/CORNING REGIONAL ....... ILS Rwy 6[12]
ILS Rwy 24,1200-3
NDB or GPS Rwy 24,1200-3
[1]Categories A,B, 1200-2; Categories C,D, 1200-3.
[2]NA when control tower closed.

**ERIE, PA**
ERIE INTL ......................................... ILS Rwy 6[1]
ILS Rwy 24[1]
NDB Rwy 6
NDB Rwy 24
RADAR-1
NA when control tower closed.
[1]ILS, 700-2.

**FARMINGDALE, NY**
REPUBLIC ........................................ ILS Rwy 14[1]
NDB or GPS Rwy 1[2]
[1]NA when control tower closed.
[2]NA when control zone not effective.

**HARRISBURG, PA**
CAPITAL CITY .................................... ILS Rwy 8
Categories A,B, 900-2; Categories C,D, 900-2¾.
NA when control tower closed.

HARRISBURG INTL ........................ ILS Rwy 13[1]
ILS Rwy 31[1]
VOR or GPS Rwy 31[2]
[1]ILS, Categories C,D, 700-2. LOC, NA.
[2]Categories A,B, 900-2, Category C, 900-2¾, Category D, 900-3.

NE-2

 **ALTERNATE MINS**

FIGURE 97B.—IFR Alternate Minimums.

**ALTERNATE MINS**

| NAME | ALTERNATE MINIMUMS |
| --- | --- |

**PHILADELPHIA, PA(CON'T)**
PHILADELPHIA INTL ...................... ILS Rwy 9L[1]
ILS Rwy 9R[2]
ILS Rwy 17[3]
ILS Rwy 27L[3]
ILS Rwy 27R[2]
NDB or GPS Rwy 27L#
RNAV or GPS Rwy 17*

[1]ILS, Category D, 700-2.
[2]ILS, 700-2.
[3]ILS, Categories A,B,C, 700-2; Category D, 700-2¼. LOC, Category D,800-2¼.
#Category C, 800-2¼; Category D, 800-2½.
*Category D, 800-2¼.

**PHILIPSBURG, PA**
MID-STATE ...................................... ILS Rwy 16[1]
NDB Rwy 16[2]
VOR Rwy 24[3]

[1]ILS, Category C, 700-2; Category D, 700-2¼. LOC, Category D, 800-2¼.
[2]Category D, 800-2¼.
[3]Categories A,B, 900-2; Category C, 900-2¼; Category D, 900-2½.

**PITTSBURGH, PA**
PITTSBURGH INTL ...................... ILS Rwy 10L[1]
ILS Rwy 10R[1]
ILS Rwy 28L[1]
ILS Rwy 28R[1]
ILS Rwy 32[1]
VOR or TACAN Rwy 28L/C[2]

[1]ILS, Category E, 700-2¼. LOC, Category E, 800-2¼.
[2]Category E, 800-2¼.

**POUGHKEEPSIE, NY**
DUTCHESS COUNTY ........................ ILS Rwy 6
ILS, Categories B,C,D, 700-2.

**READING, PA**
READING REGIONAL/CARL A.
SPAATZ FIELD .............................. ILS Rwy 36[1]#
NDB Rwy 36[2]#
RNAV or GPS Rwy 13[3]*
RNAV or GPS Rwy 18[3]*

[1]ILS, Categories A,B,C, 700-2; Category D, 800-2½. LOC, Category D, 800-2½.
[2]Category D, 800-2½.
[3]Category C, 800-2¼; Category D, 800-2½.
#NA when control tower closed.
*NA when control zone not in effect.

**REEDSVILLE, PA**
MIFFLIN COUNTY ........................... LOC Rwy 6
NA when airport unattended.
Category D, 1500-3.

**ROCHESTER, NY**
GREATER ROCHESTER INTL ......... ILS Rwy 4[1]
ILS Rwy 22[1]
ILS Rwy 28[2]
NDB or GPS Rwy 28[3]
RADAR-1#
VOR/DME or GPS Rwy 4#
VOR Rwy 4#

[1]ILS, Category D, 700-2¼. LOC, Category D, 800-2¼.
[2]Categories A,B, 800-2; Category C, 800-2¼; Category D, 800-2½.
[3]Category C, 800-2¼; Category D, 800-2½.
#Category D, 800-2¼.

**SARANAC LAKE, NY**
ADIRONDACK
REGIONAL ............... VOR/DME or GPS Rwy 5[1]
VOR or GPS Rwy 9[2][3]

[1]NA except Categories A,B, 1200-2; Categories C,D, 1200-3, for operators with approved weather reporting service.
[2]Category A, 1000-2; Category B, 1100-2; Categories C,D, 1100-3.
[3]NA except for operators with approved weather reporting service.

**STATE COLLEGE, PA**
UNIVERSITY PARK ........................ ILS Rwy 24[1][2]
VOR/DME RNAV or GPS Rwy 6[1]
VOR or GPS-B,1300-3

[1]Category D, 900-2¾.
[2]NA when airport unattended.

**UTICA, NY**
ONEIDA COUNTY .......................... NDB Rwy 33
Category D, 800-2¼.

**WATERTOWN, NY**
WATERTOWN INTL ........................ ILS Rwy 7
LOC, NA.

**WESTHAMPTON BEACH, NY**
THE FRANCIS S. GABRESKI .......... ILS Rwy 24
NDB Rwy 24
NA when control zone not in effect.

NE-2

 **ALTERNATE MINS**

FIGURE 97C.—IFR Alternate Minimums.

Form Approved: OMB No. 2120-0024

## FLIGHT PLAN

U.S. DEPARTMENT OF TRANSPORTATION
FEDERAL AVIATION ADMINISTRATION

| (FAA USE ONLY) | ☐ PILOT BRIEFING | ☐ VNR | TIME STARTED | SPECIALIST INITIALS |
| --- | --- | --- | --- | --- |
| | ☐ STOPOVER | | | |

| 1. TYPE | 2. AIRCRAFT IDENTIFICATION | 3. AIRCRAFT TYPE/ SPECIAL EQUIPMENT | 4. TRUE AIRSPEED | 5. DEPARTURE POINT | 6. DEPARTURE TIME | | 7. CRUISING ALTITUDE |
| --- | --- | --- | --- | --- | --- | --- | --- |
| ☐ VFR  X IFR  ☐ DVFR | N55JB | BE90/A | 248 KTS | DFW Dallas Ft. Worth | PROPOSED (Z) | ACTUAL (Z) | 15,000 |

**8. ROUTE OF FLIGHT**

DFW V369 BILEE, CUGAR 4 IAH

| 9. DESTINATION (Name of airport and city) | 10. EST. TIME ENROUTE | | 11. REMARKS    L/O = Level off.    PPH = Pounds Per Hour |
| --- | --- | --- | --- |
| IAH Houston Intercontinental Houston | HOURS | MINUTES | |

| 12. FUEL ON BOARD | | 13. ALTERNATE AIRPORT(S) | 14. PILOT'S NAME, ADDRESS & TELEPHONE NUMBER & AIRCRAFT HOME BASE | 15. NUMBER ABOARD |
| --- | --- | --- | --- | --- |
| HOURS | MINUTES | BPT Beaumont-Port Arthur Jefferson County | 17. DESTINATION CONTACT/TELEPHONE (OPTIONAL) | 4 |

**16. COLOR OF AIRCRAFT**
BLUE/YELLOW

CIVIL AIRCRAFT PILOTS. FAR Part 91 requires you file an IFR flight plan to operate under instrument flight rules in controlled airspace. Failure to file could result in a civil penalty not to exceed $1,000 for each violation (Section 901 of the Federal Aviation Act of 1958, as amended). Filing of a VFR flight plan is recommended as a good operating practice. See also Part 99 for requirements concerning DVFR flight plans.

FAA Form 7233-1 (8-82)

CLOSE VFR FLIGHT PLAN WITH _____ FSS ON ARRIVAL

## FLIGHT LOG

| CHECK POINTS | | ROUTE | COURSE | WIND | SPEED-KTS | | DIST | TIME | | FUEL | |
| --- | --- | --- | --- | --- | --- | --- | --- | --- | --- | --- | --- |
| FROM | TO | ALTITUDE | | TEMP | TAS | GS | NM | LEG | TOT | LEG | TOT |
| DFW | L/O | V369 Climb | | | | | 27 | | :12:00 | | 231* |
| L/O | Bilee | V369 15,000 | | 230/42 ISA | | | | | | | |
| Bilee | Cugar | Cugar 4 15,000 | | | | | | | | | |
| Cugar | Start Descent | Cugar 4 15,000 | | 230/42 ISA | | | | | | | |
| Start Descent | IAH | Descent & Approach | | | | | 25 | :14:00 | | 132 | |
| | | | | | | | | | | | |
| | | | | | | | | | | | |
| IAH | BPT | Vectors 3000 | | | | 194 | 68 | | | | |
| | | | | | | | | | | | |

**OTHER DATA:**
**NOTE:**
* Includes Taxi Fuel
Use 850 PPH Total Fuel Flow From L/O To Start Of Descent.
Use 880 PPH Total Fuel Flow For Reserve And Alternate Requirements.
A Missed Approach Requires 82# of Fuel.

**TIME and FUEL: As required by FARs.**

| TIME | FUEL (LB) | |
| --- | --- | --- |
| | | EN ROUTE |
| | | RESERVE |
| | | ALTERNATE |
| | | TOTAL |

FIGURE 98.—Flight Plan/Flight Log.

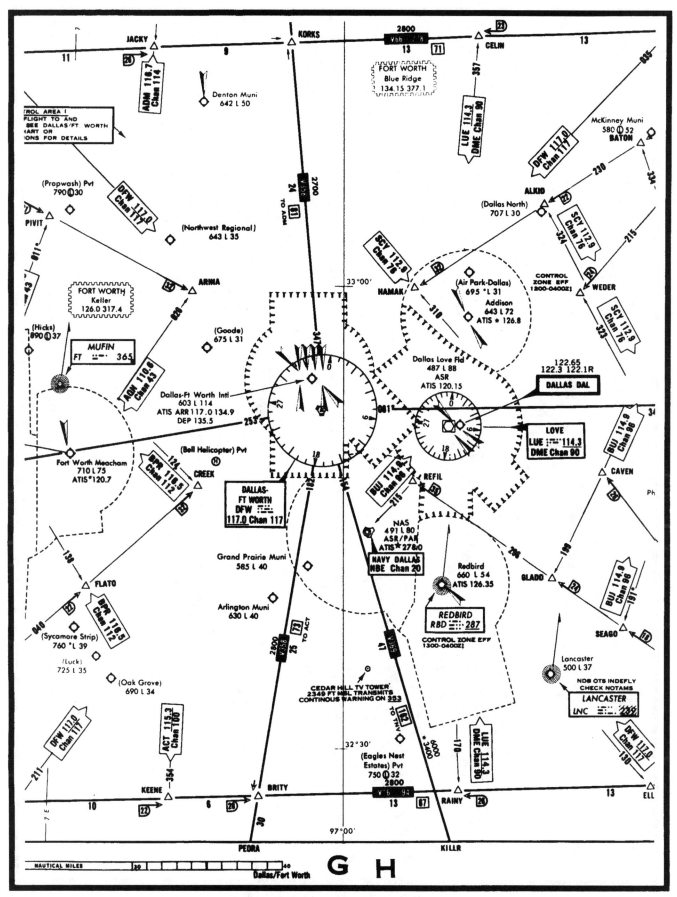

FIGURE 99.—IFR Area Chart Segment.

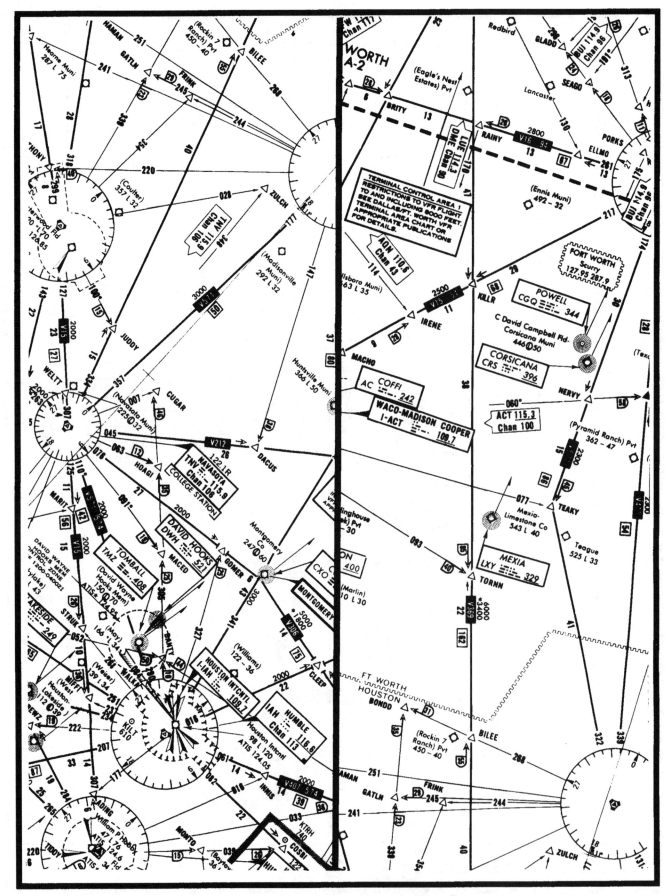

FIGURE 100.—IFR En Route Low Altitude Chart Segment.

# TEXAS

**§ DALLAS-FORT WORTH INTL** (DFW) 12 NW UTC-6(-5DT) 32°53'47"N 97°02'28"W

**DALLAS-FT. WORTH**
**H-2K, 4F, 5B, L-13C, A**
**IAP**

603 BFUEL 100LL, JET A OX 1,3 LRA CFR Index E
RWY 17L-35R: H11,388X150 (CONC-GRVD) S-120, D-200, DT-600, DDT-850 HIRL, CL
  RWY 17L: ALSF2. TDZ. RWY 35R: MALSR. TDZ.
RWY 17R-35L: H11,388X200 (CONC-GRVD) S-120, D-200, DT-600, DDT-850 HIRL, CL
  RWY 17R: SSALR TDZ. RWY 35L: TDZ. VASI(V6L).
RWY 18L-36R: H11,387X200 (CONC-GRVD) S-120, D-200, DT-600, DDT-850 HIRL, CL
  RWY 18L: SSALR.TDZ. RWY 36R: TDZ. VASI(V6L).
RWY 18R-36L: H11,388X150 (CONC-GRVD) S-120, D-200, DT-600, DDT-850 HIRL, CL
  RWY 18R: ALSF2. TDZ RWY 36L: MALSR. TDZ.
RWY 13L-31R: H9000X200 (CONC-GRVD) S-120, D-200, DT-600, DDT-850 HIRL, CL .5% up NW.
  RWY 13L: TDZ. VASI(V6L)—Upper GA 3.25°TCH 93'. Lower GA 3.0°TCH 47'.
  RWY 31 R: MALSR. TDZ.
RWY 13R-31L: H9300X150 (CONC-GRVD) S-120, D-220, DT-600, DDT-850 HIRL, CL
  RWY 13 R: MALSR. TDZ. RWY 31L: TDZ.
RWY 18S-36S: H4000X100 (CONC)
AIRPORT REMARKS: Attended continuously. Prior Permission Required from arpt ops for General Aviation acft to proceed to airline terminal gate except to General Aviation Facility. Rwy 18S-36S located on taxiway G, 4000' long 100' wide restricted to prop acft 12,500 lbs. & below and stol acft daylight VFR plus IFR departures. Prior permission required from the primary tenant airlines to operate within central terminal area, CAUTION: proper minimum clearance may not be maintained within the central terminal area. Landing fee. Clearways 500x1000 each end Rwy 17L-35R, Rwy 17R-35L, Rwy 18L-36R and Rwy 18R-36L. Flight Notification Service (ADCUS) available.
WEATHER DATA SOURCES↓LWAS
COMMUNICATIONS: ATIS 117.0 134.9 (ARR) 135.5 (DEP) UNICOM 122.95
  FORT WORTH FSS (FTW) LC 624-8471, Toll free call, dial 1-800-WX-BRIEF. NOTAM FILE DFW
  ⊕ REGIONAL APP CON 119.05(E) 119.4(E) 125.8(W) 132.1(W)
  REGIONAL TOWER 126.55 (E) 124.15 (W) GND CON 121.65 133.15(E) 121.8 (W) CLNC DEL 128.25 127.5
  ⊕ REGIONAL DEP CON 118.55 (E) 124.25 (WEST) 127.75 (NORTH-SOUTH)
  TCA Group I: See VFR Terminal Area chart.
RADIO AIDS TO NAVIGATION: NOTAM FILE DFW.
  (H) VORTACH 117.0 DFW Chan 117 32°51'57"N 97°01'40"W at fld. 560/08E.
    VOR Portion unusable 045°-050° all altitudes and distances, 350-100° beyond 30 NM below 2100'.
  ISSUE NDB (LOM) 233 PK 32°47'35"N 97°01'49"W 353° 5.1 NM to fld.
  JIFFY NDB (LOM) 219 FL 32°59'45"N 97°01'46"W 173° 5.1 NM to fld.
  ILS/DME 109.5 I-LWN Chan 32 Rwy 13R
  ILS/DME 109.1 I-FLQ Chan 28 Rwy 17L LOM JIFFY NDB
  ILS 111.5 I-JHZ Rwy 17R LOM JIFFY NDB
  ILS 111.3 I-CIX Rwy 18L
  ILS/DME 111.9 I-VYN Chan 56 Rwy 18R
  ILS 110.9 I-RRA Rwy 31R
  ILS/DME 109.1 I-PKQ Chan 28 Rwy 35R LOM ISSUE NDB
  ILS/DME 111.9 I-BXN Chan 56 Rwy 36L

---

**§ HOUSTON INTERCONTINENTAL** (IAH) 15N UTC-6(-5DT) 29°58'49"N 95°20'22"W

**HOUSTON**
**H-5B, L-17B**
**IAP**

98 B S4 FUEL 100LL, JET A OX2 LRA CFR Index D
RWY 14L-32R: H1200X150 (CONC-GRVD) S-100, D-200, DT-400, DDT-778 HIRL, CL
  RWY 14L: MALSR. VASI(V4L)—GA 3.0°TCH 54'. RWY 32R: MALSR.
RWY 09-27: H10000X150 (ASPH-GRVD) S-75, D-191, DT-400, DDT-850 HIRL, CL
  RWY 09: MALSR. TDZ. PAPI(P4L)—GA 3.0°TCH 63'.
  RWY 27: ALSF2. TDZ. PAPI(P4L)—GA 3.0°TCH 63'.
RWY 08-26: H9401X150 (CONC-GRVD) S-120, D-155, DT-265 HIRL, CL
  RWY 08: MALSR. TDZ. RWY 26: ALSF2. TDZ. VASI(V4L)—GA 3.0°TCH 53'.
RWY 14R-32L: H6038X100 (ASPH-GRVD) S-30, D-60, DT-60 MIRL
  RWY 14R: VASI(V4L)—GA 3.0°TCH 40'. Road. RWY 32L: VASI(V4L)—GA 3.0°TCH 45'.
AIRPORT REMARKS: Attended continuously. CAUTION: Birds on and in vicinity of arpt. CAUTION—Approach end of rwy 26 bright lgts approximately one mile from thld and 900' South of centerline. Caution—Deer on and in vicinity of arpt. Rwy 14R-32L CLOSED to acft over 140,000 lbs gross weight. Landing Fee. Flight Notification Service (ADCUS) available.
WEATHER DATA SOURCES↓LWAS
COMMUNICATIONS: ATIS 124.05 UNICOM 122.95
  MONTGOMERY COUNTY FSS (CXO) Toll free call, dial 1-800-WX-BRIEF. NOTAM FILE IAH.
  ⊕ APP CON 124.35 (West) 127.25 (North and East)
  TOWER 118.1 (135.15 copter control) GND CON 121.7 CLNC DEL 128.1 (135.15 copter control)
  ⊕ DEP CON 123.8 (West) 119.7 (North and East)
  TCA Group II: VFR Terminal Area chart.
RADIO AIDS TO NAVIGATION: NOTAM FILE IAH.
  HUMBLE (H) VORTACW 116.6 IAH Chan 113 29°57'24"N 95°20'44"W at fld. 90/08E. HIWAS.
  MARBE NDB (LOM) 379 HS 30°04'29"N 95°24'45"W 146° 5.9 NM to fld.
  NIXIN NDB (LOM) 326 JY 29°59'36"N 95°12'54"W 257° 6.5 NM to fld.
  ILS/DME 109.7 I-JYV Chan 34 Rwy 26 LOM NIXIN NDB
  ILS 111.9 I-HSQ Rwy 14L LOM MARBE NDB
  ILS/DME 109.7 I-IAH Chan 34 Rwy 08
  ILS/DME 110.9 I-UYO Chan 34 Rwy 09
  ILS 111.9 I-CDG Rwy 32R

FIGURE 101.—Airport/Facility Directory Excerpts.

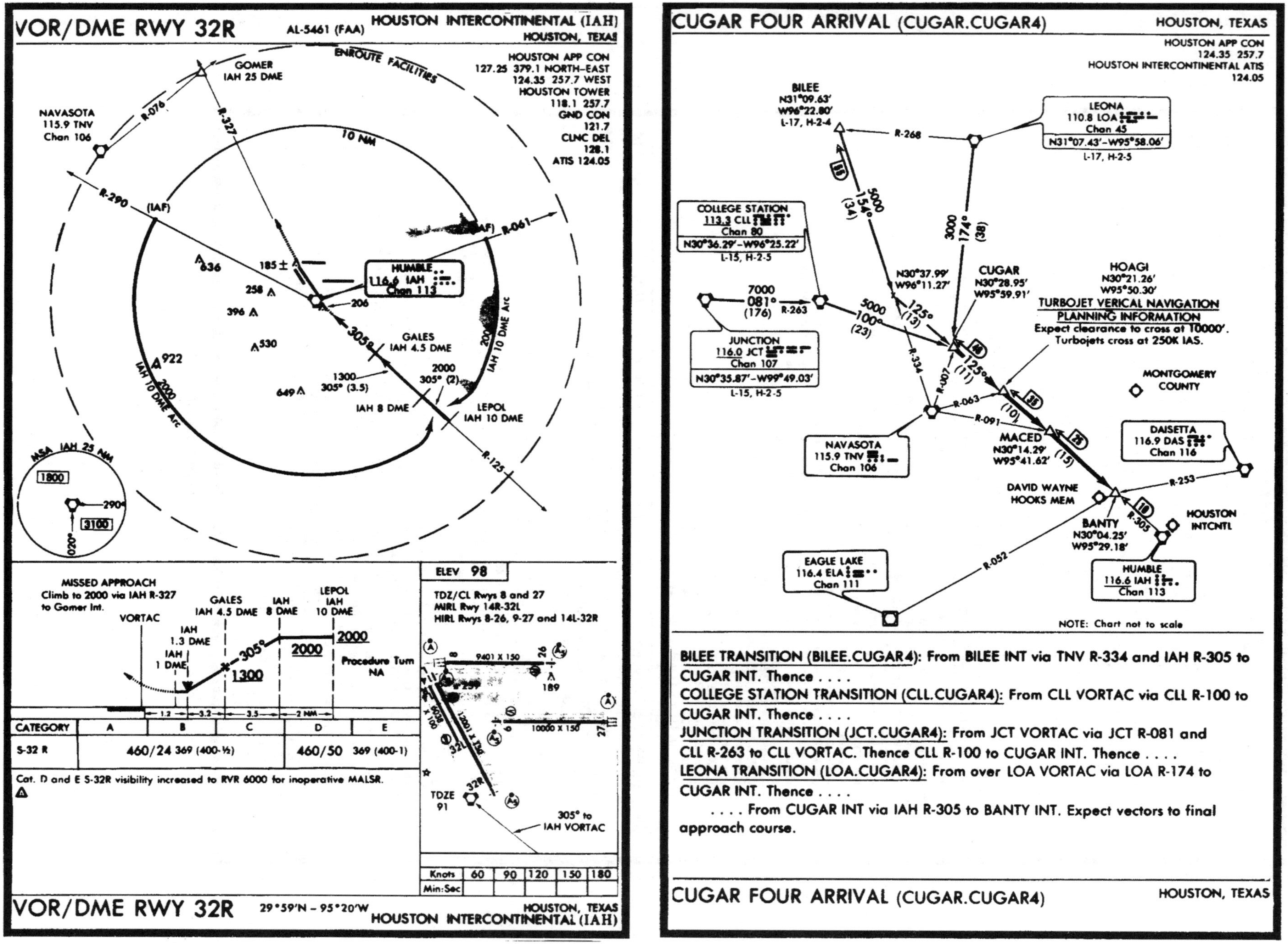


FIGURE 102.—VOR/DME RWY 32R (IAH)/Cugar Four Arrival (Cugar.Cugar4).

Form Approved: OMB No. 2120-0034

## FLIGHT PLAN

U.S. DEPARTMENT OF TRANSPORTATION
FEDERAL AVIATION ADMINISTRATION

| (FAA USE ONLY) | □ PILOT BRIEFING | □ VNR | TIME STARTED | SPECIALIST INITIALS |
|---|---|---|---|---|
| | □ STOPOVER | | | |

| 1. TYPE | 2. AIRCRAFT IDENTIFICATION | 3. AIRCRAFT TYPE/ SPECIAL EQUIPMENT | 4. TRUE AIRSPEED | 5. DEPARTURE POINT | 6. DEPARTURE TIME | | 7. CRUISING ALTITUDE |
|---|---|---|---|---|---|---|---|
| VFR | | | | | PROPOSED (Z) | ACTUAL (Z) | |
| X IFR | N91JB | BE1900/A | 233 KTS | TUS TUCSON | | | FL220 |
| DVFR | | | | | | | |

**8. ROUTE OF FLIGHT**

TUS TUS3.GBN, J104TNP, TNP.DOWNE 3 LAX

| 9. DESTINATION (Name of airport and city) | 10. EST. TIME ENROUTE | | 11. REMARKS |
|---|---|---|---|
| LAX | HOURS | MINUTES | L/O = Level Off        PPH = Pounds Per Hour |
| LOS ANGELES INT'L | | | TEC = Tower Enroute Control |
| Los Angeles | | | This flight is operating under FAR 135. |

| 12. FUEL ON BOARD | | 13. ALTERNATE AIRPORT(S) | 14. PILOT'S NAME, ADDRESS & TELEPHONE NUMBER & AIRCRAFT HOME BASE | 15. NUMBER ABOARD |
|---|---|---|---|---|
| HOURS | MINUTES | BUR | | |
| | | Burbank-Glendale- | 17. DESTINATION CONTACT/TELEPHONE (OPTIONAL) | 18 |
| | | Pasadena | | |

| 16. COLOR OF AIRCRAFT | |
|---|---|
| Maroon/White | CIVIL AIRCRAFT PILOTS. FAR Part 91 requires you file an IFR flight plan to operate under instrument flight rules in controlled airspace. Failure to file could result in a civil penalty not to exceed $1,000 for each violation (Section 901 of the Federal Aviation Act of 1958, as amended). Filing of a VFR flight plan is recommended as a good operating practice. See also Part 99 for requirements concerning DVFR flight plans. |

FAA Form 7233-1 (8-82)    CLOSE VFR FLIGHT PLAN WITH _____ FSS ON ARRIVAL

## FLIGHT LOG

| CHECK POINTS | | ROUTE | COURSE | WIND | SPEED-KTS | | DIST | TIME | | FUEL | |
|---|---|---|---|---|---|---|---|---|---|---|---|
| FROM | TO | ALTITUDE | | TEMP | TAS | GS | NM | LEG | TOT | LEG | TOT |
| TUS | L/O | TUS3.GBN Climb | | | | | 73 | :25:00 | | 350* | |
| L/O | GBN | TUS3.GBN FL220 | | 280/46 ISA-3 | | | | | | | |
| GBN | INT. J104 | J104 FL220 | | | | | | | | | |
| INT J104 | PKE | | | 280/46 ISA-3 | | | | | | | |
| PKE | TNP | | | | | | | | | | |
| TNP | Start Descent | | | | | | | | | | |
| Start Descent | Downe 3 LAX | Descent & Approach | | | | | 52 | :18:00 | | 170 | |
| | | | | | | | | | | | |
| LAX | BUR | TEC 3000 | | | | | 31 | :19:00 | | | |

OTHER DATA:    * Includes Taxi Fuel
NOTE: Use 676 PPH Total Fuel Flow From L/O To Start Of Descent.
Use 726 PPH Total Fuel Flow For Reserve And Alternate Requirements.
A Missed Approach Requires 120# of Fuel.

TIME and FUEL: As required by FARs.

| TIME | FUEL (LB) | |
|---|---|---|
| | | EN ROUTE |
| | | RESERVE |
| | | ALTERNATE |
| | | TOTAL |

FIGURE 103.—Flight Plan/Flight Log.

THIS PAGE INTENTIONALLY LEFT BLANK

## ARIZONA

**TUCSON INTL** (TUS)   6 S   UTC-7   32°06'58"N 110°56'26"W   PHOENIX
2641   B   S4   FUEL 100, 100LL, JET A   OX 1, 2, 3, 4   TPA—See Remarks   H-2M, L-4F
AOE   ARFF Index D   IAP
RWY 11L-29R: H10994X150 (ASPH-PFC)   S-160, D-200, DT-350, DDT-585   HIRL   0.6% up SE
RWY 11L: MALSR. REIL. PAPI (P4L)—GA 3.0° TCH 55'. Rgt tfc. Arresting device.
RWY 29R: REIL. VASI(V6L)—Upper GA 3.25°TCH 94'. Lower GA 3.0°TCH 50'. Arresting device.
RWY 11R-29L: H9129X75 (ASPH)   S-120, D-140, DT-220   MIRL   0.6% up SE
RWY 11R: REIL. Thld dsplcd 2109'. Pole. Rgt tfc.   RWY 29L: REIL. Pole.
RWY 03-21: H7000X150 (ASPH-PFC)   S-105, D-137, DT-230, DDT-500   MIRL
RWY 03: Thld dsplcd 841'. Railroad.
RWY 21: REIL. VASI(V4L)—GA 3.0°TCH 50'. Tree tfc. Arresting device.
**AIRPORT REMARKS:** Attended continuously. Commercial ldg fee and tiedown fee. Acft departing Rwy 11R read to attain at least 400'AGL prior to starting turn. Rwy 11L-29R has distance remaining markers on both sides. Rwy 03-21 has distance remaining markers on east side. Rwy 11R dsplcd thld not lgtd. No B-747 training except PPR: No flight training 0500-1300Z except PPR; call manager aviation svc 602-573-8152. Rwy 11L-29R gross weight limit DC-10-10 315,000 lbs. DC-10-30/40 400,000 lbs. L-1011-1 325,000 lbs. L-1011-100/200 340,000 lbs. Rwy 03-21 gross weight limit DC-10-10 300,000 lbs. DC-10-30/40 375,000 lbs. L-1011-01 310,000 lbs. L-1011-100/200 315,000 lbs. TPA-3441 (800) small acft. 4041 (1400) large/heavy turbojet acft. Portions of Taxiways C and 9 not visible from the twr due to vegetation; portions of Taxiway 2 not visible from the twr due to hangars. Note: See Special Notices—Glider Operations Northwest of Tucson, Arizona. Flight Notification Service (ADCUS) available.
**WEATHER DATA SOURCES:** LLWAS.
**COMMUNICATIONS:** ATIS 123.8   119.0   UNICOM 122.95
TUCSON FSS (TUS) on arpt. 122.2 LC 889-9689. NOTAM FILE TUS.
MOUNT LEMMON RCO 122.4 (TUCSON FSS)
® **APP/DEP CON** 125.1 (Rwy 11 090°-285°) (Rwy 29 275°-065°) 118.5 (Rwy 11 286°-089°) (Rwy 29
066°-274°)128.5
TOWER 118.3   GND CON 124.4   CLNC DEL 126.65
**RADIO AIDS TO NAVIGATION:** NOTAM FILE TUS. VHF/DF ctc FSS.
(H) VORTAC 116.0   TUS   Chan 107   32°05'42"N 110°54'51"W   301' 1.8 NM to fld. 2670'/12E.
VORTAC unusable 050°-080°beyond 30 NM below 10,500'   350°-005°beyond 30 NM below 11,200'
ILS/DME 108.5 I-TUS Chan 22 Rwy 11L

**TUCSON, AZ**
**RYAN FIELD**
DEPARTURE PROCEDURE: Rwy 8, turn right;
Rwy 24, turn left direct to Ryan NDB. Continue
climb in holding pattern (W, right turn 090°
inbound) to 5000 before proceeding on course.

**TUCSON INTL**
TAKE-OFF MINIMUMS: Rwys 3, 11L/R, 21,
29L/R, 4000-3 or std. with min. climb of 250'
per NM to 6500.
DEPARTURE PROCEDURE: Comply with
SID or radar vectors; or turn left or right as
assigned by ATC direct TUS VORTAC, climb in
holding pattern (NW, right turn, 128 inbound)
to depart TUS VORTAC at or above MCA or
MEA for assigned airway.

---

(PILOT NAV) (TUS3.TUS)   90307
## TUCSON THREE DEPARTURE
SL-430 (FAA)   TUCSON INTL
TUCSON, ARIZONA

CLNC DEL
126.65 326.2
ATIS 123.8 320.1

NOTE: Rwys 3, 11L/R, 21, 29L/R require a ceiling of 4000 feet and 3 miles visibility or standard with minimum climb of 250 ft per NM to 6500 ft.

NOTE: Gila Bend transition requires a minimum climb of 250 ft per NM to 9000 feet.

NOTE: San Simon transition requires a minimum climb of 380 ft per NM to 11,000 feet.

NOTE: DME Required.

NOTE: Chart not to scale.

## DEPARTURE ROUTE DESCRIPTION

▼ **TAKE-OFF RUNWAY 3:** Fly heading 030° for vector to appropriate transition. Maintain 17,000 feet or assigned lower altitude. Expect clearance to filed flight level 10 minutes after departure.

**TAKE-OFF RUNWAYS 11L/R, 21, 29L/R:** Fly assigned heading for vector to intercept appropriate transition. Maintain 17,000 feet, or assigned lower altitude. Expect clearance to filed flight level 10 minutes after departure.

**COCHISE TRANSITION (TUS3.CIE):** Via TUS R-107 and CIE R-245 to CIE VORTAC.
**GILA BEND TRANSITION (TUS3.GBN):** Via TUS R-280 and GBN R-109 to GBN VORTAC.
**SAN SIMON TRANSITION (TUS3.SSO):** Via TUS R-038 and SSO R-261 to SSO VORTAC.
**TOTEC TRANSITION (TUS3.TOTEC):** Via TUS R-308 to TOTEC INT.

## TUCSON THREE DEPARTURE
(PILOT NAV) (TUS3.TUS)   TUCSON, ARIZONA
TUCSON INTL

FIGURE 104.—Tucson Three Departure (Pilot Nav) (TUS3.TUS).

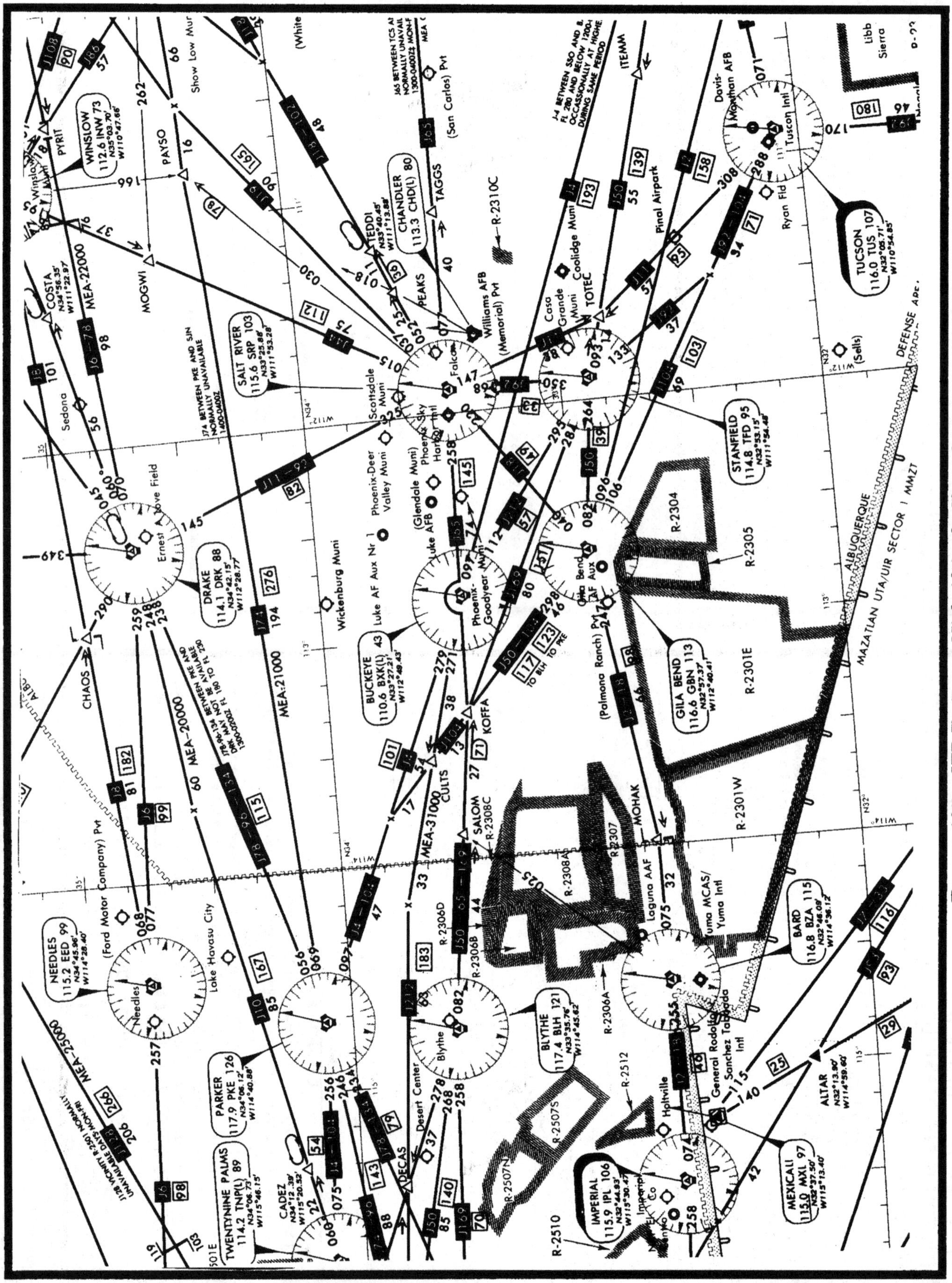

FIGURE 105.—IFR En Route High Altitude Chart Segment.

(DOWNE.DOWNE3)    89208
# DOWNE THREE ARRIVAL

LOS ANGELES INTL
LOS ANGELES, CALIFORNIA

## ARRIVAL DESCRIPTION

HECTOR TRANSITION (HEC.DOWNE3): From over HEC VORTAC via HEC R-211 and PDZ R-030 to CIVET INT, then LAX R-068 to DOWNE INT. Thence . . . .

PEACH SPRINGS TRANSITION (PGS.DOWNE3): From over PGS VORTAC via PGS R-229 and PDZ R-046 to RUST INT, then LAX R-068 to DOWNE INT. Thence . . . .

TWENTYNINE PALMS TRANSITION (TNP.DOWNE3): From over TNP VORTAC via TNP R-254 to PIONE DME, then LAX R-068 to DOWNE INT. Thence . . . .

. . . From DOWNE INT via SMO R-085 to SMO VOR/DME, then via SMO R-259 to WAKER INT, expect vector to final approach course for runways 6 and 7.

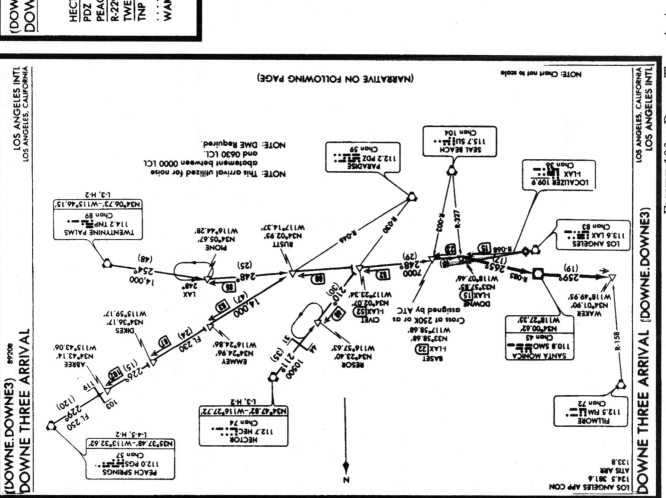

FIGURE 106.—Downe Three Arrival (Downe.Downe3).

THIS PAGE INTENTIONALLY LEFT BLANK

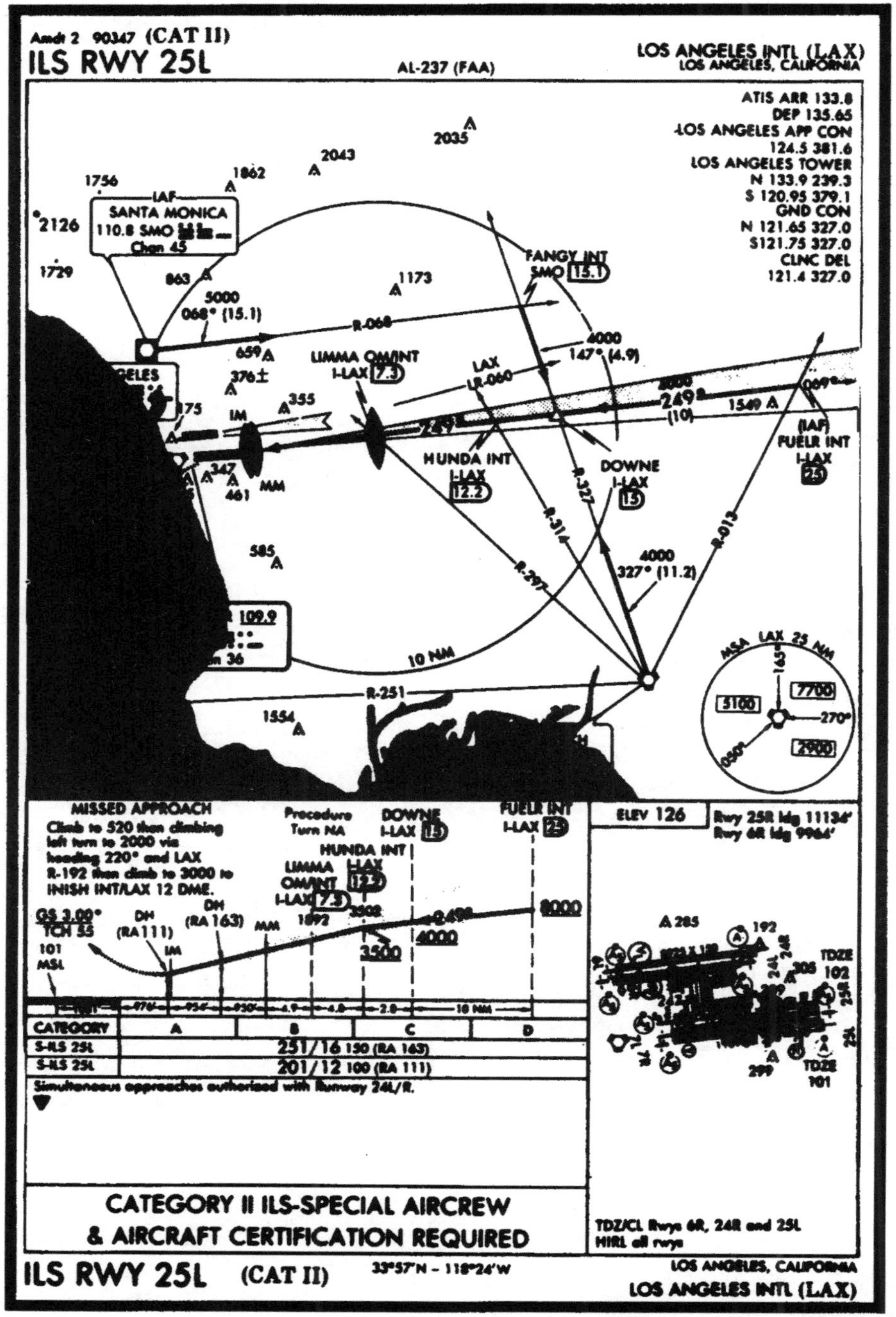

## CALIFORNIA

### LOS ANGELES
### LOS ANGELES INTL

LOS ANGELES
COPTER
H-2E, L-3B, A
IAP

LOS ANGELES INTL (LAX) 9 SW UTC-8(-7DT) 33°56'33"N 118°24'26"W
126 B S4 FUEL 100, 100LL, JET A OX 4 LRA ARFF Index E

AIRPORT REMARKS: Attended continuously. Turbulence may be deflected upward from the blast fence 180' E of Rwy 25R. CAUTION: Impaired wing clearance may exist on taxiway J between 30K and 19K when taxilane K occupied.

WEATHER DATA SOURCES: LLWAS.

COMMUNICATIONS: ATIS ARRIVAL 133.8 ATIS DEP 135.65 (213) 646-2297 UNICOM 122.95
HAWTHORNE FSS (HHR) TF 1-800-WX-BRIEF. NOTAM FILE LAX.

FIGURE 107.—ILS RWY 25L (CAT II) – LAX.

---

### ILS RWY 25L (CAT II)

Amdt 2 90J47 (CAT II)
AL-237 (FAA)

LOS ANGELES INTL (LAX)
LOS ANGELES, CALIFORNIA

ATIS ARR 133.8
DEP 135.65
LOS ANGELES APP CON 124.5 381.6
N 133.9 239.3
S 120.95 379.1
LOS ANGELES TOWER
N 133.9 327.0
GND CON
N 121.65 327.0
S 121.75 327.0
CLNC DEL
121.4 327.0

MISSED APPROACH

CATEGORY II ILS–SPECIAL AIRCREW
& AIRCRAFT CERTIFICATION REQUIRED

ILS RWY 25L (CAT II)

LOS ANGELES INTL (LAX)
LOS ANGELES, CALIFORNIA
33°57'N – 118°24'W

THIS PAGE INTENTIONALLY LEFT BLANK

Form Approved: OMB No. 2120-0034

| | | | | | | | |
|---|---|---|---|---|---|---|---|

**U.S. DEPARTMENT OF TRANSPORTATION FEDERAL AVIATION ADMINISTRATION**

**FLIGHT PLAN**

(FAA USE ONLY) ☐ PILOT BRIEFING ☐ VNR TIME STARTED SPECIALIST INITIALS

☐ STOPOVER

| 1. TYPE | 2. AIRCRAFT IDENTIFICATION | 3. AIRCRAFT TYPE/ SPECIAL EQUIPMENT | 4. TRUE AIRSPEED | 5. DEPARTURE POINT | 6. DEPARTURE TIME | | 7. CRUISING ALTITUDE |
|---|---|---|---|---|---|---|---|
| VFR | | | | | PROPOSED (Z) | ACTUAL (Z) | |
| X IFR | N131JB | BH206/A | 115 | DFW | | | 7,000 |
| DVFR | | | KTS | Dallas Ft. Worth | | | |

**8. ROUTE OF FLIGHT**

DFW V369 BILEE, CUGAR 4 IAH

| 9. DESTINATION (Name of airport and city) | 10. EST. TIME ENROUTE | | 11. REMARKS |
|---|---|---|---|
| IAH Houston Intercontinental Houston | HOURS | MINUTES | L/O = Level off.     PPH = Pounds Per Hour |

| 12. FUEL ON BOARD | | 13. ALTERNATE AIRPORT(S) | 14. PILOT'S NAME, ADDRESS & TELEPHONE NUMBER & AIRCRAFT HOME BASE | 15. NUMBER ABOARD |
|---|---|---|---|---|
| HOURS | MINUTES | HOU William P. Hobby | | 4 |
| | | | 17. DESTINATION CONTACT/TELEPHONE (OPTIONAL) | |

| 16. COLOR OF AIRCRAFT | CIVIL AIRCRAFT PILOTS. FAR Part 91 requires you file an IFR flight plan to operate under instrument flight rules in controlled airspace. Failure to file could result in a civil penalty not to exceed $1,000 for each violation (Section 901 of the Federal Aviation Act of 1958, as amended). Filing of a VFR flight plan is recommended as a good operating practice. See also Part 99 for requirements concerning DVFR flight plans. |
|---|---|
| BLUE/YELLOW | |

FAA Form 7233-1 (8-82)     CLOSE VFR FLIGHT PLAN WITH _____ FSS ON ARRIVAL

## FLIGHT LOG

| CHECK POINTS | | ROUTE | COURSE | WIND | SPEED-KTS | | DIST | TIME | | FUEL | |
|---|---|---|---|---|---|---|---|---|---|---|---|
| FROM | TO | ALTITUDE | | TEMP | TAS | GS | NM | LEG | TOT | LEG | TOT |
| DFW | L/O | V369 Climb | | | | | 23 | :14:00 | | 123' | |
| L/O | Bilee | V369 7,000 | | 220/36 ISA | | | | | | | |
| Bilee | Cugar | Cugar 4 7,000 | | | | | | | | | |
| Cugar | Start Descent | Cugar 4 7,000 | | 220/36 ISA | | | | | | | |
| Start Descent | IAH | Descent & Approach | | | | | 37 | :16:00 | | 140 | |
| | | | | | | | | | | | |
| | | | | | | | | | | | |
| IAH | HOU | Direct 3000 | | | | | 22 | :15:00 | | | |
| | | | | | | | | | | | |

**OTHER DATA:** * Includes Taxi Fuel
**NOTE:** Use 165 PPH Total Fuel Flow From L/O To Start Of Descent.
Use 172 PPH Total Fuel Flow For Reserve And Alternate Requirements.
A Missed Approach Requires 55# of Fuel.

**TIME and FUEL:** As required by FARs.

| TIME | FUEL (LB) | |
|---|---|---|
| | | EN ROUTE |
| | | RESERVE |
| | | ALTERNATE |
| | | TOTAL |

FIGURE 108.—Flight Plan/Flight Log.

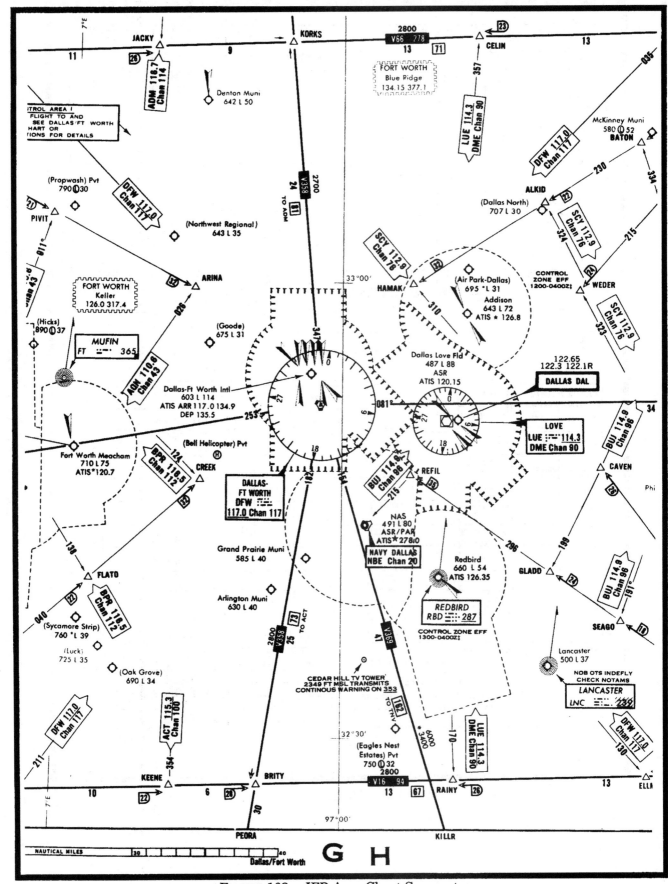

FIGURE 109.—IFR Area Chart Segment.

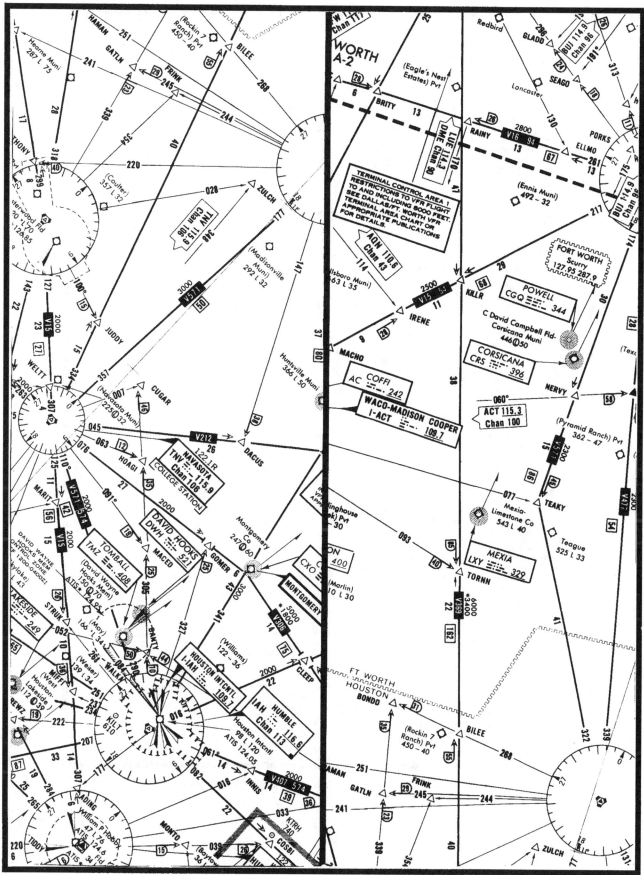

FIGURE 110.—IFR En Route Low Altitude Chart Segment.

# TEXAS

---

§ **DALLAS-FORT WORTH INTL** (DFW) 12 NW UTC-6(-5DT) 32°53'47"N 97°02'28"W **DALLAS-FT. WORTH**
603 B FUEL 100LL, JET A OX 1,3 LRA CFR Index E **H-2K, 4F, 5B, L-13C, A**
**IAP**
RWY 17L-35R: H11,388X150 (CONC-GRVD) S-120, D-200, DT-600, DDT-850 HIRL, CL
  RWY 17L: ALSF2. TDZ.   RWY 35R:MALSR. TDZ.
RWY 17R-35L: H11,388X200 (CONC-GRVD) S-120, D-200, DT-600, DDT-850 HIRL, CL
  RWY 17R: SSALR TDZ.   RWY 35L: TDZ. VASI(V6L).
RWY 18L-36R: H11,387X200 (CONC-GRVD) S-120, D-200, DT-600, DDT-850 HIRL, CL
  RWY 18L: SSALR.TDZ.   RWY 36R:TDZ. VASI(V6L).
RWY 18R-36L: H11,388X150 (CONC-GRVD) S-120, D-200, DT-600, DDT-850 HIRL, CL
  RWY 18R: ALSF2. TDZ   RWY 36L:MALSR. TDZ.
RWY 13L-31R: H9000X200 (CONC-GRVD) S-120, D-200, DT-600, DDT-850 HIRL, CL .5% up NW.
  RWY 13L: TDZ. VASI(V6L)—Upper GA 3.25°TCH 93'. Lower GA 3.0°TCH 47'.
  RWY 31 R:MALSR. TDZ.
RWY 13R-31L: H9300X150 (CONC-GRVD) S-120, D-220, DT-600, DDT-850 HIRL, CL
  RWY 13 R:MALSR. TDZ.   RWY 31L: TDZ.
RWY 18S-36S: H4000X100 (CONC)
**AIRPORT REMARKS:** Attended continuously. Prior Permission Required from arpt ops for General Aviation acft to proceed to airline terminal gate except to General Aviation Facility. Rwy 18S-36S located on taxiway G, 4000' long 100' wide restricted to prop acft 12,500 lbs. & below and stol acft daylight VFR plus IFR departures. Prior permission required from the primary tenant airlines to operate within central terminal area. CAUTION: proper minimum clearance may not be maintained within the central terminal area. Landing fee. Clearways 500x1000 each end Rwy 17L-35R, Rwy 17R-35L, Rwy 18L-36R and Rwy 18R-36L. Flight Notification Service (ADCUS) available.

**WEATHER DATA SOURCES** LLWAS.
**COMMUNICATIONS:** ATIS 117.0 134.9 (ARR) 135.5 (DEP) UNICOM 122.95
  FORT WORTH FSS (FTW) LC 624-8471, Toll free call, dial 1-800-WX-BRIEF. NOTAM FILE DFW
  ⑭ REGIONAL APP CON 19.05(E) 119.4(E) 125.8(W) 132.1(W)
  REGIONAL TOWER 126.55 (E) 124.15 (W) GND CON 121.65 133.15(E) 121.8 (W) CLNC DEL 128.25 127.5
  ⑭ REGIONAL DEP CON 118.55 (E) 124.25 (WEST) 127.75 (NORTH-SOUTH)
  TCA Group I: See VFR Terminal Area chart.
**RADIO AIDS TO NAVIGATION:** NOTAM FILE DFW.
  (H) VORTACW 117.0 DFW Chan 117 32°51'57"N97°01'40"W at fld. 560/08E.
    VOR Portion unusable 045°-050° all altitudes and distances, 350-100° beyond 30 NM below 2100'.
  ISSUE NDB (LOM) 233 PK 32°47'35"N97°01'49"W 353° 5.1 NM to fld.
  JIFFY NDB (LOM) 219 FL 32°59'45"N97°01'46"W 173° 5.1 NM to fld.
  ILS/DME 109.5 I-LWN Chan 32 Rwy 13R
  ILS/DME 109.1 I-FLQ Chan 28 Rwy 17L LOM JIFFY NDB
  ILS 111.5 I-JHZ Rwy 17R LOM JIFFY NDB
  ILS 111.3 I-CIX Rwy 18L
  ILS/DME 111.9 I-VYN Chan 56 Rwy 18R
  ILS 110.9 I-RRA Rwy 31R
  ILS/DME 109.1 I-PKQ Chan 28 Rwy 35R LOM ISSUE NDB
  ILS/DME 111.9 I-BXN Chan 56 Rwy 36L

---

§ **HOUSTON INTERCONTINENTAL** (IAH) 15N UTC-6(-5DT) 29°58'49"N 95°20'22"W **HOUSTON**
98 B S4 FUEL 100LL, JET A OX2 LRA CFR Index D **H-5B, L-17B**
**IAP**
RWY 14L-32R:H1200X150 (CONC-GRVD) S-100, D-200, DT-400, DDT-778 HIRL, CL
  RWY 14L:MALSR. VASI(V4L)—GA 3.0°TCH 54'.   RWY 32R:MALSR.
RWY 09-27: H10000X150 (ASPH-GRVD) S-75, D-191, DT-400, DDT-850 HIRL,CL
  RWY 09:MALSR. TDZ. PAPI(P4L)—GA 3.0°TCH 63'.
  RWY 27:ALSF2. TDZ. PAPI(P4L)—GA 3.0°TCH 63'.
RWY 08-26: H9401X150 (CONC-GRVD) S-120, D-155, DT-265 HIRL, CL
  RWY 08:MALSR. TDZ.   RWY 26: ALSF2. TDZ. VASI(V4L)—GA 3.0°TCH 53'.
RWY 14R-32L:H6038X100 (ASPH-GRVD) S-30, D-60, DT-60 MIRL
  RWY 14R: VASI(V4L)—GA 3.0°TCH 40'. Road.   RWY 32L: VASI(V4L)—GA 3.0°TCH 45'.
**AIRPORT REMARKS:** Attended continuously. CAUTION: Birds on and in vicinity of arpt. CAUTION—Approach end of rwy 26 bright lgts approximately one mile from thld and 900' South of centerline. Caution—Deer on and in vicinity of arpt. Rwy 14R-32L CLOSED to acft over 140,000 lbs gross weight. Landing Fee. Flight Notification Service (ADCUS) available.
**WEATHER DATA SOURCES** LLWAS.
**COMMUNICATIONS:** ATIS 124.05 UNICOM 122.95
  MONTGOMERY COUNTY FSS (CXO) Toll free call, dial 1-800-WX-BRIEF. NOTAM FILE IAH.
  ⑭ APP CON 124.35 (West) 127.25 (North and East)
  TOWER 118.1 (135.15 copter control) GND CON 121.7 CLNC DEL 128.1 (135.15 copter control)
  ⑭ DEP CON 123.8 (West) 119.7 (North and East)
  TCA Group II: VFR Terminal Area chart.
**RADIO AIDS TO NAVIGATION:** NOTAM FILE IAH.
  HUMBLE (H) VORTACW 116.6 IAH Chan 113 29°57'24"N95°20'44"W at fld. 90/08E. HIWAS.
  MARBE NDB (LOM) 379 HS 30°04'29"N 95°24'45"W 146° 5.9 NM to fld.
  NIXIN NDB (LOM) 326 JY 29°59'36"N 95°12'54"W 257° 6.5 NM to fld.
  ILS/DME 109.7 I-JYV Chan 34 Rwy 26 LOM NIXIN NDB
  ILS 111.9 I-HSQ Rwy 14L LOM MARBE NDB
  ILS/DME 109.7 I-IAH Chan 34 Rwy 08
  ILS/DME 110.9 I-UYO Chan 34 Rwy 09
  ILS 111.9 I-CDG Rwy 32R

FIGURE 111.—Airport/Facility Directory Excerpts.

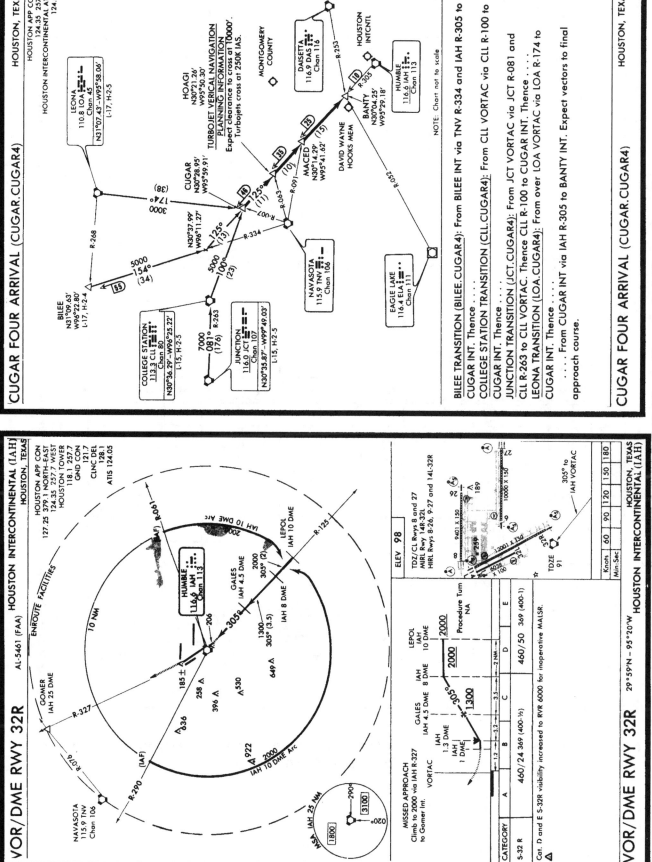

FIGURE 112.—VOR/DME RWY 32R (IAH) / Cugar Four Arrival (Cugar.Cugar4).

FIGURE 113.—Flight Plan/Flight Log.

**Form Approved: OMB No. 2120-0034**

## FLIGHT PLAN

U.S. DEPARTMENT OF TRANSPORTATION
FEDERAL AVIATION ADMINISTRATION

| (FAA USE ONLY) | ☐ PILOT BRIEFING | ☐ VNR | TIME STARTED | SPECIALIST INITIALS |
|---|---|---|---|---|
| | ☐ STOPOVER | | | |

| 1. TYPE | 2. AIRCRAFT IDENTIFICATION | 3. AIRCRAFT TYPE/ SPECIAL EQUIPMENT | 4. TRUE AIRSPEED | 5. DEPARTURE POINT | 6. DEPARTURE TIME | | 7. CRUISING ALTITUDE |
|---|---|---|---|---|---|---|---|
| | | | | | PROPOSED (Z) | ACTUAL (Z) | |
| VFR / X IFR / DVFR | N60BJ | BH214/A | 110 KTS | Ø02 Baker | | | 12,000 |

**8. ROUTE OF FLIGHT**

Hdg 270 degrees to V394, V394 POM, V210 LAX

| 9. DESTINATION (Name of airport and city) | 10. EST. TIME ENROUTE | | 11. REMARKS |
|---|---|---|---|
| LAX Los Angeles Int'l Los Angeles | HOURS | MINUTES | L/O = Level Off    PPH = Pounds Per Hour    TEC = Tower to Tower |

| 12. FUEL ON BOARD | | 13. ALTERNATE AIRPORT(S) | 14. PILOT'S NAME, ADDRESS & TELEPHONE NUMBER & AIRCRAFT HOME BASE | 15. NUMBER ABOARD |
|---|---|---|---|---|
| HOURS | MINUTES | LGB Long Beach | 17. DESTINATION CONTACT/TELEPHONE (OPTIONAL) | 15 |

| 16. COLOR OF AIRCRAFT | CIVIL AIRCRAFT PILOTS. FAR Part 91 requires you file an IFR flight plan to operate under instrument flight rules in controlled airspace. Failure to file could result in a civil penalty not to exceed $1,000 for each violation (Section 901 of the Federal Aviation Act of 1958, as amended). Filing of a VFR flight plan is recommended as a good operating practice. See also Part 99 for requirements concerning DVFR flight plans. |
|---|---|
| Brown/White | |

FAA Form 7233-1 (8-82)    CLOSE VFR FLIGHT PLAN WITH _____ FSS ON ARRIVAL

## FLIGHT LOG

| CHECK POINTS | | ROUTE | COURSE | WIND | SPEED-KTS | | DIST | TIME | | FUEL | |
|---|---|---|---|---|---|---|---|---|---|---|---|
| FROM | TO | ALTITUDE | | TEMP | TAS | GS | NM | LEG | TOT | LEG | TOT |
| Ø02 | V394 | HDG 270 Climb | | | | | 8 | | :10:00 | | 250* |
| Join V394 | DAG | V394 12000 | | 290/36 ISA-2 | | | 15 | | | | |
| DAG | POM | | | | | | | | | | |
| POM | PIRRO Int. | V210 12000 | | | | | | | | | |
| PIRRO Int. | LAX | Descent & Approach | | | | | 29 | :17:00 | | 348 | |
| | | | | | | | | | | | |
| | | | | | | | | | | | |
| LAX | LGB | TEC 3000 | | | 110 | 120 | 22 | :11:00 | | | |
| | | | | | | | | | | | |

OTHER DATA: * Includes Taxi Fuel
NOTE:
Use 1045 PPH Total Fuel Flow From L/O To Start Of Descent.
Use 1095 PPH Total Fuel Flow For Reserve / Alternate Requirements
A missed approach requires 89# of fuel.

| TIME and FUEL: As required by FARs. | | |
|---|---|---|
| TIME | FUEL (LB) | |
| | | EN ROUTE |
| | | RESERVE |
| | | ALTERNATE |
| | | TOTAL |

FIGURE 113.—Flight Plan/Flight Log.

**74**                                              **CALIFORNIA**

**LONG BEACH (DAUGHERTY FLD)**   (LGB)   3 NE   UTC–8(–7DT)   N33°49.06′ W118°09.10′         **LOS ANGELES**
    57   B   S4   **FUEL** 100LL, JET A   OX 1, 2, 3, 4   LRA   ARFF Index C                    **COPTER**
    **RWY 12-30:** H10000X200 (ASPH-GRVD)   S–30 +, D–200, DT–300   HIRL   0.4% up NW          **H–2B, L–3B, A**
        **RWY 12:** VASI(V4L)—GA 3.0° TCH 47′. Thld dsplcd 1340′. Railroad.                          **IAP**
        **RWY 30:** MALSR. PAPI(P4L)—GA 3.0° TCH 70′. Thld dsplcd 1990′. Tree.
    **RWY 07L-25R:** H6192X150 (ASPH-PFC)   S–30, D–70, DT–110   MIRL   0.3% up W
        **RWY 07L:** Thld dsplcd 1305′. Railroad.
        **RWY 25R:** REIL. VASI(V4L)—GA 4.0° TCH 57′. Thld dsplcd 531′. Road. Rgt tfc.
    **RWY 07R-25L:** H5420X150 (ASPH)   S–30, D–75   HIRL   0.4% up W
        **RWY 07R:** Tower. Rgt tfc.        **RWY 25L:** REIL. VASI(V4L)—GA 4.0° TCH 58′. Trees.
    **RWY 16R-34L:** H4470X75 (ASPH)   S–12.5
        **RWY 16R:** VASI(V4L)—GA 4.0° TCH 36′. Thld dsplcd 310′. Fence. Rgt tfc.        **RWY 34L:** Road.
    **RWY 16L-34R:** H4267X75 (ASPH)   S–12.5
        **RWY 16L:** Thld dsplcd 415′. Fence.        **RWY 34R:** Thld dsplcd 292′. Road. Rgt tfc.
    **AIRPORT REMARKS:** Attended continuously. All rwys CLOSED 0600–1500Z‡ except Rwy 12–30. Flocks of seagulls on
        and in vicinity of arpt especially during rain. Unlighted twr 152′ AGL 2500′ W and 500′ S of Rwy 07 thld. 255′
        AGL obstruction 1200′ S of Rwy 07 thld. Broken pavement on NE Police helipad between perimeter road and
        Twy F. Prior notification requested 24 hours in advance for all acft over 75,000 pounds certificated maximum
        gross weight and civilian Non-Stage III jets and all military jets, ctc Noise Abatement 310–429–6647 Mon-Fri
        1500–0100Z‡. Noise abatement information on 122.85. Noise limits (single event noise exposure level), Rwy 25
        tkf 92.0 DB–ldg 88.0 DB; Rwy 07 tkf 88.0 DB–ldg 92.0 DB; Rwys 12 and 30 tkf 102.5 DB–ldg 101.5 DB except
        0600–1500Z‡ tkf 79.0–ldg 79.0 DB. Touch and go, stop and go, low apch only permitted 1500–0300Z‡
        weekdays and 1600–2300Z‡ weekends and holidays only on Rwy 07L–25R and Rwy 07R–25L unless weather
        conditions require twr to direct such operations to Rwy 16R–34L and Rwy 16L–34R. Rwy 12–30 arpt manager
        limits gross weight to 300,000 lbs dual tandom wheel except DC–10 series 30/40 and MD11 limited to 378,000
        lbs. No twy access to Rwy 07L W of Twy D, 4897′ remaining on Rwy 07L from Twy D, Twy A clsd W of compass
        rose. Taxiway K east of Taxiway C clsd to acft with a wingspan greater than 117′. Engine run-ups other than
        preflight are limited to hours of 1500–0500Z‡ weekdays and 1700–0500Z‡ weekends and holidays. Rwy
        07R–25L limited to acft with a maximum wing span of 90′. ACTIVATE MALSR Rwy 30 when tower clsd—CTAF.
        Rwy 12–30 HIRL lighted during hours tower clsd. NOTE: See SPECIAL NOTICE—Land and Hold Short
        Operations.
    **COMMUNICATIONS: CTAF** 119.4     **ATIS** 127.75 (310) 595-8564     **UNICOM** 122.95
        **HAWTHORNE FSS (HHR)** TF 1–800–WX–BRIEF. NOTAM FILE LGB.
    Ⓡ **SOCAL APP CON** 124.65
    Ⓡ **SOCAL DEP CON** 127.2
        **LONG BEACH TOWER** 119.4 (Rwy 30 apch, Rwy 12 dep) 120.5 (Rwy 12 apch, Rwy 30 dep) (1415–0745Z‡)
            **GND CON** 133.0     **CLNC DEL** 118.15
    **AIRSPACE: CLASS D** svc effective 1415–0745Z‡ other times CLASS G.
    **RADIO AIDS TO NAVIGATION:** NOTAM FILE HHR.
        **SEAL BEACH (L) VORTACW** 115.7   SLI   Chan 104   N33°47.00′ W118°03.29′   278° 5.3 NM to fld. 20/15E.
            HIWAS.
        **BECCA NDB (LOM)** 233   LG   N33°45.40′ W118°04.64′   301° 5.2 NM to fld.
        **ILS** 110.3   I–LGB   Rwy 30.   LOM BECCA NDB. Unmonitored when twr clsd. MM unmonitored.
    •  •   •   •   •   •   •   •   •   •   •   •   •   •   •   •   •   •   •   •   •   •   •   •   •   •   •   •
    **HELIPAD H1:** H20X20 (ASPH-CONC)
    **HELIPAD H2:** H20X20 (ASPH-CONC)
    **HELIPAD H3:** H20X20 (ASPH-CONC)
    **HELIPORT REMARKS:** Training helipads H1, H2 and H3 located N of Rwy 12–30 midfield between Taxiways G and K.

---

**LONNIE POOL FLD/WEAVERVILLE**   (See WEAVERVILLE)

---

**LOS ALAMITOS AAF (ARMED FORCES RESERVE CENTER):**                                          **LOS ANGELES**
    **AIRSPACE: CLASS D** svc effective Sat–Mon 1600–0000Z‡, Tue–Fri 1500–0600Z‡ other times CLASS G.   **L–3B, A**

FIGURE 113A.—Data from Southwest U.S. Airport/Facility Directory.

**CALIFORNIA**

**AVENAL**   N35°38.82' W119°58.72'   NOTAM FILE HHR.   LOS ANGELES
   (H) VORTAC 117.1   AVE   Chan 118   080° 14.4 NM to Lost Hills–Kern Co. 710/16E.   H–2A, L–2E, 3A
   RCO 122.1R 117.1T (BAKERSFIELD FSS)

**BAKER**   (002)   2 NW   UTC–8(–7DT)   N35°17.13' W116°04.95'   LOS ANGELES
   922   B   TPA—1922(1000)   L–3C, 5B
   **RWY 15–33:** H3157X50 (ASPH)   MIRL
     **RWY 33:** P–line. Rgt tfc.
   **AIRPORT REMARKS:** Unattended. Mountain ½ mile W of arpt. Unlit towers and unmarked powerlines across apch path
     Rwy 33.
   **COMMUNICATIONS: CTAF** 122.9
     RIVERSIDE FSS (RAL) TF 1–800–WX–BRIEF. NOTAM FILE RAL.
   **RADIO AIDS TO NAVIGATION:** NOTAM FILE DAG.
     **DAGGETT (L) VORTAC** 113.2   DAG   Chan 79   N34°57.75' W116°34.69'   036° 31.1 NM to fld. 1760/15E.
     HIWAS.

**BAKERSFIELD**   N35°26.02' W119°03.41'   LOS ANGELES
   **FSS**   (BFL)   at Meadows Fld. 123.65 122.45 122.2. LD 805–399–1787.   L–3B, 5A

## BAKERSFIELD
   **BAKERSFIELD MUNI**   (L45)   3 S   UTC–8(–7DT)   N35°19.49' W118°59.75'   LOS ANGELES
    376   B   S4   **FUEL** 80, 100LL   TPA—1176(800)   L–3B, 5A
    **RWY 16–34:** H4000X75 (ASPH)   S–20   MIRL   IAP
     **RWY 16:** Road. Rgt tfc.   **RWY 34:** PAPI(P2L)—GA 4.0° TCH 54'. P–line.
    **AIRPORT REMARKS:** Attended 1500–0100Z‡. 100' pole line ½ mile south of arpt.
    **COMMUNICATIONS: CTAF/UNICOM** 122.8
     BAKERSFIELD FSS (BFL) LC 399–1787 NOTAM FILE BFL.
    Ⓡ **BAKERSFIELD APP/DEP CON** 126.45 (1400–0700Z‡)
    Ⓡ **L.A. CENTER APP/DEP CON** 127.1 (0700–1400Z‡)
    **RADIO AIDS TO NAVIGATION:** NOTAM FILE BFL.
     **SHAFTER (H) VORTACW** 115.4   EHF   Chan 101   N35°29.07' W119°05.84'   138° 10.8 NM to fld. 550/14E.
     HIWAS.

- - - - - - - - - - - - - - - - - - - - - - - - - - - - - - - - - - - - -

   **MEADOWS FLD**   (BFL)   3 NW   UTC–8(–7DT)   N35°26.02' W119°03.41'   LOS ANGELES
    507   B   S4   **FUEL** 80, 100, 100LL, JET A   ARFF Index B   H–2B, L–2E, 3B, 5A
    **RWY 12L–30R:** H10857X150 (ASPH–GRVD)   S–110, D–200, DT–500, DDT–850   HIRL   0.3% up NW   IAP
     **RWY 12L:** VASI(V4L)—GA 3.0° TCH 52'.
     **RWY 30R:** MALSR. PAPI(P4L)—GA 3.0° TCH 64'. Thld dsplcd 3428'. P–line. Rgt tfc.
    **RWY 12R–30L:** H3700X75 (ASPH)   S–18   MIRL
     **RWY 12R:** Rgt tfc.   **RWY 30L:** VASI(NSTD)—GA 3.0°. Tree.
    **AIRPORT REMARKS:** Attended 1330–0700Z‡, fee for call out service other hours. Rwy 12L 16' pump 525' from thld
     550' left. Distance remaining at the 2000' mark on Rwy 30R is actually 2850'. Noise sensitive areas S and E of
     arpt recommended turbojet training hours weekdays 1600–0600Z‡, weekends 2000–0600Z‡ no more than ten
     practice approaches per hour. Rwy 30L NSTD VASI single light source visibility 1 mile, red blo glide path. When
     twr clsd ACTIVATE PAPI Rwy 30R—CTAF. For MIRL Rwy 12R–30L and taxiway lgts when tower clsd ctc FSS—
     CTAF.
    **COMMUNICATIONS: CTAF** 118.1   **ATIS** 118.6 (805) 399–9425   **UNICOM** 122.95
     BAKERSFIELD FSS (BFL) on arpt. 123.65 122.45 122.2. LC 399–1787. NOTAM FILE BFL.
     **BAKERSFIELD APP CON** 118.9 (N) 118.8 (S) (1400–0700Z‡)
     **BAKERSFIELD DEP CON** 126.45 (N,S) (1400–0700Z‡)
    Ⓡ **L.A. CENTER APP/DEP CON** 127.1 (0700–1400Z‡)
     **BAKERSFIELD TOWER** 118.1 (1400–0700Z‡)   **GND CON** 121.7
    **AIRSPACE: CLASS D** svc effective 1400–0700Z‡ other times CLASS E.
    **RADIO AIDS TO NAVIGATION:** NOTAM FILE BFL.
     **SHAFTER (H) VORTACW** 115.4   EHF   Chan 101   N35°29.07' W119°05.84'   133° 3.6 NM to fld. 550/14E.
     HIWAS.
     **NILEY NDB (LOM)** 385   BF   N35°21.65' W118°58.12'   301° 6.1 NM to fld.
     **ILS/DME** 111.9   I–BFL   Chan 56   Rwy 30R.   LOM NILEY NDB. ILS unmonitored when twr clsd.

- - - - - - - - - - - - - - - - - - - - - - - - - - - - - - - - - - - - -

FIGURE 113B.—Data from Southwest U.S. Airport/Facility Directory.

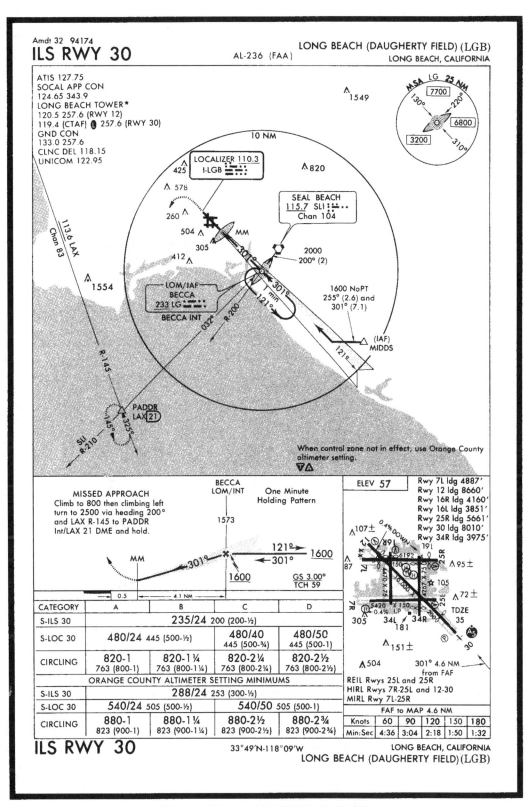

FIGURE 113C.—ILS RWY 30 (LGB).

THIS PAGE INTENTIONALLY LEFT BLANK

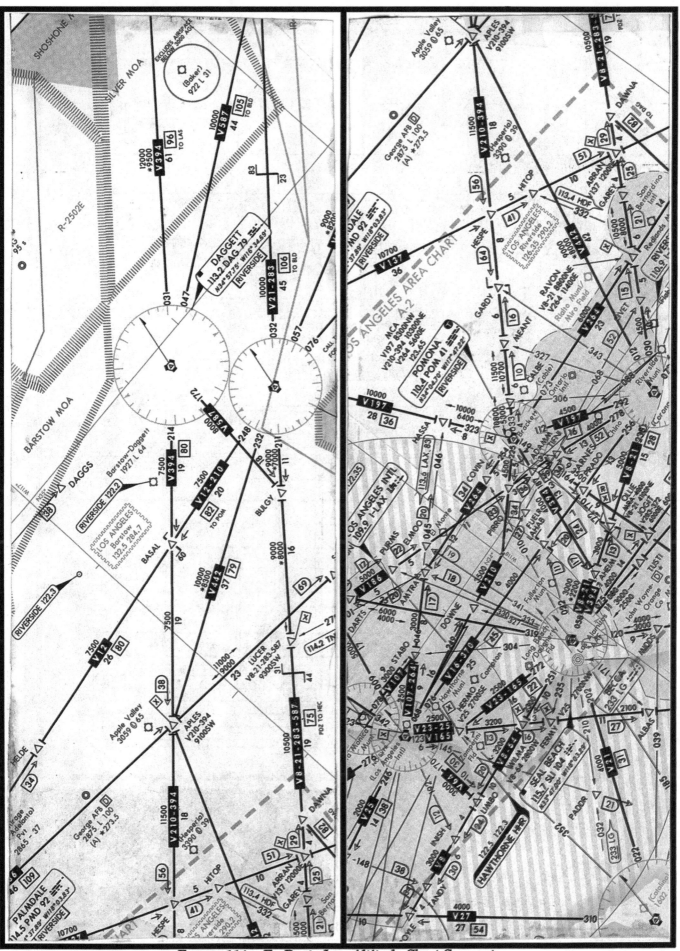

FIGURE 114.—En Route Low Altitude Chart Segment.

Form Approved: OMB No. 2120-0034

## FLIGHT PLAN

U.S. DEPARTMENT OF TRANSPORTATION
FEDERAL AVIATION ADMINISTRATION

| (FAA USE ONLY) | ☐ PILOT BRIEFING | ☐ VNR | TIME STARTED | SPECIALIST INITIALS |
|---|---|---|---|---|
| | ☐ STOPOVER | | | |

| 1. TYPE | 2. AIRCRAFT IDENTIFICATION | 3. AIRCRAFT TYPE/ SPECIAL EQUIPMENT | 4. TRUE AIRSPEED | 5. DEPARTURE POINT | 6. DEPARTURE TIME | | 7. CRUISING ALTITUDE |
|---|---|---|---|---|---|---|---|
| | | | | | PROPOSED (Z) | ACTUAL (Z) | |
| VFR | | | | | | | |
| X IFR | PTL 130 | B727/R | *** | LAX | | | FL270 |
| DVFR | | | KTS | | | | |

**8. ROUTE OF FLIGHT**

LAX INP3.IPL, J2 MOHAK, ARLIN 9 PHX

| 9. DESTINATION (Name of airport and city) | 10. EST. TIME ENROUTE | | 11. REMARKS | L/O = Level Off   PPH = Pounds Per Hour |
|---|---|---|---|---|
| PHX PHOENIX SKY HARBOR PHOENIX | HOURS | MINUTES | | ** L/O at OCN R-270/50  *** MACH .78 |

| 12. FUEL ON BOARD | | 13. ALTERNATE AIRPORT(S) | 14. PILOT'S NAME, ADDRESS & TELEPHONE NUMBER & AIRCRAFT HOME BASE | 15. NUMBER ABOARD |
|---|---|---|---|---|
| HOURS | MINUTES | TUS TUCSON INT'L | | 83 |
| | | | 17. DESTINATION CONTACT/TELEPHONE (OPTIONAL) | |

| 16. COLOR OF AIRCRAFT   RED/BLACK | CIVIL AIRCRAFT PILOTS. FAR Part 91 requires you file an IFR flight plan to operate under instrument flight rules in controlled airspace. Failure to file could result in a civil penalty not to exceed $1,000 for each violation (Section 901 of the Federal Aviation Act of 1958, as amended). Filing of a VFR flight plan is recommended as a good operating practice. See also Part 99 for requirements concerning DVFR flight plans. |
|---|---|

FAA Form 7233-1 (8-82)    CLOSE VFR FLIGHT PLAN WITH _____ FSS ON ARRIVAL

## FLIGHT LOG

| CHECK POINTS | | ROUTE | COURSE | WIND | SPEED-KTS | | DIST | TIME | | FUEL | |
|---|---|---|---|---|---|---|---|---|---|---|---|
| FROM | TO | ALTITUDE | | TEMP | TAS | GS | NM | LEG | TOT | LEG | TOT |
| LAX | L/O** | IPL3.IPL Climb | | | | | 43 | | :19:00 | | 4510* |
| L/O | IPL | IPL 3 IPL FL270 | | 300/43 ISA-2 | | | | | | | |
| IPL | BZA | J2 FL270 | | | | | | | | | |
| BZA | Mohak Int | J2 FL270 | | 300/43 ISA-2 | | | | | | | |
| Mohak | Arlin Int | Arlin 9 FL270 | | | | | | | | | |
| Arlin | PHX | Radar Vec DES/APP | | | | | | :12:00 | | 1140 | |
| | | | | | | | | | | | |
| | | | | | | | | | | | |
| PHX | TUS | Radar V FL190 | | | | | 97 | :26:00 | | | |

OTHER DATA: * Includes Taxi Fuel

NOTE: Use 9600 PPH Total Fuel Flow From L/O To Start Of Descent. Use 9250 PPH Total Fuel Flow For Reserve And Alternate Requirements. A Missed Approach Requires 416# of Fuel.

TIME and FUEL: As required by FARs.

| TIME | FUEL (LB) | |
|---|---|---|
| | | EN ROUTE |
| | | RESERVE |
| | | ALTERNATE |
| | | TOTAL |

FIGURE 115.—Flight Plan/Flight Log.

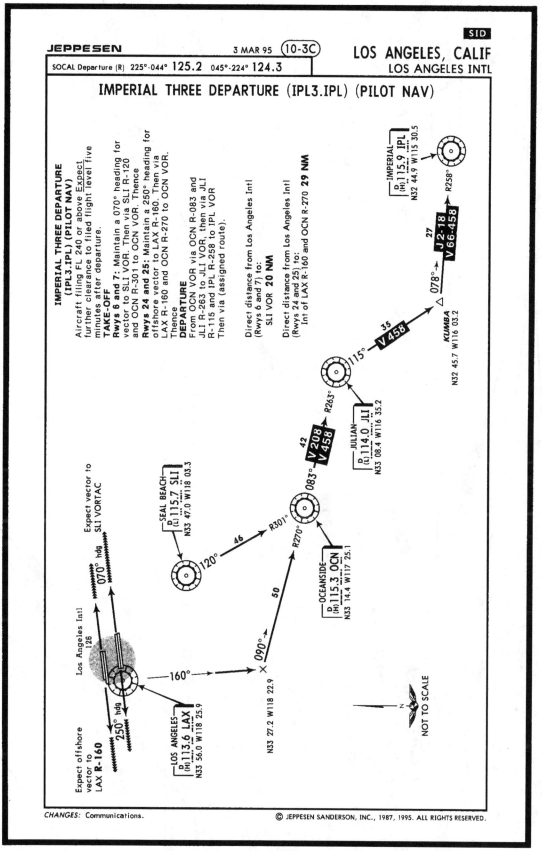

FIGURE 116.—Imperial Three Departure (IPL3.IPL) (PILOT NAV).

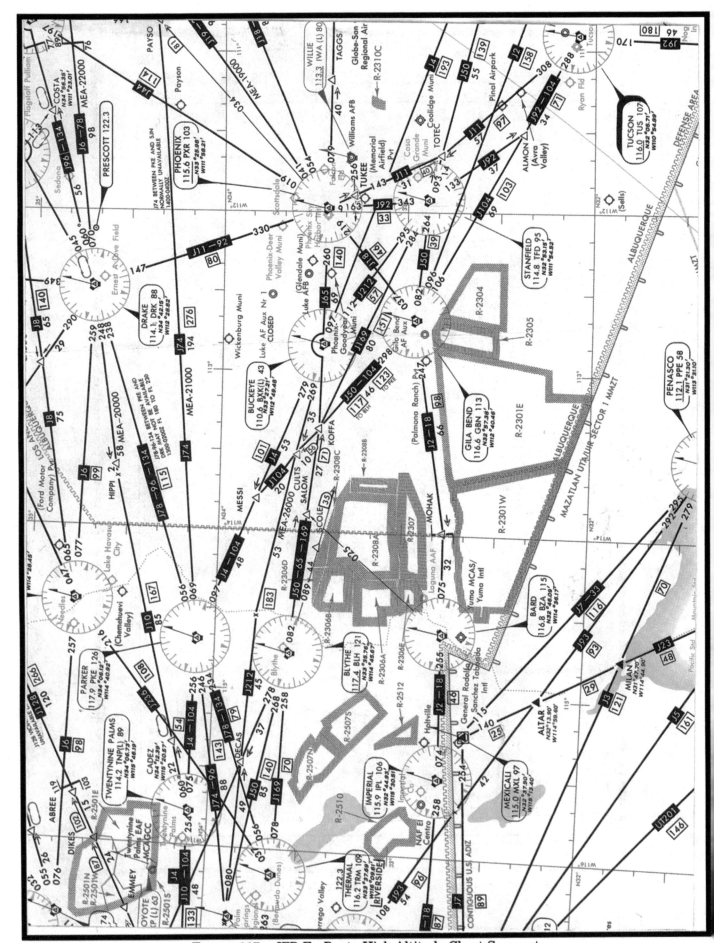

FIGURE 117.—IFR En Route High Altitude Chart Segment.

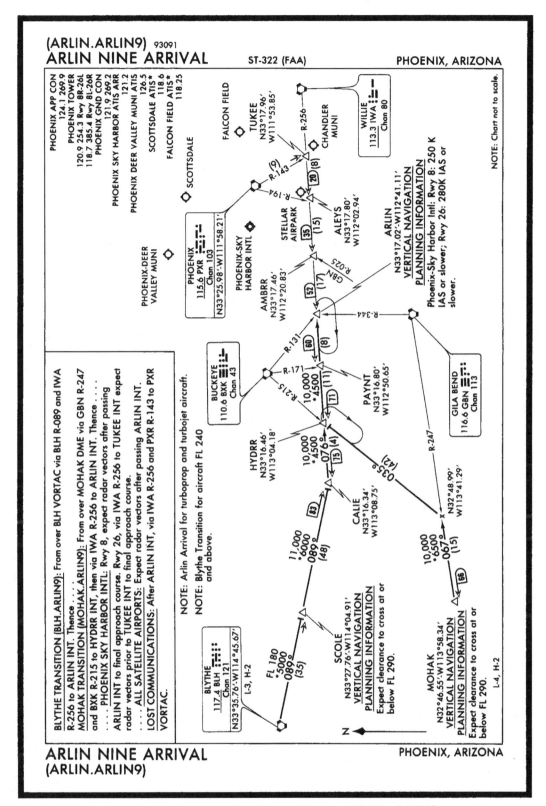

FIGURE 118.—ARLIN NINE ARRIVAL (ARLIN.ARLIN9).

THIS PAGE INTENTIONALLY LEFT BLANK

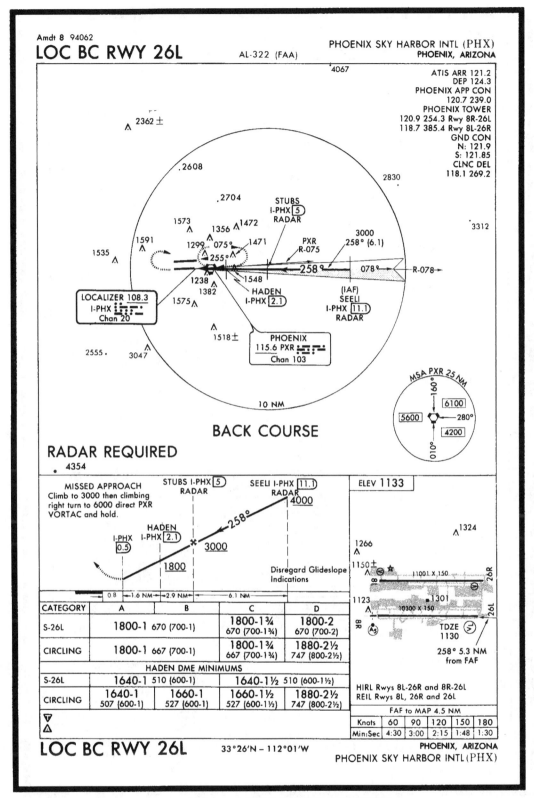

FIGURE 118A.—LOC BC RWY 26L (PHX).

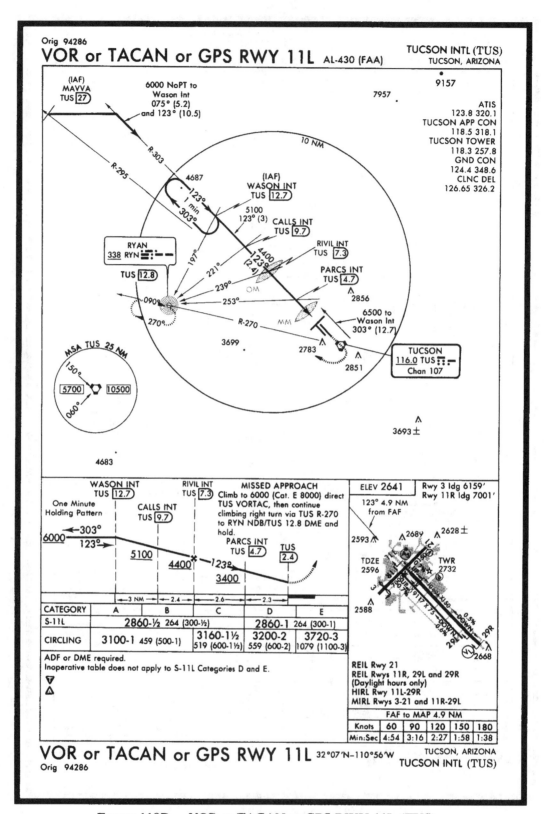

FIGURE 118B.—VOR or TACAN or GPS RWY 11L (TUS).

**PHOENIX**

**PHOENIX-DEER VALLEY MUNI** (DVT)  15 N  UTC–7  N33°41.30′ W112°04.93′  PHOENIX
  1476  B  S4  FUEL 80, 100LL, JET A  OX 1, 3  TPA—See Remarks  H-2C, L-4E
RWY 07R-25L: H8200X100 (ASPH)  S–40, D–50, DT–80  MIRL  IAP
  RWY 07R: REIL. VASI(V2L)—GA 3.0° Thld dsplcd 900′. Rgt tfc.
  RWY 25L: REIL. VASI(V2L)—GA 3.0° Thld dsplcd 920′.
RWY 07L-25R: H4500X75 (ASPH)  S–20  MIRL
  RWY 07L: REIL. PVASI(PSIL)—GA 3.0° TCH 40′.    RWY 25R: REIL. PVASI(PSIL)—GA 3.5° TCH 47′. Hill. Rgt tfc.
AIRPORT REMARKS: Attended 1300–0400Z. Fuel avbl only during hours 1400–0300Z 7 days. Lgtd hills NE, E, SE and
  W. Hot air balloon ops fall, winter, and spring months and ultralight opr South and West of arpt. Rwy 07L-25R is
  designated training rwy. Aerobatic practice area approximately 8½ miles northwest of the Deer Valley Arpt from
  the surface to 6000′ MSL. Parallel taxiway north and close proximity to Rwy 07L-25R. Rwy 07R VASI and REIL,
  Rwy 25L VASI and REIL, Rwy 07L PVASI and Rwy 25R PVASI on when twr clsd. Fee for all charters; travel clubs
  and certain revenue producing acft. TPA–2501(1025) single engine and 3001(1525) multi engine.
COMMUNICATIONS: CTAF 118.4    ATIS 126.5    UNICOM 122.95
  PRESCOTT FSS (PRC) TF 1–800–992–7433. NOTAM FILE DVT.
  PHOENIX RCO 122.6 122.2 (PRESCOTT FSS)
Ⓡ PHOENIX APP/DEP CON 120.7
  DEER VALLEY TOWER 118.4 (Rwy 07R-25L) 120.2 (Rwy 07L-25R) (1300–0400Z)    GND CON 121.8
  CLNC DEL 119.5
AIRSPACE: CLASS D svc effective 1300–0400Z other times CLASS G.
RADIO AIDS TO NAVIGATION: NOTAM FILE PRC.
  PHOENIX (H) VORTACW 115.6    PXR    Chan 103    N33°25.98′ W111°58.21′    328° 16.3 NM to fld. 1180/12E.
    HIWAS.
  SCOTTSDALE NDB (MHW) 224    SDL    N33°37.75′ W111°54.47′    279° 9.4 NM to fld. NOTAM FILE SDL.
    Unmonitored when twr closed.
COMM/NAVAID REMARKS: Emerg frequency 121.5 not available at twr.

- - - - - - - - - - - - - - - - - - - - - - - - - - - - - - - - - - - - - - - - - - -

**PHOENIX SKY HARBOR INTL** (PHX)  3 E  UTC–7  N33°26.17′ W112°00.57′  PHOENIX
  1133  B  S4  FUEL 100LL, JET A  OX 1, 2, 3, 4  TPA—See Remarks  H-2C, L-4E
  LRA  ARFF Index D  IAP
RWY 08L-26R: H11001X150 (ASPH-GRVD)    S–30, D–170, DT–280, DDT–620    HIRL
  RWY 08L: REIL. VASI(V4L)—GA 3.0° TCH 55′. Building.
  RWY 26R: REIL. VASI(V4L)—GA 3.0° TCH 60′. Road. Rgt tfc.
RWY 08R-26L: H10300X150 (ASPH-GRVD)    S–30, D–200, DT–400, DDT–620    HIRL
  RWY 08R: MALSR. Pole. Rgt tfc.
  RWY 26L: REIL. VASI(V6L)—Upper GA 3.25° TCH 90′. Lower GA 3.0° TCH 53′. Antenna.
AIRPORT REMARKS: Attended continuously. Training by civil turbojet acft prohibited except PPR. TPA—2133(1000) lgt
  acft and non-turbo jets; 2633(1500) heavy acft and turbojets. Unless advised by ATC all turbine acft and acft
  12,500 lbs and over remain at or above 3000′ MSL until established on final. Fly base leg at least 5 mile from
  arpt. Overnight parking fee. Fee for all charters; travel clubs and certain revenue producing aircraft. Taxiway
  A-6 limited to 68,000 GWT. Rwy 08L-26R FAA strength evaluation DC-10-10 505,000 pounds, DC-10-30/40
  500,000 pounds, L-1011-1 450,000 pounds, aircraft up to DDTW 620,000 pounds, DC-10-10 505,000
  pounds, DC-10-30/40 540,000 pounds, L-1011-1 450,000 pounds regularly operate on rwy. Rwy 08R-26L
  gross weight limit DC-10-10 430,000 pounds, DC-10-30/40 540,000 pounds, L-1011-1 430,000 pounds.
  Flight Notification Service (ADCUS) available.
WEATHER DATA SOURCES: ASOS (602) 231–8557. LLWAS.
COMMUNICATIONS: ATIS ARR 121.2 DEP 124.3 (602) 244–0963    UNICOM 122.95
  PRESCOTT FSS (PRC) TF 1–800–992–7433. NOTAM FILE PHX.
  RCO 122.6 122.2 (PRESCOTT FSS)
Ⓡ APP/DEP CON 126.8 (259°–309°) 124.9 (053°–146°) 124.1(147°–258° above 5500′) 123.7 (147°–258° 5500′ and
  below) 120.7 120.4 (Rwy 08L 275°–290° blo 6000′, Rwy 26R 030°–080°) (310°–052° 5500′ and below)
  119.2 (310°–052° above 5500′)
  TOWER 118.7 (Rwy 08L-26R) 120.9 (Rwy 08R-26L)    GND CON 121.9 (North) 121.85 (South)    CLNC DEL 118.1
AIRSPACE: CLASS B See VFR Terminal Area Chart.
RADIO AIDS TO NAVIGATION: NOTAM FILE PRC.
  PHOENIX (H) VORTACW 115.6    PXR    Chan 103    N33°25.98′ W111°58.21′    263° 2.0 NM to fld. 1180/12E.
    HIWAS.
  ILS 111.75    I-PZZ    Rwy 26R    (LOC only).
  ILS/DME 108.3    I-PHX    Chan 20    Rwy 08R.    GS unusable below 1280′. LOC back course unusable
    beyond 20° south of course.

- - - - - - - - - - - - - - - - - - - - - - - - - - - - - - - - - - - - - - - - - - -

FIGURE 118C.—Excerpt from Airport/Facilities Directory.

Form Approved: OMB No. 2120-0034

### U.S. DEPARTMENT OF TRANSPORTATION
### FEDERAL AVIATION ADMINISTRATION
# FLIGHT PLAN

| (FAA USE ONLY) | ☐ PILOT BRIEFING | ☐ VNR | TIME STARTED | SPECIALIST INITIALS |
|---|---|---|---|---|
| | ☐ STOPOVER | | | |

| 1. TYPE | 2. AIRCRAFT IDENTIFICATION | 3. AIRCRAFT TYPE/ SPECIAL EQUIPMENT | 4. TRUE AIRSPEED | 5. DEPARTURE POINT | 6. DEPARTURE TIME | | 7. CRUISING ALTITUDE |
|---|---|---|---|---|---|---|---|
| | | | | | PROPOSED (Z) | ACTUAL (Z) | |
| VFR | | | | | | | |
| X IFR | N130JB | B727/A | ** | BUF | | | FL310 |
| DVFR | | | KTS | Greater Buffalo Int'l | | | |

**8. ROUTE OF FLIGHT**
Buffalo One Dep. J547 FNT, FNT.PMM 2 ORD

| 9. DESTINATION (Name of airport and city) | 10. EST. TIME ENROUTE | | 11. REMARKS |
|---|---|---|---|
| O R D Chicago-Ohare Int'l Chicago | HOURS | MINUTES | L/O = Level Off     PPH = Pounds Per Hour ** MACH .78     Variation: BUF 8W, FNT 3W, ORD 2E ATC cleared N130JB to maintain FL310 until PMM R-073/15 cross PMM at FL200, cross Pivot at 10,000 feet. |

| 12. FUEL ON BOARD | | 13. ALTERNATE AIRPORT(S) | 14. PILOT'S NAME, ADDRESS & TELEPHONE NUMBER & AIRCRAFT HOME BASE | 15. NUMBER ABOARD |
|---|---|---|---|---|
| HOURS | MINUTES | RFD Greater Rockford Rockford, Ill | | 101 |
| | | | 17. DESTINATION CONTACT/TELEPHONE (OPTIONAL) | |

| 16. COLOR OF AIRCRAFT | CIVIL AIRCRAFT PILOTS. FAR Part 91 requires you file an IFR flight plan to operate under instrument flight rules in controlled airspace. Failure to file could result in a civil penalty not to exceed $1,000 for each violation (Section 901 of the Federal Aviation Act of 1958, as amended). Filing of a VFR flight plan is recommended as a good operating practice. See also Part 99 for requirements concerning DVFR flight plans. |
|---|---|
| RED/WHITE/BLUE | |

FAA Form 7233-1 (8-82)     CLOSE VFR FLIGHT PLAN WITH _____ FSS ON ARRIVAL

# FLIGHT LOG

| CHECK POINTS | | ROUTE | | | WIND | SPEED-KTS | | DIST | TIME | | FUEL | |
|---|---|---|---|---|---|---|---|---|---|---|---|---|
| FROM | TO | ALTITUDE | COURSE | | TEMP | TAS | GS | NM | LEG | TOT | LEG | TOT |
| BUF | L/O | Buffalo 1 Climb | | | | | | 70 | | :16:00 | | 4960* |
| L/O | YXU | J547 FL310 | | | 330/39 ISA-6 | | | | | | | |
| YXU | FNT | | | | | | | | | | | |
| FNT | R-073/15 PMM | FNT.PMM2 | | | 330/39 ISA-6 | | | | | | | |
| R-073/15 PMM | PMM | FNT.PMM2 Descent | 253 | | | | | 15 | :02:00 | | 216.7 | |
| PMM | ORD | FNT.PMM2 Descent & Approach | 261/216 | | | | | 89 | :13:00 | | 1408.3 | |
| | | | | | | | | | | | | |
| | | | | | | | | | | | | |
| ORD | RFD | Radar V 10,000 | | | | | | 97 | :17:00 | | | |

**OTHER DATA:** * Includes Taxi Fuel
**NOTE:** Use 9300 PPH Total Fuel Flow From L/O To Start Of Descent. Use 9550 PPH Total Fuel Flow For Reserve And Alternate Requirements. A Missed Approach Requires 450# of Fuel.

**TIME and FUEL: As required by FARs.**

| TIME | FUEL (LB) | | |
|---|---|---|---|
| | | EN ROUTE | |
| | | RESERVE | |
| | | ALTERNATE | |
| | | TOTAL | |

FIGURE 119.—Flight Plan/Flight Log.

**NEW YORK**

**BUFFALO**

§ BUFFALO AIRFIELD (9G0) 6.1 SE UTC−5(−4DT) 42°51′40″N 78°43′00″W DETROIT
670 B S2 FUEL 80, 100LL L-12H
RWY 06-24: H2665X60 (ASPH) S-8 MIRL IAP
RWY 06: Trees. RWY 24: Tree.
AIRPORT REMARKS: Attended daylight hours. CAUTION: Ultralight activity on arpt. Airport lgts opr dusk-0700Z‡. For runway lights attended after 0700Z‡ phone 716-668-4900.
COMMUNICATIONS: CTAF/UNICOM 122.8
® BUFFALO FSS (BUF) LC 631-9830. NOTAM FILE BUF.
RADIO AIDS TO NAVIGATION: NOTAM FILE BUF.
® BUFFALO (H) VORTAC 116.4 BUF Chan 111 42°55′44″N 78°38′48″W 225° 4.9 NM to fld. 730/08W.

§ GREATER BUFFALO INTL (BUF) 5.2 E UTC−5(−4DT) 42°56′26″N 78°43′57″W DETROIT
724 B S4 FUEL 100LL, JET A OX 1, 2, 3, 4 LRA CFR Index D H-3C, 6l, L-12H
RWY 05-23: H8102X150 (ASPH-GRVD) S-75, D-195, DT-450 HIRL CL 0.6% up NE IAP
RWY 05: SSALR. TDZ. Thld dsplcd 335′. Pole. RWY 23: SSALR. TDZ.
RWY 14-32: H5376X150 (ASPH) S-75, D-100, DT-160 MIRL 0.3% up SE.
RWY 14: VASI(V4L)—GA 3.0°TCH 55′. Tree. RWY 32: REIL. VASI(V4L)—GA 3.0°TCH 55′. Fence.
AIRPORT REMARKS: Attended continuously. Landing fee. CAUTION-Jet engine test stand located approximately 3600′ from approach end Rwy 32 1400′ south center line . Jet exhaust may reach altitude 100′ AGL. Ops conducted occasionally 1300-2300Z‡. CAUTION: Numerous types of birds may be encountered in holding pattern over Grand Island up to 5000′. Heavy concentration of Gulls, Blackbirds, and Starlings up to 5000′ on and in vicinity of arpt. Deer on and in vicinity of arpt. Flight Notification Service (ADCUS) available.
WEATHER DATA SOURCES: LLWAS.
COMMUNICATIONS: ATIS 135.35 UNICOM 122.95
® BUFFALO FSS (BUF) on arpt. 122.6 122.2 122.1R 116.4T DL NOTAM FILE BUF.
® BUFFALO APP DEP/CON 123.8 (055°-194°) 126.5 (195°-279°) 126.15 (280°-054°)
BUFFALO TOWER 120.5 GND CON 121.9
CLNC DEL 124.7 PRE-TAXI CLNC CLNC 124.7
ARSA ctc APP CON
RADIO AIDS TO NAVIGATION: NOTAM FILE BUF.
BUFFALO (H) VORTAC 116.4 BUF Chan 111 42°55′44″N 78°38′48″W 288° 3.5 NM to fld. 730/08W.
KLUMP NDB (LOM) 231 BU 43°00′01″N 78°39′04″W 233° 4.4 NM to fld.
PLAZZ NDB (LOM) 204 GB 42°52′26″N 78°49′00″W 053° 4.8 NM to fld.
ILS 111.3 I-BUF Rwy 23 LOM KLUMP NDB. Inner marker out of svc indefinitely. Back course unusable beyond 15 NM.
ILS 108.5 I-GBI Rwy 05 LOM PLAZZ NDB.
ASR

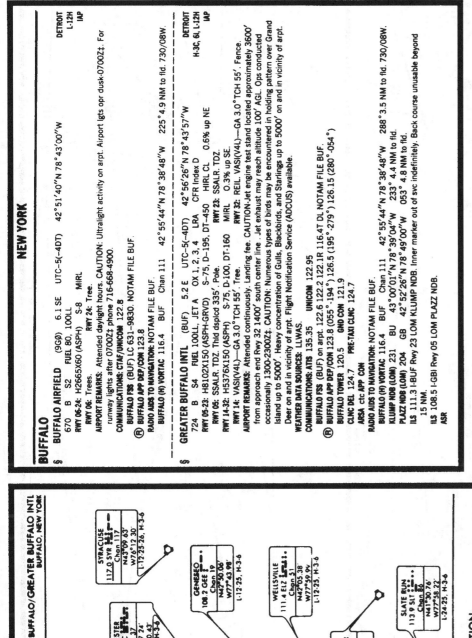

90047 SL-65 (FAA) BUFFALO/GREATER BUFFALO INTL
BUFFALO ONE DEPARTURE (VECTOR) BUFFALO, NEW YORK

ATIS 135.35
CLNC DEL
124.7
GND CON
121.9 257.8
BUFFALO TOWER
120.5 257.8

**DEPARTURE ROUTE DESCRIPTION**

All aircraft cleared as filed. Expect vectors to filed route or depicted fix. Maintain 10,000′ or assigned lower altitude. Expect further clearance to requested altitude/flight level ten minutes after departure.
All Runways: Maintain runway heading for vectors.

NOTE: Chart not to scale

BUFFALO ONE DEPARTURE (VECTOR) BUFFALO, NEW YORK
BUFFALO/GREATER BUFFALO INTL

FIGURE 120.—Buffalo One Departure (Vector).

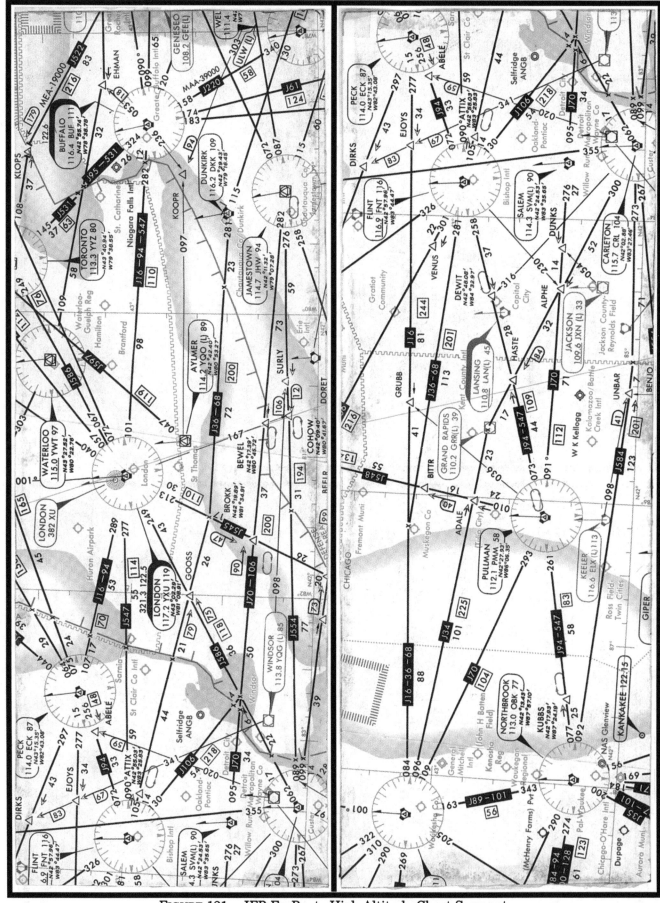

FIGURE 121.—IFR En Route High Altitude Chart Segment.

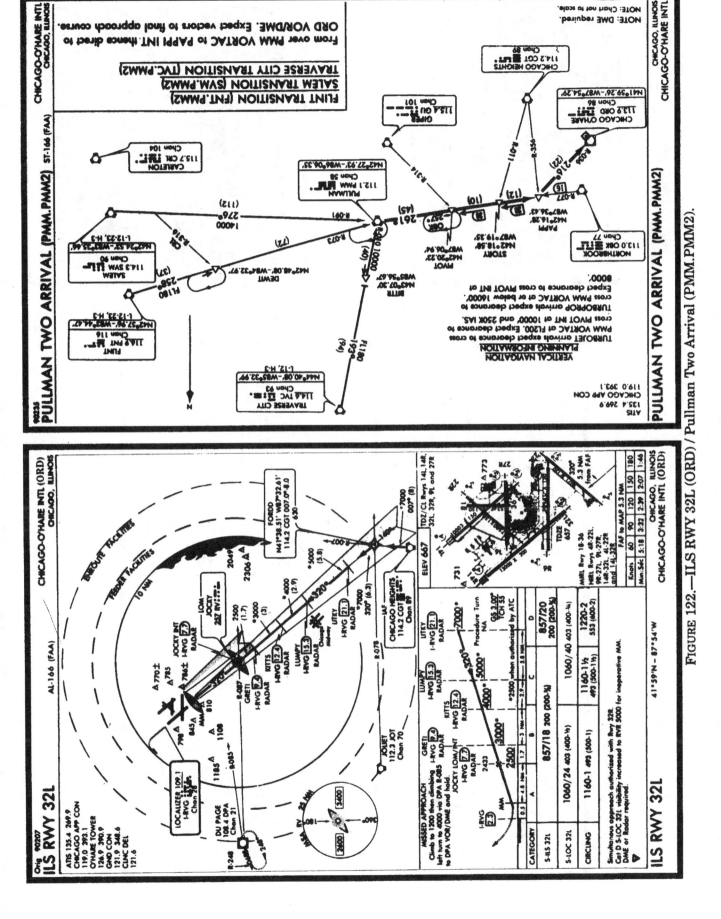

FIGURE 122.—ILS RWY 32L (ORD) / Pullman Two Arrival (PMM.PMM2).

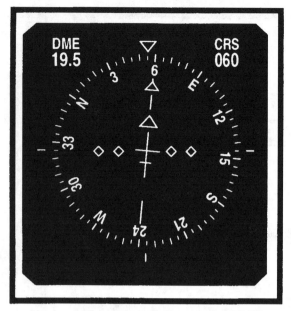

FIGURE 123.—Aircraft Course and DME Indicator.

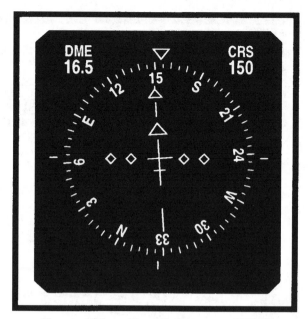

FIGURE 124.—Aircraft Course and DME Indicator.

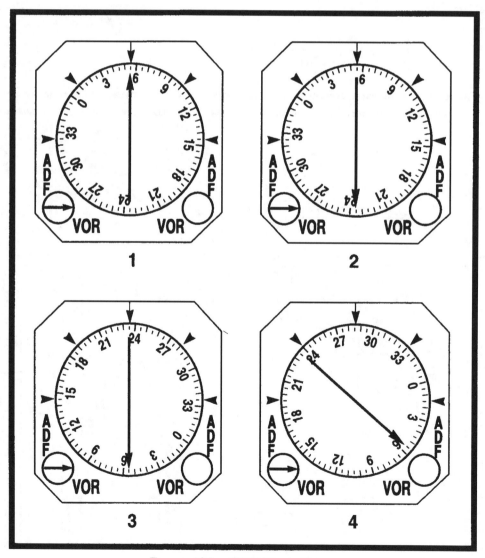

FIGURE 125.—RMI Illustrations.

# Class C Airspace

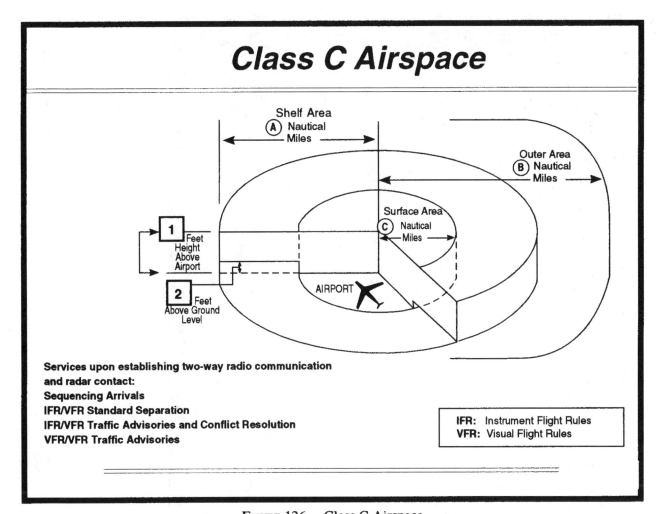

Services upon establishing two-way radio communication
and radar contact:
Sequencing Arrivals
IFR/VFR Standard Separation
IFR/VFR Traffic Advisories and Conflict Resolution
VFR/VFR Traffic Advisories

IFR: Instrument Flight Rules
VFR: Visual Flight Rules

FIGURE 126.—Class C Airspace.

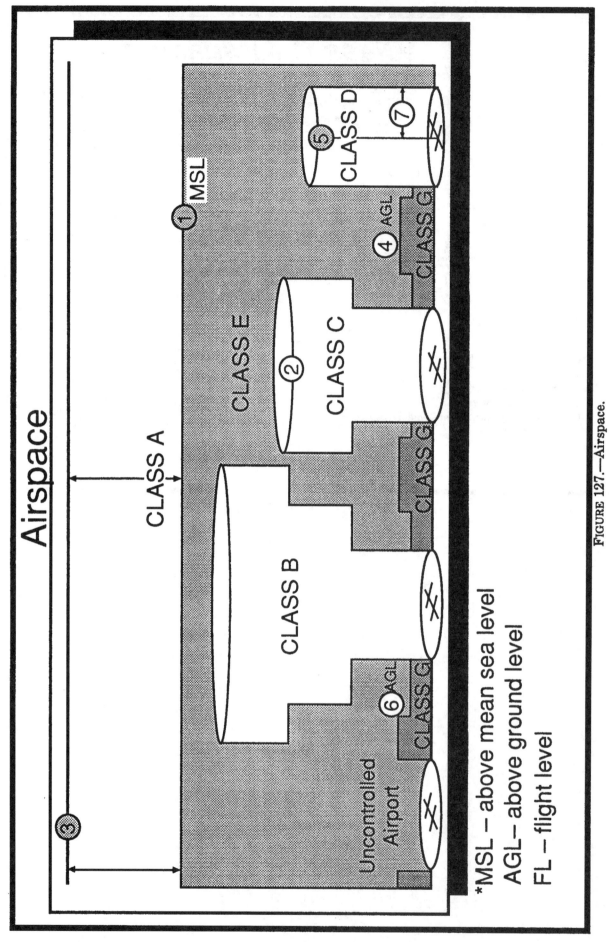

FIGURE 127.—Airspace.

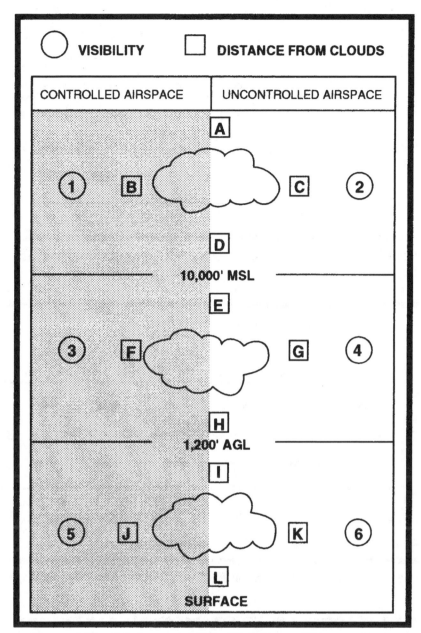

FIGURE 128.—Minimum In-Flight Visibility and Distance From Clouds.

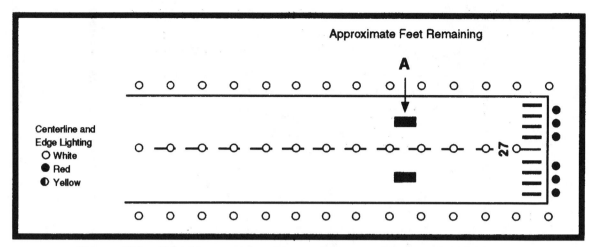

FIGURE 129.—FAA Nonprecision Approach Runway Markings and Lighting.

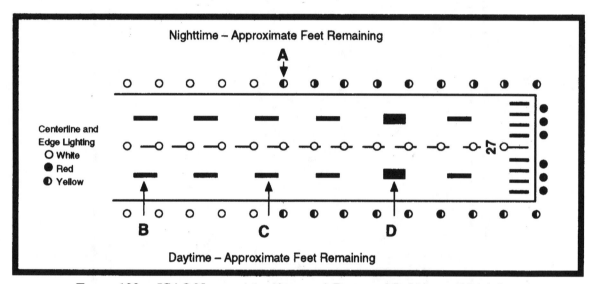

FIGURE 130.—ICAO Nonprecision Approach Runway Markings and Lighting.

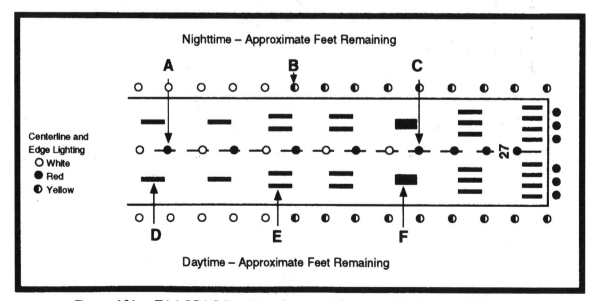

FIGURE 131.—FAA ICAO Precision Approach Runway Markings and Lighting.

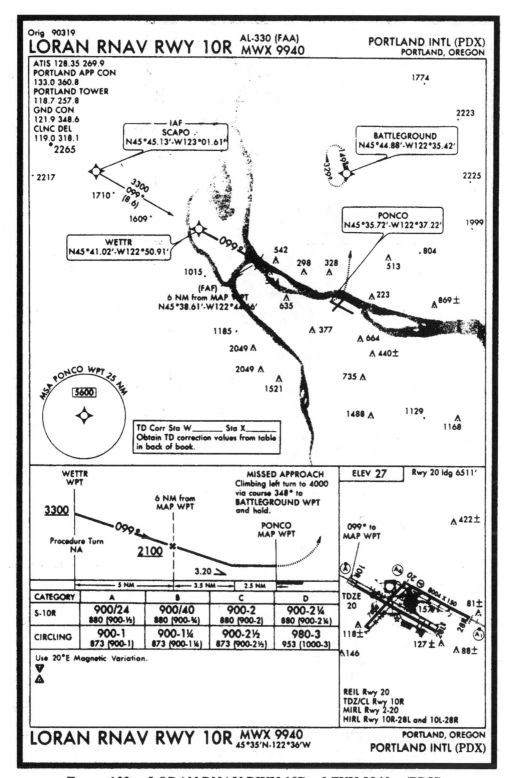

FIGURE 132.—LORAN RNAV RWY 10R – MWX 9940 – (PDX).

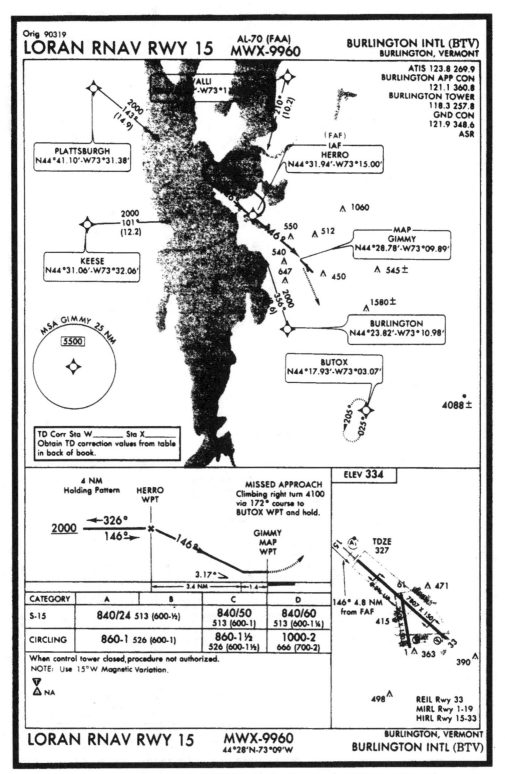

FIGURE 133.—LORAN RNAV RWY 15 – MWX-9960 – (BTV).

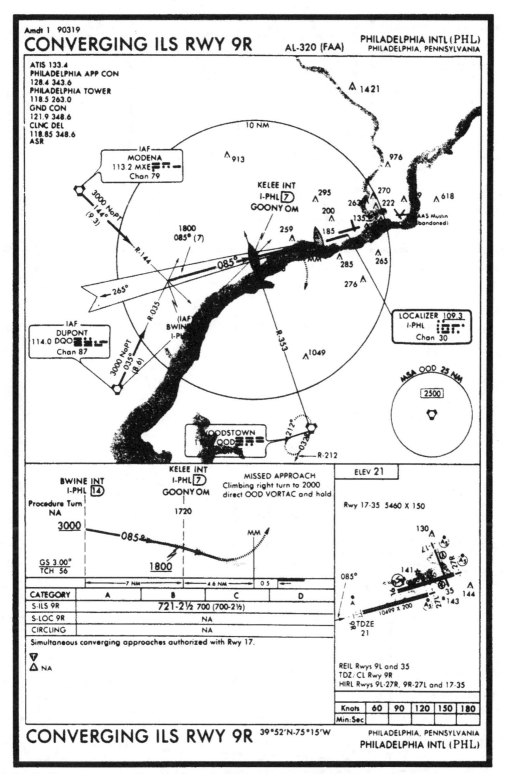

FIGURE 134.—Converging ILS RWY 9R (PHL).

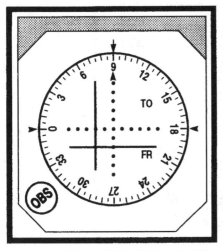

FIGURE 135.—OBS, ILS, and GS Displacement.

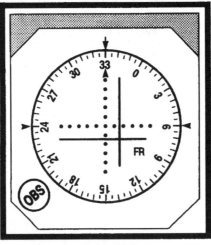

FIGURE 136.—OBS, ILS, and GS Displacement.

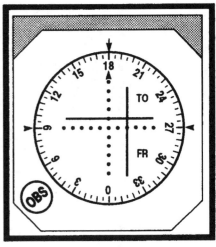

FIGURE 137.—OBS, ILS, and GS Displacement.

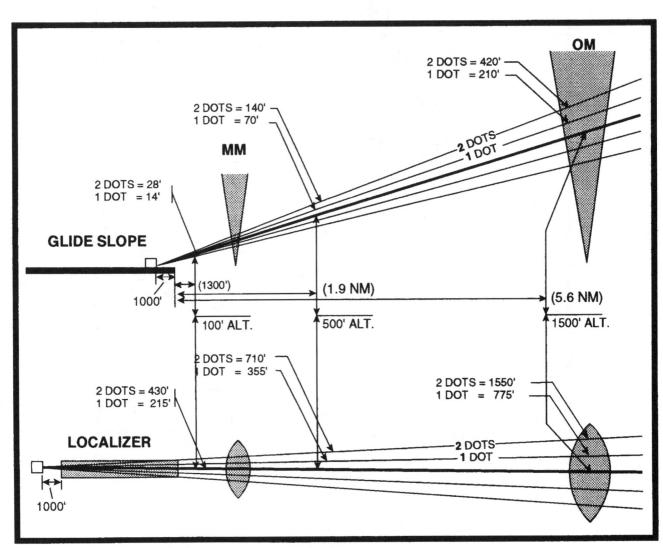

FIGURE 138.—Glide Slope and Localizer Illustration.

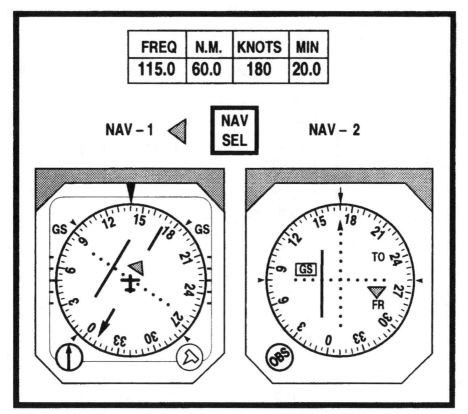

FIGURE 139.—No. 1 and No. 2 NAV Presentation.

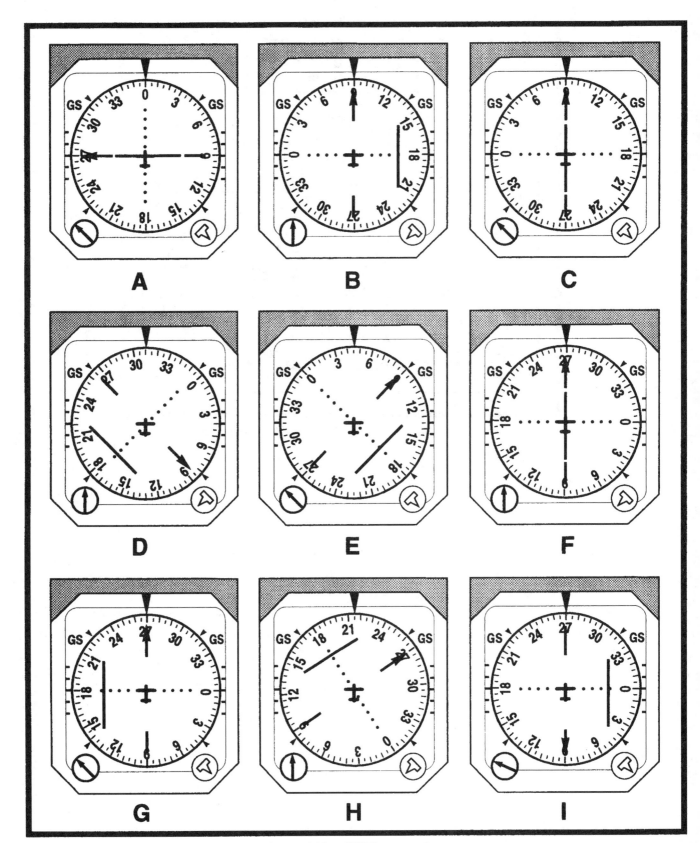

FIGURE 140.—HSI Presentation.

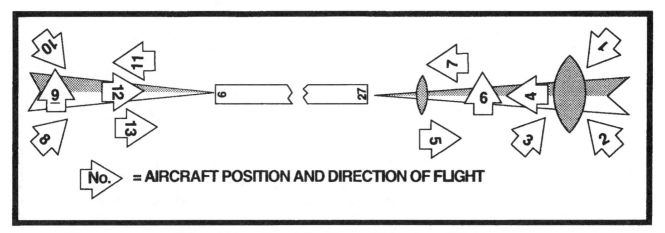

FIGURE 141.—Aircraft Position and Direction of Flight.

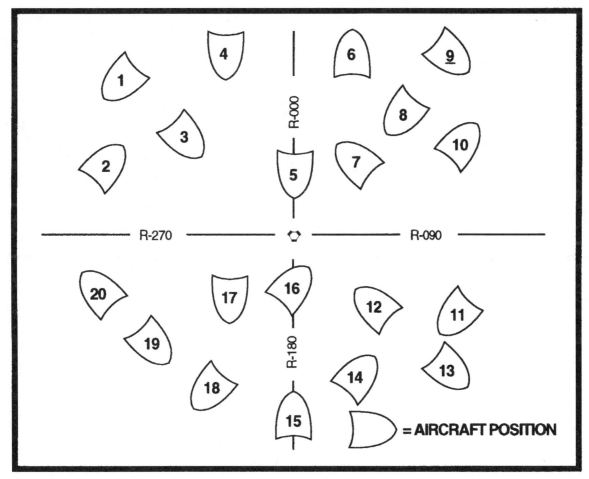

FIGURE 142.—Aircraft Position.

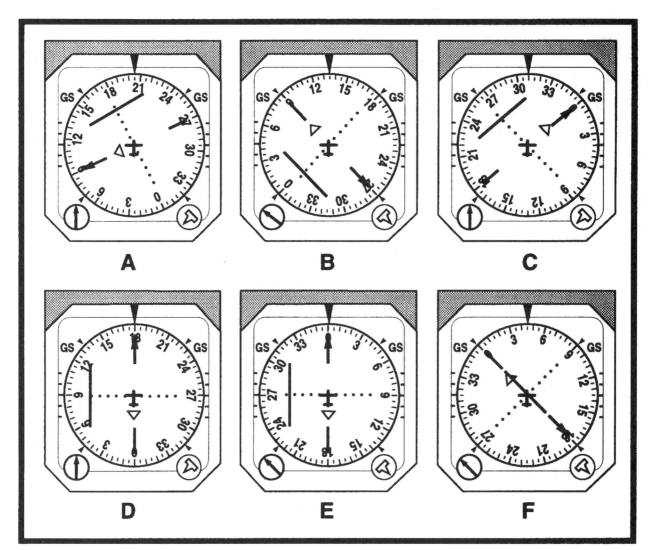

FIGURE 143.—HSI Presentation.

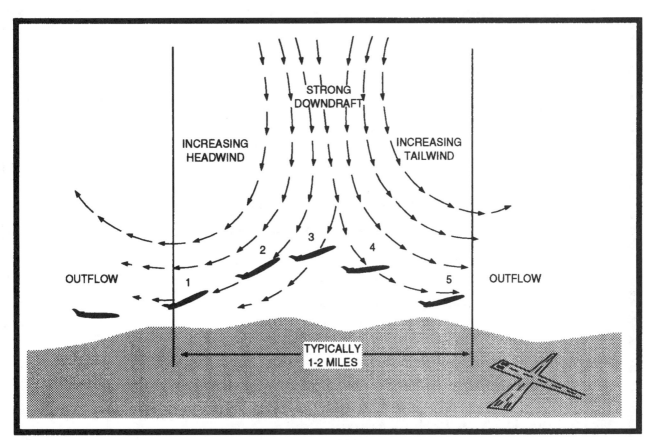

FIGURE 144.—Microburst Section Chart.

# AVIATION ROUTINE WEATHER REPORTS (METAR)

TX

METAR KAMA 131755Z 33025G35KT 3/4SM IC OVC003 M02/M01 A2952 RMK PK WND 32039/43 WSHFT 1735 PRESFR P0003.

METAR KAUS 131753Z 19011G17KT 8SM SCT040 BKN250 31/21 A3006 RMK SLPNO.

METAR KBPT 131755Z 17004KT 7SM FEW001 SCT030 BKN250 34/23 A2979 RMK VIS E 2.

METAR KBRO 131755Z 14015KT 6SM HZ SCT034 OVC250 34/30 A2985 RMK PRESRR.

METAR KCDS 131758Z 11013KT 7SM -SHRA OVC180 23/21 A3012 RMK RAB42 VIRGA SW.

METAR KCLL 131749Z 21011KT 7SM SCT003 BKN025 OVC100 34/21 A3008 RMK BKN025 V OVC.

METAR KCOT 131749Z 13010KT 10SM SCT040 SCT200 31/21 A3002 RMK RAE24.

METAR KCRP 131753Z 16016KT 10SM SCT028 BKN250 32/24 A3003.

METAR KDAL 131755Z 16005KT 7SM SCT023 OVC100 30/22 A3007.

METAR KDFW 131800Z 17007KT 10SM SCT035 OVC120 29/20 A3008.

METAR KDHT 131756Z 04014KT 15SM BKN025 22/15 A3026.

METAR KDRT 131756Z 12012KT 10SM FEW006 SCT020 BKN100 OVC250 29/22 A3000 RMK CONS LTG DSTN ESE TS SE MOVG NW VIRGA W.

METAR KELP 131755Z 09007KT 60SM VCBLDU FEW070 SCT170 BKN210 29/13 A3015.

METAR KFTW 131750Z 18007KT 7SM SCT025 OVC100 29/20 A3008.

FTW 131815Z UA /OV DFW/TM 1803/FL095/TP PA30/SK 036 OVC 060/075 OVC/RM TOPS UNKN.

METAR KGGG 131745Z 15008KT 15SM SKC 32/21 A3011.

METAR KGLS 131750Z VRB04KT 6SM VCSH SCT041 BKN093 26/22 A2995.

SPECI KGLS 131802Z 10012G21KT 060V140 2SM +SHRA SCT005 BKN035 OVC050CB 24/23 A2980 RMK RAB57 WSHFT 58 FROPA

METAR KHOU 131752Z 15008KT 7SM SCT030 OVC250 31/27 A3008.

METAR KHRL 131753Z 14015KT 8SM SKC 30/25 A3010.

METAR KIAH 131755Z VRB03KT 1/4SM R33L/1200FT BCFG VV007 27/26 A3005.

METAR KINK 131755Z 04027G36KT 2SM BLSA PO OVC015TCU 24/13 A2985.

METAR KLBB 131750Z 06029G43KT 1SM BLSNDU SQ VV010 03/M01 A2949.

LBB 131808Z UUA /OV LBB /TM 1800 /FL UNKN /TP B737 /TB MDT /RM LLWS -17 KT SFC-010 DURC RWY 36 LBB.

SPECI KLBB 131818Z 35031G40KT 1/2SM FZDZ VV030 M01/M01 A2946 RMK WSHFT 12 FROPA.

LBB 131821Z UUA /OV LBB/TM1817/FL011/TP B727/SK UNKN OVC/TA -06 /TB MOD/IC MDT CLR.

METAR KLFK 131756Z 24007KT 7SM BKN100 33/19 A3008.

METAR KMAF 131756Z 02020KT 12SM BKN025 OVC250 27/18 A3009 RMK RAE44.

METAR KMFE 131756Z 13015KT 7SM BKN125 33/19 A2998.

METAR KMRF 131752Z 09012G20KT 60SM SKC 28/14 A3000.

MRF 131801Z UUA/OV MRF/TM1758/FL450/TP B767/TB MDT CAT.

FIGURE 145.—Aviation Routine Weather Reports (METAR).

# AVIATION ROUTINE WEATHER REPORTS (METAR)

TX

METAR KABI 131755Z AUTO 21016G24KT 180V240 1SM R11/P6000FT -RA BR BKN015 OVC025 19/15 A2990 RMK AO2 PK WND 20035/25 WSHFT 1715 VIS 3/4V1 1/2 VIS 3/4 RWY11 RAB07 CIG 013V 017 CIG 014 RWY11 PRESFR SLP125 P0003 60009 T01940154 10196 20172 58033 TSNO $.

METAR KMWL 131756Z 13011KT 10SM BKN011 OVC050 25/23 A3006.

METAR KPSX 131755Z 20010KT 7SM SCT018 OVC200 31/24 A3007.

METAR KPVW 131750Z 05006KT 10SM SCT012 OVC030 30/20 A3011 RMK RAE47.

METAR KSAT 131756Z 15016KT 7SM SCT028 OVC250 30/20 A3005.

SAT 131756Z UA /OV SAT/TM 1739Z/ FL UNKN/TP UNKN/SK OVC 040.

METAR KSJT 131755Z 22012KT 7SM BKN018 OVC070 25/23 A3002.

METAR KSPS 131757Z 09014KT 6SM -RA SCT025 OVC090 24/22 A3005.

SPECI KSPS 131820Z 01025KT 2SM +RA OVC015TCU 22/21 A3000 RMK DSNT TORNADO B15 N MOV E.

SPS 131820Z UA/OV SPS/TM 1818/FL090/TP C402/SK OVC 075.

METAR KTPL 131751Z 17015KT 15SM SCT015 SCT100 OVC250 31/20 A3007.

METAR KTYR 131753Z AUTO 26029G41KT 2SM +TSRA BKN008 OVC020 31/24 A3001 RMK A02 TSB44 RAB46.

METAR KVCT 131755Z 17013KT 7SM SCT030 OVC250 30/24 A3005.

AR

METAR KARG 131753Z AUTO 22015G25KT 3/4SM R28/2400FT +RA OVC010 29/28 A2985 RMK AO2.

METAR KELD 131755Z 06005G10KT 3SM FU BKN050 OVC100 30/21 A3010.

METAR KFSM 131756Z 00000KT 5SM SKC 30/20 A2982.

FSM 131830Z UA/OV HRO-FSM/TM 1825/FL290/TP B737/SK SCT 290.

METAR KFYV 131755Z 170018G32KT 2SM +TSRA SQ SCT030 BKN060OVC100CB 28/21 A2978 RMK RAB47.

FYV 131801Z UA/OV 1 E DAK/TM 1755Z/FL 001/TP CV440/RM WS LND RWY16 FYV.

METAR KHOT 131751Z 34006KT 18SM SCT040 OVC150 32/18 A3010.

METAR KHRO 131753Z 09007KT 7SM FEW020 BKN040CB 30/27 A3001.

SPECI KHRO 131815Z 13017G26KT 2SM +TSRA SCT020 BKN045TCU 29/24A2983 RMK RAB12 FRQ LTGICCG VC PRESFR.

HRO 131830Z UUA/OV 6 S HRO/TM 1825Z/FL 001/TP DC6/RM WS TKO RWY 18.

METAR KLIT 131754Z 07004KT 10SM SCT030 BKN250 34/29 A3007.

METAR KPBF 131753Z 29007KT 5SM SCT040 BKN100 35/19 A3008.

METAR KTXK 131753Z 25003KT 7SM SCT100 BKN200 33/19 A3010.

FIGURE 146.—Aviation Routine Weather Reports (METAR).

# INTERNATIONAL TERMINAL AERODROME FORECASTS (TAF)

TX

TAF
KALI 031745Z 031818 14015KT 6SM HZ BKN012
    FM2000 15015G25KT P6SM BKN030 WS009/02045KT
    FM2200 16011G21KT 4SM SCT040 BKN250 TEMPO 2301 3SM TSGS BKN020
    FM0100 13015KT 5SM SCT015
    FM0700 12008KT 5SM BKN008 BECMG 0912 3SM BKN015

TAF
KAMA 031745Z 031818 05012KT 5SM RA BR BKN010 BKN080 TEMPO1803 03015KT 2SM +TSRA OVC010
    FM0400 03015KT 3SM BKN020 OVC080 TEMPO 0410 2SM +TSRA OVC010
    FM1100 03012KT 5SM RA BR OVC010 BECMG 1618 1/2SM RA FG OVC008

TAF
KAUS 031745Z COR 031818 17010KT P6SM BKN025 OVC100
    FM2100 15008KT 4SM BKN030 OVC100 TEMPO 2223 1SM TSPE OVC010
    FM0100 16005KT 5SM BKN014 TEMPO 0809 1SM +TSRA BKN014 BECMG 1214 3SM TSRA BKN020
    FM1500 17008KT 5SM SCT050

TAF
KCRP 031745Z 031818 15015G20KT P6SM SCT020 BKN250
    FM2300 16015G25KT 4SM SCT030 BKN250 TEMPO 0001 TSRA
    FM0100 16015KT 2SM BKN015 BECMG 0911 5SM SCT030

TAF
KDAL 031745Z 031818 00000KT P6SM SCT030 BKN100
    FM2200 17007KT 5SM BR BKN030 OVC100 PROB40 0002 2SM TSRA OVC010
    FM0200 09005KT 4SM -RA BKN020 PROB30 0407 3SM TSRA
    FM0700 07004KT 1/2SM FG OVC002 BECMG 0912 3SM TSRA SCT040

TAF AMD
KDRT 031745Z 031818 14010KT P6SM OVC014
    FM1900 VBR05KT 5SM BKN020 OVC100 TEMPO 2021 2SM +TSRA
    FM2300 14012KT 5SM HZ BKN030 BKN100 PROB40 0205 3SM TSRA BKN020
    FM0500 27006KT 6SM BR SCT035 BKN080 TEMPO 0709 2SM FU BR  BKN020
    FM1000 00000KT 4SM OVC030 BECMG 1416 3SM TSRA OVC020

TAF
KELP 031745Z 031818 08012KT P6SM SCT070 SCT100
    FM2000 13010KT 6SM SCT070 BKN120 TEMPO 2223 15026G35KT 3SM BLSA BKN050
    FM0600 07012KT 5SM BKN070 PROB40 0709 2SM -TSRA BKN025
    FM1200 07020G34KT 1SM +TSRA BKN020CB WS008/25040KT

TAF
KHOU 031745Z 031818 18010KT 6SM HZ SCT020
    FM2100 18015KT 4SM HZ SCT035 SCT250
    FM0100 19010KT 3SM HZ SCT 250
    FM0700 20005KT 1SM BR FU BKN005 OVC025
    FM1300 13007KT 4SM HZ BKN040

TAF
KIAH 031745Z 031818 18010KT 5SM HZ SCT020
    FM2000 16008KT  4SM HZ SCT015 SCT250
    FM0500 17012KT 1SM BR FU BKN008 OVC020
    FM1000 00000KT 1/4SM -RA FG BKN010 OVC031
    FM1400 14005KT 5SM BKN004 OVC080 BECMG 1618 NSW

TAF
KINK 031745Z 031818 10010KT P6SM SCT020 SCT100
    FM2100 08013KT 3SM DZ BKN025 BKN080 PROB40 0002 06026G35KT1SM +TSRAGR
    FM0400 05019KT 2SM DU BKN020 OVC050 PROB40 0709 1SM +TSRA FEW002 OVC010
    FM0900 02004KT 1/2SM RA FG SCT025 BKN045 OVC100CB
    FM1400 34035G45KT 2SM SS SKC

FIGURE 147.—International Terminal Aerodrome Forecasts (TAF).

---

**INTERNATIONAL TERMINAL AERODROME FORECASTS (TAF), CONTINUED**

TAF
KLBB 031745Z 031818 06012KT 3SM -TSRA SCT010 OVC020
    FM2100 04015KT 5SM BR BKN020 OVC060 PROB40 0103 06025G35KT 1/8SM +SHRASNPE OVC003
    FM0400 05018KT 3SM -RA BR OVC010 PROB30 0608 07020KT 1SM +TSRA
    FM0900 00000KT 1/4SM -RA FG VV002
    FM1300 01005G12KT 1SM FZRA
    FM1600 VBR04KT 1/8SM FG VV001

TAF
KSAT 031745Z 031818 17010KT 6SM HZ BKN016 OVC030
    FM2000 17015KT P6SM BKN025
    FM2200 19012KT 4SM FU BKN030 OVC250 PROB40 0104 07020G30KT 3SM TSRA BKN020
    FM0500 12015KT 3SM SG BKN010 BKN035  PROB40 0709 05015G23KT 1SM +TSRA OVC010
    FM1000 35008G16KT 4SM BLSN OVC020

TAF
KSJT 031745Z 031818 12012KT 6SM HZ BKN016
    FM2000 17018KT 4SM BR BKN025
    FM2200 14020G28KT 3SM GS BKN030 OVC250 PROB40 0103 16025G32KT 1SM +TSRA OVC008CB
    FM0900 17020G34KT 2SM RA BR OVC010CB

TAF
KSPS 031745Z 031818 07012KT 4SM -RA FG SCT030 BKN080 TEMPO 0203 09022G30KT 1SM FZDZ OVC020
    FM0900 05015KT 2SM BR SCT001 BKN005 OVC010 SNRA WS090/09035KT

FIGURE 147.—International Terminal Aerodrome Forecasts (TAF), Continued.

---

**CONVECTIVE SIGMET**

MKCC WST Ø31755
CONVECTIVE SIGMET 42C
VALID UNTIL 1955Z
TX OK
FROM 5W MLC–PEQ–SJT–5W MLC
AREA SCT EMBDD TSTMS MOVG LTL. TOPS 3ØØ.

CONVECTIVE SIGMET 43C
VALID UNTIL 1955Z
CO KS OK
FROM AKO–OSW–3ØWNW OKC–AKO
AREA SCT TSTMS OCNLY EMBDD MOVG FROM 322Ø. TOPS 38Ø.

CONVECTIVE SIGMET 44C
VALID UNTIL 1955Z
5ØNE MEM
ISOLD INSTD LVL5 TSTM DIAM 1Ø MOVG FROM 2625. TOP ABV 45Ø.

OUTLOOK VALID UNTIL 2355Z
TSTMS OVR TX AND SE OK WL MOV SEWD 15 KTS.
TSTMS OVER CO, KS, AND N OK WL CONT MOVG SEWD 2Ø KTS.
TSTM OVR TN WL CONT MOVG EWD 25 KTS.

FIGURE 148.—Convective Sigmet.

## WINDS AND TEMPERATURES ALOFT FORECASTS

DATA BASED ON Ø312ØØZ
VALID Ø4ØØØØZ  FOR USE 18ØØ–Ø3ØØZ. TEMPS NEG ABV 24ØØØ

| FT | 3ØØØ | 6ØØØ | 9ØØØ | 12ØØØ | 18ØØØ | 24ØØØ | 3ØØØØ | 34ØØØ | 39ØØØ |
|---|---|---|---|---|---|---|---|---|---|
| ABI |  | 13Ø6+16 | 16Ø7+11 | 18Ø7+Ø6 | 21Ø8-Ø7 | 22Ø8-18 | 24Ø833 | 25Ø942 | 3ØØ753 |
| ABO |  |  | Ø81Ø+14 | Ø511+Ø8 | 3415-Ø6 | 322Ø-18 | 312333 | 312543 | 3Ø2554 |
| AMA |  | Ø614 | Ø814+1Ø | Ø7Ø9+Ø5 | 321Ø-Ø7 | 2914-19 | 281934 | 282243 | 292554 |
| ATL | Ø9Ø6 | 99ØØ+17 | 99ØØ+12 | Ø2Ø5+Ø7 | 35Ø7-Ø7 | 33Ø5-19 | 29Ø534 | 28Ø543 | 99ØØ54 |
| BNA | 99ØØ | 99ØØ+17 | 32Ø5+12 | 31Ø9+Ø7 | 3Ø18-Ø7 | 2918-19 | 272134 | 262444 | 262855 |
| BRO | 151Ø | 1614+2Ø | 1611+14 | 17Ø8+Ø8 | 99ØØ-Ø7 | 99ØØ-19 | 99ØØ34 | 99ØØ43 | 99ØØ55 |
| DAL | Ø91Ø | 17Ø6+17 | 2ØØ9+11 | 2Ø11+Ø6 | 2Ø15-Ø8 | 2214-19 | 231333 | 241342 | 271153 |
| DEN |  |  | 99ØØ+Ø9 | 99ØØ+Ø4 | 3Ø2Ø-1Ø | 3Ø29-21 | 3Ø3636 | 3Ø4145 | 294756 |
| DSM | 3615 | 3315+Ø7 | 3118+Ø4 | 3Ø22+ØØ | 2835-12 | 2748-24 | 276438 | 277348 | 277957 |
| ELP |  | Ø61Ø | Ø614+13 | Ø615+Ø8 | Ø113-Ø5 | 3614-17 | 361433 | 361442 | 251354 |
| GCK |  | Ø611+11 | Ø8Ø9+Ø8 | 99ØØ+Ø3 | 2817-Ø9 | 2823-2Ø | 273135 | 273644 | 284155 |
| HLC |  | Ø4Ø9+Ø9 | Ø4Ø5+Ø7 | 31Ø6+Ø2 | 2822-1Ø | 273Ø-21 | 273936 | 274545 | 275256 |
| HOU | Ø9Ø9 | 16Ø7+19 | 16Ø6+13 | 16Ø6+Ø7 | 16Ø5-Ø8 | 99ØØ-2Ø | 99ØØ34 | 99ØØ43 | 99ØØ54 |
| ICT | Ø516 | Ø613+12 | Ø6Ø7+Ø8 | 99ØØ+Ø4 | 2718-Ø9 | 2626-2Ø | 263635 | 264144 | 274655 |
| IND | 3611 | 32Ø7+12 | 2912+Ø8 | 2818+Ø3 | 2733-Ø9 | 2643-21 | 265635 | 265944 | 256255 |
| INK |  | Ø6Ø9+16 | Ø7Ø9+12 | Ø6Ø8+Ø7 | Ø1Ø7-Ø6 | 36Ø7-18 | 35Ø833 | 34Ø842 | 35Ø855 |
| JAN | 3612 | 3613+18 | 3611+13 | 36Ø9+Ø7 | Ø1Ø5-Ø8 | 99ØØ-19 | 99ØØ34 | 99ØØ43 | 23Ø854 |
| LIT | Ø31Ø | 36Ø8+16 | 32Ø6+11 | 28Ø8+Ø6 | 2517-Ø8 | 2518-19 | 252Ø34 | 252243 | 262454 |
| LOU | Ø1Ø5 | 99ØØ+15 | 29Ø8+1Ø | 2913+Ø5 | 2825-Ø8 | 2731-2Ø | 263834 | 264143 | 254454 |
| MEM | Ø1Ø9 | Ø1Ø8+17 | 34Ø8+12 | 311Ø+Ø6 | 2916-Ø7 | 2717-19 | 261934 | 262144 | 262555 |
| MKC | Ø316 | Ø211+11 | 34Ø9+Ø7 | 3Ø13+Ø3 | 2728-1Ø | 2638-21 | 265Ø36 | 265645 | 276356 |
| MSY | Ø315 | Ø216+19 | Ø315+13 | Ø414+Ø7 | Ø51Ø-Ø8 | Ø6Ø5-2Ø | 99ØØ34 | 99ØØ43 | 21Ø854 |
| OKC | Ø715 | Ø81Ø+14 | 11Ø6+1Ø | 99ØØ+Ø5 | 2414-Ø8 | 2419-19 | 252534 | 252743 | 272754 |
| SAT | 11Ø7 | 1713+18 | 1813+13 | 1911+Ø7 | 2ØØ6-Ø7 | 19Ø6-19 | 18Ø734 | 17Ø743 | 99ØØ54 |
| SGF | Ø414 | Ø41Ø+14 | 36Ø5+Ø9 | 29Ø8+Ø4 | 2624-Ø9 | 2632-2Ø | 254135 | 264444 | 264655 |
| SHV | Ø5Ø9 | 99ØØ+18 | 99ØØ+12 | 21Ø6+Ø6 | 2Ø12-Ø8 | 21Ø9-19 | 22Ø734 | 24Ø743 | 26Ø754 |
| STL | Ø314 | Ø11Ø+12 | 321Ø+Ø8 | 2915+Ø3 | 273Ø-Ø9 | 2741-21 | 265435 | 265744 | 266Ø55 |
| TUS |  | Ø8Ø7+23 | Ø814+16 | Ø814+1Ø | Ø81Ø-Ø5 | Ø5Ø5-17 | 33Ø533 | 31Ø842 | 29Ø954 |

FIGURE 149.—Winds and Temperatures Aloft Forecast.

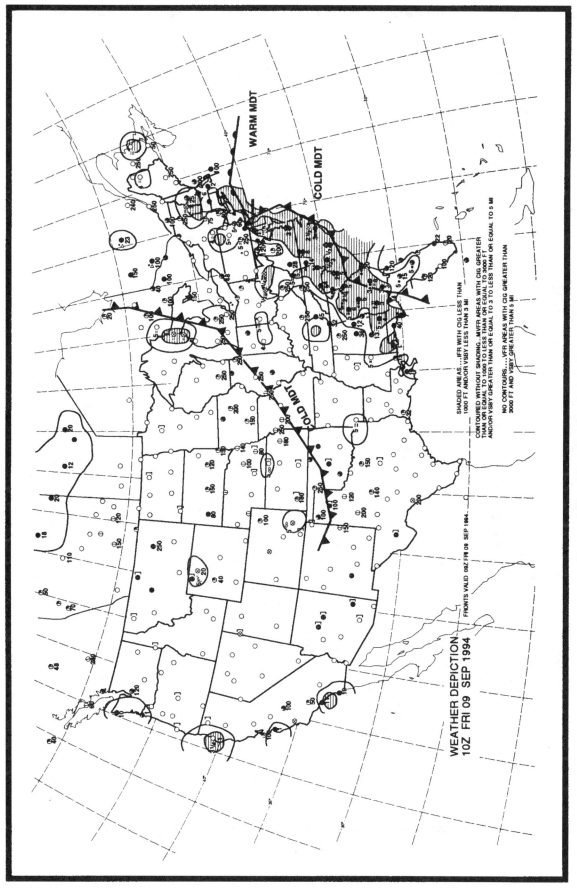

FIGURE 150.—Weather Depiction Chart.

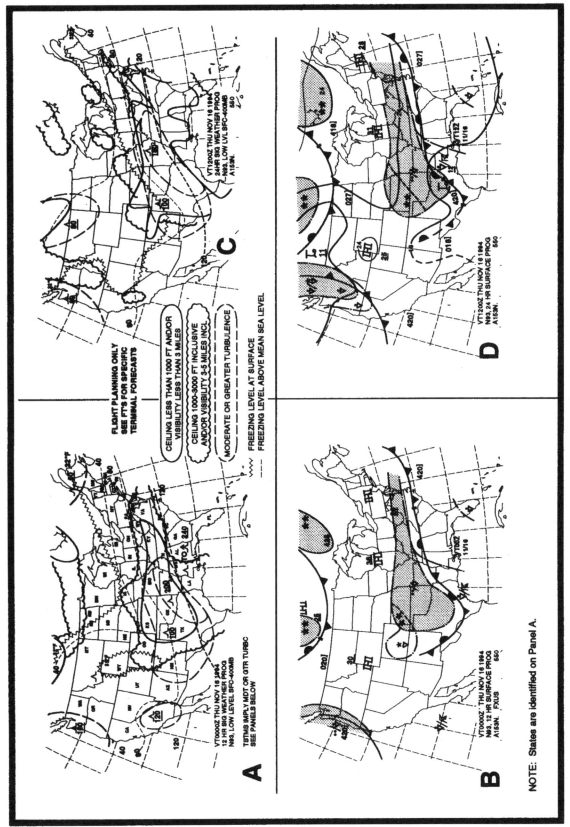

FIGURE 151.—U.S. Low-Level Significant Prog Chart.

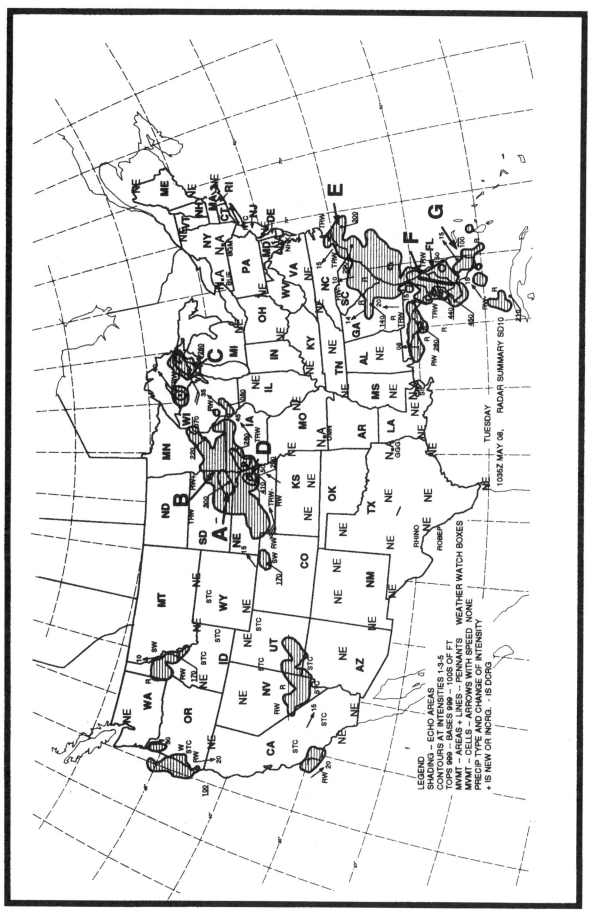

FIGURE 152.—Radar Summary Chart.

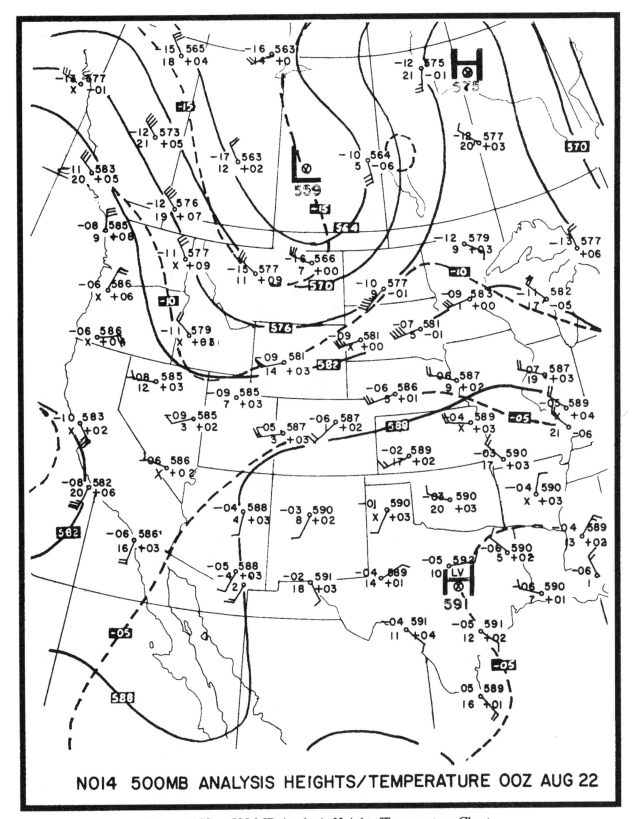

FIGURE 153.—500 MB Analysis Heights/Temperature Chart.

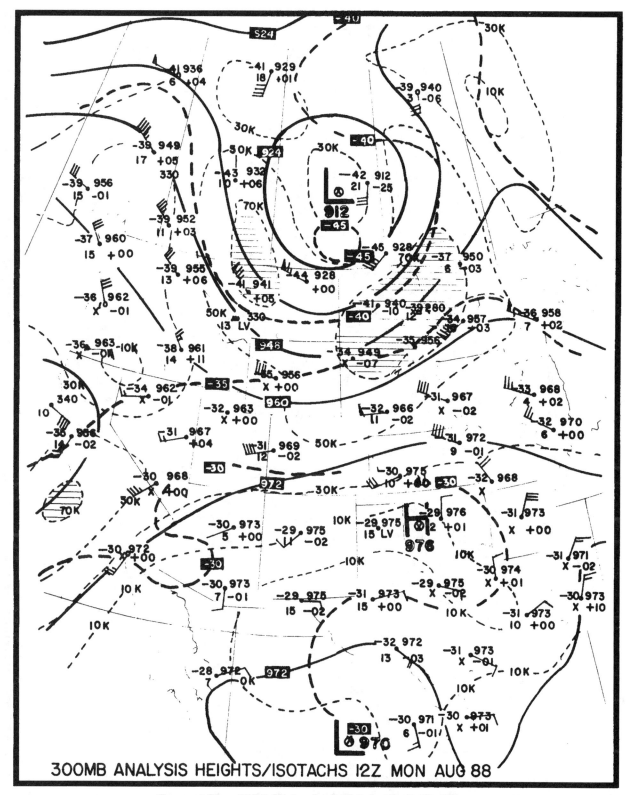

FIGURE 154.—300 MB Analysis Heights/Isotachs Chart.

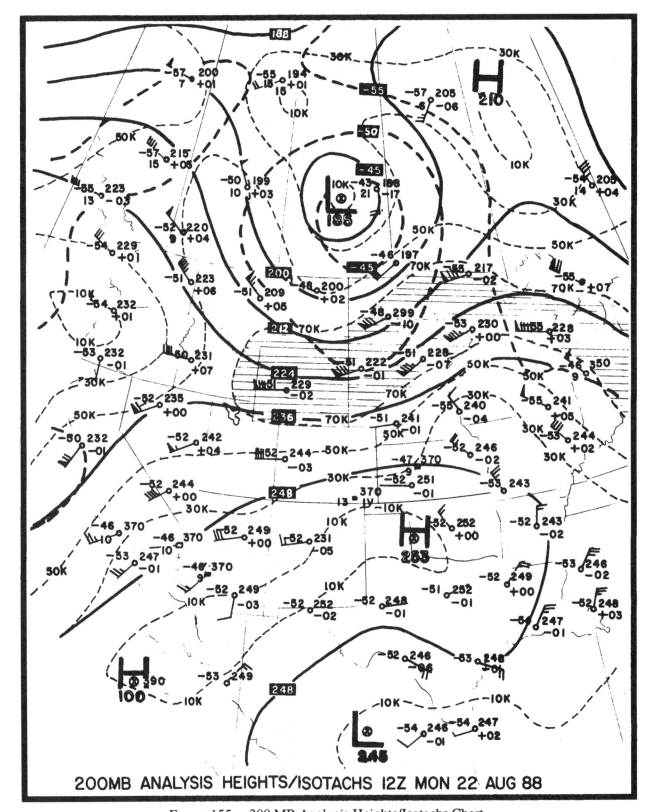

FIGURE 155.—200 MB Analysis Heights/Isotachs Chart.

FIGURE 156.—Airport Sign.

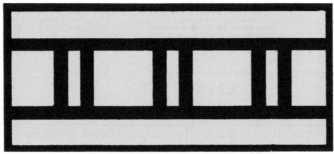

FIGURE 157.—Airport Sign.

Form Approved: OMB No. 2120-0034

| U.S. DEPARTMENT OF TRANSPORTATION FEDERAL AVIATION ADMINISTRATION **FLIGHT PLAN** | (FAA USE ONLY) | ☐ PILOT BRIEFING  ☐ STOPOVER | ☐ VNR | TIME STARTED | SPECIALIST INITIALS |
|---|---|---|---|---|---|

| 1. TYPE | 2. AIRCRAFT IDENTIFICATION | 3. AIRCRAFT TYPE/ SPECIAL EQUIPMENT | 4. TRUE AIRSPEED | 5. DEPARTURE POINT | 6. DEPARTURE TIME | | 7. CRUISING ALTITUDE |
|---|---|---|---|---|---|---|---|
| VFR  X IFR  DVFR | N711JB | G1159/A | 506 KTS | STL ST LOUIS, MO | PROPOSED (Z) | ACTUAL (Z) | FL370 |

**8. ROUTE OF FLIGHT**

STL, GATWAY2.ROD, J29 DJB, J60 PSB, PSB.MIP8, LGA

| 9. DESTINATION (Name of airport and city) LGA  LA GAURDIA NEW YORK, NY | 10. EST. TIME ENROUTE HOURS / MINUTES | 11. REMARKS L/O = LEVEL OFF   PPH = POUNDS PER HOUR   TBC = TOWER ENROUTE CONTROL   VARIATION: BIB IE, ROD IW, DJB 5W, PSB 8W, MIP 11W, SBJ 11W, LGA 12W |
|---|---|---|

| 12. FUEL ON BOARD | | 13. ALTERNATE AIRPORT(S) | 14. PILOT'S NAME, ADDRESS & TELEPHONE NUMBER & AIRCRAFT HOME BASE | 15. NUMBER ABOARD |
|---|---|---|---|---|
| HOURS 4 | MINUTES 00 | JFK NEW YORK, NY | 17. DESTINATION CONTACT/TELEPHONE (OPTIONAL) | 12 |

| 16. COLOR OF AIRCRAFT BLACK/RED | CIVIL AIRCRAFT PILOTS. FAR Part 91 requires you file an IFR flight plan to operate under instrument flight rules in controlled airspace. Failure to file could result in a civil penalty not to exceed $1,000 for each violation (Section 901 of the Federal Aviation Act of 1958, as amended). Filing of a VFR flight plan is recommended as a good operating practice. See also Part 99 for requirements concerning DVFR flight plans. |
|---|---|

FAA Form 7233-1 (8-82)     CLOSE VFR FLIGHT PLAN WITH _____ FSS ON ARRIVAL

## FLIGHT LOG

| CHECK POINTS | | ROUTE | | WIND | SPEED-KTS | | DIST | TIME | | FUEL | |
|---|---|---|---|---|---|---|---|---|---|---|---|
| FROM | TO | ALTITUDE | COURSE | TEMP | TAS | GS | NM | LEG | TOT | LEG | TOT |
| STL | BIB | GATWAY 2.ROD CLIMB | | | | | 95 | | :16:00 | | 987* |
| BIB | ROD | GATWAY2.ROD FL370 | | 350/96 ISA-1 | | | | | | | |
| ROD | DJB | J29 FL370 | | | | | | | | | |
| DJB | PSB | J60 FL370 | | | | | | | | | |
| PSB | MIP | PSB.MIP8 FL370 | | | | | | | | | |
| MIP | SBJ | | | | | | | | | | |
| SBJ | LGA | DESCENT | | | | | 52 | :16:26 | | 269 | |
| | | | | | | | | | | | |
| LGA | JFK | TEC 4000 | | | 260 | | | :15:00 | | | |

| OTHER DATA: NOTE: | * Includes Taxi Fuel Use 2389 PPH Total Fuel Flow From L/O To Start Of Descent. Use 1898 PPH Total Fuel Flow For Reserve And Alternate Requirements. A Missed Approach Requires 233# of Fuel. | TIME and FUEL: As required by FARs. |
|---|---|---|

| TIME | FUEL (LB) | |
|---|---|---|
| | | EN ROUTE |
| | | RESERVE |
| | | ALTERNATE |
| | | TOTAL |

FIGURE 158.—Flight Plan/Flight Log.

128

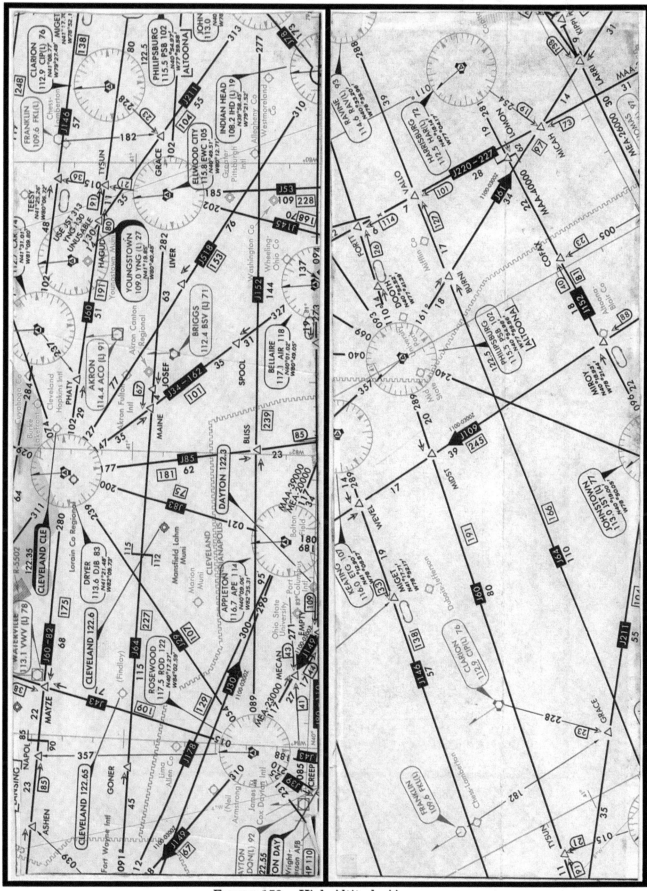

FIGURE 159.—High Altitude Airways.

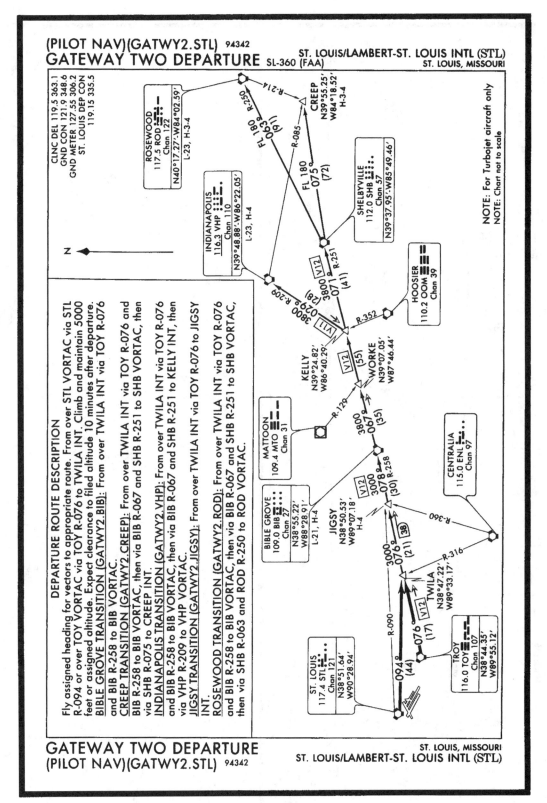

FIGURE 160.—GATEWAY TWO DEPARTURE (STL).

130

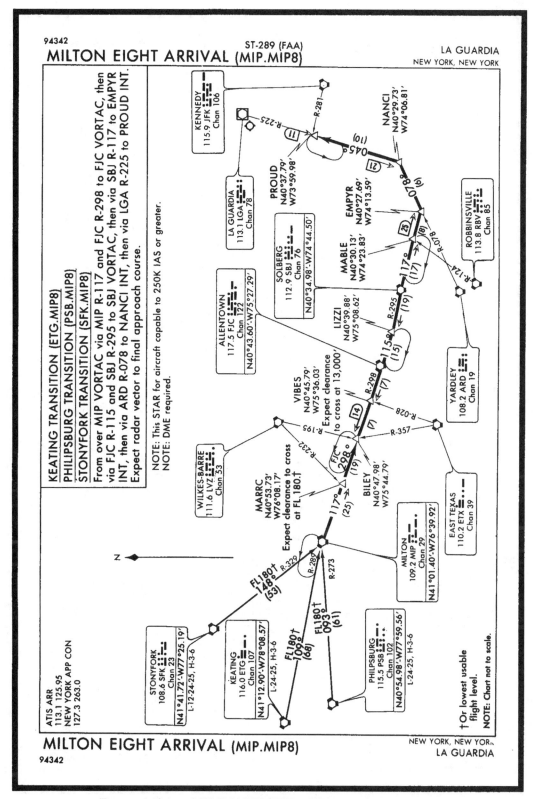

FIGURE 160A.—MILTON EIGHT ARRIVAL (MIP.MIP8).

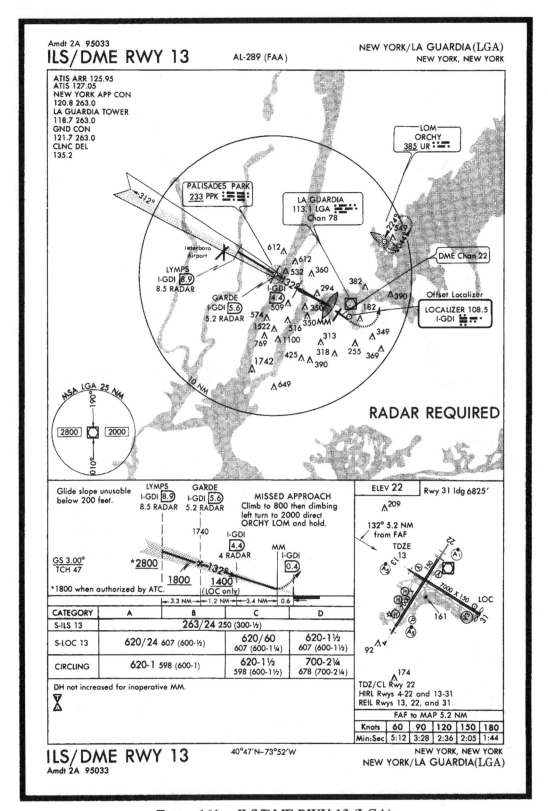

FIGURE 161.—ILS/DME RWY 13 (LGA).

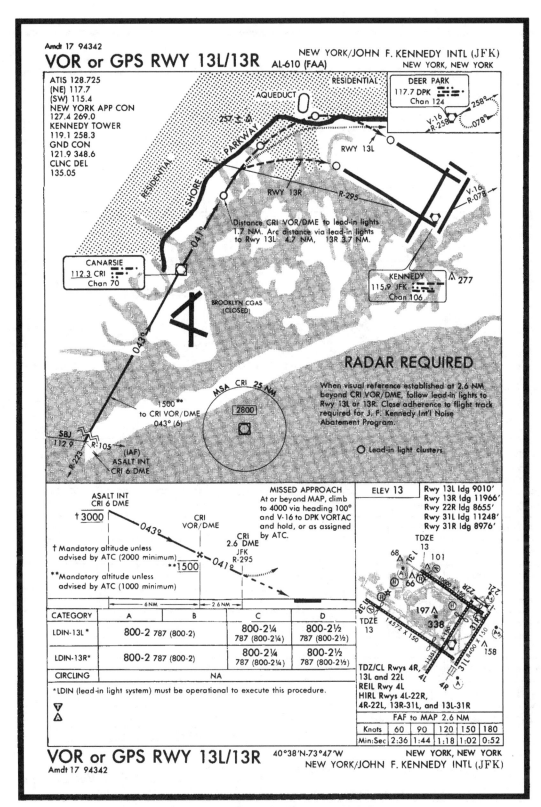

**FIGURE 161A.—VOR or GPS RWY 13L/13R (JFK).**

Form Approved: OMB No. 2120-0034

| U.S. DEPARTMENT OF TRANSPORTATION FEDERAL AVIATION ADMINISTRATION **FLIGHT PLAN** | (FAA USE ONLY) | ☐ PILOT BRIEFING ☐ STOPOVER | ☐ VNR | TIME STARTED | SPECIALIST INITIALS |
|---|---|---|---|---|---|

| 1. TYPE | 2. AIRCRAFT IDENTIFICATION | 3. AIRCRAFT TYPE/ SPECIAL EQUIPMENT | 4. TRUE AIRSPEED | 5. DEPARTURE POINT | 6. DEPARTURE TIME | 7. CRUISING ALTITUDE |
|---|---|---|---|---|---|---|
| VFR X IFR DVFR | CHIEF 4 | BH230/A | ** KTS | RYN TUCSON/RYAN FIELD | PROPOSED (Z) / ACTUAL (Z) | 11000 |

8. ROUTE OF FLIGHT

TUS, V202 SSO, V94 DMN, V110 TCS, V19 ABQ, AEG.

| 9. DESTINATION (Name of airport and city) AEG ALBUQUERQUE/DOUBLE EAGLE II | 10. EST. TIME ENROUTE HOURS / MINUTES | 11. REMARKS L/O = LEVEL OFF   PPH = POUNDS PER HOUR **CAS 125 ISA -6 TO +2 |
|---|---|---|

| 12. FUEL ON BOARD HOURS / MINUTES | 13. ALTERNATE AIRPORT(S) ABQ ALBUQERQUE INT'L | 14. PILOT'S NAME, ADDRESS & TELEPHONE NUMBER & AIRCRAFT HOME BASE 17. DESTINATION CONTACT/TELEPHONE (OPTIONAL) | 15. NUMBER ABOARD 9 |
|---|---|---|---|

| 16. COLOR OF AIRCRAFT ORANGE/BLACK | CIVIL AIRCRAFT PILOTS. FAR Part 91 requires you file an IFR flight plan to operate under instrument flight rules in controlled airspace. Failure to file could result in a civil penalty not to exceed $1,000 for each violation (Section 901 of the Federal Aviation Act of 1958, as amended). Filing of a VFR flight plan is recommended as a good operating practice. See also Part 99 for requirements concerning DVFR flight plans. |
|---|---|

FAA Form 7233-1 (8-82)    CLOSE VFR FLIGHT PLAN WITH _____ FSS ON ARRIVAL

## FLIGHT LOG

| CHECK POINTS | | ROUTE | COURSE | WIND | SPEED-KTS | | DIST | TIME | | FUEL | |
|---|---|---|---|---|---|---|---|---|---|---|---|
| FROM | TO | ALTITUDE | | TEMP | TAS | GS | NM | LEG | TOT | LEG | TOT |
| RYN | MESCA | | | | | | 38 | :17:00 | | 180* | |
| MESCA | CIE | V202 11000 | | 240/31 ISA-6 | | | | | | | |
| CIE | SSO | | | | | | | | | | |
| SSO | DMN | V94 11000 | | 250/27 ISA-1 | | | | | | | |
| DMN | TCS | V110 11000 | | | | | | | | | |
| TCS | ONM | V19 11000 | | 220/33 ISA+2 | | | | | | | |
| ONM | ABQ | | | | | | | | | | |
| ABQ | AEG | DIRECT DESCENT | | | | | 6 | :06:00 | | 49.0 | |
| AEG | ABQ | TWR-TWR 8000 | | | | | 11 | :05:00 | | | |

| OTHER DATA: NOTE: | * Includes Taxi Fuel Use 523 PPH Total Fuel Flow From L/O To Start Of Descent. Use 497 PPH Total Fuel Flow For Reserve And Alternate Requirements. A Missed Approach Requires 40# of Fuel. | TIME and FUEL: As required by FARs. |
|---|---|---|

| TIME | FUEL (LB) | |
|---|---|---|
| | | EN ROUTE |
| | | RESERVE |
| | | ALTERNATE |
| | | TOTAL |

FIGURE 162.—Flight Plan/Flight Log.

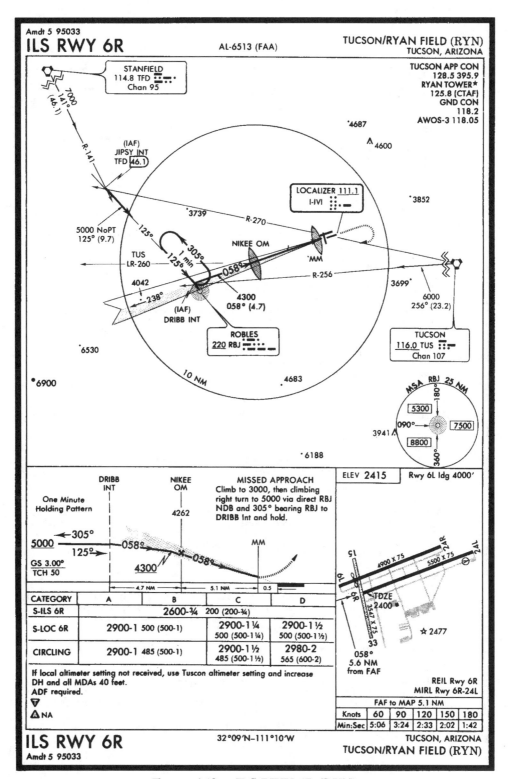

FIGURE 163.—ILS RWY 6R (RYN).

---

**TOYEI SCHOOL**   (See GANADO)

---

**TUBA CITY**   (T03)   5W   UTC–7   N36°05.57' W111°22.96'
  4513   B
  **RWY 15–33:** H6230X75 (ASPH)   S–12.5   MIRL
    **RWY 15:** PAPI(P2L)–GA 3.0° TCH 40'.     **RWY 33:** PAPI(P2L)–GA 3.0° TCH 40'.
  **AIRPORT REMARKS:** Unattended. Daylight operations only 1300–0100Z. Ngt operations not authorized. MIRL Rwy
    15–33 out of svc indefinitely. Livestock on airport.
  **COMMUNICATIONS: CTAF** 122.9
    **PRESCOTT FSS (PRC)** TF 1–800–WX–BRIEF. NOTAM FILE PRC.
    **RCO** 122.05R 113.5T (PRESCOTT FSS)
  **RADIO AIDS TO NAVIGATION:** NOTAM FILE PRC.
    **(H) VORTAC** 113.5   TBC   Chan 82   N36°07.28' W111°16.18'   238° 5.8 NM to fld. 4960/15E.

---

# TUCSON

**AVRA VALLEY**   (E14)   13 NW   UTC–7   N32°24.56' W111°13.11'
  2031   B   S3   **FUEL** 100LL, JET A
  **RWY 12–30:** H6901X100 (ASPH)
    **RWY 30:** Road. Rgt tfc.
  **RWY 03–21:** H4201X75 (ASPH)   MIRL
    **RWY 03:** VASI(V2L)–GA 3.0° TCH 43'. Thld dsplcd 295'. Road. Rgt tfc.
    **RWY 21:** VASI(V2L)–GA 3.0° TCH 31'. Tree.
  **AIRPORT REMARKS:** Attended 1400–0100Z. Parachute Jumping. Ditch apch end Rwy 21. Aerobatic activities 2–10
    miles south of arpt, surface 5000' MSL dalgt hours indefinitely. Extensive parachute training high and low levels
    all hours NW quadrant of arpt. ACTIVATE MIRL Rwy 03–21, VASI Rwy 03 and Rwy 21—CTAF. Note: See Special
    Notices—Glider Operations Northwest of Tucson, Arizona.
  **COMMUNICATIONS: CTAF/UNICOM** 123.0
    **PRESCOTT FSS (PRC)** TF 1–800–WX–BRIEF. NOTAM FILE PRC.
  **RADIO AIDS TO NAVIGATION:** NOTAM FILE PRC.
    **TUCSON (H) VORTACW** 116.0   TUS   Chan 107   N32°05.71' W110°54.89'   309° 24.3 NM to fld. 2670/12E.
      **HIWAS.**

- - - - - - - - - - - - - - - - - - - - - - - - - - - - - - - - - - - - - - - - - - - - - - - - - - -

**CASCABEL AIR PARK**   (05A)   35 N   UTC–7   N32°18.01' W110°21.91'
  3374
  **RWY 02–20:** 2750X60 (DIRT)
    **RWY 20:** Road.
  **AIRPORT REMARKS:** Unattended. Rwy 20 10' brush within primary surface. Rwy 02 25' power lines 1/2 mile south of
    rwy. –15' down slope beginning at end of Rwy 02.
  **COMMUNICATIONS: CTAF** 122.9
    **PRESCOTT FSS (PRC)** TF 1–800 WX–BRIEF. NOTAM FILE PRC.

- - - - - - - - - - - - - - - - - - - - - - - - - - - - - - - - - - - - - - - - - - - - - - - - - - -

**RYAN FLD**   (RYN)   10 SW   UTC–7   N32°08.53' W111°10.46'
  2415   B   S4   **FUEL** 80, 100LL   TPA—See Remarks
  **RWY 06R–24L:** H5500X75 (ASPH)   S–12.5, D–30   MIRL
    **RWY 06R:** REIL. Rgt tfc.     **RWY 24L:** VASI(V4L)–GA 3.0° TCH 26'.
  **RWY 06L–24R:** H4900X75 (ASPH)   S–12.5, D–30
    **RWY 06L:** Thld dsplcd 900'. Pole.     **RWY 24R:** Tree. Rgt tfc.
  **RWY 15–33:** 3547X75 (DIRT)
    **RWY 33:** Tree.
  **AIRPORT REMARKS:** Attended 1300–0100Z. Self svc fuel avbl 1300–0400Z. Rwy 06L–24R CLOSED 0100–1300Z. Rwy
    06R preferential rwy up to 10 knot tailwind. Rwy 06L–24R paved shoulders 30' wide both sides. TPA–3215(800),
    3415(1000) when twr closed. Note: See Special Notices—Glider Operations Northwest of Tucson, Arizona.
  **WEATHER DATA SOURCES: AWOS–3** 118.05 (602) 578-0269.
  **COMMUNICATIONS: CTAF** 125.8
    **PRESCOTT FSS (PRC)** TF 1–800–WX–BRIEF. NOTAM FILE PRC.
    ® **TUCSON APP/DEP CON** 128.5
    **TOWER** 125.8 NFCT (Apr–Sep 1300–0300Z, Oct–Mar 1300–0100Z)   **GND CON** 118.2
    **AIRSPACE: CLASS D** svc Apr–Sep 1300–0300Z, Oct–Mar 1300–0100Z other times **CLASS E.**
  **RADIO AIDS TO NAVIGATION:** NOTAM FILE PRC.
    **TUCSON (H) VORTACW** 116.0   TUS   Chan 107   N32°05.71' W110°54.89'   270° 13.5 NM to fld. 2670/12E.
      **HIWAS.**
    **NDB (HW–SAB)** 338   RYN   N32°08.30' W111°09.69'   at fld. TWEB avbl 1200–0500Z.
    **ILS** 111.1   I–IVI   Rwy 06R.   Unmonitored.

- - - - - - - - - - - - - - - - - - - - - - - - - - - - - - - - - - - - - - - - - - - - - - - - - - -

FIGURE 163A.—Excerpt from Airport/Facilities Directory.

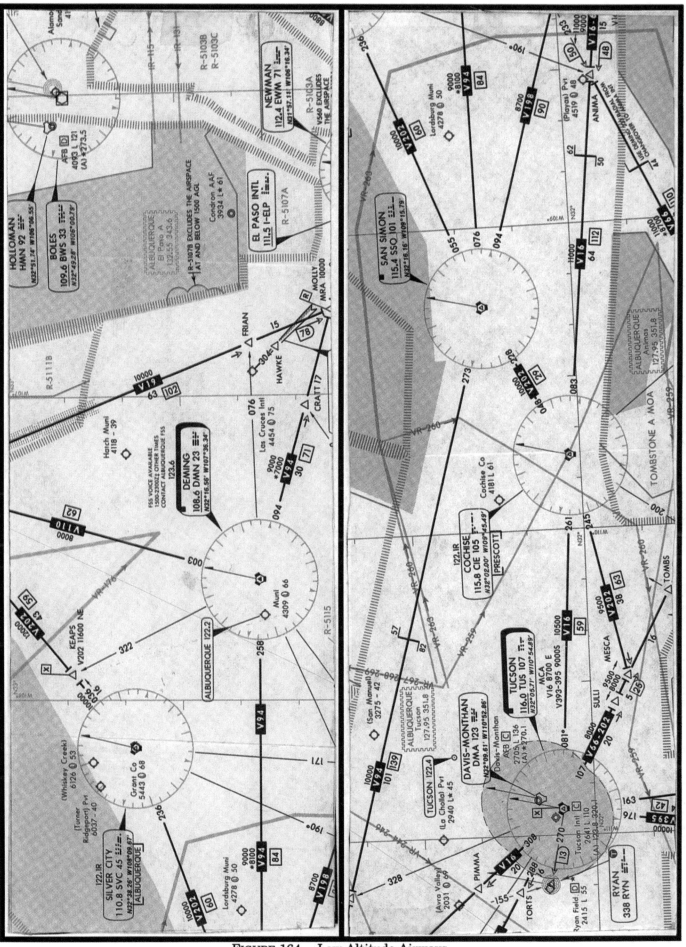

FIGURE 164.—Low Altitude Airways.

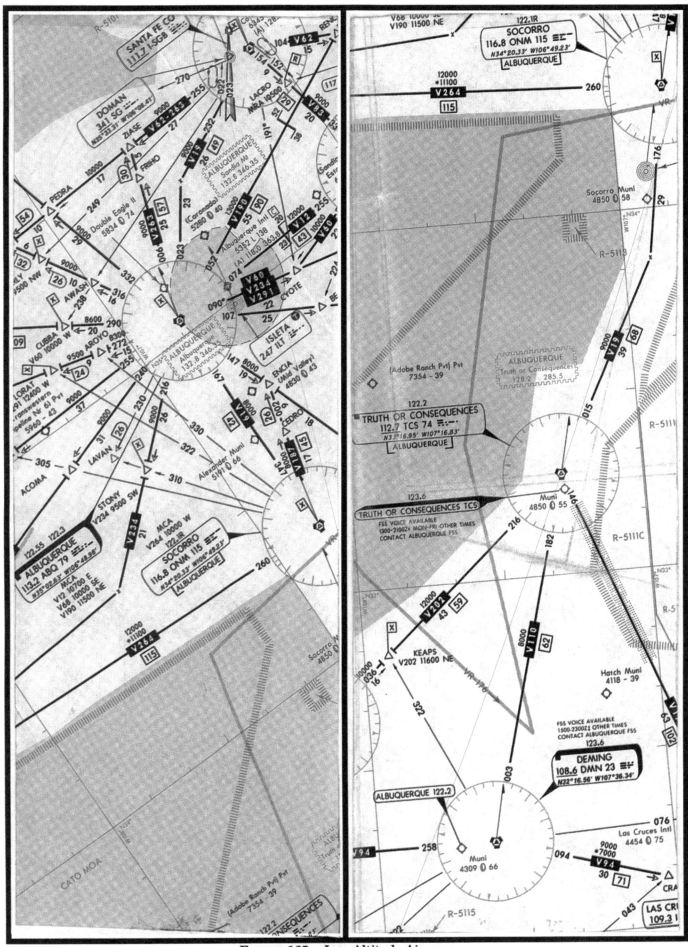

FIGURE 165.—Low Altitude Airways.

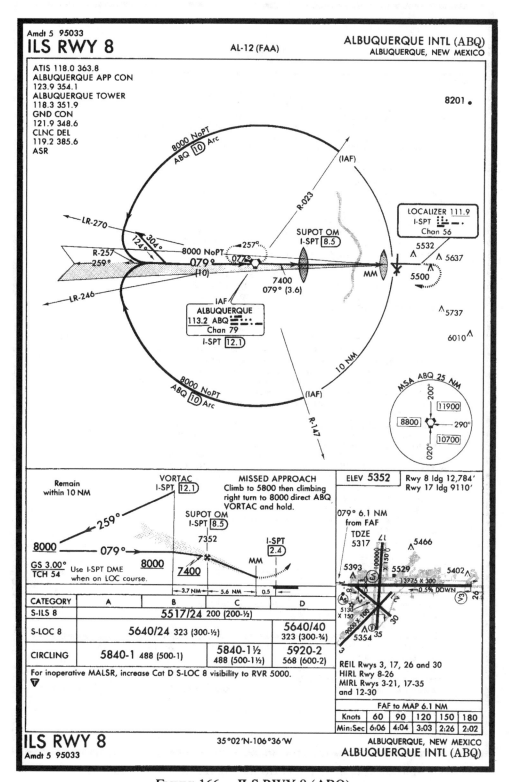

FIGURE 166.—ILS RWY 8 (ABQ).

## ALBUQUERQUE

**ALBUQUERQUE INTL** (ABQ) 3 SE UTC–7(–6DT) N35°02.45' W106°36.52'    **ALBUQUERQUE**
   5352 B S4 **FUEL** 100LL, JET A, A1, A1 + OX 1, 2, 3, 4 LRA ARFF Index C    **H–2D, L–4G, 6E**
   **RWY 08–26:** H13775X300 (ASPH–CONC–GRVD) S–100, D–210, DT–360 HIRL 0.3% up E    **IAP**
     **RWY 08:** MALSR. VASI(V6L)—GA 3.0° TCH 54'. Thld dsplcd 991'. Rgt tfc. Arresting device.
     **RWY 26:** REIL. VASI(V6L)—Upper GA 3.25° TCH 77'. Lower GA 3.0° TCH 47'. Arresting device.
   **RWY 17–35:** H10000X150 (ASPH–CONC–GRVD) S–100, D–210, DT–360 MIRL
     **RWY 17:** REIL. VASI(V4L)—GA 3.0° TCH 53'. Thld dsplcd 890'. Road. Rgt tfc.
     **RWY 35:** VASI(V4L)—GA 3.0° TCH 55'. Arresting device.
   **RWY 03–21:** H9000X100 (ASPH) S–45, D–65 MIRL
     **RWY 03:** REIL. Rgt tfc.
   **RWY 12–30:** H5130X150 (ASPH) S–45, D–65 MIRL
     **RWY 12:** Rgt tfc.    **RWY 30:** REIL.
   **RUNWAY DECLARED DISTANCE INFORMATION**

| | | | | |
|---|---|---|---|---|
| **RWY 03:** | TORA–9000 | TODA–9000 | ASDA–9000 | LDA–9000 |
| **RWY 21:** | TORA–9000 | TODA–9000 | ASDA–9000 | LDA–9000 |
| **RWY 08:** | TORA–13775 | TODA–13775 | ASDA–13775 | LDA–12784 |
| **RWY 26:** | TORA–13775 | TODA–13775 | ASDA–13775 | LDA–13775 |
| **RWY 12:** | TORA–5130 | TODA–5130 | ASDA–5130 | LDA–5130 |
| **RWY 30:** | TORA–5130 | TODA–5130 | ASDA–5130 | LDA–5130 |
| **RWY 17:** | TORA–10000 | TODA–10000 | ASDA–10000 | LDA–9110 |
| **RWY 35:** | TORA–10000 | TODA–10000 | ASDA–10000 | LDA–10000 |

   **AIRPORT REMARKS:** Attended continuously. Bird hazard Oct–Dec, and Mar–May. Heavy student copter traffic, control
     firing area S of arpt. Fighter acft depart S only, no military depart on Rwy 35. Rwy 03–21 SW 200' CLOSED to
     acft weighing over 12,500 pounds. Ramp W of Rwy 17–35 and N of Rwy 08–26 CLOSED to helicopters. Rwy
     08–26 and 17–35 grooved 130' wide. Takeoff Rwy 03 prohibited except for emergency conditions on fld.
     Takeoff Rwy 35 requires prior coordination with twr. Twy H closed between Twy G and Rwy 17–35 indefinitely.
     Twy F S of freight ramp closed to acft over 65,000 pounds. Twy F between Twy F1 and Twy C restricted to
     maximum wing span 108' B727 or smaller acft. Portions of Twy D N of Twy D–3 not visible from twr. Arresting
     cables at Rwy 26 thld. Recessed arresting cables at Rwy 08 and Rwy 35 thld. Flight Notification Service (ADCUS)
     available. NOTE: See Land and Hold Short Operations Section.
   **WEATHER DATA SOURCES:** LLWAS.
   **COMMUNICATIONS:** ATIS 118.0 (505) 856–4928   **UNICOM** 122.95
     ALBUQUERQUE FSS (ABQ) on arpt. 122.55 122.3 TF 1–800–WX–BRIEF. LC 505–243–7831. NOTAM FILE ABQ.
   Ⓡ **APP CON** 124.4 (on or N of V12 and W of SANDIA MTNS) 134.8 (S of V12 and W of Manzano Mtns) 123.9 (S of V12
     and E of Manzano Mtns) 127.4 (on or N of V12 and E of Sandia Mtns) 126.3
   Ⓡ **DEP CON** 127.4 (on or N of V12 and E of Sandia Mtns) 124.4 (on or N of V12 and W of Sandia Mtns) 123.9 (S of V12
     and E of Manzano Mtns) 134.8 (S of V12 and W of Manzano Mtns)
   **TOWER** 118.3 120.3   **GND CON** 121.9   **CLNC DEL** 119.2
   **AIRSPACE: CLASS C** svc ctc **APP CON**
   **RADIO AIDS TO NAVIGATION:** NOTAM FILE ABQ.
     **(H) VORTACW** 113.2 ABQ Chan 79 N35°02.63' W106°48.98' 078° 10.2 NM to fld. 5740/13E. **HIWAS.**
     **ISLETA NDB (HW)** 247 ILT N34°59.22' W106°37.22' 359° 3.3 NM to fld.
     **ILS/DME** 111.9 I–SPT Chan 56 Rwy 08.
     **ASR**

- - - - - - - - - - - - - - - - - - - - - - - - - - - - - - - - - - - - - - - - - - - -

  **CORONADO** (4AC) 6 NE UTC–7(–6DT) N35°11.75' W106°34.40'    **ALBUQUERQUE**
   5280 B S4 **FUEL** 100LL OX 3    **L–4G, 6E**
   **RWY 17–35:** H4010X60 (ASPH) S–22, D–28 LIRL (NSTD)
     **RWY 17:** Thld dsplcd 200'. Hill. Rgt tfc.    **RWY 35:** Thld dsplcd 200'. Trees.
   **RWY 03–21:** H3500X40 (ASPH) S–22, D–28
     **RWY 03:** Building.
   **AIRPORT REMARKS:** Attended continuously. Rising terrain East of airport. Rwy 03 rgt tfc for ultralight operations below
     300' and E of Rwy 17–35. Rwy 03–21 cracked and heavily weeded. ACTIVATE LIRL Rwy 17–35—CTAF.
   **COMMUNICATIONS: CTAF/UNICOM** 122.8
     ALBUQUERQUE FSS (ABQ) LC 243–7831 NOTAM FILE ABQ.
   **RADIO AIDS TO NAVIGATION:** NOTAM FILE ABQ.
     **ALBUQUERQUE (H) VORTACW** 113.2 ABQ Chan 79 N35°02.63' W106°48.98' 040° 15 NM to fld. 5740/13E.
     **HIWAS.**

- - - - - - - - - - - - - - - - - - - - - - - - - - - - - - - - - - - - - - - - - - - -

FIGURE 166A.—Excerpt from Airport/Facilities Directory.

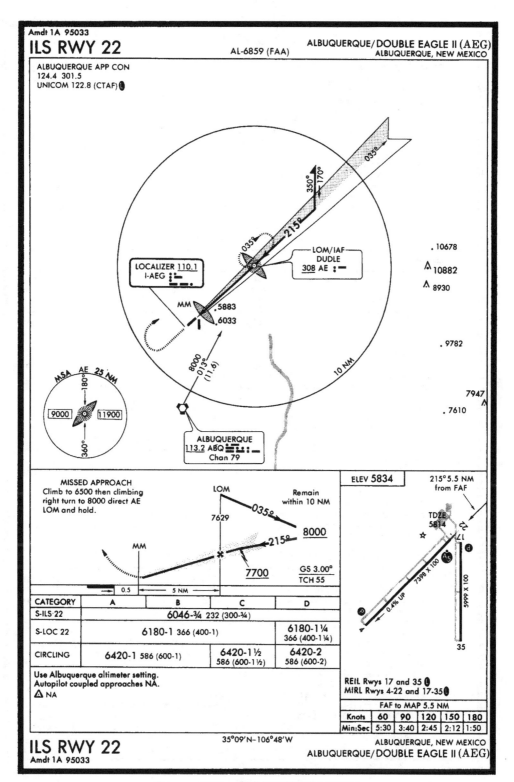

FIGURE 167.—ILS RWY 22 (AEG).

**DOUBLE EAGLE II**   (AEG)   7 NW   UTC–7(–6DT)   N35°08.71' W106°47.71'                   ALBUQUERQUE
  5834   B   S4   FUEL 100LL, JET A   OX 3                                                  H–2D, L–4G, 6E
  **RWY 04–22:** H7398X100 (ASPH)   S–30   MIRL   0.4% up SW                                IAP
    **RWY 04:** PAPI(P4L).   **RWY 22:** MALSR. Rgt tfc.
  **RWY 17–35:** H5999X100 (ASPH) S–30   MIRL
    **RWY 17:** REIL. PAPI(P4L).   **RWY 35:** REIL. Rgt tfc.
  **AIRPORT REMARKS:** Attended continuously. Fixed-base operator and arpt services 505–842–7007 or 505–836–7717.
    ACTIVATE MIRL Rwy 04–22 and Rwy 17–35, REIL Rwy 17 and Rwy 35 and MALSR Rwy 22 and PAPI Rwy 04
    and Rwy 17—CTAF.
  **COMMUNICATIONS: CTAF/UNICOM** 122.8
    ALBUQUERQUE FSS (ABQ) LC 243–7831. NOTAM FILE ABQ
  ® **ALBUQUERQUE APP/DEP CON** 124.4
  **RADIO AIDS TO NAVIGATION:** NOTAM FILE ABQ.
    **ALBUQUERQUE (H) VORTACW** 113.2   ABQ   Chan 79   N35°02.63' W106°48.98'   357° 6.2 NM to fld.
      5740/13E.   **HIWAS.**
    **DUDLE NDB (LOM)** 308   AE   N35°13.04' W106°42.77'   212° 5.9 NM to fld.
    **ILS** 110.1   I–AEG   Rwy 22   LOM DUDLE NDB. ILS unmonitored.

**ALEXANDER MUNI**   (See BELEN)

**ANTON CHICO**   N35°06.70' W105°02.40'   NOTAM FILE ABQ.                                  ALBUQUERQUE
  **(H) VORTAC** 117.8   ACH   Chan 125   105° 22.3 NM to Santa Rosa Muni. 5450/12E.        H–2D, L–4G, 6E
  **RCO** 122.1R 117.8T (ALBUQUERQUE FSS)

**ANGEL FIRE**   (AXX)   1 N   UTC–7(–6DT)   N36°25.24' W105°17.40'                          DENVER
  8382   S4   FUEL 100LL, JET A                                                             H–2D, L–6E
  **RWY 17–35:** H8900X100 (ASPH)   S–22   0.6% up S
    **RWY 17:** Ground.   **RWY 35:** Road.
  **AIRPORT REMARKS:** Attended dalgt hours. Airport located in mountain valley, rising terrain in all directions. Aerobatics
    will be conducted adjacent to and east of arpt 14,500' and below. Ramp asph surfaces deteriorated with
    numerous cracks and soft spots. Dirt berm located approximately 1700' up NW from rwy end 17 250 ft E of E
    NW edge.
  **COMMUNICATIONS: CTAF/UNICOM** 122.8
    ALBUQUERQUE FSS (ABQ) TF 1–800–WX–BRIEF. NOTAM FILE ABQ.
  **RADIO AIDS TO NAVIGATION:** NOTAM FILE ABQ.
    **TAOS (L) VORTAC** 117.6   TAS   Chan 123   N36°36.53' W105°54.38'   098° 31.9 NM to fld. 7860/13E.

**APACHE CREEK**
  **JEWETT MESA**   (Q13)   10 N   UTC–7(–6DT)   N34°00.20' W108°40.69'                      ALBUQUERQUE
  7681
  **RWY 06–24:** 5200X40 (DIRT)
    **RWY 06:** Pole.   **RWY 24:** Fence.
  **AIRPORT REMARKS:** Unattended. Arpt open May–Sep; other times CLOSED. Livestock on runway. Rwy 06–24
    recommend visual inspection before using, infrequent maintenance. Rwy 06–24 heavily weeded with large rocks
    on rwy edges + 2' rocks 45' from rwy centerline.
  **COMMUNICATIONS: CTAF** 122.9
    ALBUQUERQUE FSS (ABQ) TF 1–800–WX–BRIEF. NOTAM FILE ABQ.

**ARTESIA MUNI**   (ATS)   3 W   UTC–7(–6DT)   N32°51.15' W104°28.06'                        ALBUQUERQUE
  3548   B   S4   FUEL 100LL, JET A1                                                         H–2D, 5A, L–4H
  **RWY 03–21:** H6300X150 (ASPH–PFC)   S–40, D–57   MIRL   0.4% up SW                       IAP
    **RWY 03:** P-line.   **RWY 21:** PVASI(PSIL)—GA 3.0° TCH 25'. Road.
  **RWY 12–30:** H5399X150 (ASPH–PFC)   S–40, D–57   MIRL   0.5% up NW
    **RWY 12:** Fence.
  **AIRPORT REMARKS:** Attended 1400–0100Z‡. Fuel on call after hours 505–748–9053, 746–4196, 457–2399/2268, fee
    charged. MIRL Rwy 03–21 and Rwy 12–30 preset at low ints dusk–0800Z‡, ACTIVATE higher ints—CTAF. Rwys
    03–21 and 12–30 PFC center 75' width only.
  **WEATHER DATA SOURCES:** AWOS-3 126.725 (505) 748–2103.
  **COMMUNICATIONS: CTAF/UNICOM** 122.8
    ALBUQUERQUE FSS (ABQ) TF 1–800–WX–BRIEF. NOTAM FILE ABQ.
    **ROSWELL APP/DEP CON** 119.6 (1300–0400Z‡)   ® **ALBUQUERQUE CENTER APP/DEP CON** 132.65 (0400–1300Z‡)
  **RADIO AIDS TO NAVIGATION:** NOTAM FILE ROW.
    **CHISUM (H) VORTACW** 116.1   CME   Chan 108   N33°20.25' W104°37.28'   153° 30.1 NM to fld. 3770/12E.
      **HIWAS.**
    **NDB (MHW)** 414   ATS   N32°51.16' W104°27.70'   at fld. NOTAM FILE ABQ.

FIGURE 167A.—Excerpt from Airport/Facilities Directory.

Form Approved: OMB No. 2120-0034

## FLIGHT PLAN

U.S. DEPARTMENT OF TRANSPORTATION
FEDERAL AVIATION ADMINISTRATION

| (FAA USE ONLY) | ☐ PILOT BRIEFING | ☐ VNR | TIME STARTED | SPECIALIST INITIALS |
|---|---|---|---|---|
| | ☐ STOPOVER | | | |

| 1. TYPE | 2. AIRCRAFT IDENTIFICATION | 3. AIRCRAFT TYPE/ SPECIAL EQUIPMENT | 4. TRUE AIRSPEED | 5. DEPARTURE POINT | 6. DEPARTURE TIME | | 7. CRUISING ALTITUDE |
|---|---|---|---|---|---|---|---|
| ☐ VFR ☒ IFR ☐ DVFR | PTZ 70 | BE 1900/R | 247 KTS | KPWK CHICAGO/ PAL-WAUKEE | PROPOSED (Z) | ACTUAL (Z) | FL190 |

**8. ROUTE OF FLIGHT**

PAL-WAUKEE TWO DEPARTURE, PMM J547 BUF

| 9. DESTINATION (Name of airport and city) | 10. EST. TIME ENROUTE | | 11. REMARKS |
|---|---|---|---|
| BUF GREATER BUFFALO INT'L BUFFALO | HOURS | MINUTES | L/O = LEVEL OFF  PPH = POUNDS PER HOUR |

L/O PMM R-261/47
VARIATION: PWK 1W, FNT 3W, BUF 8W

| 12. FUEL ON BOARD | | 13. ALTERNATE AIRPORT(S) | 14. PILOT'S NAME, ADDRESS & TELEPHONE NUMBER & AIRCRAFT HOME BASE | 15. NUMBER ABOARD |
|---|---|---|---|---|
| HOURS | MINUTES | SYR | | |
| 3 | 35 | SYRACUSE HANCOCK INT'L | 17. DESTINATION CONTACT/TELEPHONE (OPTIONAL) | 13 |

| 16. COLOR OF AIRCRAFT | CIVIL AIRCRAFT PILOTS. FAR Part 91 requires you file an IFR flight plan to operate under instrument flight rules in controlled airspace. Failure to file could result in a civil penalty not to exceed $1,000 for each violation (Section 901 of the Federal Aviation Act of 1958, as amended). Filing of a VFR flight plan is recommended as a good operating practice. See also Part 99 for requirements concerning DVFR flight plans. |
|---|---|
| WHITE/BLACK | |

FAA Form 7233-1 (8-82)          CLOSE VFR FLIGHT PLAN WITH _____ FSS ON ARRIVAL

## FLIGHT LOG

| CHECK POINTS | | ROUTE | COURSE | WIND | SPEED-KTS | | DIST | TIME | | FUEL | |
|---|---|---|---|---|---|---|---|---|---|---|---|
| FROM | TO | ALTITUDE | | TEMP | TAS | GS | NM | LEG | TOT | LEG | TOT |
| PWK | L/O | VECTORS CLIMB | | | | | 49 | | :24:00 | 410* | |
| L/O | PMM | J547 FL190 | | 020/61 ISA | | | | | | | |
| PMM | FNT | | | | | | | | | | |
| FNT | YXU | | | | | | | | | | |
| YXU | BUF R-282/40 | | | | | | | | | | |
| BUF R-282/40 | BUF | J547 DESCENT | | | | | 40 | :19:00 | | 163 | |
| BUF | SYR | VECTORS 4000 | | | | | 112 | :30:00 | | | |
| | | | | | | | | | | | |

| OTHER DATA: NOTE: | * Includes Taxi Fuel | TIME and FUEL: As required by FARs. | | |
|---|---|---|---|---|
| | Use 676 PPH Total Fuel Flow From L/O To Start Of Descent. Use 726 PPH Total Fuel Flow for Reserve And Alternate Requirements. A Missed Approach Requires 76# of Fuel. | TIME | FUEL (LB) | |
| | | | | EN ROUTE |
| | | | | RESERVE |
| | | | | ALTERNATE |
| | | | | TOTAL |

FIGURE 168.—Flight Plan/Flight Log.

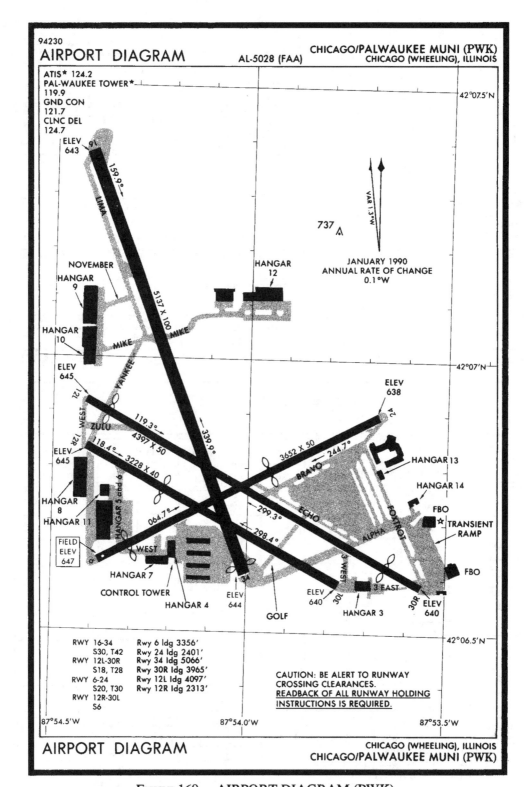

FIGURE 169.—AIRPORT DIAGRAM (PWK).

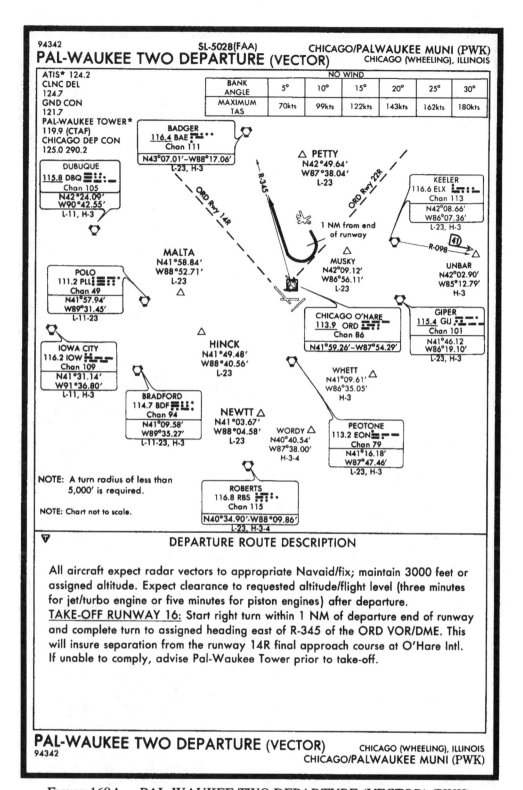

94342
SL-5028(FAA)
## PAL-WAUKEE TWO DEPARTURE (VECTOR)
CHICAGO/PALWAUKEE MUNI (PWK)
CHICAGO (WHEELING), ILLINOIS

ATIS* 124.2
CLNC DEL 124.7
GND CON 121.7
PAL-WAUKEE TOWER* 119.9 (CTAF)
CHICAGO DEP CON 125.0 290.2

| BANK ANGLE | NO WIND | | | | | |
|---|---|---|---|---|---|---|
| | 5° | 10° | 15° | 20° | 25° | 30° |
| MAXIMUM TAS | 70kts | 99kts | 122kts | 143kts | 162kts | 180kts |

BADGER
116.4 BAE
Chan 111
N43°07.01'–W88°17.06'
L-23, H-3

PETTY
N42°49.64'
W87°38.04'
L-23

KEELER
116.6 ELX
Chan 113
N42°08.66'
W86°07.36'
L-23, H-3

DUBUQUE
115.8 DBQ
Chan 105
N42°24.09'
W90°42.55'
L-11, H-3

ORD Rwy 14R
R-345
ORD Rwy 22R

1 NM from end of runway

R-098

MALTA
N41°58.84'
W88°52.71'
L-23

MUSKY
N42°09.12'
W86°56.11'
L-23

UNBAR
N42°02.90'
W85°12.79'
H-3

POLO
111.2 PLL
Chan 49
N41°57.94'
W89°31.45'
L-11-23

CHICAGO O'HARE
113.9 ORD
Chan 86
N41°59.26'–W87°54.29'

GIPER
115.4 GIJ
Chan 101
N41°46.12
W86°19.10'
L-23, H-3

HINCK
N41°49.48'
W88°40.56'
L-23

IOWA CITY
116.2 IOW
Chan 109
N41°31.14'
W91°36.80'
L-11, H-3

WHETT
N41°09.61'
W86°35.05'
H-3

BRADFORD
114.7 BDF
Chan 94
N41°09.58'
W89°35.27'
L-11-23, H-3

NEWTT
N41°03.67'
W88°04.58'
L-23

WORDY
N40°40.54'
W87°38.00'
H-3-4

PEOTONE
113.2 EON
Chan 79
N41°16.18'
W87°47.46'
L-23, H-3

NOTE: A turn radius of less than 5,000' is required.

NOTE: Chart not to scale.

ROBERTS
116.8 RBS
Chan 115
N40°34.90'-W88°09.86'
L-23, H-3-4

## DEPARTURE ROUTE DESCRIPTION

All aircraft expect radar vectors to appropriate Navaid/fix; maintain 3000 feet or assigned altitude. Expect clearance to requested altitude/flight level (three minutes for jet/turbo engine or five minutes for piston engines) after departure.

TAKE-OFF RUNWAY 16: Start right turn within 1 NM of departure end of runway and complete turn to assigned heading east of R-345 of the ORD VOR/DME. This will insure separation from the runway 14R final approach course at O'Hare Intl. If unable to comply, advise Pal-Waukee Tower prior to take-off.

## PAL-WAUKEE TWO DEPARTURE (VECTOR)
94342
CHICAGO (WHEELING), ILLINOIS
CHICAGO/PALWAUKEE MUNI (PWK)

FIGURE 169A.—PAL-WAUKEE TWO DEPARTURE (VECTOR) (PWK).

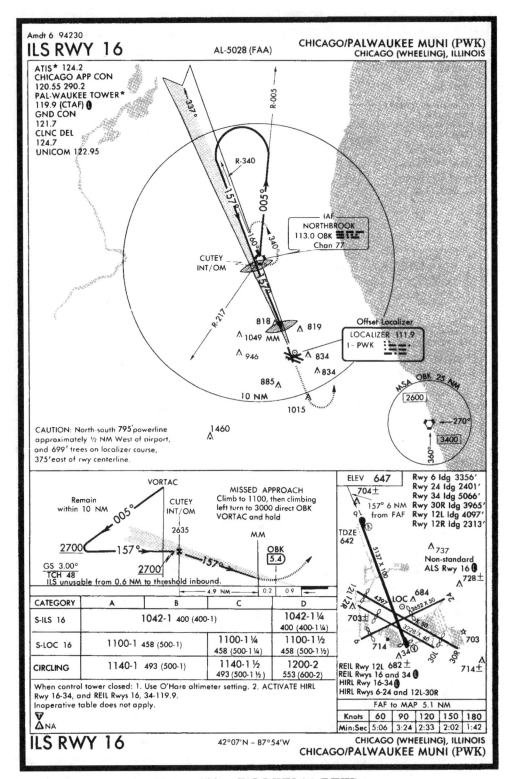

FIGURE 170.—ILS RWY 16 (PWK).

# ▽ TAKE-OFF MINS

94286

## CHICAGO, IL

### CHICAGO MIDWAY

TAKE-OFF MINIMUMS: Rwys 13R, 31L, 300-1. Rwy 13L, 300-1 or std. with min. climb of 300' per NM to 900. Rwy 31C, 300-1 or std. with min. climb of 330' per NM to 900. Rwy 31R, 300-1 or std. with min. climb of 225' per NM to 900. Rwy 22L, 300-1 or std. with min. climb of 400' per NM to 900. Rwy 22R, 300-1 or std. with min. climb of 340' per NM to 900.
DEPARTURE PROCEDURE: Rwys 4L, 4R, Northbound Departures (360° CW 080°), climbing right turn to 2400 heading 100° before proceeding on course. Rwys 22L, 22R, 31C, 31R, 31L, 13R, 13L, 13C, climb runway heading to 1300' before turning.

### CHICAGO-O'HARE INTL

TAKE-OFF MINIMUMS: Rwy 22R, 300-1. Rwy 32L, straight out or right turn, std.; left turn 1000-3 or std. with a min. climb of 240' per NM to 1800. Rwy 18, NA. Rwy 36, 500-1.

### LANSING MUNI

DEPARTURE PROCEDURE: Rwy 9, 300-1. Rwy 36, 400-1.

## CHICAGO/ROMEOVILLE, IL

### LEWIS UNIVERSITY

DEPARTURE PROCEDURE: Rwy 6, climb on heading 065° to 1200 before proceeding on course.

## CHICAGO/WAUKEGAN, IL

### WAUKEGAN REGIONAL

TAKE-OFF MINIMUMS: Rwy 14, 300-1.

## CHICAGO (WHEELING), IL

### PALWAUKEE MUNI

TAKE-OFF MINIMUMS: Rwys 6, 12L/R, 24, 30L/R, 34, 300-1.

## CLINTONVILLE, WI

### CLINTONVILLE MUNI

DEPARTURE PROCEDURE: Rwys 4, 9, climb on runway heading to 2000 before turning on course.

## DE KALB, IL

### DE KALB TAYLOR MUNI

TAKE-OFF MINIMUMS: Rwys 9, 27, 300-1.

## DECATUR, IL

### DECATUR

DEPARTURE PROCEDURE: Northbound Departures; Rwy 36, left turn, climb to 3000 via DEC R-340 before proceeding North. Rwy 30, right turn, climb to 3000 via DEC R-340 before proceeding North. Rwy 18, climb runway heading to 1200 before turning North. Rwys 6, 12, 24, climb runway heading to 1600 before turning North.

## DELAVAN, WI

### LAKE LAWN

TAKE-OFF MINIMUMS: Rwys 18, 36, 300-1.

## DIXON, IL

### DIXON MUNI-CHARLES R. WALGREEN FIELD

TAKE-OFF MINIMUMS: Rwys 26, 30, 300-1.

## EAU CLAIRE, WI

### CHIPPEWA VALLEY REGIONAL

TAKE-OFF MINIMUMS: Rwy 14, 500-1.
DEPARTURE PROCEDURE: Rwys 14, 22, climb runway heading to 2500 before turning southbound.

## EFFINGHAM, IL

### EFFINGHAM COUNTY MEMORIAL

TAKE-OFF MINIMUMS: Rwy 1, 500-1.
DEPARTURE PROCEDURE: Rwy 29, climb runway heading to 2100 before turning right.

## FAIRFIELD, IL

### FAIRFIELD MUNI

TAKE-OFF MINIMUMS: Rwy 9, 400-1.
DEPARTURE PROCEDURE: Rwy 36, climb runway heading to 2100 before turning right. Rwy 18, climb runway heading to 2100 before turning left. Rwy 27, climb runway heading to 1500 before turning eastbound. Rwy 9, climb to 2100 on heading 120° before proceeding eastbound or northbound.

## FLORA, IL

### FLORA MUNI

DEPARTURE PROCEDURE: Rwys 3, 33, climb runway heading to 1100' before turning left. Rwy 21, climb runway heading to 1100 before turning right.

## FOND DU LAC, WI

### FOND DU LAC COUNTY

DEPARTURE PROCEDURE: Rwy 9, climb runway heading to 2000 before turning North. Rwy 36, climb runway heading to 2000 before turning East.

## FRANKFORT, IL

### FRANKFORT

TAKE-OFF MINIMUMS: Rwy 27, 300-1.
DEPARTURE PROCEDURE: Rwy 9, climb runway heading to 1200 before turning northbound.

## GRANTSBURG, WI

### GRANTSBURG MUNI

TAKE-OFF MINIMUMS: Rwy 23, 300-1.

## GRAYSLAKE, IL

### CAMPBELL

TAKE-OFF MINIMUMS: Rwy 24, 300-1.
DEPARTURE PROCEDURE: Rwy 9, climb runway heading to 1200 before turning.

94286

EC-3

# ▽ TAKE-OFF MINS

FIGURE 170A.—TAKE-OFF MINS.

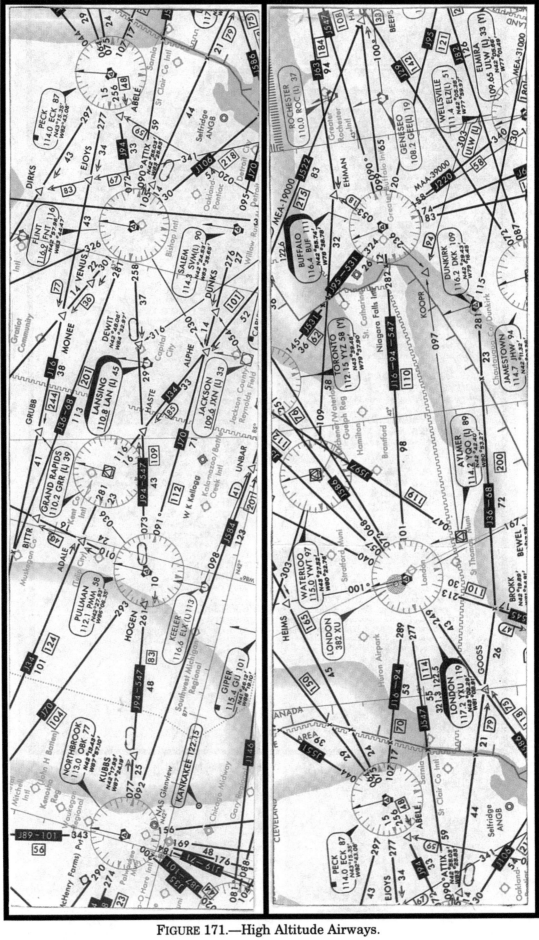

FIGURE 171.—High Altitude Airways.

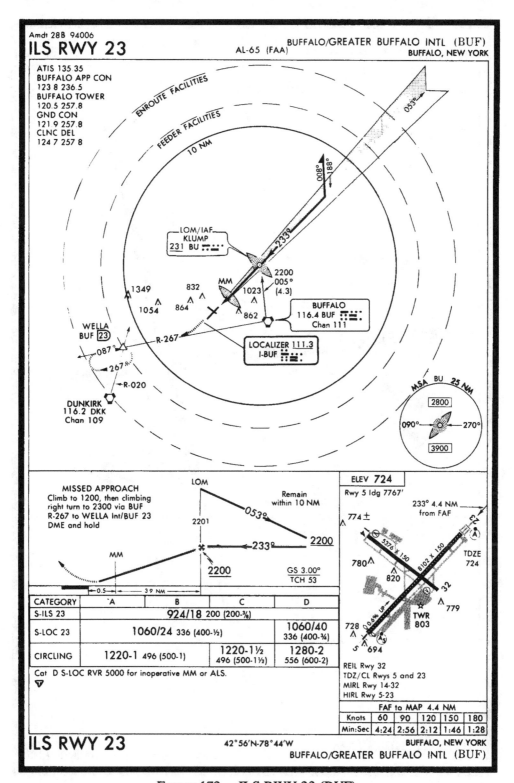

FIGURE 172.—ILS RWY 23 (BUF).

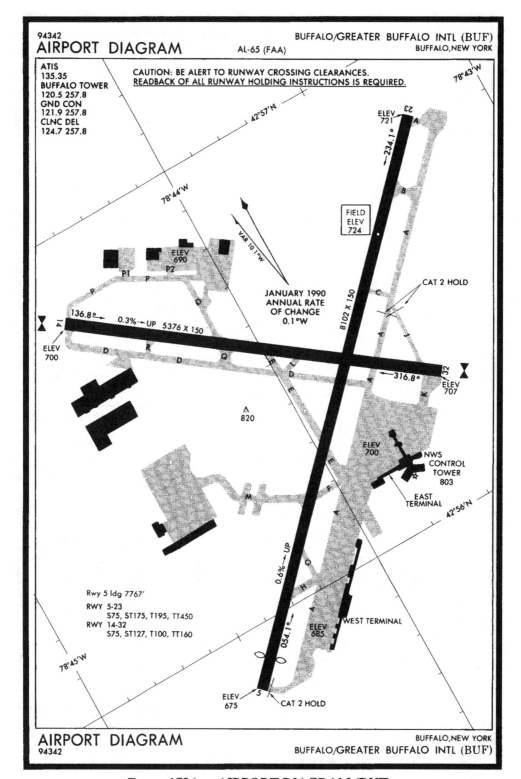

FIGURE 172A.—AIRPORT DIAGRAM (BUF).

**A** **ALTERNATE MINS** **A**
95033

INSTRUMENT APPROACH PROCEDURE CHARTS

**A** **IFR ALTERNATE MINIMUMS**
(NOT APPLICABLE TO USA/USN/USAF)

Standard alternate minimums for non precision approaches are 800-2 (NDB, VOR, LOC, TACAN, LDA, VORTAC, VOR/DME or ASR); for precision approaches 600-2 (ILS or PAR). Airports within this geographical area that require alternate minimums other than standard or alternate minimums with restrictions are listed below. NA - means alternate minimums are not authorized due to unmonitored facility or absence of weather reporting service. Civil pilots see FAR 91. USA/USN/USAF pilots refer to appropriate regulations.

| NAME | ALTERNATE MINIMUMS |
|---|---|

**ALBANY, NY**
ALBANY COUNTY ............................. ILS Rwy 1[1]
ILS Rwy 19[1]
VOR/DME or GPS Rwy 1[1]
VOR Rwy 1[2]
VOR or GPS Rwy 19[1]
VOR or GPS Rwy 28[1]
[1]Category D, 800-2½.
[2]Category C, 800-2¼; Category D, 800-2½.

**ALLENTOWN, PA**
LEHIGH VALLEY INTL ..................... ILS Rwy 13
ILS, Categories A,B,C, 700-2; Category D, 700-2¼. LOC, Category D, 800-2¼.

**ALTOONA, PA**
ALTOONA-BLAIR COUNTY ............ ILS Rwy 20[1]
VOR or GPS-A[2]
[1]Categories A,B,C, 900-2½, Category D, 1100-3.
[2]Category D, 1100-3.

**BRADFORD, PA**
BRADFORD
REGIONAL ............... VOR/DME or GPS Rwy 14
NA when BFD FSS closed.

**CORTLAND, NY**
CORTLAND COUNTY-
CHASE FIELD ............................ VOR or GPS-A
Categories A,B, 1100-2,Categories C,D, 1100-3.

**DUBOIS, PA**
DUBOIS-JEFFERSON COUNTY ..... ILS Rwy 25
LOC, NA.

**ELMIRA, NY**
ELMIRA/CORNING REGIONAL ....... ILS Rwy 6[12]
ILS Rwy 24,1200-3
NDB or GPS Rwy 24,1200-3
[1]Categories A,B, 1200-2; Categories C,D, 1200-3.
[2]NA when control tower closed.

**ERIE, PA**
ERIE INTL ........................................ ILS Rwy 6[1]
ILS Rwy 24[1]
NDB Rwy 6
NDB Rwy 24
RADAR-1
NA when control tower closed.
[1]ILS, 700-2.

**FARMINGDALE, NY**
REPUBLIC ...................................... ILS Rwy 14[1]
NDB or GPS Rwy 1[2]
[1]NA when control tower closed.
[2]NA when control zone not effective.

**HARRISBURG, PA**
CAPITAL CITY .................................. ILS Rwy 8
Categories A,B, 900-2; Categories C,D, 900-2¾.
NA when control tower closed.

HARRISBURG INTL ........................ ILS Rwy 13[1]
ILS Rwy 31[1]
VOR or GPS Rwy 31[2]
[1]ILS, Categories C,D, 700-2. LOC, NA.
[2]Categories A,B, 900-2, Category C, 900-2¾, Category D, 900-3.

NE-2

**A** **ALTERNATE MINS** **A**
95033

FIGURE 173.—IFR ALTERNATE MINIMUMS.

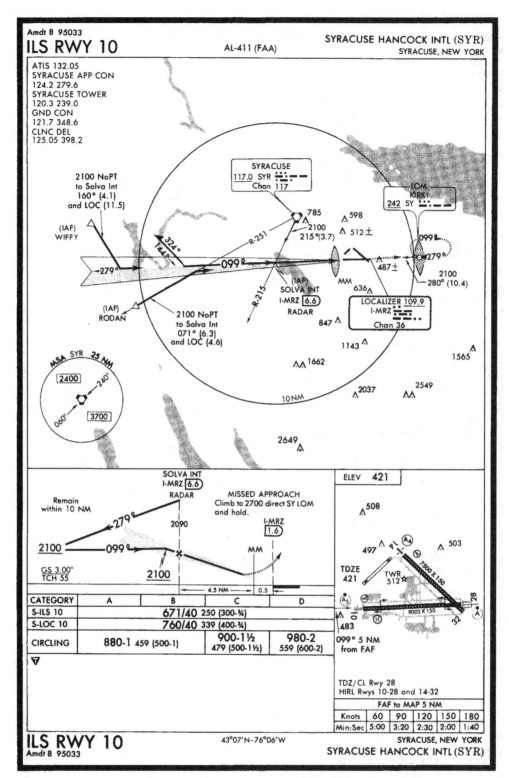

FIGURE 173A.—ILS RWY 10 (SYR).

Form Approved: OMB No. 2120-0034

| U.S. DEPARTMENT OF TRANSPORTATION FEDERAL AVIATION ADMINISTRATION **FLIGHT PLAN** | (FAA USE ONLY) | ☐ PILOT BRIEFING ☐ STOPOVER | ☐ VNR | TIME STARTED | SPECIALIST INITIALS |
|---|---|---|---|---|---|

| 1. TYPE | 2. AIRCRAFT IDENTIFICATION | 3. AIRCRAFT TYPE/ SPECIAL EQUIPMENT | 4. TRUE AIRSPEED | 5. DEPARTURE POINT | 6. DEPARTURE TIME | | 7. CRUISING ALTITUDE |
|---|---|---|---|---|---|---|---|
| VFR / X IFR / DVFR | SEA HAWK 1 | BH230/R | ** KTS | LWS LEWISTON-ZEZ PERCE CO. | PROPOSED (Z) | ACTUAL (Z) | *** 12000 |

**8. ROUTE OF FLIGHT**

POTOR2.CLOVA, V520PSC, V204YKM, V4 SEA, V27 ULESS, HQ, HQM

| 9. DESTINATION (Name of airport and city) HQM BOWERMAN HOQUIAM, WA | 10. EST. TIME ENROUTE | | 11. REMARKS L/O = LEVEL OFF   PPH = POUNDS PER HOUR |
|---|---|---|---|
| | HOURS | MINUTES | **CAS 132   ISA - 8 TO ±0  *** AFTER SEA DESCEND TO 4000 FEET |

| 12. FUEL ON BOARD | | 13. ALTERNATE AIRPORT(S) OLM OLYMPIA, WA | 14. PILOT'S NAME, ADDRESS & TELEPHONE NUMBER & AIRCRAFT HOME BASE | 15. NUMBER ABOARD |
|---|---|---|---|---|
| HOURS | MINUTES | | 17. DESTINATION CONTACT/TELEPHONE (OPTIONAL) | 8 |

| 16. COLOR OF AIRCRAFT YELLOW/BLACK | CIVIL AIRCRAFT PILOTS. FAR Part 91 requires you file an IFR flight plan to operate under instrument flight rules in controlled airspace. Failure to file could result in a civil penalty not to exceed $1,000 for each violation (Section 901 of the Federal Aviation Act of 1958, as amended). Filing of a VFR flight plan is recommended as a good operating practice. See also Part 99 for requirements concerning DVFR flight plans. |
|---|---|

FAA Form 7233-1 (8-82)      CLOSE VFR FLIGHT PLAN WITH _____ FSS ON ARRIVAL

---

## FLIGHT LOG

| CHECK POINTS | | ROUTE | | WIND | SPEED-KTS | | DIST | TIME | | FUEL | |
|---|---|---|---|---|---|---|---|---|---|---|---|
| FROM | TO | ALTITUDE | COURSE | TEMP | TAS | GS | NM | LEG | TOT | LEG | TOT |
| LWS | MQG | POTOR2.CLOVA CLIMB | | | | | 15 | :15:00 | | 191* | |
| MQG | ALW | V520 12000 | | 340/40 ISA-8 | | | | | | | |
| ALW | PSC | V520 12000 | | 340/40 ISA-3 | | | | | | | |
| PSC | YKM | V204 12000 | | 320/35 ISA-3 | | | | | | | |
| YKM | SEA | V4 12000 | | 300/29 ISA+1 | | | | | | | |
| SEA | ULESS | V27 4000 | | 280/7 ISA | | | | | | | |
| ULESS | HQ | DIRECT DESCENT | | | | | | :02:00 | | 16.0 | |
| HQ | HQM | DIRECT DESCENT | | | | | | :04:00 | | 32.0 | |
| HQM | OLM | V204 5000 | | 270/16 ISA | 158 | 42 | | | | | |

| OTHER DATA: | * Includes Taxi Fuel | TIME and FUEL: As required by FARs. |
|---|---|---|

NOTE: Use 525 PPH Total Fuel Flow From L/O To Start Of Descent. Use 499 PPH Total Fuel Flow For Reserve And Alternate Requirements.

A Missed Approach Requires 40# of Fuel.

| TIME | FUEL (LB) | |
|---|---|---|
| | | EN ROUTE |
| | | RESERVE |
| | | ALTERNATE |
| | | TOTAL |

FIGURE 174.—Flight Plan/Flight Log.

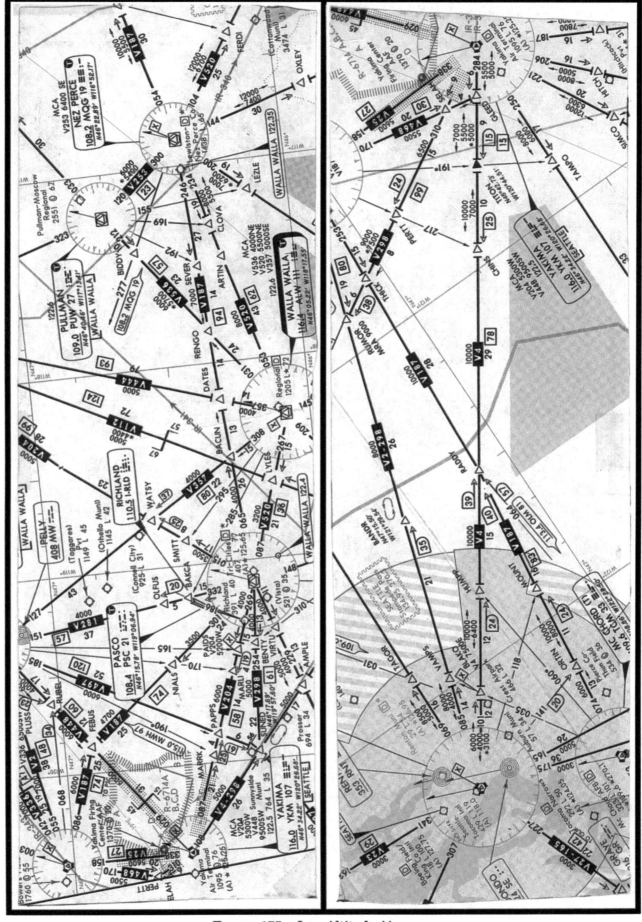

**FIGURE 175.—Low Altitude Airways.**

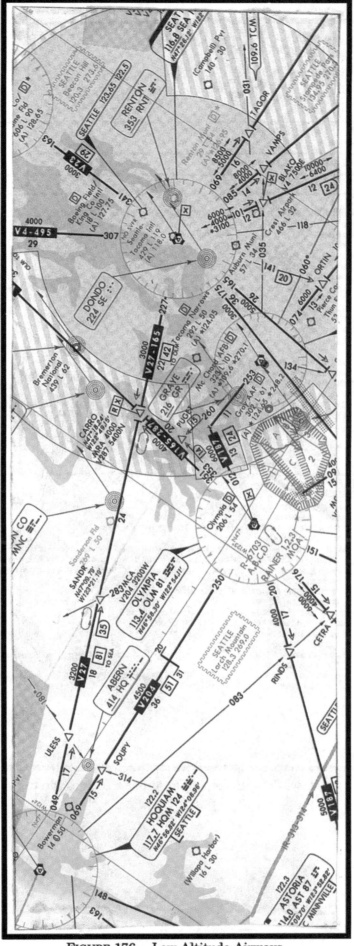

FIGURE 176.—Low Altitude Airways.

26                                          IDAHO                                          GREAT FALLS

**LEENY**   N47°44.57' W116°57.66'.   NOTAM FILE COE.
NDB (LOM) 347   CO   053° 6.0 NM to Coeur D'Alene Air Terminal.

**LEE WILLIAMS MEM**   (See MIDVALE)

**LEMHI CO**   (See SALMON)

# LEWISTON
**LEWISTON-NEZ PERCE CO**   (LWS)   2 S   UTC−8(−7DT)   N46°22.47' W117°00.92'                    SEATTLE
   1438   B   S4   FUEL 100, 100LL, JET A   TPA—See Remarks   ARFF Index A                        H−1B, L−9A
   RWY 08−26: H6512X150 (ASPH−PFC)   S−150, D−180, DT−400   HIRL                                    IAP
      RWY 08: REIL. VASI(V4R)—GA 3.0° TCH 45'. Antenna. Rgt tfc.        RWY 26: MALSR. Tree.
   RWY 11−29: H5001X100 (ASPH)   S−70, D−94, DT−150   MIRL
      RWY 11: REIL. Rgt tfc.        RWY 29: VASI(V4R)—GA 3.0° TCH 47'.
   AIRPORT REMARKS: Attended 1330−0500Z‡. CLOSED to unscheduled air carrier ops with more than 30 passenger
      seats 1500−0100Z‡ except PPR call arpt manager 208−746−7962 other times call station number 4
      208−743−0172. TPA—turbine powered heavy acft 3000 (1562) all others 2500 (1062). When twr clsd ACTIVATE
      MALSR Rwy 26, REIL Rwy 08 and Rwy 11—CTAF.
   WEATHER DATA SOURCES: LAWRS.
   COMMUNICATIONS: CTAF 119.4   UNICOM 122.95
      BOISE FSS (BOI) TF 1−800−WX−BRIEF. NOTAM FILE LWS.
      RCO 122.35 (BOISE FSS)
      SEATTLE CENTER APP/DEP CON 120.05
      TOWER 119.4 (1400−0600Z‡)   GND CON 121.9
   AIRSPACE: CLASS D svc effective 1400−0600Z‡ other times CLASS G.
   RADIO AIDS TO NAVIGATION: NOTAM FILE LWS.
      NEZ PERCE (L) VORW/DME 108.2   MQG   Chan 19   N46°22.89' W116°52.17'   246° 6.1 NM to fld. 1720/20E.
      ILS 109.7   I−LWS   Rwy 26.   ILS unmonitored when tower closed.

                                        WASHINGTON                                          105

# HOQUIAM
**BOWERMAN**   (HQM)   2 W   UTC−8(−7DT)   N46°58.27' W123°56.19'                              SEATTLE
   14   B   S4   FUEL 80, 100LL, JET A1+   LRA                                                    L−1C
   RWY 06−24: H4999X150 (ASPH)   S−30, D−40, DT−80   HIRL                                         IAP
      RWY 06: MALSR. REIL. VASI(V4L)—GA 3.0° TCH 52'. Antenna. Rgt tfc.
      RWY 24: VASI(V4L)—GA 3.0° TCH 50'. Sign.
   AIRPORT REMARKS: Attended 1600−0200Z‡. Fuel avbl between 0100−1700Z‡, call 533−6655, call−out fee required.
      CAUTION—Flocks of waterfowl on and in vicinity of arpt. Service road south of rwy in primary surface. Ultralights
      prohibited without written permission from arpt manager. ACTIVATE HIRL Rwy 06−24 and REIL Rwy 06—CTAF.
   COMMUNICATIONS: CTAF/UNICOM 122.7
      SEATTLE FSS (SEA) TF 1−800−WX−BRIEF. NOTAM FILE HQM.
      RCO 122.2 (SEATTLE FSS)
   AIRSPACE: CLASS E svc effective 1400−0600Z‡ other times CLASS G.
   RADIO AIDS TO NAVIGATION: NOTAM FILE HQM. VHF/DF ctc FSS.
      HOQUIAM (H) VORTACW 117.7   HQM   Chan 124   N46°56.82' W124°08.96'   062° 8.9 NM to fld. 10/19E.
      HIWAS.
      ABERN NDB (LOM) 414   HQ   N46°59.26' W123°47.86'   241° 5.8 NM to fld. Unmonitored 0600−1400Z‡. Out of
      service indefinitely.
      ILS/DME 108.7   I−HQM   Chan 24   Rwy 24   LOM ABERN NDB. LOM out of service indefinitely.
      LOC/LOM/DME unmonitored 0600−1400Z‡.

FIGURE 177.—Excerpt from Airport/Facilities Directory.

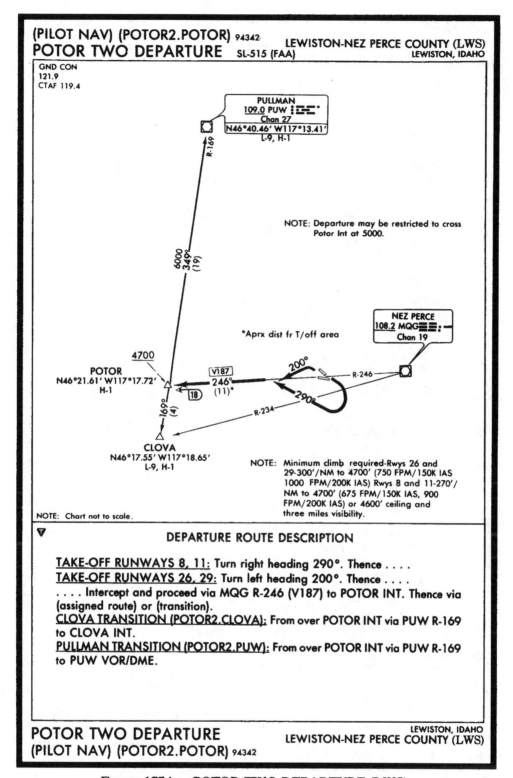

**(PILOT NAV) (POTOR2.POTOR)** 94342   LEWISTON-NEZ PERCE COUNTY (LWS)
**POTOR TWO DEPARTURE**   SL-515 (FAA)   LEWISTON, IDAHO

GND CON
121.9
CTAF 119.4

PULLMAN
109.0 PUW
Chan 27
N46°40.46' W117°13.41'
L-9, H-1

R-169

6000
349°
(19)

NOTE: Departure may be restricted to cross
Potor Int at 5000.

NEZ PERCE
108.2 MQG
Chan 19

*Aprx dist fr T/off area

4700

200°

POTOR
N46°21.61' W117°17.72'
H-1

V187
246°
(11)*

R-246

18

169°
(4)

290°

R-234

CLOVA
N46°17.55' W117°18.65'
L-9, H-1

NOTE: Minimum climb required-Rwys 26 and
29-300'/NM to 4700' (750 FPM/150K IAS
1000 FPM/200K IAS) Rwys 8 and 11-270'/
NM to 4700' (675 FPM/150K IAS, 900
FPM/200K IAS) or 4600' ceiling and
three miles visibility.

NOTE: Chart not to scale.

## DEPARTURE ROUTE DESCRIPTION

**TAKE-OFF RUNWAYS 8, 11:** Turn right heading 290°. Thence . . . .
**TAKE-OFF RUNWAYS 26, 29:** Turn left heading 200°. Thence . . . .
. . . . Intercept and proceed via MQG R-246 (V187) to POTOR INT. Thence via
(assigned route) or (transition).
**CLOVA TRANSITION (POTOR2.CLOVA):** From over POTOR INT via PUW R-169
to CLOVA INT.
**PULLMAN TRANSITION (POTOR2.PUW):** From over POTOR INT via PUW R-169
to PUW VOR/DME.

**POTOR TWO DEPARTURE**   LEWISTON, IDAHO
**(PILOT NAV) (POTOR2.POTOR)** 94342   LEWISTON-NEZ PERCE COUNTY (LWS)

FIGURE 177A.—POTOR TWO DEPARTURE (LWS).

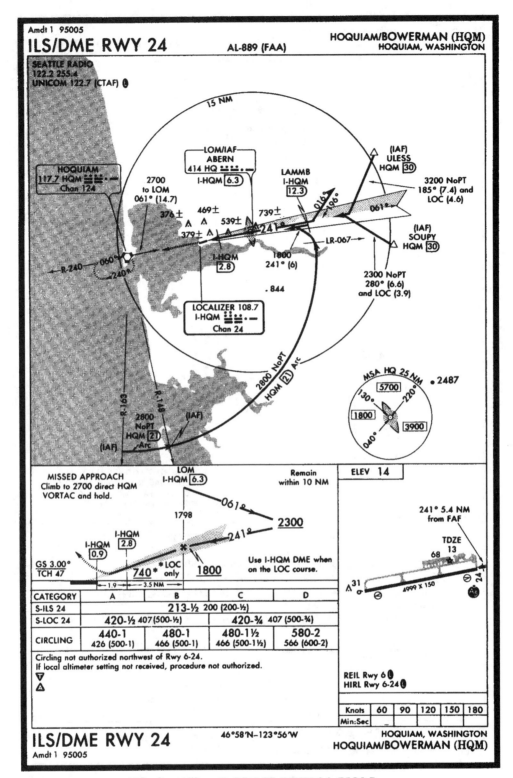

FIGURE 178.—ILS/DME RWY 24 (HQM).

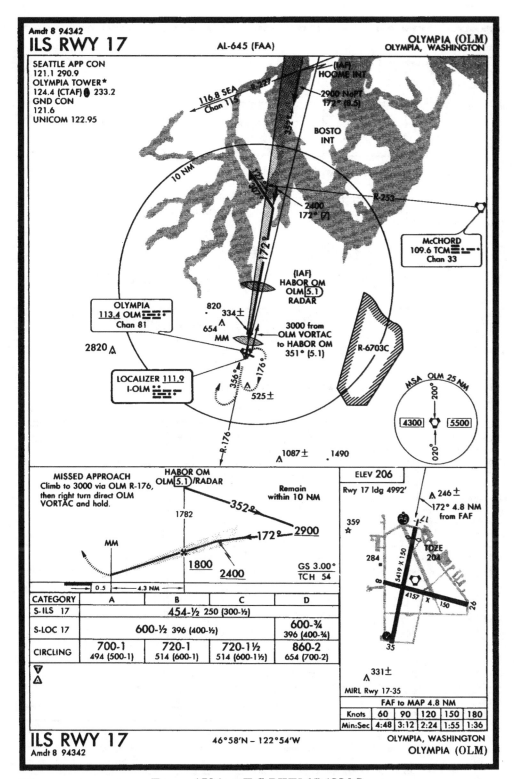

FIGURE 178A.—ILS RWY 17 (OLM).

Form Approved: OMB No. 2120-0034

## FLIGHT PLAN

U.S. DEPARTMENT OF TRANSPORTATION
FEDERAL AVIATION ADMINISTRATION

| (FAA USE ONLY) | ☐ PILOT BRIEFING | ☐ VNR | TIME STARTED | SPECIALIST INITIALS |
|---|---|---|---|---|
| | ☐ STOPOVER | | | |

| 1. TYPE | 2. AIRCRAFT IDENTIFICATION | 3. AIRCRAFT TYPE/ SPECIAL EQUIPMENT | 4. TRUE AIRSPEED | 5. DEPARTURE POINT | 6. DEPARTURE TIME | | 7. CRUISING ALTITUDE |
|---|---|---|---|---|---|---|---|
| VFR | | | | KPHF | PROPOSED (Z) | ACTUAL (Z) | |
| X IFR | BAB 90 | BE1900/A | 236 | | | | FL190 |
| DVFR | | | KTS | NEWPORT NEWS, VA | | | |

**8. ROUTE OF FLIGHT**

HENRY ONE ORF, J121 SIE, SIE. VCN5 PHL.

| 9. DESTINATION (Name of airport and city) KPHL PHILADELPHIA INT'L PHILADELPHIA | 10. EST. TIME ENROUTE | | 11. REMARKS |
|---|---|---|---|
| | HOURS | MINUTES | VARIATION: PHF 7°W, PHL 10°W. |
| | | | TEC = TOWER ENROUTE CONTROL   PPH = Pounds Per Hour |

| 12. FUEL ON BOARD | | 13. ALTERNATE AIRPORT(S) | 14. PILOT'S NAME, ADDRESS & TELEPHONE NUMBER & AIRCRAFT HOME BASE | 15. NUMBER ABOARD |
|---|---|---|---|---|
| HOURS | MINUTES | KACY ATLANTIC CITY INT'L | | |
| 2 | 45 | | 17. DESTINATION CONTACT/TELEPHONE (OPTIONAL) | 13 |

| 16. COLOR OF AIRCRAFT BLUE/RED | CIVIL AIRCRAFT PILOTS. FAR Part 91 requires you file an IFR flight plan to operate under instrument flight rules in controlled airspace. Failure to file could result in a civil penalty not to exceed $1,000 for each violation (Section 901 of the Federal Aviation Act of 1958, as amended). Filing of a VFR flight plan is recommended as a good operating practice. See also Part 99 for requirements concerning DVFR flight plans. |
|---|---|

FAA Form 7233-1 (8-82)       CLOSE VFR FLIGHT PLAN WITH _____ FSS ON ARRIVAL

## FLIGHT LOG

| CHECK POINTS | | ROUTE | COURSE | WIND | SPEED-KTS | | DIST | TIME | | FUEL | |
|---|---|---|---|---|---|---|---|---|---|---|---|
| FROM | TO | ALTITUDE | | TEMP | TAS | GS | NM | LEG | TOT | LEG | TOT |
| PHF | ORF | VECTORS CLIMB | | | | | 40 | | :19:00 | | 312* |
| ORF | SAWED | J/21 FL190 | | 300/70 ISA+5 | | | | | | | |
| SAWED | SWL | | | | | | | | | | |
| SWL | SIE | | | | | | | | | | |
| SIE | VCN | | | | | | | | | | |
| VCN | OOD | | | | | | | | | | |
| OOD | PHL | DESCENT & APPROACH | | | | | 30 | :16:00 | | 177 | |
| | | | | | | | | | | | |
| PHL | ACY | TEC 3000 | | | | | 46 | :18:00 | | | |

| OTHER DATA: NOTE: | * Includes Taxi Fuel Use 689 PPH Total Fuel Flow From L/O To Start Of Descent. Use 739 PPH Total Fuel Flow For Reserve And Alternate Requirements. A Missed Approach Requires 95# of Fuel. | TIME and FUEL: As required by FARs. |
|---|---|---|

| TIME | FUEL (LB) | |
|---|---|---|
| | | EN ROUTE |
| | | RESERVE |
| | | ALTERNATE |
| | | TOTAL |

FIGURE 179.—Flight Plan/Flight Log.

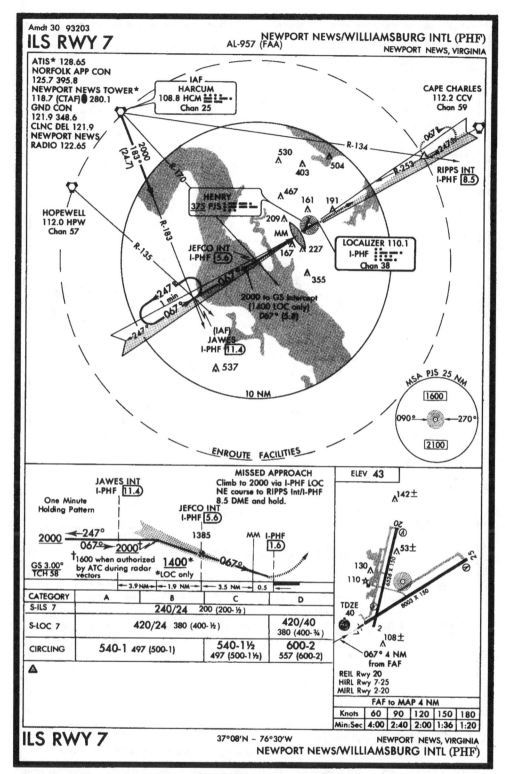

FIGURE 180.—ILS RWY 7 (PHF).

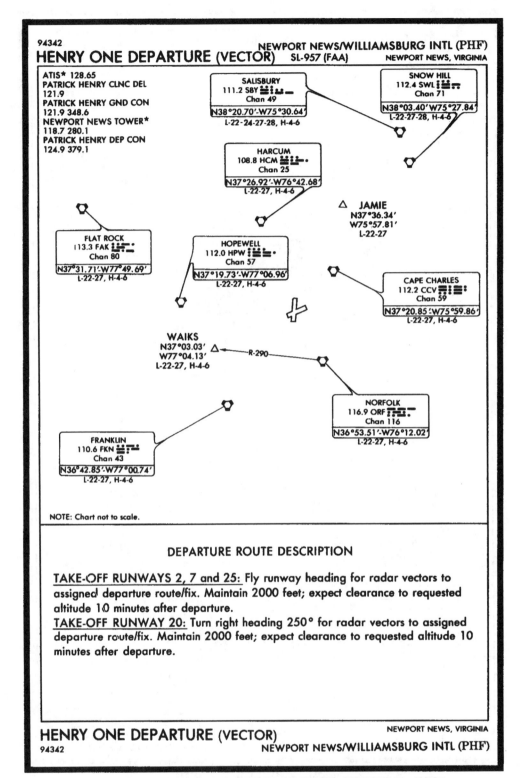

FIGURE 180A.—HENRY ONE DEPARTURE (VECTOR) (PHF).

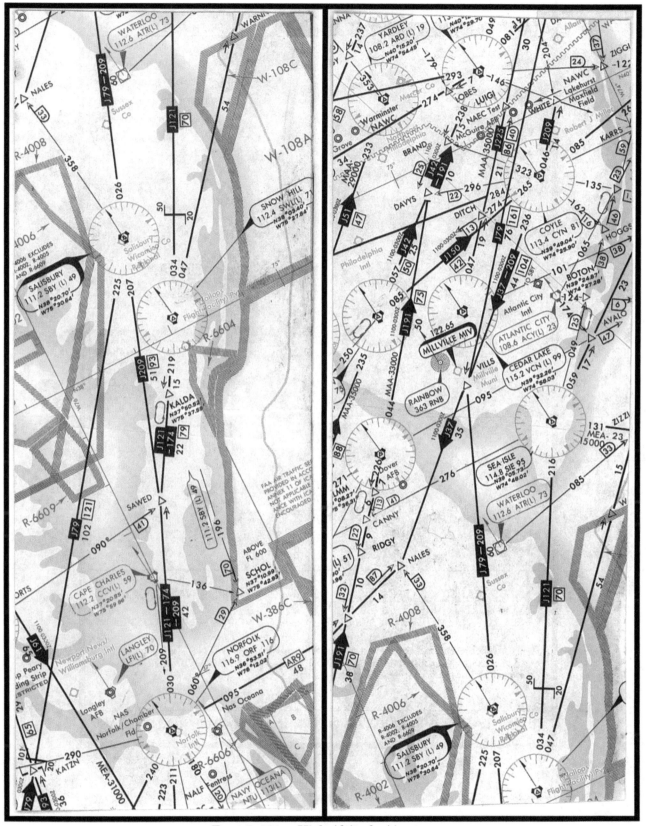

FIGURE 181.—High Altitude Airways.

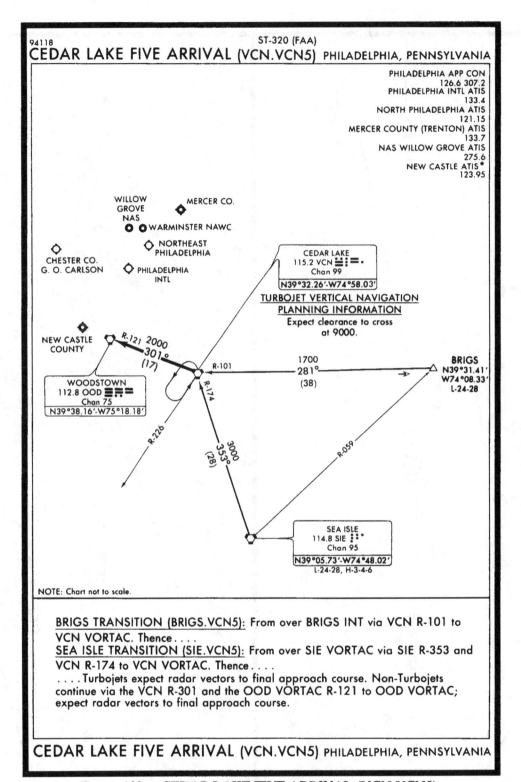

FIGURE 182.—CEDAR LAKE FIVE ARRIVAL (VCN.VCN5).

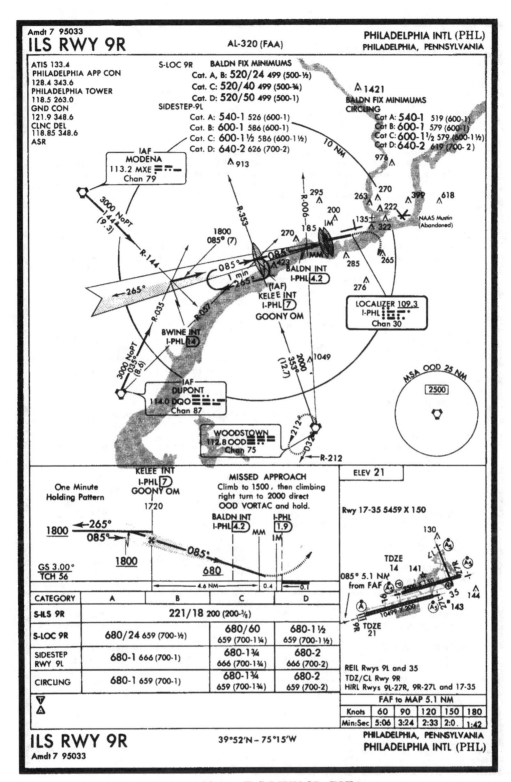

FIGURE 182A.—ILS RWY 9R (PHL).

**Appendix 2**

INSTRUMENT APPROACH PROCEDURE CHARTS

 IFR  ALTERNATE MINIMUMS

(NOT APPLICABLE TO USA/USN/USAF)

Standard alternate minimums for non precision approaches are 800-2 (NDB, VOR, LOC, TACAN, LDA, VORTAC, VOR/DME or ASR); for precision approaches 600-2 (ILS or PAR). Airports within this geographical area that require alternate minimums other than standard or alternate minimums with restrictions are listed below. NA - means alternate minimums are not authorized due to unmonitored facility or absence of weather reporting service. Civil pilots see FAR 91. USA/USN/USAF pilots refer to appropriate regulations.

| NAME | ALTERNATE MINIMUMS |
|---|---|

**ATLANTIC CITY, NJ**
ATLANTIC CITY INTL ..................... ILS Rwy 13[1]
RADAR-1[2]
VOR/DME or GPS Rwy 22[3]
VOR or GPS Rwy 4[3]
VOR or GPS Rwy 13[3]
VOR or GPS Rwy 31[3]
[1]ILS, Category D, 700-2; Category E, 700-2½.
  LOC, Category E, 800-2½.
[2]Category D, 700-2; Category E, 800-2½.
[3]Category E, 800-2½.

**BALTIMORE, MD**
BALTIMORE-WASHINGTON
INTL ....................... VOR or GPS Rwy 10,1000-3

MARTIN STATE ............................. ILS Rwy 33[1]
VOR/DME or TACAN 1 Rwy 15[2]
[1]ILS, Category D, 700-2.
[2]Categories A,B, 900-2; Categories C,D,
  900-2¾.

**BECKLEY, WV**
RALEIGH COUNTY MEMORIAL ..... ILS Rwy 19[1]
VOR or GPS Rwy 19[2]
[1]ILS, Categories B,C,D, 700-2. LOC, NA.
[2]Category D, 800-2¼.

**BLUEFIELD, WV**
MERCER COUNTY ......................... ILS Rwy 23[1]
VOR/DME or GPS Rwy 23
VOR Rwy 23
NA when FSS is closed.
[1]ILS, Categories C,D, 700-2.

**CHARLESTON, WV**
YEAGER .................................. ILS Rwy 5, 700-2
ILS Rwy 23, 700-2
VOR/DME RNAV or GPS Rwy 33[1]
VOR or GPS-A[1]
[1]Category D, 800-2¼.

| NAME | ALTERNATE MINIMUMS |
|---|---|

**CHARLOTTESVILLE, VA**
CHARLOTTESVILLE-ALBEMARLE .. ILS Rwy 3[1]
NDB Rwy 3[2]
NA when control tower closed.
[1]ILS, Category D, 900-2¾. LOC, NA.
[2]Category D, 900-2¾.

**CLARKSBURG, WV**
BENEDUM ....................................... ILS Rwy 21[1]
VOR or GPS Rwy 3[2]
NA when control tower is closed, except for
operators with approved weather reporting
service.
[1]Categories A,B, 800-2; Category C, 900-2½;
Category D, 900-2¾.
[2]Category C, 900-2½; Category D, 900-2¾.

**DANVILLE, VA**
DANVILLE REGIONAL ................. RNAV Rwy 20
NA when control zone not in effective.

**ELKINS, WV**
ELKINS-RANDOLPH COUNTY JENNINGS-
RANDOLPH FIELD ................................. LDA-C[1]
VOR/DME-B[2]
NA at night.
[1]Categories A,B, 1200-2; Categories C,D,
1500-3.
[2]Categories A,B, 1500-2; Categories C,D,
1500-3.

**HAGERSTOWN, MD**
WASHINGTON COUNTY
REGIONAL ...................................... ILS Rwy 27[1]
VOR or GPS Rwy 9[2]
[1]NA when control zone not in effect.
[2]NA when control zone not in effect except for
operators with approved weather reporting
service.

NE-3

FIGURE 183.—IFR ALTERNATE MINIMUMS.

166

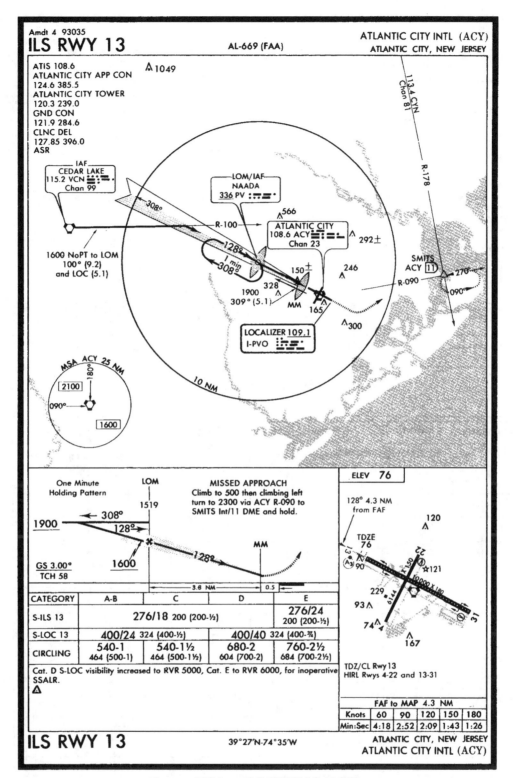

FIGURE 183A.—ILS RWY 13 (ACY).

Form Approved: OMB No. 2120-0034

| U.S. DEPARTMENT OF TRANSPORTATION<br>FEDERAL AVIATION ADMINISTRATION<br>**FLIGHT PLAN** | (FAA USE ONLY) | ☐ PILOT BRIEFING | ☐ VNR | TIME STARTED | SPECIALIST INITIALS |
| --- | --- | --- | --- | --- | --- |
| | | ☐ STOPOVER | | | |

| 1. TYPE | 2. AIRCRAFT IDENTIFICATION | 3. AIRCRAFT TYPE/ SPECIAL EQUIPMENT | 4. TRUE AIRSPEED | 5. DEPARTURE POINT | 6. DEPARTURE TIME | | 7. CRUISING ALTITUDE |
| --- | --- | --- | --- | --- | --- | --- | --- |
| ☐ VFR<br>☒ IFR<br>☐ DVFR | HOSS 1 | A109K2/A | ** KTS | LAS | PROPOSED (Z) | ACTUAL (Z) | 15000 |

**8. ROUTE OF FLIGHT**

LAS, ACLAM, V8 MMM, V21 REEKA, PVU

| 9. DESTINATION (Name of airport and city) PVU<br>PROVO MUNI<br>PROVO, UTAH | 10. EST. TIME ENROUTE | | 11. REMARKS   L/O = LEVEL OFF    PPH = POUNDS PER HOUR |
| --- | --- | --- | --- |
| | HOURS | MINUTES | **CAS 135, ISA -10 |

| 12. FUEL ON BOARD | | 13. ALTERNATE AIRPORT(S) | 14. PILOT'S NAME, ADDRESS & TELEPHONE NUMBER & AIRCRAFT HOME BASE | 15. NUMBER ABOARD |
| --- | --- | --- | --- | --- |
| HOURS | MINUTES | SLC<br>SALT LAKE CITY | 17. DESTINATION CONTACT/TELEPHONE (OPTIONAL) | 8 |

| 16. COLOR OF AIRCRAFT<br>GREEN/GOLD | CIVIL AIRCRAFT PILOTS. FAR Part 91 requires you file an IFR flight plan to operate under instrument flight rules in controlled airspace. Failure to file could result in a civil penalty not to exceed $1,000 for each violation (Section 901 of the Federal Aviation Act of 1958, as amended). Filing of a VFR flight plan is recommended as a good operating practice. See also Part 99 for requirements concerning DVFR flight plans. |
| --- | --- |

FAA Form 7233-1(8-82)        CLOSE VFR FLIGHT PLAN WITH _____ FSS ON ARRIVAL

## FLIGHT LOG

| CHECK POINTS | | ROUTE | COURSE | WIND | SPEED-KTS | | DIST | TIME | | FUEL | |
| --- | --- | --- | --- | --- | --- | --- | --- | --- | --- | --- | --- |
| FROM | TO | ALTITUDE | | TEMP | TAS | GS | NM | LEG | TOT | LEG | TOT |
| LAS | ACLAM | DIRECT CLIMB | | | | | 31 | | :15:00 | | 152* |
| ACLAM | MMM | V-8 15000 | | 210/71 ISA-10 | | | | | | | |
| MMM | REEKA | V-21 15000 | | | | | | | | | |
| REEKA | PVU | DESCENT & APPROACH | | | | | 19 | :10:00 | | 87 | |
| | | | | | | | | | | | |
| | | | | | | | | | | | |
| | | | | | | | | | | | |
| | | | | | | | | | | | |
| PVU | SLC | DIRECT 7000 | | | | | 41 | :17:20 | | | |

| OTHER DATA:<br>NOTE: | * Includes Taxi Fuel<br>Use 496 PPH Total Fuel Flow From L/O<br>To Start Of Descent.<br>Use 480 PPH Total Fuel Flow For<br>Reserve And Alternate Requirements.<br><br>A Missed Approach Requires 40# of Fuel. |
| --- | --- |

**TIME and FUEL: As required by FARs.**

| TIME | FUEL (LB) | |
| --- | --- | --- |
| | | EN ROUTE |
| | | RESERVE |
| | | ALTERNATE |
| | | TOTAL |

FIGURE 184.—Flight Plan/Flight Log.

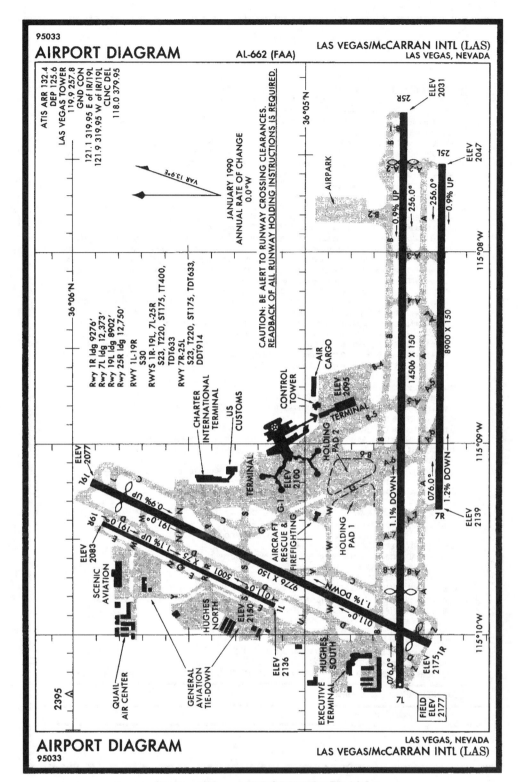

FIGURE 185.—AIRPORT DIAGRAM.

**McCARRAN INTL** (LAS) 5 S UTC−8(−7DT) N36°04.82′ W115°09.02′      LAS VEGAS
2177 B S4 FUEL 100, 100LL, JET A1 + OX 1, 2, 3 LRA ARFF Index D      H−2B, L−5B
RWY 07L−25R: H14506X150 (ASPH−PFC) S−23, D−220, DT−633 HIRL 1.0% up W      IAP
  RWY 07L: VASI(V6L)—Upper GA 3.25° TCH 94′. Lower GA 3.0° TCH 47′. Thld dsplcd 2133′. Hangar.
  RWY 25R: MALSR. Thld dsplcd 1400′.
RWY 01R−19L: H9776X150 (ASPH−PFC) S−23, D−220, DT−633 MIRL 1.0% up S
  RWY 01R: VASI(V4L)—GA 3.0° TCH 50′. Thld dsplcd 500′. Railroad. Rgt tfc.
  RWY 19L: VASI(V6L)—Upper GA 3.25° TCH 66′. Lower GA 3.0° TCH 35′. Thld dsplcd 874′. Pole.
RWY 07R−25L: H8900X150 (ASPH−PFC) S−23, D−220, DT−633, DDT−914 HIRL
  RWY 07R: REIL. Pole.      RWY 25L: MALSF.
RWY 01L−19R: H5001X75 (ASPH) S−30 MIRL 1.1% up S
  RWY 01L: REIL. VASI(V4L)—GA 3.0° TCH 35′. Antenna.
  RWY 19R: REIL. VASI(V4L)—GA 3.0° TCH 60′. Pole. Rgt tfc.
AIRPORT REMARKS: Attended continuously. Rwy 19R CLOSED arrival, Rwy 01L CLOSED departure Mon−Fri
1500−2300Z‡. Extensive glider/soaring operations weekends and holidays. Sunrise to sunset, LAS 187020,
altitudes up to but not including FL180. Gliders remain clear of the CLASS B airspace but otherwise operate
within the entire SW quadrant of the CLASS B airspace Veil. Lgtd crane 950′ AGL 4 miles N of arpt. Rotating bcn
not visible 115°−240° NE to SW from McCarran Twr. Acft may experience reflection of sun from glass pyramid
located NW of arpt. Reflection may occur at various altitudes, headings and distances from arpt. Rwy 07R−25L
DDT GWT 521,000 lbs for L−1011, 620,000 lbs for DC−10, 633,000 lbs for MD−11. PAEW between Rwy
01R−19L and Twy D north of Twy N. PAEW west of Rwy 01L−19R. PAEW west of Twy D. Twy E clsd between Twy
Q and Twy R. Twy N, Twy S and Twy T clsd between Rwy 01L−19R and Twy D. Twy Y acft be alert keep
nosewheel on centerline and acft with wing span greater than 70′ prohibited north of New Quail Gate. Twy D clsd
to B747 and clsd to all acft with wingspan 171′ or greater north of Rwy 07L−25R. All non−standard rwy
operations PPR from Department of Aviation. Turbojet operations not permitted Rwy 01R−19L and Rwy
01L−19R between 0400−1600Z‡. Exceptions will be made due to weather. Rwy 07L VASI out of svc indefinitely.
Rwy 25 MALSR out of svc indefinitely. Tiedown fee. Flight Notification Service (ADCUS) available. NOTE: See
Land and Hold Short Operations Section.
WEATHER DATA SOURCES: LLWAS.
COMMUNICATIONS: ATIS 132.4 (ARR) 125.6 (DEP)   UNICOM 122.95
  RENO FSS (RNO) TF 1−800−WX−BRIEF. NOTAM FILE LAS.
Ⓡ LAS VEGAS APP CON 127.15
Ⓡ LAS VEGAS DEP CON 133.95 (North) 125.9 (South)
  LAS VEGAS TOWER 119.9   GND CON 121.9 (West of Rwy 01R−19L) 121.1 (East of Rwy 01R−19L)   CLNC DEL 118.0
AIRSPACE: CLASS B See VFR Terminal Area Chart.
RADIO AIDS TO NAVIGATION: NOTAM FILE LAS.
  LAS VEGAS (H) VORTACW 116.9   LAS   Chan 116   N36°04.78′ W115°09.59′   at fld. 2140/15E.
  ILS 110.3   I−LAS   Rwy 25R.
  ILS 111.75   I−RLE   Rwy 25L.   Loc unusable byd 19° South of course.

**NORTH LAS VEGAS AIR TERMINAL** (VGT) 3 NW UTC−8(−7DT)      LAS VEGAS
  N36°12.75′ W115°11.82′      H−2B, L−5B
2207 B S4 FUEL 100LL, JET A OX 2 TPA—3007(800)
RWY 07−25: H5005X75 (ASPH) S−30 MIRL
  RWY 07: PAPI(P4L)—GA 3.0° TCH 37′. Pole.      RWY 25: PAPI(P4L)—GA 3.0° TCH 36′.
RWY 12−30: H5000X75 (ASPH) S−30 MIRL
  RWY 12: PAPI(P4L)—GA 3.0° TCH 25′.
  RWY 30: MIRL. PAPI(P4L)—GA 3.0° TCH 45′. Thld dsplcd 290′. P−line.
AIRPORT REMARKS: Attended 1400−0630Z‡. Rwy 30 PAPI OTS indef. When twr clsd ACTIVATE MIRL Rwy 07−25 and
Rwy 12−30—CTAF. NOTE: See Land and Hold Short Operations Section.
COMMUNICATIONS: CTAF 125.7   ATIS 118.05 (1400−0400Z‡)   UNICOM 122.95
  RENO FSS (RNO) TF 1−800−WX−BRIEF. NOTAM FILE RNO.
  TOWER 125.7 (1400−0400Z‡)   GND CON 121.7
AIRSPACE: CLASS D svc effective 1400−0400Z‡ other times CLASS G.
RADIO AIDS TO NAVIGATION: NOTAM FILE LAS.
  LAS VEGAS (H) VORTACW 116.9   LAS   Chan 116   N36°04.78′ W115°09.59′   332° 8.2 NM to fld. 2140/15E.

**LIDA JUNCTION**   (See GOLDFIELD)

**LINCOLN CO**   (See PANACA)

FIGURE 185A.—Excerpt from Airport/Facilities Directory.

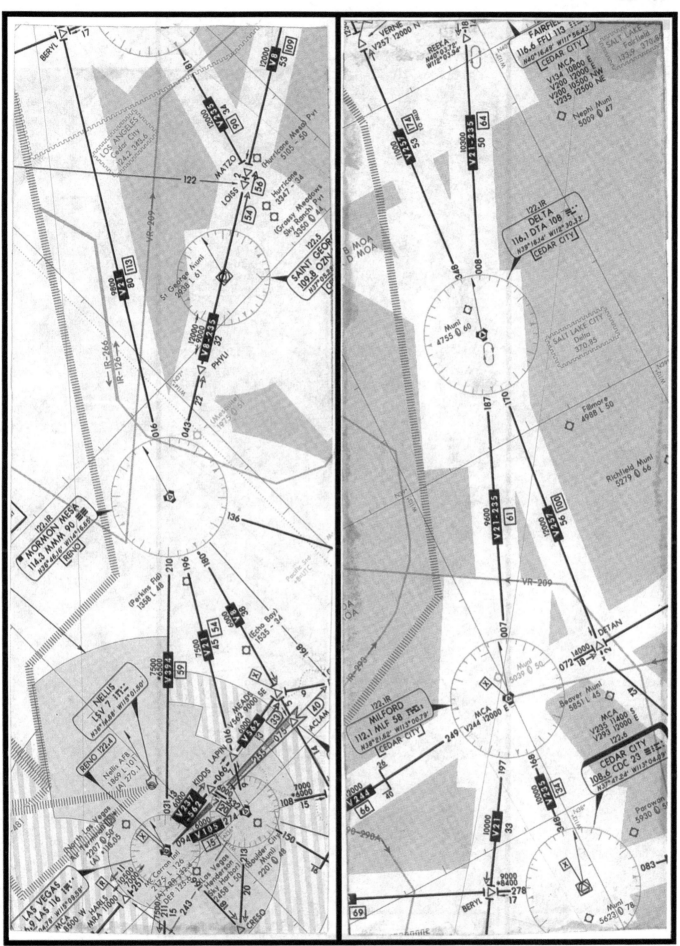

FIGURE 186.—Low Altitude Airways.

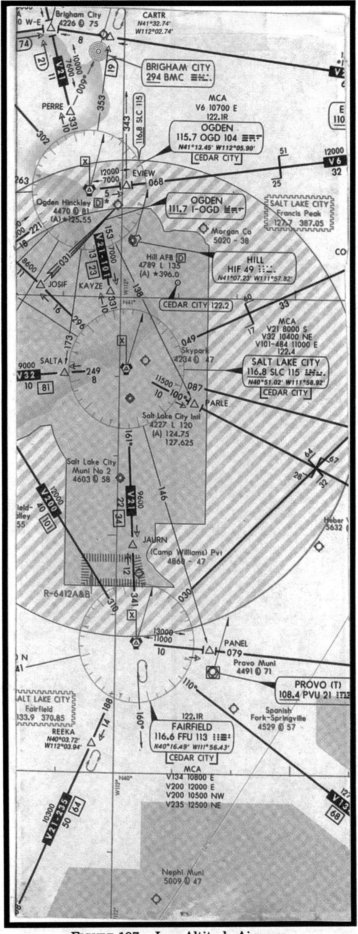

FIGURE 187.—Low Altitude Airways.

## UTAH

**PROVO MUNI** (PVU)  2 SW  UTC – 7( – 6DT)  N40°12.94' W111°43.29'  
  4491  B  S4  **FUEL** 100, JET A  OX 2  
  **RWY 13-31:** H7091X150 (ASPH–PFC)  S–65, D–85, DT–140  MIRL  
    **RWY 13:** MALSF. VASI(V2L)—GA 3.0°TCH 40'. Thld dsplcd 438'. Road.  
    **RWY 31:** VASI(V2L)—GA 3.0°TCH 56'. Thld dsplcd 290'. Road.  
  **RWY 18-36:** H6937X150 (ASPH)  S–50, D–70, DT–110  MIRL  
    **RWY 18:** VASI(V2L)—GA 3.0°TCH 55'. Thld dsplcd 373'. Road.  
    **RWY 36:** VASI(V2L)—GA 3.0°TCH 55'. Thld dsplcd 334'. Road.  
  **RWY 06-24:** H5596X150 (ASPH)  S–50, D–70, DT–110  
    **RWY 06:** Thld dsplcd 611'. Brush.  **RWY 24:** Thld dsplcd 598'. Road.  
  **AIRPORT REMARKS:** Attended 1400–0200Z‡. ACTIVATE ALS Rwy 13, MIRL and VASI Rwys 13–31 and 18–36 122.8.  
  **WEATHER DATA SOURCES:** AWOS-3 135.175 (801) 373–9782.  
  **COMMUNICATIONS: CTAF/UNICOM** 122.8  
    **CEDAR CITY FSS** (CDC) TF 1–800–WX–BRIEF. NOTAM FILE PVU.  
  Ⓡ **SALT LAKE CITY APP CON** 124.3  
  Ⓡ **SALT LAKE CITY DEP CON** 118.85  
  **AIRSPACE: CLASS E** svc effective 1400–0200Z‡ other times CLASS G.  
  **RADIO AIDS TO NAVIGATION:** NOTAM FILE PVU.  
    (T) **VORW/DME** 108.4  PVU  Chan 21  N40°12.90' W111°43.28'  at fld. 4490/15E.  
      Unusable 330°–170°beyond 10 NM below 13,000'  
    **ILS/DME** 110.3  I-PVU  Chan 40  Rwy 13.  LOC unusable inside threshold. ILS unmonitored  
    0200–1400Z‡.  

• • • • • • • • • • • • • • • • • • • • • • • • • • • •

  **HELIPAD H1:** H40X40 (CONC)  
  **HELIPAD H2:** H40X40 (CONC)

---

**RICHFIELD MUNI** (RIF)  1 SW  UTC – 7( – 6DT)  N38°44.50' W112°05.71'  
  5279  B  **FUEL** 100, JET A  
  **RWY 01-19:** H6645X75 (ASPH)  S–19  MIRL  
  **RWY 01:** Rgt tfc.  
  **AIRPORT REMARKS:** Attended Mon–Fri 1530–0000Z‡. For fuel after hours call 801–896–8918/7258. ACTIVATE MIRL  
  Rwy 01–19—CTAF.  
  **COMMUNICATIONS: CTAF/UNICOM** 122.8  
    **CEDAR CITY FSS** (CDC) TF 1–800–WX–BRIEF. NOTAM FILE CDC.  
    **RCO** 122.5 (CEDAR CITY FSS)  
  **RADIO AIDS TO NAVIGATION:** NOTAM FILE CDC.  
    **DELTA (H) VORTAC** 116.1  DTA  Chan 108  N39°18.14' W112°30.33'  134° 38.7 NM to fld. 4600/16E.

---

**ROOSEVELT MUNI** (74V)  3 SW  UTC – 7( – 6DT)  N40°16.70' W110°03.08'  
  5172  B  **FUEL** 100, JET A, MOGAS  
  **RWY 07-25:** H6500X75 (ASPH)  S–12  MIRL  1.0% up W  
    **RWY 07:** VASI(V2L)—GA 3.0° TCH 34'.  **RWY 25:** VASI(V2L)—GA 3.0° TCH 27'.  
  **AIRPORT REMARKS:** Attended on call. For svc call 801–722–4741. ACTIVATE MIRL and VASI Rwy 07–25—CTAF.  
  **COMMUNICATIONS: CTAF/UNICOM** 122.8  
    **CEDAR CITY FSS** (CDC) TF 1–800–WX–BRIEF. NOTAM FILE CDC.  
    **MYTON RCO** 122.1R 112.7T (CEDAR CITY FSS)  
  **RADIO AIDS TO NAVIGATION:** NOTAM FILE CDC.  
    **MYTON (H) VORTAC** 112.7  MTU  Chan 74  N40°08.70' W110°07.66'  010° 8.7 NM to fld. 5332/14E.

---

**ST GEORGE MUNI** (SGU)  1 W  UTC – 7( – 6DT)  N37°05.48' W113°35.58'  
  2938  B  S4  **FUEL** 100, 100LL, JET A, MOGAS  OX 2  ARFF Index Ltd.  
  **RWY 16-34:** H6101X100 (ASPH–PFC)  S–26  MIRL  1.1% up N  
    **RWY 16:** VASI(V2R)—GA 4.0° TCH 44'. Road.  **RWY 34:** REIL. VASI(V2L)—GA 3.0° TCH 43'.  
  **AIRPORT REMARKS:** Attended 1330–0230Z‡. CLOSED to Air Carrier ops with more than 30 passenger seat except  
  PPR. Call arpt manager 801–634–5800. ACTIVATE REIL Rwy 34—CTAF.  
  **WEATHER DATA SOURCES:** AWOS-3 135.075 (801) 634–0940.  
  **COMMUNICATIONS: CTAF/UNICOM** 122.8  
    **CEDAR CITY FSS** (CDC) TF 1–800–WX–BRIEF. NOTAM FILE SGU.  
    **RCO** 122.5 (CEDAR CITY FSS)  
  **RADIO AIDS TO NAVIGATION:** NOTAM FILE CDC.  
    (T) **VORW/DME** 109.8  OZN  Chan 35  N37°05.28' W113°35.51'  at fld. 2898/15E.  
      VOR/DME unusable:  
        210°–235° beyond 15 NM below 8500'      270°–350° all altitudes and distances;  
        235°–270° beyond 15 NM below 9700'      350°–020° beyond 10 NM below 14000'.

Right column labels:

SALT LAKE CITY  
H-2C, L-8E, 7D, 5C  
IAP

LAS VEGAS  
H-2C, L-5C

SALT LAKE CITY  
H-2C, L-8E, 5C  
IAP

LAS VEGAS  
H-2B, L-5B  
IAP

FIGURE 188.—Excerpt from Airport/Facilities Directory.

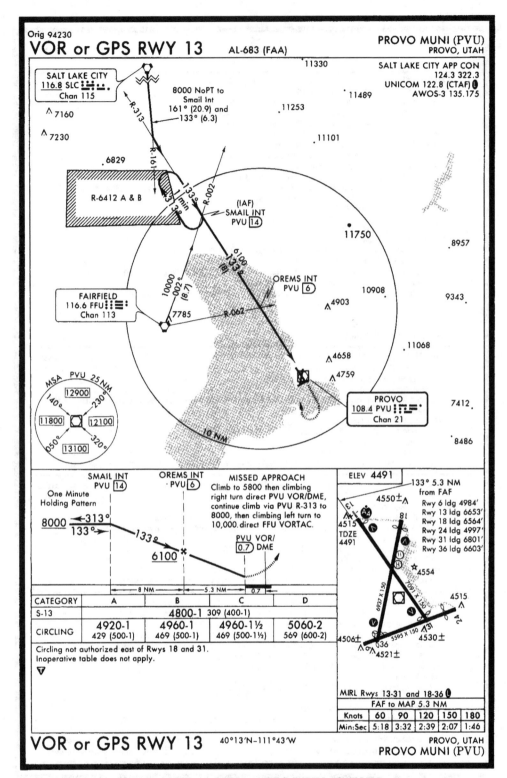

FIGURE 188A.—VOR or GPS RWY 13 (PVU).

178  UTAH

**SALINA-GUNNISON**  (44U)  5 NE  UTC–7(–6DT)  N39°01.75' W111°50.30'  **LAS VEGAS**<br>**L-5C**
5159  B
**RWY 02-20:** H3815X60 (ASPH)  S-6  MIRL
**AIRPORT REMARKS:** Unattended. ACTIVATE MIRL Rwy 02-20—CTAF.
**COMMUNICATIONS: CTAF** 122.9
   **CEDAR CITY FSS** (CDC) TF 1–800–WX–BRIEF. NOTAM FILE CDC.
  **RADIO AIDS TO NAVIGATION:** NOTAM FILE CDC.
   **DELTA (H) VORTAC** 116.1  DTA  Chan 108  N39°18.14' W112°30.33'  102° 35.2 NM to fld. 4600/16E.

---

# SALT LAKE CITY

**SALT LAKE CITY INTL**  (SLC)  3 W  UTC–7(–6DT)  N40°47.21' W111°58.13'  **SALT LAKE CITY**<br>**H-1C, L-7D**<br>**IAP**
4227  B  S4  **FUEL** 100, 100LL, JET A1  OX 1, 2, 3, 4  LRA  ARFF Index D
**RWY 16-34:** H12003X150 (ASPH–PFC)  S-60 +, D-200 +, DT-350  HIRL CL
  **RWY 16:** ALSF2. TDZ. REIL. PAPI(P4L).    **RWY 34:** ALSF2. TDZ. REIL. PAPI(P4L).
**RWY 17-35:** H9596X150 (ASPH–PFC)  S-60 +, D-170, DT-320  HIRL
  **RWY 17:** MALSR. PAPI(P4R)—GA 3.0° TCH 55'.    **RWY 35:** PAPI(P4L)—GA 3.0° TCH 75'.
**RWY 14-32:** H4758X150 (ASPH–PFC)  S-60 +, D-170, DT-320  MIRL
  **RWY 14:** Thld dsplcd 202'.    **RWY 32:** Thld dsplcd 479'. Road.
**AIRPORT REMARKS:** Attended continuously. CAUTION: Flocks of birds on and in vicinity of arpt. Preferential rwys, use
  Rwy 34 and Rwy 35 when wind and temperature permit. Rwy 14–32 GWT strengths for S, D, DT apply to center
  75' only. 180° turns by acft over 12,500 lbs, prohibited on all rwys and taxiways. Rwy 17–35 tfc on Twy K not
  visible from twr. Due to the high volume of tfc at SLC arpt during the following time periods: 1800–1845Z‡,
  2200–2230Z‡, 0145–0230Z‡ and 0300–0330Z‡ local departures and arrivals are discouraged. Greater than
  normal delays can be expected during these time periods. Rwy 16R–34L under construction. Flight Notification
  Service (ADCUS) available. NOTE: See Land and Hold Short Operations Section. NOTE: See Special Notice—
  Runway Under Construction.
**WEATHER DATA SOURCES:** LLWAS.
**COMMUNICATIONS: ATIS** 127.625 124.75 (801) 539–2581  **UNICOM** 122.95
  **CEDAR CITY FSS** (CDC) TF 1–800–WX–BRIEF. NOTAM FILE SLC.
   **RCO** 122.4 (CEDAR CITY FSS)
ⓡ **APP/DEP CON** 121.1 (North of 41° latitude blo 8000') 124.3 (105°–249°) 124.9 (297°–005° N of 41° N latitude
  above 8000') 135.5 (250°–296° and 006°–104°) 125.7
   **TOWER** 118.3 (E of Rwy 17–35) 119.05 (W of Rwy 16–34) 127.3  **GND CON** 121.9  **CLNC DEL** 127.3
   **PRE-TAXI CLNC** 127.3
**AIRSPACE: CLASS B** See VFR Terminal Area Chart. Ctc **APP CON** 134.35 (West) all other quadrants 120.9.
**RADIO AIDS TO NAVIGATION:** NOTAM FILE SLC.
  **(H) VORTACW** 116.8  SLC  Chan 115  N40°51.02' W111°58.92'  155° 3.9 NM to fld. 4220/16E.
   Unusable:
    100°–140°beyond 30 NM below 13,000'      315°–330°beyond 20 NM below 8600'.
    200°–230°beyond 25 NM below 10,800'      330°–345°beyond 24 NM below 7000'.
    280°–290°beyond 30 NM below 8,100'      360°–070°beyond 20 NM below 11,200'
    290°–315°beyond 35 NM below 8600'.
  **KERNN NDB (LOM)** 338  SL  N40°40.87' W111°57.78'  343° 6.3 NM to fld.
  **ILS/DME** 110.7  I-MOY  Chan 44  Rwy 16.
  **ILS** 109.5  I-SLC  Rwy 34  LOM KERNN NDB.
  **ILS/DME** 111.5  I-BNT  Chan 52  Rwy 17.
  **ILS** 110.1  I-UTJ  Rwy 35 LOM KERNN NOB. Localizer unusable byd 25° west of rwy centerline.
  **ASR**
• • • • • • • • • • • • • • • • • • • • • • • • • • •
**HELIPAD H1:** H100X75 (ASPH)
**HELIPAD H2:** H60X60 (ASPH)
**HELIPAD H3:** H60X60 (ASPH)
**HELIPAD H4:** H60X60 (ASPH)
**HELIPAD H5:** H60X60 (ASPH)
**HELIPAD H6:** H60X60 (ASPH)
**HELIPORT REMARKS:** Helipads H1 through H4 located on general aviation side of arpt and Helipads H5 and H6 located
  on air carrier side of arpt.

- - - - - - - - - - - - - - - - - - - - - - - - - - - - - -

FIGURE 189.—Excerpt from Airport/Facilities Directory.

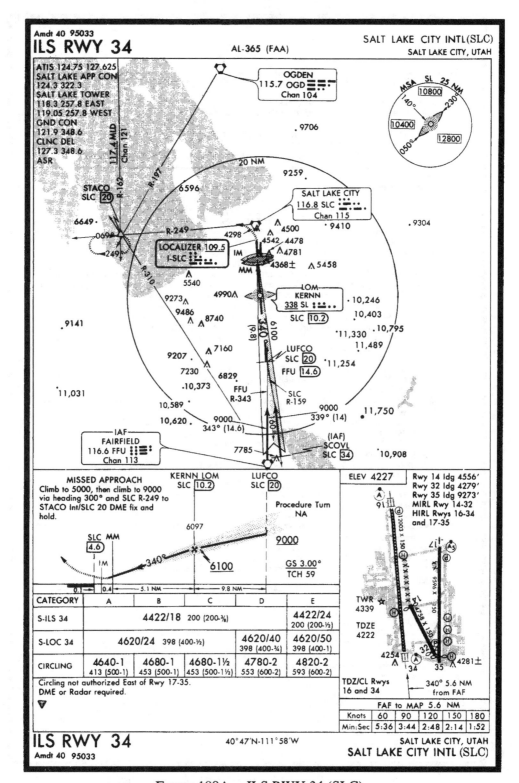

FIGURE 189A.—ILS RWY 34 (SLC).

Form Approved: OMB No. 2120-0034

## FLIGHT PLAN

U.S. DEPARTMENT OF TRANSPORTATION
FEDERAL AVIATION ADMINISTRATION

(FAA USE ONLY)  □ PILOT BRIEFING  □ VNR  TIME STARTED  SPECIALIST INITIALS

□ STOPOVER

| 1. TYPE | 2. AIRCRAFT IDENTIFICATION | 3. AIRCRAFT TYPE/ SPECIAL EQUIPMENT | 4. TRUE AIRSPEED | 5. DEPARTURE POINT | 6. DEPARTURE TIME | | 7. CRUISING ALTITUDE |
|---|---|---|---|---|---|---|---|
| | | | | | PROPOSED (Z) | ACTUAL (Z) | |
| X IFR  VFR  DVFR | PIL 10 | B767/G | 456 KTS | MSP | | | FL430 |

**8. ROUTE OF FLIGHT**

MINNEAPOLIS FOUR  DEPARTURE FSD, J197 OBH, J10 LBF, SAYGE.SAYGE1

| 9. DESTINATION (Name of airport and city) DEN | 10. EST. TIME ENROUTE | | 11. REMARKS L/O = LEVEL OFF   PPH = POUNDS PER HOUR |
|---|---|---|---|
| | HOURS | MINUTES | L/O FSD R-048/90   VARIATION: FSD 9E, LBF 10E, MSP 3E |

| 12. FUEL ON BOARD | | 13. ALTERNATE AIRPORT(S) | 14. PILOT'S NAME, ADDRESS & TELEPHONE NUMBER & AIRCRAFT HOME BASE | 15. NUMBER ABOARD |
|---|---|---|---|---|
| HOURS | MINUTES | ABQ ALBUQUERQUE | 17. DESTINATION CONTACT/TELEPHONE (OPTIONAL) | 190 |

16. COLOR OF AIRCRAFT  SILVER/RED

CIVIL AIRCRAFT PILOTS. FAR Part 91 requires you file an IFR flight plan to operate under instrument flight rules in controlled airspace. Failure to file could result in a civil penalty not to exceed $1,000 for each violation (Section 901 of the Federal Aviation Act of 1958, as amended). Filing of a VFR flight plan is recommended as a good operating practice. See also Part 99 for requirements concerning DVFR flight plans.

FAA Form 7233-1 (8-82)  CLOSE VFR FLIGHT PLAN WITH _____ FSS ON ARRIVAL

## FLIGHT LOG

| CHECK POINTS | | ROUTE | | WIND | SPEED-KTS | | DIST | TIME | | FUEL | |
|---|---|---|---|---|---|---|---|---|---|---|---|
| FROM | TO | ALTITUDE | COURSE | TEMP | TAS | GS | NM | LEG | TOT | LEG | TOT |
| MSP | FSD R-048/90 | VECTORS CLIMB | | | | | 90 | :19:00 | | 4170* | |
| FSD R-048/90 | FSD | DIRECT FL430 | | 290/89 ISA-6 | | | | | | | |
| FSD | OBH | J197 FL430 | | | | | | | | | |
| OBH | LBF | J10 FL410 | | 300/83 ISA-5 | | | | | | | |
| LBF | MODES | SAUGE.SAUGE.1 FL410 | | | | | | | | | |
| MODES | AMWAY | SAUGE.SAUGE.1 FL410 | | | | | | | | | |
| AMWAY | DEN | DESCENT & APPROACH | | | | | 97 | :25:00 | | 3107 | |
| DEN | ABQ | VECTORS FL410 | | | | | | :36:00 | | | |

**OTHER DATA:** * Includes Taxi Fuel
NOTE: Use 9026 PPH Total Fuel Flow From L/O To Start Of Descent.
Use 7688 PPH Total Fuel Flow For Reserve And Alternate Requirements.
A Missed Approach Requires 1050# of Fuel.

TIME and FUEL: As required by FARs.

| TIME | FUEL (LB) | |
|---|---|---|
| | | EN ROUTE |
| | | RESERVE |
| | | ALTERNATE |
| | | TOTAL |

FIGURE 190.—Flight Plan/Flight Log.

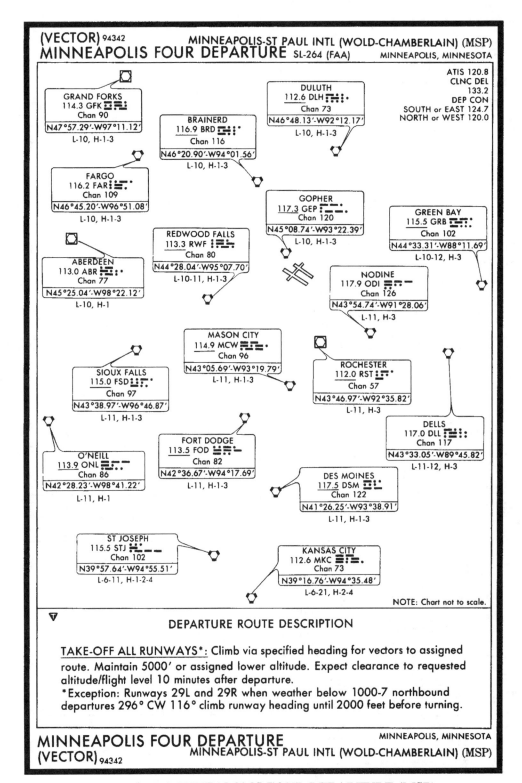

**FIGURE 191.—MINNEAPOLIS FOUR DEPARTURE (MSP).**

## MINNESOTA 105

- - - - - - - - - - - - - - - - - - - - - - - - - - - - - - - - - - - - - - - - - -

**FLYING CLOUD** (FCM)   11 SW   UTC–6(–5DT)   N44°49.63' W93°27.43'   **TWIN CITIES**
906   B   S4   **FUEL** 100, 100LL, JET A   OX 3, 4   TPA–1906(1000)   **L–10G, A**
**RWY 09R–27L:** H3909X75 (ASPH)   S–30   HIRL   **IAP**
  **RWY 09R:** MALSR. VASI(V4L)—GA 3.0° TCH 41' Rgt tfc.
  **RWY 27L:** REIL. VASI(V4L)—GA 3.0° TCH 45'. Thld dsplcd 200'. Road.
**RWY 09L–27R:** H3599X75 (ASPH)   S–30
  **RWY 27R:** Road. Rgt tfc.
**RWY 18–36:** H2691X75 (ASPH)   S–23   MIRL
  **RWY 18:** VASI(V4L)—GA 3.0° TCH 37'. Barn.   **RWY 36:** REIL. VASI(V4L)—GA 3.0° TCH 31'. Road.
**AIRPORT REMARKS:** Attended 1300–0400Z‡. Rwy 09L–27R CLOSED when twr clsd. Arpt CLOSED to jet acft not
  meeting FAR 36, jet training and jet acft over 20,000 lbs. Deer and waterfowl on and in vicinity of arpt. Rwy 09R
  and Rwy 27R rgt tfc during twr hours only. When twr clsd ACTIVATE VASI Rwy 09R, VASI Rwy 18, MALSR Rwy
  09R, HIRL Rwy 09R–27L and MIRL Rwy 18–36–118.1.
**WEATHER DATA SOURCES:** LAWRS
**COMMUNICATIONS: CTAF** 118.1   **ATIS** 124.9 (612) 944–2970   **UNICOM** 122.95
  **PRINCETON FSS (PNM) TF** 1–800–WX–BRIEF. NOTAM FILE FCM
  Ⓡ **MINNEAPOLIS APP/DEP CON** 125.0
  **MINNEAPOLIS CLNC DEL** 121.7 (When twr closed)
  **TOWER** 118.1 125.2 (Apr–Oct 1300–0400Z‡, Nov–Mar 1300–0300Z‡)   **GND CON** 121.7   **CLNC DEL** 121.7
**AIRSPACE: CLASS D** svc effective Apr–Oct 1300–0400Z‡ Nov–Mar 1300–0300Z‡ other times CLASS G.
**RADIO AIDS TO NAVIGATION:** NOTAM FILE FCM.
  **(L) ABVORW/DME** 111.8   FCM   Chan 55   N44°49.54' W93°27.41'   at fld. 900/6E.
    Route forecast only on TWEB 0400–1100Z‡.
  **ILS** 109.7   I–FCM   RWY 09R.   LOC unusable byd 30 degrees either side of centerline. GS unusable byd 5
    degrees left of course.

- - - - - - - - - - - - - - - - - - - - - - - - - - - - - - - - - - - - - - - - - -

**MINNEAPOLIS–ST PAUL INTL (WOLD–CHAMBERLAIN)** (MSP)   6 SW   UTC–6(–5DT)   **TWIN CITIES**
  N44°53.05' W93°12.90'   **H–1E, 3G, L–10G, A**
841   B   S4   **FUEL** 100, JET A, A1 +   OX 1, 2, 3, 4   LRA   ARFF Index E   **IAP**
**RWY 11R–29L:** H10000X200 (ASPH–CONC–GRVD)   S–65, D–85, DT–145   HIRL CL   0.3% up W
  **RWY 11R:** MALSR. PAPI(P4L)—GA 3.0° TCH 65'. Tree.
  **RWY 29L:** ALSF1. TDZ. PAPI(P4L)—GA 3.0° TCH 73'. Pole.
**RWY 04–22:** H8256X150 (CONC–GRVD)   S–65, D–85, DT–145   HIRL
  **RWY 04:** SSALR. PAPI(P4L)—GA 3.0° TCH 76'.
  **RWY 22:** MALSR. PAPI(P4L)—GA 3.0° TCH 42'. Thld dsplcd 988'. Fence.
**RWY 11L–29R:** H8200X150 (ASPH–CONC–GRVD)   S–100, D–125, DT–210   HIRL
  **RWY 11L:** MALSR. PAPI(P4L)—GA 3.0° TCH 75'. Tree.   0.3% down.
  **RWY 29R:** REIL. PAPI(P4L)—GA 3.0° TCH 73'.
**AIRPORT REMARKS:** Attended continuously. Birds on and in vicinity of arpt. Training prohibited. Only Initial departure
  and full stop termination training flights permitted. PPR for noise abatement procedures —call 612–726–9411.
  No stage 1 noise Category Civil acft. Landing fee. Flight Notification Service (ADCUS) available. NOTE: See Land
  and Hold Short Operations Section.
**WEATHER DATA SOURCES:** LLWAS.
**COMMUNICATIONS: ATIS** 135.35 (612) 726–9240. 120.8 (TCA ARR INFO)   **UNICOM** 122.95
  **PRINCETON FSS (PNM) TF** 1–800–WX–BRIEF. NOTAM FILE MSP.
  **RCO** 122.55 122.3 (PRINCETON FSS)   **RCO** 122.1R 115.3T (PRINCETON FSS)
  Ⓡ **APP CON** 119.3 (N or E of arrival rwy) 126.95 (S or W of arrival rwy and Rwys 04, 11R and 29L)
  **TOWER** 126.7 (Rwys 11R–29L and 04–22) 123.95 (Rwy 11L–29R)   **GND CON** 121.9 (S) 121.8 (N)   **CLNC DEL** 133.2
  Ⓡ **DEP CON** 127.925 (N or E of arrival rwy) 124.7 (S or W of arrival rwy)
**AIRSPACE: CLASS B:** See VFR Terminal Area Chart.
**RADIO AIDS TO NAVIGATION:** NOTAM FILE MSP.
  **(H) VORTAC** 115.3   MSP   Chan 100   N44°52.92' W93°13.99'   at fld. 850/3E.
    VOR portion unusable below 3000', beyond 20 NM below 4000', 205°–235°/265°–025° all distances and
    altitudes, 235°–265° below 7000'.
  **NARCO NDB (MH–SAB/LOM)** 266   MS   N44°49.55' W93°05.48'   299° 6.3 NM to fld.
    Route forecast only on TWEB 0400–1100Z‡.
  **VAGEY NDB (LOM)** 338   AP   N44°49.45' W93°18.36'   042° 5.3 NM to fld. Unmonitored.
  **ILS** 109.9   I–INN   Rwy 29R
  **ILS/DME** 110.3   I–MSP   Chan 40   Rwy 29L   LOM NARCO NDB.
  **ILS** 109.3   I–APL   Rwy 04   LOM VAGEY NDB. Glide slope unusable for coupled approaches below 1085.
  **ILS/DME** 110.3   I–HKZ   Chan 40   Rwy 11R.
  **ILS** 110.7   I–PJL   Rwy 11L.
  **ILS** 110.5   I–SIJ   Rwy 22.

**MOBERG AIR BASE SPB**   (See BEMIDJI)

FIGURE 191A.——Excerpt from Airport/Facilities Directory.

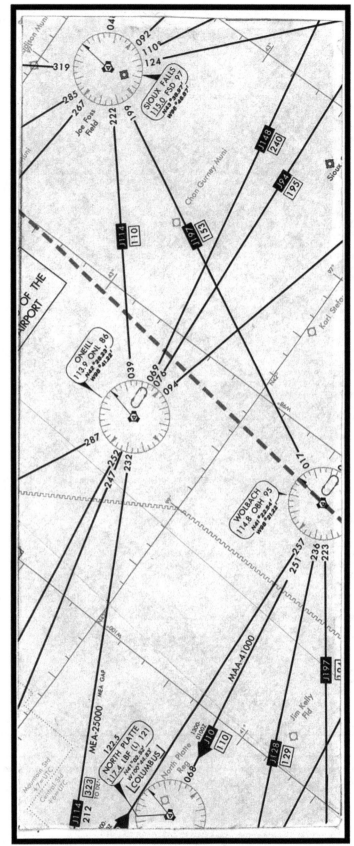

FIGURE 192.—High Altitude Airways.

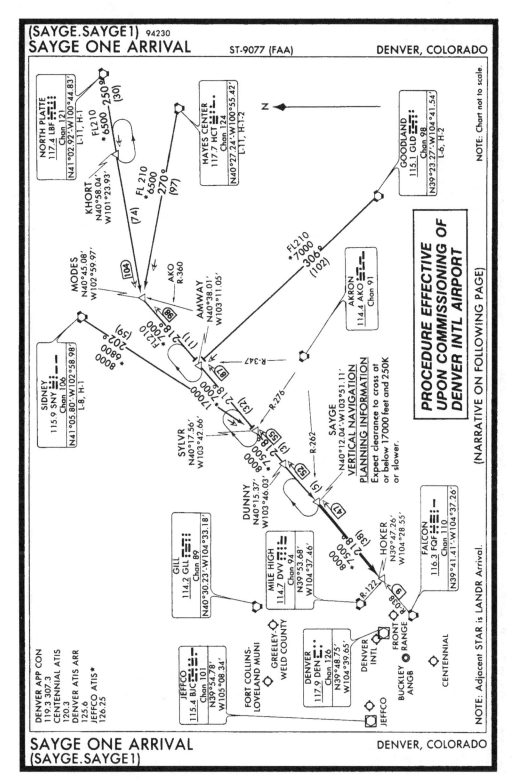

FIGURE 193.—SAYGE ONE ARRIVAL (SAYGE.SAYGE1).

(SAYGE.SAYGE1) 93315
**SAYGE ONE ARRIVAL**     ST-9077 (FAA)     DENVER, COLORADO

ARRIVAL DESCRIPTION

<u>GOODLAND TRANSITION (GLD.SAYGE1):</u> From over GLD VORTAC via GLD
R-306 and FQF R-038 to SAYGE INT. Thence . . . .
<u>HAYES CENTER TRANSITION (HCT.SAYGE1):</u> From over HCT VORTAC via HCT
R-270 and FQF R-038 to SAYGE INT. Thence . . . .
<u>NORTH PLATTE TRANSITION (LBF.SAYGE1):</u> From over LBF VORTAC via LBF
R-250 and FQF R-038 to SAYGE INT. Thence . . . .
<u>SIDNEY TRANSITION (SNY.SAYGE1):</u> From over SNY VORTAC via SNY R-202
and FQF R-038 to SAYGE INT. Thence . . . .
. . . . From over SAYGE INT via FQF R-038 to HOKER INT. Expect radar vectors to
the final approach course at or before HOKER INT.

**PROCEDURE EFFECTIVE
UPON COMMISSIONING OF
DENVER INTL AIRPORT**

**SAYGE ONE ARRIVAL**     DENVER, COLORADO
(SAYGE.SAYGE1)

FIGURE 193A.—SAYGE ONE ARRIVAL (SAYGE.SAYGE1).

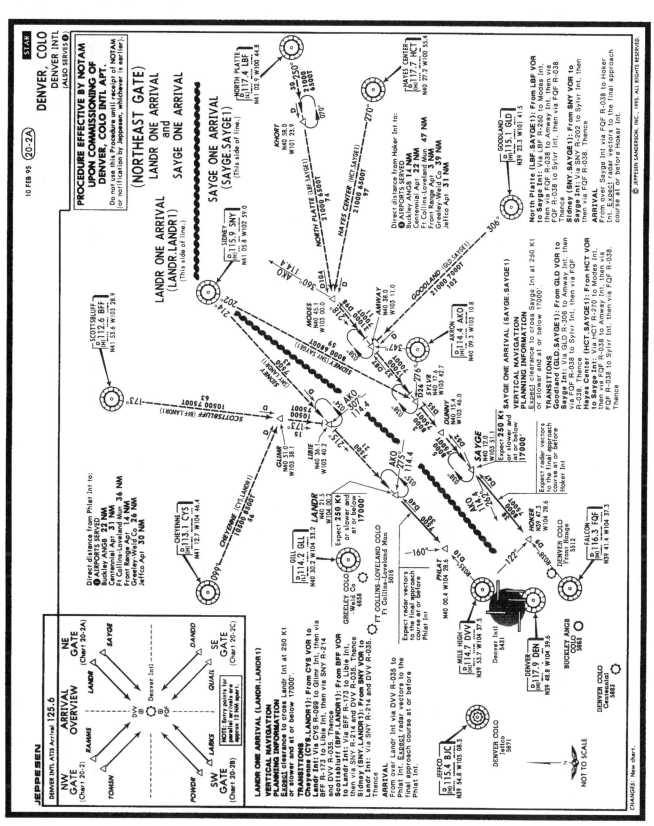

FIGURE 194.—Landr One Arrival/Sayge One Arrival.

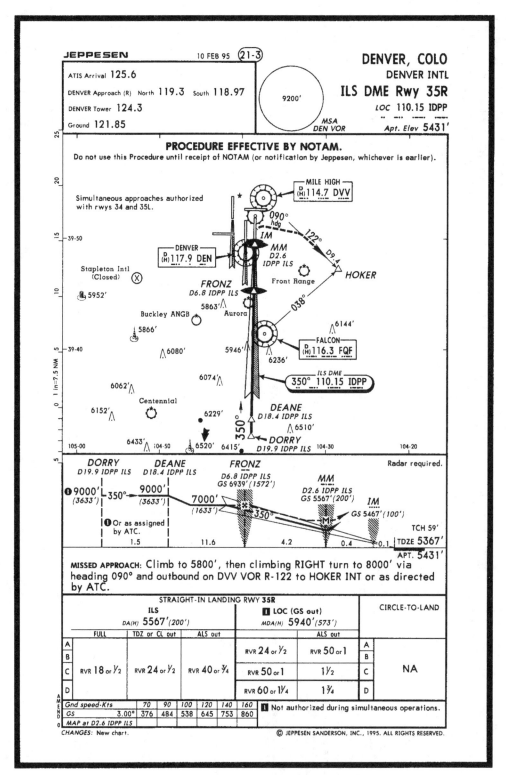

FIGURE 195.—ILS DME RWY 35R.

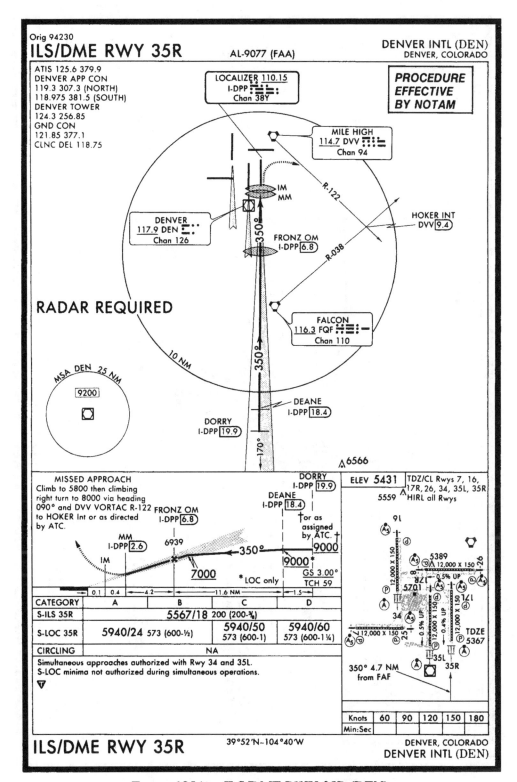

FIGURE 195A.—ILS/DME RWY 35R (DEN).

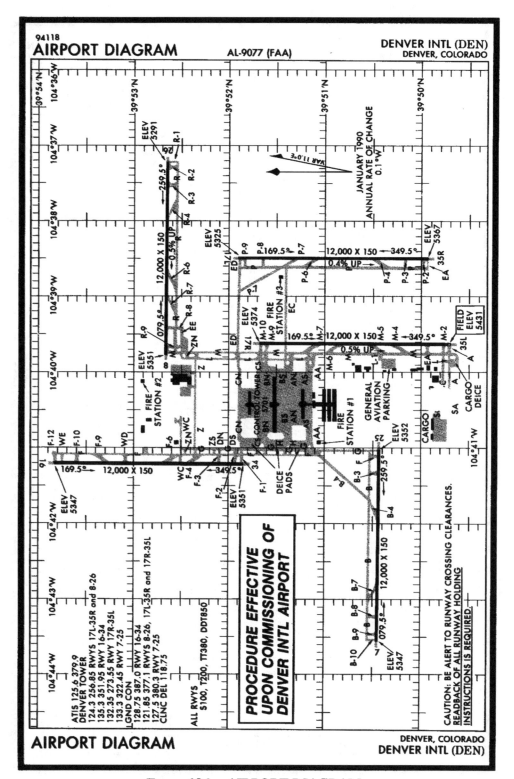

FIGURE 196.—AIRPORT DIAGRAM.

**DENVER INTL**    (DEN)    16 NE    UTC–7 (–6DT)    N39°51.51' W104°40.02'          **DENVER**

5431   B   S4   **FUEL** 100, 100LL, MOGAS   OX 1, 3          **H–2D, L–6E, 8G, A**

RWY 07-25: H12000X150 (CONC–GRVD)    S–100, D–200, DT–380, DDT–850   HIRL   CL       **IAP**

   RWY 07: MALSR. TDZ. PAPI(P4R)---GA 3.0° TCH 55'.      RWY 25: MALSR. PAPI(P4L)---GA 3.0° TCH 55'.

RWY 08-26: H12000X150 (CONC–GRVD)    S–100, D–200, DT–380, DDT–850   HIRL   CL

   RWY 08: MALSR. PAPI(P4L)---GA 3.0° TCH 55'.     RWY 26: MALSR. TDZ. PAPI(P4L)---GA 3.0° TCH 55'.

RWY 16-34: H12000X150 (CONC–GRVD)    S–100, D–200, DT–380, DDT–850   HIRL   CL

   RWY 16: MALSR. TDZ. PAPI(P4L)---GA 3.0° TCH 55'.      RWY 34: ALSF2. TDZ. PAPI(P4L)---GA 3.0° TCH 55'.

RWY 17R-35L: H12000X150 (CONC–GRVD)    S–100, D–200, DT–380, DDT–850   HIRL   CL

   RWY 17R: MALSR. TDZ. PAPI(P4L)---GA 3.0° TCH 55'.     RWY 35L: ALSF2. TDZ. PAPI(P4R)---GA 3.0° TCH 55'.

RWY 17L-35R: H12000X150 (CONC–GRVD)    S–100, D–200, DT–380, DDT–850   HIRL   CL

   RWY 17L: MALSR. PAPI(P4L)---GA 3.0° TCH 55'.     RWY 35R: ALSF2. TDZ. PAPI(P4R)---GA 3.0° TCH 55'.

**AIRPORT REMARKS:** Attended continuously. Overhead walk-way on South side of concourse 'A' provides 44 ft high tail and 117 ft wide wing span clearance. Insufficient twy corner fillet pavement in the SE corner of the Twy M/M2 intersection for acft with wingspan over 107 ft. Noise abatement: Stage III or quieter acft only allowed to depart Rwy 25. Ldg fee.

**WEATHER DATA SOURCES:** ASOS (303)342-0838. LLWAS.

**COMMUNICATIONS: ATIS** 125.6 (Arr) (303) 342-0819    134.025 (Dep) (303) 342-0820    **UNICOM** 122.95

   **FSS** (DEN) TF 1-800-WX-BRIEF. NOTAM FILE DEN.

Ⓡ **APP CON** 119.3 (North) 118.975 (South)    **FINAL CON** 120.8

   **TOWER** 135.3 (Rwy 16–34) 133.3 (Rwy 07–25) 132.35 (Rwy 17R–35L) 124.3 (Rwys 08–26 and 17L–35R)

   **GND CON** 128.75 (Rwy 16–34) 127.5 (Rwy 07–25) 121.85 (Rwys 08–26, 17L–35R and 17R–35L)    **CLNC DEL** 118.75

Ⓡ **DEP CON** 128.25 (East/South) 127.05 (North) 126.1 (West/South)

**AIRSPACE: CLASS B** See VFR Terminal Area Chart.

**RADIO AIDS TO NAVIGATION:** NOTAM FILE DEN.

   **(H) VORW/DME** 117.9      DEN      Chan 126     N39°48.75' W104°39.65'     343° 2.8 NM to fld. 5440/11E.

| | | | | |
|---|---|---|---|---|
| ILS/DME | 111.1 | I-LTT | Chan 48 | Rwy 16. |
| ILS/DME | 111.1 | I-OUF | Chan 48 | Rwy 34. |
| ILS/DME | 108.9 | I-FUI | Chan 26 | Rwy 08. |
| ILS/DME | 108.9 | I-JOY | Chan 26 | Rwy 26. |
| ILS/DME | 108.5 | I-ACX | Chan 22 | Rwy 17R. |
| ILS/DME | 108.5 | I-AQD | Chan 22 | Rwy 35L. |
| ILS/DME | 110.15 | I-BXP | Chan 38(Y) | Rwy 17L. |
| ILS/DME | 110.15 | I-DPP | Chan 38(Y) | Rwy 35R. |
| ILS/DME | 111.55 | I-DZG | Chan 52(Y) | Rwy 07. |
| ILS/DME | 111.55 | I-ERP | Chan 52(Y) | Rwy 25. |

**COMM/NAVAID REMARKS:** Emerg frequency 121.5 not avbl at twr.

## SATELLITE AIRPORT COMMUNICATIONS

DENVER, CENTENNIAL (APA)

   DENVER APP/DEP CON 126.375

DENVER, FRONT RANGE (FTG)

   DENVER APP/DEP CON 128.45

DENVER, JEFFCO (BJC)

   DENVER APP/DEP CON 128.45

ERIE, TRI-COUNTY (48V)

   DENVER APP/DEP CON 128.45

FORT COLLINS, DOWNTOWN FORT COLLINS AIRPARK (3V5)

   DENVER APP/DEP CON 134.85

FORT COLLINS-LOVELAND MUNI (FNL)

   DENVER APP/DEP CON 134.85    CLNC DEL 120.25

GREELEY-WELD COUNTY (GXY)

   DENVER APP/DEP CON 134.85    CLNC DEL 126.65

LONGMONT, VANCE BRAND (2V2)

   DENVER APP/DEP CON 128.45

FIGURE 196A.—Excerpt from Airport/Facilities Directory.

Form Approved: OMB No. 2120-0034

| U.S. DEPARTMENT OF TRANSPORTATION FEDERAL AVIATION ADMINISTRATION **FLIGHT PLAN** | (FAA USE ONLY) | ☐ PILOT BRIEFING ☐ STOPOVER | ☐ VNR | TIME STARTED | SPECIALIST INITIALS |
|---|---|---|---|---|---|

| 1. TYPE | 2. AIRCRAFT IDENTIFICATION | 3. AIRCRAFT TYPE/ SPECIAL EQUIPMENT | 4. TRUE AIRSPEED | 5. DEPARTURE POINT | 6. DEPARTURE TIME | | 7. CRUISING ALTITUDE |
|---|---|---|---|---|---|---|---|
| VFR ☐ <br> IFR ☒ <br> DVFR ☐ | HOSS 2 | A109K2/A | ** KTS | EGE EAGLE CO. REGIONAL | PROPOSED (Z) | ACTUAL (Z) | 14000 |

**8. ROUTE OF FLIGHT**

DBL, VI34 FFU, V21 JAURN, SL, SLC

| 9. DESTINATION (Name of airport and city) SLC SALT LAKE CITY INT'L | 10. EST. TIME ENROUTE | | 11. REMARKS L/O = LEVEL OFF    PPH = POUNDS PER HOUR **CAS 139 ISA +20 TO +14 VARIATION: PUC 14E. |
|---|---|---|---|
| | HOURS | MINUTES | |

| 12. FUEL ON BOARD | | 13. ALTERNATE AIRPORT(S) | 14. PILOT'S NAME, ADDRESS & TELEPHONE NUMBER & AIRCRAFT HOME BASE | 15. NUMBER ABOARD |
|---|---|---|---|---|
| HOURS | MINUTES | OGD OGDEN HINCKLEY | 17. DESTINATION CONTACT/TELEPHONE (OPTIONAL) | 8 |

| 16. COLOR OF AIRCRAFT ORANGE/BLUE | CIVIL AIRCRAFT PILOTS. FAR Part 91 requires you file an IFR flight plan to operate under instrument flight rules in controlled airspace. Failure to file could result in a civil penalty not to exceed $1,000 for each violation (Section 901 of the Federal Aviation Act of 1958, as amended). Filing of a VFR flight plan is recommended as a good operating practice. See also Part 99 for requirements concerning DVFR flight plans. |
|---|---|

FAA Form 7233-1 (8-82)      CLOSE VFR FLIGHT PLAN WITH _____ FSS ON ARRIVAL

## FLIGHT LOG

| CHECK POINTS | | ROUTE | COURSE | WIND | SPEED-KTS | | DIST | TIME | | FUEL | |
|---|---|---|---|---|---|---|---|---|---|---|---|
| FROM | TO | ALTITUDE | | TEMP | TAS | GS | NM | LEG | TOT | LEG | TOT |
| EGE | DBL | | | | | | 13 | | :10:00 | | 101* |
| DBL | JNC | V-134 <br> 14000 | | 100/41 <br> ISA+20 | | | | | | | |
| JNC | PUC | V134 <br> 14000 | | | | | | | | | |
| PUC | FFU | V134 <br> 1400 | | 120/34 <br> ISA+14 | | | | | | | |
| FFU | JAURN | V21 <br> 14000 | | | | | | | | | |
| JAURN | SLC | DESCENT & APPROACH | | | | | 18 | :10:00 | | 92 | |
| | | | | | | | | | | | |
| | | | | | | | | | | | |
| SLC | OGD | | | | | | 160 | 24 | :09:00 | | |

| OTHER DATA: NOTE: | * Includes Taxi Fuel <br> Use 495 PPH Total Fuel Flow From L/O To Start Of Descent. <br> Use 469 PPH Total Fuel Flow For Reserve And Alternate Requirements. <br> A Missed Approach Requires 33# of Fuel. | TIME and FUEL: As required by FARs. | | |
|---|---|---|---|---|
| | | TIME | FUEL (LB) | |
| | | | | EN ROUTE |
| | | | | RESERVE |
| | | | | ALTERNATE |
| | | | | TOTAL |

FIGURE 197.—Flight Plan/Flight Log.

## COLORADO

**EAGLE CO REGIONAL**   (EGE)   4 W   UTC–7(–6DT)   N39°38.55' W106°55.06'   **DENVER**
  6535   B   S4   **FUEL** 100, 100LL, JET A1, JET A1 +   OX 1, 3   ARFF Index C   **H–2C, L–5D, 6E, 8F**
  **RWY 07–25:** H8000X150 (ASPH)   S–60, D–115   MIRL   **IAP**
   **RWY 07:** REIL. Tree. Rgt tfc.       **RWY 25:** MALSR. REIL. PAPI(P4L)—GA 3.0° TCH 45'.
  **AIRPORT REMARKS:** Attended 1400–0200Z‡. CLOSED to unscheduled air carrier operations with more than 30
    passenger seats except PPR call arpt manager 303–524–9490. High unmarked terrain all quadrants. Ngt ops
    discouraged to pilots unfamiliar with arpt. Rwy 07 mountain top 10:1 clearance 12000' from thld 1500' left of
    rwy centerline extended. Recommend all acft departing Rwy 25 initiate a left turn as soon as altitude and safety
    permit to avoid high terrain. Extensive military helicopter training operations surface to 1000' AGL within 25 NM
    radius Eagle County Arpt 1330–0500Z‡. Wildlife in vicinity of arpt. No snow removal at nights. Rwy 25 PAPI only
    visible to 6° left of centerline due to terrain. After 0300Z‡ ACTIVATE MALSR Rwy 25 MIRL Rwy 07–25, PAPI
    Rwy 25 and REIL Rwy 07 and Rwy 25—CTAF.
  **WEATHER DATA SOURCES:** AWOS-3 135.575 (303) 524–7386. Frequency 135.575 out of svc 1400–0200Z‡.
  **COMMUNICATIONS: CTAF** 118.2   **UNICOM** 122.95
   **DENVER FSS (DEN)** TF 1–800–WX–BRIEF. NOTAM FILE EGE.
   **RCO** 122.2 (DENVER FSS)
   **DENVER CENTER APP/DEP CON** 134.5
   **TOWER** 118.2 NFCT (1400–0200Z‡) VFR only. **GND CON** 121.8
  **AIRSPACE: CLASS D** svc effective 1400–0200Z‡ other times CLASS E.
  **RADIO AIDS TO NAVIGATION:** NOTAM FILE DEN.
   **SNOW (L) VORW/DME** 109.2   SXW   Chan 29   N39°37.77' W106°59.47'   065° 3.5 NM to fld. 8060/12E.
    Unmonitored.
   **ILS/DME** 110.1   I–EGE   Chan 38   Rwy 25   (LOC only). LOC/DME unmonitored.

---

**EASTON (VALLEY VIEW)**   (See GREELEY)

---

# ECKERT/ORCHARD CITY
## DOCTORS MESA   (E00)   3 W   UTC–7(–6DT)   N38°51.17' W108°01.04'   **DENVER**
  5600   **FUEL** 100, MOGAS                      Not insp.
  **RWY 08–26:** 6750X110 (DIRT–TURF)
   **RWY 08:** Hill.       **RWY 26:** Tree.
  **AIRPORT REMARKS:** Attended continuously. Powerlines across middle of rwy 2352' from Rwy 26 end perpendicular to
    centerline, marked with 3 red powerline marker balls. Vegetation/grass on and in vicinity of rwy. +200'
    mountains 3 miles west of arpt. Wildlife on and in vicinity of arpt. Rwy 26 has end reflectors. Takeoffs to the east
    and landings to the west preferred, SW winds predominant. Rwy 08–26 soft when wet.
  **COMMUNICATIONS: CTAF/UNICOM** 122.8
   **DENVER FSS (DEN)** TF 1–800–WX–BRIEF. NOTAM FILE DEN.

---

# ELLICOTT
## COLORADO SPRINGS EAST   (CO50)   3 NW   UTC–7(–6DT)   N38°52.47' W104°24.60'   **DENVER**
  6145   S2   **FUEL** 100LL   **H–2D, L–6E**
  **RWY 17–35:** H5000X60 (ASPH)   RWY LGTS (NSTD)
   **RWY 35:** Rgt tfc.
  **RWY 08–26:** 3440X60 (GRVL)
   **RWY 08:** Fence.
  **AIRPORT REMARKS:** Attended 1500–0000Z‡. P–line runs perpendicular to Rwy 08 1500' from rwy end. Rwy 17–35
    asph broken and loose in areas. Rwy 08–26 rough at intersection of Rwy 17–35. 4' fence 125' from centerline
    both sides of Rwy 08–26 W of Rwy 17–35. Rwy 17–35 lights on E side of rwy only. For NSTD rwy lights call
    719–683–2701. Fee for commercial acft ctc arpt manager 719–683–2701.
  **COMMUNICATIONS: CTAF** 122.9
   **DENVER FSS (DEN)** TF 1–800–WX–BRIEF. NOTAM FILE DEN.
  **RADIO AIDS TO NAVIGATION:** NOTAM FILE COS.
   **COLORADO SPRINGS (L) VORTACW** 112.5   COS   Chan 72   N38°56.67' W104°38.01'   099° 11.3 NM to fld.
    6930/13E.

FIGURE 198.—Excerpt from Airport/Facilities Directory.

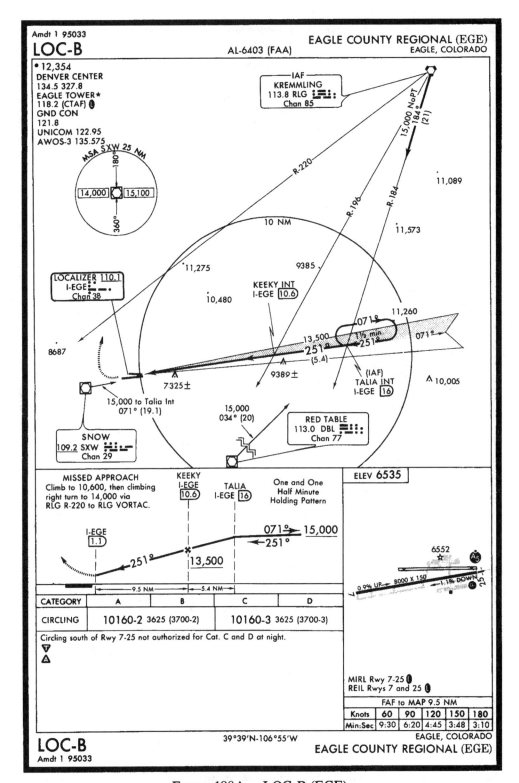

FIGURE 198A.—LOC-B (EGE).

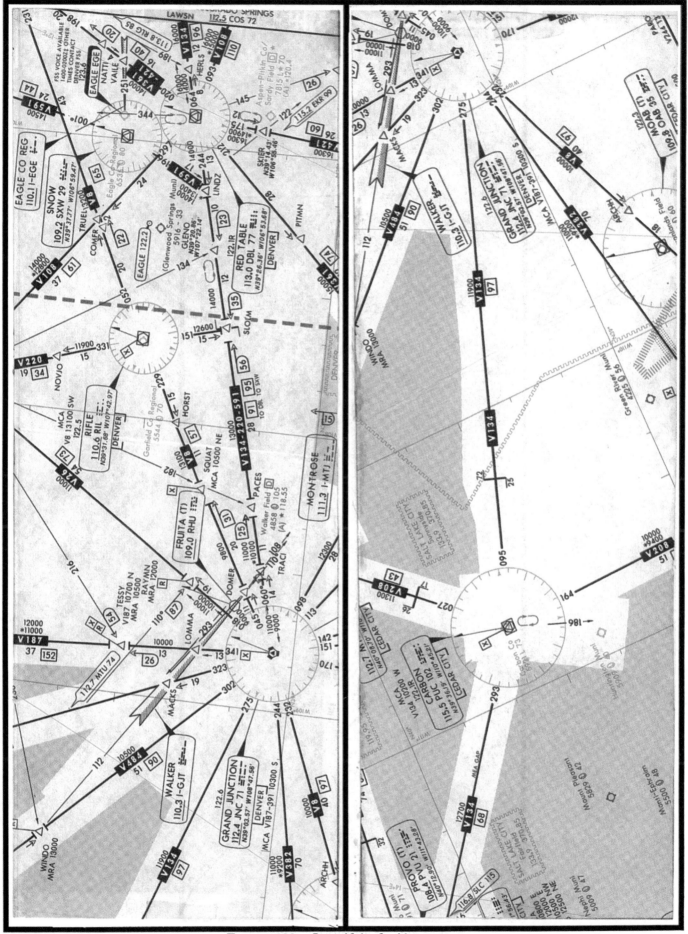

FIGURE 199.—Low Altitude Airways.

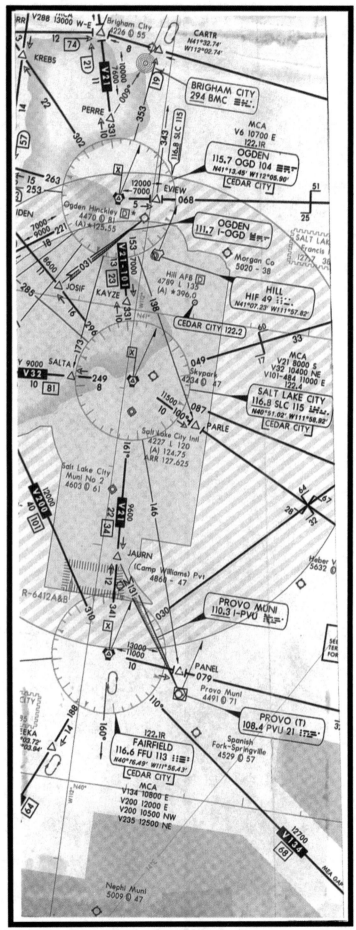

FIGURE 200.—Low Altitude Airways.

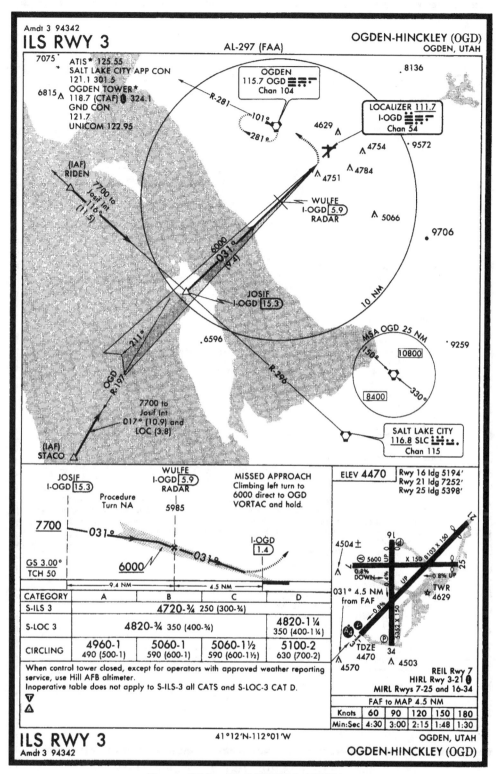

FIGURE 201.—ILS RWY 3 (OGD).

**MOUNT PLEASANT** (43U) 2 SW UTC–7(–6DT) N39°31.48′ W111°28.51′     **LAS VEGAS**
  5829 B     **L-5C**
  **RWY 02-20:** H4260X60 (ASPH)   MIRL
    **RWY 20:** Road.
  **AIRPORT REMARKS:** Unattended. Rwy 02–20 marked by stripes. For runway lights key 122.8 7 times.
  **COMMUNICATIONS:** CTAF 122.9
    **CEDAR CITY FSS (CDC)** TF 1–800–WX–BRIEF. NOTAM FILE CDC.
  **RADIO AIDS TO NAVIGATION:** NOTAM FILE CDC.
    **DELTA (H) VORTAC** 116.1   DTA   Chan 108   N39°18.14′ W112°30.33′   058° 49.7 NM to fld. 4600/16E.

**MYTON**   N40°08.70′ W110°07.66′   NOTAM FILE CDC.     **SALT LAKE CITY**
  **(H) VORTAC** 112.7   MTU   Chan 74   270° 12.0 NM to Duchesne Muni. 5332/14E.   **H-2C, L-5C, 8E**
  **RCO** 122.1R 112.7T (CEDAR CITY FSS)

**NEPHI MUNI** (U14) 3 NW UTC–7(–6DT) N39°44.33′ W111°52.30′′     **LAS VEGAS**
  5009 B  S4 **FUEL** 100LL, JET A     **L-5C, 7D, 8E**
  **RWY 16-34:** H4700X75 (ASPH)   S–21   MIRL
    **RWY 16:** Thld dsplcd 200′.     **RWY 34:** Thld dsplcd 400′.
  **AIRPORT REMARKS:** Attended continuously. Rwy 16–34 cracking and loose chips on apron and rwy. Rwy 16 thld
    relocated 200′ for ngt operations, Rwy 34 thld relocated 400′ for ngt operations, 4100′ of rwy avbl for ngt
    operations. ACTIVATE MIRL Rwy 16–34—CTAF.
  **COMMUNICATIONS:** CTAF/UNICOM 122.8
    **CEDAR CITY FSS (CDC)** TF 1–800–WX–BRIEF. NOTAM FILE CDC.
  **RADIO AIDS TO NAVIGATION:** NOTAM FILE PVU.
    **PROVO (T) VORW/DME** 108.4   PVU   Chan 21   N40°12.90′ W111°43.28′   179° 29.4 NM to fld. 4490/15E.

**OGDEN-HINCKLEY** (OGD) 3 SW UTC–7(–6DT) N41°11.76′ W112°00.73′     **SALT LAKE CITY**
  4470 B  S4 **FUEL** 80, 100, JET A1 +   OX 1, 2   TPA—5215(745)   ARFF Index Ltd.   **H-1C, L-7D**
  **RWY 03-21:** H8103X150 (ASPH-PFC)   S–75, D–100, DT–170   HIRL   0.8% up SW   **IAP**
    **RWY 03:** MALS. VASI(V2L). Trees.     **RWY 21:** Thld dsplcd 851′. Signs. Rgt tfc.
  **RWY 07-25:** H5600X150 (ASPH)   S–20, D–50, DT–70   MIRL   0.3% up W
    **RWY 07:** REIL. VASI(V4L)—GA 3.5° TCH 50′. Tree.     **RWY 25:** Thld dsplcd 202′. Road. Rgt tfc.
  **RWY 16-34:** H5352X150 (ASPH)   S–50, D–75, DT–120   MIRL   0.4% up S
    **RWY 16:** PAPI(P2L)—GA 3.0° TCH 40′. Thld dsplcd 158′. Ditch. Rgt tfc.
    **RWY 34:** PAPI(P2L)—GA 3.0° TCH 40′. Sign.
  **AIRPORT REMARKS:** Attended continuously. Parachute jumping on arpt between Rwys 21 and 25. Rwy 07–25 CLOSED
    indefinitely. Flocks of birds on and in vicinity of arpt. No multiple approaches. No practice approaches—full stop
    ldgs only from 0500–1400Z‡. CLOSED to air carrier ops with more than 30 passenger seats except PPR call arpt
    manager or twr 801–629–8251/625–5569. Be alert parking lot lgts off the apch end of Rwy 34 can be confused
    for rwy lgts. Acft exceeding S–50, D–75 and DT–120 use Taxiway C and conc apron except PPR call arpt
    manager 801–629–8251/625–5569. Air carriers use Rwy 03–21 and Taxiway C only. No snow removal after twr
    closes. When twr clsd ACTIVATE HIRL Rwy 03–21 and taxiway lights—CTAF. MIRL Rwys 07–25 and 16–34 and
    REIL Rwy 07 not avbl when twr closed. NOTE: See Land and Hold Short Operations Section.
  **WEATHER DATA SOURCE:** LAWRS.
  **COMMUNICATIONS:** CTAF 118.7   **ATIS** 125.55 (1400–0500Z‡)   **UNICOM** 122.95
    **CEDAR CITY FSS (CDC)** TF 1–800–WX–BRIEF. NOTAM FILE OGD.
  **RCO** 122.1R 115.7T (CEDAR CITY FSS)
  ® **SALT LAKE CITY APP/DEP CON** 121.1
    **TOWER** 118.7 (1400–0500Z‡)   **GND CON** 121.7
  **AIRSPACE: CLASS D** svc effective 1400–0500Z‡ other times CLASS G.
  **RADIO AIDS TO NAVIGATION:** NOTAM FILE OGD.
    **(L) VORTAC** 115.7   OGD   Chan 104   N41°13.45′ W112°05.90′   099° 4.3 NM to fld. 4220/14E.
      VORTAC unusable 010°–130° beyond 25 NM below 11,300′   350°–010° beyond 38 NM below 11,000′
    **ILS/DME** 111.7   I–OGD   Chan 54   Rwy 03. ILS/DME unmonitored when twr clsd.
  **COMM/NAVAID REMARKS:** Emerg frequency 121.5 not avbl at twr.

FIGURE 201A.—Excerpt from Airport/Facilities Directory.

Form Approved: OMB No. 2120-0034

| U.S. DEPARTMENT OF TRANSPORTATION FEDERAL AVIATION ADMINISTRATION **FLIGHT PLAN** | (FAA USE ONLY) | ☐ PILOT BRIEFING  ☐ STOPOVER | ☐ VNR | TIME STARTED | SPECIALIST INITIALS |
|---|---|---|---|---|---|

| 1. TYPE | 2. AIRCRAFT IDENTIFICATION | 3. AIRCRAFT TYPE/ SPECIAL EQUIPMENT | 4. TRUE AIRSPEED | 5. DEPARTURE POINT | 6. DEPARTURE TIME | | 7. CRUISING ALTITUDE |
|---|---|---|---|---|---|---|---|
| ☐ VFR  X IFR  ☐ DVFR | PTL 55 | B/B747/R | 460 KTS | LAS  LAS VEGAS | PROPOSED (Z) | ACTUAL (Z) | FL390 |

**8. ROUTE OF FLIGHT**

LAS OASIS8.BTY, J92 OAL, OAL.LOCKE SFO

| 9. DESTINATION (Name of airport and city)  SFO  SAN FRANCISCO INT'L. | 10. EST. TIME ENROUTE | | 11. REMARKS  L/O = LEVEL OFF    PPH = POUNDS PER HOUR |
|---|---|---|---|
| | HOURS | MINUTES | |

| 12. FUEL ON BOARD | | 13. ALTERNATE AIRPORT(S) | 14. PILOT'S NAME, ADDRESS & TELEPHONE NUMBER & AIRCRAFT HOME BASE | 15. NUMBER ABOARD |
|---|---|---|---|---|
| HOURS | MINUTES | OAK  METROPOLITAN OAKLAND INT'L | | |
| 4 | 30 | | 17. DESTINATION CONTACT/TELEPHONE (OPTIONAL) | 339 |

| 16. COLOR OF AIRCRAFT  WHITE/GREEN | CIVIL AIRCRAFT PILOTS. FAR Part 91 requires you file an IFR flight plan to operate under instrument flight rules in controlled airspace. Failure to file could result in a civil penalty not to exceed $1,000 for each violation (Section 901 of the Federal Aviation Act of 1958, as amended). Filing of a VFR flight plan is recommended as a good operating practice. See also Part 99 for requirements concerning DVFR flight plans. |
|---|---|

FAA Form 7233-1 (8-82)    CLOSE VFR FLIGHT PLAN WITH _____ FSS ON ARRIVAL

## FLIGHT LOG

| CHECK POINTS | | ROUTE | | WIND | | SPEED-KTS | | DIST | TIME | | FUEL | |
|---|---|---|---|---|---|---|---|---|---|---|---|---|
| FROM | TO | ALTITUDE | COURSE | TEMP | | TAS | GS | NM | LEG | TOT | LEG | TOT |
| LAS | L/O | OASIS8.BTY CLIMB | | | | | | 65 | | :21:00 | | 5600* |
| L/O | BTY | BTY R-126 FL390 | | 340/53 ISA+4 | | | | | | | | |
| BTY | OAL | J92 FL390 | | | | | | | | | | |
| OAL | GROAN | OAL LOCKE.1 FL390 | | | | | | | | | | |
| GROAN | SFO | DESCENT | | | | | | 75 | :26:00 | | 4500 | |
| | | | | | | | | | | | | |
| SFO | OAK | VECTORS 3000 | | | | | | 29 | :09:00 | | | |
| | | | | | | | | | | | | |

| OTHER DATA: NOTE: | * Includes Taxi Fuel  Use 12,000 PPH Total Fuel Flow From L/O To Start Of Descent.  Use 11,000 PPH Total Fuel Flow For Reserve/Alternate Requirements.  A Missed Approach Requires 1133# of Fuel | TIME and FUEL: As required by FARs. | | |
|---|---|---|---|---|
| | | TIME | FUEL (LB) | |
| | | | | EN ROUTE |
| | | | | RESERVE |
| | | | | ALTERNATE |
| | | | | TOTAL |

FIGURE 202.—Flight Plan/Flight Log.

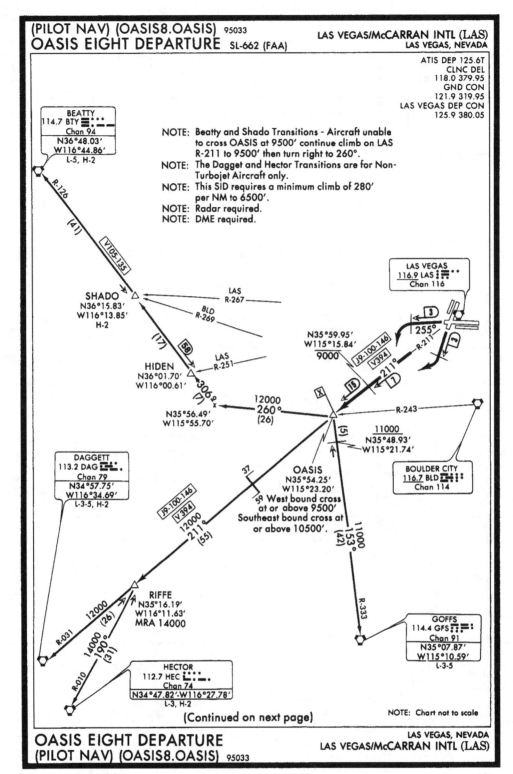

FIGURE 203.—OASIS EIGHT DEPARTURE (LAS).

(PILOT NAV) (OASIS8.OASIS) 95033
OASIS EIGHT DEPARTURE SL-662 (FAA)

LAS VEGAS/McCARRAN INTL (LAS)
LAS VEGAS, NEVADA

▽

DEPARTURE ROUTE DESCRIPTION

TAKE-OFF RUNWAYS 19L/R: Climb on runway heading until reaching 3 DME, then turn right to intercept and proceed via the LAS R-211, thence. . . .
TAKE-OFF RUNWAYS 25L/R: Fly heading 255° until reaching 3 DME, then turn left to intercept and proceed via the LAS R-211, thence. . . .
. . . . cross the LAS R-211 7 DME at or below 9000′, then climb via LAS R-211 to OASIS INT, then via (transition) or (assigned route).
ALL RUNWAYS: Aircraft filing 17000 or above expect filed altitude/flight level 10 minutes after departure.
BEATTY TRANSITION (OASIS8.BTY): From over OASIS INT via heading 260° to intercept BTY R-126 to BTY VORTAC.
DAGGETT TRANSITION (OASIS8.DAG): From over OASIS INT via LAS R-211 and DAG R-031 to DAG VORTAC.
GOFFS TRANSITION (OASIS8.GFS): From over OASIS INT via GFS R-333 to GFS VORTAC.
HECTOR TRANSITION (OASIS8.HEC): From over OASIS INT via LAS R-211 and DAG R-031 to RIFFE INT, then via HEC R-010 to HEC VORTAC.
SHADO TRANSITION (OASIS8.SHADO): From over OASIS INT via heading 260° to intercept BTY R-126 to SHADO INT.

OASIS EIGHT DEPARTURE
(PILOT NAV) (OASIS8.OASIS) 95033

LAS VEGAS, NEVADA
LAS VEGAS/McCARRAN INTL (LAS)

FIGURE 203A.—OASIS EIGHT DEPARTURE (DEPARTURE ROUTE DESCRIPTIONS).

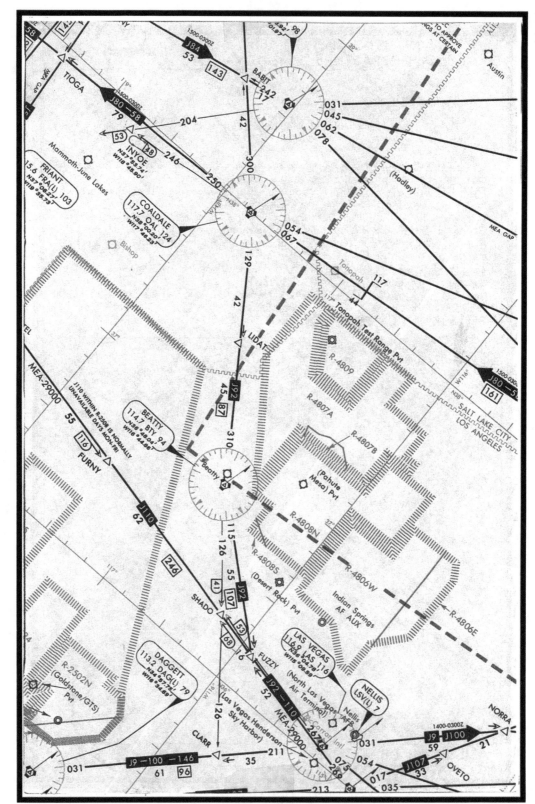

FIGURE 204.—High Altitude Airways.

Appendix 2

**SAN FRANCISCO INTL**  (SFO)  8 SE  UTC−8(−7DT)  N37°37.14′ W122°22.49′    SAN FRANCISCO
11  B  S4  **FUEL** 100, 100LL  OX 1, 2, 3, 4  ARFF Index E    H−2A, L−2F, A
  **RWY 10L−28R:** H11870X200 (ASPH−GRVD)  S−60, D−200, DT−355, DDT−710  HIRL CL    IAP
    **RWY 10L:** REIL. VASI(V6L)—Upper GA 3.25° TCH 109′, Lower GA 3.0° TCH 69′. Transmission twr.
    **RWY 28R:** ALSF2. TDZ. PAPI(P4L)—GA 3.0° TCH 51′. Rgt tfc.
  **RWY 10R−28L:** H10600X200 (ASPH−GRVD)  S−60, D−200, DT−355, DDT−710  HIRL CL
    **RWY 10R:** VASI(V6L)—Upper GA 3.25° TCH 101′, Lower GA 3.0° TCH 60′. Transmission twr. Rgt tfc.
    **RWY 28L:** SSALR.
  **RWY 01R−19L:** H8901X200 (ASPH−GRVD)  S−60, D−195, DT−325, DDT−710  HIRL CL
    **RWY 01R:** REIL. Thld dsplcd 492′. Blast fence.  **RWY 19L:** SSALS. TDZ.
  **RWY 01L−19R:** H7001X200 (ASPH)  S−60, D−170, DT−270, DDT−710  HIRL
    **RWY 01L:** REIL. Trees.  **RWY 19R:** VASI(V6L)—Upper GA 3.25° TCH 79′, Lower GA 3.0° TCH 47′.
**AIRPORT REMARKS:** Attended continuously. Rwy 19L SALSF are only 1100′ long with only one flasher on the last light station. Flocks of birds feeding along shoreline adjacent to arpt; on occasions fly across various parts of arpt. Noise sensitive arpt. For noise abatement procedures ctc arpt noise office Monday–Friday 1600–0100Z‡ by calling 415-876-2220. Ldg fee. Rubber accumulated on first 3000 feet of Rwys 28L−28R. No grooving exists at arpt rwy intersections. Rwy 01R−19L is grooved full length except area between Rwys 28L and 28R and 535′ from Taxiway Charlie north. Rwy 10L−28R grooved full length except from Taxiway Tango to Rwy 10L thld. Rwy 10R−28L grooved full length except from east edge of Rwy 01R−19L to Taxiway Kilo. Rwy 01L−19R grooved full length except from south edge of Taxiway Foxtrot to north edge of Rwy 10L−28R. Widebody acft restricted on Taxiway M west of Taxiway A. Several rwy hold position signs are on the right rather than the left side of the taxiways. Rwys 01L−19R, 01R−19L, 10L−28R and 10R−28L gross weight limit DC−10−10 430,000 pounds, DC−10−30 555,000 pounds, L−1011−100 450,000 pounds, L−1011−200 466,000 pounds, B−747 710,000 pounds. 747−400's shall taxi at a speed of less than 10 miles per hour on all non−restricted taxiways on the terminal side of the intersecting rwys. Movement speed of not more than 5 miles per hour is required when two 747−400's pass or overtake each other on parallel taxiways A and B. 747−400 are restricted from using Twy E to or from Twy B. Airline pilots shall strictly follow the painted nose−gear lines and no oversteering adjustment is permitted. Acft with wingspan of 140−156′ must be under tow with wing walkers on Twy R southwest of the fix−base operator, acft with wingspan exceeding 156′ are prohibited. B747 and larger acft are prohibited from using Twy A between Twy S and the United Airline Freedom area. Twy M clsd west of Gate 16 to acft exceeding a wingspan of 125′. Flight Notification Service (ADCUS) available. NOTE: See Land and Hold Short Operations Section.
**WEATHER DATA SOURCES:** AWOS−1 118.05 (San Bruno Hill). LLWAS.
**COMMUNICATIONS: ATIS (ARR)** 118.85 113.7 108.9 (415) 877−3585 **(DEP)** 135.45 (415) 877−8422/8423
  **UNICOM** 122.95
  **OAKLAND FSS (OAK)** TF 1−800−WX−BRIEF. NOTAM FILE SFO.
Ⓡ **BAY APP CON** 134.5 132.55 135.65
Ⓡ **BAY DEP CON** 135.1 (SE−W) 120.9 (NW−E)
  **TOWER** 120.5  **GND CON** 121.8 (Gates 53−90 W side) 124.25 (Gates 1−52 E side)  **CLNC DEL** 118.2
  **PRE TAXI CLNC** 118.2
**AIRSPACE: CLASS B** See VFR Terminal Area Chart.
**RADIO AIDS TO NAVIGATION:** NOTAM FILE SFO.
  **(L) VORW/DME** 115.8  SFO  Chan 105  N37°37.17′ W122°22.43′  at fld. 10/17E.
    VOR/DME unusable:
      035−055°beyond 15 NM below 6500′    190−260°beyond 10 NM below 4500′
      025−065°beyond 30 NM    260−295°beyond 35 NM below 3000′
      150−190°beyond 25 NM below 4500′    295−330°beyond 20 NM below 4000′
  **BRIJJ NDB (LOM)** 379  SF  N37°34.33′ W122°15.59′  280° 6.2 NM to fld.
    Unusable 160°−195° byd 6 NM all altitudes.
  **ILS/DME** 109.55  I−SFO  Chan 32Y  Rwy 28L.  LOM BRIJJ NDB. LOM unusable 160°−195° byd 6 NM all altitudes.
  **ILS/DME** 111.7  I−GWQ  Chan 54  Rwy 28R.  LOM BRIJJ NDB. LOM unusable 160°−195° byd 6 NM all altitudes.
  **ILS/DME** 108.9  I−SIA  Chan 26  Rwy 19L.
  **LDA/DME** 110.75  Chan 44(Y)  Rwy 28R.
**COMM/NAVID REMARKS:** ILS Rwy 19L−pilots be alert for momentary LOC course excursions due to large acft opr in vicinity of LOC antenna. ATIS frequency 108.9 avbl when SFO VOR out of service 415−877−3585.

---

**SAN JACINTO**  N33°47.70′ W116°59.96′  NOTAM FILE RAL.    LOS ANGELES
  **NDB (MHW)** 227  SJY  184° 3.8 NM to Hemet−Ryan. NDB unmonitored.    L−3C

FIGURE 205.—Excerpt from Airport/Facilities Directory.

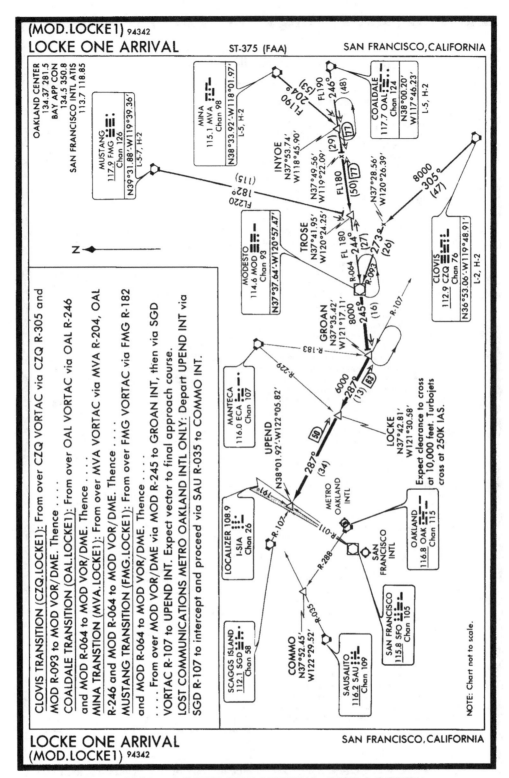

FIGURE 205A.—LOCKE ONE ARRIVAL (MOD.LOCKE1).

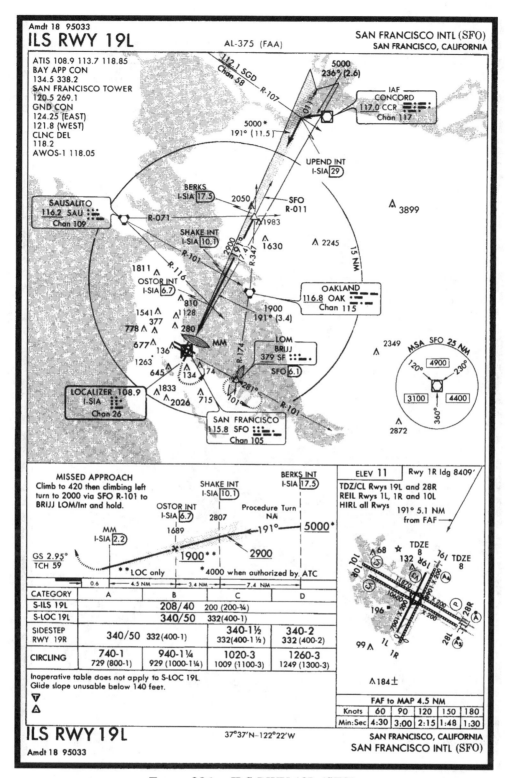

FIGURE 206.—ILS RWY 19L (SFO).

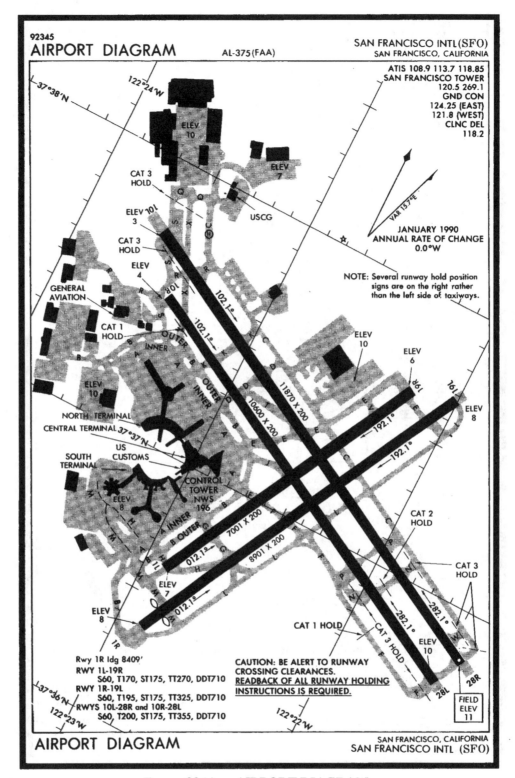

FIGURE 206A.—AIRPORT DIAGRAM.

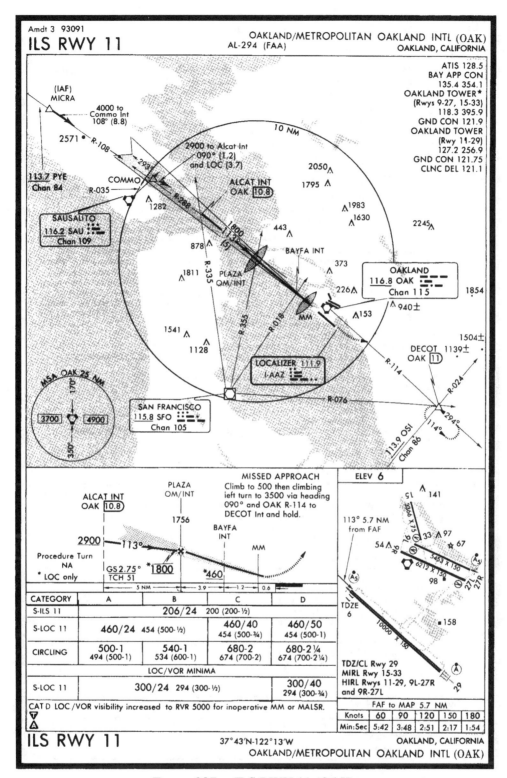

FIGURE 207.—ILS RWY 11 (OAK).

| 84 | **CALIFORNIA** | |
|---|---|---|

**OAKLAND**

**METROPOLITAN OAKLAND INTL** (OAK) 4 S UTC–8(–7DT) N37°43.28' W122°13.24'    **SAN FRANCISCO**
06   B   S4   FUEL 100LL, JET A   OX 1, 2, 3, 4   TPA—See Remarks   LRA   ARFF Index D    **H–2A, L–2F, A**
RWY 11–29: H10000X150 (ASPH–PFC)   S–200, D–200, DT–400, DDT–900   HIRL CL    **IAP**
  RWY 11: MALSR. Rgt tfc.   RWY 29: ALSF2. TDZ.
RWY 09R–27L: H6212X150 (ASPH–PFC)   S–75, D–200, DT–400, DDT–800   HIRL
  RWY 09R: VASI(V4L)—GA 3.0° TCH 46'. Tree.   RWY 27L: VASI(V4L)—GA 3.0° TCH 55'.
RWY 09L–27R: H5453X150 (ASPH)   S–75, D–115, DT–180   HIRL
  RWY 09L: VASI(V4L)—GA 3.0° TCH 38'.   RWY 27R: MALSR. Building. Rgt tfc.
RWY 15–33: H3366X75 (ASPH)   S–12.5, D–65, DT–100   MIRL
  RWY 33: Rgt tfc.
AIRPORT REMARKS: Attended continuously. Fee Rwy 11–29 and tiedown  Birds on and in vicinity of arpt. Rwy 09L–27R
  and Rwy 15–33 CLOSED to air carrier acft, except air carrier acft may use Rwy 09L and 27R for taxiing. Rwy
  09L–27R and Rwy 09R–27L CLOSED to 4 engine wide body acft except Rwy 09R–27L operations avbl PPR call
  operations supervisor 510–577–4067. All turbo–jet/fan acft, all 4–engine acft and turbo–prop acft with
  certificated gross weight over 12,500 pounds are prohibited from tkf Rwys 27R/27L or ldg Rwy 09L and Rwy
  09R. Preferential rwy use program in effect 0600–1400Z‡: All acft preferred north fld arrive Rwys 27R/27L or
  Rwy 33; all acft preferred north fld dep Rwys 09R/09L or Rwy 15. If these rwys unacceptable for safety or ATC
  instructions then Rwy 11–29 must be used. Prohibitions not applicable in emerg or whenever Rwy 11–29 is
  closed due to maintenance, construction or safety. For noise abatement information ctc noise abatement office at
  510–577–4276. 400' blast pad Rwy 29 and 500' blast pad Rwy 11. Rwy 29 and Rwy 27L distance remaining
  signs left side. Acft with experimental or limited certification having over 1,000 horsepower or 4,000 pounds are
  restricted to Rwy 11–29. Rwy 09R–27L FAA gross weight strength DC 10–10 350,000 pounds, DC 10–30
  450,000 pounds, L–1011 350,000 pounds. Rwy 11–29 FAA gross weight strength DC 10–10 600,000 pounds,
  DC 10–30 700,000 pounds, L–1011 600,000 pounds. TPA—Rwy 27L 606(600), TPA—Rwy 27R 1006(1000). Rwy
  29 centerline lgts 6500'. Flight Notification Service (ADCUS) available.
COMMUNICATIONS: ATIS 128.5 (510) 635–5850 (N and S Complex)   UNICOM 122.95
  OAKLAND FSS (OAK) on arpt. 122.5 122.2. TF 1–800–WX–BRIEF. NOTAM FILE OAK.
Ⓡ BAY APP CON 135.65 133.95 (South) 135.4 134.5 (East) 135.1 (West) 127.0 (North) 120.9 (Northwest) 120.1
  (Southeast)
Ⓡ BAY DEP CON 135.4 (East) 135.1 (West) 127.0 (North) 120.9 (Northwest)
  OAKLAND TOWER 118.3 (N Complex) 127.2 (S Complex) 124.9
  GND CON 121.75 (S Complex) 121.9 (N Complex)   CLNC DEL 121.1
AIRSPACE: CLASS C svc ctc APP CON
RADIO AIDS TO NAVIGATION: NOTAM FILE OAK.
  OAKLAND (H) VORTACW 116.8   OAK   Chan 115   N37°43.55' W122°13.42'   at fld. 10/17E.   HIWAS.
  RORAY NDB (LMM) 341   AK   N37°43.28' W122°11.65'   253° 1.3 NM to fld.
  ILS 108.7   I–INB   Rwy 29
  ILS 111.9   I–AAZ   Rwy 11
  ILS 109.9   I–OAK   Rwy 27R   LMM RORAY NDB.

**OAKLAND** N37°43.56' W122°13.42'   NOTAM FILE OAK.    **SAN FRANCISCO**
(H) VORTACW 116.8   OAK   Chan 115   at Metropolitan Oakland Intl. 10/17E.   HIWAS.    **H–2A, L–2F, A**
  VOR unusable: 307°–323° byd 10 NM blo 5,000'   307°–323° byd 17 NM blo 12,500'
  DME unusable:
    307°–323° byd 30 NM blo 1,500'                       040°–065° byd 30 NM blo 4,100'
    350°–030° byd 20 NM blo 3,500'
FSS   (OAK)   at Metropolitan Oakland Intl. 122.5 122.2 TF 1–800–WX–BRIEF.

**OCEANO CO** (L52)   1 W   UTC–8(–7DT)   N35°06.08' W120°37.33'    **LOS ANGELES**
14   B   S4   FUEL 100LL   TPA—1000(986)
RWY 11–29: H2325X50 (ASPH)   S–12.5   MIRL
  RWY 11: P–line. Rgt tfc.   RWY 29: Pole.
AIRPORT REMARKS: Attended 1600–0100Z‡. Arpt unattended Christmas day. For fuel after hours call 805–481–6100.
  Ultralight activity on and in vicinity of arpt. Recurring flocks of waterfowl on and in vicinity of arpt. Be alert for
  kites flown along beach 1/2 mile west of rwy. Unsurfaced areas soft and unusable. Taxilanes very narrow near
  buildings and parked acft. Extremely noise sensitive arpt and community, for tkf Rwy 29 pilots are requested to
  maintain rwy heading until crossing the shoreline. ACTIVATE MIRL Rwy 11–29—CTAF.
COMMUNICATIONS: CTAF/UNICOM 122.7
  HAWTHORNE FSS (HHR) TF 1–800–WX–BRIEF. NOTAM FILE HHR.

**OCEAN RIDGE**   (See GUALALA)

**OCEANSIDE** N33°14.44' W117°25.06'   NOTAM FILE CRQ.    **LOS ANGELES**
(H) VORTAC 115.3   OCN   Chan 100   097° 3.6 NM to Oceanside Muni. 90/15E.    **H–2B, L–3C**
  VOR unusable 260°–265° byd 20NM.

FIGURE 207A.—Excerpt from Airport/Facilities Directory.

Form Approved: OMB No. 2120-0034

| U.S. DEPARTMENT OF TRANSPORTATION FEDERAL AVIATION ADMINISTRATION **FLIGHT PLAN** | (FAA USE ONLY) | ☐ PILOT BRIEFING ☐ STOPOVER | ☐ VNR | TIME STARTED | SPECIALIST INITIALS |
|---|---|---|---|---|---|

| 1. TYPE | 2. AIRCRAFT IDENTIFICATION | 3. AIRCRAFT TYPE/ SPECIAL EQUIPMENT | 4. TRUE AIRSPEED | 5. DEPARTURE POINT | 6. DEPARTURE TIME | | 7. CRUISING ALTITUDE |
|---|---|---|---|---|---|---|---|
| VFR **X** IFR DVFR | SLING 2 | S76/A | ** KTS | EYW KEY WEST INT'L | PROPOSED (Z) | ACTUAL (Z) | 9000 |

**8. ROUTE OF FLIGHT**
TIGAR, V157 MIA, V51 PHK, V437 MLB, V3 SMYRA, DA, DAB

| 9. DESTINATION (Name of airport and city) DAB DAYTONA BEACH | 10. EST. TIME ENROUTE HOURS / MINUTES | 11. REMARKS PPH = POUNDS PER HOUR **CAS 120 TEMP ISA+10 TO ISA+1 |
|---|---|---|

| 12. FUEL ON BOARD HOURS / MINUTES | 13. ALTERNATE AIRPORT(S) SGJ ST. AUGUSTINE | 14. PILOT'S NAME, ADDRESS & TELEPHONE NUMBER & AIRCRAFT HOME BASE | 15. NUMBER ABOARD |
|---|---|---|---|
| | | 17. DESTINATION CONTACT/TELEPHONE (OPTIONAL) | 6 |

| 16. COLOR OF AIRCRAFT GREY/RED | CIVIL AIRCRAFT PILOTS. FAR Part 91 requires you file an IFR flight plan to operate under instrument flight rules in controlled airspace. Failure to file could result in a civil penalty not to exceed $1,000 for each violation (Section 901 of the Federal Aviation Act of 1958, as amended). Filing of a VFR flight plan is recommended as a good operating practice. See also Part 99 for requirements concerning DVFR flight plans. |
|---|---|

FAA Form 7233-1 (8-82)         CLOSE VFR FLIGHT PLAN WITH _____ FSS ON ARRIVAL

# FLIGHT LOG

| CHECK POINTS | | ROUTE | | WIND | SPEED-KTS | | DIST | TIME | | FUEL | |
|---|---|---|---|---|---|---|---|---|---|---|---|
| FROM | TO | ALTITUDE | COURSE | TEMP | TAS | GS | NM | LEG | TOT | LEG | TOT |
| EYW | TIGAR | DIRECT CLIMB | | | | | 28 | | :14:00 | | 205.4* |
| TIGAR | MIA | V157 9000 | | 220/23 ISA+10 | | | | | | | |
| MIA | PHK | V51 | | 200/19 ISA+10 | | | | | | | |
| PHK | MLB | V437 | | 180/17 ISA+1 | | | | | | | |
| MLB | SMYRA | V3 | | 190/19 ISA+1 | | | | | | | |
| SMYRA | DAB | DESCENT APPROACH | | | | | 16 | :09:08 | | 139.3 | |
| | | | | | | | | | | | |
| | | | | | | | | | | | |
| DAB | SGJ | DIRECT 4000 | | | | | 48 | :21:00 | | | |

| OTHER DATA: NOTE: | * Includes Taxi Fuel Use 740 PPH Total Fuel Flow From L/O To Start Of Descent. Use 705 PPH Total Fuel Flow For Reserve And Alternate Requirements. A Missed Approach Requires 51# of Fuel. | TIME and FUEL: As required by FARs. | |  |
|---|---|---|---|---|
| | | TIME | FUEL (LB) | |
| | | | | EN ROUTE |
| | | | | RESERVE |
| | | | | ALTERNATE |
| | | | | TOTAL |

FIGURE 208.—Flight Plan/Flight Log.

**56**                                                          **FLORIDA**

**KEYSTONE HEIGHTS**
  **KEYSTONE AIRPARK**  (42J)  3 N  UTC–5(–4DT)  N29°50.66' W82°03.01'     JACKSONVILLE
    196  B  S4  FUEL 100LL, JET A  TPA 1196 (1000)                 H–5E, L–18H, 19B
    RWY 04-22: H5025X100 (ASPH)  S–40, D–80  MIRL                          IAP
      RWY 04: PAPI(P2L)—GA 3.0° TCH 40'. Trees.      RWY 22: PAPI(P2L)—GA 3.0° TCH 40'. Trees.
    RWY 10-28: H4900X75 (ASHP)  S–30, D–60
      RWY 10: Trees.      RWY 28: Trees.
    RWY 16-34: H4400X150 (ASPH)  S–25
      RWY 16: Thld dsplcd 200'. Trees.      RWY 34: Trees.
    AIRPORT REMARKS: Attended 1300–2300Z‡. Parachute Jumping. CAUTION: Ultralgt activity on and in vicinity of arpt.
      CAUTION—Animals on and in vicinity of arpt. ACTIVATE MIRL Rwy 04–22—CTAF. Rwy 16–34 cracked with loose
      grvl and weeds growing thru cracks.
    COMMUNICATIONS: CTAF/UNICOM 122.7
      GAINESVILLE FSS (GNV) TF 1–800–WX–BRIEF. NOTAM FILE GNV.
    Ⓡ JACKSONVILLE APP/DEP CON 123.8
    RADIO AIDS TO NAVIGATION: NOTAM FILE GNV.
      GAINESVILLE (L) VORTAC 116.2  GNV  Chan 109  N29°34.33' W82°21.76'  044° 23.1 NM to fld. 60/01E.
      HIWAS.

---

  **KEY WEST**  N24°35.15' W81°48.03'  NOTAM FILE EYW.                     MIAMI
    (H) VORTAC 113.5  EYW  Chan 82  128° 2.8 NM to Key West Intl. 10/01E.  HIWAS.   H–5E, L–19D
    RCO 123.65 122.2 122.1R 113.5T (MIAMI FSS)
      FSS freqs 123.65 and 122.2 unusable 330°–015° byd 20 NM blo 1500'.

---

  **KEY WEST INTL**  (EYW)  2 E  UTC–5(–4DT)  N24°33.37' W81°45.57'        MIAMI
    4  B  S4  FUEL 100, JET A  AOE  ARFF Index A                           L–19D
    RWY 09-27: H4800X100 (ASPH–GRVD)  S–40, D–95, DT–130  MIRL             IAP
      RWY 09: REIL. VASI(V4L)—GA 3.0° TCH 34'. Tree.    RWY 27: REIL. VASI(V4L)—GA 3.0° TCH 34'. Tree.
    AIRPORT REMARKS: Attended 1300–2300Z‡. CAUTION: Numerous flocks of birds on and in the vicinity of airport.
      CAUTION—Restricted area R-2916 14 NM NE of arpt has strobe–lgtd and marked balloon and cable to 14,000
      ft. Noise Sensitive Area: all jet acft use NBAA close in noise abatement procedures. PPR for unscheduled air
      carrier operations with more than 30 passenger seats 0430–1045Z‡; Call arpt manager 305–296–7223.
      ACTIVATE MIRL Rwy 09–27, VASI/REIL Rwys 09–27—CTAF. Intensive military jet tfc S and E of arpt; acft
      entering arpt tfc area from SE through W. Enter arpt tfc area blo 2000'; refer to MIAMI VFR Terminal Area Chart
      for suggested VFR flyway routes. Flight Notification Service (ADCUS) available.
    COMMUNICATIONS: CTAF 118.2  UNICOM 122.95
      MIAMI FSS (MIA) TF 1–800–WX–BRIEF. NOTAM FILE EYW.
      RCO 123.65 122.2 122.1R 113.5T (MIAMI FSS)
    Ⓡ NAVY KEY WEST APP/DEP CON 124.45 (1200–0500Z‡)      ⓇMIAMI CENTER APP/DEP CON 132.2 (0500–1200Z‡)
      TOWER 118.2 (1100–0300Z‡)  GND CON 121.9  CLNC DEL 121.9
    AIRSPACE: CLASS D svc effective 1100–0300Z‡ other times CLASS G.
    RADIO AIDS TO NAVIGATION: NOTAM FILE EYW.  VHF/DF ctc MIAMI FSS.
      (H) VORTAC 113.5  EYW  Chan 82  N24°35.15' W81°48.03'  127° 2.9 NM to fld. 10/01E.  HIWAS.
      FISH HOOK NDB (H) 332  FIS  N24°32.90' W81°47.18'  073° 1.5 NM to fld.
      ASR
    COMM/NAVAID REMARKS: FSS freqs 123.65 and 122.2 unusable 330°–015° beyond 20 NM below 1500'.

---

  **KEY WEST NAS**  AIRSPACE: CLASS D svc effective 1100–0300Z‡ other times CLASS G.

---

  **KISSIMMEE MUNI**  (See ORLANDO)

---

  **KNIGHT**  N27°54.50' W82°27.26'  NOTAM FILE PIE.                        MIAMI
    NDB (MHW) 270  TPF  at Peter O'Knight. NDB unusable byd 20NM.             L–19B

---

  **KOBRA**  N30°51.19' W86°32.20'  NOTAM FILE CEW.                         NEW ORLEANS
    NDB (LOM) 201  CE  170° 4.5 NM to Bob Sikes.

---

  **LA BELLE**  N26°49.69' W81°23.49'  NOTAM FILE MIA                       MIAMI
    (L) VORTAC 110.4  LBV  Chan 41  205° 5.2 NM to La Belle Muni. 30/01E.     H–5E, L–19C
    RCO 122.1R 110.4T (MIAMI FSS)

FIGURE 209.—Excerpt from Airport/Facilities Directory.

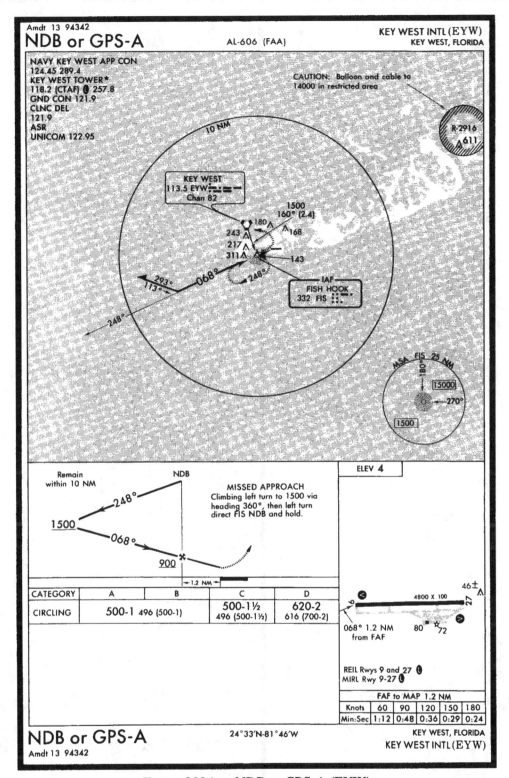

FIGURE 209A.—NDB or GPS-A (EYW).

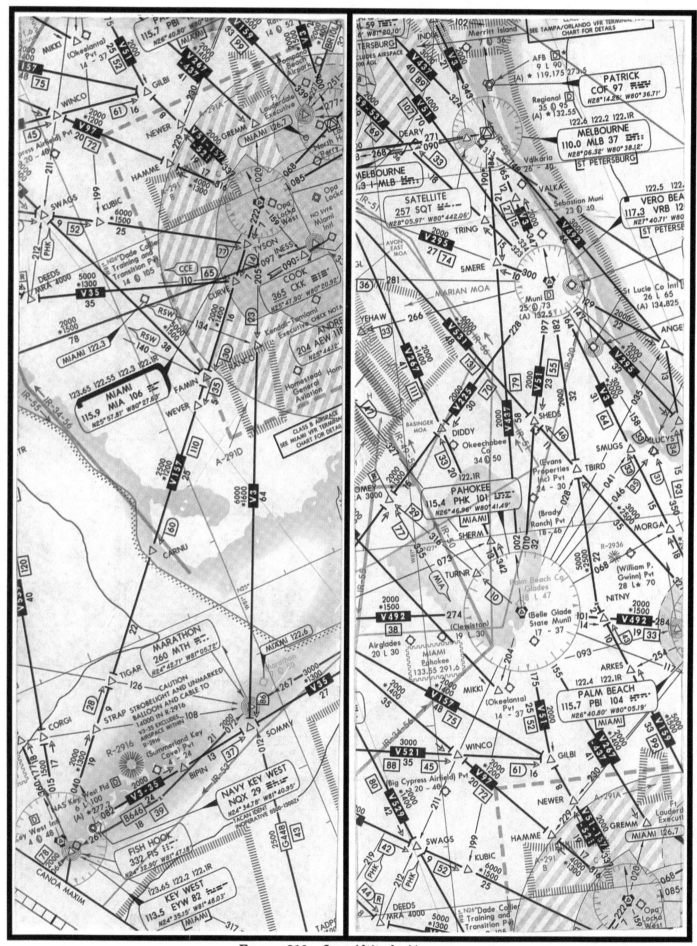

FIGURE 210.—Low Altitude Airways.

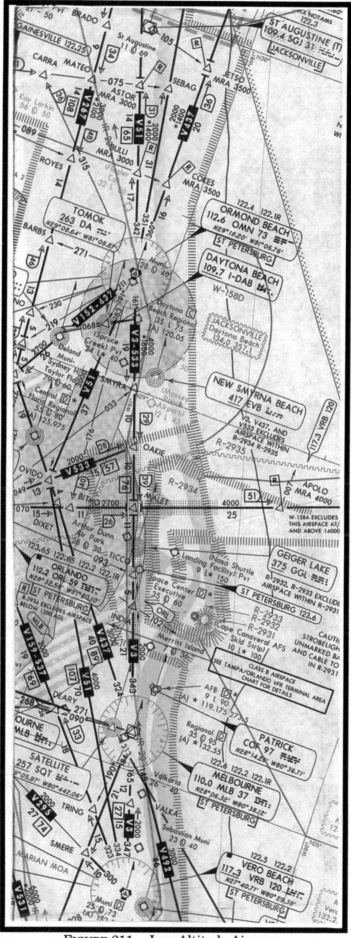

FIGURE 211.—Low Altitude Airways.

**46**                                                          **FLORIDA**

**CROSS CITY** (CTY)   1 E   UTC−5(−4DT)   N29°38.07′ W83°06.34′                    JACKSONVILLE
  42   B   FUEL 100LL                                                                H−5D, L−18G, 19B
  RWY 13−31: H5001X150 (ASPH)   S−13   MIRL                                          IAP
    RWY 13: Trees.        RWY 31: Trees.
  RWY 04−22: H4050X150 (ASPH)   S−13   MIRL
    RWY 04: Trees.        RWY 22: Trees.
  AIRPORT REMARKS: Attended continuously. ACTIVATE MIRL Rwy 13−31 and 04−22—CTAF.
  COMMUNICATIONS: CTAF/UNICOM 122.8
    GAINESVILLE FSS (GNV) TF 1−800−WX−BRIEF. NOTAM FILE GNV.
    RCO 122.1R 112.0T (GAINESVILLE FSS)
  ® JAX CENTER APP/DEP CON 127.8
  RADIO AIDS TO NAVIGATION: NOTAM FILE GNV.
    (L) VORTAC 112.0   CTY   Chan 57   N29°35.94′ W83°02.92′   308° 3.7 NM to fld. 30/02W.

**CRYSTAL RIVER** (X31)   3 SE   UTC−5(−4DT)   N28°52.07′ W82°34.47′                JACKSONVILLE
  10   B   S2   FUEL 100LL, JET A                                                    L−19B
  RWY 09−27: H4297X60 (ASPH)   LIRL                                                  IAP
    RWY 09: PAPI(P2R)—GA 3.0° TCH 38′. P-line.        RWY 27: REIL. Trees.
  RWY 18−36: 3020X57 (TURF)
    RWY 18: Thld dsplcd 517′. Building.        RWY 36: Thld dsplcd 748′. Road.
  AIRPORT REMARKS: Attended 1200−0000Z‡. Aerobatic activity along N side of Rwy 09−27 and 4 NM SW of arpt. Ctc
    unicom for tfc info and ST PETERSBURG FSS for specific times. Rwy 18−36 dsplcd thld marked with green pipes.
    Rwy 18−36 marked with white pipes every 200′. Rwy 18−36 acft parked 45′ from rwy W edge. ACTIVATE LIRL
    Rwy 09−27—CTAF. Glider ops within 25 NM.
  COMMUNICATIONS: CTAF/UNICOM 122.7
    ST PETERSBURG FSS (PIE) TF 1−800−WX−BRIEF. NOTAM FILE PIE.
  ® JAX CENTER APP/DEP CON 135.75
  RADIO AIDS TO NAVIGATION: NOTAM FILE OCF.
    OCALA (L) VORTAC 113.7   OCF   Chan 84   N29°10.65′ W82°13.58′   225° 26 NM to fld. 80/00E.

**CYPRESS**   N26°09.21′ W81°46.69′   NOTAM FILE APF.                                MIAMI
  (T) VORW/DME 108.6   CCE   Chan 23   at Naples Muni. 10/00E.                        H−5E, L−19C

**DADE−COLLIER TRAINING AND TRANSITION**   (See MIAMI)

**DAVIE**   N26°04.34′ W80°14.69′                                                   MIAMI
  RCO 126.7 (MIAMI FSS)                                                              L−19C, A

**DAYTONA BEACH INTL** (DAB)   3 SW   UTC−5(−4DT)   N29°10.80′ W81°03.48′            JACKSONVILLE
  35   B   S4   FUEL 100LL, JET A   OX 2   TPA—See Remarks   ARFF Index C            H−5E, L−18H, 19B
  RWY 07L−25R: H10500X150 (ASPH−GRVD)   S−75, D−140, DT−220   HIRL                   IAP
    RWY 07L: MALSR. Thld dsplcd 700′.
    RWY 25R: REIL. VASI(V6L)—Upper GA 3.25° TCH 95.3′. Lower GA 2.75° TCH 53.4′. Rgt tfc.
  RWY 16−34: H6000X150 (ASPH−GRVD)   S−75, D−150, DT−260   MIRL
    RWY 16: REIL. PAPI(P4L)—GA 3.0° TCH 45′. Road. Rgt tfc.
    RWY 34: REIL. PAPI(P4L)—GA 3.0° TCH 45′. Trees.
  RWY 07R−25L: H3197X100 (ASPH)   S−30   MIRL
    RWY 07R: PAPI(P2L)—GA 2.86° TCH 40′. Trees. Rgt tfc.        RWY 25L: PAPI(P2L)—GA 2.86° TCH 32′. Ground.
  AIRPORT REMARKS: Attended continuously. Heavy migratory bird activity on and in vicinity of arpt. TPA—835(800) lgt
    acft; 1235(1200) high performance acft. E end of Twy S is non-movement area. NOTE: See Land and Hold Short
    Operations Section.
  WEATHER DATA SOURCES: LLWAS.
  COMMUNICATIONS: ATIS 120.05   UNICOM 122.95
    ST PETERSBURG FSS (PIE) TF 1−800−WX−BRIEF. NOTAM FILE DAB.
  ® APP CON 135.57 (9000′ and above) 118.85 (N 4000′−8500′) 127.07 (S 4000′−8500′) 125.8 (N 3500′ and blo)
    125.35 (S 3500′ and blo)
    TOWER 120.7 118.1   GND CON 121.9   CLNC DEL 119.3
  ® DEP CON 123.9
  AIRSPACE: CLASS C svc continuous ctc APP CON
  RADIO AIDS TO NAVIGATION: NOTAM FILE PIE.
    ORMOND BEACH (H) VORTAC 112.6   OMN   Chan 73   N29°18.20′ W81°06.76′   159° 7.9 NM to fld. 20/00E.
    TOMOK NDB (LOM) 263   DA   N29°08.66′ W81°08.87′   069° 5.2 NM to fld.
    ILS 109.7   I−DAB   Rwy 07L.   LOM TOMOK NDB.
    ASR

FIGURE 212.—Excerpt from Airport/Facilities Directory.

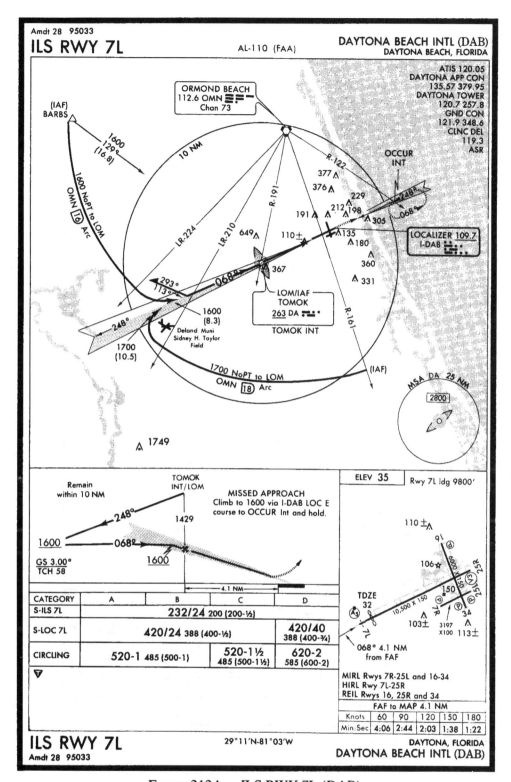

FIGURE 212A.—ILS RWY 7L (DAB).

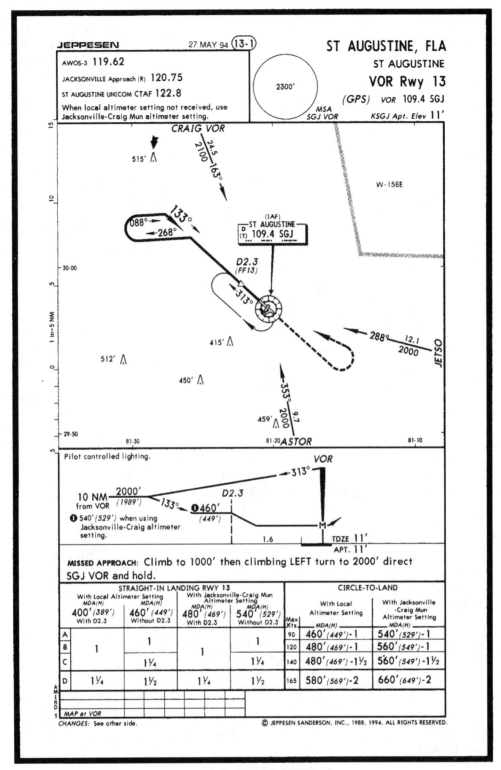

FIGURE 213.—VOR RWY 13.

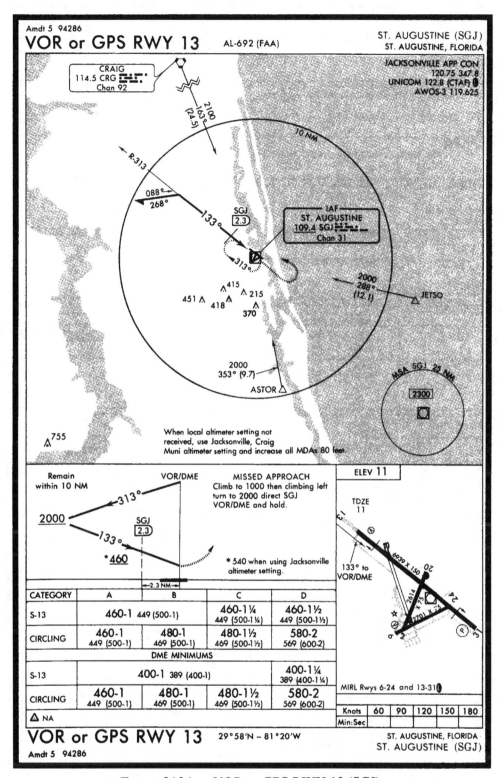

FIGURE 213A.—VOR or GPS RWY 13 (SGJ).

Form Approved: OMB No. 2120-0034

## FLIGHT PLAN

| U.S. DEPARTMENT OF TRANSPORTATION FEDERAL AVIATION ADMINISTRATION | (FAA USE ONLY) | ☐ PILOT BRIEFING | ☐ VNR | TIME STARTED | SPECIALIST INITIALS |
|---|---|---|---|---|---|
| **FLIGHT PLAN** | | ☐ STOPOVER | | | |

| 1. TYPE | 2. AIRCRAFT IDENTIFICATION | 3. AIRCRAFT TYPE/ SPECIAL EQUIPMENT | 4. TRUE AIRSPEED | 5. DEPARTURE POINT | 6. DEPARTURE TIME | | 7. CRUISING ALTITUDE |
|---|---|---|---|---|---|---|---|
| | | | | | PROPOSED (Z) | ACTUAL (Z) | |
| VFR | | | | | | | |
| X IFR | TNA 90 | MD90/G | 440 | KBDL | | | FL330 |
| DVFR | | | KTS | Bradley Int'l | | | |

**8. ROUTE OF FLIGHT**

CSTL.SHERL, J121 BRIGS, BRIGS.VCN 5 PHL

| 9. DESTINATION (Name of airport and city) | 10. EST. TIME ENROUTE | | 11. REMARKS | | |
|---|---|---|---|---|---|
| KPHL PHILADELPHIA INT'L PHILADELPHIA | HOURS | MINUTES | L/O = Level Off    PPH = Pounds Per Hour TEC = Tower to Tower  Variation: BDL 14W, PHL 10W | | |

| 12. FUEL ON BOARD | | 13. ALTERNATE AIRPORT(S) | 14. PILOT'S NAME, ADDRESS & TELEPHONE NUMBER & AIRCRAFT HOME BASE | 15. NUMBER ABOARD |
|---|---|---|---|---|
| HOURS | MINUTES | KACY ATLANTIC CITY INT'L | | 99 |
| 2 | 20 | | 17. DESTINATION CONTACT/TELEPHONE (OPTIONAL) | |

| 16. COLOR OF AIRCRAFT BLACK/RED | CIVIL AIRCRAFT PILOTS. FAR Part 91 requires you file an IFR flight plan to operate under instrument flight rules in controlled airspace. Failure to file could result in a civil penalty not to exceed $1,000 for each violation (Section 901 of the Federal Aviation Act of 1958, as amended). Filing of a VFR flight plan is recommended as a good operating practice. See also Part 99 for requirements concerning DVFR flight plans. |
|---|---|

FAA Form 7233-1 (8-82)          CLOSE VFR FLIGHT PLAN WITH _____ FSS ON ARRIVAL

## FLIGHT LOG

| CHECK POINTS | | ROUTE | | WIND | SPEED-KTS | | DIST | TIME | | FUEL | |
|---|---|---|---|---|---|---|---|---|---|---|---|
| FROM | TO | ALTITUDE | COURSE | TEMP | TAS | GS | NM | LEG | TOT | LEG | TOT |
| BDL | YODER INTER | CSTL1.SHERL CLIMB | | | | | 45 | :15:00 | | | 2560* |
| Yoder Inter | SHERL INTER | CSTL1.SHERL FL330 | | 340/55 ISA | | | | | | | |
| Sherl Inter | BRIGS INTER | J121 FL330 | | | | | | | | | |
| Brigs Inter | VCN | BRIGS.VCN5 FL300 | | | | | | | | | |
| VCN | PHL | BRIGS.VCN5 DESCENT & APPROACH | | | | | 46 | :14:00 | | 1190 | |
| | | | | | | | | | | | |
| | | | | | | | | | | | |
| PHL | ACY | TEC 3000 | | | | | 44 | :12:00 | | | |
| | | | | | | | | | | | |

| OTHER DATA: NOTE: | * Includes Taxi Fuel Use 6150 PPH Total Fuel Flow From L/O To Start Of Descent. Use 5900 PPH Total Fuel Flow For Reserve And Alternate Requirements. A Missed Approach Requires 244# of Fuel. | TIME and FUEL: As required by FARs. |
|---|---|---|

| TIME | FUEL (LB) | |
|---|---|---|
| | | EN ROUTE |
| | | RESERVE |
| | | ALTERNATE |
| | | TOTAL |

FIGURE 214.—Flight Plan/Flight Log.

214

## 20 CONNECTICUT

**WINDSOR LOCKS**

**BRADLEY INTL** (BDL)  3 W  UTC–5(–4DT)  N41°56.33′ W72°40.99′  **NEW YORK**

174  B  S4  **FUEL** 100LL, JET A  OX 1, 2, 3, 4  TPA—See Remarks  H–3J, 6J, L–25C, 28I

LRA  ARFF Index D  **IAP**

**RWY 06–24:** H9502X200 (ASPH–GRVD)  S–200, D–200, DT–350,DDT–710  HIRL  CL

**RWY 06:** ALSF2 TDZ.  **RWY 24:** MALSR. VASI(V4L)—GA 3.0°TCH 56′. Trees.

**RWY 15–33:** H6846X150 (ASPH–GRVD)  S–200, D–200, DT–350  HIRL

**RWY 15:** REIL. VASI(V4L)—GA 3.5°TCH 59′. Trees.  **RWY 33:** MALSF. VASI(V4R)—GA 3.0°TCH 59′. Trees.

**RWY 01–19:** H5145X100 (ASPH)  S–60, D–190, DT–328  MIRL

**RWY 01:** Building.  **RWY 19:** Trees.

**AIRPORT REMARKS:** Attended continuously. Numerous birds frequently on or in vicinity or arpt. TPA—1174(1000) light acft, 1874(1700) heavy acft. Landing fee for business, corporate and revenue producing aircraft. Flight Notification Service (ADCUS) available. NOTE: See Land and Hold Short Operations Section.

**WEATHER DATA SOURCES:** LLWAS.

**COMMUNICATIONS: ATIS** 118.15 (203–627–3423)  **UNICOM** 122.95

**BRIDGEPORT FSS** (BDR) TF 1–800–WX–BRIEF. NOTAM FILE BDL.

**WINDSOR LOCKS RCO** 122.3 (BRIDGEPORT FSS)

®  **BRADLEY APP CON** 125.8 (within 20 miles)

®  **BRADLEY DEP CON** 127.8 (South) 125.35 (North and West) 123.95 (Northeast)

**TOWER** 120.3  **GND CON** 121.9  **CLNC DEL** 121.75

**AIRSPACE: CLASS C** svc continuous ctc **APP CON**

**RADIO AIDS TO NAVIGATION:** NOTAM FILE BDL.

(T) **VORTACW** 109.0  BDL  Chan 27  N41°56.45′ W72°41.32′  at fld. 160/14W.

VOR portion unusable:

093°–103° byd 24 NM blo 5000′  140°–170° byd 15 NM blo 6000′

104°–139° byd 10 NM blo 6000′  260°–290° byd 15 NM blo 6000′

DME unusable 250°–290° byd 18 NN blo 6000′.

**CHUPP NDB (LOM)** 388  BD  N41°52.64′ W72°45.98′  059° 5.2 NM to fld.

**ILS/DME** 111.1  I–BDL  Chan 48  Rwy 06.  LOM CHUPP NDB.

**ILS/DME** 108.55  I–IKX  Chan 22Y  Rwy 33.

**ILS/DME** 111.1  I–MYQ  Chan 48  Rwy 24.

▽  **TAKE-OFF MINS**  ▽

94286

### INSTRUMENT APPROACH PROCEDURE CHARTS
## ▽ IFR TAKE-OFF MINIMUMS AND DEPARTURE PROCEDURES
### Civil Airports and Selected Military Airports

CIVIL USERS: FAR 91 prescribes take-off rules and establishes take-off minimums for certain operators as follows: (1) Aircraft having two engines or less - one statute mile. (2) Aircraft having more than two engines - one-half statute mile. Airports with IFR take-off minimums other than standard are listed below. Departure procedures and/or ceiling visibility minimums are established to assist all pilots conducting IFR flight in avoiding obstacles during climb to the minimum enroute altitude. Take-off minimums and departures apply to all runways unless otherwise specified. Altitudes, unless otherwise indicated, are minimum altitudes in feet MSL.

MILITARY USERS: Special IFR departures not published as Standard Instrument Departure (SIDS) and civil take-off minima are included below and are established to assist pilots in obstacle avoidance. Refer to appropriate service directives for take-off minimums.

### WINDSOR LOCKS, CT
**BRADLEY INTL**

TAKE-OFF MINIMUMS: Rwy 15, 300-1 or std. with a min. climb of 350′ per NM to 300. Rwy 33, 700-1 or std. with a min. climb of 300′ per NM to 1000.

DEPARTURE PROCEDURE: Rwy 1, climb to 1000 via runway heading before turning westbound.

FIGURE 215.—Excerpts from Airport/Facilities Directory.

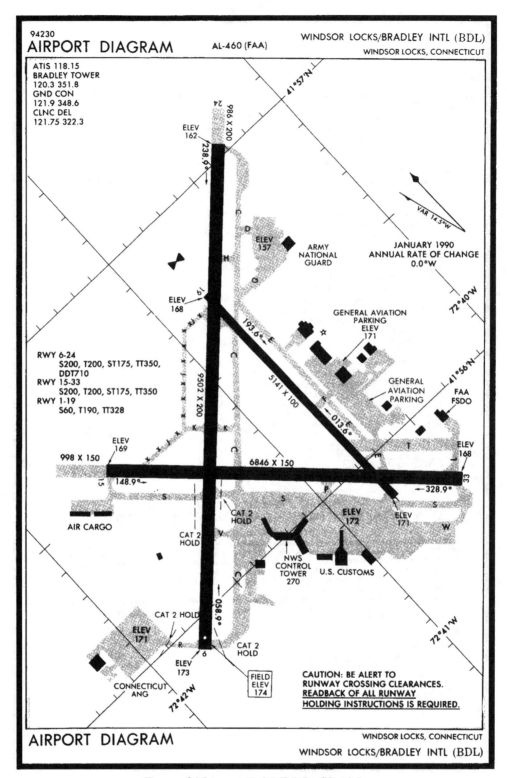

FIGURE 215A.—AIRORT DIAGRAM.

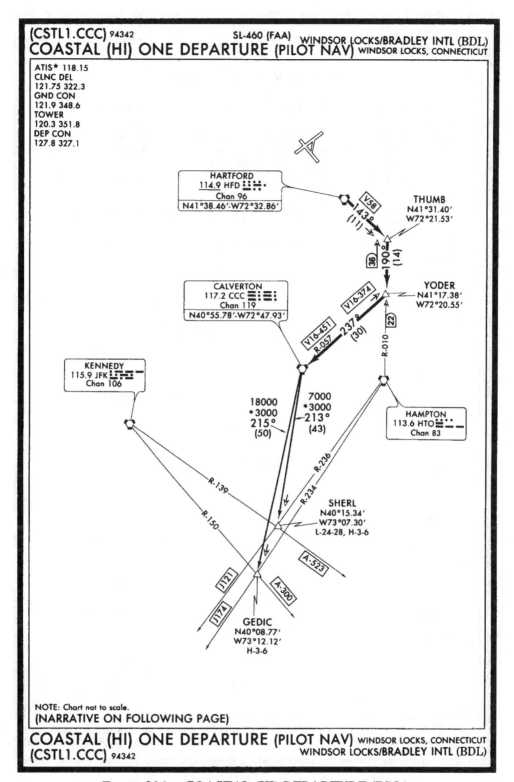

(CSTL1.CCC) 94342      SL-460 (FAA)    WINDSOR LOCKS/BRADLEY INTL (BDL)
**COASTAL (HI) ONE DEPARTURE (PILOT NAV)** WINDSOR LOCKS, CONNECTICUT

ATIS* 118.15
CLNC DEL
121.75 322.3
GND CON
121.9 348.6
TOWER
120.3 351.8
DEP CON
127.8 327.1

HARTFORD
114.9 HFD
Chan 96
N41°38.46'-W72°32.86'

THUMB
N41°31.40'
W72°21.53'

V58
143°
(11)

190°
(14)

36

CALVERTON
117.2 CCC
Chan 119
N40°55.78'-W72°47.93'

YODER
N41°17.38'
W72°20.55'

V16-374

V16-451
R-057

237°
(30)

22
R-010

KENNEDY
115.9 JFK
Chan 106

18000
*3000
215°
(50)

7000
*3000
213°
(43)

HAMPTON
113.6 HTO
Chan 83

R-139

R-236

R-234

SHERL
N40°15.34'
W73°07.30'
L-24-28, H-3-6

R-150

A-523

J121

A-300

J174

GEDIC
N40°08.77'
W73°12.12'
H-3-6

NOTE: Chart not to scale.
(NARRATIVE ON FOLLOWING PAGE)

**COASTAL (HI) ONE DEPARTURE (PILOT NAV)** WINDSOR LOCKS, CONNECTICUT
WINDSOR LOCKS/BRADLEY INTL (BDL)
(CSTL1.CCC) 94342

FIGURE 216.—COASTAL (HI) DEPARTURE (BDL).

## DEPARTURE ROUTE DESCRIPTION

<u>TAKE-OFF RWY 6:</u> Turn right heading 075° or as assigned for radar vectors to HFD VORTAC.

<u>TAKE-OFF ALL OTHER RUNWAYS:</u> Fly runway heading or as assigned for radar vectors to HFD VORTAC. Maintain 4000 feet or assigned altitude. Expect clearance to requested flight level ten (10) minutes after departure.

. . . . From over HFD VORTAC proceed via the HFD R-143 to THUMB INT, then proceed via the HTO R-010 to YODER INT, then via the CCC R-057 to CCC VORTAC. Then via (transition) or (assigned route).

<u>GEDIC TRANSITION (CSTL1.GEDIC):</u> From over CCC VORTAC via CCC R-215 to GEDIC INT.

<u>SHERL TRANSITION (CSTL1.SHERL):</u> From over CCC VORTAC via CCC R-213 to SHERL INT.

FIGURE 216A.—Departure Route Description.

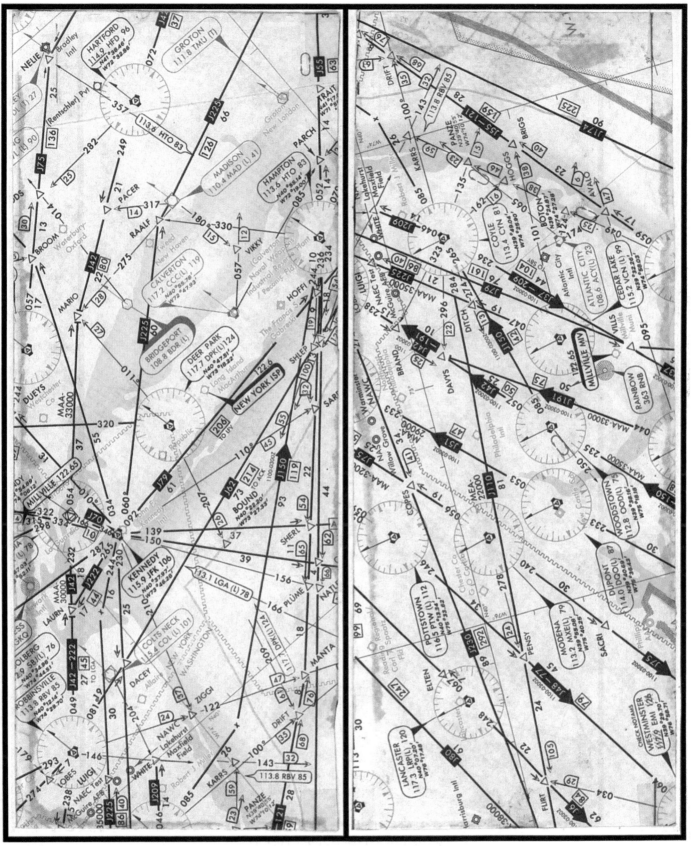

FIGURE 217.—High Altitude Airways.

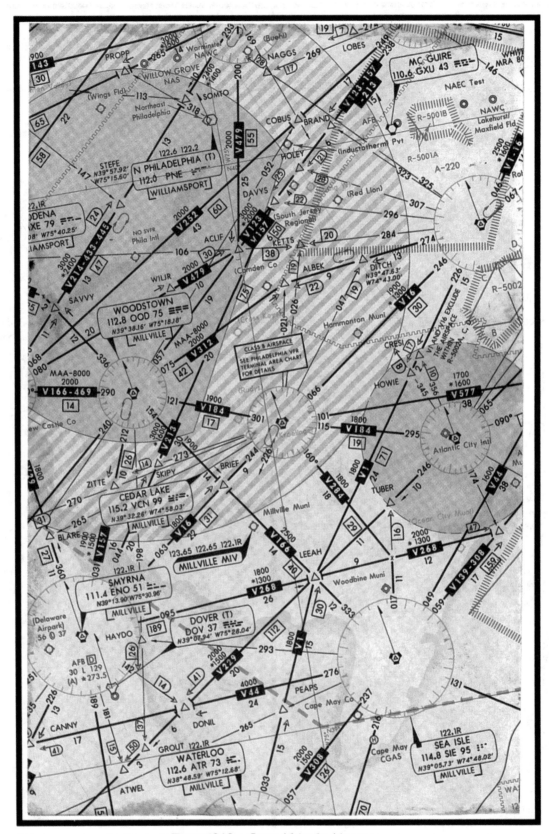

FIGURE 218.—Low Altitude Airways.

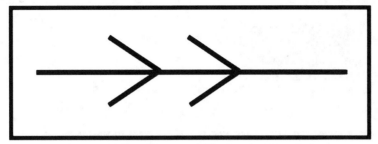

Figure 219.—Chart and Navigation Symbol.

Figure 220.—Chart and Navigation Symbol.

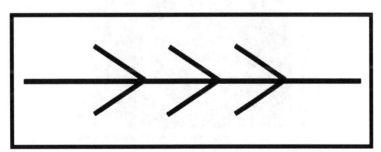

Figure 221.—Chart and Navigation Symbol.

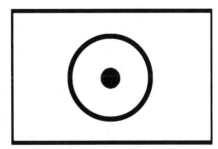

Figure 222.—Chart and Navigation Symbol.

FIGURE 223.—Holding Position Markings.

FIGURE 224.—ILS Critical Area Markings.

FIGURE 225.—No Entry.

FIGURE 226.—Outbound Destination.

FIGURE 227.—Taxiway End Marker.

FIGURE 228.—TWY-RWY Hold Position.

## Takeoff Field Limit - Dry Runway
### Flaps 10
**Based on engine bleed for packs on and anti-ice off**

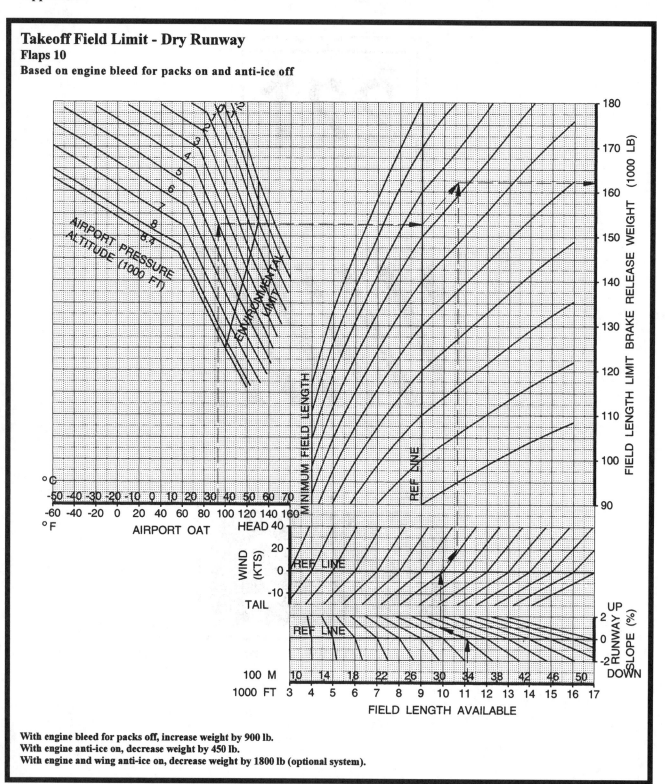

With engine bleed for packs off, increase weight by 900 lb.
With engine anti-ice on, decrease weight by 450 lb.
With engine and wing anti-ice on, decrease weight by 1800 lb (optional system).

FIGURE 229.—Takeoff Field Limit—Dry Runway.

## Takeoff Field Limit - Dry Runway
### Flaps 15
**Based on engine bleed for packs on and anti-ice off**

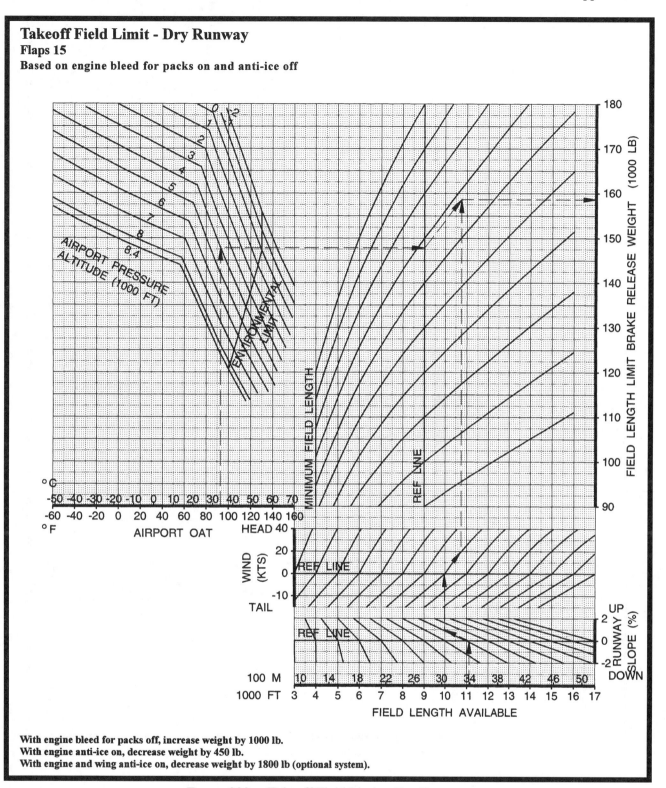

With engine bleed for packs off, increase weight by 1000 lb.
With engine anti-ice on, decrease weight by 450 lb.
With engine and wing anti-ice on, decrease weight by 1800 lb (optional system).

FIGURE 230.—Takeoff Field Limit—Dry Runway.

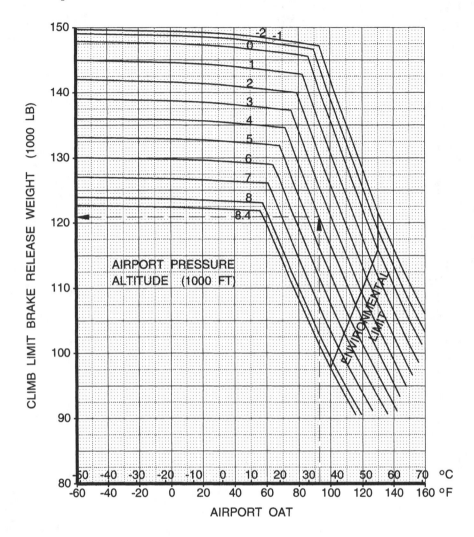

**Takeoff Climb Limit**
**Flaps 15**
**Based on engine bleed for packs on and anti-ice off**

With engine bleed for packs off, increase weight by 2400 lb.
With engine anti-ice on, decrease weight by 400 lb.
With engine and wing anti-ice on, decrease weight by 2300 lb (optional system).

FIGURE 231.—Takeoff Climb Limit.

**Takeoff Climb Limit**
**Flaps 25**
**Based on engine bleed for packs on and anti-ice off**

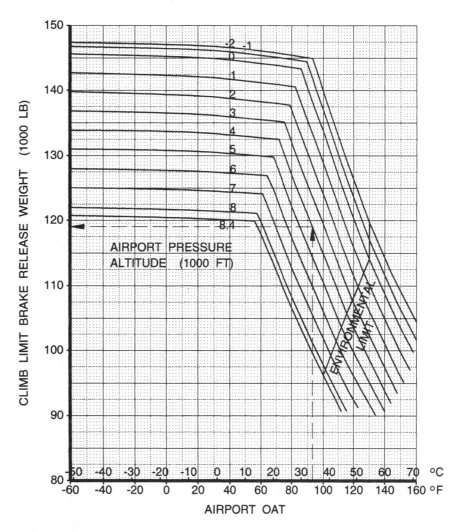

With engine bleed for packs off, increase weight by 2300 lb.
With engine anti-ice on, decrease weight by 400 lb.
With engine and wing anti-ice on, decrease weight by 2300 lb (optional system).

FIGURE 232.—Takeoff Climb Limit.

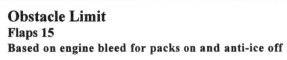

## Obstacle Limit
### Flaps 15
### Based on engine bleed for packs on and anti-ice off

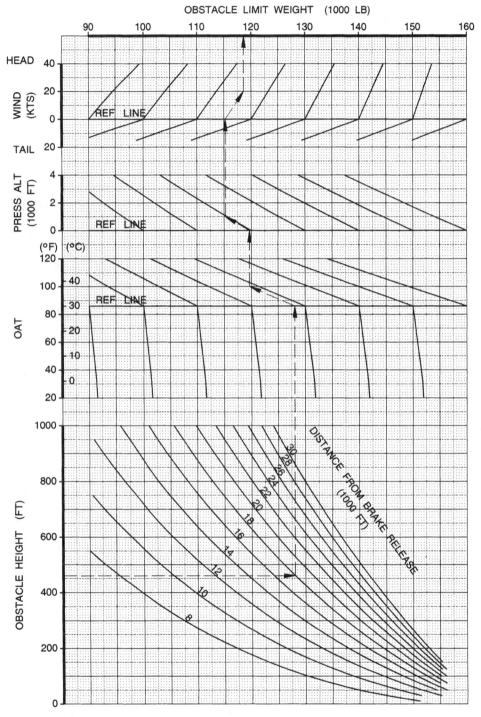

**Obstacle height must be calculated from the lowest point of the runway to conservatively account for runway slope.**
**With engine bleed for packs off, increase weight by 1900 lb.**
**With engine anti-ice on, decrease weight by 400 lb.**
**With engine and wing anti-ice on, decrease weight by 2000 lb (optional system).**

FIGURE 233.—Obstacle Limit.

## Brake Energy Limits VMBE

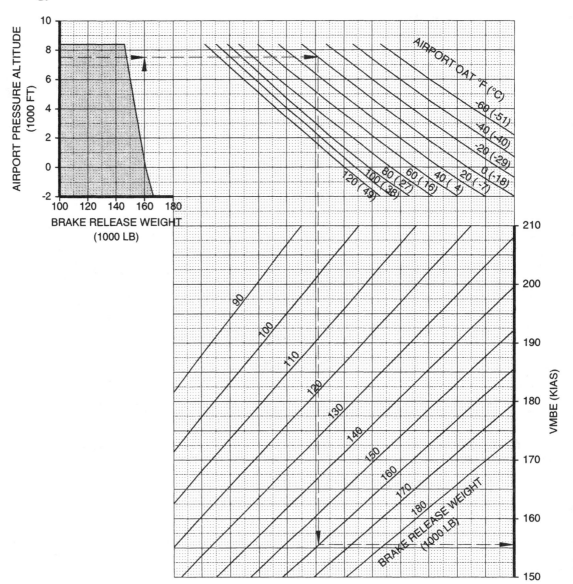

Check VMBE when outside shaded area or when operating with tailwind.
Increase VMBE by 2 knots per 1% uphill runway slope. Decrease VMBE by 3 knots per 1% downhill runway slope.
Increase VMBE by 4 knots per 10 knots headwind. Decrease VMBE by 18 knots per 10 knots tailwind.

Normal takeoff:
Decrease brake release weight by 1100 lb for each knot V1 exceeds VMBE.
Determine normal V1, VR, V2 speeds for lower brake release weight.

Improved climb takeoff:
Decrease climb weight improvement by 550 lb for each knot V1 exceeds VMBE.
Determine V1, VR, V2 speed increments for the lower climb weight improvement.

FIGURE 234.—Brake Energy Limits VMBE.

**ADVISORY INFORMATION**

## Slush/Standing Water Takeoff
**No Reverse Thrust**
**Weight Adjustments (1000 LB)**

| DRY FIELD/OBSTACLE LIMIT WEIGHT (1000 LB) | SLUSH/STANDING WATER DEPTH | | | | | | | | |
|---|---|---|---|---|---|---|---|---|---|
| | 0.12 INCHES (3 mm) | | | 0.25 INCHES (6 mm) | | | 0.50 INCHES (13 mm) | | |
| | PRESSURE ALTITUDE (FT) | | | PRESSURE ALTITUDE (FT) | | | PRESSURE ALTITUDE (FT) | | |
| | S.L. | 5000 | 10000 | S.L. | 5000 | 10000 | S.L. | 5000 | 10000 |
| 180 | -26.4 | -34.9 | -43.4 | -30.8 | -39.3 | -47.8 | -39.8 | -48.3 | -56.8 |
| 170 | -23.4 | -31.9 | -40.4 | -27.0 | -35.5 | -44.0 | -34.4 | -42.9 | -51.4 |
| 160 | -20.7 | -29.2 | -37.7 | -23.6 | -32.1 | -40.6 | -29.6 | -38.1 | -46.6 |
| 150 | -18.3 | -26.8 | -35.3 | -20.6 | -29.1 | -37.6 | -25.5 | -34.0 | -42.5 |
| 140 | -16.2 | -24.7 | -33.2 | -18.0 | -26.5 | -35.0 | -22.0 | -30.5 | -39.0 |
| 130 | -14.4 | -22.9 | -31.4 | -15.9 | -24.4 | -32.9 | -19.3 | -27.8 | -36.3 |
| 120 | -12.9 | -21.4 | -29.9 | -14.2 | -22.7 | -31.2 | -17.2 | -25.7 | -34.2 |
| 110 | -11.6 | -20.1 | -28.6 | -12.8 | -21.3 | -29.8 | -15.6 | -24.1 | -32.6 |
| 100 | -10.4 | -18.9 | -27.4 | -11.4 | -19.9 | -28.4 | -14.1 | -22.6 | -31.1 |
| 90 | -9.1 | -17.6 | -26.1 | -10.1 | -18.6 | -27.1 | -12.5 | -21.0 | -29.5 |

### V1(MCG) Limit Weight (1000 LB)

| ADJUSTED FIELD LENGTH (FT) | SLUSH/STANDING WATER DEPTH | | | | | | | | |
|---|---|---|---|---|---|---|---|---|---|
| | 0.12 INCHES (3 mm) | | | 0.25 INCHES (6 mm) | | | 0.50 INCHES (13 mm) | | |
| | PRESSURE ALTITUDE (FT) | | | PRESSURE ALTITUDE (FT) | | | PRESSURE ALTITUDE (FT) | | |
| | S.L. | 5000 | 10000 | S.L. | 5000 | 10000 | S.L. | 5000 | 10000 |
| 5800 | | | | | | | 86.8 | | |
| 6200 | | | | 78.7 | | | 105.6 | | |
| 6600 | 81.1 | | | 99.7 | | | 125.0 | 86.8 | |
| 7000 | 103.5 | | | 120.8 | 78.7 | | 145.2 | 105.6 | |
| 7400 | 125.9 | 81.1 | | 142.1 | 99.7 | | 166.1 | 125.0 | 86.8 |
| 7800 | 148.3 | 103.5 | | 163.6 | 120.8 | 78.7 | 188.0 | 145.2 | 105.6 |
| 8200 | 170.6 | 125.9 | 81.1 | 185.2 | 142.1 | 99.7 | | 166.1 | 125.0 |
| 8600 | 192.9 | 148.3 | 103.5 | | 163.6 | 120.8 | | 188.0 | 145.2 |
| 9000 | | 170.6 | 125.9 | | 185.2 | 142.1 | | | 166.1 |
| 9400 | | 192.9 | 148.3 | | | 163.6 | | | 188.0 |
| 9800 | | | 170.6 | | | 185.2 | | | |
| 10200 | | | 192.9 | | | | | | |

1. Enter Weight Adjustment table with slush/standing water depth and dry field/obstacle limit weight to obtain slush/standing water weight adjustment.
2. Adjust field length available by -150 ft/+140 ft for every 5°C above/below 4°C.
3. Find V1(MCG) limit weight for adjusted field length and pressure altitude.
4. Max allowable slush/standing water limited weight is lesser of weights from 1 and 3.

### V1 Adjustment (KIAS)

| WEIGHT (1000 LB) | SLUSH/STANDING WATER DEPTH | | | | | | | | |
|---|---|---|---|---|---|---|---|---|---|
| | 0.12 INCHES (3 mm) | | | 0.25 INCHES (6 mm) | | | 0.50 INCHES (13 mm) | | |
| | PRESSURE ALTITUDE (FT) | | | PRESSURE ALTITUDE (FT) | | | PRESSURE ALTITUDE (FT) | | |
| | S.L. | 5000 | 10000 | S.L. | 5000 | 10000 | S.L. | 5000 | 10000 |
| 180 | -21 | -16 | -11 | -12 | -7 | -2 | 0 | 0 | 0 |
| 170 | -22 | -17 | -12 | -14 | -9 | -4 | 0 | 0 | 0 |
| 160 | -23 | -18 | -13 | -17 | -12 | -7 | -3 | 0 | 0 |
| 150 | -24 | -19 | -14 | -19 | -14 | -9 | -7 | -2 | 0 |
| 140 | -25 | -20 | -15 | -21 | -16 | -11 | -10 | -5 | 0 |
| 130 | -26 | -21 | -16 | -22 | -17 | -12 | -14 | -9 | -4 |
| 120 | -27 | -22 | -17 | -24 | -19 | -14 | -17 | -12 | -7 |
| 110 | -28 | -23 | -18 | -25 | -20 | -15 | -20 | -15 | -10 |
| 100 | -29 | -24 | -19 | -27 | -22 | -17 | -22 | -17 | -12 |
| 90 | -29 | -24 | -19 | -28 | -23 | -18 | -25 | -20 | -15 |

1. Obtain V1, VR and V2 for the actual weight using the Dry Runway Takeoff Speeds table.
2. If V1(MCG) limited, set V1 = V1(MCG). If not V1(MCG) limited, enter V1 Adjustment table with the actual weight to obtain V1 speed adjustment. If adjusted V1 is less than V1(MCG), set V1 = V1(MCG).

FIGURE 235.—Slush/Standing Water Takeoff.

# ADVISORY INFORMATION

## Slush/Standing Water Takeoff
### Maximum Reverse Thrust
### Weight Adjustments (1000 LB)

| DRY FIELD/OBSTACLE LIMIT WEIGHT (1000 LB) | SLUSH/STANDING WATER DEPTH | | | | | | | | |
| --- | --- | --- | --- | --- | --- | --- | --- | --- | --- |
| | 0.12 INCHES (3 mm) | | | 0.25 INCHES (6 mm) | | | 0.50 INCHES (13 mm) | | |
| | PRESSURE ALTITUDE (FT) | | | PRESSURE ALTITUDE (FT) | | | PRESSURE ALTITUDE (FT) | | |
| | S.L. | 5000 | 10000 | S.L. | 5000 | 10000 | S.L. | 5000 | 10000 |
| 180 | -21.9 | -27.4 | -32.9 | -26.4 | -31.9 | -37.4 | -37.5 | -43.0 | -48.5 |
| 170 | -19.3 | -24.8 | -30.3 | -22.8 | -28.3 | -33.8 | -31.1 | -36.6 | -42.1 |
| 160 | -17.0 | -22.5 | -28.0 | -19.7 | -25.2 | -30.7 | -25.8 | -31.3 | -36.8 |
| 150 | -15.0 | -20.5 | -26.0 | -17.2 | -22.7 | -28.2 | -21.7 | -27.2 | -32.7 |
| 140 | -13.3 | -18.8 | -24.3 | -15.1 | -20.6 | -26.1 | -18.8 | -24.3 | -29.8 |
| 130 | -11.9 | -17.4 | -22.9 | -13.4 | -18.9 | -24.4 | -16.6 | -22.1 | -27.6 |
| 120 | -10.5 | -16.0 | -21.5 | -11.7 | -17.2 | -22.7 | -14.4 | -19.9 | -25.4 |
| 110 | -9.1 | -14.6 | -20.1 | -10.0 | -15.5 | -21.0 | -12.2 | -17.7 | -23.2 |
| 100 | -7.6 | -13.1 | -18.6 | -8.2 | -13.7 | -19.2 | -10.0 | -15.5 | -21.0 |
| 90 | -6.2 | -11.7 | -17.2 | -6.5 | -12.0 | -17.5 | -7.8 | -13.3 | -18.8 |

### V1(MCG) Limit Weight (1000 LB)

| ADJUSTED FIELD LENGTH (FT) | SLUSH/STANDING WATER DEPTH | | | | | | | | |
| --- | --- | --- | --- | --- | --- | --- | --- | --- | --- |
| | 0.12 INCHES (3 mm) | | | 0.25 INCHES (6 mm) | | | 0.50 INCHES (13 mm) | | |
| | PRESSURE ALTITUDE (FT) | | | PRESSURE ALTITUDE (FT) | | | PRESSURE ALTITUDE (FT) | | |
| | S.L. | 5000 | 10000 | S.L. | 5000 | 10000 | S.L. | 5000 | 10000 |
| 4600 | | | | | | | 74.3 | | |
| 5000 | 75.8 | | | 82.9 | | | 93.3 | | |
| 5400 | 94.0 | | | 100.9 | | | 111.9 | | |
| 5800 | 112.6 | | | 119.4 | 73.9 | | 130.1 | 83.9 | |
| 6200 | 131.5 | 84.9 | | 138.2 | 91.9 | | 147.9 | 102.7 | |
| 6600 | 150.8 | 103.2 | | 157.4 | 110.1 | | 165.4 | 121.1 | 74.3 |
| 7000 | 170.6 | 122.0 | 75.8 | 177.0 | 128.7 | 82.9 | 182.6 | 139.1 | 93.3 |
| 7400 | 190.9 | 141.1 | 94.0 | 197.0 | 147.7 | 100.9 | 199.5 | 156.7 | 111.9 |
| 7800 | | 160.7 | 112.6 | | 167.1 | 119.4 | | 174.0 | 130.1 |
| 8200 | | 180.7 | 131.5 | | 186.9 | 138.2 | | 191.0 | 147.9 |
| 8600 | | | 150.8 | | | 157.4 | | | 165.4 |
| 9000 | | | 170.6 | | | 177.0 | | | 182.6 |
| 9400 | | | 190.9 | | | 197.0 | | | 199.5 |

1. Enter Weight Adjustment table with slush/standing water depth and dry field/obstacle limit weight to obtain slush/standing water weight adjustment.
2. Adjust field length available by -120 ft/+110 ft for every 5°C above/below 4°C.
3. Find V1(MCG) limit weight for adjusted field length and pressure altitude.
4. Max allowable slush/standing water limited weight is lesser of weights from 1 and 3.

### V1 Adjustment (KIAS)

| WEIGHT (1000 LB) | SLUSH/STANDING WATER DEPTH | | | | | | | | |
| --- | --- | --- | --- | --- | --- | --- | --- | --- | --- |
| | 0.12 INCHES (3 mm) | | | 0.25 INCHES (6 mm) | | | 0.50 INCHES (13 mm) | | |
| | PRESSURE ALTITUDE (FT) | | | PRESSURE ALTITUDE (FT) | | | PRESSURE ALTITUDE (FT) | | |
| | S.L. | 5000 | 10000 | S.L. | 5000 | 10000 | S.L. | 5000 | 10000 |
| 180 | -15 | -12 | -10 | -8 | -5 | -3 | -3 | 0 | 0 |
| 170 | -16 | -13 | -11 | -10 | -7 | -5 | -3 | -1 | 0 |
| 160 | -17 | -15 | -12 | -12 | -10 | -7 | -4 | -2 | 0 |
| 150 | -18 | -16 | -13 | -14 | -11 | -9 | -6 | -3 | -1 |
| 140 | -19 | -16 | -14 | -15 | -13 | -10 | -8 | -5 | -3 |
| 130 | -20 | -17 | -15 | -17 | -14 | -12 | -10 | -7 | -5 |
| 120 | -20 | -18 | -15 | -18 | -16 | -13 | -12 | -10 | -7 |
| 110 | -21 | -19 | -16 | -19 | -17 | -14 | -15 | -12 | -10 |
| 100 | -23 | -20 | -18 | -21 | -18 | -16 | -17 | -14 | -12 |
| 90 | -24 | -21 | -19 | -22 | -20 | -17 | -19 | -17 | -14 |

1. Obtain V1, VR and V2 for the actual weight using the Dry Runway Takeoff Speeds table.
2. If V1(MCG) limited, set V1 = V1(MCG). If not V1(MCG) limited, enter V1 Adjustment table with the actual weight to obtain V1 speed adjustment. If adjusted V1 is less than V1(MCG), set V1 = V1(MCG).

FIGURE 236.—Slush/Standing Water Takeoff.

## Takeoff Speeds - Dry Runway
### Flaps 10, 15 and 25
### V1, VR, V2 for Max Takeoff Thrust

| WEIGHT (1000 LB) | FLAPS 10 | | | FLAPS 15 | | | FLAPS 25 | | |
|---|---|---|---|---|---|---|---|---|---|
| | V1 | VR | V2 | V1 | VR | V2 | V1 | VR | V2 |
| 170 | 138 | 140 | 145 | 136 | 136 | 141 | | | |
| 160 | 134 | 135 | 141 | 132 | 132 | 138 | 131 | 131 | 136 |
| 150 | 129 | 131 | 137 | 128 | 128 | 135 | 126 | 126 | 133 |
| 140 | 124 | 126 | 133 | 123 | 123 | 131 | 121 | 122 | 129 |
| 130 | 118 | 121 | 129 | 117 | 118 | 127 | 116 | 117 | 125 |
| 120 | 112 | 115 | 124 | 111 | 113 | 122 | 109 | 111 | 121 |
| 110 | 106 | 109 | 119 | 105 | 107 | 117 | 103 | 106 | 116 |
| 100 | 99 | 103 | 114 | 98 | 101 | 113 | 97 | 100 | 111 |
| 90 | 92 | 97 | 109 | 91 | 95 | 107 | 90 | 94 | 106 |

Check V1(MCG).

### V1, VR, V2 Adjustments*

| TEMP | | V1 | | | | | | VR | | | | | | V2 | | | | | |
|---|---|---|---|---|---|---|---|---|---|---|---|---|---|---|---|---|---|---|---|
| | | PRESSURE ALTITUDE (1000 FT) | | | | | | PRESSURE ALTITUDE (1000 FT) | | | | | | PRESSURE ALTITUDE (1000 FT) | | | | | |
| °F | °C | -2 | 0 | 2 | 4 | 6 | 8 | -2 | 0 | 2 | 4 | 6 | 8 | -2 | 0 | 2 | 4 | 6 | 8 |
| 140 | 60 | 5 | 6 | 7 | 9 | | | 3 | 4 | 5 | 6 | | | -2 | -2 | -2 | -3 | | |
| 120 | 49 | 3 | 4 | 5 | 7 | 8 | 10 | 2 | 3 | 4 | 5 | 6 | 6 | -1 | -1 | -2 | -2 | -3 | -3 |
| 100 | 38 | 1 | 2 | 3 | 5 | 6 | 8 | 1 | 1 | 2 | 3 | 4 | 5 | 0 | -1 | -1 | -2 | -2 | -3 |
| 80 | 27 | 0 | 0 | 1 | 3 | 5 | 6 | 0 | 0 | 1 | 2 | 3 | 4 | 0 | 0 | 0 | -1 | -1 | -2 |
| 60 | 16 | 0 | 0 | 1 | 2 | 3 | 4 | 0 | 0 | 1 | 1 | 2 | 3 | 0 | 0 | 0 | 0 | -1 | -1 |
| -60 | -51 | 0 | 0 | 1 | 2 | 3 | 3 | 0 | 0 | 1 | 1 | 2 | 3 | 0 | 0 | 0 | 0 | -1 | -1 |

### Slope and Wind V1 Adjustments*

| WEIGHT (1000 LB) | SLOPE (%) | | | | | WIND (KTS) | | | | | | | | |
|---|---|---|---|---|---|---|---|---|---|---|---|---|---|---|
| | -2 | -1 | 0 | 1 | 2 | -15 | -10 | -5 | 0 | 10 | 20 | 30 | 40 |
| 170 | -3 | -1 | 0 | 1 | 1 | -1 | -1 | -1 | 0 | 0 | 1 | 1 | 1 |
| 160 | -3 | -1 | 0 | 1 | 2 | -1 | -1 | -1 | 0 | 0 | 1 | 1 | 1 |
| 150 | -3 | -1 | 0 | 1 | 2 | -1 | -1 | -1 | 0 | 0 | 1 | 1 | 1 |
| 140 | -2 | -1 | 0 | 1 | 2 | -2 | -1 | -1 | 0 | 0 | 1 | 1 | 1 |
| 130 | -2 | -1 | 0 | 1 | 2 | -2 | -1 | -1 | 0 | 0 | 1 | 1 | 1 |
| 120 | -2 | -1 | 0 | 1 | 2 | -2 | -1 | -1 | 0 | 0 | 1 | 1 | 1 |
| 110 | -2 | -1 | 0 | 1 | 2 | -2 | -1 | -1 | 0 | 0 | 1 | 1 | 2 |
| 100 | -2 | -1 | 0 | 1 | 2 | -2 | -1 | -1 | 0 | 0 | 1 | 2 | 2 |
| 90 | -1 | -1 | 0 | 1 | 1 | -2 | -1 | -1 | 0 | 0 | 1 | 2 | 2 |

### Clearway and Stopway V1 Adjustments*

| NORMAL V1 (KIAS) | CLEARWAY MINUS STOPWAY (FT) | | | | | | | | |
|---|---|---|---|---|---|---|---|---|---|
| | 800 | 600 | 400 | 200 | 0 | -200 | -400 | -600 | -800 |
| 140 | -3 | -3 | -3 | -2 | 0 | 2 | 2 | 2 | 2 |
| 120 | -3 | -3 | -3 | -2 | 0 | 2 | 2 | 2 | 2 |
| 100 | -3 | -3 | -2 | -1 | 0 | 1 | 1 | 1 | 1 |

*V1 not to exceed VR.

### Max Allowable Clearway for V1 Adjustment

| FIELD LENGTH (FT) | 4000 | 6000 | 8000 | 10000 | 12000 | 14000 |
|---|---|---|---|---|---|---|
| MAX ALLOWABLE CLEARWAY (FT) | 450 | 650 | 850 | 1000 | 1450 | 1550 |

### V1(MCG)
### Max Takeoff Thrust

| TEMP | | PRESSURE ALTITUDE (FT) | | | | | | |
|---|---|---|---|---|---|---|---|---|
| °F | °C | -2000 | 0 | 2000 | 4000 | 6000 | 8000 | 10000 |
| 160 | 71 | 102 | | | | | | |
| 140 | 60 | 102 | 99 | 97 | 96 | | | |
| 120 | 49 | 104 | 102 | 98 | 96 | 94 | 92 | 90 |
| 100 | 38 | 110 | 107 | 103 | 100 | 96 | 92 | 90 |
| 80 | 27 | 112 | 111 | 109 | 105 | 101 | 97 | 93 |
| 60 | 16 | 112 | 112 | 109 | 107 | 104 | 101 | 97 |
| -60 | -51 | 113 | 113 | 110 | 108 | 105 | 102 | 100 |

FIGURE 237.—Takeoff Speeds—Dry Runway.

# Takeoff Speeds - Wet Runway
## Flaps 10, 15 and 25
## V1, VR, V2 for Max Takeoff Thrust

| WEIGHT (1000 LB) | FLAPS 10 | | | FLAPS 15 | | | FLAPS 25 | | |
|---|---|---|---|---|---|---|---|---|---|
| | V1 | VR | V2 | V1 | VR | V2 | V1 | VR | V2 |
| 170 | 133 | 139 | 145 | 133 | 136 | 141 | | | |
| 160 | 128 | 135 | 141 | 128 | 132 | 138 | 126 | 131 | 136 |
| 150 | 123 | 131 | 137 | 122 | 128 | 135 | 121 | 126 | 133 |
| 140 | 117 | 126 | 133 | 117 | 123 | 131 | 115 | 122 | 129 |
| 130 | 111 | 121 | 129 | 111 | 118 | 127 | 109 | 117 | 125 |
| 120 | 105 | 115 | 124 | 104 | 113 | 122 | 103 | 111 | 121 |
| 110 | 99 | 109 | 119 | 98 | 107 | 117 | 97 | 106 | 116 |
| 100 | 92 | 103 | 114 | 92 | 101 | 112 | 91 | 100 | 111 |
| 90 | 86 | 97 | 109 | 85 | 95 | 107 | 84 | 94 | 106 |

Check V1(MCG).

## V1, VR, V2 Adjustments*

| TEMP | | V1 | | | | | | VR | | | | | | V2 | | | | | |
|---|---|---|---|---|---|---|---|---|---|---|---|---|---|---|---|---|---|---|---|
| | | PRESSURE ALTITUDE (1000 FT) | | | | | | PRESSURE ALTITUDE (1000 FT) | | | | | | PRESSURE ALTITUDE (1000 FT) | | | | | |
| °F | °C | -2 | 0 | 2 | 4 | 6 | 8 | -2 | 0 | 2 | 4 | 6 | 8 | -2 | 0 | 2 | 4 | 6 | 8 |
| 140 | 60 | 6 | 7 | 9 | 10 | | | 3 | 4 | 5 | 6 | | | -2 | -2 | -2 | -3 | | |
| 120 | 49 | 4 | 4 | 6 | 8 | 9 | 11 | 2 | 3 | 4 | 4 | 5 | 6 | -1 | -1 | -2 | -2 | -3 | -3 |
| 100 | 38 | 1 | 2 | 3 | 5 | 7 | 9 | 1 | 1 | 2 | 3 | 4 | 5 | 0 | -1 | -1 | -2 | -2 | -2 |
| 80 | 27 | 0 | 0 | 1 | 3 | 4 | 6 | 0 | 0 | 1 | 2 | 3 | 4 | 0 | 0 | 0 | -1 | -1 | -2 |
| 60 | 16 | 0 | 0 | 1 | 2 | 3 | 4 | 0 | 0 | 1 | 1 | 2 | 3 | 0 | 0 | 0 | 0 | -1 | -1 |
| -60 | -51 | 0 | 0 | 1 | 2 | 3 | 4 | 0 | 0 | 1 | 1 | 2 | 3 | 0 | 0 | 0 | 0 | -1 | -1 |

## Slope and Wind V1 Adjustments*

| WEIGHT (1000 LB) | SLOPE (%) | | | | | WIND (KTS) | | | | | | | |
|---|---|---|---|---|---|---|---|---|---|---|---|---|---|
| | -2 | -1 | 0 | 1 | 2 | -15 | -10 | -5 | 0 | 10 | 20 | 30 | 40 |
| 170 | -4 | -2 | 0 | 2 | 4 | -3 | -2 | -1 | 0 | 1 | 1 | 2 | 3 |
| 160 | -4 | -2 | 0 | 2 | 4 | -3 | -2 | -1 | 0 | 1 | 1 | 2 | 3 |
| 150 | -4 | -2 | 0 | 2 | 4 | -3 | -2 | -1 | 0 | 1 | 1 | 2 | 3 |
| 140 | -4 | -2 | 0 | 2 | 3 | -4 | -2 | -1 | 0 | 1 | 1 | 2 | 3 |
| 130 | -3 | -1 | 0 | 1 | 3 | -4 | -3 | -1 | 0 | 1 | 2 | 2 | 3 |
| 120 | -3 | -1 | 0 | 1 | 3 | -4 | -3 | -1 | 0 | 1 | 2 | 2 | 3 |
| 110 | -2 | -1 | 0 | 1 | 2 | -4 | -3 | -1 | 0 | 1 | 2 | 2 | 3 |
| 100 | -2 | -1 | 0 | 1 | 2 | -4 | -3 | -1 | 0 | 1 | 2 | 2 | 3 |
| 90 | -2 | -1 | 0 | 1 | 2 | -4 | -3 | -1 | 0 | 1 | 2 | 3 | 3 |

## Stopway V1 Adjustments*

| NORMAL V1 (KIAS) | STOPWAY (FT) | | | | |
|---|---|---|---|---|---|
| | 0 | 200 | 400 | 600 | 800 |
| 160 | 0 | 1 | 2 | 2 | 3 |
| 140 | 0 | 1 | 2 | 2 | 3 |
| 120 | 0 | 1 | 2 | 3 | 4 |
| 100 | 0 | 1 | 2 | 3 | 4 |

Use of clearway not allowed on wet runways.
*V1 not to exceed VR.

## V1(MCG)
## Max Takeoff Thrust

| TEMP | | PRESSURE ALTITUDE (FT) | | | | | | |
|---|---|---|---|---|---|---|---|---|
| °F | °C | -2000 | 0 | 2000 | 4000 | 6000 | 8000 | 10000 |
| 160 | 71 | 102 | | | | | | |
| 140 | 60 | 102 | 99 | 97 | 96 | | | |
| 120 | 49 | 104 | 102 | 98 | 96 | 94 | 92 | 90 |
| 100 | 38 | 110 | 107 | 103 | 100 | 96 | 92 | 90 |
| 80 | 27 | 112 | 111 | 109 | 105 | 101 | 97 | 93 |
| 60 | 16 | 112 | 112 | 109 | 107 | 104 | 101 | 97 |
| -60 | -51 | 113 | 113 | 110 | 108 | 105 | 102 | 100 |

FIGURE 238.—Takeoff Speeds—Wet Runway.

## Takeoff %N1
### Based on engine bleeds for packs on, engine and wing anti-ice on or off

| OAT (°F) | AIRPORT PRESSURE ALTITUDE (FT) | | | | | | | | | | | | |
|---|---|---|---|---|---|---|---|---|---|---|---|---|---|
| | -2000 | -1000 | 0 | 1000 | 2000 | 3000 | 4000 | 5000 | 6000 | 7000 | 8000 | 9000 | 10000 |
| 170 | 87.6 | 88.0 | 88.9 | 89.4 | 89.8 | 90.4 | 91.0 | 91.7 | 92.4 | 92.9 | 93.4 | 93.5 | 93.6 |
| 160 | 88.5 | 89.0 | 89.3 | 89.2 | 89.1 | 89.7 | 90.3 | 91.0 | 91.7 | 92.2 | 92.6 | 92.8 | 92.9 |
| 150 | 89.4 | 89.9 | 90.3 | 90.2 | 90.1 | 90.1 | 90.0 | 90.3 | 91.0 | 91.4 | 91.9 | 92.0 | 92.1 |
| 140 | 90.3 | 90.8 | 91.2 | 91.2 | 91.1 | 91.1 | 91.0 | 91.1 | 91.2 | 91.0 | 91.2 | 91.3 | 91.4 |
| 130 | 91.1 | 91.7 | 92.1 | 92.1 | 92.0 | 92.0 | 92.0 | 92.0 | 92.0 | 91.9 | 91.8 | 91.4 | 90.9 |
| 120 | 92.0 | 92.6 | 93.0 | 93.0 | 93.0 | 92.9 | 92.9 | 92.9 | 92.9 | 92.8 | 92.7 | 92.4 | 92.0 |
| 110 | 92.9 | 93.5 | 93.9 | 93.9 | 93.8 | 93.8 | 93.8 | 93.7 | 93.7 | 93.6 | 93.6 | 93.4 | 93.1 |
| 100 | 93.8 | 94.3 | 94.8 | 94.7 | 94.7 | 94.7 | 94.6 | 94.6 | 94.5 | 94.4 | 94.4 | 94.3 | 94.2 |
| 90 | 94.2 | 95.3 | 95.7 | 95.7 | 95.7 | 95.6 | 95.6 | 95.5 | 95.4 | 95.4 | 95.3 | 95.2 | 95.2 |
| 80 | 93.3 | 94.5 | 95.6 | 96.1 | 96.5 | 96.5 | 96.4 | 96.4 | 96.3 | 96.2 | 96.2 | 96.1 | 96.1 |
| 70 | 92.5 | 93.7 | 94.8 | 95.3 | 95.8 | 96.4 | 97.1 | 97.4 | 97.3 | 97.2 | 97.1 | 97.1 | 97.0 |
| 60 | 91.6 | 92.8 | 93.9 | 94.4 | 95.0 | 95.6 | 96.2 | 96.9 | 97.6 | 98.3 | 98.5 | 98.4 | 98.3 |
| 50 | 90.8 | 92.0 | 93.0 | 93.6 | 94.1 | 94.7 | 95.3 | 96.0 | 96.7 | 97.5 | 98.2 | 99.1 | 100.0 |
| 40 | 89.9 | 91.1 | 92.2 | 92.7 | 93.2 | 93.8 | 94.4 | 95.1 | 95.8 | 96.6 | 97.4 | 98.3 | 99.2 |
| 30 | 89.1 | 90.2 | 91.3 | 91.8 | 92.3 | 92.9 | 93.6 | 94.2 | 94.9 | 95.7 | 96.5 | 97.4 | 98.3 |
| 20 | 88.2 | 89.3 | 90.4 | 90.9 | 91.4 | 92.0 | 92.7 | 93.4 | 94.0 | 94.8 | 95.6 | 96.6 | 97.5 |
| 10 | 87.3 | 88.4 | 89.5 | 90.0 | 90.5 | 91.1 | 91.7 | 92.4 | 93.1 | 93.9 | 94.7 | 95.7 | 96.6 |
| 0 | 86.4 | 87.5 | 88.6 | 89.1 | 89.6 | 90.2 | 90.8 | 91.5 | 92.2 | 93.0 | 93.8 | 94.8 | 95.8 |
| -10 | 85.5 | 86.6 | 87.6 | 88.1 | 88.6 | 89.3 | 89.9 | 90.6 | 91.3 | 92.1 | 92.9 | 94.0 | 94.9 |
| -20 | 84.6 | 85.7 | 86.7 | 87.2 | 87.7 | 88.3 | 89.0 | 89.7 | 90.4 | 91.2 | 92.0 | 93.1 | 94.0 |
| -30 | 83.6 | 84.7 | 85.7 | 86.2 | 86.7 | 87.4 | 88.0 | 88.7 | 89.4 | 90.2 | 91.1 | 92.2 | 93.1 |
| -40 | 82.7 | 83.8 | 84.8 | 85.3 | 85.8 | 86.4 | 87.0 | 87.8 | 88.5 | 89.3 | 90.1 | 91.2 | 92.2 |
| -50 | 81.7 | 82.8 | 83.8 | 84.3 | 84.8 | 85.4 | 86.1 | 86.8 | 87.5 | 88.3 | 89.2 | 90.3 | 91.3 |
| -60 | 80.8 | 81.8 | 82.8 | 83.3 | 83.8 | 84.4 | 85.1 | 85.8 | 86.5 | 87.3 | 88.2 | 89.4 | 90.3 |

### %N1 Adjustments for Engine Bleeds

| BLEED CONFIGURATION | PRESSURE ALTITUDE (FT) | | | | | | | | | | | | |
|---|---|---|---|---|---|---|---|---|---|---|---|---|---|
| | -2000 | -1000 | 0 | 1000 | 2000 | 3000 | 4000 | 5000 | 6000 | 7000 | 8000 | 9000 | 10000 |
| PACKS OFF | 0.7 | 0.7 | 0.7 | 0.7 | 0.7 | 0.7 | 0.8 | 0.8 | 0.8 | 0.8 | 0.8 | 0.9 | 1.0 |

FIGURE 239.—Takeoff % N1.

## Stab Trim Setting
### Max Takeoff Thrust
### Flaps 1 and 5

| WEIGHT (1000 LB) | C.G. (%MAC) | | | | | | | | |
|---|---|---|---|---|---|---|---|---|---|
| | 9 | 11 | 13 | 16 | 20 | 24 | 28 | 30 | 33 |
| 160-180 | 8 1/2 | 8 1/2 | 8 1/2 | 7 3/4 | 6 3/4 | 6 | 5 1/4 | 4 3/4 | 4 1/4 |
| 140 | 8 1/2 | 8 1/2 | 8 | 7 1/4 | 6 1/2 | 5 1/2 | 4 3/4 | 4 1/2 | 3 3/4 |
| 120 | 8 1/2 | 8 | 7 1/2 | 6 1/2 | 5 3/4 | 5 | 4 1/4 | 4 | 3 1/4 |
| 80-100 | 6 3/4 | 6 1/2 | 6 | 5 1/2 | 5 | 4 1/4 | 3 1/2 | 3 1/4 | 2 3/4 |

### Flaps 10, 15 and 25

| WEIGHT (1000 LB) | C.G. (%MAC) | | | | | | | | |
|---|---|---|---|---|---|---|---|---|---|
| | 9 | 11 | 13 | 16 | 20 | 24 | 28 | 30 | 33 |
| 160-180 | 8 1/2 | 8 1/2 | 8 1/2 | 7 1/4 | 6 1/2 | 5 1/2 | 4 1/2 | 4 1/4 | 3 1/2 |
| 140 | 8 1/2 | 8 1/2 | 7 3/4 | 6 3/4 | 6 | 5 | 4 1/4 | 3 3/4 | 3 |
| 120 | 8 1/2 | 7 3/4 | 7 | 6 | 5 1/4 | 4 1/2 | 3 3/4 | 3 1/4 | 2 3/4 |
| 80-100 | 6 1/4 | 6 | 5 1/2 | 5 | 4 1/2 | 3 3/4 | 3 | 2 3/4 | 2 3/4 |

FIGURE 240.—Stab Trim Setting.

# ADDENDUM
## COMPUTER TESTING
## SUPPLEMENT
## FOR
## AIRLINE TRANSPORT PILOT
## AND
## AIRCRAFT DISPATCHER

U.S. Department of Transportation
**Federal Aviation Administration**

# Table of Contents

## ADDENDUM C

# COMPUTER TESTING SUPPLEMENT
## FOR
## AIRLINE TRANSPORT PILOT
## AND
## AIRCRAFT DISPATCHER

## ADDENDUM A
## JULY 2011

U.S. DEPARTMENT OF TRANSPORTATION
**FEDERAL AVIATION ADMINISTRATION**
Flight Standards Service

11069

## HOT SPOTS

An "airport surface hot spot" is a location on an aerodrome movement area with a history or potential risk of collision or runway incursion, and where heightened attention by pilots/drivers is necessary.

A "hot spot" is a runway safety related problem area on an airport that presents increased risk during surface operations. Typically it is a complex or confusing taxiway/taxiway or taxiway/runway intersection. The area of increased risk has either a history of or potential for runway incursions or surface incidents, due to a variety of causes, such as but not limited to: airport layout, traffic flow, airport marking, signage and lighting, situational awareness, and training. Hot spots are depicted on airport diagrams as open circles or polygons designated as "HS 1", "HS 2", etc. and tabulated in the list below with a brief description of each hot spot. Hot spots will remain charted on airport diagrams until such time the increased risk has been reduced or eliminated.

| CITY/AIRPORT | HOT SPOT | DESCRIPTION* |
|---|---|---|
| CARLSBAD, CA | | |
| MC CLELLAN-PALOMAR (CRQ) | HS 1 | Large Jets may obscure twr visibility of small aircraft. |
| CHINO, CA | | |
| CHINO (CNO) | HS 1 | Twy D close proximity to Rwy 08L-26R. |
| | HS 2 | Twy L close proximity to Rwy 03-21. |
| HAWTHORNE, CA | | |
| JACK NORTHROP FIELD/ HAWTHORNE MUNI (HHR) | HS 1 | Rwy 25 run-up area. |
| LONG BEACH, CA | | |
| LONG BEACH (DAUGHERTY FLD) (LGB) | HS 1 | Rwy 30 and Rwy 07L-25R, Twy A and Twy D. |
| | HS 2 | Rwy 12-30 and Rwy 07L-25R, Twy B and Twy K. |
| | HS 3 | Rwy 07R-25L, Twy B. |
| | HS 4 | Rwy 07R-25L and Rwy 12-30, Twy J and Twy D. |
| | HS 5 | Rwy 16R-34L, southwest ramp, Twy F and Twy B. |
| | HS 6 | Rwy 34R and Rwy 07R-25L. |
| | HS 7 | Rwy 12-30 cross every other rwy. |
| LOS ANGELES, CA | | |
| LOS ANGELES INTL (LAX) | HS 1 | Twy R not visible from the control twr. |
| PALM SPRINGS, CA | | |
| PALM SPRINGS INTL (PSP) | HS 1 | Twy C mistaken for Rwy 13R-31L or Rwy 13L-31R. |
| | HS 2 | Int of Twy B and Twy C. |
| | HS 3 | Twy B and Rwy 31R. |
| | HS 4 | Twy C and Twy J. |
| RIVERSIDE, CA | | |
| RIVERSIDE MUNI (RAL) | HS 1 | Rwy 27, Twy C. |
| | HS 2 | ATC non-visibility area. |
| SAN DIEGO, CA | | |
| MONTGOMERY FLD (MYF) | HS 1 | Rwy 10R-28L, Twy G and Twy H. |
| | HS 2 | Rwy 28R and Rwy 28L, Twys G. |
| | HS 3 | Rwy 28R and Rwy 28L, Twys F. |
| SANTA ANA, CA | | |
| JOHN WAYNE ARPT-ORANGE COUNTY (SNA) | HS 1 | Rwy 19L and Rwy 19R, Twy L and Twy K. |
| | HS 2 | Rwy 19L and Rwy 19R, Twy H. |
| | HS 3 | Twy A,Twy H, and Twy C. |

10 MAR 2011 to 07 APR 2011

(SEE CONTINUATION PAGE FOR MORE LISTINGS)

11069

FAA-CT-8080-7C

**Figure 241—Hot Spots.**

11069

## HOT SPOTS

### (CONTINUED)

| CITY/AIRPORT | HOT SPOT | DESCRIPTION* |
|---|---|---|
| SANTA BARBARA, CA | | |
| SANTA BARBARA MUNI (SBA) | HS 1 | Rwy 07-25, Twy C. |
| | HS 2 | Rwy 15L and Rwy 15R, Twy C, wide pavement. |
| | HS 3 | Rwy 15L-33R, Rwy 15R-33L, Rwy 07-25. Rwy 15L-33R and Rwy 15R-33L utilized for taxi. |
| | HS 4 | Rwy 25, Twy H and Twy J. |
| SANTA MARIA, CA | | |
| CAPTAIN G. ALLAN HANCOCK FLD (SMX) | HS 1 | Twy A, Twy C, and Twy D. |
| | HS 2 | Rwy 20 and Twy A. |
| | HS 3 | Rwy 12 and Twy B. |
| VICTORVILLE, CA | | |
| SOUTHERN CALIFORNIA LOGISTICS (VCV) | HS 1 | Wrong rwy departure risk. |

10 MAR 2011 to 07 APR 2011

*See appropriate A/FD, Alaska or Pacific Supplement HOT SPOT table for additional information.

11069

FAA-CT-8080-7C

**Figure 241—Hot Spots, continued.**

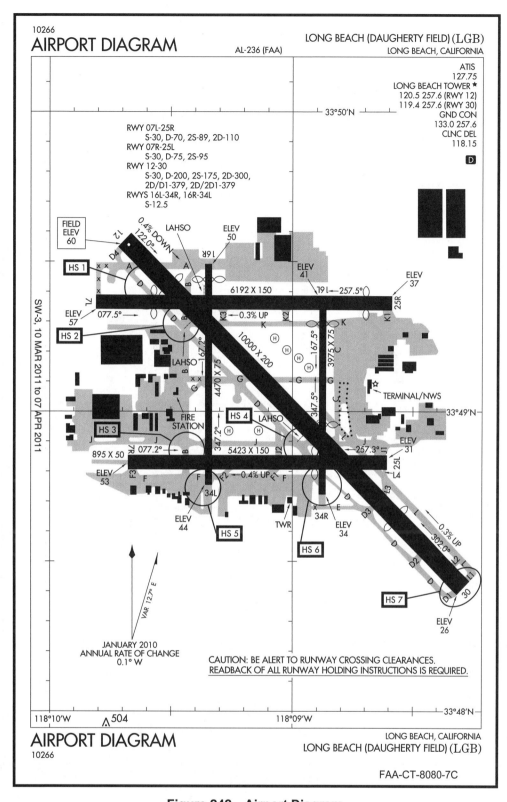

**Figure 242—Airport Diagram.**

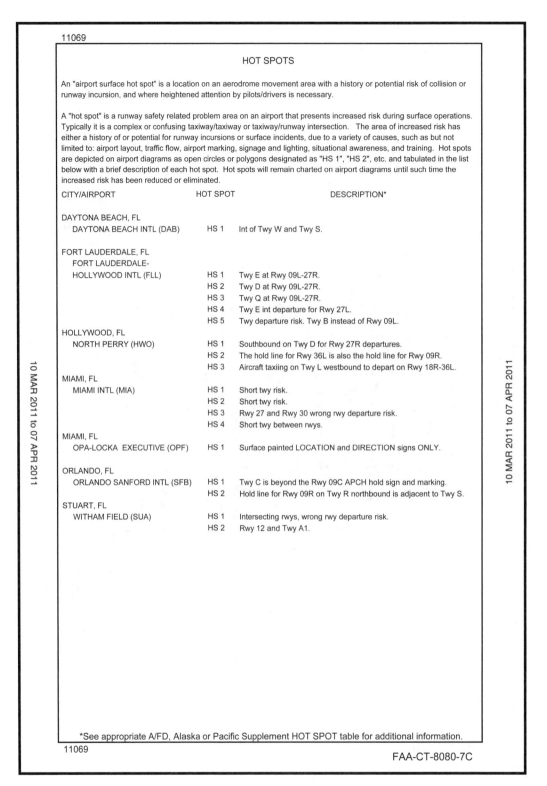

11069

## HOT SPOTS

An "airport surface hot spot" is a location on an aerodrome movement area with a history or potential risk of collision or runway incursion, and where heightened attention by pilots/drivers is necessary.

A "hot spot" is a runway safety related problem area on an airport that presents increased risk during surface operations. Typically it is a complex or confusing taxiway/taxiway or taxiway/runway intersection. The area of increased risk has either a history of or potential for runway incursions or surface incidents, due to a variety of causes, such as but not limited to: airport layout, traffic flow, airport marking, signage and lighting, situational awareness, and training. Hot spots are depicted on airport diagrams as open circles or polygons designated as "HS 1", "HS 2", etc. and tabulated in the list below with a brief description of each hot spot. Hot spots will remain charted on airport diagrams until such time the increased risk has been reduced or eliminated.

| CITY/AIRPORT | HOT SPOT | DESCRIPTION* |
|---|---|---|
| **DAYTONA BEACH, FL** | | |
| DAYTONA BEACH INTL (DAB) | HS 1 | Int of Twy W and Twy S. |
| | | |
| **FORT LAUDERDALE, FL** | | |
| FORT LAUDERDALE- | | |
| HOLLYWOOD INTL (FLL) | HS 1 | Twy E at Rwy 09L-27R. |
| | HS 2 | Twy D at Rwy 09L-27R. |
| | HS 3 | Twy Q at Rwy 09L-27R. |
| | HS 4 | Twy E int departure for Rwy 27L. |
| | HS 5 | Twy departure risk. Twy B instead of Rwy 09L. |
| **HOLLYWOOD, FL** | | |
| NORTH PERRY (HWO) | HS 1 | Southbound on Twy D for Rwy 27R departures. |
| | HS 2 | The hold line for Rwy 36L is also the hold line for Rwy 09R. |
| | HS 3 | Aircraft taxiing on Twy L westbound to depart on Rwy 18R-36L. |
| **MIAMI, FL** | | |
| MIAMI INTL (MIA) | HS 1 | Short twy risk. |
| | HS 2 | Short twy risk. |
| | HS 3 | Rwy 27 and Rwy 30 wrong rwy departure risk. |
| | HS 4 | Short twy between rwys. |
| **MIAMI, FL** | | |
| OPA-LOCKA EXECUTIVE (OPF) | HS 1 | Surface painted LOCATION and DIRECTION signs ONLY. |
| | | |
| **ORLANDO, FL** | | |
| ORLANDO SANFORD INTL (SFB) | HS 1 | Twy C is beyond the Rwy 09C APCH hold sign and marking. |
| | HS 2 | Hold line for Rwy 09R on Twy R northbound is adjacent to Twy S. |
| **STUART, FL** | | |
| WITHAM FIELD (SUA) | HS 1 | Intersecting rwys, wrong rwy departure risk. |
| | HS 2 | Rwy 12 and Twy A1. |

*See appropriate A/FD, Alaska or Pacific Supplement HOT SPOT table for additional information.

11069

FAA-CT-8080-7C

10 MAR 2011 to 07 APR 2011

**Figure 243—Hot Spots.**

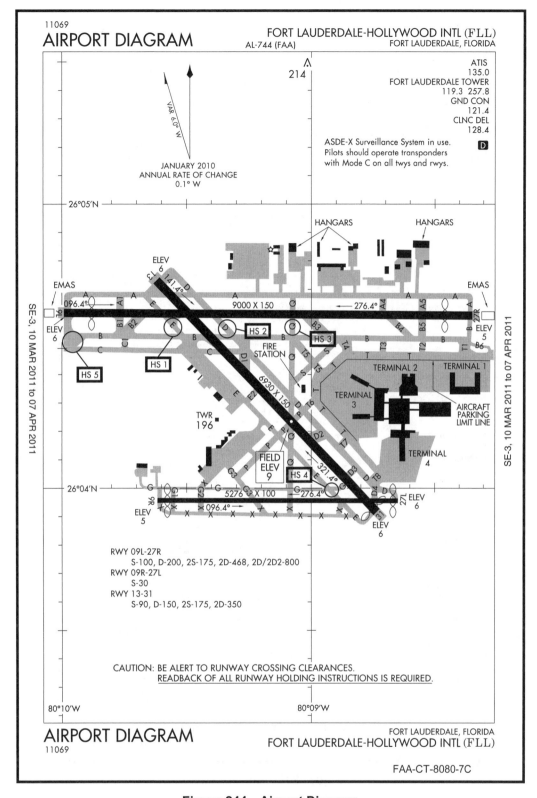

**Figure 244—Airport Diagram.**

11069

## HOT SPOTS

An "airport surface hot spot" is a location on an aerodrome movement area with a history or potential risk of collision or runway incursion, and where heightened attention by pilots/drivers is necessary.

A "hot spot" is a runway safety related problem area on an airport that presents increased risk during surface operations. Typically it is a complex or confusing taxiway/taxiway or taxiway/runway intersection. The area of increased risk has either a history of or potential for runway incursions or surface incidents, due to a variety of causes, such as but not limited to: airport layout, traffic flow, airport marking, signage and lighting, situational awareness, and training. Hot spots are depicted on airport diagrams as open circles or polygons designated as "HS 1", "HS 2", etc. and tabulated in the list below with a brief description of each hot spot. Hot spots will remain charted on airport diagrams until such time the increased risk has been reduced or eliminated.

| CITY/AIRPORT | HOT SPOT | DESCRIPTION* |
|---|---|---|
| CHANDLER, AZ | | |
| CHANDLER MUNI (CHD) | HS 1 | Rwy 22R may be used as an alternate taxi route. |
| LAS VEGAS, NV | | |
| HENDERSON | HS 1 | Twy H, Twy G, and Rwy 17R. |
| EXECUTIVE (HND) | HS 2 | Twy E and ramp area. High volume of traffic. |
| | HS 3 | Twy A and run up area. Twy A being confused for Rwy 35L. |
| LAS VEGAS, NV | | |
| McCARRAN INTL (LAS) | HS 1 | Rwy 01R-19L, Twy S and the ramp. |
| | HS 2 | Rwy 01R-19L and Rwy 01L-19R, Twy U. |
| | HS 3 | Rwy 01R-19L and Rwy 01L-19R, Twy Y. |
| | HS 4 | Rwy 07L and Rwy 01L, co-located rwy holding position markings. |
| | HS 5 | Twy E. |
| LAS VEGAS, NV | | |
| NORTH LAS VEGAS (VGT) | HS 1 | Rwy 07, Twy G and Twy F. |
| | HS 2 | Rwy 12R, Twy G. |
| | HS 3 | Rwy 12R, Twy A and Twy B. |
| | HS 4 | Rwy 12L, Twy A. |
| MESA, AZ | | |
| FALCON FIELD (FFZ) | HS 1 | Rwy 04R-22L, Twy B and Twy D. |
| MINDEN, NV | | |
| MINDEN-TAHOE (MEV) | HS 1 | Complex int. |
| | HS 2 | Frequent crossings for sailplane operations. |
| OGDEN, UT | | |
| OGDEN-HINCKLEY (OGD) | HS 1 | Twy D intersects Rwy 25 at north edge of Rwy 03-21. Wrong rwy departure risk. |
| | HS 2 | Confusing twy int in close proximity to rwy. |
| PHOENIX, AZ | | |
| PHOENIX DEER VALLEY (DVT) | HS 1 | Inadvertent Rwy 07R-25L crossings from Twy B5. |
| | HS 2 | Inadvertent Rwy 07R-25L crossings from Twy B9. |
| PHOENIX, AZ | | |
| PHOENIX-MESA | | |
| GATEWAY (IWA) | HS 1 | Twy V, Twy B, and Twy K complex int. |
| PHOENIX, AZ | | |
| PHOENIX SKY HARBOR | HS 1 | Pilots sometimes mistake Twy F for Rwy 07L or Rwy 07R. |
| INTL (PHX) | HS 2 | Pilots sometimes cross Rwy 07L-25R at Twy F8, Twy F9, or Twy F10, without authorization. |
| | HS 3 | Aircraft taxiing from southern ramps have turned onto Rwy 25L when given instructions to cross Rwy 25L at Twy H3. |

(SEE CONTINUATION PAGE FOR MORE LISTINGS)

11069

FAA-CT-8080-7C

**Figure 245—Hot Spots.**

11069

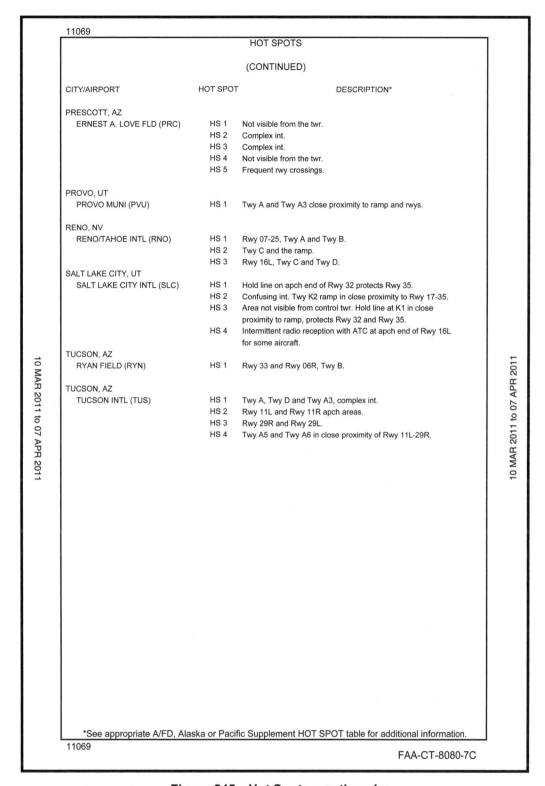

### HOT SPOTS

### (CONTINUED)

| CITY/AIRPORT | HOT SPOT | DESCRIPTION* |
|---|---|---|
| **PRESCOTT, AZ** | | |
| ERNEST A. LOVE FLD (PRC) | HS 1 | Not visible from the twr. |
| | HS 2 | Complex int. |
| | HS 3 | Complex int. |
| | HS 4 | Not visible from the twr. |
| | HS 5 | Frequent rwy crossings. |
| **PROVO, UT** | | |
| PROVO MUNI (PVU) | HS 1 | Twy A and Twy A3 close proximity to ramp and rwys. |
| **RENO, NV** | | |
| RENO/TAHOE INTL (RNO) | HS 1 | Rwy 07-25, Twy A and Twy B. |
| | HS 2 | Twy C and the ramp. |
| | HS 3 | Rwy 16L, Twy C and Twy D. |
| **SALT LAKE CITY, UT** | | |
| SALT LAKE CITY INTL (SLC) | HS 1 | Hold line on apch end of Rwy 32 protects Rwy 35. |
| | HS 2 | Confusing int. Twy K2 ramp in close proximity to Rwy 17-35. |
| | HS 3 | Area not visible from control twr. Hold line at K1 in close proximity to ramp, protects Rwy 32 and Rwy 35. |
| | HS 4 | Intermittent radio reception with ATC at apch end of Rwy 16L for some aircraft. |
| **TUCSON, AZ** | | |
| RYAN FIELD (RYN) | HS 1 | Rwy 33 and Rwy 06R, Twy B. |
| **TUCSON, AZ** | | |
| TUCSON INTL (TUS) | HS 1 | Twy A, Twy D and Twy A3, complex int. |
| | HS 2 | Rwy 11L and Rwy 11R apch areas. |
| | HS 3 | Rwy 29R and Rwy 29L. |
| | HS 4 | Twy A5 and Twy A6 in close proximity of Rwy 11L-29R. |

10 MAR 2011 to 07 APR 2011

10 MAR 2011 to 07 APR 2011

*See appropriate A/FD, Alaska or Pacific Supplement HOT SPOT table for additional information.

11069

FAA-CT-8080-7C

**Figure 245—Hot Spots, continued.**

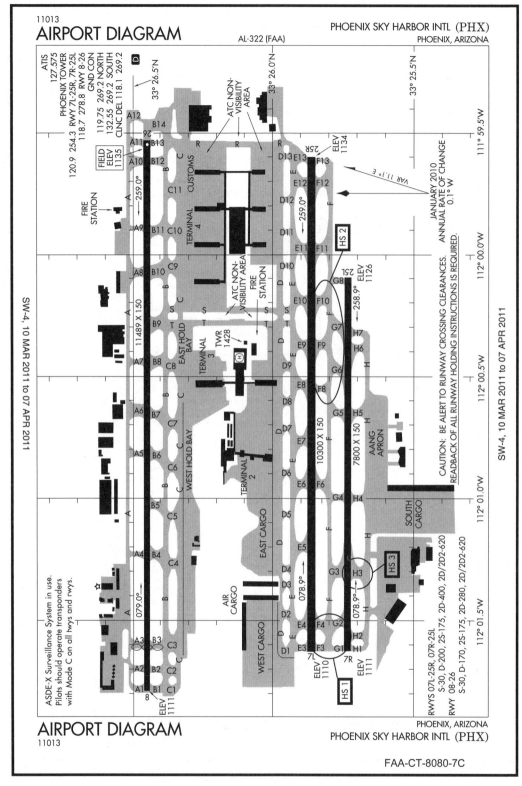

Figure 246—Airport Diagram.

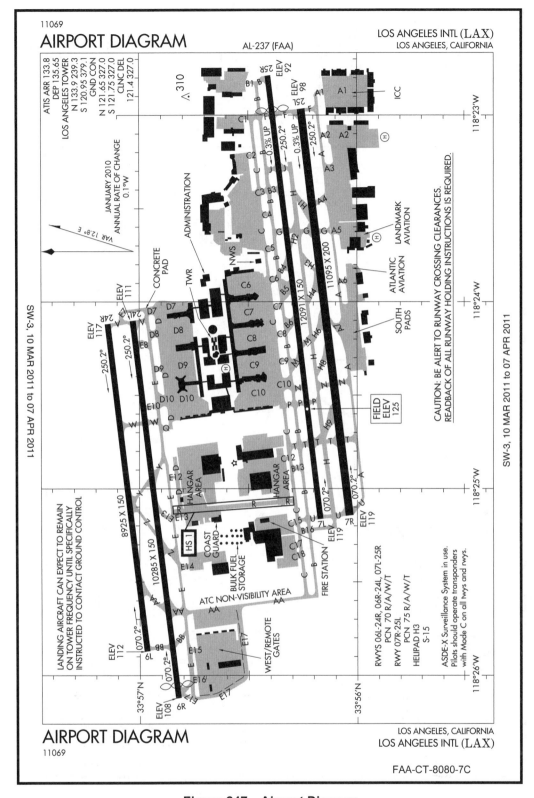

Figure 247—Airport Diagram.

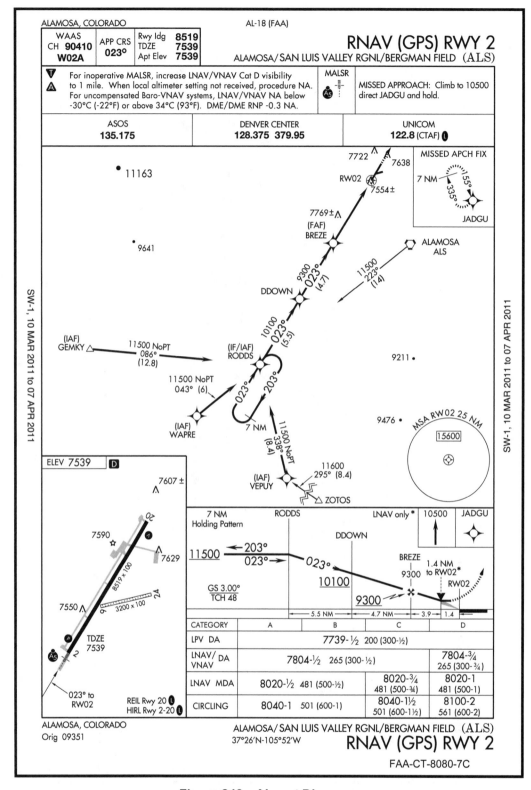

**Figure 248—Airport Diagram.**

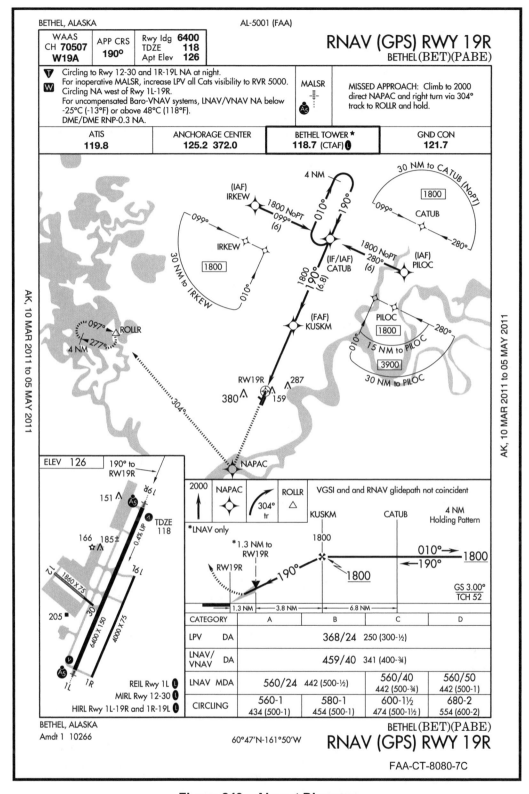

**Figure 249—Airport Diagram.**

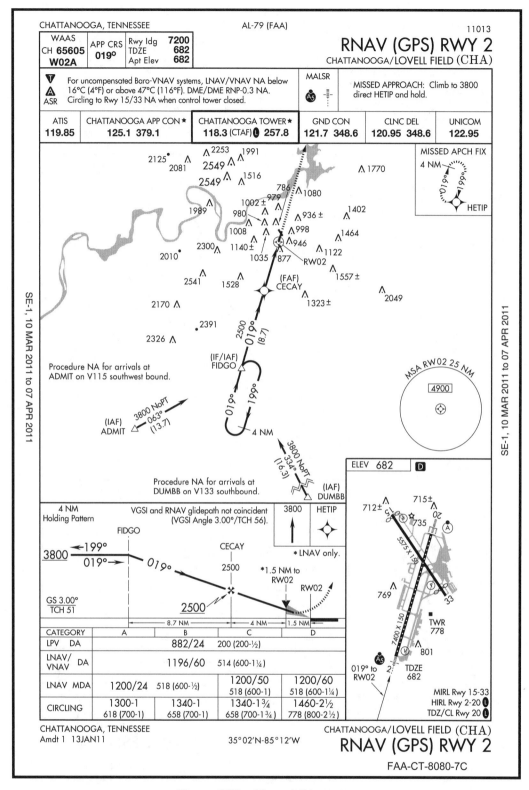

**Figure 250—Airport Diagram.**

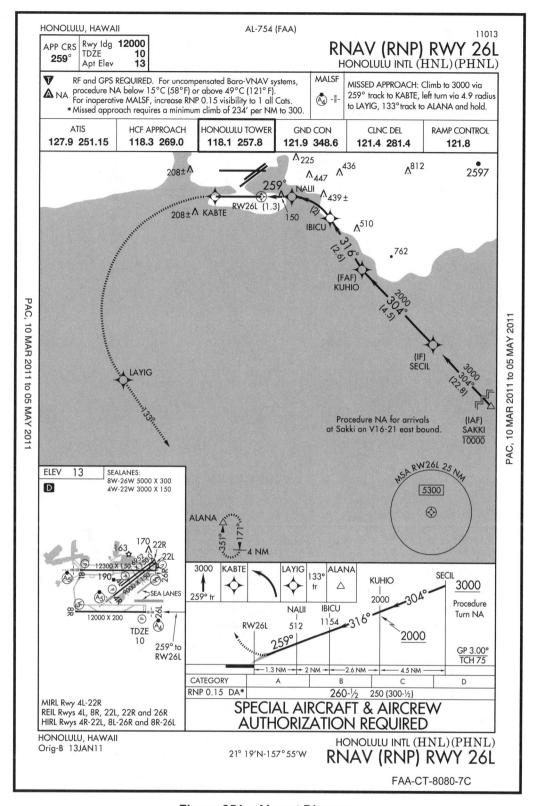

**Figure 251—Airport Diagram.**

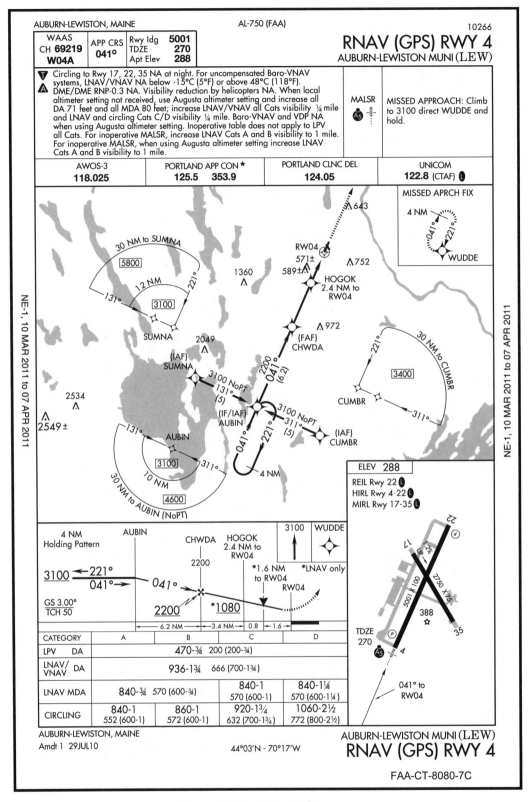

**Figure 252—Airport Diagram.**

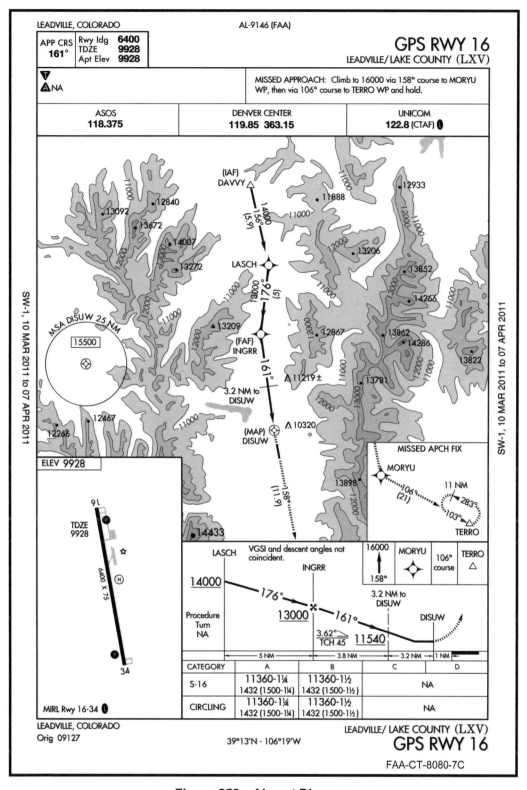

**Figure 253—Airport Diagram.**

# COMPUTER TESTING SUPPLEMENT
## FOR
## AIRLINE TRANSPORT PILOT
## AND
## AIRCRAFT DISPATCHER

## ADDENDUM B
## MAY 2012

U.S. DEPARTMENT OF TRANSPORTATION
**FEDERAL AVIATION ADMINISTRATION**
Flight Standards Service

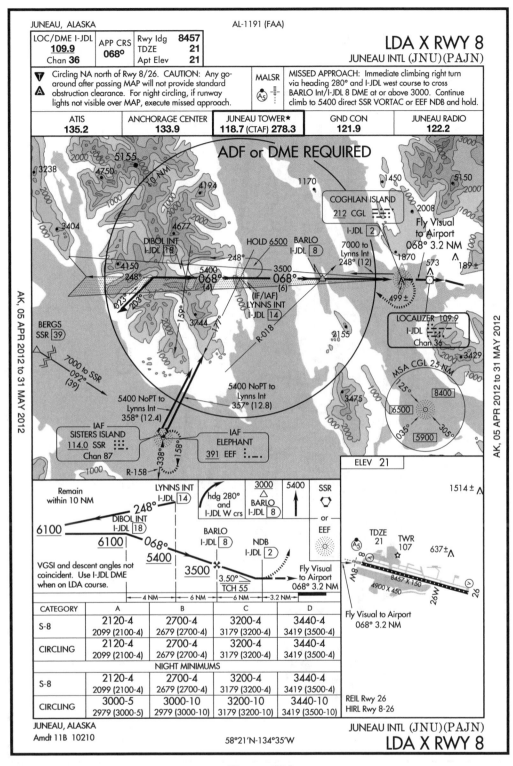

**Figure 254**

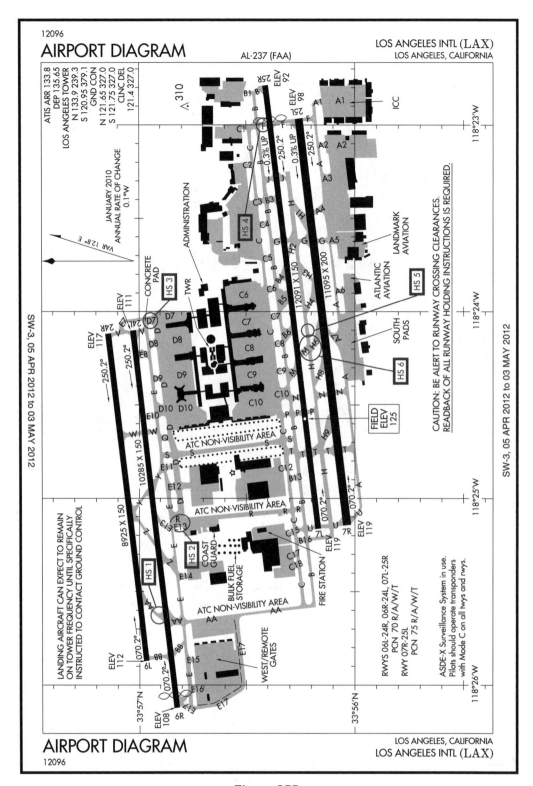

**Figure 255**

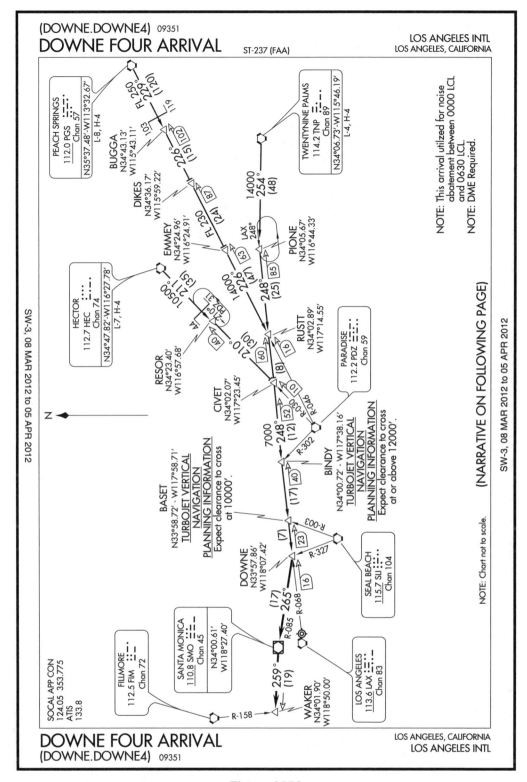

**Figure 255A**

(DOWNE.DOWNE4) 02276

# DOWNE FOUR ARRIVAL

ST-237 (FAA)

LOS ANGELES INTL
LOS ANGELES, CALIFORNIA

SW-3, 08 MAR 2012 to 05 APR 2012

ARRIVAL DESCRIPTION

HECTOR TRANSITION (HEC.DOWNE4): From over HEC VORTAC via HEC R-211 and PDZ R-030 to CIVET INT, then LAX R-068 to DOWNE INT. Thence....
PEACH SPRINGS TRANSITION (PGS.DOWNE4): From over PGS VORTAC via PGS R-229 and PDZ R-046 to RUSTT INT, then LAX R-068 to DOWNE INT. Thence....
TWENTYNINE PALMS TRANSITION (TNP.DOWNE4): From over TNP VORTAC via TNP R-254 to PIONE DME, then LAX R-068 to DOWNE INT.Thence....
....From DOWNE INT via SMO R-085 to SMO VOR/DME, then via SMO R-259 to WAKER INT, expect vector to final approach course for runways 6 and 7.

SW-3, 08 MAR 2012 to 05 APR 2012

DOWNE FOUR ARRIVAL
(DOWNE.DOWNE4) 02276

LOS ANGELES, CALIFORNIA
LOS ANGELES INTL

**Figure 255B**

---

## CALIFORNIA 133

## LOS ANGELES

### LOS ANGELES INTL (LAX) 9 SW UTC–8(–7DT) N33°56.55′ W118°24.48′

LOS ANGELES
COPTER
H-4I, L-3E, 4G, 7B, A
IAP, AD

125 B S4 **FUEL** JET A OX 1, 3 LRA Class I, ARFF Index E NOTAM FILE LAX

**RWY 07L–25R:** H12091X150 (CONC–GRVD) PCN 70 R/A/W/T HIRL CL
    **RWY 07L:** MALSR. TDZL. PAPI(P4L)—GA 3.0° TCH 59′. Rgt tfc.
    **RWY 25R:** MALSR. Thld dsplcd 957′. Railroad. 0.3% up.
**RWY 07R–25L:** H11095X200 (CONC–GRVD) PCN 75 R/A/W/T HIRL CL
    **RWY 07R:** MALSR. PAPI(P4L)—GA 3.0° TCH 57′. Pole. Rgt tfc.
    **RWY 25L:** ALSF2. TDZL. Railroad. 0.3% up.
**RWY 06R–24L:** H10285X150 (CONC–GRVD) PCN 70 R/A/W/T HIRL CL
    **RWY 06R:** MALSR. TDZL. PAPI(P4L)—GA 3.0° TCH 78′. Thld dsplcd 331′. Pole.
    **RWY 24L:** MALSR. PAPI(P4R)—GA 3.0° TCH 79′. Rgt tfc.
**RWY 06L–24R:** H8925X150 (CONC–GRVD) PCN 70 R/A/W/T HIRL CL
    **RWY 06L:** MALSR. PAPI(P4L)—GA 3.0° TCH 77′. Pole.
    **RWY 24R:** ALSF2. PAPI(P4L)—GA 3.0° TCH 73′. Sign. Rgt tfc.

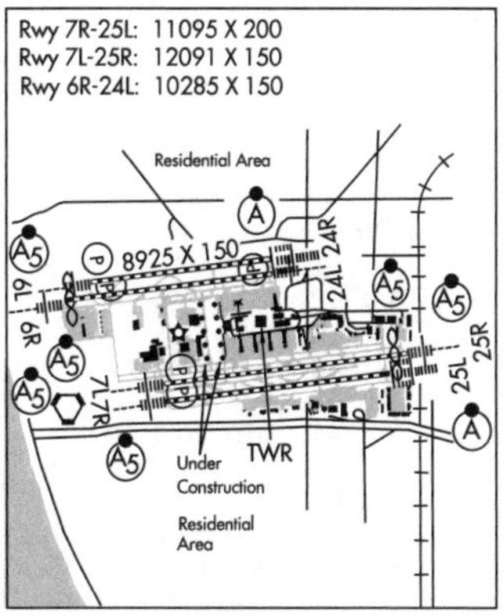

**AIRPORT REMARKS:** Attended continuously. Rwy 25L preferred emerg rwy. Numerous birds on and invof airport. Turbulence may be deflected upward from the blast fence 180′ E of Rwy 25R. ASDE–X Surveillance System in use: Pilots should operate transponders with Mode C on all twys and rwys. Tom Bradley International Gates: check LAWA (Los Angeles World Airport) rules and regulations for latest operating procedures. For B–777–300 and 300ER/A340–600 acft ops restrictions ctc LAX afld ops (310) 646–4265. Practice instrument approaches and touch and go landings are prohibited. Noise sensitive arpt. On westerly tkfs no turns before crossing shoreline. Over–ocean apchs utilized 0800–1430Z‡. Rwy 24R ALSF2 operates as SSALR till weather goes below VFR. Rwy 25L ALSF2 operates as SSALR until weather goes below VFR. Westbound B747–400 acft on Twy C prohibited from southbound turns onto Twy P. (Twy C–7, C–8, C–9 north of Twy C) and Twy D–7 south of Twy E will not accommodate B747 200 and larger acft. Twy D between Twy D–7 and D–8 (north of terminal one) restricted to B–767–300 and smaller acft. Taxilane D7 south of Twy E Rstd to 767–300 acft and smaller. Twy E–17, A340–600, B777–300/300ER acft northbound turn onto Twy E–17 from westbound Twy E prohibited. Twy E, A340–600, B777–300/300ER acft westbound turn onto Twy E from southbound Twy BB prohibited. Twy C–8, A340–600, B777–300/300ER acft prohibited on Twy C–8 between Twy B and Twy C. Twy C–9, A340–600, B777–300/300ER acft prohibited on Twy C–9 between Twy B and Twy C. A–380 ops ctc LAX afld opr (310) 646–4265 for acft movement procedures. West remote gates: acft use of open gates as taxi path is prohibited (gates 206, 207, 208, 209). A 700′X500′ clearway has been reestablished at west end of Rwy 24R. Touchdown, midpoint and rollout runway visual range avbl Rwy 06L, Rwy 24R, Rwy 06R, Rwy 24L, Rwy 07R, Rwy 25L, Rwy 07L, Rwy 25R. Simultaneous acft ops prohibited on Twy T and Twy H9 between Rwy 07L–25R and Rwy 07R–25L. Simultaneous acft ops prohibited on Twy H2 and Twy G between Rwy 07L–25R and Rwy 07R–25R. Overnight storage fee. Flight Notification Service (ADCUS) available. NOTE: See Special Notices—Noise Abatement Procedures, Continuous Power Facilities.

**WEATHER DATA SOURCES:** ASOS (310) 568-1486

**COMMUNICATIONS: D-ATIS ARR** 133.8 **D-ATIS DEP** 135.65 310-646-2297 **UNICOM** 122.95
    ®**SOCAL APP CON** 128.5 (045°-089°), 124.9 (090°-224°), 124.5 (225°-044°) 124.3 (App from west)
    **TOWER** 133.9 (N. complex), 120.95 (S. complex) 119.8
    **GND CON** 121.75 (S. complex) 121.65 (N. complex) **CLNC DEL** 121.4 120.35
    ®**SOCAL DEP CON** 125.2 (225°-044°) 124.3 (045°-224°) (Dep to west)

**AIRSPACE: CLASS B** See VFR Terminal Area Chart

**RADIO AIDS TO NAVIGATION:** NOTAM FILE LAX.
    **(H) VORTACW** 113.6 LAX Chan 83 N33°55.99′ W118°25.92′ 050° 1.3 NM to fld. 182/15E.
    VOR portion unusable:
        270°-277° byd 25 NM blo 8,000′
        277°-300° byd 10 NM blo 8,000′
        277°-300° byd 28 NM blo 12,000′
    VOR portion unusable:
        175°-205° byd 10 NM blo 3,000′

**CONTINUED ON NEXT PAGE**

---

**Figure 256**

134                                    **CALIFORNIA**
                                    **CONTINUED FROM PRECEDING PAGE**

    **ILS/DME** 108.5  I-UWU  Chan 22  Rwy 06L.  Class IE.  DME also serves Rwy 24R.
    **ILS/DME** 111.7  I-GPE  Chan 54  Rwy 06R.  Class IE.  MM OTS indef. DME also serves Rwy 24L.
    **ILS/DME** 111.1  I-IAS  Chan 48  Rwy 07L.  Class ID.  MM OTS indef. Glideslope unusable byd 5° right of localizer
       course. DME also serves Rwy 25R.
    **ILS/DME** 109.9  I-MKZ  Chan 36  Rwy 07R.  Class IT.  GS unuseable 5° left and 4° right of course. Coupled
       approaches not applicable below 264 ' MSL. DME also serves Rwy 25L.
    **ILS/DME** 111.7  I-HQB  Chan 54  Rwy 24L.  Class IE.  DME also serves Rwy 06R.
    **ILS/DME** 108.5  I-OSS  Chan 22  Rwy 24R.  Class IIIE.  DME also serves Rwy 06L.
    **ILS/DME** 109.9  I-LAX  Chan 36  Rwy 25L.  Class IIIE.
    **ILS/DME** 111.1  I-CFN  Chan 48  Rwy 25R.  Class IE.  DME also serves Rwy 07L.

- - - - - - - - - - - - - - - - - - - - - - - - - - - - - - - - - - - - - - - - - - - - - - - -

  **WHITEMAN**  (WHP)  1 E  UTC–8(–7DT)  N34°15.56´ W118°24.81´      LOS ANGELES
    1003   B  S4  **FUEL** 100LL, JET A  **OX** 1, 3  TPA—2003(1000)  NOTAM FILE WHP    COPTER
    **RWY 12–30:** H4120X75 (ASPH)  S–12.5  MIRL  1.0% up NW           L-3E, 4G, 7B, A
      **RWY 12:** REIL. PAPI(P2R)—GA 3.8° TCH 40´. Thld dsplcd 729´. P-line.      IAP, AD
      **RWY 30:** REIL. PAPI(P2L)—GA 3.8° TCH 40´. Thld dsplcd 478´. P-line.
      Rgt tfc.
    **RUNWAY DECLARED DISTANCE INFORMATION**
      **RWY 12:** TORA–3442  TODA–4120  ASDA–3910  LDA–3181
      **RWY 30:** TORA–3191  TODA–4120  ASDA–3940  LDA–3462
    **AIRPORT REMARKS:** Attended continuously. Birds on and invof arpt.
      Helicopter ops 2500´ MSL (1500´ AGL) and below. Arpt CLOSED to
      helicopter training/pattern opr 0400–1600Z‡. Dirt infield areas.
      Helicopters advised to use care to prevent blasting dirt and debris onto
      movement areas.
    **WEATHER DATA SOURCES:** AWOS-3PT 132.1 (818) 899-9820.
    **COMMUNICATIONS: CTAF** 135.0  **ATIS** 132.1 818-899-9820
      **UNICOM** 122.95
    Ⓡ**SOCAL APP/DEP CON** 120.4  134.2 (VNY 280°-BUR 050°) 134.2 (VNY
      160°-VNY 280°)
      **TOWER** 135.0  (1600-0400Z‡)  **GND CON** 125.0
    **CLNC DEL** For clnc del when  ATCT clsd call Socal App 800-448-3724.
    **AIRSPACE: CLASS D** svc 1600-0400Z‡ other times **CLASS G**
    **RADIO AIDS TO NAVIGATION:** NOTAM FILE VNY.
      **VAN NUYS (L) VORW/DME** 113.1   VNY  Chan 78  N34°13.41´ W118°29.50´   046° 4.4 NM to fld. 812/15E.
      VOR/DME unusable:
        010°-030° byd 20 NM blo 6,700´
        030°-050° byd 25 NM blo 8,600´
        330°-350° byd 25 NM blo 5,500´
        350°-010° byd 15 NM blo 6,100´
      DME unusable:
        094°-096° byd 35 NM blo 5,000´
      **PACOIMA NDB (MHW)** 370   PAI  N34°15.58´ W118°24.80´  at fld.  NOTAM FILE HHR. VFR only.
    **COMM/NAV/WEATHER REMARKS:** Whiteman arpt altimeter setting not avbl.

 **LOS BANOS**

  **LOS BANOS MUNI**  (LSN)  1 W  UTC–8(–7DT)  N37°03.83´ W120°52.19´     SAN FRANCISCO
    121   B  S2  **FUEL** 100LL, JET A  TPA—921(800)  NOTAM FILE RIU         L–3B
    **RWY 14–32:** H3801X75 (ASPH)  S–23  MIRL                 IAP
      **RWY 14:** REIL. PAPI(P2L)—GA 3.0° TCH 30´. Tree. Rgt tfc.
      **RWY 32:** REIL. PAPI(P2L)—GA 3.0° TCH 38´. Tree.
    **AIRPORT REMARKS:** Unattended. For cash fuel after hours call 209–827–7070. 24 hour automated fuel avbl with major credit
      card. Avoid overflight of houses south of arpt. No departures over housing areas to east of arpt. MIRL Rwy 14–32 preset
      low intensity until 0800Z‡. To increase intensity and ACTIVATE MIRL Rwy 14–32, REIL Rwy 14 and Rwy 32, and PAPI
      Rwy 14 and Rwy 32—CTAF.
    **WEATHER DATA SOURCES:** AWOS-3 118.675 (209) 827-7084.
    **COMMUNICATIONS: CTAF/UNICOM** 122.8
      **PANOCHE RCO** 122.1R 112.6T (FRESNO RADIO)
    Ⓡ**NORCAL APP/DEP CON** 120.95
    **RADIO AIDS TO NAVIGATION:** NOTAM FILE RIU.
      **PANOCHE (L) VORTAC** 112.6   PXN  Chan 73  N36°42.93´ W120°46.72´   332° 21.3 NM to fld. 2060/16E.
      VOR unusable:
        230°-280° byd 7NM blo 9,000´

- - - - - - - - - - - - - - - - - - - - - - - - - - - - - - - - - - - - - - - - - - - - - - - -

**Figure 257**

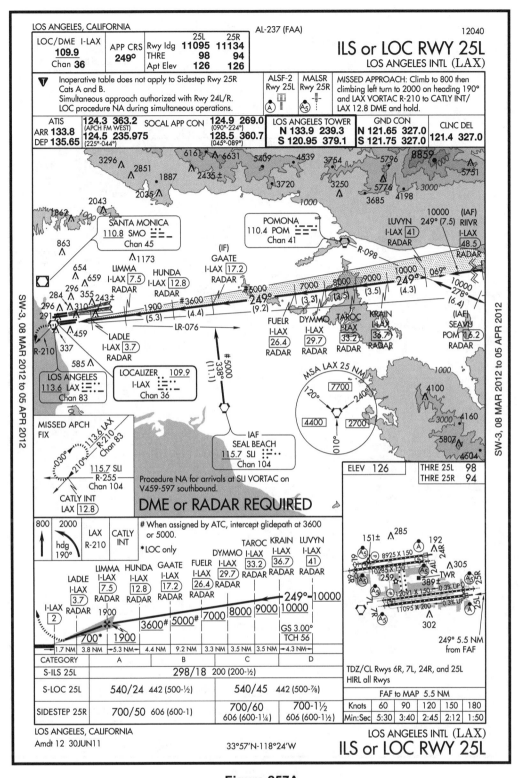

**Figure 257A**

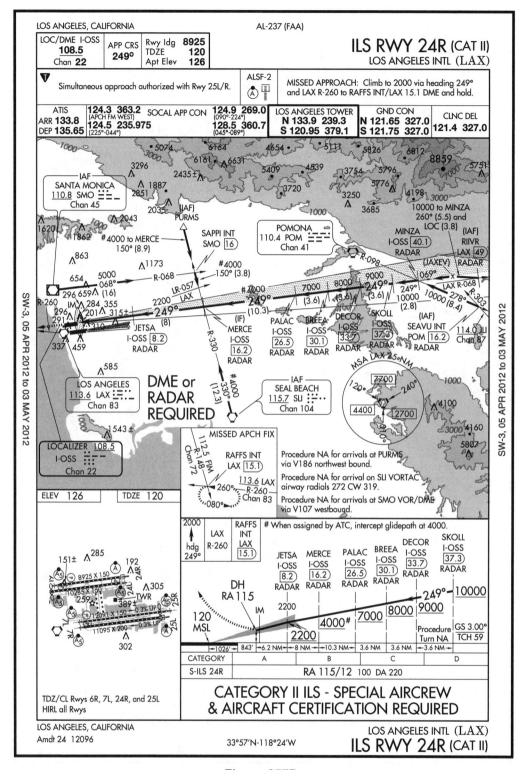

**Figure 257B**

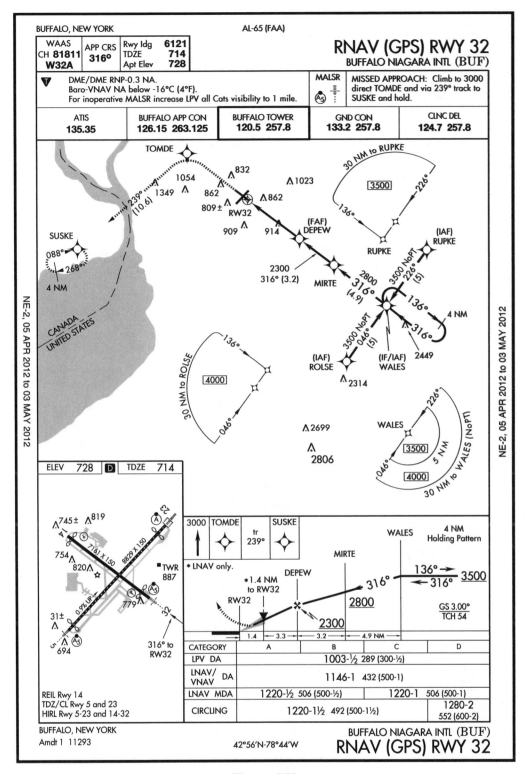

**Figure 258**

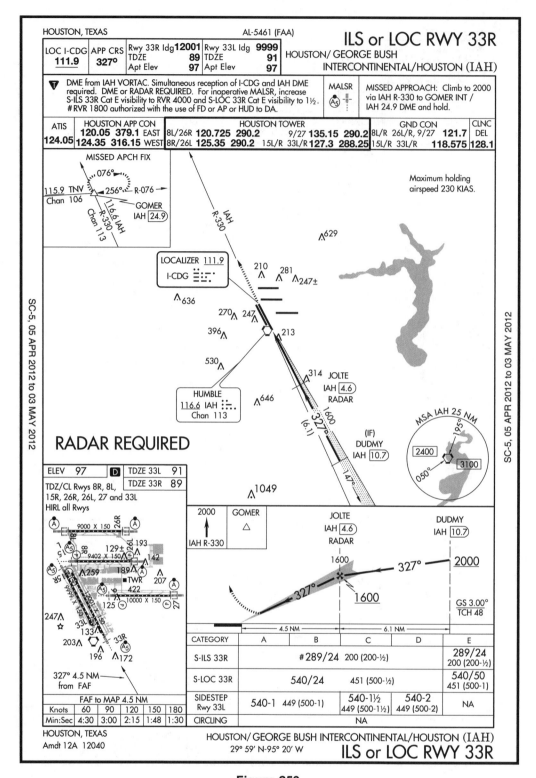

**Figure 259**

L3

▽▽ TAKE-OFF MINIMUMS AND (OBSTACLE) DEPARTURE PROCEDURES ▽▽

11349

## CROCKETT, TX
HOUSTON COUNTY (DKR)
ORIG 11349 (FAA)
TAKE-OFF MINIMUMS: **Rwy 2,** 400-2 or std. w/min. climb of 280' per NM to 800. **Rwy 20,** 300-1½ or std. w/ min. climb of 459' per NM to 700.
NOTE: **Rwy 2,** multiple trees beginning 57' from DER, 61' right of centerline, up to 50' AGL/399' MSL. Multiple trees and terrain beginning 27' from DER, 109' left of centerline, up to 50' AGL/409' MSL. Tower 1.5 NM from DER, 2864' left of centerline 233' AGL/ 623' MSL. **Rwy 20,** multiple towers beginning 4567' from DER, 1025' right of centerline, up to 200' AGL/ 529' MSL.

## EAGLE LAKE, TX
EAGLE LAKE
TAKE-OFF MINIMUMS: **Rwy 17,** 200-1, or std. with a min. climb of 420' per NM to 500.
NOTE: **Rwy 17,** tower 3068' from departure end of runway, 793' left of centerline, 192' AGL/317' MSL.

## GALVESTON, TX
SCHOLES INTL AT GALVESTON (GLS)
AMDT 4 08157 (FAA)
TAKE-OFF MINIMUMS: **Rwy 17,** 300-1 or std. w/ min. climb of 502' per NM to 300.
NOTE: **Rwy 13,** bush 381' from departure end of runway, 533' left of centerline, 15' AGL/20' MSL. Fence 201' from departure end of runway, 490' left of centerline, 6' AGL/ 11' MSL. Tree 343' from departure end of runway, 468' right of centerline, 12' AGL/17' MSL. **Rwy 17,** building 3057' from departure end of runway, 339' left of centerline, 123' AGL/130' MSL. Multiple poles beginning 2034' from departure end of runway, 87' right of centerline, up to 60' AGL/70' MSL. Multiple transmission towers beginning 636' from departure end of runway, 551' right of centerline, up to 55' AGL/60' MSL. Tree 460' from departure end of runway, 316' right of centerline, 22' AGL/29' MSL. **Rwy 31,** multiple cranes beginning 4341' from departure end of runway, 1017' left of centerline, up to 131' AGL/ 131' MSL. **Rwy 35,** tree 730' from departure end of runway, 501' right of centerline, 27' AGL/32' MSL.

## GIDDINGS, TX
GIDDINGS-LEE COUNTY (GYB)
ORIG 10210 (FAA)
NOTE: **Rwy 17,** numerous trees beginning 720' from DER, 58' right of centerline, up to 50' AGL/479' MSL. Numerous trees beginning 754' from DER, 340' left of centerline, up to 50' AGL/479' MSL. **Rwy 35,** numerous trees beginning 613' from DER, 272' right of centerline, up to 50' AGL/539' MSL. Numerous trees beginning 558' from DER, 265' left of centerline, up to 50' AGL/559' MSL. Vehicle on road 516' from DER, 246' left of centerline, 15' AGL/514' MSL.

## HOUSTON, TX
DAN JONES INTL (T51)
ORIG 11321 (FAA)
TAKE-OFF MINIMUMS: **Rwy 17,** NA - numerous trees. **Rwy 35,** NA - numerous trees.

## HOUSTON, TX (CON'T)
DAVID WAYNE HOOKS MEMORIAL (DWH)
AMDT 3 08157 (FAA)
TAKE-OFF MINIMUMS: **Rwys 17L, 35R,** NA-Environmental. **Waterways 17, 35,** NA - air traffic.
NOTE: **Rwy 17R,** multiple trees beginning 708' from departure end of runway, 68' left of centerline, up to 71' AGL/220' MSL. Multiple hangars beginning 433' from departure end of runway, 515' left of centerline, up to 37' AGL/182' MSL. DME antenna 653' from departure end of runway, 256' left of centerline, 13' AGL/162' MSL. Multiple trees and pole beginning 85' from departure end of runway, 294' right of centerline, up to 45' AGL/ 189' MSL. **Rwy 35L,** multiple trees and poles beginning 144' from departure end of runway, 32' left of centerline, up to 79' AGL/238' MSL. Multiple hangars and buildings beginning 85' from departure end of runway, 9' left of centerline, up to 53' AGL/202' MSL. Multiple trees, towers and pole beginning 100' from departure end of runway, 124' right of centerline, up to 93' AGL/247' MSL. Vehicle and road 315' from departure end of runway, on centerline 15' AGL/166' MSL. Building 894' from departure end of runway, 231' right of centerline, 23' AGL/173' MSL.

ELLINGTON FIELD (EFD)
AMDT 2 08157 (FAA)
NOTE: **Rwy 17R,** pole 1489' from departure end of runway, 817' right of centerline, 40' AGL/74' MSL. **Rwy 22,** antenna on building 1998' from departure end of runway, 598' right of centerline, 54' AGL/83' MSL. Obstruction light on glide slope 327' from departure end of runway, 543' left of centerline, 39' AGL/68' MSL. **Rwy 35R,** tree 1597' from departure end of runway, 32' left of centerline, 33' AGL/80' MSL. **Rwy 35L,** multiple trees beginning 1118' from departure end of runway, 679' right of centerline, up to 37' AGL/ 77' MSL. Crane 2352' from departure end of runway, 1024' left of centerline, 37' AGL/97' MSL.

GEORGE BUSH INTERCONTINENTAL/ HOUSTON (IAH)
AMDT 2 08157 (FAA)
NOTE: **Rwy 8L,** tree 2866' from departure end of runway, 921' left of centerline, 107' AGL/201' MSL. Multiple trees beginning 2750' from departure end of runway, 106' right of centerline, up to 80' AGL/174' MSL. **Rwy 15L,** multiple trees 2638' from departure end of runway, 758' right of centerline, up to 76' AGL/160' MSL. **Rwy 15R,** tower 1431' from departure end of runway, 591' left of centerline, 48' AGL/133' MSL. Antenna on glideslope 1469' from departure end of runway, 621' left of centerline, 49' AGL/133' MSL. **Rwy 26R,** pole 950' from departure end of runway, 660' right of centerline, 40' AGL/129' MSL. **Rwy 33R,** tree 2868' from departure end of runway, 1027' right of centerline, 73' AGL/172' MSL.

HOUSTON EXECUTIVE (TME)
DEPARTURE PROCEDURE: **Rwy 36,** Climb heading 355° to 700 before turning east.
NOTE: **Rwy 36,** power poles from left to right beginning 703' from departure end of runway, 623' left to 685' right of centerline, up to 32' AGL/196' MSL.

05 APR 2012 to 03 MAY 2012

05 APR 2012 to 03 MAY 2012

11349

▽▽ TAKE-OFF MINIMUMS AND (OBSTACLE) DEPARTURE PROCEDURES ▽▽

L3                                                                                                    SC-5

Figure 260

L4

▽ **TAKE-OFF MINIMUMS AND (OBSTACLE) DEPARTURE PROCEDURES** ▽

11349

### HOUSTON, TX (CON'T)

HOUSTON-SOUTHWEST (AXH)
AMDT 5 08157 (FAA)
  DEPARTURE PROCEDURE: **Rwy 9,** climb heading 089°
  to 2000 before turning left. **Rwy 27,** climb heading 269° to
  2200 before turning right.
  NOTE: **Rwy 9,** multiple hangars beginning 239' from
  departure end of runway, 360' right of centerline, up to 42'
  AGL/106' MSL. Multiple trees beginning 501' from
  departure end of runway, 355' right of centerline, up to 43'
  AGL/111' MSL. Multiple hangars beginning 119' from
  departure end of runway, 498' left of centerline, up to 41'
  AGL/105' MSL. Pole 332' from departure end of runway,
  299' left of centerline, 43' AGL/97' MSL. Antenna 1172'
  from departure end of runway, 658' left of centerline, 51'
  AGL/115' MSL. Multiple trees beginning 558' from
  departure end of runway, 68' left of centerline, up to 58'
  AGL/122' MSL. **Rwy 27,** multiple trees beginning 1050'
  from departure end of runway, 40' left of centerline, up to
  71' AGL/140' MSL. Vehicle and road 99' from departure
  end of runway, 291' right of centerline, 15' AGL/83' MSL.
  Multiple trees beginning 873' from departure end of
  runway, 514' right of centerline, up to 59' AGL/130' MSL.
  Multiple transmission poles beginning 1304' from
  departure end of runway, 131' right of centerline, up to 41'
  AGL/110' MSL.

LONE STAR EXECUTIVE (CXO)
AMDT 3 10266 (FAA)
  NOTE: **Rwy 1,** trees beginning 194' from DER, 130' right of
  centerline, up to 100' AGL/374' MSL. Trees beginning 817'
  from DER, 15' left of centerline, up to 100' AGL/359' MSL.
  **Rwy 14,** trees and obstruction light on DME beginning
  399' from DER, 80' right of centerline, up to 100' AGL/329'
  MSL. Trees beginning 640' from DER, 408' left of
  centerline, up to 100' AGL/329' MSL. **Rwy 19,** trees
  beginning 68' from DER, 64' right of centerline, up to 100'
  AGL/344' MSL. Trees beginning 1' from DER, 159' left of
  centerline, up to 100' AGL/339' MSL. **Rwy 32,** trees
  beginning 1785' from DER, 973' right of centerline, up to
  100' AGL/339' MSL. Trees and vehicles on road beginning
  603' from DER, 458' left of centerline, up to 100' AGL/354'
  MSL.

PEARLAND RGNL
  DEPARTURE PROCEDURE: **Rwy 14,** climb heading 139°
  to 1600 before proceeding south through southwest. **Rwy
  32,** climb heading 319° to 900 before proceeding on
  course.
  NOTE: **Rwy 14,** multiple trees beginning 199' from
  departure end of runway, 226' right of centerline, up to 66'
  AGL/100' MSL. Vehicle on road 398' from departure end of
  runway, 405' left of centerline, 9' AGL/55' MSL. Trees
  1287' from departure end of runway, 453' left of centerline,
  up to 56' AGL/90' MSL. **Rwy 32,** multiple trees beginning
  690' from departure end of runway, 81' left of centerline, up
  to 79' AGL/128' MSL. Multiple poles beginning 745' from
  departure end of runway, 24' left of centerline, up to 40'
  AGL/80' MSL. Multiple trees and poles beginning 29' from
  departure end of runway, 11' right of centerline, up to 64'
  AGL/104' MSL. Building 237' from departure end of
  runway, 520' right of centerline, 32' AGL/72' MSL.

### HOUSTON, TX (CON'T)

SUGAR LAND RGNL (SGR)
AMDT 7 08157 (FAA)
  DEPARTURE PROCEDURE: **Rwy 17,** climb heading
  170° to 1500 before turning eastbound. **Rwy 35,** climb
  heading 350° to 1100 before turning southbound.
  NOTE: **Rwy 17,** multiple poles beginning 436' from
  departure end of runway, 172' right of centerline, up to 44'
  AGL/124' MSL. Railroad 110' from departure end of
  runway, 10' left of centerline, 23' AGL/104' MSL. Multiple
  poles beginning 135' from departure end of runway, 270'
  left of centerline, up to 44' AGL/111' MSL. **Rwy 35,**
  vehicle and road 65' from departure end of runway, 2'
  right of centerline, 15' AGL/96' MSL. Multiple trees
  beginning 37' from departure end of runway, 275' right of
  centerline, up to 81' AGL/164' MSL. DME antenna 380'
  from departure end of runway, 253' right of centerline, 24'
  AGL/100' MSL. Multiple trees beginning 83' from
  departure end of runway, 65' left of centerline, up to 81'
  AGL/155' MSL.

WEISER AIR PARK (EYQ)
AMDT 2 08157 (FAA)
  TAKE-OFF MINIMUMS: **Rwy 9,** 200-1 or std. w/ min.
  climb of 399' per NM to 400.
  NOTE: **Rwy 9,** tank 4127' from departure end of runway,
  1455' left of centerline, 147' AGL/282' MSL. **Rwy 27,**
  railroad 462' from departure end of runway, 555' left of
  centerline, 23' AGL/165' MSL. Vehicle and road 650' from
  departure end of runway, 7' left of centerline, 17' AGL/159'
  MSL.

WEST HOUSTON (IWS)
AMDT 3 09295 (FAA)
  NOTE: **Rwy 15,** vehicles on roadway beginning abeam
  DER, left and right of centerline, up to 15' AGL/124' MSL.
  Building 177' from DER, 398' left of centerline, 18' AGL/
  126' MSL. Trees beginning 178' from DER, 289' right of
  centerline, up to 100' AGL/209' MSL. **Rwy 33,** building
  265' from DER, 364' left of centerline, 33' AGL/143' MSL.
  Trees beginning 2706' from DER, 700' left of centerline,
  up to 100' AGL/214' MSL. Trees beginning 3159' from
  DER, 747' right of centerline, up to 100' AGL/216' MSL.

05 APR 2012 to 03 MAY 2012

05 APR 2012 to 03 MAY 2012

11349

▽ **TAKE-OFF MINIMUMS AND (OBSTACLE) DEPARTURE PROCEDURES** ▽

SC-5

L4

**Figure 261**

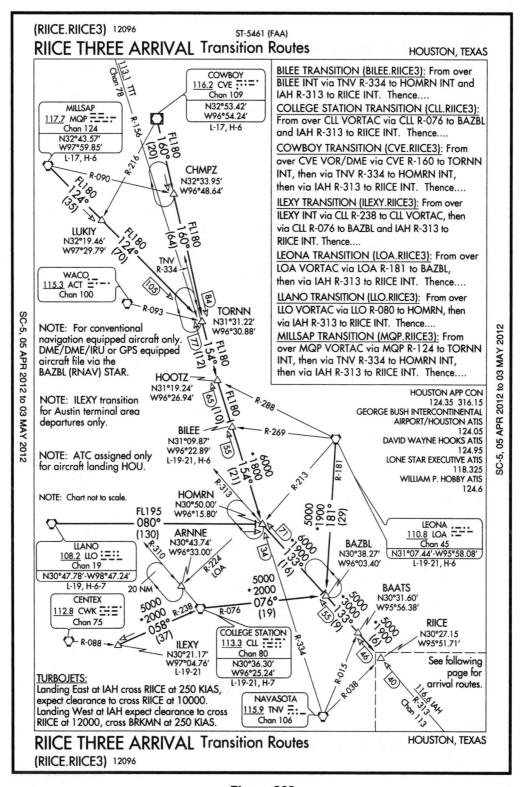

**Figure 262**

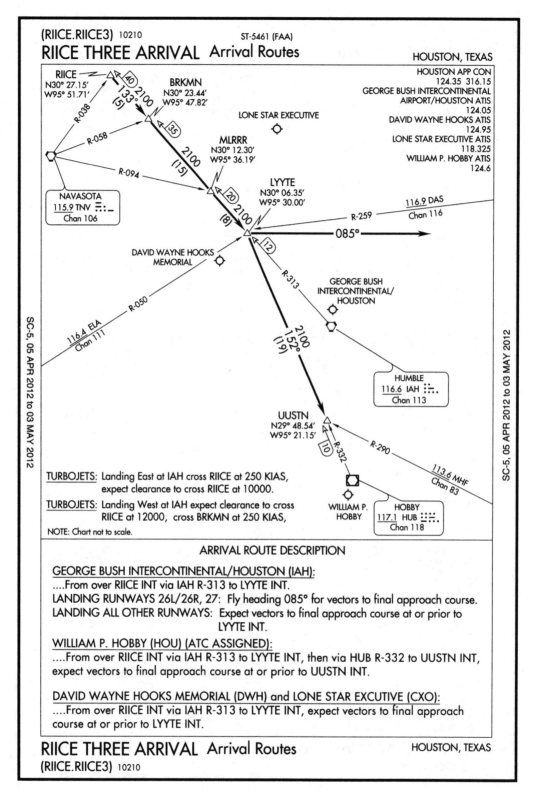

(RIICE.RIICE3) 10210
RIICE THREE ARRIVAL Arrival Routes
ST-5461 (FAA)
HOUSTON, TEXAS

HOUSTON APP CON
124.35  316.15
GEORGE BUSH INTERCONTINENTAL
AIRPORT/HOUSTON ATIS
124.05
DAVID WAYNE HOOKS ATIS
124.95
LONE STAR EXECUTIVE ATIS
118.325
WILLIAM P. HOBBY ATIS
124.6

RIICE
N30° 27.15'
W95° 51.71'

BRKMN
N30° 23.44'
W95° 47.82'

LONE STAR EXECUTIVE

MLRRR
N30° 12.30'
W95° 36.19'

LYYTE
N30° 06.35'
W95° 30.00'

NAVASOTA
115.9 TNV
Chan 106

116.9 DAS
Chan 116

085°

DAVID WAYNE HOOKS
MEMORIAL

GEORGE BUSH
INTERCONTINENTAL/
HOUSTON

116.4 ELA
Chan 111

HUMBLE
116.6 IAH
Chan 113

UUSTN
N29° 48.54'
W95° 21.15'

113.6 MHF
Chan 83

TURBOJETS: Landing East at IAH cross RIICE at 250 KIAS,
expect clearance to cross RIICE at 10000.

TURBOJETS: Landing West at IAH expect clearance to cross
RIICE at 12000, cross BRKMN at 250 KIAS,

NOTE: Chart not to scale.

WILLIAM P.
HOBBY

HOBBY
117.1 HUB
Chan 118

SC-5, 05 APR 2012 to 03 MAY 2012

SC-5, 05 APR 2012 to 03 MAY 2012

### ARRIVAL ROUTE DESCRIPTION

GEORGE BUSH INTERCONTINENTAL/HOUSTON (IAH):
....From over RIICE INT via IAH R-313 to LYYTE INT.
LANDING RUNWAYS 26L/26R, 27:  Fly heading 085° for vectors to final approach course.
LANDING ALL OTHER RUNWAYS:  Expect vectors to final approach course at or prior to
LYYTE INT.

WILLIAM P. HOBBY (HOU) (ATC ASSIGNED):
....From over RIICE INT via IAH R-313 to LYYTE INT, then via HUB R-332 to UUSTN INT,
expect vectors to final approach course at or prior to UUSTN INT.

DAVID WAYNE HOOKS MEMORIAL (DWH) and LONE STAR EXECUTIVE (CXO):
....From over RIICE INT via IAH R-313 to LYYTE INT, expect vectors to final approach
course at or prior to LYYTE INT.

RIICE THREE ARRIVAL Arrival Routes                                  HOUSTON, TEXAS
(RIICE.RIICE3) 10210

**Figure 263**

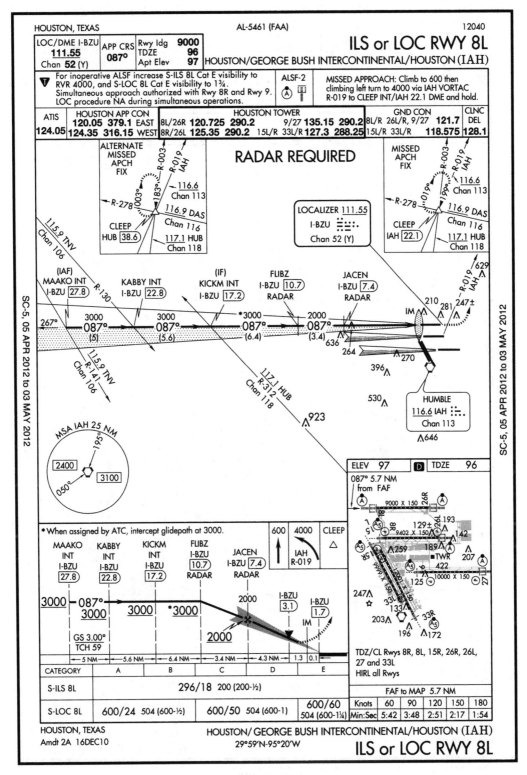

Figure 264

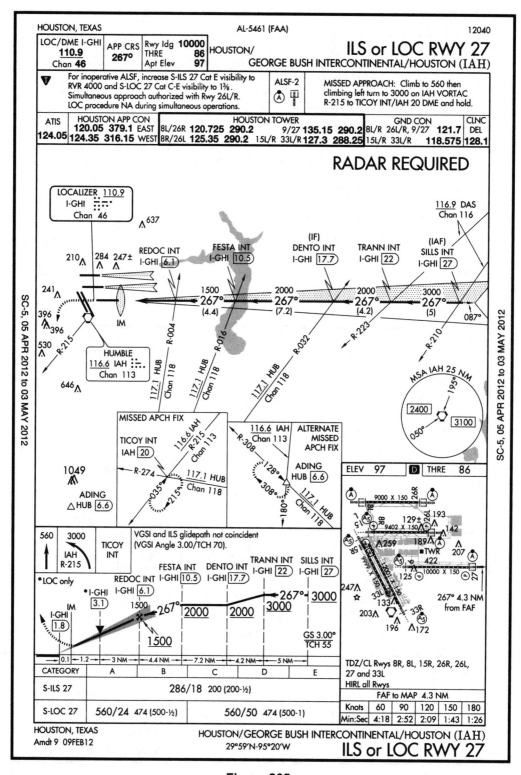

**Figure 265**

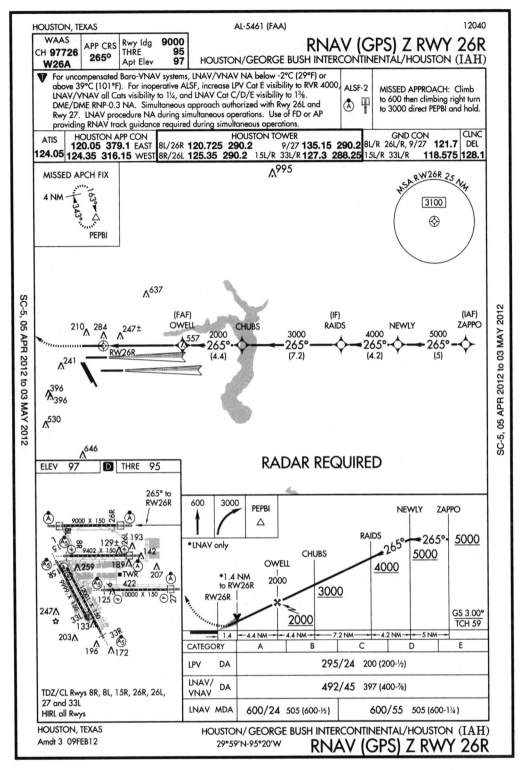

Figure 266

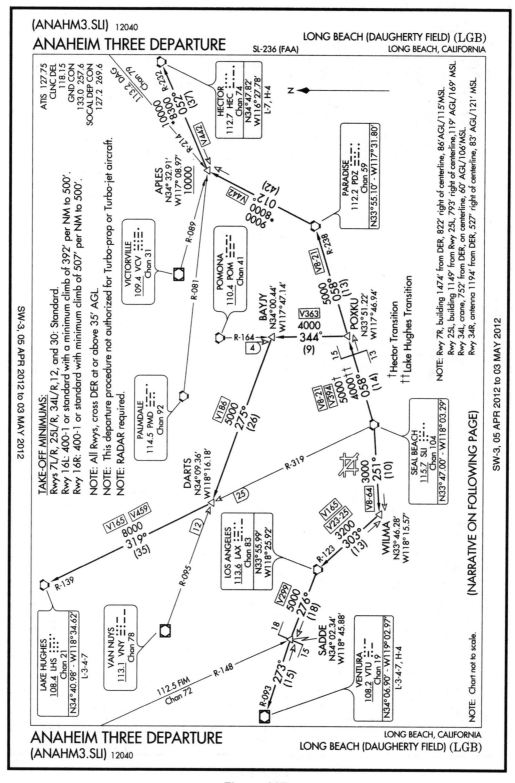

**Figure 267**

(ANAHM3.SLI) 08045

**ANAHEIM THREE DEPARTURE**    SL-236 (FAA)

LONG BEACH (DAUGHERTY FIELD) (LGB)
LONG BEACH, CALIFORNIA

### DEPARTURE ROUTE DESCRIPTION

<u>HECTOR or LAKE HUGHES TRANSITION:</u> Climb runway heading to 800' then fly assigned heading for radar vectors to SLI VORTAC. Thence. . . .

<u>VENTURA TRANSITION:</u> Climb runway heading to 800' then fly assigned heading for radar vectors to LAX VORTAC. Thence. . . .

. . . .via (transition) or (assigned route). Maintain assigned altitude. Expect clearance to filed altitude 10 minutes after departure.

<u>HECTOR TRANSITION (ANAHM3.HEC):</u> From over SLI VORTAC via SLI R-058 and PDZ R-238 to PDZ VORTAC, then via PDZ R-012 and HEC R-232 to HEC VORTAC.

<u>LAKE HUGHES TRANSITION (ANAHM3.LHS):</u> From over SLI VORTAC via SLI R-058 and PDZ R-238 to POXKU INT, then via POM R-164 to BAYJY INT, then via VNY R-095 to DARTS INT. Thence via SLI R-319 and LHS R-139 to LHS VORTAC.

<u>VENTURA TRANSITION (ANAHM3.VTU):</u> From over SLI VORTAC via SLI R-251 to WILMA INT, then via LAX R-123 to LAX VORTAC, then via LAX R-276 and VTU R-093 to VTU VOR/DME.

SW-3, 05 APR 2012 to 03 MAY 2012

SW-3, 05 APR 2012 to 03 MAY 2012

**ANAHEIM THREE DEPARTURE**
(ANAHM3.SLI) 08045

LONG BEACH, CALIFORNIA
LONG BEACH (DAUGHERTY FIELD) (LGB)

**Figure 268**

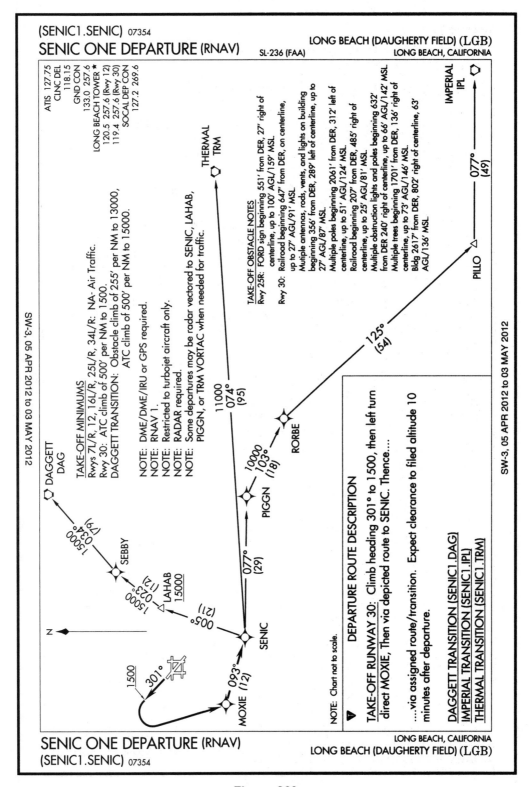

**Figure 269**

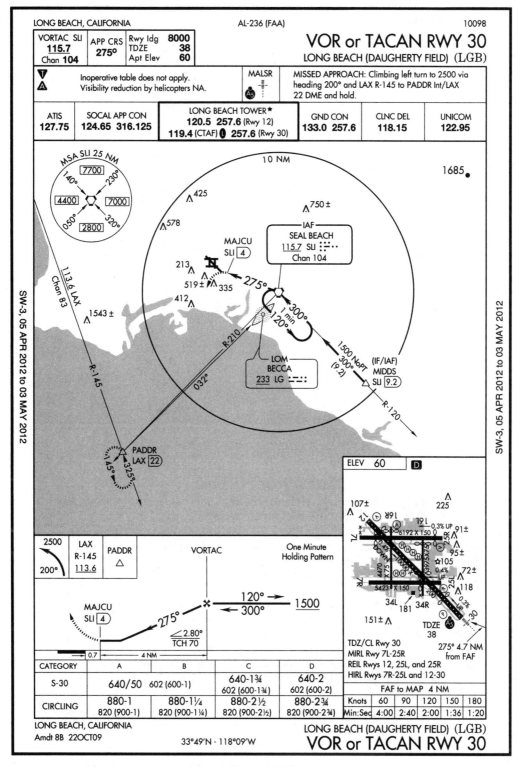

**Figure 270**

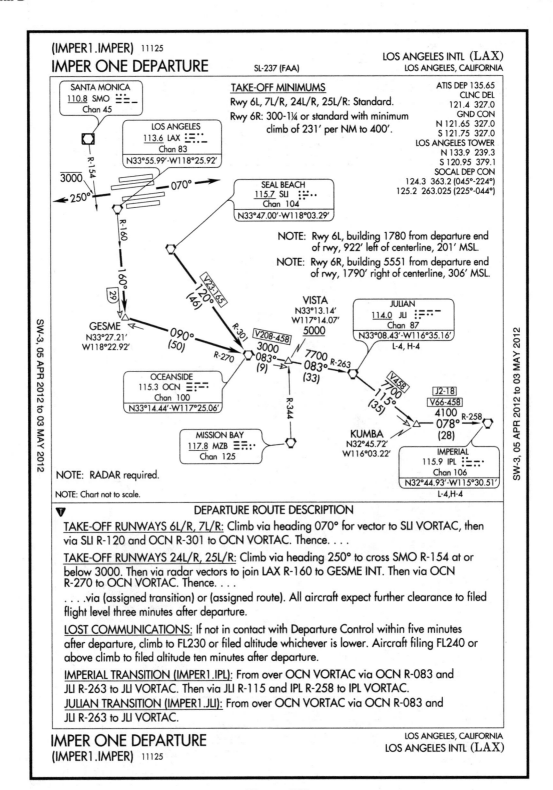

**DEPARTURE ROUTE DESCRIPTION**

<u>TAKE-OFF RUNWAYS 6L/R, 7L/R:</u> Climb via heading 070° for vector to SLI VORTAC, then via SLI R-120 and OCN R-301 to OCN VORTAC. Thence. . . .

<u>TAKE-OFF RUNWAYS 24L/R, 25L/R:</u> Climb via heading 250° to cross SMO R-154 at or below 3000. Then via radar vectors to join LAX R-160 to GESME INT. Then via OCN R-270 to OCN VORTAC. Thence. . . .

. . . .via (assigned transition) or (assigned route). All aircraft expect further clearance to filed flight level three minutes after departure.

<u>LOST COMMUNICATIONS:</u> If not in contact with Departure Control within five minutes after departure, climb to FL230 or filed altitude whichever is lower. Aircraft filing FL240 or above climb to filed altitude ten minutes after departure.

<u>IMPERIAL TRANSITION (IMPER1.IPL):</u> From over OCN VORTAC via OCN R-083 and JLI R-263 to JLI VORTAC. Then via JLI R-115 and IPL R-258 to IPL VORTAC.

<u>JULIAN TRANSITION (IMPER1.JLI):</u> From over OCN VORTAC via OCN R-083 and JLI R-263 to JLI VORTAC.

**Figure 271**

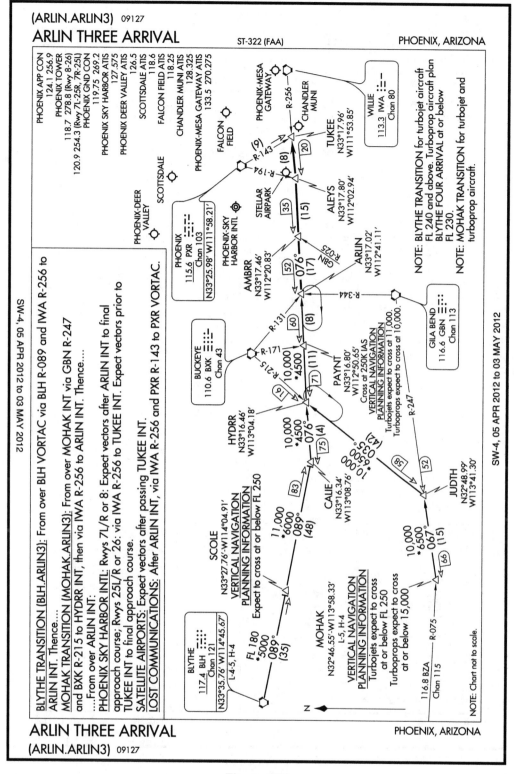

**Figure 272**

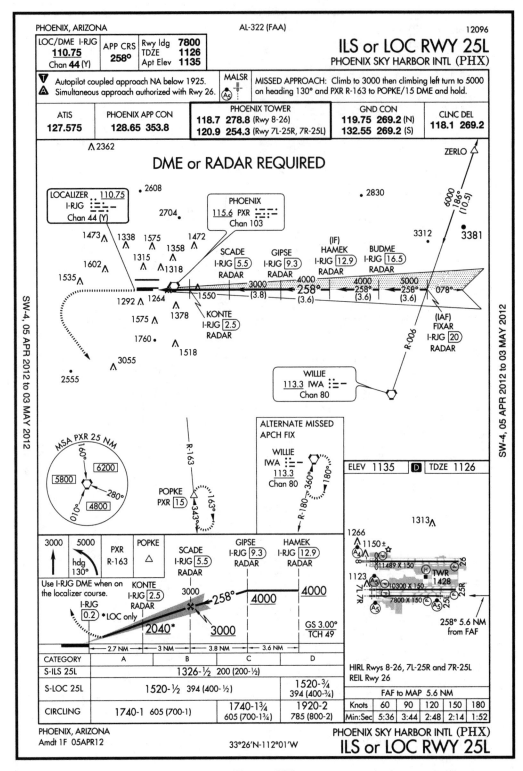

**Figure 273**

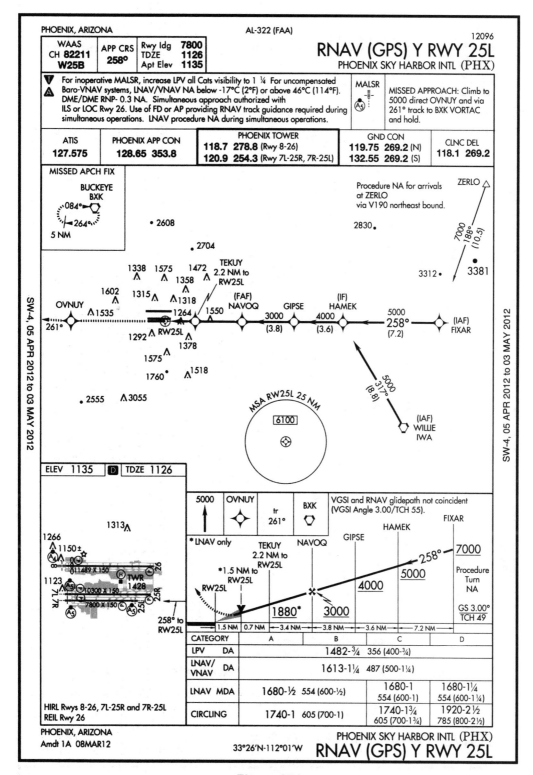

**Figure 274**

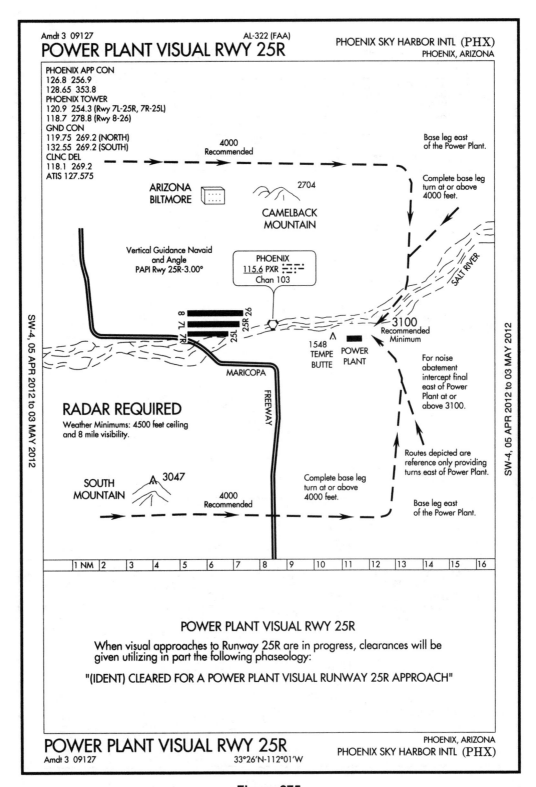

**Figure 275**

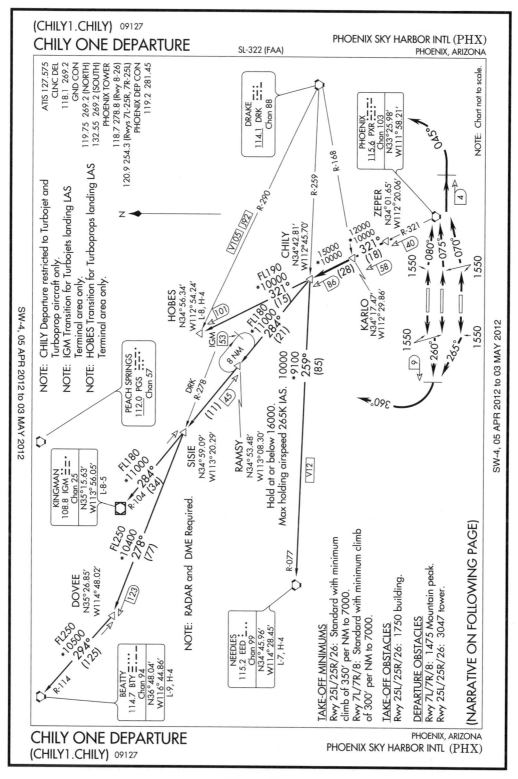

**Figure 276**

(CHILY1.CHILY)  02052
## CHILY ONE DEPARTURE
SL-322 (FAA)

PHOENIX SKY HARBOR (PHX)
PHOENIX, ARIZONA

▼                    DEPARTURE ROUTE DESCRIPTION

TAKE-OFF RUNWAY 7L:  Climb runway heading to 1550, then climbing left  turn heading 075°, at 4 DME east of PXR VORTAC, climbing left turn heading 045°. Thence....

TAKE-OFF RUNWAY 7R:  Climb runway heading to 1550, then climbing left turn heading 070°, at 4 DME east of PXR VORTAC, climbing left turn heading 045°. Thence....

TAKE-OFF RUNWAY 8:  Climb runway heading to 1550, then climbing right turn heading 080°, at 4 DME east of PXR VORTAC, climbing left turn heading 045°. Thence....

TAKE-OFF RUNWAY 25L:  Climb runway heading to 1550, then climbing right turn heading 265°, at 9 DME west of PXR VORTAC, climbing right turn heading 360°. Thence....

TAKE-OFF RUNWAY 25R:  Climb runway heading to 1550, then climbing right turn heading 260°, at 9 DME west of PXR VORTAC, climbing right turn heading 360°. Thence....

TAKE-OFF RUNWAY 26:  Climb runway heading to 1550, then climbing right turn heading 260°, at 9 DME west of PXR VORTAC, climbing right turn heading 360°. Thence....

....maintain 7000.  Expect radar vectors to PXR R-321 to ZEPER INT then CHILY INT. Then via (transition).  Expect filed altitude 3 minutes after departure.

BEATTY TRANSITION (CHILY1.BTY):  From over CHILY INT via IGM R-104 to SISIE INT, then via DRK R-278 to DOVEE INT, then via BTY R-114 to BTY VORTAC.

HOBES TRANSITION (CHILY1.HOBES):  From over CHILY INT via PXR R-321 to HOBES INT.

KINGMAN TRANSITION (CHILY1.IGM):  From over CHILY INT via IGM R-104 to IGM VOR/DME.

NEEDLES TRANSITION (CHILY1.EED):  From over CHILY INT via DRK R-259 and EED R-077 to EED VORTAC.

SW-4, 05 APR 2012 to 03 MAY 2012

SW-4, 05 APR 2012 to 03 MAY 2012

## CHILY ONE DEPARTURE
(CHILY1.CHILY)  02052

PHOENIX, ARIZONA
PHOENIX SKY HARBOR (PHX)

**Figure 277**

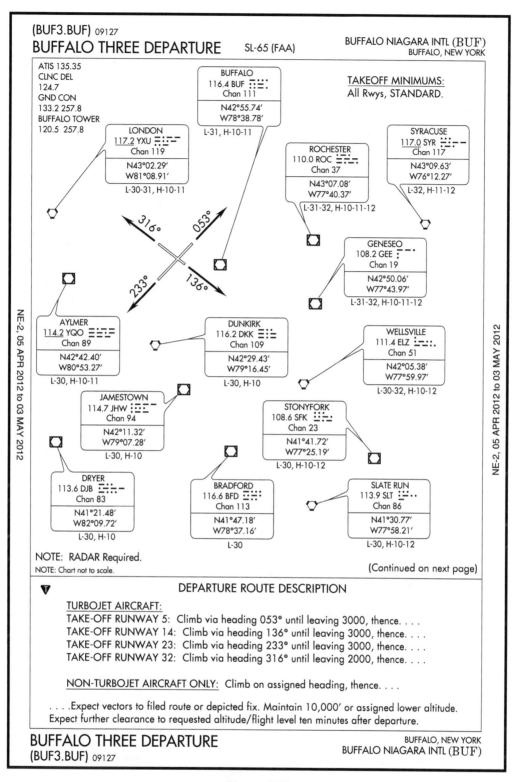

(BUF3.BUF) 09127
## BUFFALO THREE DEPARTURE

SL-65 (FAA)

BUFFALO NIAGARA INTL (BUF)
BUFFALO, NEW YORK

ATIS 135.35
CLNC DEL
124.7
GND CON
133.2 257.8
BUFFALO TOWER
120.5 257.8

**BUFFALO**
116.4 BUF
Chan 111
N42°55.74'
W78°38.78'
L-31, H-10-11

**TAKEOFF MINIMUMS:**
All Rwys, STANDARD.

**LONDON**
117.2 YXU
Chan 119
N43°02.29'
W81°08.91'
L-30-31, H-10-11

**ROCHESTER**
110.0 ROC
Chan 37
N43°07.08'
W77°40.37'
L-31-32, H-10-11-12

**SYRACUSE**
117.0 SYR
Chan 117
N43°09.63'
W76°12.27'
L-32, H-11-12

316°   053°
233°   136°

**GENESEO**
108.2 GEE
Chan 19
N42°50.06'
W77°43.97'
L-31-32, H-10-11-12

**AYLMER**
114.2 YQO
Chan 89
N42°42.40'
W80°53.27'
L-30, H-10-11

**DUNKIRK**
116.2 DKK
Chan 109
N42°29.43'
W79°16.45'
L-30, H-10

**WELLSVILLE**
111.4 ELZ
Chan 51
N42°05.38'
W77°59.97'
L-30-32, H-10-12

**JAMESTOWN**
114.7 JHW
Chan 94
N42°11.32'
W79°07.28'
L-30, H-10

**STONYFORK**
108.6 SFK
Chan 23
N41°41.72'
W77°25.19'
L-30, H-10-12

**DRYER**
113.6 DJB
Chan 83
N41°21.48'
W82°09.72'
L-30, H-10

**BRADFORD**
116.6 BFD
Chan 113
N41°47.18'
W78°37.16'
L-30

**SLATE RUN**
113.9 SLT
Chan 86
N41°30.77'
W77°58.21'
L-30, H-10-12

NOTE:  RADAR Required.
NOTE: Chart not to scale.

(Continued on next page)

### DEPARTURE ROUTE DESCRIPTION

<u>TURBOJET AIRCRAFT:</u>
TAKE-OFF RUNWAY 5:  Climb via heading 053° until leaving 3000, thence. . . .
TAKE-OFF RUNWAY 14:  Climb via heading 136° until leaving 3000, thence. . . .
TAKE-OFF RUNWAY 23:  Climb via heading 233° until leaving 3000, thence. . . .
TAKE-OFF RUNWAY 32:  Climb via heading 316° until leaving 2000, thence. . . .

<u>NON-TURBOJET AIRCRAFT ONLY:</u>  Climb on assigned heading, thence. . . .

. . . .Expect vectors to filed route or depicted fix. Maintain 10,000' or assigned lower altitude.
Expect further clearance to requested altitude/flight level ten minutes after departure.

## BUFFALO THREE DEPARTURE
(BUF3.BUF) 09127

BUFFALO, NEW YORK
BUFFALO NIAGARA INTL (BUF)

**Figure 278**

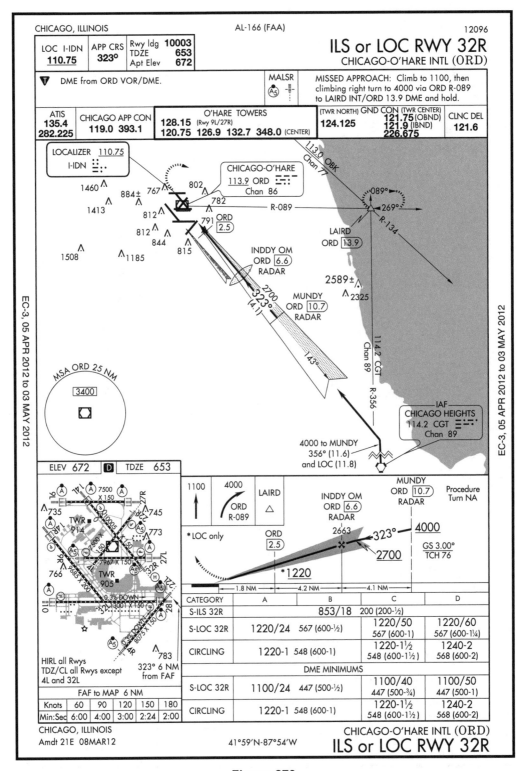

**Figure 279**

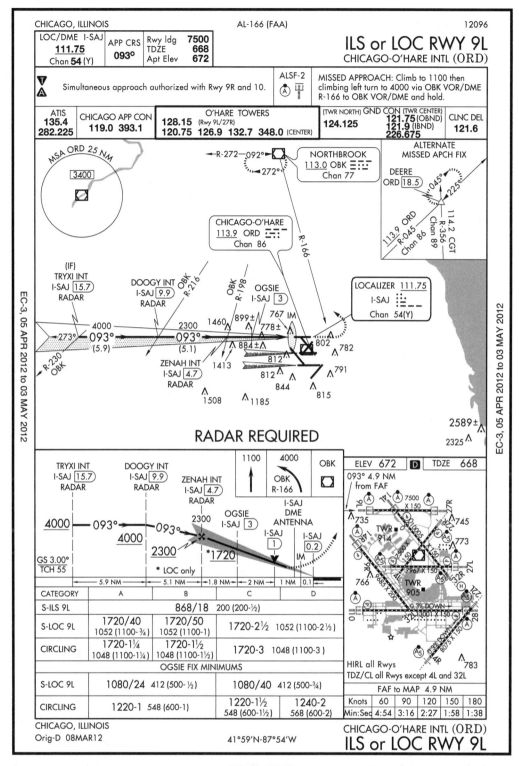

**Figure 280**

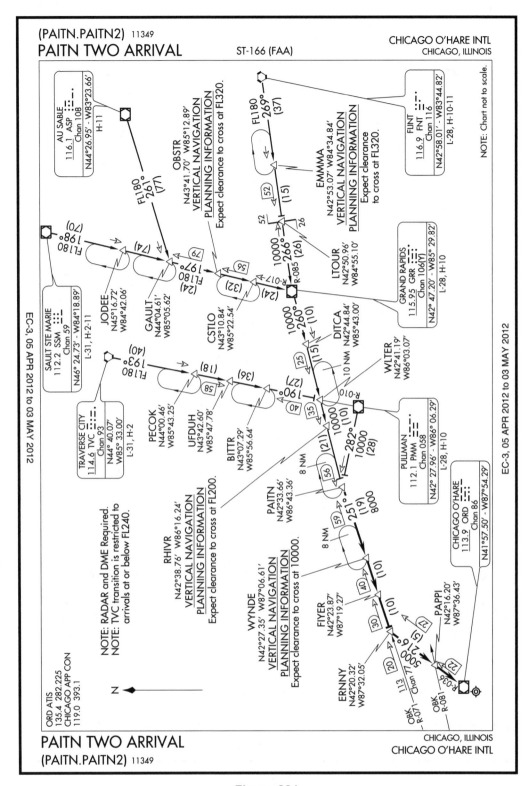

**Figure 281**

## PAITN TWO ARRIVAL

ST-166 (FAA)

CHICAGO O'HARE INTL
CHICAGO, ILLINOIS

### ARRIVAL ROUTE DESCRIPTION

AU SABLE TRANSITION (ASP.PAITN2): From over ASP VOR/DME via ASP R-261 to GAULT then via GRR R-017 to GRR VOR/DME then via GRR R-260 to PAITN. Thence....
FLINT TRANSITION (FNT.PAITN2): From over FNT VORTAC via FNT R-269 to LTOUR and GRR R-085 to GRR VOR/DME then via GRR R-260 to PAITN. Thence....
GRAND RAPIDS TRANSITION (GRR.PAITN2): From over GRR VOR/DME via GRR R-260 to PAITN. Thence....
PULLMAN TRANSITION (PMM.PAITN2): From over PMM VOR/DME via PMM R-282 to PAITN. Thence....
SAULT STE MARIE TRANSITION (SSM.PAITN2): From over SSM VOR/DME via SSM R-198 to GAULT then via GRR R-017 to GRR VOR/DME then via GRR R-260 to PAITN. Thence....
TRAVERSE CITY TRANSITION (TVC.PAITN2): From over TVC VORTAC via TVC R-193 to BITTR then via PMM R-010 to WLTER then via GRR R-260 to PAITN. Thence....

....From over PAITN via OBK VOR/DME R-071 to WYNDE/OBK 40 DME, then via OBK VOR/DME R-071 to FIYER/OBK 30 DME, then via OBK VOR/DME R-071 to ERNNY/OBK 20 DME, then via ORD VOR/DME R-036 to PAPPI/ORD 22 DME, then via ORD VOR/DME R-036 to ORD VOR/DME. Expect radar vectors to final approach course.

EC-3, 05 APR 2012 to 03 MAY 2012

EC-3, 05 APR 2012 to 03 MAY 2012

## PAITN TWO ARRIVAL
(PAITN.PAITN2) 11013

CHICAGO, ILLINOIS
CHICAGO O'HARE INTL

**Figure 282**

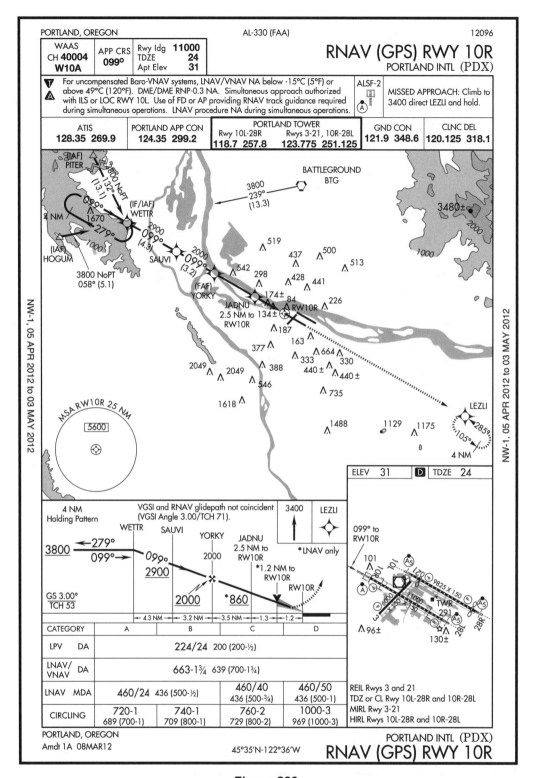

**Figure 283**

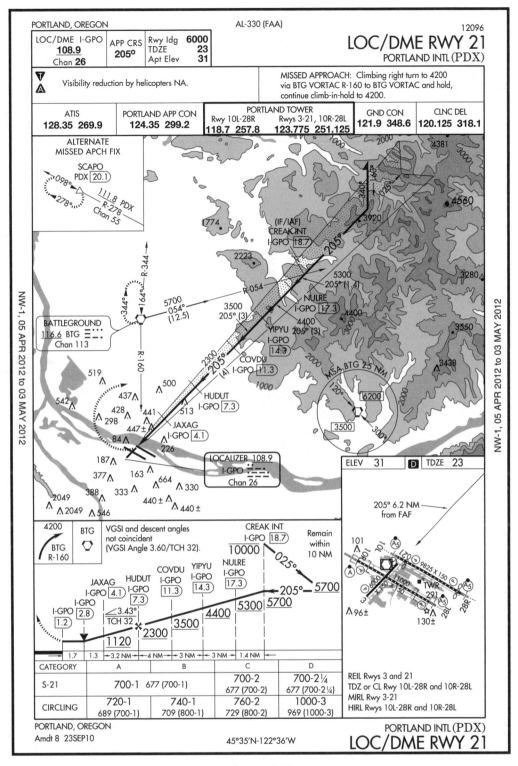

**Figure 284**

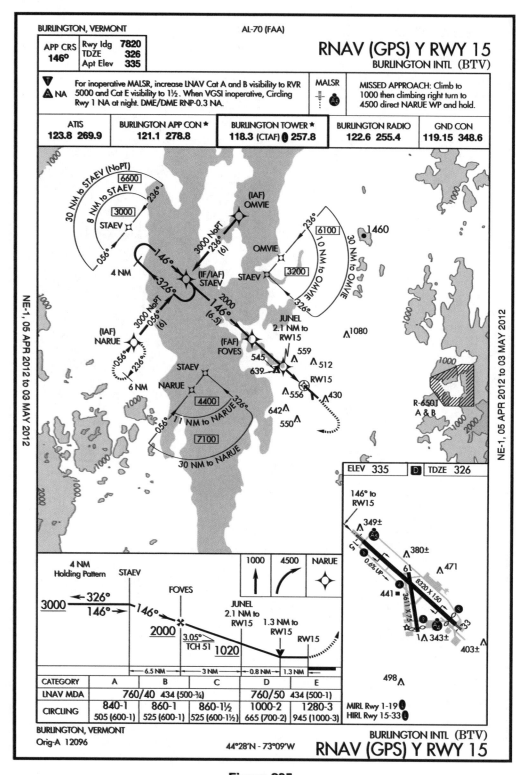

**Figure 285**

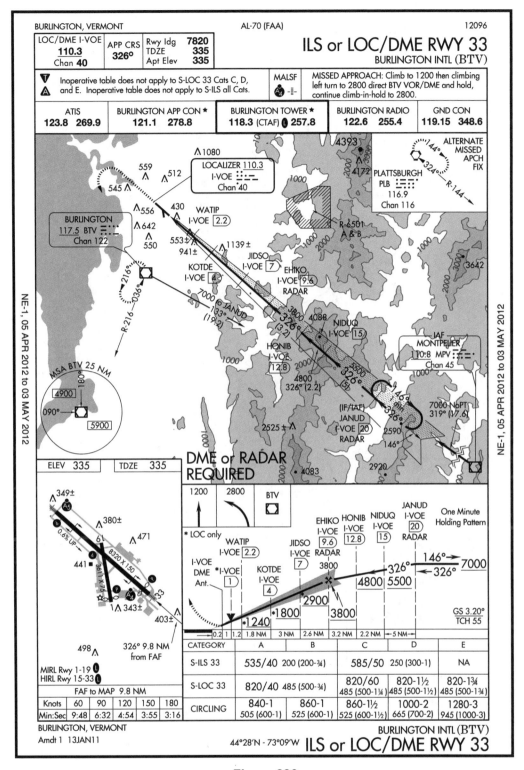

Figure 286

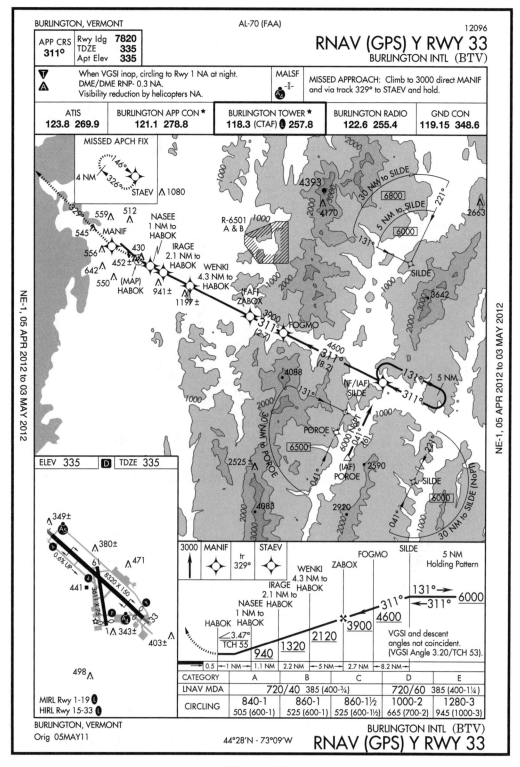

**Figure 287**

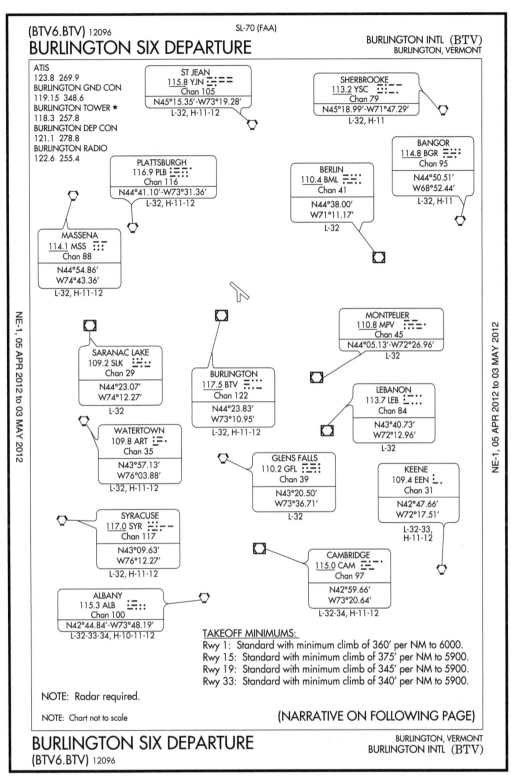

Figure 288

(BTV6.BTV) 10210                    SL-70 (FAA)                 BURLINGTON INTL  (BTV)
## BURLINGTON SIX DEPARTURE                              BURLINGTON, VERMONT

DEPARTURE ROUTE DESCRIPTION

<u>TAKEOFF RUNWAYS 1, 15, 19, 33:</u> Climb on assigned heading for vectors to filed navaid, fix, or airway to 10000 or assigned lower altitude.  Expect filed altitude ten minutes after departure.

<u>TAKEOFF OBSTACLE NOTES:</u>
Rwy 1:    Trees beginning 1396' from DER, 216' right of centerline, up to 64' AGL/384' MSL.
          Trees 1694' from DER, 200' left of centerline, up to 80' AGL/380' MSL.
Rwy 15:   Bush 318' from DER, 292' left of centerline, up to 23' AGL/343' MSL.
          Trees beginning 1418' from DER, 358' right of centerline, up to 27' AGL/387' MSL.
          Hopper and trees beginning 1801' from DER, 377' left of centerline, up to 63'
          AGL/403' MSL.
          Building 3453' from DER, 1145' left of centerline, 110' AGL/430' MSL.
Rwy 19:   Trees beginning 168' from DER, 24' right of centerline, up to 56' AGL/436' MSL.
          Trees beginning 172' from DER, 184' left of centerline, up to 93' AGL/413'  MSL.
Rwy 33:   Pole and trees beginning 971' from DER, 755' left of centerline, up to 97' AGL/357' MSL.
          Trees beginning 1091' from DER, 590' right of centerline, up to 34' AGL/334' MSL.

NE-1, 05 APR 2012 to 03 MAY 2012

NE-1, 05 APR 2012 to 03 MAY 2012

## BURLINGTON SIX DEPARTURE                              BURLINGTON, VERMONT
(BTV6.BTV) 10210                                         BURLINGTON INTL  (BTV)

**Figure 289**

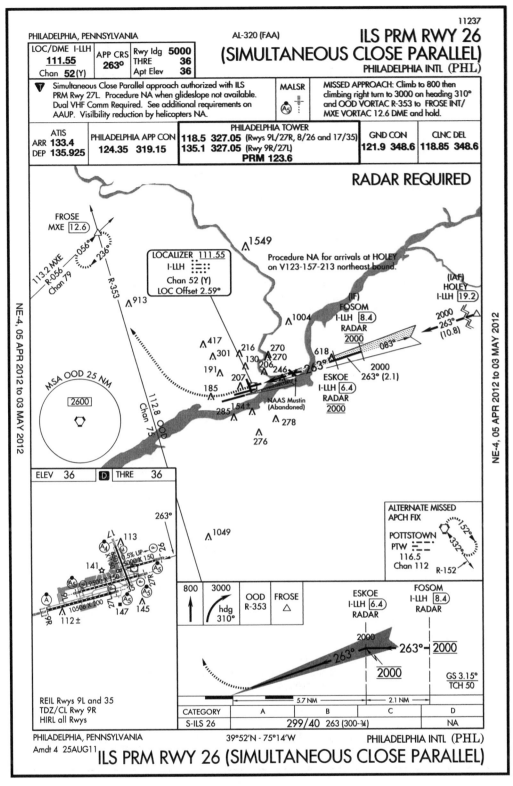

Figure 290

ILS PRM RWY 26 Amdt 4 11237
(SIMULTANEOUS CLOSE PARALLEL)   AL-320 (FAA)

PHILADELPHIA INTL (PHL)
PHILADELPHIA, PENNSYLVANIA

## ATTENTION ALL USERS OF ILS PRECISION RUNWAY MONITOR (PRM)

Condensed Briefing Point:
*When instructed, immediately switch to the tower frequency and select the monitor frequency audio.

1. **ATIS.** When the ATIS broadcast advises that simultaneous ILS/PRM and LDA/PRM approaches are in progress, pilots should brief to fly the ILS/PRM 26 approach. If later advised to expect an ILS 26 approach, the ILS/PRM 26 chart may be used after completing the following briefing items:
   (a) Minimums and missed approach procedures are unchanged.
   (b) Monitor frequency no longer required.

2. **Dual VHF Communication required.** To avoid blocked transmissions, each runway will have two frequencies, a primary and a monitor frequency. The tower controller will transmit on both frequencies. The monitor controller's transmissions, if needed, will override both frequencies. Pilots will ONLY transmit on the tower controller's frequency, but will listen to both frequencies. Select the monitor frequency audio only when instructed by ATC to contact the tower. The volume levels should be set about the same on both radios so that the pilots will be able to hear transmissions on at least one frequency if the other is blocked.

3. **ALL "Breakouts"** are to be hand flown to assure that the manuever is accomplished in the shortest amount of time. Pilots, when directed by ATC to break off an approach, must assume that an aircraft is blundering toward their course and a breakout must be initiated immediately.

   (a) ATC Directed "Breakouts": ATC directed breakouts will consist of a turn and a climb or descent. Pilots must always initiate the breakout in response to an air traffic controller instruction. Controllers will give a descending breakout only when there are no other reasonable options available, but in no case will the descent be below minimum vectoring altitude (MVA) which provides at least 1000 feet required obstruction clearance. The MVA in the final approach segment is 1800 feet at Philadelphia Intl Airport.

   (b) Phraseology - "TRAFFIC ALERT": If an aircraft enters the "NO TRANSGRESSION ZONE" (NTZ), the controller will breakout the threatened aircraft on the adjacent approach. The phraseology for the breakout will be:

      "TRAFFIC ALERT, (aircraft call sign) TURN (left/right) IMMEDIATELY, HEADING (degrees), CLIMB/DESCEND AND MAINTAIN (altitude)".

4. **ILS Navigation** Decending on ILS glideslope ensures complying with any charted crossing restrictions.

Special pilot training required. Pilots who are unable to participate will be afforded appropriate arrival services as operational conditions permit and must notify the controlling ARTCC as soon as practical, but at least 100 miles from destination.

(SIMULTANEOUS CLOSE PARALLEL)   39° 52'N-75° 14'W

PHILADELPHIA, PENNSYLVANIA
PHILADELPHIA INTL (PHL)

ILS PRM RWY 26 Amdt 4 11237

**Figure 291**

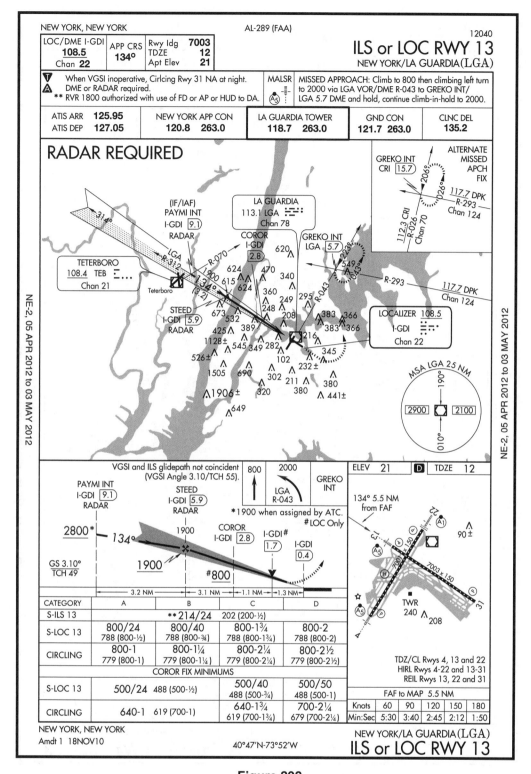

**Figure 292**

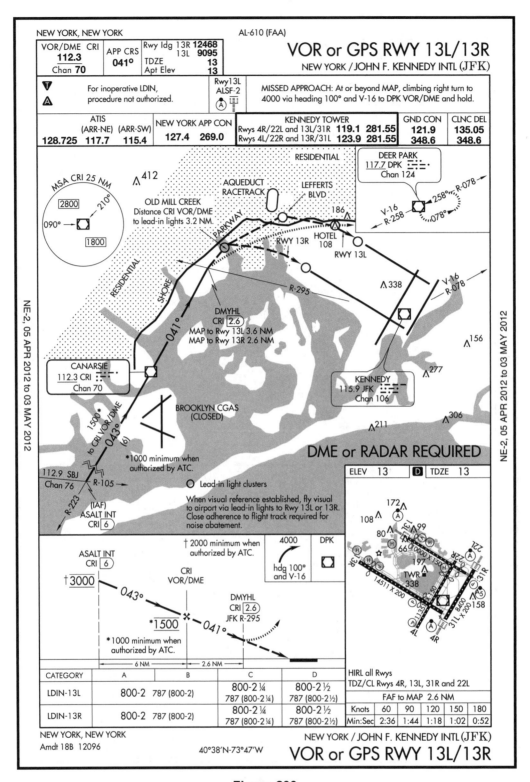

**Figure 293**

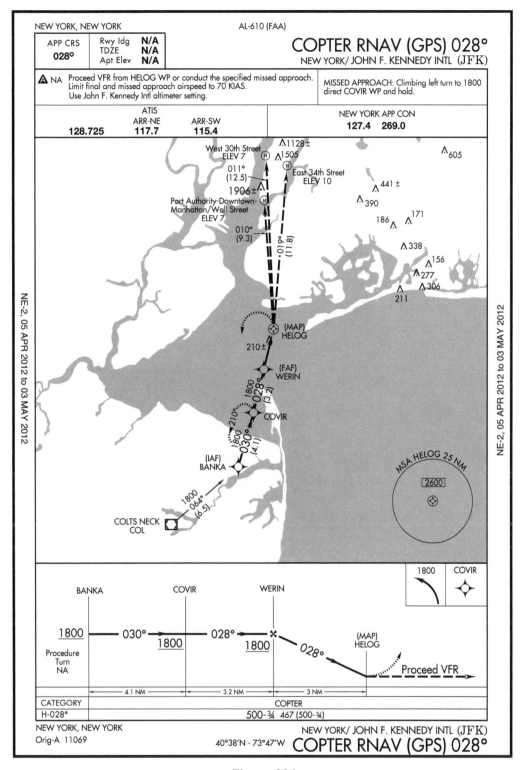

NEW YORK, NEW YORK
AL-610 (FAA)

## COPTER RNAV (GPS) 028°
NEW YORK/ JOHN F. KENNEDY INTL (JFK)

| APP CRS | Rwy Idg | N/A |
|---------|---------|-----|
| **028°** | TDZE | N/A |
| | Apt Elev | N/A |

⚠ NA  Proceed VFR from HELOG WP or conduct the specified missed approach.
Limit final and missed approach airspeed to 70 KIAS.
Use John F. Kennedy Intl altimeter setting.

MISSED APPROACH: Climbing left turn to 1800 direct COVIR WP and hold.

| ATIS | ARR-NE | ARR-SW | NEW YORK APP CON |
|------|--------|--------|------------------|
| 128.725 | 117.7 | 115.4 | 127.4   269.0 |

NE-2, 05 APR 2012 to 03 MAY 2012

West 30th Street ELEV 7
011° (12.5)
1906±
Port Authority-Downtown-Manhattan/Wall Street ELEV 7
010° (9.3)
017° (11.8)

1128±
1505
East 34th Street ELEV 10
605
441±
390
186  171
338
156
277  306
211

(MAP) HELOG
210±
(FAF) WERIN
1800  028° (3.2)
210°  COVIR
1800  030° (4.1)
(IAF) BANKA
1800  064° (6.5)
COLTS NECK COL

MSA HELOG 25 NM
2600

| | BANKA | COVIR | WERIN | (MAP) HELOG | | COVIR |
|---|---|---|---|---|---|---|

1800   030° →   1800   028° →   1800   ✕   028°   (MAP) HELOG
Procedure Turn NA
Proceed VFR
|← 4.1 NM →|← 3.2 NM →|← 3 NM →|

| CATEGORY | COPTER |
|----------|--------|
| H-028° | 500-¾  467 (500-¾) |

NEW YORK, NEW YORK
Orig-A  11069
40°38'N - 73°47'W

NEW YORK/ JOHN F. KENNEDY INTL (JFK)
## COPTER RNAV (GPS) 028°

**Figure 294**

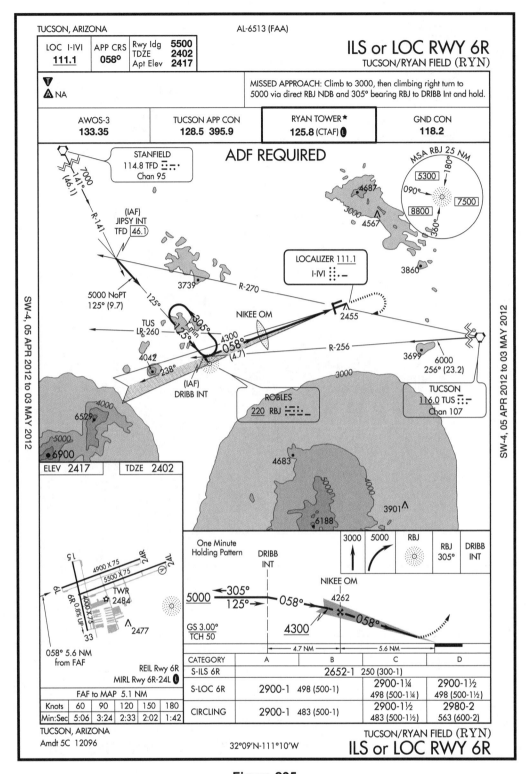

**Figure 295**

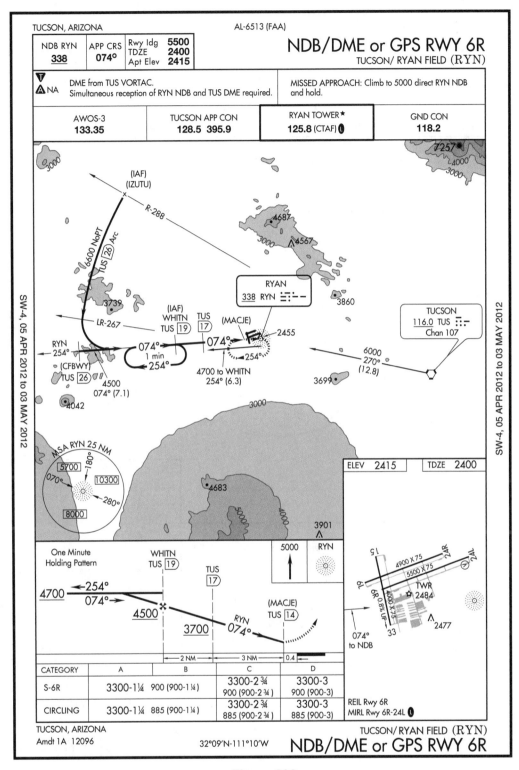

**Figure 296**

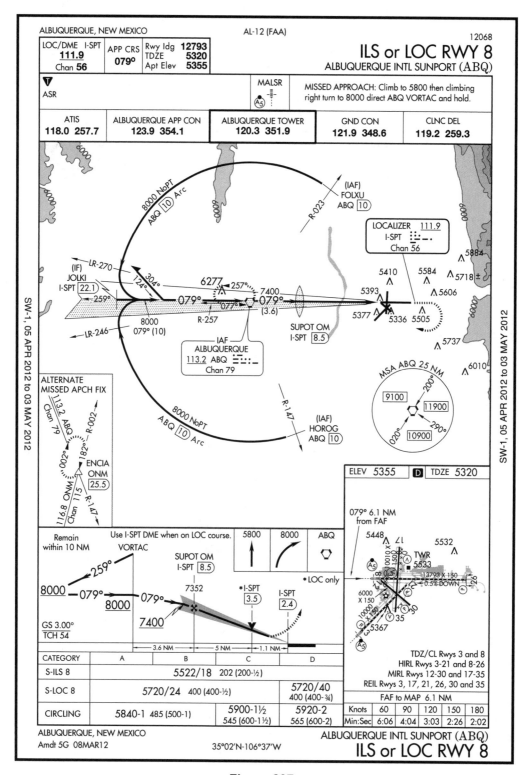

**Figure 297**

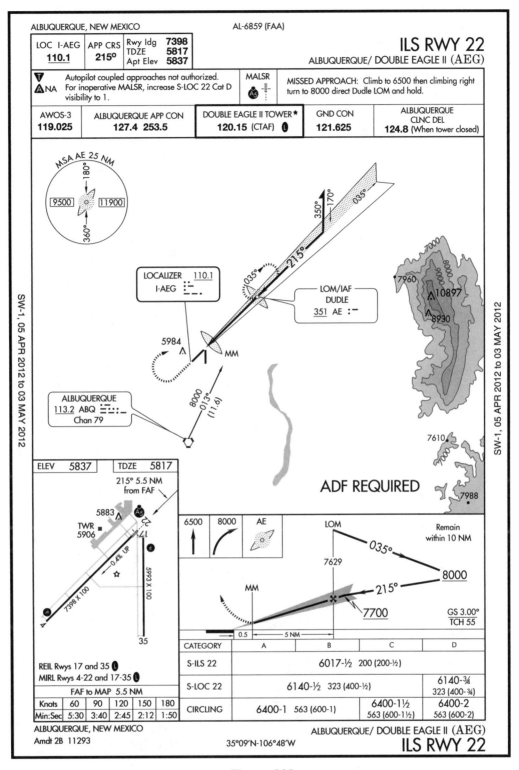

**Figure 298**

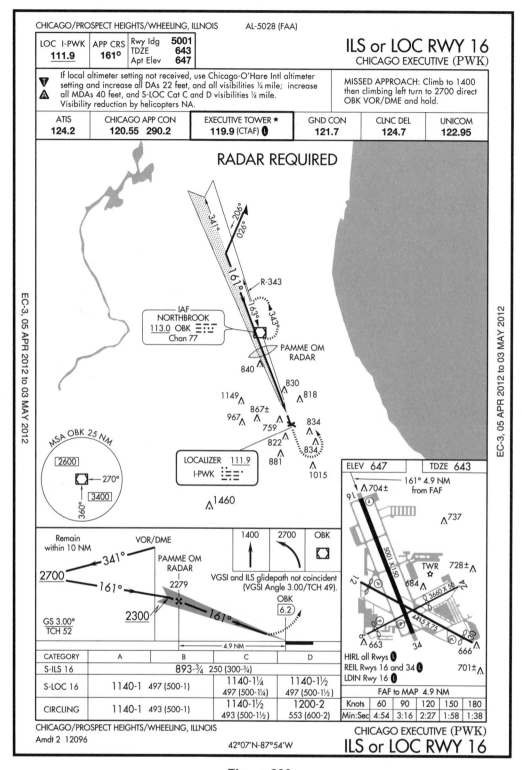

**Figure 299**

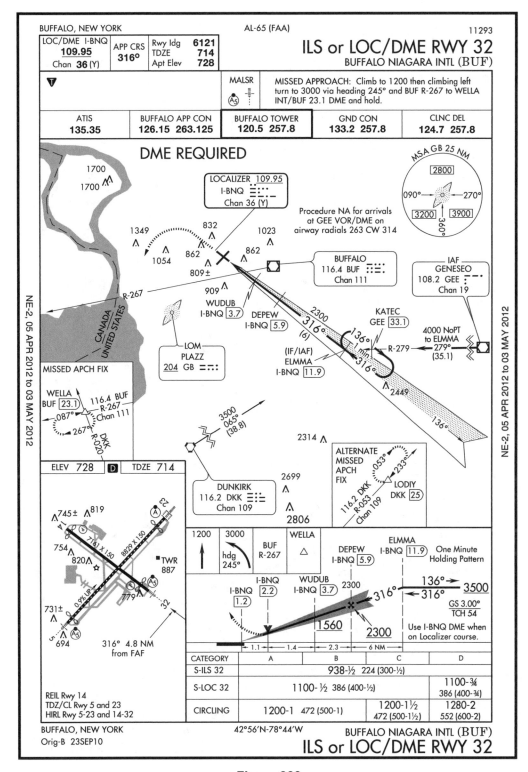

**Figure 300**

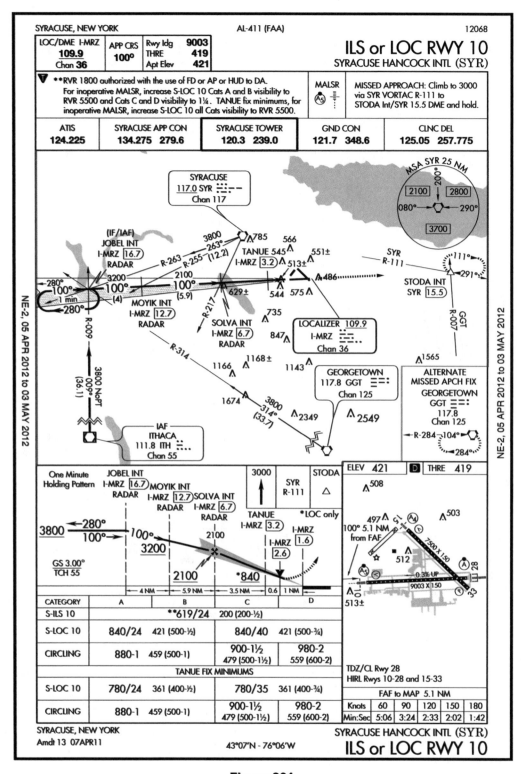

**Figure 301**

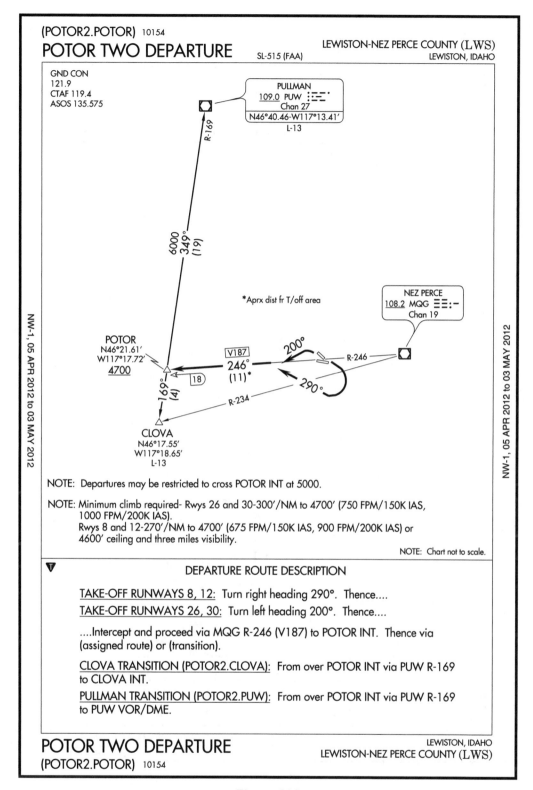

POTOR TWO DEPARTURE    SL-515 (FAA)    LEWISTON-NEZ PERCE COUNTY (LWS)
LEWISTON, IDAHO

GND CON
121.9
CTAF 119.4
ASOS 135.575

PULLMAN
109.0 PUW
Chan 27
N46°40.46'-W117°13.41'
L-13

R-169

6000
349°
(19)

*Aprx dist fr T/off area

NEZ PERCE
108.2 MQG
Chan 19

POTOR
N46°21.61'
W117°17.72'
4700

V187
246°
(11)*

18

200°

R-246

290°

169°
(4)

R-234

CLOVA
N46°17.55'
W117°18.65'
L-13

NW-1, 05 APR 2012 to 03 MAY 2012

NOTE: Departures may be restricted to cross POTOR INT at 5000.

NOTE: Minimum climb required- Rwys 26 and 30-300'/NM to 4700' (750 FPM/150K IAS, 1000 FPM/200K IAS).
Rwys 8 and 12-270'/NM to 4700' (675 FPM/150K IAS, 900 FPM/200K IAS) or 4600' ceiling and three miles visibility.

NOTE: Chart not to scale.

DEPARTURE ROUTE DESCRIPTION

TAKE-OFF RUNWAYS 8, 12: Turn right heading 290°. Thence....
TAKE-OFF RUNWAYS 26, 30: Turn left heading 200°. Thence....

....Intercept and proceed via MQG R-246 (V187) to POTOR INT. Thence via (assigned route) or (transition).

CLOVA TRANSITION (POTOR2.CLOVA): From over POTOR INT via PUW R-169 to CLOVA INT.

PULLMAN TRANSITION (POTOR2.PUW): From over POTOR INT via PUW R-169 to PUW VOR/DME.

POTOR TWO DEPARTURE    LEWISTON, IDAHO
LEWISTON-NEZ PERCE COUNTY (LWS)
(POTOR2.POTOR) 10154

**Figure 302**

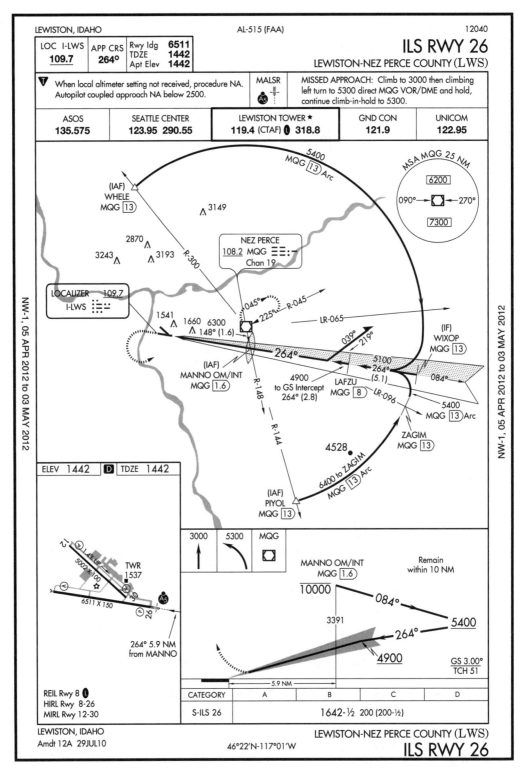

**Figure 303**

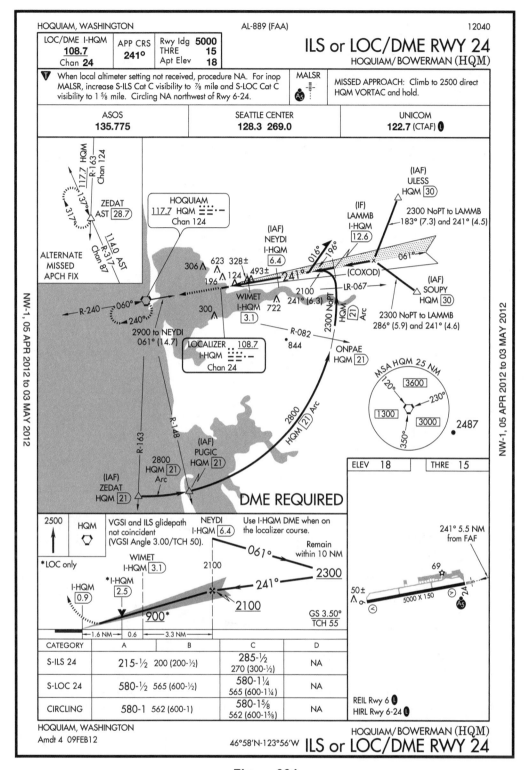

**Figure 304**

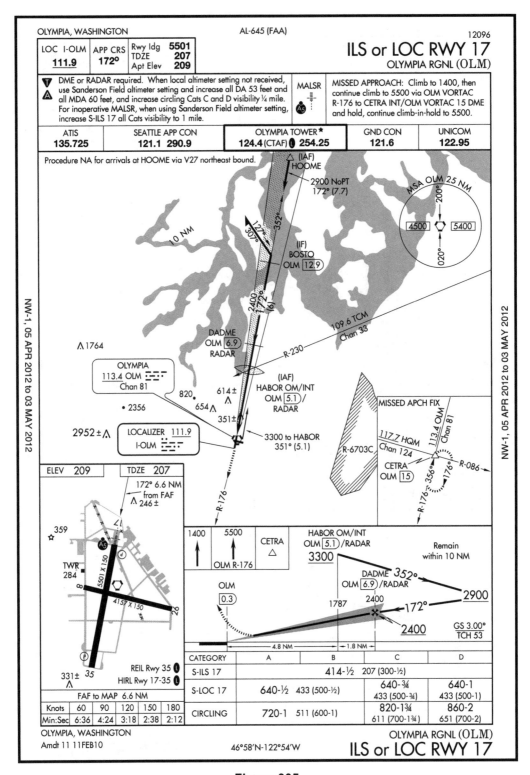

**Figure 305**

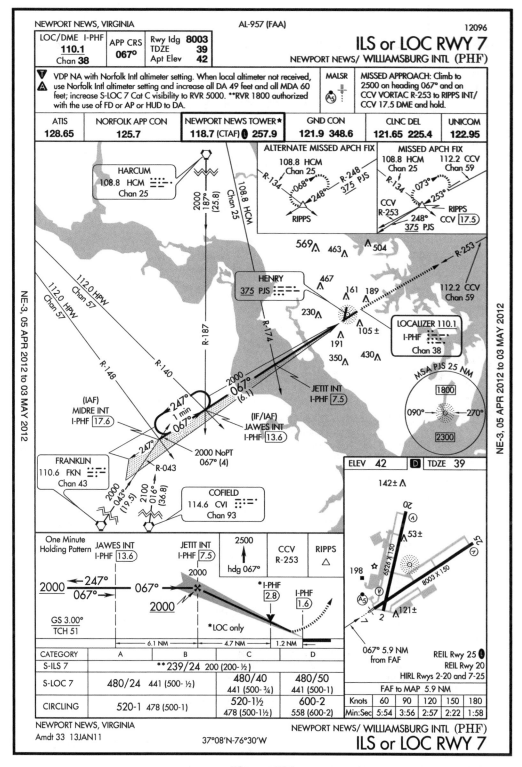

**Figure 306**

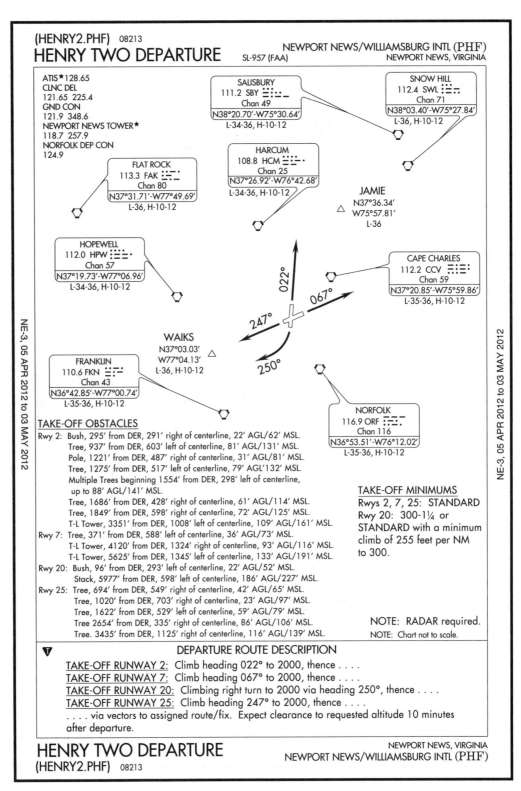

# HENRY TWO DEPARTURE
SL-957 (FAA)

NEWPORT NEWS/WILLIAMSBURG INTL (PHF')
NEWPORT NEWS, VIRGINIA

ATIS ★128.65
CLNC DEL
121.65 225.4
GND CON
121.9 348.6
NEWPORT NEWS TOWER ★
118.7 257.9
NORFOLK DEP CON
124.9

SALISBURY
111.2 SBY
Chan 49
N38°20.70'-W75°30.64'
L-34-36, H-10-12

SNOW HILL
112.4 SWL
Chan 71
N38°03.40'-W75°27.84'
L-36, H-10-12

HARCUM
108.8 HCM
Chan 25
N37°26.92'-W76°42.68'
L-34-36, H-10-12

JAMIE
N37°36.34'
W75°57.81'
△
L-36

FLAT ROCK
113.3 FAK
Chan 80
N37°31.71'-W77°49.69'
L-36, H-10-12

HOPEWELL
112.0 HPW
Chan 57
N37°19.73'-W77°06.96'
L-34-36, H-10-12

CAPE CHARLES
112.2 CCV
Chan 59
N37°20.85'-W75°59.86'
L-35-36, H-10-12

022°
067°
247°
250°

WAIKS
N37°03.03'
W77°04.13'
△
L-36, H-10-12

FRANKLIN
110.6 FKN
Chan 43
N36°42.85'-W77°00.74'
L-35-36, H-10-12

NORFOLK
116.9 ORF
Chan 116
N36°53.51'-W76°12.02'
L-35-36, H-10-12

## TAKE-OFF OBSTACLES
Rwy 2: Bush, 295' from DER, 291' right of centerline, 22' AGL/62' MSL.
Tree, 937' from DER, 603' left of centerline, 81' AGL/131' MSL.
Pole, 1221' from DER, 487' right of centerline, 31' AGL/81' MSL.
Tree, 1275' from DER, 517' left of centerline, 79' AGL/132' MSL.
Multiple Trees beginning 1554' from DER, 298' left of centerline,
up to 88' AGL/141' MSL.
Tree, 1686' from DER, 428' right of centerline, 61' AGL/114' MSL.
Tree, 1849' from DER, 598' right of centerline, 72' AGL/125' MSL.
T-L Tower, 3351' from DER, 1008' left of centerline, 109' AGL/161' MSL.
Rwy 7: Tree, 371' from DER, 588' left of centerline, 36' AGL/73' MSL.
T-L Tower, 4120' from DER, 1324' right of centerline, 93' AGL/116' MSL.
T-L Tower, 5625' from DER, 1345' left of centerline, 133' AGL/191' MSL.
Rwy 20: Bush, 96' from DER, 293' left of centerline, 22' AGL/52' MSL.
Stack, 5977' from DER, 598' left of centerline, 186' AGL/227' MSL.
Rwy 25: Tree, 694' from DER, 549' right of centerline, 42' AGL/65' MSL.
Tree, 1020' from DER, 703' right of centerline, 23' AGL/97' MSL.
Tree, 1622' from DER, 529' left of centerline, 59' AGL/79' MSL.
Tree 2654' from DER, 335' right of centerline, 86' AGL/106' MSL.
Tree. 3435' from DER, 1125' right of centerline, 116' AGL/139' MSL.

### TAKE-OFF MINIMUMS
Rwys 2, 7, 25: STANDARD
Rwy 20: 300-1¼ or
STANDARD with a minimum
climb of 255 feet per NM
to 300.

NOTE: RADAR required.
NOTE: Chart not to scale.

NE-3, 05 APR 2012 to 03 MAY 2012

## DEPARTURE ROUTE DESCRIPTION
TAKE-OFF RUNWAY 2: Climb heading 022° to 2000, thence . . . .
TAKE-OFF RUNWAY 7: Climb heading 067° to 2000, thence . . . .
TAKE-OFF RUNWAY 20: Climbing right turn to 2000 via heading 250°, thence . . . .
TAKE-OFF RUNWAY 25: Climb heading 247° to 2000, thence . . . .
. . . . via vectors to assigned route/fix. Expect clearance to requested altitude 10 minutes
after departure.

# HENRY TWO DEPARTURE
(HENRY2.PHF) 08213

NEWPORT NEWS, VIRGINIA
NEWPORT NEWS/WILLIAMSBURG INTL (PHF')

**Figure 307**

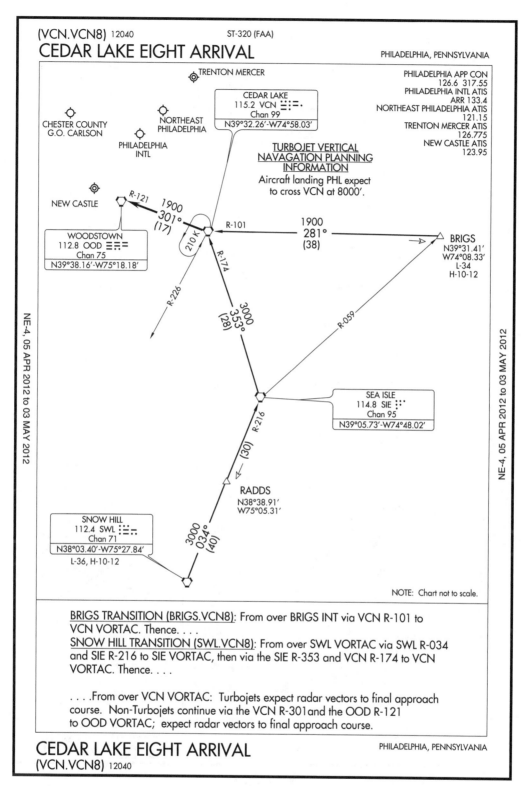

# CEDAR LAKE EIGHT ARRIVAL

PHILADELPHIA, PENNSYLVANIA

PHILADELPHIA APP CON
126.6 317.55
PHILADELPHIA INTL ATIS
ARR 133.4
NORTHEAST PHILADELPHIA ATIS
121.15
TRENTON MERCER ATIS
126.775
NEW CASTLE ATIS
123.95

TRENTON MERCER

CEDAR LAKE
115.2 VCN
Chan 99
N39°32.26'-W74°58.03'

CHESTER COUNTY
G.O. CARLSON

NORTHEAST
PHILADELPHIA

PHILADELPHIA
INTL

TURBOJET VERTICAL
NAVAGATION PLANNING
INFORMATION
Aircraft landing PHL expect
to cross VCN at 8000'.

NEW CASTLE

R-121 1900
301°
(17)

R-101

1900
281°
(38)

210 K

BRIGS
N39°31.41'
W74°08.33'
L-34
H-10-12

WOODSTOWN
112.8 OOD
Chan 75
N39°38.16'-W75°18.18'

R-174

R-226

3000
353°
(28)

R-059

SEA ISLE
114.8 SIE
Chan 95
N39°05.73'-W74°48.02'

R-216

(30)

RADDS
N38°38.91'
W75°05.31'

SNOW HILL
112.4 SWL
Chan 71
N38°03.40'-W75°27.84'
L-36, H-10-12

3000
034°
(40)

NOTE: Chart not to scale.

BRIGS TRANSITION (BRIGS.VCN8): From over BRIGS INT via VCN R-101 to
VCN VORTAC. Thence. . . .
SNOW HILL TRANSITION (SWL.VCN8): From over SWL VORTAC via SWL R-034
and SIE R-216 to SIE VORTAC, then via the SIE R-353 and VCN R-174 to VCN
VORTAC. Thence. . . .

. . . .From over VCN VORTAC: Turbojets expect radar vectors to final approach
course. Non-Turbojets continue via the VCN R-301 and the OOD R-121
to OOD VORTAC; expect radar vectors to final approach course.

# CEDAR LAKE EIGHT ARRIVAL

PHILADELPHIA, PENNSYLVANIA

(VCN.VCN8) 12040

**Figure 308**

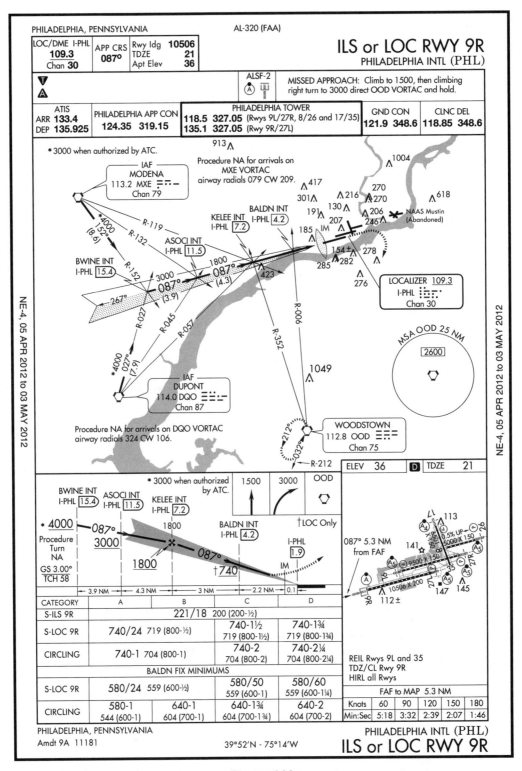

**Figure 309**

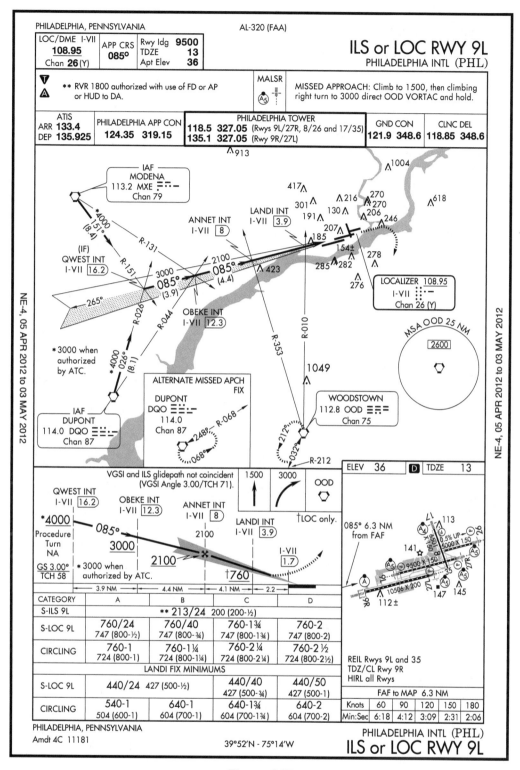

**Figure 310**

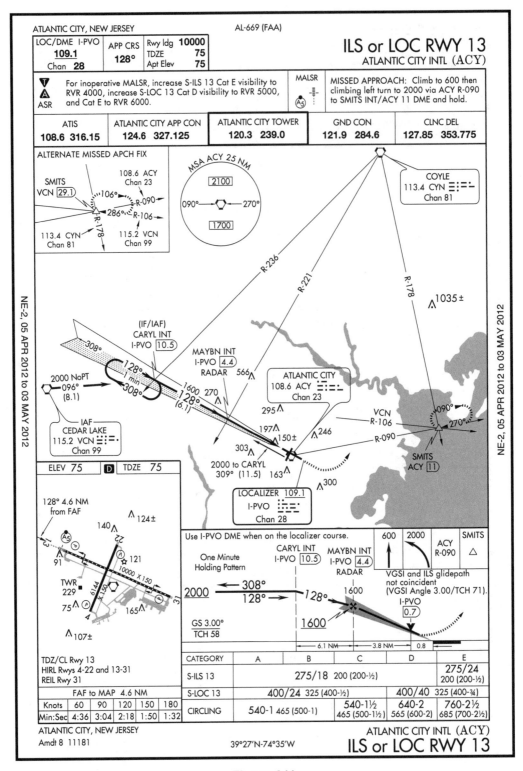

**Figure 311**

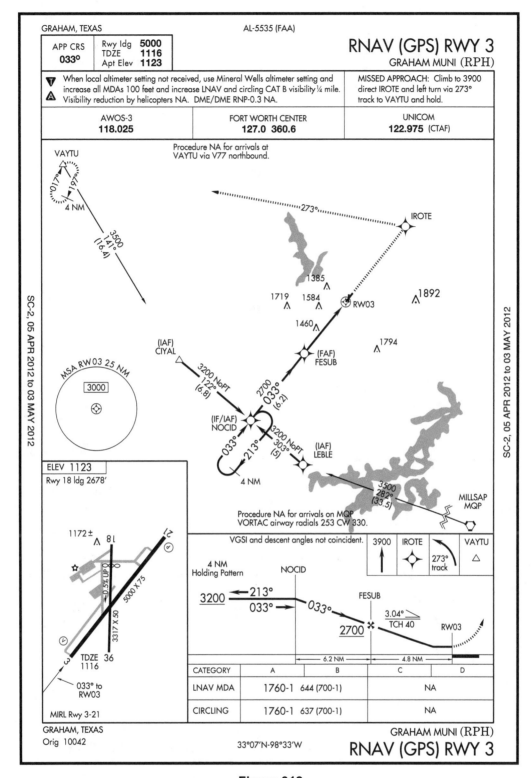

**Figure 312**

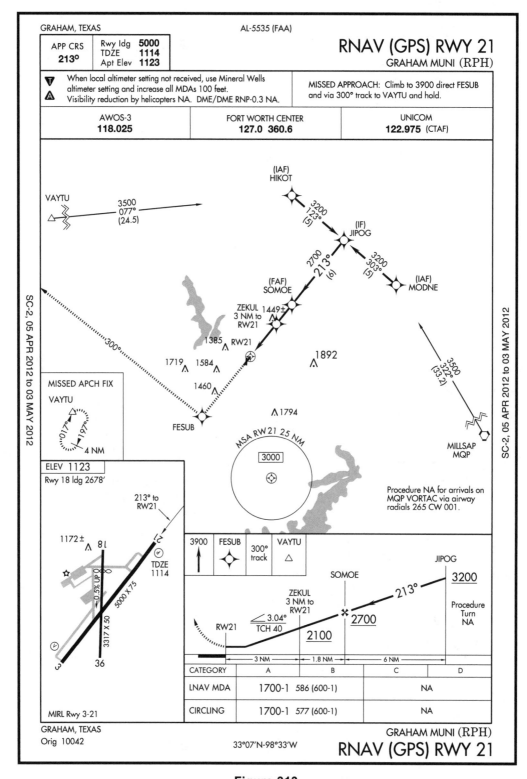

**Figure 313**

L7

## ▼ TAKE-OFF MINIMUMS AND (OBSTACLE) DEPARTURE PROCEDURES ▼
12096

### FORT WORTH, TX (CON'T)
FORT WORTH SPINKS
TAKE-OFF MINIMUMS: **Rwys 17L,35R**, NA.
(Environmental)
DEPARTURE PROCEDURE: **Rwy 17R** climb heading
173° to 1200 before turning right.
NOTE: **Rwy 17R,** tree 4909' from departure end of runway,
1556' left of centerline, 60' AGL/830' MSL.

### FORT WORTH NAS JRB (CARSWELL FLD)(KNFW)
FORT WORTH, TX . . . . . . . . . 10014
**Rwy 17,** Cross DER at or above 6' AGL/656' MSL.
TAKE-OFF OBSTACLES: **Rwy 17,** rising terrain up to 670'
MSL, 200'-600' from DER, 500'-560' right of centerline.

### GAINESVILLE, TX
GAINESVILLE MUNI (GLE)
ORIG 09127 (FAA)
NOTE: **Rwy 17,** trees and poles beginning 1' from DER,
472' right and left of centerline, up to 25' AGL/819' MSL.
**Rwy 30,** taxiways beginning 651' from DER, crossing
centerline left to right 859' MSL. Trees and terrain
beginning 2' from DER, 14' left and right of centerline, up
to 64' AGL/890' MSL. **Rwy 35,** terrain, trees, poles, road,
and vehicle beginning 149' from DER, 51' left of
centerline, up to 95' AGL/940' MSL. Terrain and poles
beginning 13' from DER, 85' right of centerline, up to 37'
AGL/882' MSL.

### GILMER, TX
FOX STEPHENS FIELD-GILMER MUNI (JXI)
ORIG 11293 (FAA)
DEPARTURE PROCEDURE: **Rwy 18,** climb heading 177°
to 1000 before turning left.
NOTE: **Rwy 18,** trees beginning abeam the DER left and
right of centerline, up to 100' AGL/500' MSL. **Rwy 36,**
trees beginning abeam the DER left and right of
centerline, up to 50' AGL/505' MSL.

### GLADEWATER, TX
GLADEWATER MUNI (07F)
AMDT 1 11153 (FAA)
TAKE-OFF MINIMUMS: **Rwy 17,** 300-1¾ or std. w/min.
climb of 285' per NM to 600. **Rwy 32,** 300-1. **Rwy 35,**
Std. w/min. climb of 280' per NM to 1300 or 1100-2 ½
for climb in visual conditions.
DEPARTURE PROCEDURE: **Rwy 32,** climb heading
320° to 1100 before turning right. **Rwy 35,** for climb in
visual conditions cross Gladewater Municipal Airport at
or above 1200 before proceeding on course.
NOTE: **Rwy 14,** vehicles on roadway beginning 450' from
DER, left and right of centerline, up to 17' AGL/311'
MSL. Trees beginning 770' from DER, left and right of
centerline, up to 100' AGL/394' MSL. Power lines 3524'
from DER, left to right of centerline, 150' AGL/420'
MSL. **Rwy 17,** vehicles on roadway beginning 212' from
DER, left and right of centerline, up to 17' AGL/311'
MSL. Trees beginning 624' from DER, left and right of
centerline, up to 100' AGL/509' MSL. Power lines 1807'
from DER, left to right of centerline, 150' AGL/439'
MSL. **Rwy 32,** trees beginning 12' from DER, left and
right of centerline, up to 100' AGL/429' MSL. **Rwy 35,**
trees beginning 47' from DER, left and right of
centerline, up to 100' AGL/429' MSL. Power lines 1.4
12096 NM from DER, 844' right of centerline, 75' AGL/520'
MSL.

### GRAFORD, TX
POSSUM KINGDOM (F35)
ORIG-A 10154 (FAA)
TAKE-OFF MINIMUMS: **Rwy 20,** 400-2½ or std. w/a
min. climb of 212' per NM to 1500 or alternatively, with
standard takeoff minimums and a normal 200' per NM
climb gradient, takeoff must occur no later than 1600'
prior to DER.
DEPARTURE PROCEDURE: **Rwy 20,** climb heading
204° to 1500 before turning left.
NOTE: **Rwy 2,** trees beginning 31' from DER, 22' left of
centerline, up to 100' AGL/1099' MSL. Trees beginning
1023' from DER, 114' right of centerline, up to 100'
AGL/1129' MSL. **Rwy 20,** vehicle on roadway 116' from
DER, 498' right of centerline, 15' AGL/1024' MSL.
Trees beginning 494' from DER, 126' right of
centerline, up to 100' AGL/1109' MSL. Trees beginning
977' from DER, 115' left of centerline, up to 100' AGL/
1109' MSL. Trees beginning 2.29 miles from DER,
1679' left of centerline, up to 100' AGL/1329' MSL.

### GRAHAM, TX
GRAHAM MUNI
DEPARTURE PROCEDURE: **Rwys 17, 21,** climb
runway heading to 2000 before proceeding on course.
NOTE: **Rwy 17,** light pole 21' from departure end of
runway, 195' left of centerline, 30' AGL/1141' MSL.
Light pole 86' from departure end of runway, 381' left of
centerline, 50' AGL/1168' MSL.

### GRANBURY, TX
GRANBURY RGNL (GDJ)
AMDT 2 11125 (FAA)
TAKE-OFF MINIMUMS: **Rwy 14,** 300-1.
DEPARTURE PROCEDURE: **Rwy 14,** climb heading
144° to 1700 before turning right.
NOTE: **Rwy 14,** vehicles on road beginning 1020' from
DER, on centerline, 15' AGL/814' MSL. Trees and
power poles beginning at DER, 75' right of centerline,
up to 100' AGL/879' MSL. Trees, power poles, light
poles and vehicles on road beginning at DER, 251' left
of centerline, up to 100' AGL/899' MSL. **Rwy 32,** train
on railroad tracks, transmission poles and tree
beginning 339' from DER, 107' right of centerline,
76' AGL/845' MSL. Trees, vehicles on road and bush
beginning 14' from DER, 198' left of centerline, up to
46' AGL/815' MSL.

### GRAND PRAIRIE, TX
GRAND PRAIRIE MUNI (GPM)
AMDT 4 09295 (FAA)
DEPARTURE PROCEDURE: **Rwy 17,** climbing right
turn to 2000 via heading 200° and TTT R-180 to NINAE/
TTT 24 DME before proceeding on course. DME
Required. **Rwy 35,** climb heading 356° to 1400 before
turning south.
NOTE: **Rwy 17,** antenna 190' from DER, 456' right of
centerline, 26' AGL/615' MSL. Road, multiple poles and
signs beginning 570' from DER, 410' right of
centerline, up to 31' AGL/620' MSL. Tree 1506' from
DER, 517' right of centerline, 37' AGL/617' MSL.
**Rwy 35,** tree 837' from DER, 204' left of centerline, up
to 100' AGL/665' MSL. Pole 2687' from DER, 122' left of
centerline, up to 75' AGL/653' MSL.

12096
## ▼ TAKE-OFF MINIMUMS AND (OBSTACLE) DEPARTURE PROCEDURES ▼
SC-2

L7

**Figure 314**

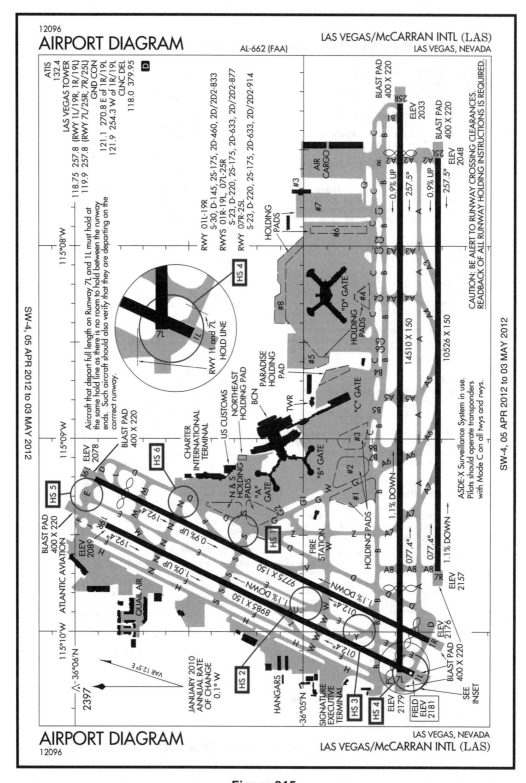

**Figure 315**

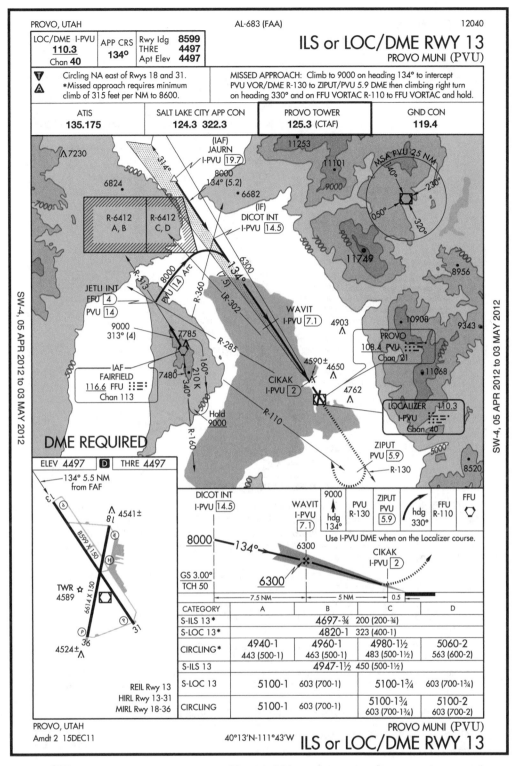

**Figure 316**

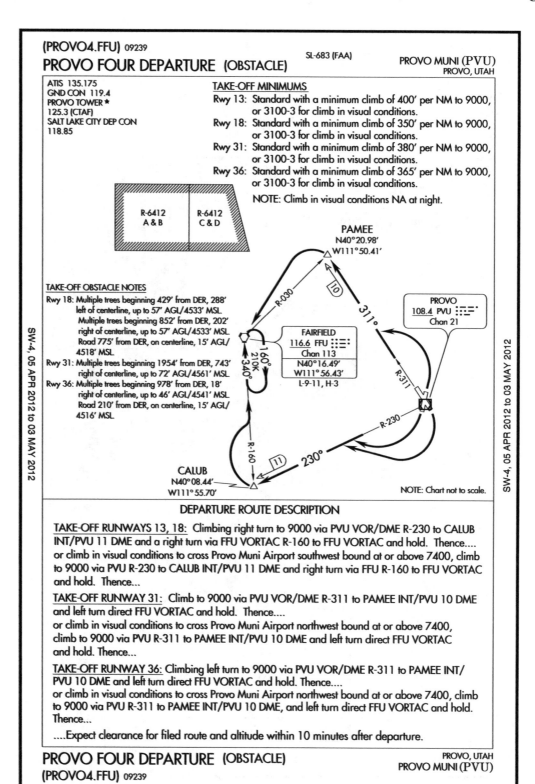

**(PROVO4.FFU)** 09239

# PROVO FOUR DEPARTURE (OBSTACLE)

SL-683 (FAA)

PROVO MUNI (PVU)
PROVO, UTAH

ATIS 135.175
GND CON 119.4
PROVO TOWER ★
125.3 (CTAF)
SALT LAKE CITY DEP CON
118.85

**TAKE-OFF MINIMUMS**

Rwy 13: Standard with a minimum climb of 400' per NM to 9000, or 3100-3 for climb in visual conditions.

Rwy 18: Standard with a minimum climb of 350' per NM to 9000, or 3100-3 for climb in visual conditions.

Rwy 31: Standard with a minimum climb of 380' per NM to 9000, or 3100-3 for climb in visual conditions.

Rwy 36: Standard with a minimum climb of 365' per NM to 9000, or 3100-3 for climb in visual conditions.

NOTE: Climb in visual conditions NA at night.

R-6412
A & B

R-6412
C & D

**TAKE-OFF OBSTACLE NOTES**

Rwy 18: Multiple trees beginning 429' from DER, 288' left of centerline, up to 57' AGL/4533' MSL. Multiple trees beginning 852' from DER, 202' right of centerline, up to 57' AGL/4533' MSL. Road 775' from DER, on centerline, 15' AGL/ 4518' MSL.

Rwy 31: Multiple trees beginning 1954' from DER, 743' right of centerline, up to 72' AGL/4561' MSL.

Rwy 36: Multiple trees beginning 978' from DER, 18' right of centerline, up to 46' AGL/4541' MSL. Road 210' from DER, on centerline, 15' AGL/ 4516' MSL.

PAMEE
N40°20.98'
W111°50.41'

PROVO
108.4 PVU
Chan 21

FAIRFIELD
116.6 FFU
Chan 113
N40°16.49'
W111°56.43'
L-9-11, H-3

CALUB
N40°08.44'
W111°55.70'

NOTE: Chart not to scale.

SW-4, 05 APR 2012 to 03 MAY 2012

SW-4, 05 APR 2012 to 03 MAY 2012

## DEPARTURE ROUTE DESCRIPTION

**TAKE-OFF RUNWAYS 13, 18:** Climbing right turn to 9000 via PVU VOR/DME R-230 to CALUB INT/PVU 11 DME and a right turn via FFU VORTAC R-160 to FFU VORTAC and hold. Thence.... or climb in visual conditions to cross Provo Muni Airport southwest bound at or above 7400, climb to 9000 via PVU R-230 to CALUB INT/PVU 11 DME and right turn via FFU R-160 to FFU VORTAC and hold. Thence...

**TAKE-OFF RUNWAY 31:** Climb to 9000 via PVU VOR/DME R-311 to PAMEE INT/PVU 10 DME and left turn direct FFU VORTAC and hold. Thence.... or climb in visual conditions to cross Provo Muni Airport northwest bound at or above 7400, climb to 9000 via PVU R-311 to PAMEE INT/PVU 10 DME and left turn direct FFU VORTAC and hold. Thence...

**TAKE-OFF RUNWAY 36:** Climbing left turn to 9000 via PVU VOR/DME R-311 to PAMEE INT/ PVU 10 DME and left turn direct FFU VORTAC and hold. Thence.... or climb in visual conditions to cross Provo Muni Airport northwest bound at or above 7400, climb to 9000 via PVU R-311 to PAMEE INT/PVU 10 DME, and left turn direct FFU VORTAC and hold. Thence...

....Expect clearance for filed route and altitude within 10 minutes after departure.

# PROVO FOUR DEPARTURE (OBSTACLE)
**(PROVO4.FFU)** 09239

PROVO, UTAH
PROVO MUNI (PVU)

**Figure 317**

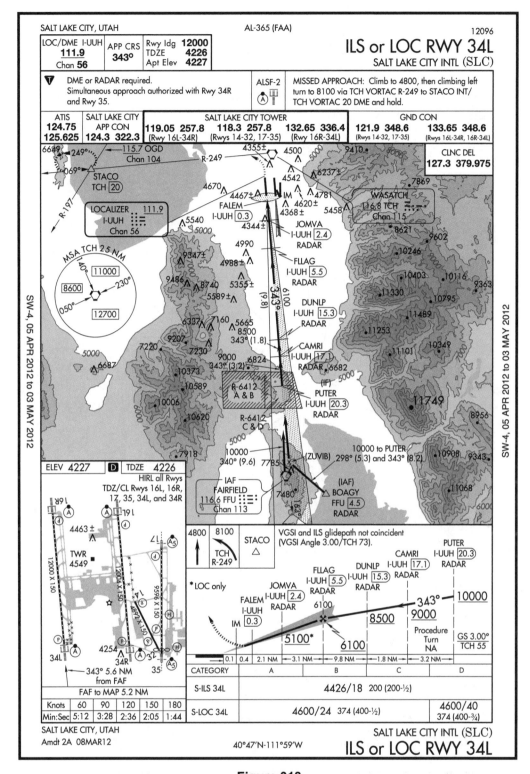

**Figure 318**

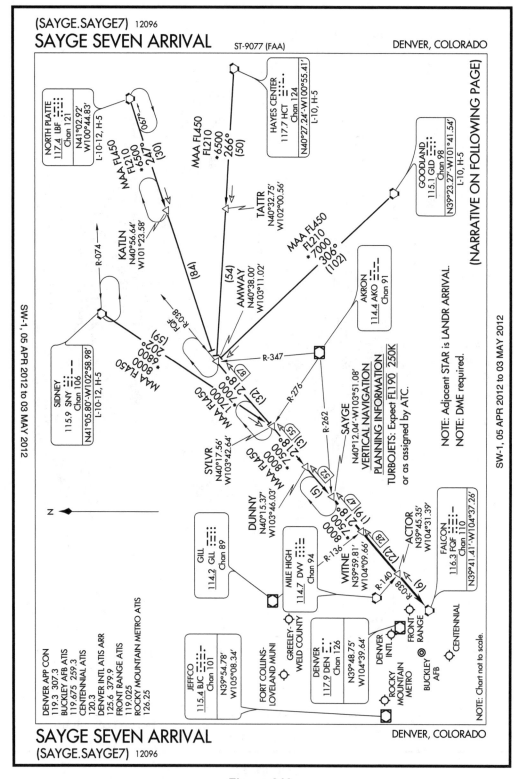

Figure 319

(SAYGE.SAYGE7) 12096
## SAYGE SEVEN ARRIVAL   ST-9077 (FAA)                    DENVER, COLORADO

ARRIVAL ROUTE DESCRIPTION

<u>GOODLAND TRANSITION (GLD.SAYGE7):</u>  From over GLD VORTAC via GLD R-306
and FQF R-038 to SAYGE INT.  Thence....
<u>HAYES CENTER TRANSITION (HCT.SAYGE7):</u>  From over HCT VORTAC via HCT R-266
and FQF R-038 to SAYGE INT.  Thence....
<u>NORTH PLATTE TRANSITION (LBF.SAYGE7):</u>  From over LBF VORTAC via LBF R-247
and FQF R-038 to SAYGE INT.  Thence....
<u>SIDNEY TRANSITION (SNY.SAYGE7):</u>  From over SNY VORTAC via SNY R-202
and FQF R-038 to SAYGE INT.  Thence....

....From over SAYGE INT via FQF R-038 to FQF VORTAC.  Expect RADAR vectors to
the final approach course at or before FQF VORTAC.

SW-1, 05 APR 2012 to 03 MAY 2012

SW-1, 05 APR 2012 to 03 MAY 2012

## SAYGE SEVEN ARRIVAL                               DENVER, COLORADO
(SAYGE.SAYGE7) 12096

**Figure 320**

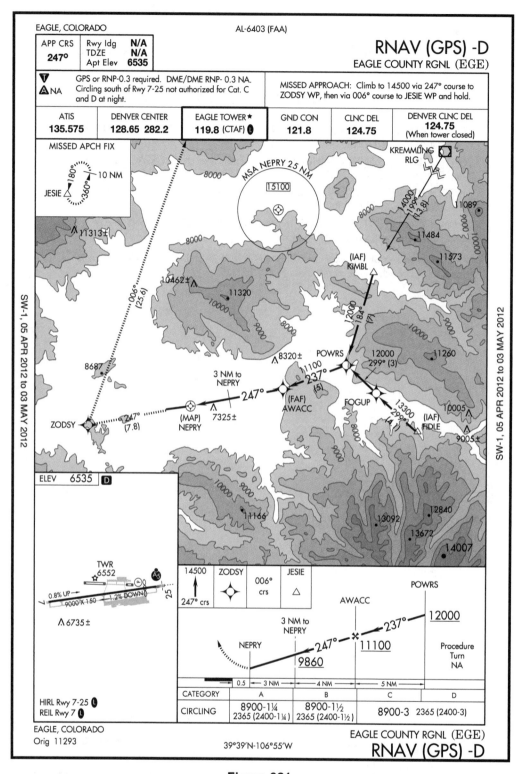

Figure 321

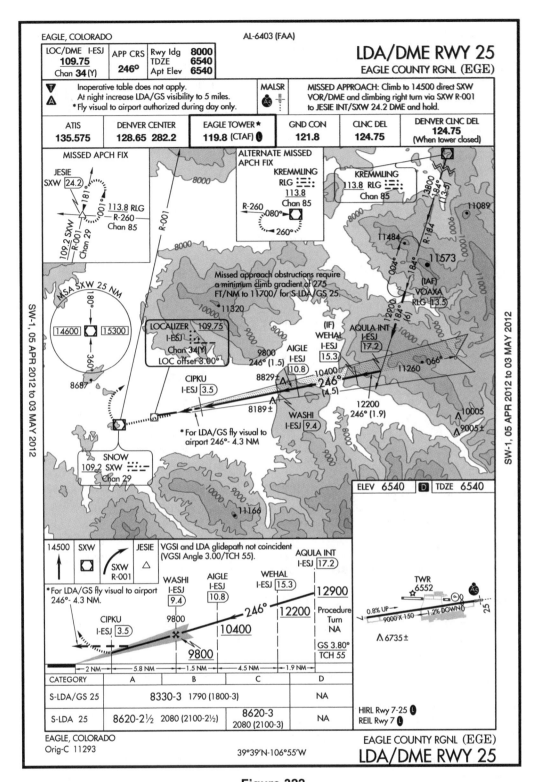

**Figure 322**

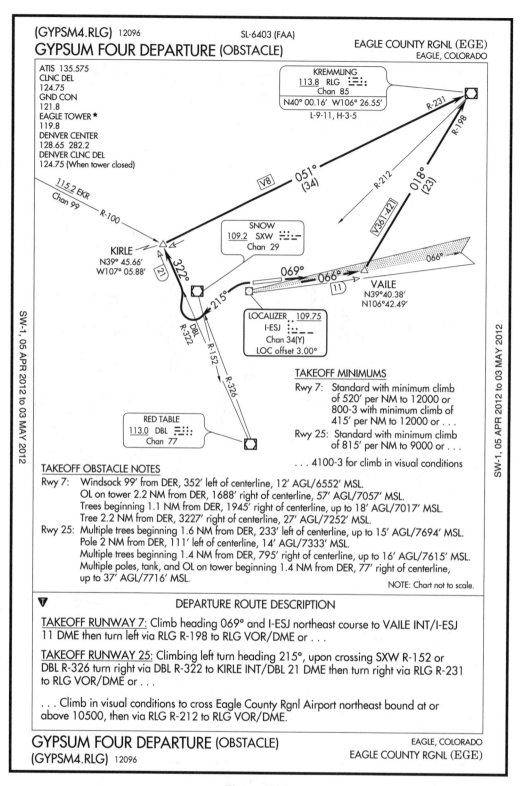

(GYPSM4.RLG) 12096    SL-6403 (FAA)    EAGLE COUNTY RGNL (EGE)
## GYPSUM FOUR DEPARTURE (OBSTACLE)    EAGLE, COLORADO

ATIS 135.575
CLNC DEL
124.75
GND CON
121.8
EAGLE TOWER ★
119.8
DENVER CENTER
128.65  282.2
DENVER CLNC DEL
124.75 (When tower closed)

KREMMLING
113.8 RLG
Chan 85
N40° 00.16'  W106° 26.55'
L-9-11, H-3-5

115.2 EKR
Chan 99    R-100

V8    051°
(34)

R-231
R-198
R-212
018°
(23)
V361-421

SNOW
109.2 SXW
Chan 29

KIRLE
N39° 45.66'
W107° 05.88'

322°
21

069°
066°
066°

11

VAILE
N39°40.38'
N106°42.49'

215°
DBL
R-322
R-152
R-326

LOCALIZER  109.75
I-ESJ
Chan 34(Y)
LOC offset 3.00°

RED TABLE
113.0 DBL
Chan 77

TAKEOFF MINIMUMS
Rwy 7:  Standard with minimum climb
of 520' per NM to 12000 or
800-3 with minimum climb of
415' per NM to 12000 or . . .
Rwy 25:  Standard with minimum climb
of 815' per NM to 9000 or . . .

. . . 4100-3 for climb in visual conditions

TAKEOFF OBSTACLE NOTES
Rwy 7:  Windsock 99' from DER, 352' left of centerline, 12' AGL/6552' MSL.
OL on tower 2.2 NM from DER, 1688' right of centerline, 57' AGL/7057' MSL.
Trees beginning 1.1 NM from DER, 1945' right of centerline, up to 18' AGL/7017' MSL.
Tree 2.2 NM from DER, 3227' right of centerline, 27' AGL/7252' MSL.
Rwy 25:  Multiple trees beginning 1.6 NM from DER, 233' left of centerline, up to 15' AGL/7694' MSL.
Pole 2 NM from DER, 111' left of centerline, 14' AGL/7333' MSL.
Multiple trees beginning 1.4 NM from DER, 795' right of centerline, up to 16' AGL/7615' MSL.
Multiple poles, tank, and OL on tower beginning 1.4 NM from DER, 77' right of centerline,
up to 37' AGL/7716' MSL.
NOTE: Chart not to scale.

▼    DEPARTURE ROUTE DESCRIPTION

TAKEOFF RUNWAY 7: Climb heading 069° and I-ESJ northeast course to VAILE INT/I-ESJ
11 DME then turn left via RLG R-198 to RLG VOR/DME or . . .

TAKEOFF RUNWAY 25: Climbing left turn heading 215°, upon crossing SXW R-152 or
DBL R-326 turn right via DBL R-322 to KIRLE INT/DBL 21 DME then turn right via RLG R-231
to RLG VOR/DME or . . .

. . . Climb in visual conditions to cross Eagle County Rgnl Airport northeast bound at or
above 10500, then via RLG R-212 to RLG VOR/DME.

## GYPSUM FOUR DEPARTURE (OBSTACLE)    EAGLE, COLORADO
(GYPSM4.RLG) 12096    EAGLE COUNTY RGNL (EGE)

SW-1, 05 APR 2012 to 03 MAY 2012

**Figure 323**

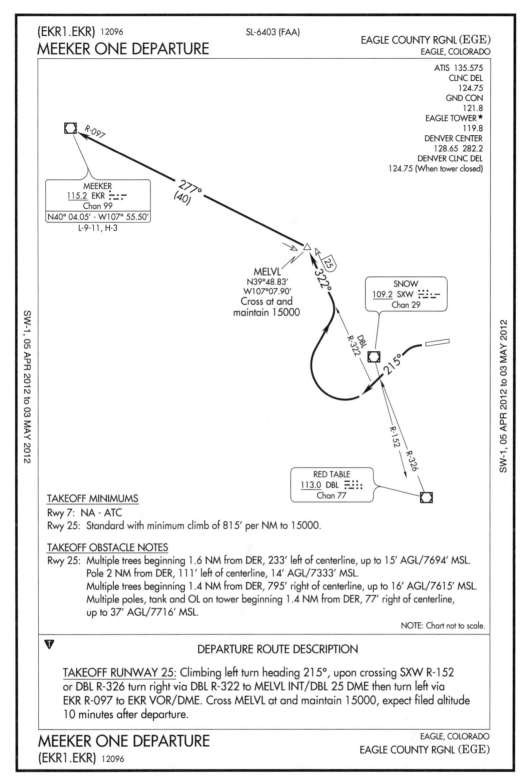

(EKR1.EKR) 12096

MEEKER ONE DEPARTURE

SL-6403 (FAA)

EAGLE COUNTY RGNL (EGE)
EAGLE, COLORADO

ATIS 135.575
CLNC DEL
124.75
GND CON
121.8
EAGLE TOWER ★
119.8
DENVER CENTER
128.65 282.2
DENVER CLNC DEL
124.75 (When tower closed)

MEEKER
115.2 EKR
Chan 99
N40° 04.05' - W107° 55.50'
L-9-11, H-3

277°
(40)

R-097

322°
25

MELVL
N39°48.83'
W107°07.90'
Cross at and
maintain 15000

SNOW
109.2 SXW
Chan 29

DBL
R-322

215°

R-152    R-326

RED TABLE
113.0 DBL
Chan 77

SW-1, 05 APR 2012 to 03 MAY 2012

SW-1, 05 APR 2012 to 03 MAY 2012

TAKEOFF MINIMUMS

Rwy 7: NA - ATC
Rwy 25: Standard with minimum climb of 815' per NM to 15000.

TAKEOFF OBSTACLE NOTES

Rwy 25: Multiple trees beginning 1.6 NM from DER, 233' left of centerline, up to 15' AGL/7694' MSL.
Pole 2 NM from DER, 111' left of centerline, 14' AGL/7333' MSL.
Multiple trees beginning 1.4 NM from DER, 795' right of centerline, up to 16' AGL/7615' MSL.
Multiple poles, tank and OL on tower beginning 1.4 NM from DER, 77' right of centerline,
up to 37' AGL/7716' MSL.

NOTE: Chart not to scale.

DEPARTURE ROUTE DESCRIPTION

TAKEOFF RUNWAY 25: Climbing left turn heading 215°, upon crossing SXW R-152
or DBL R-326 turn right via DBL R-322 to MELVL INT/DBL 25 DME then turn left via
EKR R-097 to EKR VOR/DME. Cross MELVL at and maintain 15000, expect filed altitude
10 minutes after departure.

MEEKER ONE DEPARTURE
(EKR1.EKR) 12096

EAGLE, COLORADO
EAGLE COUNTY RGNL (EGE)

**Figure 324**

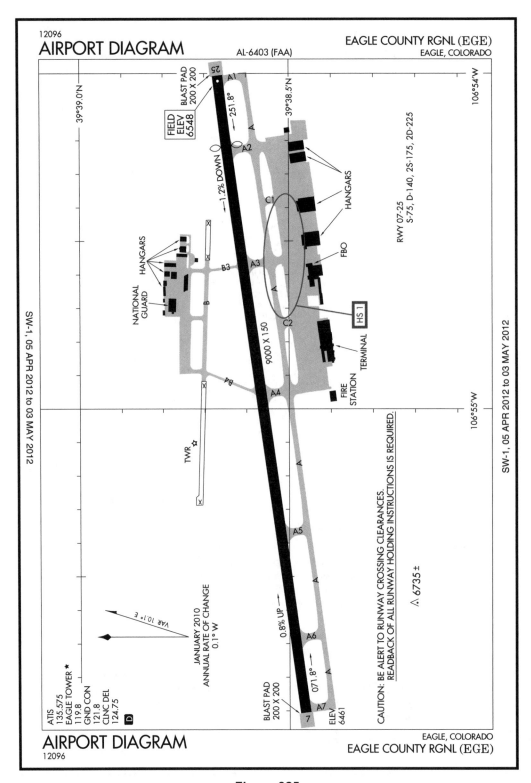

**Figure 325**

🔺 **ALTERNATE MINS**    M2    🔺
12096

NAME                     ALTERNATE MINIMUMS
**DENVER, CO**
CENTENNIAL (APA) ...... **ILS or LOC Rwy 35R[1]**
**NDB Rwy 35R[2]**
**RNAV (GPS) Rwy 28[34]**
**RNAV (GPS) Rwy 35R[14]**
[1]Categories A,B, 900-2; Category C, 900-2½,
  Category D, 900-2¾.
[2]Categories A,B, 1000-2; Categories C,D,
  1000-3.
[3]Category D, 800-2¼.
[4]NA when local weather not available.

ROCKY MOUNTAIN METROPOLITAN
(BJC) ........................ **ILS or LOC Y Rwy 29R[123]**
**ILS or LOC Z Rwy 29R[23]**
**RNAV (GPS) Rwy 29L[3]**
**RNAV (GPS) Rwy 29R[3]**
**VOR/DME Rwy 29L/R[2]**
[1]ILS, Categories A, B, C, D, 700-2.
[2]NA when control tower closed.
[3]NA when local weather not available.

**EAGLE, CO**
EAGLE COUNTY
RGNL (EGE) .......................... **LDA/DME Rwy 25**
Categories A,B, 2100-2; Category C, 2100-3.
NA when control tower closed.
NA when local weather not available.

**FARMINGTON, NM**
FOUR CORNERS
RGNL (FMN) ................... **ILS or LOC Rwy 25[12]**
**RNAV (GPS) Rwy 5[3]**
**RNAV (GPS) Rwy 7[3]**
**RNAV (GPS) Rwy 23[4]**
**RNAV (GPS) Rwy 25[3]**
[1]NA when control tower closed.
[2]ILS, Categories B,C,D, 700-2.
[3]NA when local weather not available.
[4]Category D, 800-2¼.

**FORT COLLINS/LOVELAND, CO**
FORT COLLINS-LOVELAND
MUNI (FNL) ...................... **RNAV (GPS) Rwy 15**
**RNAV (GPS) Rwy 33**
**VOR/DME-A**
NA when local weather not available.

**GALLUP, NM**
GALLUP MUNI (GUP) ....... **RNAV (GPS) Rwy 6[12]**
**RNAV (GPS) Rwy 24[3]**
**VOR Rwy 6[4]**
[1]Categories A, B, 900-2; Category C, 900-2½;
  Category D, 900-3.
[2]NA when local weather not available.
[3]Category D, 900-3.
[4]Category C, 800-2¼; Category D, 900-3.

NAME                     ALTERNATE MINIMUMS
**GRAND JUNCTION, CO**
GRAND JUNCTION
RGNL (GJT) .................... **ILS or LOC Rwy 11[12]**
**LDA/DME Rwy 29[3]**
**RNAV (GPS) Y Rwy 11[3]**
[1]ILS, Category D, 700-2¼.
[2]NA when local weather not available.
[3]Category D, 800-2¼.

**GREELEY, CO**
GREELEY-WELD
COUNTY (GXY) ................. **ILS or LOC Rwy 34**
**RNAV (GPS) Rwy 16**
**RNAV (GPS) Rwy 27**
**RNAV (GPS) Rwy 34**
**VOR-A**
NA when local weather not available.

**GUNNISON, CO**
GUNNISON-CRESTED
BUTTE RGNL (GUC) .......... **ILS or LOC Rwy 6[1]**
**RNAV (RNP) Rwy 6, 800-2¼**
**VOR or GPS-A[23]**
[1]ILS,LOC, Categories A, B, C, 1600-3.
[2]Categories A,B,C, 1700-3;Cat D, 2300-3.
[3]NA when local altimeter setting not available
  except for operators with approved weather
  reporting service.

**HAYDEN, CO**
YAMPA
VALLEY (HDN) .... **ILS or LOC/DME Y Rwy 10[12]**
**RNAV (GPS) Y Rwy 10[12]**
**RNAV (RNP) Z Rwy 10, 800-2¼[1]**
**VOR/DME-B[3]**
[1]NA when local weather not availalbe.
[2]Categories A, B, 1200-2; Categories C, D,
  1200-3.
[3]Categories A, B, 1300-2; Categories C, D,
  1300-3.

**HOBBS, NM**
LEA COUNTY
RGNL (HOB) ...................... **ILS or LOC Rwy 3[1]**
**LOC/DME BC Rwy 21[2]**
**RNAV (GPS) Rwy 3[3]**
**RNAV (GPS) Rwy 21[2]**
**RNAV (GPS) Rwy 30[2]**
**VOR/DME or TACAN Rwy 21[2]**
**VOR or TACAN Rwy 3[2]**
[1]NA when control tower closed.
[2]NA when control tower closed, except
  standard for operators with approved weather
  reporting service.
[3]NA when local weather not available.

🔺 **ALTERNATE MINS**    SW-1 🔺
12096    M2

05 APR 2012 to 03 MAY 2012

**Figure 326**

97

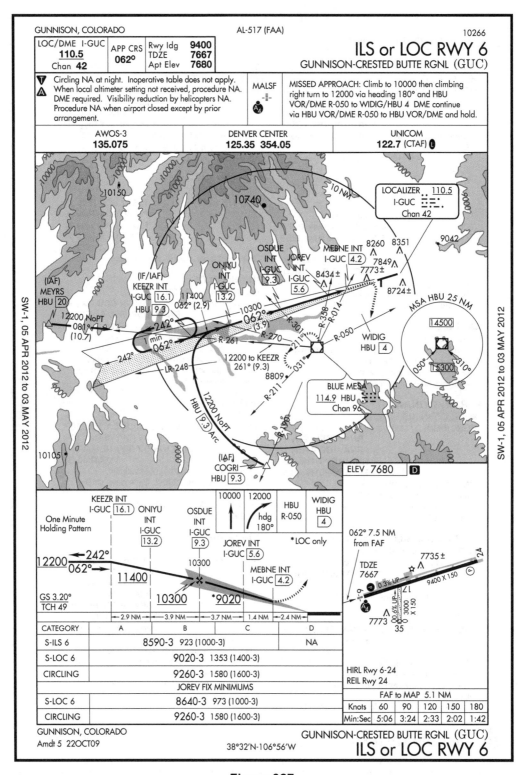

GUNNISON, COLORADO                          AL-517 (FAA)                                    10266

| LOC/DME I-GUC **110.5** Chan **42** | APP CRS **062°** | Rwy Idg **9400** TDZE **7667** Apt Elev **7680** |
|---|---|---|

ILS or LOC RWY 6
GUNNISON-CRESTED BUTTE RGNL (GUC)

Circling NA at night. Inoperative table does not apply. When local altimeter setting not received, procedure NA. DME required. Visibility reduction by helicopters NA. Procedure NA when airport closed except by prior arrangement.

MISSED APPROACH: Climb to 10000 then climbing right turn to 12000 via heading 180° and HBU VOR/DME R-050 to WIDIG/HBU 4 DME continue via HBU VOR/DME R-050 to HBU VOR/DME and hold.

| AWOS-3 **135.075** | DENVER CENTER **125.35 354.05** | UNICOM **122.7** (CTAF) |
|---|---|---|

GUNNISON, COLORADO
Amdt 5 22OCT09                          38°32'N-106°56'W

GUNNISON-CRESTED BUTTE RGNL (GUC)
ILS or LOC RWY 6

| CATEGORY | A | B | C | D |
|---|---|---|---|---|
| S-ILS 6 | 8590-3 | 923 (1000-3) | | NA |
| S-LOC 6 | 9020-3 | 1353 (1400-3) | | |
| CIRCLING | 9260-3 | 1580 (1600-3) | | |
| JOREV FIX MINIMUMS | | | | |
| S-LOC 6 | 8640-3 | 973 (1000-3) | | |
| CIRCLING | 9260-3 | 1580 (1600-3) | | |

ELEV 7680

HIRL Rwy 6-24
REIL Rwy 24

| FAF to MAP 5.1 NM | | | | | |
|---|---|---|---|---|---|
| Knots | 60 | 90 | 120 | 150 | 180 |
| Min:Sec | 5:06 | 3:24 | 2:33 | 2:02 | 1:42 |

**Figure 327**

98

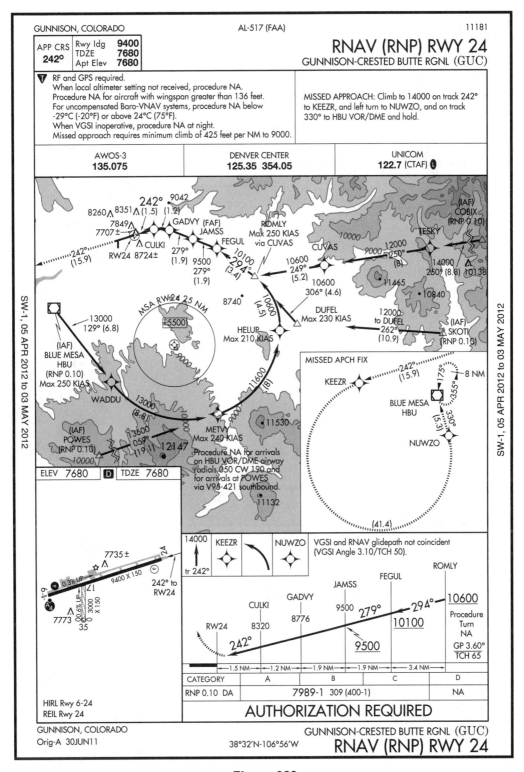

**Figure 328**

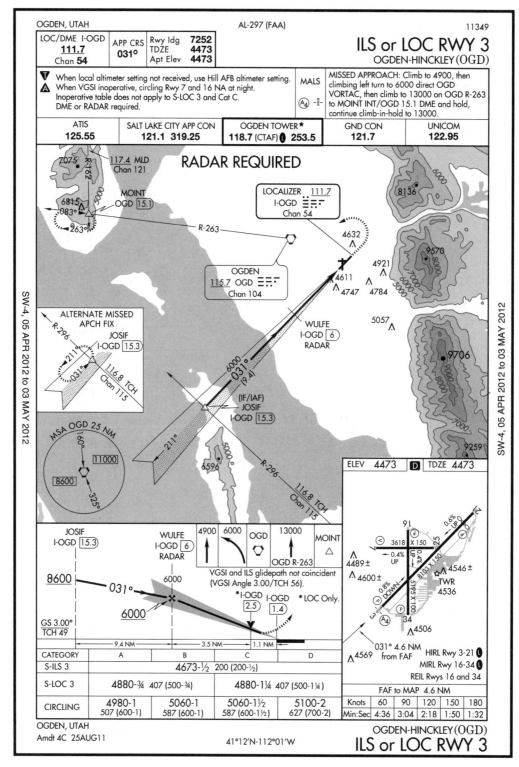

**Figure 329**

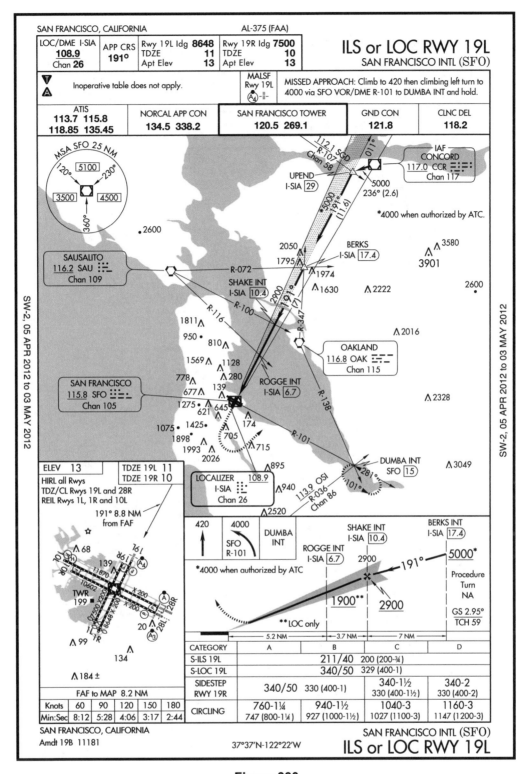

**Figure 330**

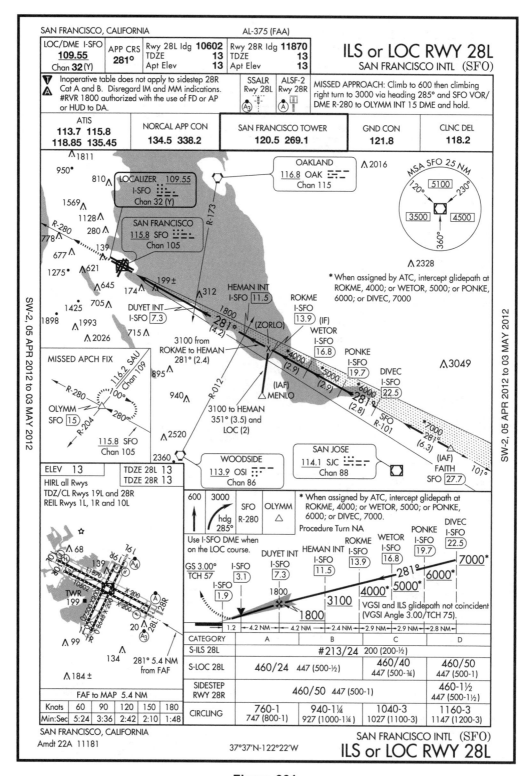

**Figure 331**

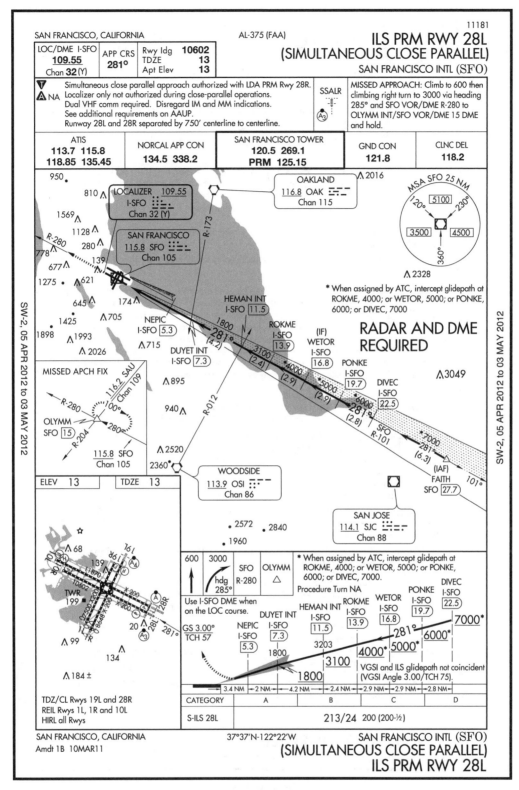

**Figure 332**

ILS PRM RWY 28L  Amdt 1B 11069          AL-375 (FAA)
(SIMULTANEOUS CLOSE PARALLEL)                    SAN FRANCISCO INTL (SFO)
                                                 SAN FRANCISCO, CALIFORNIA

## ATTENTION ALL USERS PAGE (AAUP)

Condensed Briefing Points:
- Listen to the PRM monitor frequency when communicating with NORCAL approach control (135.65), no later than LOC intercept.
- Expect to be switched to SFO Tower (120.5) at NEPIC (I-SFO 5.3 DME).
- PRM monitor frequency may be de-selected after determining that the aircraft is on the tower frequency.

1. **ATIS.** When the ATIS broadcast advises that simultaneous ILS/PRM and LDA/PRM approaches are in progress, pilots should brief to fly the ILS/PRM 28L approach. If later advised to expect an ILS 28L approach, the ILS/PRM 28L chart may be used after completing the following briefing items:

   (a) Minimums and missed approach procedures are unchanged.
   (b) Monitor frequency no longer required.
   (c) A different glideslope intercept altitude may be assigned when advised to expect the ILS 28L approach.

Simultaneous parallel approaches will only be offered/conducted when the weather is at least 2100 feet (ceiling) and 4 miles (visibility).

2. **Dual VHF Communication required.** To avoid blocked transmissions, each runway will have two frequencies, a primary and a PRM monitor frequency. The NORCAL approach controller will transmit on both frequencies. The PRM Monitor controller's transmissions, if needed, will override both frequencies. Pilots will ONLY transmit on the approach controller's frequency (135.65), but will listen to both frequencies. Select the PRM monitor frequency audio only when in contact with NORCAL approach control (135.65). The volume levels should be set about the same on both radios so that the pilots will be able to hear transmissions on at least one frequency if the other is blocked. The PRM monitor frequency may be de-selected passing NEPIC.

3. **ALL "Breakouts"** are to be hand flown to assure that the maneuver is accomplished in the shortest amount of time. Pilots, when directed by ATC to break off an approach, must assume that an aircraft is blundering toward their course and a breakout must be initiated immediately.

   (a) ATC Directed "Breakouts:" ATC directed breakouts will consist of a turn and a climb or descent. Pilots must always initiate the breakout in response to an air traffic controller instruction. Controllers will give a descending breakout only when there are no other reasonable options available, but in no case will the descent be below minimum vectoring altitude (MVA) which provides at least 1000 feet required obstruction clearance. The MVA in the final approach segment is 1600 feet at San Francisco International Airport.

   (b) Phraseology - "TRAFFIC ALERT:" If an aircraft enters the "NO TRANSGRESSION ZONE" (NTZ), the controller will breakout the threatened aircraft on the adjacent approach. The phraseology for the breakout will be:

      "TRAFFIC ALERT, (aircraft call sign) TURN (left/right) IMMEDIATELY, HEADING (degrees), CLIMB/DESCEND AND MAINTAIN (altitude)".

4. Descending on (not above) the ILS glideslope ensures complying with any charted crossing restrictions and assists traffic on the LDA PRM 28R approach to mitigate possible wake turbulence encounters without destabilizing the LDA approach and creating a go-around.

5. **LDA Traffic:** While conducting this ILS/PRM approach to Runway 28L, other aircraft may be conducting the offset LDA/PRM approach to Runway 28R. These aircraft will approach from the right-rear and will re-align with 28R after making visual contact with the ILS traffic.

Special pilot training required. Pilots who are unable to participate will be afforded appropriate arrival services as operational conditions permit and must notify the controlling ARTCC as soon as practical, but at least 100 miles from destination.

SW-2, 05 APR 2012 to 03 MAY 2012

(SIMULTANEOUS CLOSE PARALLEL)                    SAN FRANCISCO, CALIFORNIA
ILS PRM RWY 28L  Amdt 1B 11069   37°37'N-122°22'W   SAN FRANCISCO INTL (SFO)

**Figure 333**

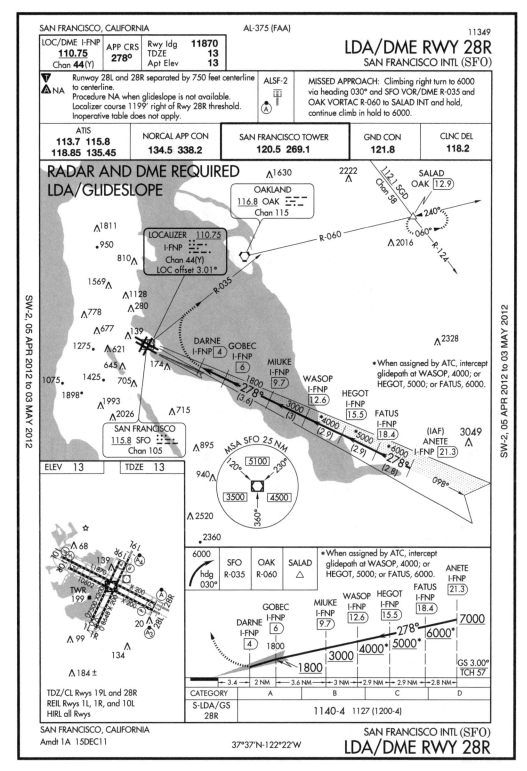

**Figure 334**

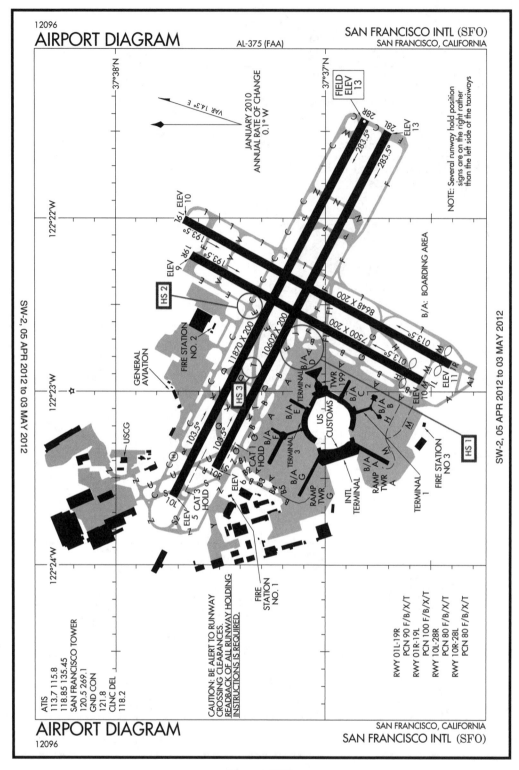

**Figure 335**

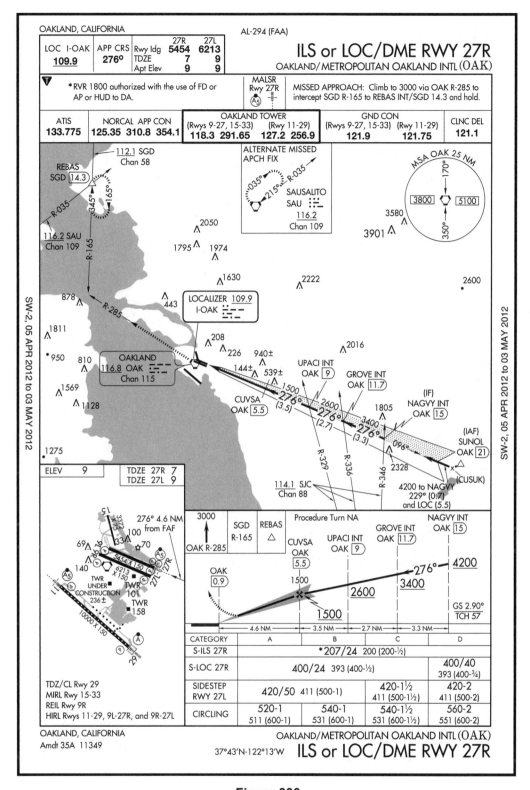

**Figure 336**

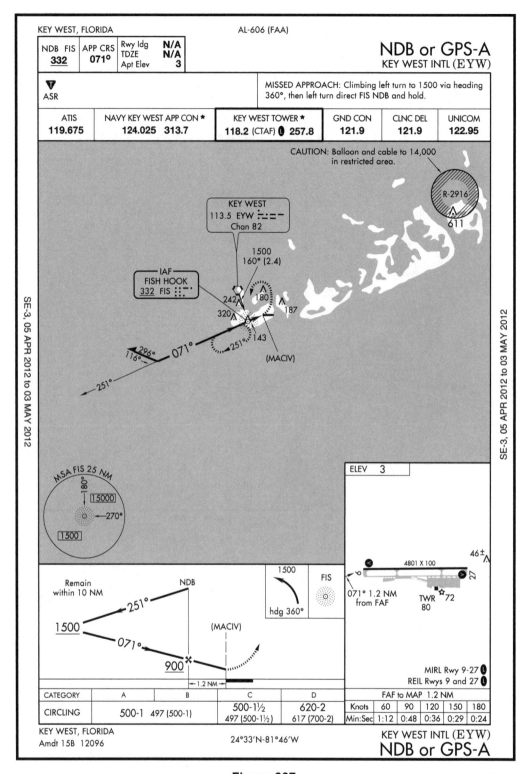

KEY WEST, FLORIDA AL-606 (FAA)

**NDB or GPS-A**
KEY WEST INTL (EYW)

| NDB FIS | APP CRS | Rwy ldg | N/A |
|---|---|---|---|
| **332** | **071°** | TDZE | N/A |
| | | Apt Elev | 3 |

MISSED APPROACH: Climbing left turn to 1500 via heading 360°, then left turn direct FIS NDB and hold.

| ATIS | NAVY KEY WEST APP CON ★ | KEY WEST TOWER ★ | GND CON | CLNC DEL | UNICOM |
|---|---|---|---|---|---|
| **119.675** | **124.025 313.7** | **118.2** (CTAF) **257.8** | **121.9** | **121.9** | **122.95** |

| CATEGORY | A | B | C | D |
|---|---|---|---|---|
| CIRCLING | 500-1 | 497 (500-1) | 500-1½ 497 (500-1½) | 620-2 617 (700-2) |

KEY WEST, FLORIDA
Amdt 15B 12096

24°33'N-81°46'W

KEY WEST INTL (EYW)
**NDB or GPS-A**

FAF to MAP 1.2 NM

| Knots | 60 | 90 | 120 | 150 | 180 |
|---|---|---|---|---|---|
| Min:Sec | 1:12 | 0:48 | 0:36 | 0:29 | 0:24 |

**Figure 337**

108

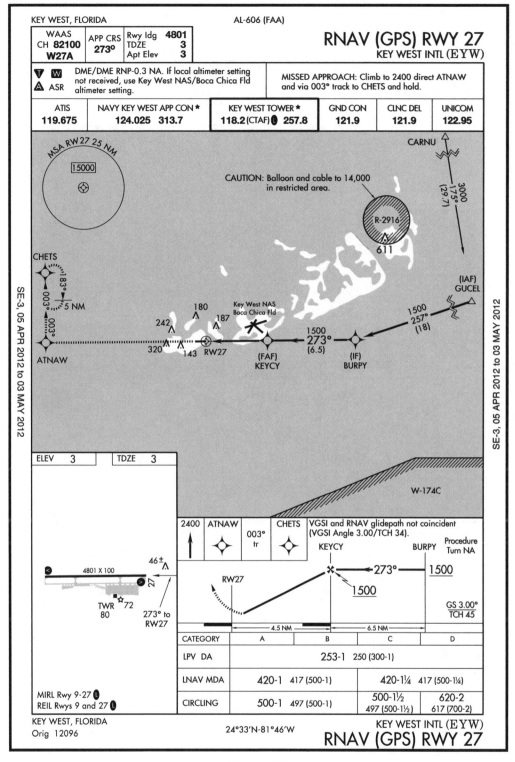

**Figure 338**

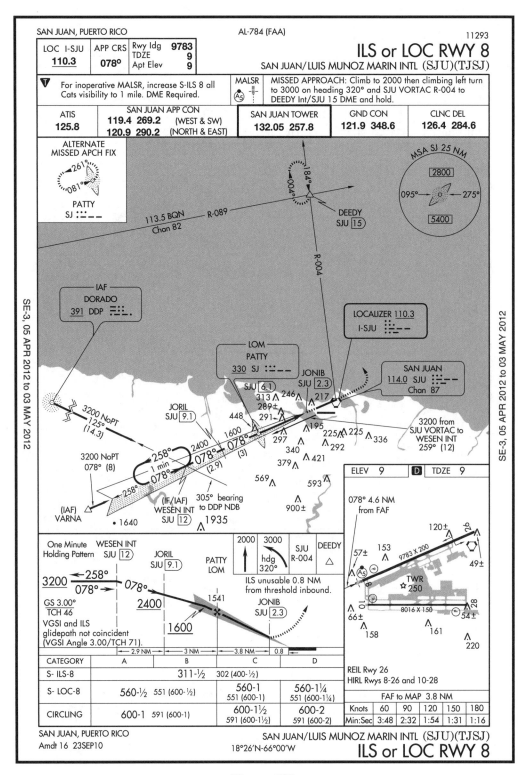

SAN JUAN, PUERTO RICO
AL-784 (FAA)
11293

| LOC I-SJU | APP CRS | Rwy Idg | 9783 |
| 110.3 | 078° | TDZE | 9 |
| | | Apt Elev | 9 |

**ILS or LOC RWY 8**

SAN JUAN/LUIS MUNOZ MARIN INTL (SJU)(TJSJ)

For inoperative MALSR, increase S-ILS 8 all Cats visibility to 1 mile. DME Required.

MALSR

MISSED APPROACH: Climb to 2000 then climbing left turn to 3000 on heading 320° and SJU VORTAC R-004 to DEEDY Int/SJU 15 DME and hold.

| ATIS | SAN JUAN APP CON | | SAN JUAN TOWER | GND CON | CLNC DEL |
| 125.8 | 119.4 269.2 (WEST & SW) | 120.9 290.2 (NORTH & EAST) | 132.05 257.8 | 121.9 348.6 | 126.4 284.6 |

ALTERNATE MISSED APCH FIX

261°
081°

PATTY
SJ

MSA SJ 25 NM
2800
095° — 275°
5400

113.5 BQN
Chan 82
R-089

004°
184°

DEEDY
SJU 15

R-004

IAF
DORADO
391 DDP

LOCALIZER 110.3
I-SJU

LOM
PATTY
330 SJ

JONIB
SJU 2.3

SAN JUAN
114.0 SJU
Chan 87

SJU 6.1

313
246
289±
217
291

JORIL
SJU 9.1

448

3200 NoPT
125°
(14.3)

1600

258°
2400
078°
(2.9)

078°
(3)

297
340
379
195
225 225 336
292
421

3200 from SJU VORTAC to WESEN INT
259° (12)

ELEV 9     D     TDZE 9

078° 4.6 NM from FAF

3200 NoPT
078° (8)

258°
1 min
078°
078°

305° bearing to DDP NDB

(IF/IAF)
WESEN INT
SJU 12

569
593

900±

120±
57±  153
9783 X 200
49±

(IAF)
VARNA

1640

1935

TWR 250

8016 X 150

66±
54±
158   161
220

One Minute Holding Pattern

WESEN INT
SJU 12

JORIL
SJU 9.1

PATTY
LOM

2000  3000
hdg 320°

SJU R-004

DEEDY

ILS unusable 0.8 NM from threshold inbound.

3200  258°
078°

078°
2400

GS 3.00°
TCH 46
VGSI and ILS glidepath not coincident (VGSI Angle 3.00/TCH 71).

1541

1600

JONIB
SJU 2.3

REIL Rwy 26
HIRL Rwys 8-26 and 10-28

| | | 2.9 NM | 3 NM | 3.8 NM | 0.8 | |

| CATEGORY | A | B | C | D |
|---|---|---|---|---|
| S- ILS-8 | 311-½ | | 302 (400-½) | |
| S- LOC-8 | 560-½ 551 (600-½) | | 560-1 551 (600-1) | 560-1¼ 551 (600-1¼) |
| CIRCLING | 600-1 591 (600-1) | | 600-1½ 591 (600-1½) | 600-2 591 (600-2) |

FAF to MAP 3.8 NM

| Knots | 60 | 90 | 120 | 150 | 180 |
|---|---|---|---|---|---|
| Min:Sec | 3:48 | 2:32 | 1:54 | 1:31 | 1:16 |

SAN JUAN, PUERTO RICO
Amdt 16  23SEP10

18°26'N-66°00'W

SAN JUAN/LUIS MUNOZ MARIN INTL (SJU)(TJSJ)

**ILS or LOC RWY 8**

SE-3, 05 APR 2012 to 03 MAY 2012

**Figure 339**

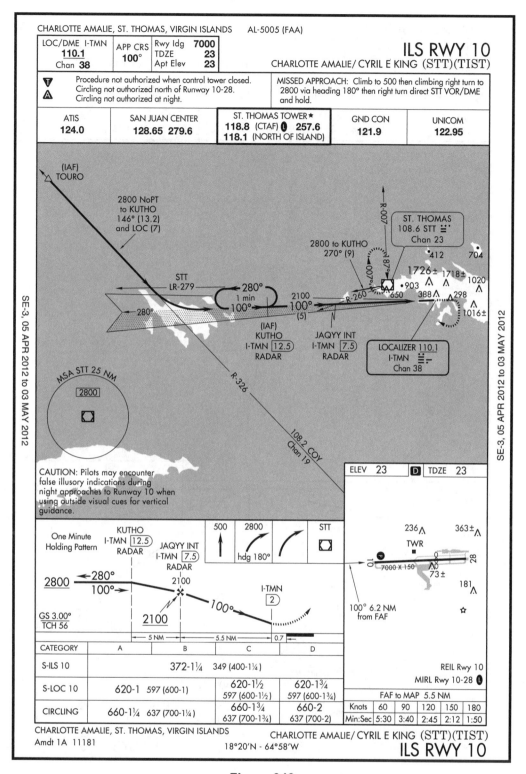

**Figure 340**

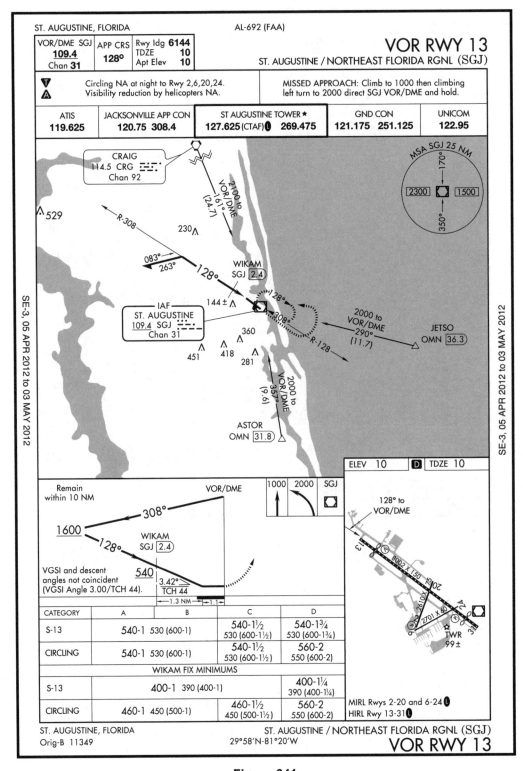

**Figure 341**

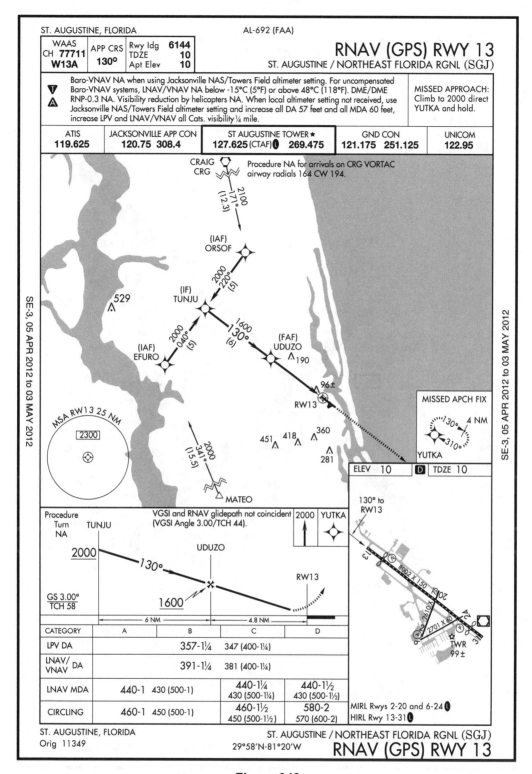

**Figure 342**

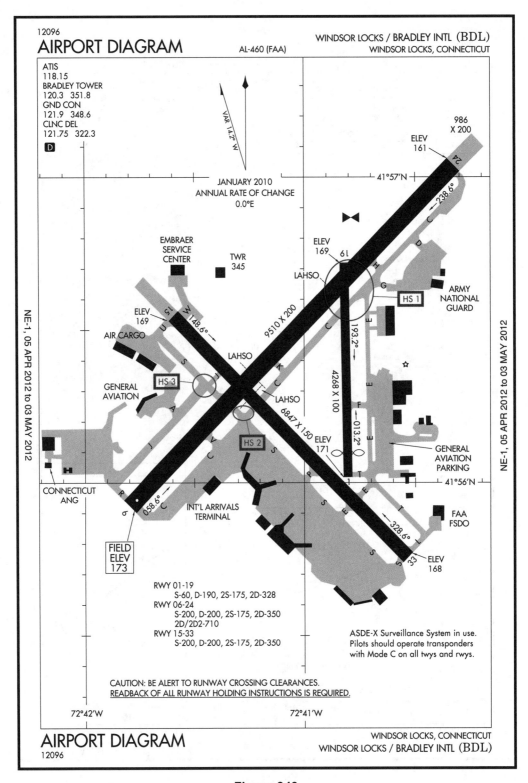

**Figure 343**

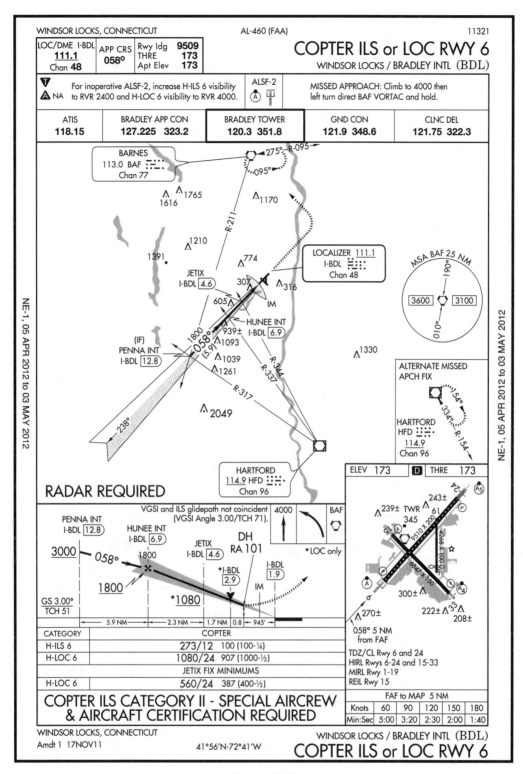

**Figure 344**

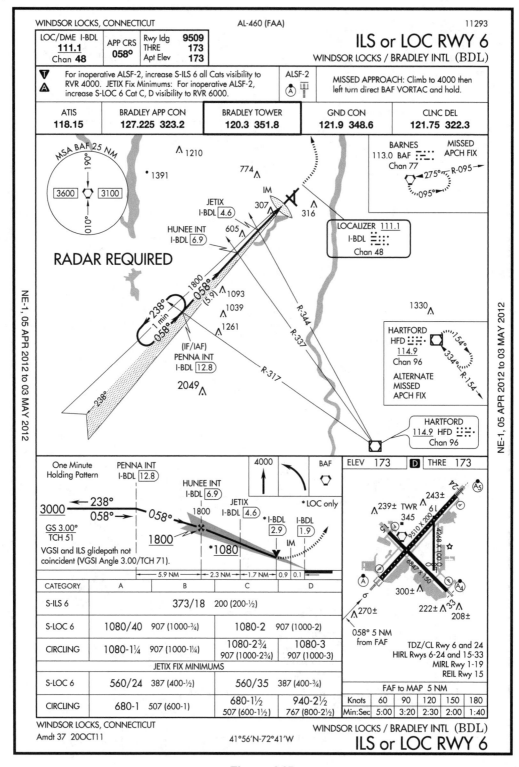

**Figure 345**

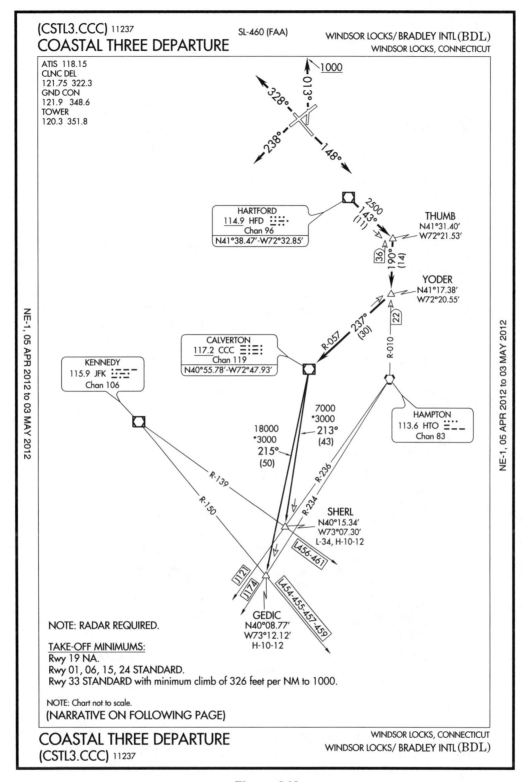

**Figure 346**

(CSTL3.CCC) 10154        SL-460 (FAA)       WINDSOR LOCKS/ BRADLEY INTL (BDL)
## COASTAL THREE DEPARTURE
WINDSOR LOCKS, CONNECTICUT

▼             DEPARTURE ROUTE DESCRIPTION

NOTE: INITIAL DEPARTURE HEADINGS ARE PREDICATED ON AVOIDING NOISE SENSITIVE AREAS. FLIGHT CREW AWARENESS AND COMPLIANCE IS IMPORTANT IN MINIMIZING NOISE IMPACTS ON SURROUNDING COMMUNITIES.

NOTE: APPROPRIATE DEPARTURE CONTROL FREQUENCY TO BE ASSIGNED BY ATC.

TAKE-OFF RWY 1: Climb heading 013° to 1000 or as assigned for radar vectors to HFD VOR/DME, thence . . .
TAKE-OFF RWY 6: Fly assigned heading for radar vectors to HFD VOR/DME, thence . . .
TAKE-OFF RWY 15: Climb heading 148° or as assigned for radar vectors to HFD VOR/DME, thence . . .
TAKE-OFF RWY 24: Climb heading 238° or as assigned for radar vectors to HFD VOR/DME, thence . . .
TAKE-OFF RWY 33: Climb heading 328° or as assigned for radar vectors to HFD VOR/DME, thence . . .
. . . . From over HFD VOR/DME proceed via HFD R-143 to THUMB INT, then proceed via HTO R-010 to YODER INT, then proceed via CCC R-057 to CCC VOR/DME. Then via (transition) or (assigned route). Maintain 4000 or assigned altitude. Expect clearance to requested flight level ten minutes after departure.

GEDIC TRANSITION (CSTL3.GEDIC): From over CCC VOR/DME via CCC R-215 to GEDIC.
SHERL TRANSITION (CSTL3.SHERL): From over CCC VOR/DME via CCC R-213 to SHERL.

TAKE-OFF OBSTACLE NOTES:
Rwy 1: Vehicle on road 342' from DER, 564' left of centerline, 15' AGL/184' MSL. Trees beginning 441' from DER, 493' left of centerline, up to 100' AGL/269' MSL. Trees beginning 1884' from DER, 45' right of centerline, up to 100' AGL/299' MSL.
Rwy 6: Trees beginning 21' from DER, 464' left of centerline, up to 100' AGL/249' MSL. Trees beginning 1956' from DER, 921' right of centerline, up to 100' AGL/239' MSL.
Rwy 15: Vehicle on roadway 531' from DER, 606' left of centerline, up to 15' AGL/186' MSL. Trees beginning 2341' from DER, 767' left of centerline, up to 100' AGL/244' MSL. Vehicle on roadway 429' from DER, 572' right of centerline, up to 15' AGL/186' MSL. Tree 1520' from DER, 786' right of centerline, up to 100' AGL/259' MSL.
Rwy 24: Trees beginning 3066' from DER, 599' left of centerline, up to 100' AGL/269' MSL. OL on fence 1239' DER, 784' left of centerline, up to 45' AGL/215' MSL. Trees beginning 2345' from DER, 489' right of centerline, up to 100' AGL/299' MSL.
Rwy 33: Trees beginning 1590' from DER, 275' left of centerline, up to 100' AGL/256' MSL. Tower 2.4 NM from DER, 3534' left of centerline, 104' AGL/774' MSL. Trees beginning 1618' from DER, 264' right of centerline, up to 100' AGL/263' MSL.

## COASTAL THREE DEPARTURE
(CSTL3.CCC) 10154
WINDSOR LOCKS, CONNECTICUT
WINDSOR LOCKS/ BRADLEY INTL (BDL)

**Figure 347**

64                                    **ARIZONA**

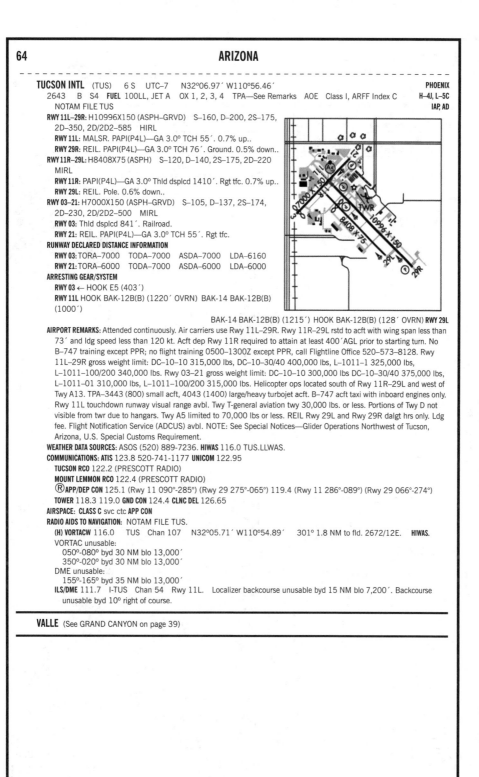

**TUCSON INTL** (TUS)  6 S  UTC–7  N32°06.97´ W110°56.46´                       PHOENIX
2643  B  S4  **FUEL** 100LL, JET A  OX 1, 2, 3, 4  TPA—See Remarks  AOE  Class I, ARFF Index C    H–4J, L–5C
NOTAM FILE TUS                                                                  IAP, AD
**RWY 11L–29R:** H10996X150 (ASPH–GRVD)  S–160, D–200, 2S–175,
2D–350, 2D/2D2–585  HIRL
 **RWY 11L:** MALSR. PAPI(P4L)—GA 3.0° TCH 55´. 0.7% up..
 **RWY 29R:** REIL. PAPI(P4L)—GA 3.0° TCH 76´. Ground. 0.5% down..
**RWY 11R–29L:** H8408X75 (ASPH)  S–120, D–140, 2S–175, 2D–220
MIRL
 **RWY 11R:** PAPI(P4L)—GA 3.0° Thld dsplcd 1410´. Rgt tfc. 0.7% up..
 **RWY 29L:** REIL. Pole. 0.6% down..
**RWY 03–21:** H7000X150 (ASPH–GRVD)  S–105, D–137, 2S–174,
2D–230, 2D/2D2–500  MIRL
 **RWY 03:** Thld dsplcd 841´. Railroad.
 **RWY 21:** REIL. PAPI(P4L)—GA 3.0° TCH 55´. Rgt tfc.
**RUNWAY DECLARED DISTANCE INFORMATION**
 **RWY 03:** TORA–7000  TODA–7000  ASDA–7000  LDA–6160
 **RWY 21:** TORA–6000  TODA–7000  ASDA–6000  LDA–6000
**ARRESTING GEAR/SYSTEM**
 **RWY 03** ← HOOK E5 (403´)
 **RWY 11L** HOOK BAK-12B(B) (1220´ OVRN) BAK-14 BAK-12B(B)
 (1000´)
        BAK-14 BAK-12B(B) (1215´) HOOK BAK-12B(B) (128´ OVRN) **RWY 29L**
**AIRPORT REMARKS:** Attended continuously. Air carriers use Rwy 11L–29R. Rwy 11R–29L rstd to acft with wing span less than
73´ and ldg speed less than 120 kt. Acft dep Rwy 11R required to attain at least 400´ AGL prior to starting turn. No
B–747 training except PPR; no flight training 0500–1300Z except PPR, call Flightline Office 520–573–8128. Rwy
11L–29R gross weight limit: DC–10–10 315,000 lbs, DC–10–30/40 400,000 lbs, L–1011–1 325,000 lbs,
L–1011–100/200 340,000 lbs. Rwy 03–21 gross weight limit: DC–10–10 300,000 lbs DC–10–30/40 375,000 lbs,
L–1011–01 310,000 lbs, L–1011–100/200 315,000 lbs. Helicopter ops located south of Rwy 11R–29L and west of
Twy A13. TPA–3443 (800) small acft, 4043 (1400) large/heavy turbojet acft. B–747 acft taxi with inboard engines only.
Rwy 11L touchdown runway visual range avbl. Twy T–general aviation twy 30,000 lbs. or less. Portions of Twy D not
visible from twr due to hangars. Twy A5 limited to 70,000 lbs or less. REIL Rwy 29L and Rwy 29R dalgt hrs only. Ldg
fee. Flight Notification Service (ADCUS) avbl. NOTE: See Special Notices—Glider Operations Northwest of Tucson,
Arizona, U.S. Special Customs Requirement.
**WEATHER DATA SOURCES:** ASOS (520) 889-7236. **HIWAS** 116.0 TUS.LLWAS.
**COMMUNICATIONS: ATIS** 123.8 520-741-1177 **UNICOM** 122.95
 **TUCSON RCO** 122.2 (PRESCOTT RADIO)
 **MOUNT LEMMON RCO** 122.4 (PRESCOTT RADIO)
 Ⓡ**APP/DEP CON** 125.1 (Rwy 11 090°-285°) (Rwy 29 275°-065°) 119.4 (Rwy 11 286°-089°) (Rwy 29 066°-274°)
 **TOWER** 118.3 119.0 **GND CON** 124.4 **CLNC DEL** 126.65
**AIRSPACE: CLASS C** svc ctc **APP CON**
**RADIO AIDS TO NAVIGATION:** NOTAM FILE TUS.
 **(H) VORTACW** 116.0  TUS  Chan 107  N32°05.71´ W110°54.89´    301° 1.8 NM to fld. 2672/12E.  **HIWAS.**
 VORTAC unusable:
  050°-080° byd 30 NM blo 13,000´
  350°-020° byd 30 NM blo 13,000´
 DME unusable:
  155°-165° byd 35 NM blo 13,000´
 **ILS/DME** 111.7  I-TUS  Chan 54  Rwy 11L.  Localizer backcourse unusable byd 15 NM blo 7,200´. Backcourse
 unusable byd 10° right of course.

**VALLE** (See GRAND CANYON on page 39)

**Figure 348**

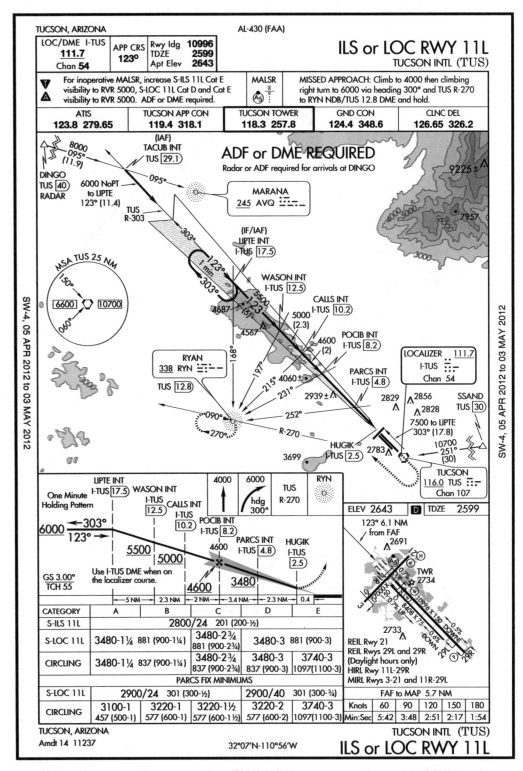

**Figure 349**

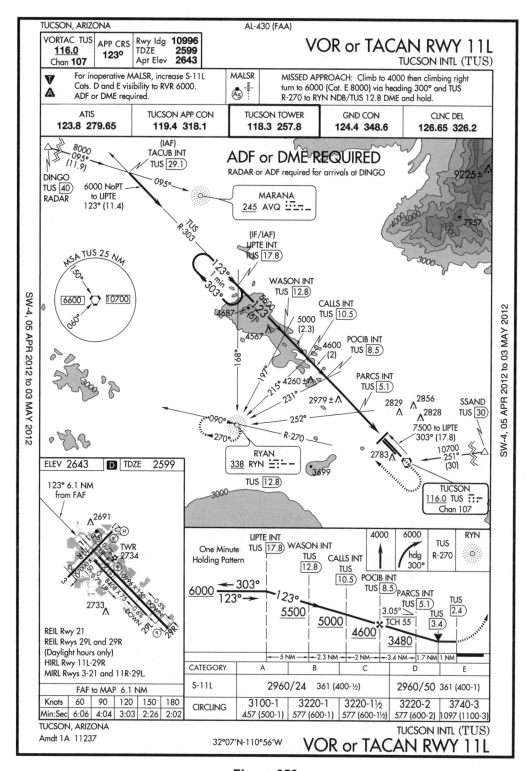

**Figure 350**

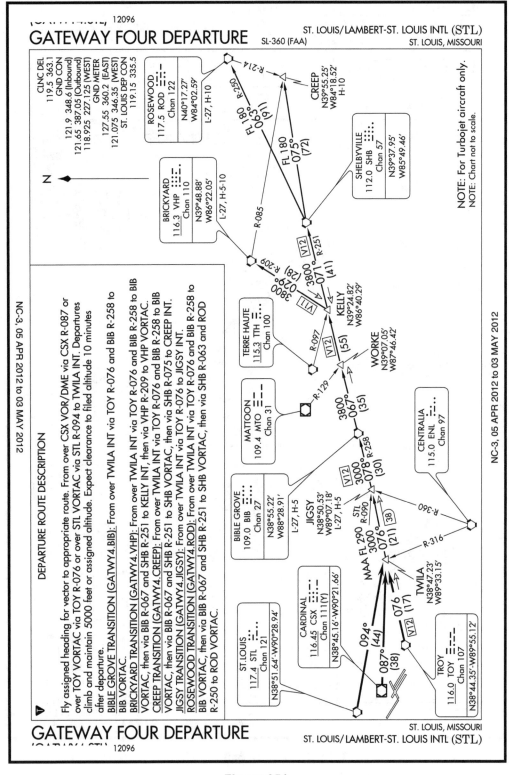

**Figure 351**

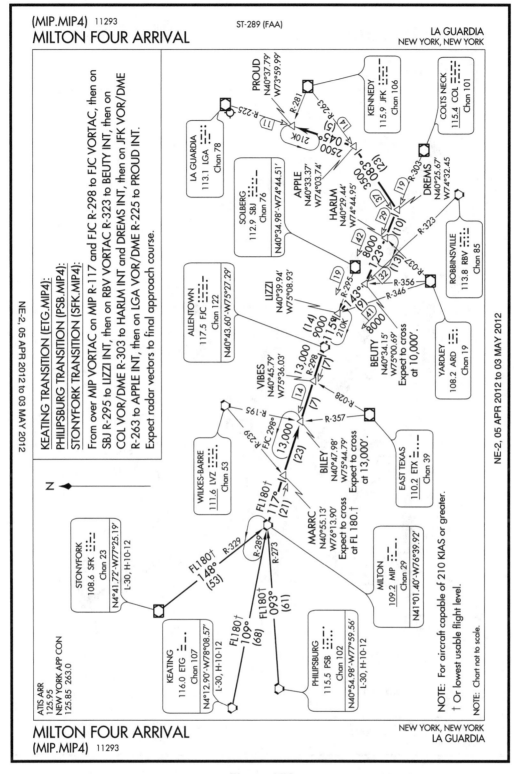

Figure 352

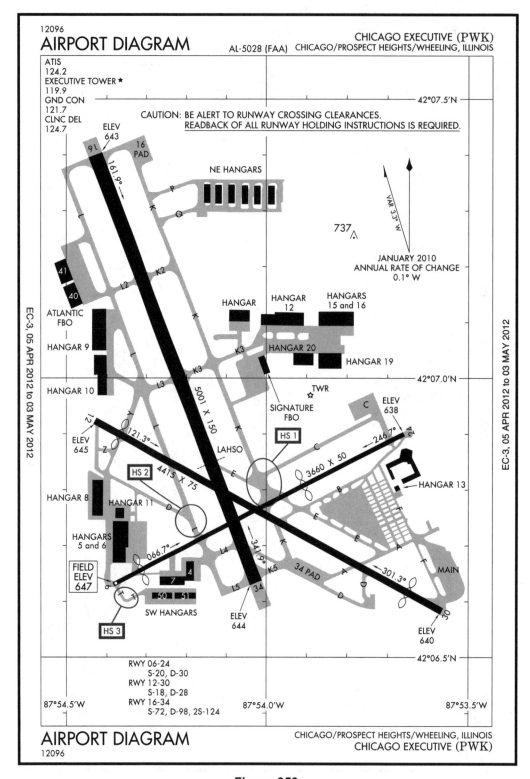

Figure 353

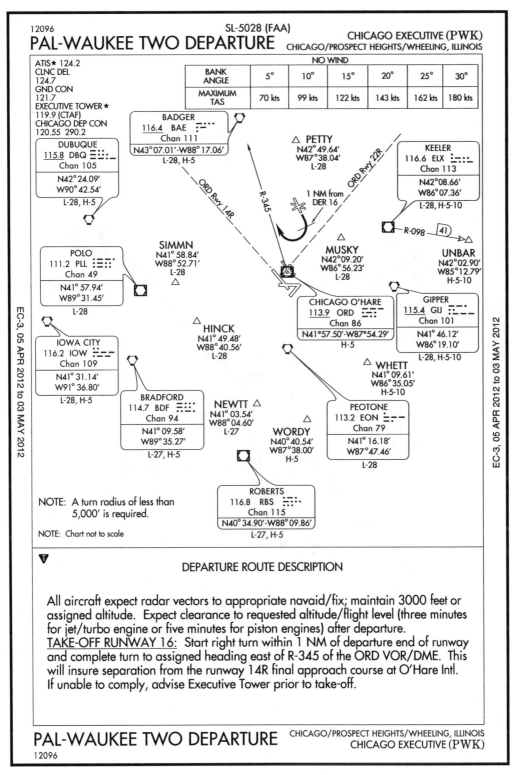

EC-3, 05 APR 2012 to 03 MAY 2012

**Figure 354**

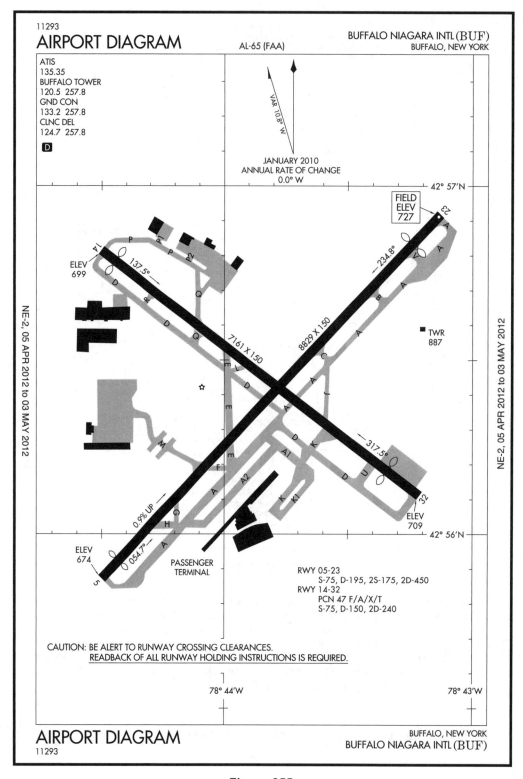

# AIRPORT DIAGRAM

AL-65 (FAA)

BUFFALO NIAGARA INTL (BUF)
BUFFALO, NEW YORK

ATIS
135.35
BUFFALO TOWER
120.5  257.8
GND CON
133.2  257.8
CLNC DEL
124.7  257.8

VAR 10.8° W

JANUARY 2010
ANNUAL RATE OF CHANGE
0.0° W

42° 57'N

FIELD
ELEV
727

ELEV
699

137.5°

234.8°

7161 X 150

8829 X 150

TWR
887

317.5°

ELEV
709

42° 56'N

ELEV
674

0.9% UP

054.7°

PASSENGER
TERMINAL

RWY 05-23
S-75, D-195, 2S-175, 2D-450
RWY 14-32
PCN 47 F/A/X/T
S-75, D-150, 2D-240

CAUTION: BE ALERT TO RUNWAY CROSSING CLEARANCES.
READBACK OF ALL RUNWAY HOLDING INSTRUCTIONS IS REQUIRED.

78° 44'W

78° 43'W

NE-2, 05 APR 2012 to 03 MAY 2012

NE-2, 05 APR 2012 to 03 MAY 2012

AIRPORT DIAGRAM

BUFFALO, NEW YORK
BUFFALO NIAGARA INTL (BUF)

**Figure 355**

**BUFFALO NIAGARA INTL**  (BUF)  5 E  UTC−5(−4DT)  N42°56.43′ W78°43.84′            **DETROIT**
727  B  S4  **FUEL** 100LL, JET A   OX 1, 2, 3, 4   LRA   Class I, ARFF Index D           **H−10I, 11B, L−31E**
NOTAM FILE BUF                                                                            **IAP, AD**
RWY 05−23: H8829X150 (ASPH−GRVD)   S−75, D−195, 2S−175,
   2D−450   HIRL CL
  RWY 05: MALSR. TDZL. Thld dsplcd 535′. Bldg.   0.9% up.
  RWY 23: ALSF2. TDZL. Thld dsplcd 725′. Tree.
RWY 14−32: H7161X150 (ASPH−GRVD)   S−75, D−150, 2D−240
   PCN 47 F/A/X/T   HIRL
  RWY 14: REIL. PAPI(P4L)—GA 3.0° TCH 45′. Thld dsplcd 320′. Tree.
  RWY 32: MALSR. REIL. PAPI(P4L)—GA 3.0° TCH 54′. Thld dsplcd
   720′. Sign.
RUNWAY DECLARED DISTANCE INFORMATION
  RWY 05: TORA−8827  TODA−8827  ASDA−8292  LDA−7757
  RWY 14: TORA−7161  TODA−7161  ASDA−6441  LDA−6121
  RWY 23: TORA−8827  TODA−8827  ASDA−8292  LDA−7567
  RWY 32: TORA−7161  TODA−7161  ASDA−6841  LDA−6121
AIRPORT REMARKS: Attended continuously. Heavy concentration of gulls,
  blackbirds, and starlings up to 5000 ft on and invof arpt. Deer on
  and invof arpt. Twy K1 clsd 0200−1300Z‡ daily. Twy A SW runup
  area/holding bay marked design group 3 acft (generally B727 or
  smaller), unavbl design group 4 (includes but not limited to B757,
  DC8). For fixed−base operator svcs ctc 131.75; for cargo svcs ctc 122.95. Rwy 23 ALSF2 unmonitored. Ldg fee.
  Flight Notification Service (ADCUS) available.
WEATHER DATA SOURCES: ASOS (716) 635−0532. WSP.
COMMUNICATIONS: D−ATIS 135.35
  RCO 122.6 122.2 122.1R (BUFFALO RADIO)
Ⓡ APP DEP/CON 126.15 (053°−233°) 126.5 (234°−052°)
  TOWER 120.5   GND CON 133.2   CLNC DEL 124.7   PRE−TAXI CLNC 124.7
AIRSPACE: CLASS C svc continuous, ctc APP CON
RADIO AIDS TO NAVIGATION: NOTAM FILE BUF.
  (H) VOR/DME 116.4   BUF   Chan 111   N42°55.74′ W78°38.78′   288° 3.8 NM to fld. 730/08W.
    VOR/DME unusable:
     036°−261° blo 11,000′                         276°−305° blo 6000′
     262°−275° blo 2300′
  KLUMP NDB (LOM) 231   BU   N43°00.02′ W78°39.05′   233° 5.0 NM to fld.
  PLAZZ NDB (LOM) 204   GB   N42°52.43′ W78°48.99′   053° 5.5 NM to fld.
  ILS 111.3   I−BUF   Rwy 23.   Class IE.   LOM KLUMP NDB. Glideslope unusable byd 5° rgt of course.
  ILS 108.5   I−GBI   Rwy 05.   Class IA.   LOM PLAZZ NDB.
  ILS/DME 109.95   I−BNQ   Chan 36(Y)   Rwy 32.

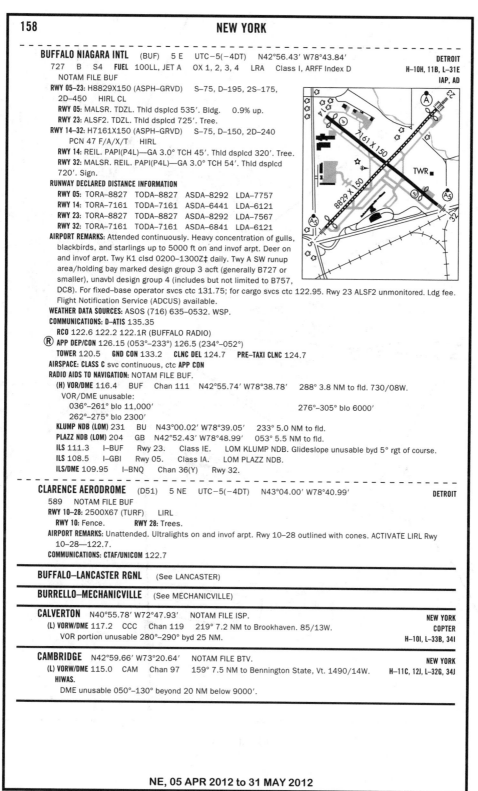

**CLARENCE AERODROME**  (D51)  5 NE  UTC−5(−4DT)  N43°04.00′ W78°40.99′            **DETROIT**
589   NOTAM FILE BUF
RWY 10−28: 2500X67 (TURF)   LIRL
  RWY 10: Fence.      RWY 28: Trees.
AIRPORT REMARKS: Unattended. Ultralights on and invof arpt. Rwy 10−28 outlined with cones. ACTIVATE LIRL Rwy
  10−28—122.7.
COMMUNICATIONS: CTAF/UNICOM 122.7

**BUFFALO−LANCASTER RGNL**   (See LANCASTER)

**BURRELLO−MECHANICVILLE**   (See MECHANICVILLE)

**CALVERTON**  N40°55.78′ W72°47.93′   NOTAM FILE ISP.                           **NEW YORK**
(L) VORW/DME 117.2   CCC   Chan 119   219° 7.2 NM to Brookhaven. 85/13W.       **COPTER**
  VOR portion unusable 280°−290° byd 25 NM.                                 **H−10I, L−33B, 34I**

**CAMBRIDGE**  N42°59.66′ W73°20.64′   NOTAM FILE BTV.                          **NEW YORK**
(L) VORW/DME 115.0   CAM   Chan 97   159° 7.5 NM to Bennington State, Vt. 1490/14W.   **H−11C, 12J, L−32G, 34J**
HIWAS.
  DME unusable 050°−130° beyond 20 NM below 9000′.

**NE, 05 APR 2012 to 31 MAY 2012**

**Figure 356**

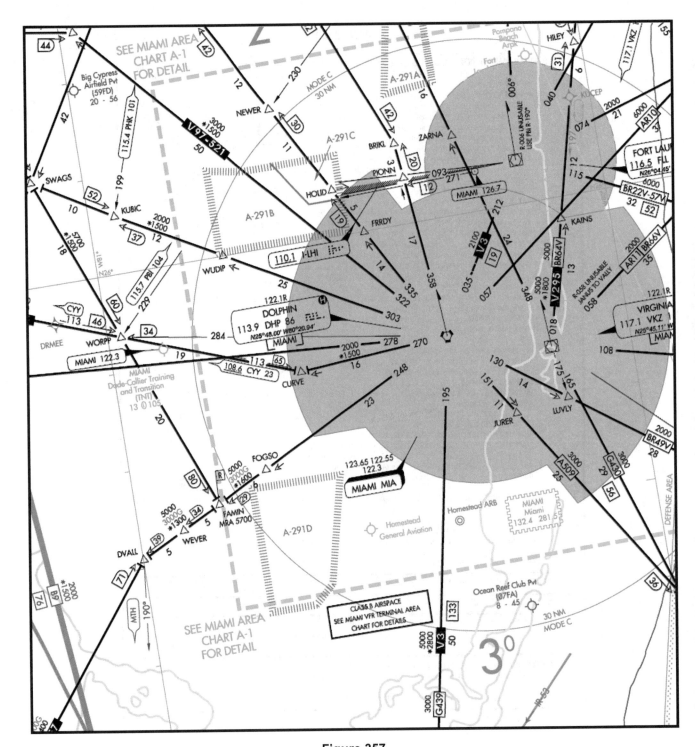

**Figure 357**

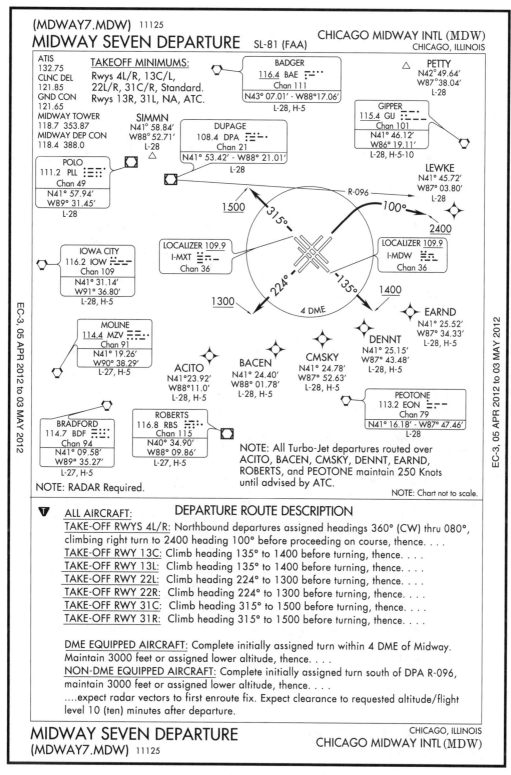

**(MDWAY7.MDW)** 11125
# MIDWAY SEVEN DEPARTURE  SL-81 (FAA)
CHICAGO MIDWAY INTL (MDW)
CHICAGO, ILLINOIS

ATIS
132.75
CLNC DEL
121.85
GND CON
121.65
MIDWAY TOWER
118.7 353.87
MIDWAY DEP CON
118.4 388.0

TAKEOFF MINIMUMS:
Rwys 4L/R, 13C/L,
22L/R, 31C/R, Standard.
Rwys 13R, 31L, NA, ATC.

BADGER
116.4 BAE
Chan 111
N43° 07.01' - W88°17.06'
L-28, H-5

PETTY
N42° 49.64'
W87° 38.04'
L-28

GIPPER
115.4 GIJ
Chan 101
N41° 46.12'
W86° 19.11'
L-28, H-5-10

SIMMN
N41° 58.84'
W88° 52.71'
L-28

DUPAGE
108.4 DPA
Chan 21
N41° 53.42' - W88° 21.01'
L-28

POLO
111.2 PLL
Chan 49
N41° 57.94'
W89° 31.45'
L-28

LEWKE
N41° 45.72'
W87° 03.80'
L-28

R-096
1500
315°
100°
2400

IOWA CITY
116.2 IOW
Chan 109
N41° 31.14'
W91° 36.80'
L-28, H-5

LOCALIZER 109.9
I-MXT
Chan 36

LOCALIZER 109.9
I-MDW
Chan 36

224°
135°
4 DME
1300
1400

EARND
N41° 25.52'
W87° 34.33'
L-28, H-5

MOLINE
114.4 MZV
Chan 91
N41° 19.26'
W90° 38.29'
L-27, H-5

DENNT
N41° 25.15'
W87° 43.48'
L-28, H-5

ACITO
N41°23.92'
W88°11.0'
L-28, H-5

BACEN
N41° 24.40'
W88° 01.78'
L-28, H-5

CMSKY
N41° 24.78'
W87° 52.63'
L-28, H-5

PEOTONE
113.2 EON
Chan 79
N41° 16.18' - W87° 47.46'
L-28

BRADFORD
114.7 BDF
Chan 94
N41° 09.58'
W89° 35.27'
L-27, H-5

ROBERTS
116.8 RBS
Chan 115
N40° 34.90'
W88° 09.86'
L-27, H-5

NOTE: All Turbo-Jet departures routed over
ACITO, BACEN, CMSKY, DENNT, EARND,
ROBERTS, and PEOTONE maintain 250 Knots
until advised by ATC.

NOTE: RADAR Required.

NOTE: Chart not to scale.

EC-3, 05 APR 2012 to 03 MAY 2012

EC-3, 05 APR 2012 to 03 MAY 2012

## DEPARTURE ROUTE DESCRIPTION

▼ ALL AIRCRAFT:
TAKE-OFF RWYS 4L/R: Northbound departures assigned headings 360° (CW) thru 080°,
climbing right turn to 2400 heading 100° before proceeding on course, thence. . . .
TAKE-OFF RWY 13C: Climb heading 135° to 1400 before turning, thence. . . .
TAKE-OFF RWY 13L: Climb heading 135° to 1400 before turning, thence. . . .
TAKE-OFF RWY 22L: Climb heading 224° to 1300 before turning, thence. . . .
TAKE-OFF RWY 22R: Climb heading 224° to 1300 before turning, thence. . . .
TAKE-OFF RWY 31C: Climb heading 315° to 1500 before turning, thence. . . .
TAKE-OFF RWY 31R: Climb heading 315° to 1500 before turning, thence. . . .

DME EQUIPPED AIRCRAFT: Complete initially assigned turn within 4 DME of Midway.
Maintain 3000 feet or assigned lower altitude, thence. . . .
NON-DME EQUIPPED AIRCRAFT: Complete initially assigned turn south of DPA R-096,
maintain 3000 feet or assigned lower altitude, thence. . . .
....expect radar vectors to first enroute fix. Expect clearance to requested altitude/flight
level 10 (ten) minutes after departure.

# MIDWAY SEVEN DEPARTURE
(MDWAY7.MDW) 11125
CHICAGO, ILLINOIS
CHICAGO MIDWAY INTL (MDW)

**Figure 358**

(MDWAY7.MDW) 08325

## MIDWAY SEVEN DEPARTURE   SL-81 (FAA)

CHICAGO MIDWAY INTL (MDW)
CHICAGO, ILLINOIS

### TAKEOFF OBSTACLE NOTES:

NOTE: RWY 4L, Fence 18 feet from DER, 257 feet left of centerline, 12 feet AGL/616 feet MSL. Vehicle plus road 143 feet from DER, 163 feet left of centerline, 16 feet AGL/620 feet MSL. Bldg 251 feet from DER, 217 feet left of centerline, 26 feet AGL/630 feet MSL. Sign 1,912 feet from DER, 330 feet left of centerline, 88 feet AGL/692 feet MSL. Multiple Lt poles and trees beginning 375 feet from DER, 98 feet right of centerline, up to 75 feet AGL/679 feet MSL.

NOTE: RWY 4R, LOC 300 feet from DER, on centerline, 10 feet AGL/614 feet MSL. Lt pole and multiple trees beginning 40 feet from DER, 369 feet left of centerline, up to 75 feet AGL/679 feet MSL. Blast fence 277 feet from DER, 45 feet left of centerline, 9 feet AGL/613 feet MSL. Tower 3,983 feet from DER, 1,142 feet left of centerline, 109 feet AGL/708 feet MSL. Multiple lt poles and trees beginning 96 feet from DER, 21 feet right of centerline, up to 53 feet AGL/657 feet MSL. Train beginning 1,483 feet from DER, 570 feet right of centerline, 48 feet AGL/654 feet MSL.

NOTE: RWY 13C, LOC 248 feet from DER, on centerline, 8 feet AGL/619 feet MSL. Bldg 101 feet from DER, 254 feet left of centerline, 14 feet AGL/625 feet MSL. Trees beginning 288 feet from DER, 459 feet left of centerline, up to 76 feet AGL/680 feet MSL. Trees beginning 109 feet from DER, 402 feet right of centerline, up to 86 feet AGL/700 feet MSL.

NOTE: RWY 13L, Multiple poles and trees beginning 362 feet from DER, 215 feet left of centerline, up to 71 feet AGL/675 feet MSL. Trees beginning 1,136 feet from DER, 54 feet right of centerline, up to 76 feet AGL/680 feet MSL.

NOTE: RWY 22L, Multiple poles and trees beginning 74 feet from DER, 375 feet left of centerline, up to 70 feet AGL/689 feet MSL. Multiple poles and trees beginning 465 feet from DER, 49 feet right of centerline, up to 60 feet AGL/679 feet MSL. Tank 4,100 feet from DER, 161 feet right of centerline, 109 feet AGL/728 feet MSL.

NOTE: RWY 22R, Multiple poles and trees beginning 575 feet from DER, 168 feet left of centerline, up to 58 feet AGL/677 feet MSL. Tank 4,100 feet from DER, 161 feet left of centerline, 109 feet AGL/728 feet MSL. Fence 198 feet from DER, 3 feet right of centerline, 12 feet AGL/630 feet MSL. Trees beginning 183 feet from DER, 65 feet right of centerline, up to 72 feet AGL/686 feet MSL.

NOTE: RWY 31C, LOC 239 feet from DER, on centerline, 10 feet AGL/617 feet MSL. Trees beginning 452 feet from DER, 454 feet left of centerline, up to 63 feet AGL/667 feet MSL. Spire 2,207 feet from DER, 699 feet left of centerline, 78 feet AGL/684 feet MSL. Multiple poles and trees beginning 142 feet from DER, 28 feet right of centerline, up to 73 feet AGL/672 feet MSL. DME 183 feet from DER, 309 feet right of centerline, 17 feet AGL/624 feet MSL. Sign 1,528 feet from DER, 270 feet right of centerline, 52 feet AGL/652 feet MSL. Tank 5,576 feet from DER, 1,430 feet right of centerline, 162 feet AGL/756 feet MSL.

NOTE: RWY 31R, Multiple poles and trees beginning 379 feet from DER, 49 feet left of centerline, up to 65 feet AGL/664 feet MSL. Pole and trees beginning 70 feet from DER, 50 feet right of centerline, up to 68 feet AGL/667 feet MSL.

EC-3, 05 APR 2012 to 03 MAY 2012

EC-3, 05 APR 2012 to 03 MAY 2012

## MIDWAY SEVEN DEPARTURE
(MDWAY7.MDW) 08325

CHICAGO, ILLINOIS
CHICAGO MIDWAY INTL (MDW)

**Figure 359**

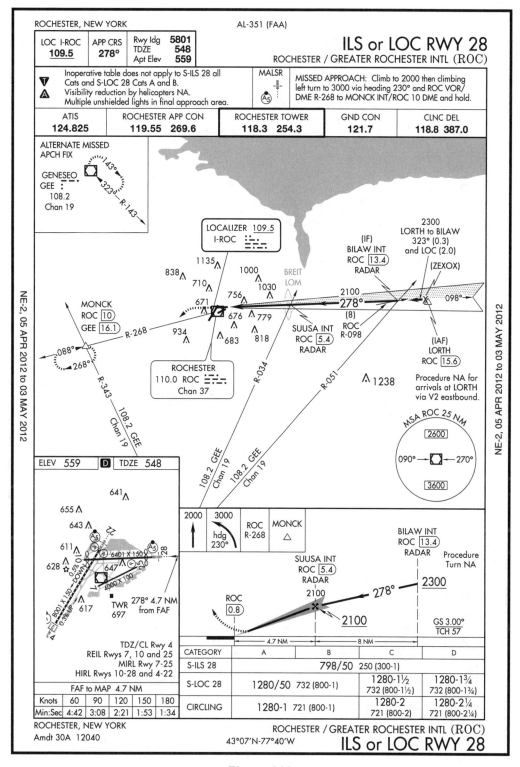

**Figure 360**

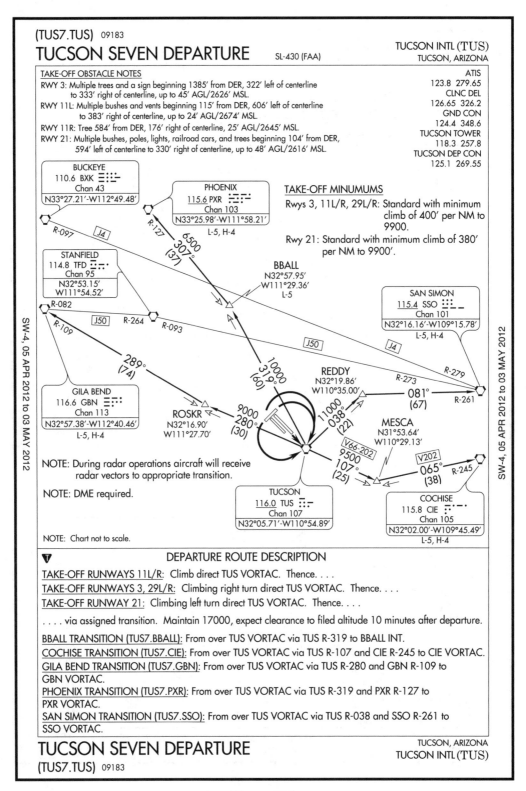

**(TUS7.TUS)** 09183

# TUCSON SEVEN DEPARTURE    SL-430 (FAA)

TUCSON INTL (TUS)
TUCSON, ARIZONA

TAKE-OFF OBSTACLE NOTES

RWY 3: Multiple trees and a sign beginning 1385' from DER, 322' left of centerline to 333' right of centerline, up to 45' AGL/2626' MSL.

RWY 11L: Multiple bushes and vents beginning 115' from DER, 606' left of centerline to 383' right of centerline, up to 24' AGL/2674' MSL.

RWY 11R: Tree 584' from DER, 176' right of centerline, 25' AGL/2645' MSL.

RWY 21: Multiple bushes, poles, lights, railroad cars, and trees beginning 104' from DER, 594' left of centerline to 330' right of centerline, up to 48' AGL/2616' MSL.

ATIS
123.8 279.65
CLNC DEL
126.65 326.2
GND CON
124.4 348.6
TUCSON TOWER
118.3 257.8
TUCSON DEP CON
125.1 269.55

TAKE-OFF MINUMUMS

Rwys 3, 11L/R, 29L/R: Standard with minimum climb of 400' per NM to 9900.

Rwy 21: Standard with minimum climb of 380' per NM to 9900'.

NOTE: During radar operations aircraft will receive radar vectors to appropriate transition.

NOTE: DME required.

NOTE: Chart not to scale.

SW-4, 05 APR 2012 to 03 MAY 2012

## DEPARTURE ROUTE DESCRIPTION

TAKE-OFF RUNWAYS 11L/R: Climb direct TUS VORTAC. Thence. . . .

TAKE-OFF RUNWAYS 3, 29L/R: Climbing right turn direct TUS VORTAC. Thence. . . .

TAKE-OFF RUNWAY 21: Climbing left turn direct TUS VORTAC. Thence. . . .

. . . . via assigned transition. Maintain 17000, expect clearance to filed altitude 10 minutes after departure.

BBALL TRANSITION (TUS7.BBALL): From over TUS VORTAC via TUS R-319 to BBALL INT.

COCHISE TRANSITION (TUS7.CIE): From over TUS VORTAC via TUS R-107 and CIE R-245 to CIE VORTAC.

GILA BEND TRANSITION (TUS7.GBN): From over TUS VORTAC via TUS R-280 and GBN R-109 to GBN VORTAC.

PHOENIX TRANSITION (TUS7.PXR): From over TUS VORTAC via TUS R-319 and PXR R-127 to PXR VORTAC.

SAN SIMON TRANSITION (TUS7.SSO): From over TUS VORTAC via TUS R-038 and SSO R-261 to SSO VORTAC.

# TUCSON SEVEN DEPARTURE
TUCSON, ARIZONA
TUCSON INTL (TUS)

(TUS7.TUS) 09183

**Figure 361**

L12

## ▼ TAKE-OFF MINIMUMS AND (OBSTACLE) DEPARTURE PROCEDURES ▼

12096

### TONOPAH TEST RANGE (KTNX)
TONOPAH, NV. . . . . . . . . AMDT 1 12096
DEPARTURE PROCEDURE: **Rwy 14:** 1000-3 with minimum climb of 320 ft/NM to 10,700 or 2700-3 for Climb in Visual Conditions. Climb on a heading between 325° CW to 155° from departure end of runway or Climb in Visual Conditions to cross KZ-KTNX airport at or above 8100 MSL before proceeding on course. **Rwy 32:** 1000-3 with minimum climb of 260 ft/NM to 5900 or 2700-3 for Climb in Visual Conditions. Climb on a heading between 295° CW to 005° from departure end of runway or Climb in Visual Conditions to cross KZ-KTNX airport at or above 8100 MSL before proceeding on course.
TAKE-OFF OBSTACLES: **Rwy 14,** Terrain, 5582' MSL, 1204' from DER, 823' right of centerline. Terrain, 5565' MSL, 63' from DER, 517' right of centerline. Terrain, 5564' MSL, 46' from DER, 480' right of centerline. Terrain, 5561' MSL, 0' from DER, 353' right of centerline. Terrain, 5558' MSL, 62' from DER, 200' right of centerline. Terrain, 5561' MSL, 14' from DER, 292' right of centerline. Terrain, 5561' MSL, 0' from DER, 287' right of centerline. Terrain, 5559' MSL, 0' from DER, 222' right of centerline. Surveyed terrain, 5560' MSL, 215' from DER, 427' right of centerline. **Rwy 32,** Terrain, 5476' MSL, 0' from DER, 500' left of centerline. Terrain, 5476' MSL, 19' from DER, 465' left of centerline. Terrain, 5476' MSL, 110' from DER, 529' left of centerline.

### TOOELE, UT
BOLINDER FIELD-TOOELE VALLEY
TAKE-OFF MINIMUMS: **Rwy 17,** std. with a min. climb of 490' per NM to 11000. **Rwy 35,** std. with a min. climb of 360' per NM to 9000.
DEPARTURE PROCEDURE: Use STACO DEPARTURE.
NOTE: **Rwy 17,** tree 794' from departure end of runway, 277' right of centerline, 35' AGL/4380' MSL. Tree 967' from departure end of runway, 432' right of centerline, 35' AGL/4394' MSL. Tree 1023' from departure end of runway, 313' right of centerline, 35' AGL/4395' MSL.

### TUCSON, AZ
MARANA RGNL
TAKE-OFF MINIMUMS: **Rwys 3, 12,** N/A-Obstacles
DEPARTURE PROCEDURE: **Rwy 21,** climb to 6500 via heading 360° and TUS R-308 to TOTEC Int/TUS 57 DME, then as filed. **Rwy 30,** climb to 6500 via heading 303° intercept TUS R-308 above 3500, to TOTEC INT/TUS 57 DME, then as filed.
NOTE: **Rwy 21,** road 192' from departure end of runway, 527' left of centerline 15' AGL/2034' MSL.

RYAN FIELD (RYN)
AMDT 3 10210 (FAA)
TAKE-OFF MINIMUMS: **Rwys 6L, 15, 24R, 33,** NA, ATC.
DEPARTURE PROCEDURE: **Rwys 6R, 24L,** use ALMON DEPARTURE.

### TUCSON, AZ (CON'T)
TUCSON INTL (TUS)
AMDT 4A 08241 (FAA)
TAKE-OFF MINIMUMS: **Rwy 3,** 300-1¾ or std. w/min. climb of 228' per NM to 3000.
DEPARTURE PROCEDURE: **Rwys 3, 29L, 29R,** climbing right turn direct to TUS VORTAC. **Rwys 11L, 11R** climb via runway heading to 4000 then climbing left turn direct TUS VORTAC. **Rwy 21,** climbing left turn direct to TUS VORTAC. **All aircraft** continue climbing in holding pattern (NW, right turns, 128° inbound) to depart TUS VORTAC at or above 9000.
NOTE: **Rwy 3,** tower 9215' from departure end of runway, 1689' left of centerline, 246' AGL/2831' MSL.

### VERNAL, UT
VERNAL RGNL
TAKE-OFF MINIMUMS: **Rwy 16,** 1500-2 or std with a min. climb of 250' per NM to 7000'. **Rwy 25,** 1500-2 or std. with a min. climb of 390' per NM to 7000. **Rwy 34,** 1600-2 pr std. with a min. climb of 330' per NM to 7000'.
DEPARTURE PROCEDURE: **Rwys 7, 34,** turn right. **Rwys 16, 25,** turn left. **All aircraft** climb direct VEL. Aircraft departing V391 S-bound climb on course. All others climb in holding pattern (SE, right turns, 322° inbound). Aircraft SW-bound V208 depart VEL at or above 8400', all others depart VEL at or above 9500'. Continue climb on course to MEA or assigned altitude.

### WENDOVER, UT
WENDOVER
TAKE-OFF MINIMUMS: **Rwy 26,** standard with a min. climb of 300' per NM to 7000. **Rwy 30,** NA.
DEPARTURE PROCEDURE: **Rwys 8, 12, 26,** climbing left turn direct BVL VORTAC. Aircraft departing BVL VORTAC R-330 CW R-150 climb on course. All others continue climb in BVL VORTAC holding pattern (Hold NE right turns, 247° inbound) to cross at or above 7400, then climb on course.

### WILLCOX, AZ
COCHISE COUNTY
DEPARTURE PROCEDURE: **Rwy 3,** turn right. **Rwy 21,** turn left. **All aircraft** climb direct CIE VORTAC.

### WINDOW ROCK, AZ
WINDOW ROCK
TAKE-OFF MINIMUMS: **Rwy 2,** 700-2 or std. with a min. climb of 500' per NM to 8000. **Rwy 20,** 600-2 or std. with a min. climb of 260' per NM to 8200.
DEPARTURE PROCEDURE: **Rwy 2,** turn right. **Rwy 20,** turn left direct to GUP VORTAC before proceeding on course.
NOTE: **Rwy 2,** terrain 3832' from departure end of runway, 1025' right of centerline, 6926' MSL. Poles 5220' from departure end of runway, 245' right of centerline, 180' AGL/6922' MSL. Tower 7067' from departure end of runway, 3072' left of centerline, 71' AGL/7316' MSL. Terrain 7449' from departure end of runway, 1612' left of centerline, 6991' MSL. Terrain 8776' from departure end of runway, 1851' left of centerline, 7109' MSL. Tree 9665' from departure end of runway, 1326' right of centerline, 7340' MSL. Tree 11326' from departure end of runway, 355' left of centerline, 7351' MSL. **Rwy 20,** trees 1018' from departure end of runway, 620' left of centerline, 30' AGL/6768' MSL.

05 APR 2012 to 03 MAY 2012

05 APR 2012 to 03 MAY 2012

12096

## ▼ TAKE-OFF MINIMUMS AND (OBSTACLE) DEPARTURE PROCEDURES ▼

L12                                                                SW-4

Figure 362

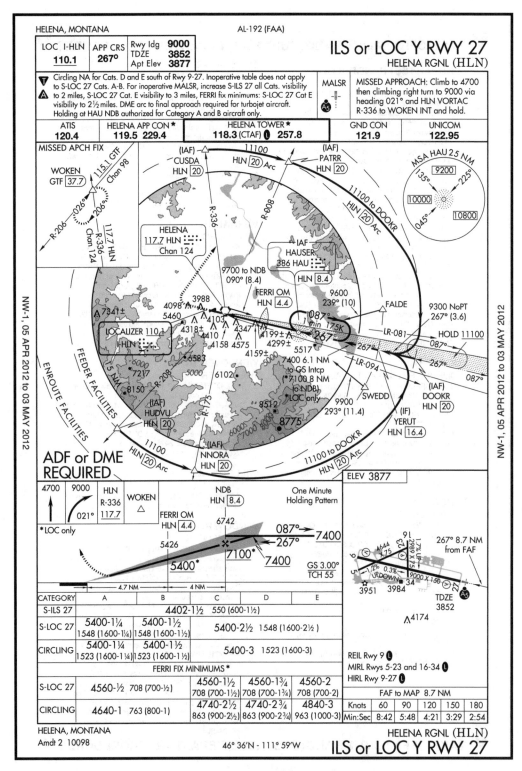

**Figure 363**

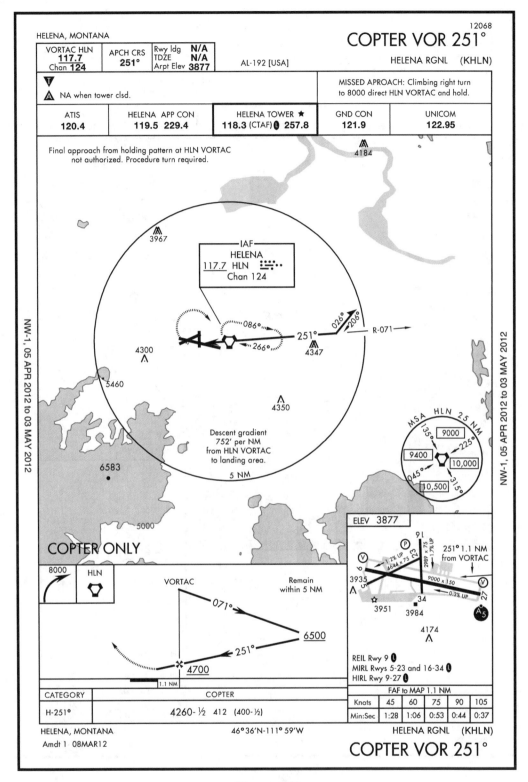

**Figure 364**

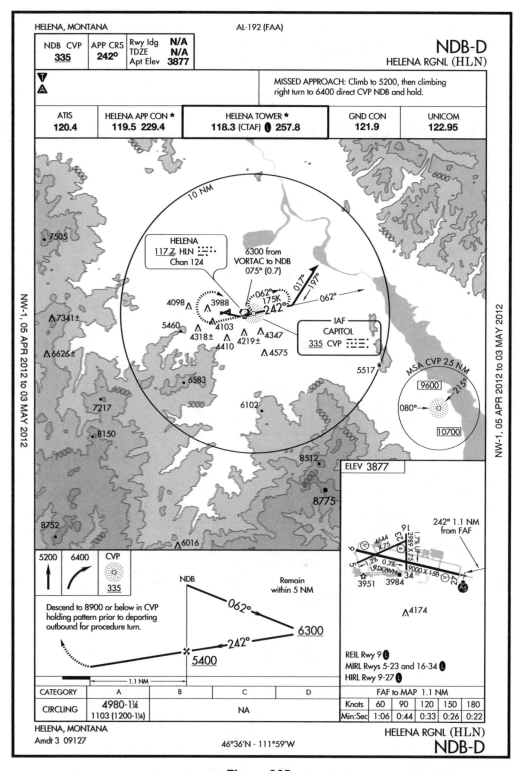

HELENA, MONTANA                          AL-192 (FAA)

| NDB CVP | APP CRS | Rwy Idg | N/A | NDB-D |
| 335 | 242° | TDZE | N/A | HELENA RGNL (HLN) |
| | | Apt Elev | 3877 | |

MISSED APPROACH: Climb to 5200, then climbing right turn to 6400 direct CVP NDB and hold.

| ATIS | HELENA APP CON ★ | HELENA TOWER ★ | GND CON | UNICOM |
| 120.4 | 119.5  229.4 | 118.3 (CTAF) ● 257.8 | 121.9 | 122.95 |

HELENA, MONTANA
Amdt 3  09127                          46°36'N - 111°59'W

HELENA RGNL (HLN)
NDB-D

**Figure 365**

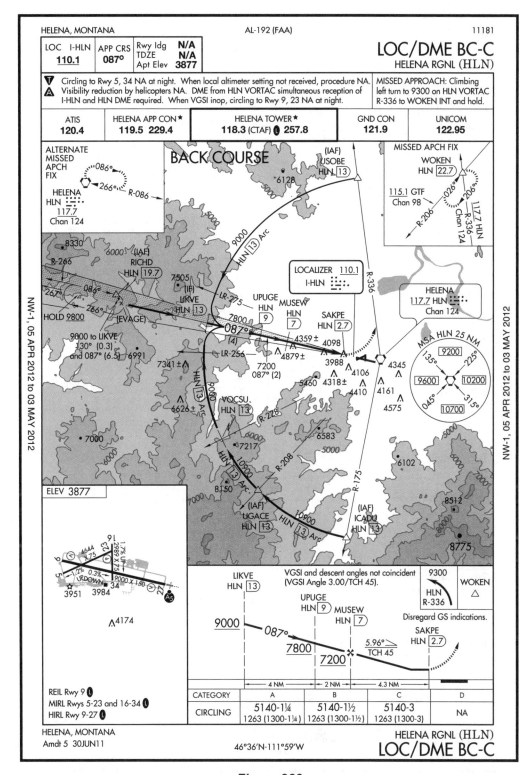

Figure 366

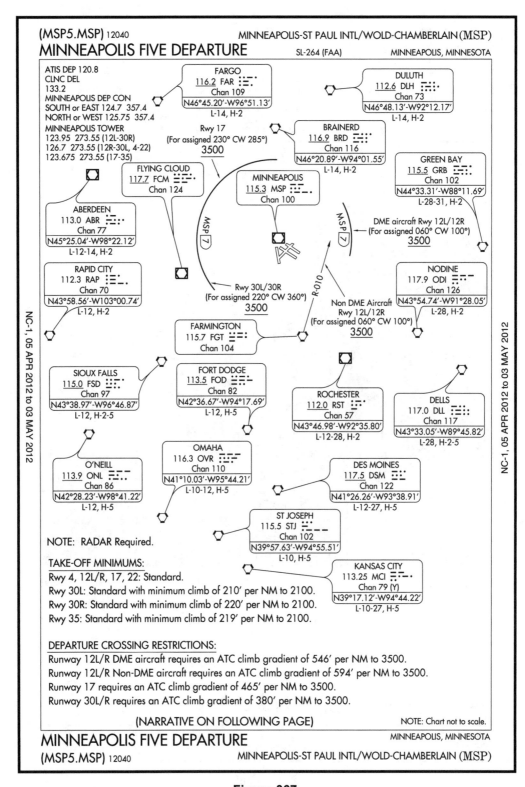

**(MSP5.MSP)** 12040     MINNEAPOLIS-ST PAUL INTL/WOLD-CHAMBERLAIN (MSP)

# MINNEAPOLIS FIVE DEPARTURE
SL-264 (FAA)      MINNEAPOLIS, MINNESOTA

ATIS DEP 120.8
CLNC DEL
133.2
MINNEAPOLIS DEP CON
SOUTH or EAST 124.7 357.4
NORTH or WEST 125.75 357.4
MINNEAPOLIS TOWER
123.95 273.55 (12L-30R)
126.7 273.55 (12R-30L, 4-22)
123.675 273.55 (17-35)

FARGO
116.2 FAR
Chan 109
N46°45.20'-W96°51.13'
L-14, H-2

DULUTH
112.6 DLH
Chan 73
N46°48.13'-W92°12.17'
L-14, H-2

BRAINERD
116.9 BRD
Chan 116
N46°20.89'-W94°01.55'
L-14, H-2

GREEN BAY
115.5 GRB
Chan 102
N44°33.31'-W88°11.69'
L-28-31, H-2

Rwy 17
(For assigned 230° CW 285°)
3500

FLYING CLOUD
117.7 FCM
Chan 124

MINNEAPOLIS
115.3 MSP
Chan 100

MSP 7

MSP 7

DME aircraft Rwy 12L/12R
(For assigned 060° CW 100°)
3500

ABERDEEN
113.0 ABR
Chan 77
N45°25.04'-W98°22.12'
L-12-14, H-2

RAPID CITY
112.3 RAP
Chan 70
N43°58.56'-W103°00.74'
L-12, H-2

Rwy 30L/30R
(For assigned 220° CW 360°)
3500

R-010

NODINE
117.9 ODI
Chan 126
N43°54.74'-W91°28.05'
L-28, H-2

Non DME Aircraft
Rwy 12L/12R
(For assigned 060° CW 100°)
3500

FARMINGTON
115.7 FGT
Chan 104

SIOUX FALLS
115.0 FSD
Chan 97
N43°38.97'-W96°46.87'
L-12, H-2-5

FORT DODGE
113.5 FOD
Chan 82
N42°36.67'-W94°17.69'
L-12, H-5

ROCHESTER
112.0 RST
Chan 57
N43°46.98'-W92°35.80'
L-12-28, H-2

DELLS
117.0 DLL
Chan 117
N43°33.05'-W89°45.82'
L-28, H-2-5

OMAHA
116.3 OVR
Chan 110
N41°10.03'-W95°44.21'
L-10-12, H-5

DES MOINES
117.5 DSM
Chan 122
N41°26.26'-W93°38.91'
L-12-27, H-5

O'NEILL
113.9 ONL
Chan 86
N42°28.23'-W98°41.22'
L-12, H-5

ST JOSEPH
115.5 STJ
Chan 102
N39°57.63'-W94°55.51'
L-10, H-5

KANSAS CITY
113.25 MCI
Chan 79 (Y)
N39°17.12'-W94°44.22'
L-10-27, H-5

NOTE: RADAR Required.

TAKE-OFF MINIMUMS:
Rwy 4, 12L/R, 17, 22: Standard.
Rwy 30L: Standard with minimum climb of 210' per NM to 2100.
Rwy 30R: Standard with minimum climb of 220' per NM to 2100.
Rwy 35: Standard with minimum climb of 219' per NM to 2100.

DEPARTURE CROSSING RESTRICTIONS:
Runway 12L/R DME aircraft requires an ATC climb gradient of 546' per NM to 3500.
Runway 12L/R Non-DME aircraft requires an ATC climb gradient of 594' per NM to 3500.
Runway 17 requires an ATC climb gradient of 465' per NM to 3500.
Runway 30L/R requires an ATC climb gradient of 380' per NM to 3500.

(NARRATIVE ON FOLLOWING PAGE)     NOTE: Chart not to scale.

# MINNEAPOLIS FIVE DEPARTURE
MINNEAPOLIS, MINNESOTA
**(MSP5.MSP)** 12040     MINNEAPOLIS-ST PAUL INTL/WOLD-CHAMBERLAIN (MSP)

NC-1, 05 APR 2012 to 03 MAY 2012

NC-1, 05 APR 2012 to 03 MAY 2012

**Figure 367**

(MSP5.MSP) 11349      MINNEAPOLIS-ST PAUL INTL/WOLD-CHAMBERLAIN (MSP)

## MINNEAPOLIS FIVE DEPARTURE

SL-264 (FAA)      MINNEAPOLIS, MINNESOTA

▼

### DEPARTURE ROUTE DESCRIPTION

<u>ALL RUNWAYS:</u> Fly assigned heading for radar vectors to join filed/assigned route. Turbojet aircraft maintain 7000 or lower assigned altitude, all other aircraft maintain 5000 or lower assigned altitude. Expect clearance to assigned altitude/flight level 10 (ten) minutes after departure.

<u>DME EQUIPPED AIRCRAFT RWY 12L/12R DEPARTURES:</u> For assigned heading from 060° clockwise to 100°, cross MSP 7 DME at or above 3500, maintain assigned altitude. If unable to comply advise ATC as soon as possible prior to departure.

<u>NON-DME EQUIPPED AIRCRAFT RWY 12L/12R DEPARTURES:</u> For assigned headings from 060° clockwise to 100°, cross FGT R-010 at or above 3500, maintain assigned altitude. If unable to comply, advise ATC as soon as possible prior to departure.

<u>TAKE-OFF RWY 17 DEPARTURES:</u> For assigned headings from 230° clockwise to 285° cross MSP 7 DME at or above 3500, maintain assigned altitude. If unable to comply, advise ATC as soon as possible prior to departure.

<u>TAKE-OFF RWYS 30L/30R DEPARTURES:</u> For assigned headings from 220° clockwise to 360° cross MSP 7 DME at or above 3500, maintain assigned altitude. If unable to comply, advise ATC as soon as possible prior to departure.

<u>TAKE-OFF OBSTACLE NOTES:</u>

RWY 04: Multiple trees beginning 800' from DER, 264' left of centerline, up to 75' AGL/921' MSL.
Rod on building 2528' from DER, 1175' left of centerline, 78' AGL/922' MSL.
Fence 803' from DER, 585' left of centerline, 15' AGL/860' MSL.
Ant on OL building 456' from DER, 319' left of centerline, 13' AGL/850' MSL.
LT poles 1932' from DER, 718' left of centerline, 45' AGL/885' MSL.
Stack 4535' from DER, 481' left of centerline, 139' AGL/949' MSL.

RWY 12R: Multiple trees beginning 1477' from DER, 407' left of centerline, up to 86' AGL/851' MSL.
Multiple trees beginning 1426' from DER, 124' right of centerline, up to 111' AGL/847' MSL.
LT pole 1408' from DER, 746' right of centerline, 85' AGL/843' MSL.
Radar reflector 983' from DER, 32' left of centerline, 15' AGL/829' MSL.
Pipe on bldg, 826' from DER, 576' left of centerline, 10' AGL/825' MSL.
OL on LOC 766' from DER, on centerline, 7' AGL/821' MSL.

RWY 17: Antenna 1272' from DER, 562' right of centerline, 57' AGL/891' MSL.
Pole 409' from DER, 530' right of centerline, 29' AGL/866' MSL.
Wind direction indicator on bldg 2619' from DER, 881' left of centerline, 97' AGL/918' MSL.
Bldg 2619' from DER, 859' left of centerline, 84' AGL/905' MSL.
LT 1176' from DER, 291' right of centerline, 11' AGL/875' MSL.
Tree 2619' from DER, on centerline, 79' AGL/900' MSL.

RWY 22: Tree 2906' from DER, 833' right of centerline, 94' AGL/934' MSL.
Hopper 1717' from DER, 456' left of centerline, 48' AGL/888' MSL.

RWY 30L: Multiple trees beginning 1113' from DER, 701' left of centerline, up to 80' AGL/919' MSL.
Tree 1230' from DER, 633' right of centerline, 30' AGL/877' MSL.
Ground 28' from DER, 490' right of centerline, 0' AGL/844' MSL.

RWY 30R: Bldg 1056' from DER, 198' left of centerline, 13' AGL/853' MSL.
Multiple trees beginning 3010' from DER, 334' left of centerline, up to 94' AGL/940' MSL.
LT pole 1849' from DER, 698' right of centerline, 17' AGL/871' MSL.
Fence 1327' from DER, 667' right of centerline, 8' AGL/857' MSL.
Tree 3703' from DER, 350' right of centerline, 67' AGL/914' MSL.
Rod on pole 3143' from DER, 47' right of centerline, 38' AGL/898' MSL.

RWY 35: Tree 175' from DER, 398' right of centerline, 73' AGL/883' MSL.
Multiple trees beginning 1989' from DER, 351' left of centerline, up to 65' AGL/902' MSL.
Multiple buildings beginning 5.5 NM from DER, 1787' left of centerline, up to 811' AGL/1743' MSL.

NC-1, 05 APR 2012 to 03 MAY 2012

NC-1, 05 APR 2012 to 03 MAY 2012

## MINNEAPOLIS FIVE DEPARTURE

MINNEAPOLIS, MINNESOTA

(MSP5.MSP) 11349      MINNEAPOLIS-ST PAUL INTL/WOLD-CHAMBERLAIN (MSP)

**Figure 368**

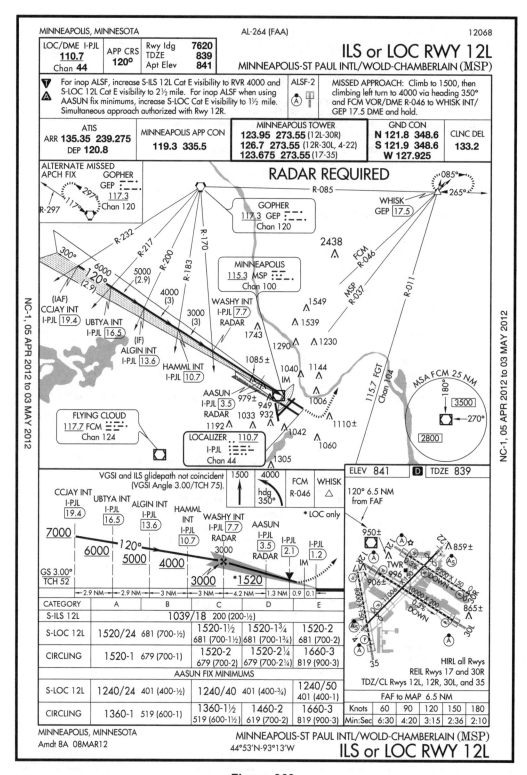

Figure 369

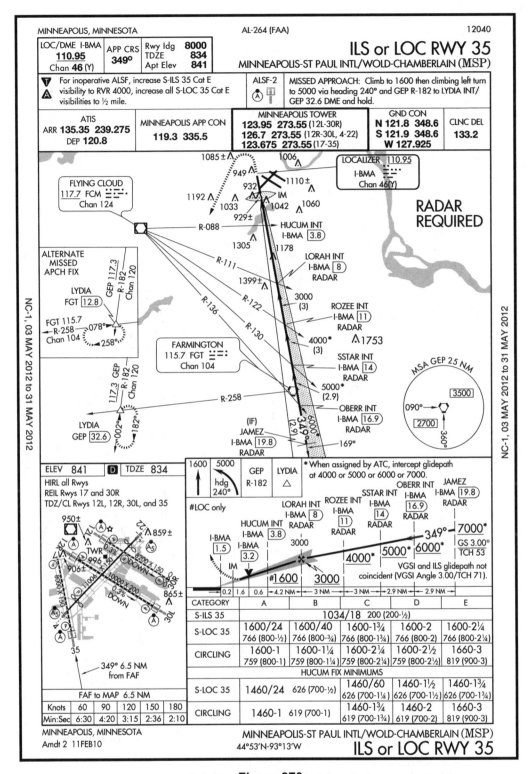

**Figure 370**

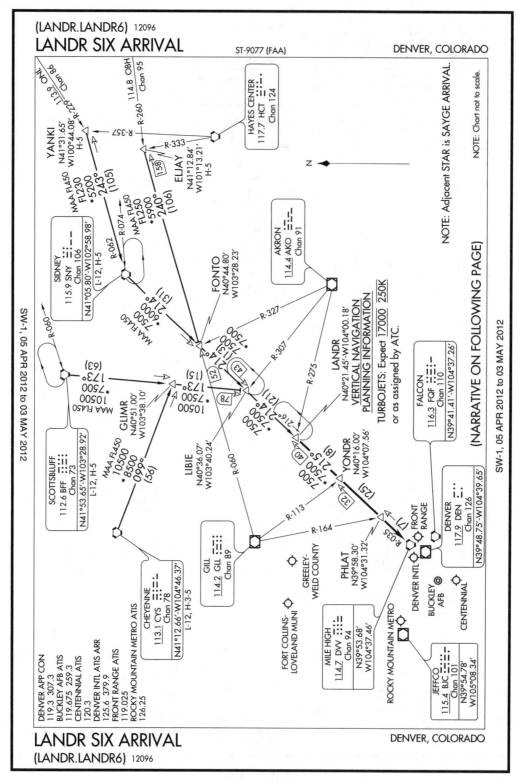

**Figure 371**

(LANDR.LANDR6) 12096
# LANDR SIX ARRIVAL                    ST-9077 (FAA)                    DENVER, COLORADO

## ARRIVAL ROUTE DESCRIPTION

<u>CHEYENNE TRANSITION (CYS.LANDR6):</u> From over CYS VORTAC via CYS R-099 and BFF R-173 to LIBIE INT; then via SNY R-214 and DVV R-035 to LANDR INT. Thence . . . .

<u>ELJAY TRANSITION (ELJAY.LANDR6):</u> From over ELJAY INT via GLL R-060 to FONTO INT, then via SNY R-214 and DVV R-035 to LANDR INT. Thence . . . .

<u>SCOTTSBLUFF TRANSITION (BFF.LANDR6):</u> From over BFF VORTAC via BFF R-173 to LIBIE INT; then via SNY R-214 and DVV R-035 to LANDR INT. Thence . . . .

<u>SIDNEY TRANSITION (SNY.LANDR6):</u> From over SNY VORTAC via SNY R-214 to FONTO INT, then via SNY R-214 and DVV R-035 to LANDR INT. Thence . . . .

<u>YANKI TRANSITION (YANKI.LANDR6):</u> From over YANKI INT via SNY R-062 to SNY VORTAC; then via SNY R-214 and DVV R-035 to LANDR INT. Thence . . . .

. . . . From over LANDR INT via DVV R-035 to DVV VORTAC. Expect RADAR vectors to the final approach course at or before DVV VORTAC.

SW-1, 05 APR 2012 to 03 MAY 2012

SW-1, 05 APR 2012 to 03 MAY 2012

# LANDR SIX ARRIVAL                                              DENVER, COLORADO
(LANDR.LANDR6) 12096

**Figure 372**

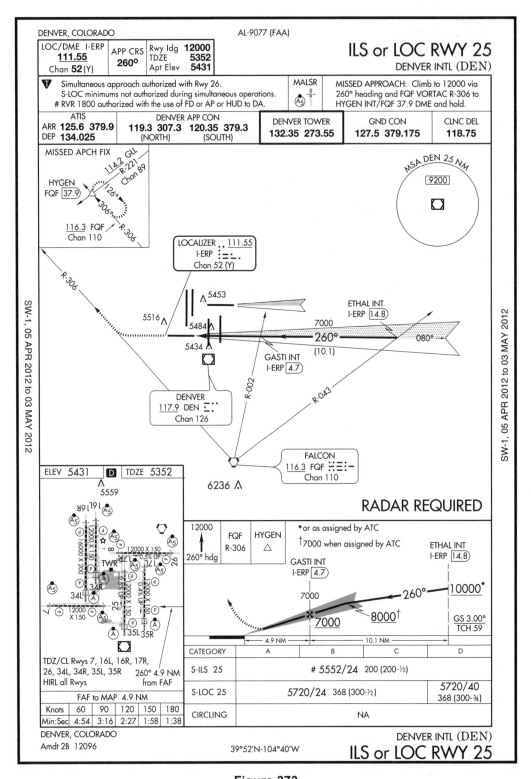

**Figure 373**

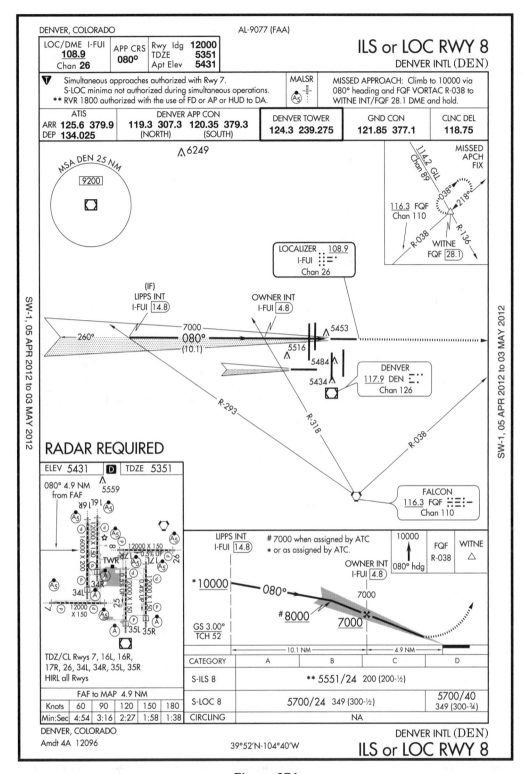

**Figure 374**

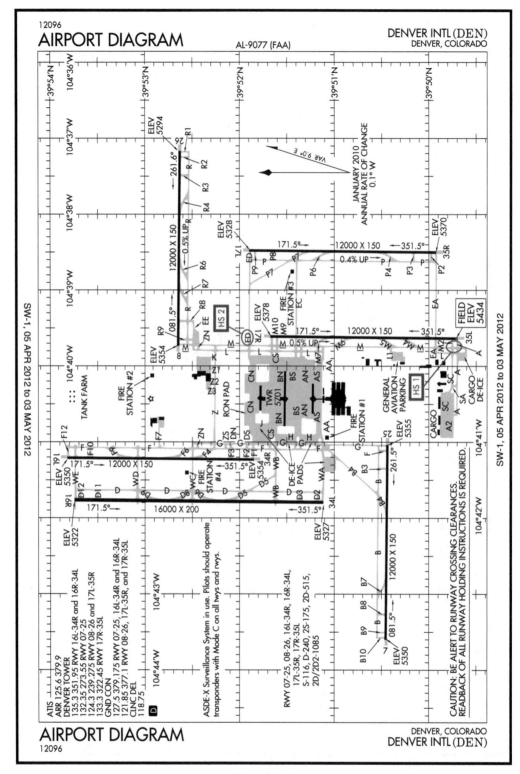

**Figure 375**

---

**DENVER INTL** (DEN) 16 NE UTC–7(–6DT) N39°51.70′ W104°40.39′      **DENVER**
5434 B S4 **FUEL** 100, 100LL, JET A, MOGAS OX 1, 3 Class I, ARFF Index E    H–3F, 5A, L–10F, A
NOTAM FILE DEN      IAP, AD

**RWY 16R–34L:** H16000X200 (CONC–GRVD) S–116, D–240, 2S–175,
   2D–515, 2D/2D2–1085 PCN 92 R/B/W/T HIRL CL
  **RWY 16R:** MALSR. TDZL. PAPI(P4R)—GA 3.0° TCH 55′.
  **RWY 34L:** ALSF2. TDZL. PAPI(P4L)—GA 3.0° TCH 50′.
**RWY 07–25:** H12000X150 (CONC–GRVD) S–116, D–240, 2S–175,
   2D–515, 2D/2D2–1085 PCN 92 R/B/W/T HIRL CL
  **RWY 07:** MALSR. TDZL. PAPI(P4R)—GA 3.0° TCH 55′.
  **RWY 25:** PAPI(P4L)—GA 3.0° TCH 59′.
**RWY 08–26:** H12000X150 (CONC–GRVD) S–116, D–240, 2S–175,
   2D–515, 2D/2D2–1085 PCN 92 R/B/W/T HIRL CL
  **RWY 08:** MALSR. PAPI(P4L)—GA 3.0° TCH 52′.
  **RWY 26:** MALSR. TDZL. PAPI(P4L)—GA 3.0° TCH 55′. 0.5% up.
**RWY 16L–34R:** H12000X150 (CONC–GRVD) S–116, D–240, 2S–175,
   2D–515, 2D/2D2–1085 PCN 92 R/B/W/T HIRL CL
  **RWY 16L:** MALSR. TDZL. PAPI(P4L)—GA 3.0° TCH 60′.
  **RWY 34R:** ALSF2. TDZL. PAPI(P4L)—GA 3.0° TCH 59′.
**RWY 17L–35R:** H12000X150 (CONC–GRVD) S–116, D–240, 2S–175,
   2D–515, 2D/2D2–1085 PCN 92 R/B/W/T HIRL CL
  **RWY 17L:** MALSR. PAPI(P4L)—GA 3.0° TCH 55′. 0.4% up.
  **RWY 35R:** ALSF2. TDZL. PAPI(P4R)—GA 3.0° TCH 59′.
**RWY 17R–35L:** H12000X150 (CONC–GRVD) S–116, D–240, 2S–175, 2D–515, 2D/2D2–1085 PCN 92 R/B/W/T HIRL
   CL
  **RWY 17R:** MALSR. TDZL. PAPI(P4L)—GA 3.0° TCH 60′. 0.5% up.
  **RWY 35L:** ALSF2. TDZL. PAPI(P4R)—GA 3.0° TCH 57′.

**RUNWAY DECLARED DISTANCE INFORMATION**
  **RWY 07:** TORA–12000 TODA–12000 ASDA–12000 LDA–12000
  **RWY 08:** TORA–12000 TODA–13000 ASDA–12000 LDA–12000
  **RWY 16L:** TORA–12000 TODA–12000 ASDA–12000 LDA–12000
  **RWY 16R:** TORA–16000 TODA–16000 ASDA–16000 LDA–16000
  **RWY 17L:** TORA–12000 TODA–12000 ASDA–12000 LDA–12000
  **RWY 17R:** TORA–12000 TODA–12000 ASDA–12000 LDA–12000
  **RWY 25:** TORA–12000 TODA–13000 ASDA–12000 LDA–12000
  **RWY 26:** TORA–12000 TODA–12000 ASDA–12000 LDA–12000
  **RWY 34L:** TORA–16000 TODA–16000 ASDA–16000 LDA–16000
  **RWY 34R:** TORA–12000 TODA–13000 ASDA–12000 LDA–12000
  **RWY 35L:** TORA–12000 TODA–12000 ASDA–12000 LDA–12000
  **RWY 35R:** TORA–12000 TODA–12000 ASDA–12000 LDA–12000

**AIRPORT REMARKS:** Attended continuously. Waterfowl and migratory bird activity invof arpt year round. ASDE–X Surveillance System in use: Pilots should opr transponders with Mode C on all twys and rwys. Arpt maintains clearways (500′ X 1000′). 1.25% slope) on departure Rwy 08, Rwy 26, and Rwy 34R. RVR Rwy 07 touchdown, rollout, RVR Rwy 25 touchdown, rollout, RVR Rwy 08 touchdown, rollout, RVR Rwy 26 touchdown, rollout, RVR Rwy 16L touchdown, midfield, rollout, RVR Rwy 34R touchdown, midfield, rollout, RVR Rwy 17L touchdown, midfield, rollout, RVR Rwy 35R touchdown, midfield, rollout, RVR Rwy 17R touchdown, midfield, rollout, RVR Rwy 35L touchdown, midfield, rollout. RVR Rwy 16R touchdown, midfield, rollout, RVR Rwy 34L touchdown, midfield, rollout. Overhead passenger bridge on South side of concourse `A′ provides 42 ft tail and 118 ft wingspan clearance when on twy centerline. Insufficient twy corner fillet pavement in the SE corner of the Twy M/M2 intersection for acft with wingspan over 107 ft. Informal rwy use program is in effect 24 hours a day. For additional noise abatement information contact airport management at 303–342–4200. Customs avbl with prior permission. Ldg fee. Flight Notification Service (ADCUS) avbl. NOTE: See Special Notices—Continuous Power Facilities.
**WEATHER DATA SOURCES:** ASOS (303) 342-0838 LLWAS-NE. TDWR.
**COMMUNICATIONS:** D-ATIS ARR 125.6 303-342-0819 D-ATIS DEP 134.025 303-342-0820 **UNICOM** 122.95
  **RCO** 122.2 122.35 (DENVER RADIO)
  **RCO** 123.65 (DENVER RADIO)
  ®**APP CON** 119.3 124.95 (North) 120.35 126.55 (South) **FINAL CON** 120.8
  **TOWER** 132.35 (Rwy 07-25) 135.3 (Rwy 16L-34R, Rwy 16R-34L) 133.3 (Rwy 17R-35L) 124.3 (Rwy 08-26 and 17L-35R)
  **GND CON** 127.5 (Rwy 07-25, Rwy 16L-34R and Rwy 16R-34L) 121.85 (Rwys 08-26, 17L-35R and 17R-35L)
  **CLNC DEL** 118.75
  ®**DEP CON** 128.25 (East) 127.05 (North) 126.1 (West) 128.45 (South)
**AIRSPACE: CLASS B** See VFR Terminal Area Chart
**RADIO AIDS TO NAVIGATION:** NOTAM FILE DEN.

**CONTINUED ON NEXT PAGE**

Figure 376

## 232 COLORADO
### CONTINUED FROM PRECEDING PAGE

(H) VORW/DME 117.9   DEN   Chan 126   N39°48.75′ W104°39.64′   338° 3.0 NM to fld. 5452/11E.
ILS/DME 111.55  I-DZG  Chan 52(Y)  Rwy 07.   Class IE.
ILS/DME 108.9  I-FUI  Chan 26  Rwy 08.
ILS/DME 111.1  I-LTT  Chan 48  Rwy 16L.   Class IE.
ILS/DME 111.9  I-DQQ  Chan 56  Rwy 16R.
ILS/DME 110.15  I-BXP  Chan 38(Y)  Rwy 17L.   Class IE.
ILS/DME 108.5  I-ACX  Chan 22  Rwy 17R.   Class IE.
ILS/DME 111.55  I-ERP  Chan 52(Y)  Rwy 25.   Class IE.
ILS/DME 108.9  I-JOY  Chan 26  Rwy 26.   Class IE.
ILS/DME 111.9  I-DXU  Chan 56  Rwy 34L.   Class IIIE.
ILS/DME 111.1  I-OUF  Chan 48  Rwy 34R.   Class IIIE.
ILS/DME 108.5  I-AQD  Chan 22  Rwy 35L.
ILS/DME 110.15  I-DPP  Chan 38(Y)  Rwy 35R.   Class IIIE.
COMM/NAV/WEATHER REMARKS: Emerg frequency 121.5 not avbl at twr.

- - - - - - - - - - - - - - - - - - - - - - - - - - - - - - - - - - - - - - - - - -

**FRONT RANGE**  (FTG)  19 E   UTC−7(−6DT)   N39°47.12′ W104°32.59′                    DENVER
5512   B  S4  **FUEL** 100LL, JET A   OX 1, 2   TPA—6500(988)   NOTAM FILE FTG         H−5A, L−10F, A
RWY 08−26: H8000X100 (ASPH)   S−28, D−40   HIRL                                        IAP, AD
  RWY 08: REIL. PAPI(P2L)—GA 3.0° TCH 50′. Rgt tfc. 0.5% up.
  RWY 26: MALSR. PAPI(P2L)—GA 3.0° TCH 50′. 0.4% down.
RWY 17−35: H8000X100 (ASPH)   S−34, D−75   MIRL
  RWY 17: REIL. PAPI(P4L)—GA 3.0° TCH 50′. 0.5% up.
  RWY 35: MALSR. PAPI(P4L)—GA 3.0° TCH 50′. Rgt tfc.
AIRPORT REMARKS: Attended 1400−0400Z‡. For svc after hrs call
  303−208−8536. 24 hr credit card 100LL self fueling station. Be alert,
  intensive USAF student training invof Colorado Springs and Pueblo
  Colorado. Noise sensitive areas SE, S and SW of arpt. Avoid flights blo
  1,000 ft over populated areas. Blue and yellow reflectors along Twy A,
  B, C, E edges. ACTIVATE MIRL Rwy 17−35, HIRL Rwy 08−26, PAPI
  Rwy 08, Rwy 26, Rwy 17 and Rwy 35 and REIL Rwy 08 and Rwy
  17, MALSR Rwy 26 and Rwy 35—CTAF. See Special Notices—USAF
  306 FTG Flight Training Areas, Vicinity of Colorado Springs and Pueblo
  Colorado.
WEATHER DATA SOURCES: AWOS-3 119.025 (303) 261-9104.
COMMUNICATIONS: CTAF 120.2   ATIS 119.025   UNICOM 122.95
  DENVER APP/DEP CON 128.2
  TOWER 120.2 (1400-0400Z‡)   GND CON 124.7   CLNC DEL 124.7
  DENVER CLNC DEL 121.75 (0400-1400Z‡)
AIRSPACE: CLASS D svc 1400-0400Z‡ other times CLASS G
RADIO AIDS TO NAVIGATION: NOTAM FILE DEN.
  DENVER (H) VORW/DME 117.9   DEN   Chan 126   N39°48.75′ W104°39.64′   096° 5.7 NM to fld. 5452/11E.
  SKIPI NDB (LOM) 321   FT   N39°47.51′ W104°26.05′ 255° 5.1 NM to fld. Unmonitored.
  ILS/DME 110.9  I-FZR  Chan 46  Rwy 17.
  ILS/DME 109.3  I-FTG  Chan 30  Rwy 26.   LOM SKIPI NDB. Unmonitored.
  ILS/DME 110.9  I-VWT  Chan 46  Rwy 35.

- - - - - - - - - - - - - - - - - - - - - - - - - - - - - - - - - - - - - - - - - -

**Figure 377**

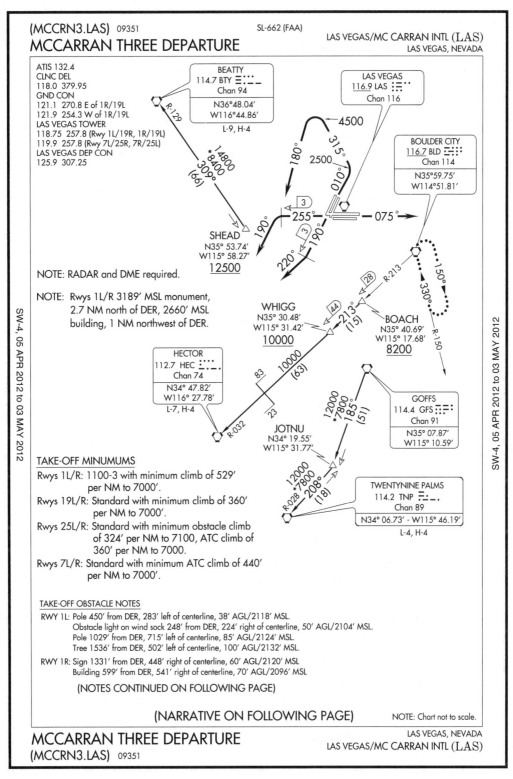

**Figure 378**

(MCCRN3.LAS) 09351                    SL-662 (FAA)

## MCCARRAN THREE DEPARTURE

LAS VEGAS/MC CARRAN INTL (LAS)
LAS VEGAS, NEVADA

▼                    DEPARTURE ROUTE DESCRIPTION

TAKE-OFF RUNWAYS 1L/R:  Climb via heading 010° to 2500', then climbing left turn via heading 315° to 4500', then climbing left turn heading 180°, thence ....

TAKE-OFF RUNWAYS 7L/R:  Climb via heading 075°, thence ....

TAKE-OFF RUNWAYS 19L/R: Climb via heading 190° until LAS VORTAC 3 DME, then right turn via heading 220°, thence ....

TAKE-OFF RUNWAYS 25L/R: Climb via heading 255° until LAS VORTAC 3 DME, then left turn via heading 190°, thence ....

....via radar vectors to transition or assigned route, maintain 7000', expect clearance to filed altitude 2 minutes after departure.

LOST COMMUNICATIONS:  If no contact with ATC upon reaching 7000', proceed direct BLD VORTAC, then climb in BLD VORTAC holding pattern to the appropriate MEA for route of flight.

BEATTY TRANSITION (MCCRN3.BTY): From over SHEAD INT via BTY R-129 to BTY VORTAC.

HECTOR TRANSITION (MCCRN3.HEC): From over BOACH INT via BLD R-213 and HEC R-032 to HEC VORTAC.

TWENTY NINE PALMS TRANSITION (MCCRN3.TNP): From over GFS VORTAC via GFS R-185 to JOTNU INT, then via TNP R-028 to TNP VORTAC.

TAKE-OFF OBSTACLE NOTES (CONTINUED)

RWY 25R:  Light pole 3115' from DER, 1033' right of centerline, 109' AGL/2301' MSL.
          Light on pole 1.5 NM from DER, 2836' left of centerline, 124' AGL/2457' MSL.
          Light pole 1.7 NM from DER, 2965' left of centerline, 139' AGL/2469' MSL.
          Light on pole 1100' from DER, 508' left of centerline, 47' AGL/2226' MSL.
          Building 1822' from DER, 652' left of centerline, 46' AGL/2238' MSL.
          Building 2202' from DER, 596' left of centerline, 44' AGL/2246' MSL.
          Rod on building 534' from DER, 369' left of centerline, 33' AGL/2202' MSL.
          Road 678' from DER, 16' right of centerline, 35' AGL/2201' MSL.
          Light on localizer antenna 533' from DER, 32' AGL/2195' MSL.

RWY 25L:  Pole 2860' from DER, 813' left of centerline, 57' AGL/2236' MSL.
          Sign 3672' from DER, 1302' left of centerline, 57' AGL/2256' MSL.
          Antenna on building 1002' from DER, 251' left of centerline, 34' AGL/2183' MSL.
          Pole 3677' from DER, 145' left of centerline, 67' AGL/2249' MSL.

RWY 7L:   Tree 1257' from DER, 789' left of centerline, 85' AGL/2077' MSL.
          Light pole 747' from DER, 441' right of centerline, 62' AGL/2057' MSL.
          Tree 1007' from DER, 557' right of centerline, 70' AGL/2062' MSL.

RWY 7R:   Light on wind sock 102' from DER, 300' right of centerline, 30' AGL/2051' MSL.

RWY 19L:  Pole 1394' from DER, 533' right of centerline, 36' AGL/2236' MSL.
          Sign 2181' from DER, 1062' right of centerline, 50' AGL/2256' MSL.
          Rod on building 2921' from DER, 581' right of centerline, 50' AGL/2262' MSL.
          Pole 2633' from DER, 319' right of centerline, 40' AGL/2246' MSL.

RWY 19R:  Pole 1135' from DER, 619' right of centerline, 65' AGL/2249' MSL.
          Pole 756' from DER, 618' left of centerline, 50' AGL/2231' MSL.
          Sign 2182' from DER, 125' right of centerline, 50' AGL/2256' MSL.
          Pole 1396' from DER, 403' left of centerline, 55' AGL/2236' MSL.
          Rod on building 197' from DER, 441' right of centerline, 30' AGL/2202' MSL.
          Rod on building 2922' from DER, 356' left of centerline, 50' AGL/2262' MSL.

SW-4, 05 APR 2012 to 03 MAY 2012

SW-4, 05 APR 2012 to 03 MAY 2012

## MCCARRAN THREE DEPARTURE
(MCCRN3.LAS)  09351

LAS VEGAS, NEVADA
LAS VEGAS/MC CARRAN INTL (LAS)

**Figure 379**

184  CALIFORNIA

**SAN FRANCISCO INTL** (SFO)  8 SE  UTC–8(–7DT)  N37°37.14´ W122°22.49´

SAN FRANCISCO
H–3B, L–2F, 3B, A
IAP, AD

13  B  S4  **FUEL** 100, 100LL, JET A  OX 1, 2, 3, 4  LRA  Class I, ARFF Index E
NOTAM FILE SFO

RWY 10L–28R: H11870X200 (ASPH–GRVD)  PCN 80 F/B/X/T  HIRL
CL

Rwy 01L–19R: 7500 X 200

RWY 10L: REIL. PAPI(P4L)—GA 3.0° TCH 80´. Tower.
RWY 28R: ALSF2. TDZL. PAPI(P4L)—GA 3.0° TCH 70´. Rgt tfc.

RWY 10R–28L: H10602X200 (ASPH–GRVD)  PCN 80 F/B/X/T  HIRL
CL

RWY 10R: PAPI(P4L)—GA 3.0° TCH 75´. Tower. Rgt tfc.
RWY 28L: SSALR. PAPI(P4L)—GA 3.0° TCH 75´.

RWY 01R–19L: H8648X200 (ASPH–GRVD)  PCN 100F/B/X/T  HIRL  CL
RWY 01R: REIL. Thld dsplcd 238´. Tree.
RWY 19L: MALSF. TDZL. PAPI(P4L)—GA 3.0° TCH 75´.

RWY 01L–19R: H7500X200 (ASPH–CONC–GRVD)  PCN 90 F/B/X/T
HIRL  CL

RWY 01L: REIL. Thld dsplcd 491´.
RWY 19R: PAPI(P4L)—GA 3.0° TCH 73´.

**AIRPORT REMARKS:** Attended continuously. PAEW AER 28L, Rwy 28R and
Rwy 19L indef. Flocks of birds feeding along shoreline adjacent to arpt,
on occasions fly across various parts of arpt. Due to obstructed vision,
SFO twr is able to provide only limited arpt tfc control svc on Twy A
between gates 88 and 89. Twr personnel are unable to determine whether this area is clear of traffic or obstructions. Rwy
10 preferred rwy between 0900–1400Z‡ weather and flight conditions permitting. Simultaneous ops in effect all rwys.
Helicopter ldg area marked on Twy (C) west of Twy (R) opr for civil and military use. Noise sensitive arpt. For noise
abatement procedures ctc arpt noise office Monday–Friday 1600–0100Z‡ by calling 650–821–5100. Airline pilots shall
strictly follow the painted nose gear lines and no oversteering adjustment is permitted. No grooving exists at arpt rwy
intersections. Rwy 01L–19R, 01R–19L, Rwy 10R–28L, Rwy 10L–28R grooved full length except at rwy intersections.
B747, B777, A330, A340 or larger acft are restricted from using Twy A1 when B747–400, A340–600 or larger acft are
holding short of Rwy 01R on Twy A. 747–400´s shall taxi at a speed of less than 10 miles per hour on all non–restricted
taxiways on the terminal side of the intersecting rwys. All outbound Twy Y heavy aircraft with a wingspan of 171´ or
greater under power prohibited from entering westbound Twy Z. Ramp clsd to acft with wingspan over 117´ at Terminal
1, gate C41 indef. Movement speed of not more than 5 miles per hour is required when two 747–400´s pass or overtake
each other on parallel taxiways A and B. Rwy 19L MALSF has a NSTD length of 1115´ with 3 sequenced flashers. Ldg
fee. Flight Notification Service (ADCUS) available. NOTE: See Special Notices—Intersection Departures During Period of
Darkness, Expanded Charted Visual Flight Procedures. Continuous Power Facilities, Special Noise Abatement Procedures,
Special Noise Abatement Procedures—Preferential Runways.

**WEATHER DATA SOURCES:** ASOS (650) 872-0246 LLWAS.
**COMMUNICATIONS:** D-ATIS 135.45 118.85 115.8 113.7 650-877-3585/8422 **UNICOM** 122.95
Ⓡ**NORCAL APP CON** 135.65 (S) 133.95
**TOWER** 120.5 **GND CON** 121.8 **CLNC DEL** 118.2 **PRE TAXI CLNC** 118.2
Ⓡ**NORCAL DEP CON** 135.1 (SE-W) 120.9 (NW-E)
**AIRSPACE: CLASS B** See VFR Terminal Area Chart
**RADIO AIDS TO NAVIGATION:** NOTAM FILE SFO.
(L) VORW/DME 115.8  SFO  Chan 105  N37°37.17´ W122°22.43´  at fld. 13/17E.
VOR DME unusable:
  025°-065° byd 30 NM blo 18,000´
  035°-055° byd 12 NM blo 6,500´
  150°-190° byd 25 NM blo 4,500´
  190°-260° byd 10 NM blo 4,500´
  260°-295° byd 35 NM blo 3,000´
  295°-330° byd 20 NM blo 8,000´
BRIJJ NDB (LOM) 379  GW  N37°34.33´ W122°15.59´ 282° 6.2 NM to fld. LOM unusable 160°-195° byd 6 NM.
ILS/DME 108.9  I-SIA  Chan 26  Rwy 19L.  Class IE.  Ry 19L glideslope deviations are possible when critical areas
  are not required to be protected.  Acft operating invof glideslope transmitter. Pilots should be alert for momentary
  localizer course excursions due to large aircraft operating in vicinity of localizer antenna.
ILS/DME 109.55  I-SFO  Chan 32(Y)  Rwy 28L.  Class IE.
ILS/DME 111.7  I-GWQ  Chan 54  Rwy 28R.  Class IIIE.  LOM BRIJJ NDB. LOM unusable 160°-195° byd 6 NM.
LDA/DME 110.75  I-FNP  Chan 44(Y)  Rwy 28R.

**Figure 380**

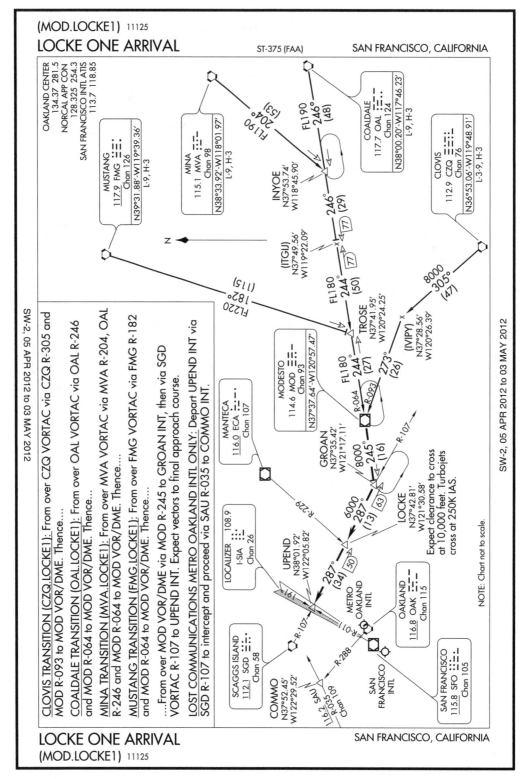

**Figure 381**

**CALIFORNIA**

## OAKLAND
**METROPOLITAN OAKLAND INTL** (OAK)   4 S   UTC–8(–7DT)   N37°43.28′ W122°13.24′   **SAN FRANCISCO**
   9   B   S4   **FUEL** 100LL, JET A   OX 1, 2, 3, 4   TPA—See Remarks   LRA   Class I, ARFF Index D   **H–3B, L–2F, 3B, A**
   NOTAM FILE OAK   **IAP, AD**
   RWY 11–29: H10000X150 (ASPH–GRVD)   PCN 71 F/A/W/T   HIRL   CL
   RWY 11: MALSR. PAPI(P4L)—GA 2.75° TCH 65′. Rgt tfc.
   RWY 29: ALSF2. TDZL. PAPI(P4L)—GA 3.0° TCH 71′.
   RWY 09R–27L: H6213X150 (ASPH–GRVD)   PCN 97 F/B/W/T   HIRL
   RWY 09R: REIL. PAPI(P4R)—GA 3.0° TCH 50′.
   RWY 27L: PAPI(P4L)—GA 3.0° TCH 71′.
   RWY 09L–27R: H5454X150 (ASPH–GRVD)   PCN 69 F/C/W/T   HIRL
   RWY 09L: PAPI(P4R)—GA 3.0° TCH 49′.
   RWY 27R: MALSR. PAPI(P4L)—GA 2.9° TCH 57′. Bldg. Rgt tfc.
   RWY 15–33: H3372X75 (ASPH)   S–12.5   MIRL
   RWY 33: Rgt tfc. 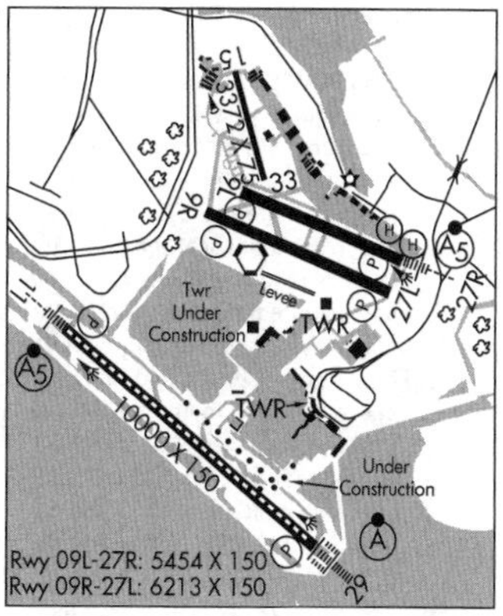
   AIRPORT REMARKS: Attended continuously. Rwy 15–33 CLOSED to air
   carrier acft. Birds on and invof arpt. Acft with experimental or limited
   certification having over 1,000 horsepower or 4,000 pounds are
   restricted to Rwy 11–29. 24 hr Noise abatement procedure–turbojet
   and turbofan powered acft, turborops over 17,000 lbs, four engine
   reciprocating powered acft, and surplus Military acft over 12,500 lbs
   should not depart Rwy 27L and Rwy 27R or land on Rwy 09L and Rwy
   09R. For noise abatement information ctc noise abatement office at
   510–563–6463. Intersection of Twy B, Twy W and Twy V not visible from twr. Twy K between Rwy 33 and Twy D and
   portions of Twy D not visible from twr. Twy A, Twy E, Twy G, Twy H between Rwy 27R and Twy C max acft weight 150,000
   lbs. Twy G and Twy H between Rwy 27L and Rwy 27R, max acft weight 12,500 lbs. Twy P max acft weight 24,000 lbs
   single, 40,000 lbs dual. Twy C between Rwy 27R and Twy G and Twy B, Twy J, and Twy D max acft weight 9,000,000
   lbs. Twy C between Twy G and Twy J max acft weight 25,000 lbs single, 175,000 lbs dual, 4,000,000 lbs tandem. Twy
   C between Twy J and Twy F max acft weight 25,000 lbs single, 150,000 lbs dual. 155,000 lbs tandem (dual tandem
   not authorized). Twy K between Twy D and intersection Twy F, Twy L, Twy K max acft weight 25,000 lbs single, 115,000
   lbs dual, 140,000 lbs tandem. Twy K between Rwy 9R and intersection Twy F, Twy L, Twy K max acft weight 25,000 lbs
   single, 115,000 lbs dual, 140,000 lbs tandem. Twy K between Rwy 9R and intersection Twy F, Twy L, Twy K max acft
   weight 25,000 lbs single, 45,000 lbs dual, tandem not authorized. Preferential rwy use program in effect 0600–1400Z‡.
   North fld preferred arrival Rwy 27L, north fld preferred departure Rwys 09L or 27R. If these Rwys unacceptable for safety
   or twr instruction then Rwy 11–29 must be used. Noise prohibitions not applicable in emerg or whenever Rwy 11–29 is
   closed due to maintenance, safety, winds or weather. 400′ blast pad Rwy 29 and 500′ blast pad Rwy 11. Rwys 29, 27R
   and 27L distance remaining signs left side. TPA—Rwy 27L 606(597), TPA—Rwy 27R 1006(997). Ldg fee may apply
   for Rwy 11–29, rwy commercial ops and tiedown, ctc afld ops 510–563–3361. Flight Notification Service (ADCUS) avbl.
   WEATHER DATA SOURCES: ASOS (510) 383-9514 **HIWAS** 116.8 OAK.
   COMMUNICATIONS: D-ATIS 133.775 (510) 635-5850 (N and S Complex) **UNICOM** 122.95
      OAKLAND RCO 122.2 122.5 (OAKLAND RADIO)
      ®NORCAL APP CON 125.35 (East) 135.65 (South) 135.1 (West) 134.5 120.9
      ®NORCAL DEP CON 135.1 (West) 120.9 (Northwest)
      OAKLAND TOWER 118.3 (N Complex) 127.2 (S Complex) 124.9
      GND CON 121.75 (S Complex) 121.9 (N Complex) **CLNC DEL** 121.1
   AIRSPACE: CLASS C svc ctc APP CON
   RADIO AIDS TO NAVIGATION: NOTAM FILE OAK.
      OAKLAND (H) VORTACW 116.8   OAK   Chan 115   N37°43.56′ W122°13.42′   at fld. 10/17E.   **HIWAS.**
      DME unusable:
         335°-065° byd 30 NM blo 8,000′
      ILS 111.9   I-AAZ   Rwy 11.   Class IE.   Glideslope deviations are possible when critical areas are not required to be
         protected. Acft operating invof glideslope transmitter.
      ILS 109.9   I-OAK   Rwy 27R.   Class IE.
      ILS 108.7   I-INB   Rwy 29.   Class IIIE.
   COMM/NAV/WEATHER REMARKS: Emerg frequency 121.5 not avbl at twr.

**OAKLAND**   N37°43.56′ W122°13.42′   NOTAM FILE OAK.   **SAN FRANCISCO**
   (H) VORTACW 116.8   OAK   Chan 115   at Metropolitan Oakland Intl. 10/17E.   **HIWAS.**   **H–3A, L–2F, 3B, A**
   DME unusable:
      335°-065° byd 30 NM blo 8,000′
   RCO 122.2 122.5 (OAKLAND RADIO)
   ASOS   OAK   N37°43.28′ W122°13.24′. (510) 383-9514.

**OCEAN RIDGE** (See GUALALA on page 113)

**Figure 382**

## 96            FLORIDA

**KEY WEST INTL** (EYW)  2 E  UTC−5(−4DT)  N24°33.37′ W81°45.57′        **MIAMI**
  3   B   S4  **FUEL** 100, JET A   AOE   Class I, ARFF Index IB   NOTAM FILE EYW    **L−21D, 23C**
  **RWY 09−27:** H4801X100 (ASPH−GRVD)   S−75, D−125, 2D−195   MIRL        **IAP, AD**
     **RWY 09:** REIL. VASI(V4L)—GA 3.0° TCH 34′. Rgt tfc.
     **RWY 27:** REIL. VASI(V4L)—GA 3.0° TCH 34′.
  **ARRESTING GEAR/SYSTEM**
     **RWY 09:** EMAS
  **AIRPORT REMARKS:** Attended 1200−0400Z‡. Parachute Jumping.
     Numerous flocks of birds on and in the vicinity of airport.
     Departing VFR acft requested to maintain rwy heading until
     reaching fld boundary, then execute turns for N or S dep.
     Restricted area R−2916 located 14 NM NE of arpt has strobe−lgtd
     and marked balloon and cable to 14,000 ft. Extremely noise
     sensitive area. Urge no ops 0400−1200Z‡. Use NBAA close in
     noise abatement procedures other times. Local ordinance rqr
     engine runups in designated area on N side commercial ramp
     from 0400−1200Z‡ and fines. PPR for unscheduled air carrier
     operations with more than 30 passenger seats 0430−1045Z‡;
     Call arpt manager 305−809−5200. PPR for acft exceeding rwy
     weight bearing capacity; call arpt manager 305−809−5200.
     Intensive military jet tfc S and E of arpt; acft entering arpt tfc area
     from SE through W. Enter arpt tfc area blo 2000′; refer to MIAMI
     VFR Terminal Area Chart for suggested VFR flyway routes. Twy A5 and Twy A6 not visible from twr. ACTIVATE
     MIRL Rwy 09−27, VASI/REIL Rwys 09−27—CTAF. Flight Notification Service (ADCUS) available. NOTE: See
     Special Notices—U.S. Special Customs Requirement.
  **WEATHER DATA SOURCES:** ASOS 119.65 (305) 292−4046. **HIWAS** 113.5 EYW.
  **COMMUNICATIONS: CTAF** 118.2    **ATIS** 119.675    **UNICOM** 122.95
     **RCO** 122.1R 113.5T (MIAMI RADIO)
     **RCO** 123.65 122.2 (MIAMI RADIO)
  Ⓡ **NAVY KEY WEST APP/DEP CON** 124.025 126.575 (1200−0300Z‡)    Ⓡ**MIAMI CENTER APP/DEP CON** 133.5
     (0300−1200Z‡)
     **TOWER** 118.2 (1200−0200Z‡)    **GND CON** 121.9    **CLNC DEL** 121.9
  **AIRSPACE: CLASS D** svc 1200−0200Z‡ other times CLASS G.
  **RADIO AIDS TO NAVIGATION:** NOTAM FILE EYW.
     **(H) VORTAC** 113.5    EYW    Chan 82    N24°35.15′ W81°48.03′    127° 2.9 NM to fld. 10/01E.
     **HIWAS.** VOR unusable 040°−050°, 210°−240°.
     **FISH HOOK NDB (HW)** 332    FIS    N24°32.90′ W81°47.18′    076° 1.5 NM to fld.
     **ASR** (1100−0300Z‡)
  **COMM/NAV/WEATHER REMARKS:** FSS freqs 123.65 and 122.2 unusable 330°−015° beyond 20 NM below 1500′. VORTAC
     unusable 121°−139°. Acft overflying SIMPL, ACRUZ, CANOA, and MAXIM shall ctc Miami Center 10 minutes prior
     to crossing the Miami flight information region 132.2.

**SE, 05 APR 2012 to 31 MAY 2012**

**Figure 383**

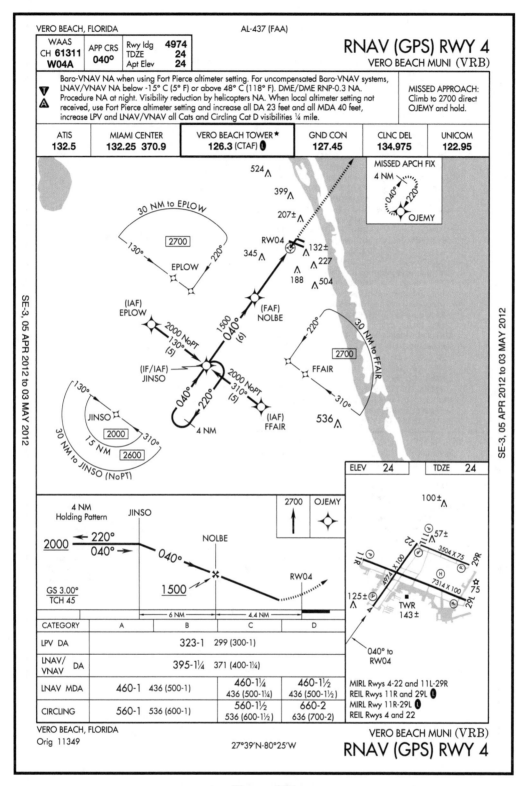

Figure 384

## FLORIDA                                                                    143

- - - - - - - - - - - - - - - - - - - - - - - - - - - - - - - - - - - - - - - - - - -

**VERO BEACH MUNI** (VRB)  1 NW  UTC−5(−4DT)  N27°39.33′ W80°25.08′                **MIAMI**
  24  B  S4  **FUEL** 100, JET A  OX 1, 2  TPA—See Remarks  Class IV, ARFF Index A    **H−8I, L−24F**
  NOTAM FILE VRB                                                                          **IAP, AD**
  **RWY 11R−29L:** H7314X100 (ASPH−GRVD)
    S−85, D−115, 2S−146, 2D−220    MIRL
    **RWY 11R:** REIL. PAPI (P4L)—GA 3.0° TCH 41′. Trees.
    **RWY 29L:** REIL. PAPI(P4L) TCH 58′.
  **RWY 04−22:** H4974X100 (ASPH−GRVD)  S−30, D−115, 2S−146,
    2D−220    MIRL
    **RWY 04:** REIL. VASI(V4L)—GA 3.0° TCH 45′.Trees.
    **RWY 22:** REIL. PAPI(P4L)—GA 3.0° TCH 42′. Trees.
  **RWY 11L−29R:** H3504X75 (ASPH)  S−12.5    MIRL
    **RWY 11L:** PAPI(P2L)—GA 3.0° TCH 37′. Tree.
    **RWY 29R:** PAPI(P2L)—GA 3.5° TCH 35′. Poles.
  **LAND AND HOLD SHORT OPERATIONS**

| LANDING | HOLD SHORT POINT | DIST AVBL |
|---------|------------------|-----------|
| RWY 29L | 04/22 | 4700 |

  **AIRPORT REMARKS:** Attended 1200−0200Z‡. Rwy 04−22 CLOSED when
  twr clsd. TPA 1024(1000) large acft 1524(1500). Rwy 11L−29R
  CLOSED when twr clsd. CLOSED to air carrier ops with more than
  30 passenger seats except 24 hrs PPR, call arpt manager
  772−978−4930. No intersection departures except by ATC req.
  Noise sensitive arpt. Jet acft use NBAA noise abatement
  procedures. Voluntary local noise abatement procedures in effect call 772−978−4930. No touch and go ops
  0300−1200Z‡ except PPR. Extensive flight training. ACTIVATE MIRL Rwy 11R−29L and REIL Rwy 11R and Rwy
  29L—CTAF.
  **WEATHER DATA SOURCES:** ASOS (772) 978−9535. **HIWAS** 117.3 VRB.
  **COMMUNICATIONS:** CTAF 126.3    **ATIS** 132.5    **UNICOM** 122.95
    RCO 122.1R 117.3T (ST PETERSBURG RADIO)
    RCO 122.5 122.2 (ST PETERSBURG RADIO)
  Ⓡ **MIAMI CENTER APP/DEP CON** 132.25
    **TOWER** 126.3 133.15 (1200−0200Z‡)    **GND CON** 127.45    **CLNC DEL** 134.975
  **AIRSPACE: CLASS D** svc 1200−0200Z‡ other times CLASS E.
  **RADIO AIDS TO NAVIGATION:** NOTAM FILE VRB.
    **(H) VORTAC** 117.3    VRB    Chan 120    N27°40.71′ W80°29.38′    114° 4.1 NM to fld. 11/04W.    **HIWAS.**

**VIRGINIA KEY**  N25°45.11′ W80°09.27′    NOTAM FILE MIA.                        **MIAMI**
  **(H) VOR/DME** 117.1    VKZ    Chan 118    293° 7.8 NM to Miami Intl. 12/04W.    **H−8I, L−23C, A**
    VOR portion unusable 020°−064° byd 20 NM blo 4500′, 091°−104° byd 30 NM blo 3000′, 279°−284° byd 25
    NM blo 7500′, 285°−319° byd 15 NM blo 7500′, 320°−335° byd 25 NM blo 3000′.
  RCO 122.1R 117.1T (MIAMI RADIO)

**WAKUL**  N30°19.57′ W84°21.50′    NOTAM FILE TLH.                               **JACKSONVILLE**
  **NDB (HW/LOM)** 379    TL    007° 4.2 NM to Tallahassee Rgnl.                   **H−8G, L−21D, 22I**

**WAKULLA CO**  (See PANACEA)

**WARRINGTON**  N30°28.69′ W86°31.25′    NOTAM FILE CEW.                          **NEW ORLEANS**
  **(T) TACAN**    Chan 2 DWG (134.5)    at Eglin AFB 118/00°E.                    **L−21C, 22H**

**Figure 385**

**WINDSOR LOCKS**
**BRADLEY INTL**    (BDL)   3 W   UTC–5(–4DT)   N41°56.35' W72°41.00'                      NEW YORK
173   B   S4   **FUEL** 100LL, JET A   OX 1, 2, 3, 4   TPA—See Remarks        H–10I, 11D, 12K, L–33C, 34I
      LRA   Class I, ARFF Index D   NOTAM FILE BDL                                        IAP, AD
**RWY 06–24:** H9510X200 (ASPH–GRVD)   S–200, D–200, 2S–175,
   2D–350, 2D/2D2–710   HIRL   CL
   **RWY 06:** ALSF2. TDZL. PAPI(P4L)—GA 3.0° TCH 71'. Trees.
   **RWY 24:** MALSR. TDZL. PAPI(P4L)—GA 3.0° TCH 71'. Trees.
**RWY 15–33:** H6847X150 (ASPH–GRVD)   S–200, D–200, 2S–175,
   2D–350   HIRL
   **RWY 15:** REIL. PAPI(P4L)—GA 3.5°TCH 61'. Trees.
   **RWY 33:** MALSF. PAPI(P4R)—GA 3.0°TCH 72'. Trees.
**RWY 01–19:** H4268X100 (ASPH)   S–60, D–190, 2S–175, 2D–328
   MIRL
   **RWY 01:** Thld dsplcd 475'. Acft.        **RWY 19:** Trees.

Rwy 1-19: 4268 X 100

**LAND AND HOLD SHORT OPERATIONS**

| LANDING | HOLD SHORT POINT | DIST AVBL |
|---------|------------------|-----------|
| RWY 06  | 01–19            | 6000      |
| RWY 24  | 15–33            | 5850      |
| RWY 33  | 06–24            | 4550      |

**RUNWAY DECLARED DISTANCE INFORMATION**

| RWY 01: | TORA–4268 | TODA–4268 | ASDA–4268 |           |
|---------|-----------|-----------|-----------|-----------|
| RWY 06: | TORA–9509 | TODA–9509 | ASDA–9509 | LDA–9509  |
| RWY 15: | TORA–6847 | TODA–6847 | ASDA–6847 | LDA–6847  |
| RWY 19: |           |           |           | LDA–4268  |
| RWY 24: | TORA–9509 | TODA–9509 | ASDA–9509 | LDA–9509  |
| RWY 33: | TORA–6847 | TODA–6847 | ASDA–6847 | LDA–6847  |

**AIRPORT REMARKS:** Attended continuously. Numerous birds frequently on or invof arpt. No training flights; no practice
   apchs; no touch and go ldgs between: Mon–Sat 0400–1200Z‡ and Sun 0400–1700Z‡. Rwy 01–19 open for acft
   with wingspan less than 79'. Rwy 01 CLOSED for arrivals to all fixed wing acft. Rwy 19 CLOSED for departures
   to all fixed wing acft. Twy J clsd between S and R to acft with wing spans in excess of 171 ft. Air National
   Guard ramp PAEW barricaded adjacent northeast side. ASDE–X Surveilance System in Use. Pilots should
   operate transponders with Mode C on all twys and rwys. Rwy 33 touchdown RVR avbl. TPA—1873(1700) heavy
   acft. Rwy 06 visual glideslope indicator and glidepath not coincident. Rwy 24 visual glideslope indicator and
   glidepath not coincident. Rwy 33 visual glideslope indicator and glidepath not coincident. Ldg fee for
   business, corporate and revenue producing acft. Flight Notification Service (ADCUS) available. NOTE: See
   Special Notices–Land and Hold Short Lights.
**WEATHER DATA SOURCES:** ASOS (860) 627–9732. WSP.
**COMMUNICATIONS:** D-ATIS 118.15 (860–386–3570)   **UNICOM** 122.95
   **WINDSOR LOCKS RCO** 122.3 (BRIDGEPORT RADIO)
Ⓡ **BRADLEY APP CON** 123.95 (176°–240°) 125.35 (241°–060°) 127.8 (061°–175° and HFD area)
Ⓡ **BRADLEY DEP CON** 123.95 (176°–240°) 125.35 (241°–060°) 127.8 (061°–175° and HFD area)
   **TOWER** 120.3   **GND CON** 121.9   **CLNC DEL** 121.75
**AIRSPACE: CLASS C** svc continuous ctc **APP CON**
**RADIO AIDS TO NAVIGATION:** NOTAM FILE BDL.
   **(T) VORTACW** 109.0   BDL   Chan 27   N41°56.46' W72°41.32'   at fld. 160/14W.
   **ILS/DME** 111.1   I–BDL   Chan 48   Rwy 06.   Class IIIE.
   **ILS/DME** 108.55   I–IKX   Chan 22(Y)   Rwy 33.   Class IE.
   **ILS/DME** 111.1   I–MYQ   Chan 48   Rwy 24.   Class IT.   DME unusable from .4 NM inbound to Rwy 24.

**YALESVILLE HELIPORT**   (4C3)   2 N   UTC–5(–4DT)   N41°29.51' W72°48.67'
65   B   **FUEL** 100LL, JET A   NOTAM FILE BDR
**HELIPAD H1:** H65X65 (CONC)
**HELIPORT REMARKS:** Attended 1400–2300Z‡. Pilots unfamiliar with heliport ctc 203–294–8800 prior to arrival for a
   briefing on current procedures. ACTIVATE rotating bcn—123.5
**COMMUNICATIONS:** CTAF/UNICOM 123.05

NE, 05 APR 2012 to 31 MAY 2012

**Figure 386**

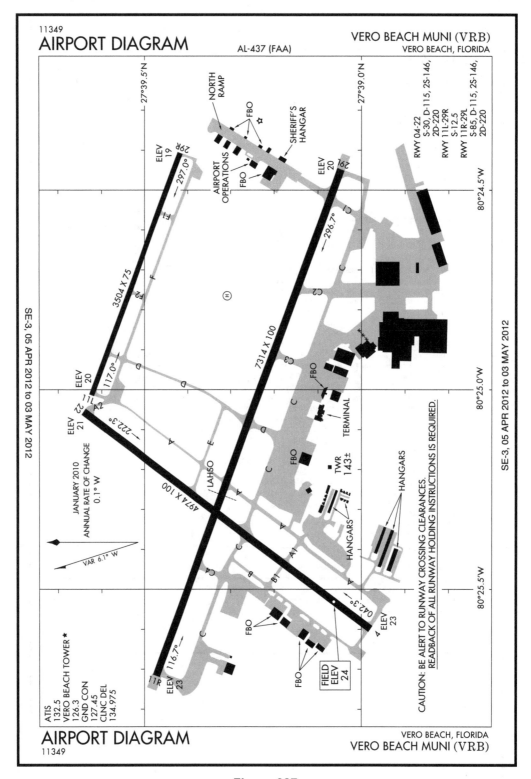

**Figure 387**

Addendum B

ALTERNATE MINS          M4
12096

NAME                    ALTERNATE MINIMUMS
**ROCHESTER, NY**
GREATER ROCHESTER
INTL (ROC) ........................ **ILS or LOC Rwy 4**[1]
                        **ILS or LOC Rwy 22**[1]
                        **ILS or LOC Rwy 28**[2]
                        **RNAV (GPS) Rwy 4**[3]
                        **RNAV (GPS) Rwy 22**[3]
                        **RNAV (GPS) Rwy 25**[3]
                        **RNAV (GPS) Rwy 28**[4]
                        **VOR Rwy 4**[3]
                        **VOR/DME Rwy 4**[3]
[1]ILS, Category D, 700-2¼. LOC, Category D, 800-2¼.
[2]ILS, Categories A,B,C, 800-2; Category D, 800-2¼. LOC, Category D, 800-2¼.
[3]Category D, 800-2¼.
[4]Category C, 800-2¼; Category D, 800-2½.

**ROME, NY**
GRIFFISS INTL (RME) .... **ILS or LOC Rwy 33**[12]
                        **RNAV (GPS) Rwy 15**[3]
                        **RNAV (GPS ) Rwy 33**[3]
NA when local weather not available.
[1]NA when control tower closed.
[2]ILS, Categories A, B, 700-2; Category C, 800-2; Category D, 800-2½. LOC, Category D, 800-2½.
[3]Category D, 800-2½.

**SARANAC LAKE, NY**
ADIRONDACK
RGNL (SLK) .......................... **VOR/DME Rwy 5**[1]
                        **VOR or GPS Rwy 9**[2]
[1]Category A, 1100-2; Category B, 1200-2; Categories C,D, 1200-3.
[2]Categories A,B, 1400-2; Categories C,D, 1400-3.

**SHIRLEY, NY**
BROOKHAVEN (HWV) ....... **RNAV (GPS) Rwy 6**
                        **RNAV (GPS) Rwy 15**
                        **RNAV (GPS) Y Rwy 24**
                        **RNAV (GPS) Z Rwy 24**
                        **RNAV (GPS) Rwy 33**
                        **VOR Rwy 6**
NA when local weather not available.

**SUSSEX, NJ**
SUSSEX (FWN) ............... **RNAV (GPS) Rwy 3**[1]
                        **VOR-A**[2]
NA when local weather not available.
[1]Categories A, B, 900-2; Category C, 900-2½.
[2]Categories A, B, 1400-2; Category C, 1400-3.

NAME                    ALTERNATE MINIMUMS
**TETERBORO, NJ**
TETERBORO (TEB) ............ **ILS or LOC Rwy 6**[1]
                        **ILS RWY 19**[1]
                        **RNAV (GPS) Y Rwy 6**[3]
                        **RNAV (RNP) Z Rwy 6,** 800-2¼
                        **VOR/DME-A**[2]
                        **VOR/DME-B**[2]
                        **VOR/DME Rwy 6**[3]
                        **VOR Rwy 24**[4]
[1]ILS, Categories A,B, 800-2; Category C, 800-2¼; Category D, 900-2¾. LOC, Category C, 800-2¼; Category D, 900-2¾.
[2]Categories A,B, 1000-2; Categories C,D, 1000-3.
[3]Category C, 800-2¼; Category D, 900-2¾.
[4]Categories B,C,D, 1000-3.

**TRENTON, NJ**
TRENTON MERCER (TTN) ............... **ILS Rwy 6**
                        **NDB or GPS Rwy 6**
                        **VOR or GPS-A**
                        **VOR or GPS Rwy 24**
NA when control tower closed.

**WATERTOWN, NY**
WATERTOWN
INTL (ART) ........................ **ILS or LOC Rwy 7**[1]
                        **RNAV (GPS) Rwy 7**[2]
                        **RNAV (GPS) Rwy 10**[3]
                        **RNAV (GPS) Rwy 28**[3]
                        **VOR Rwy 7**[2]
[1]ILS, Categories A, B, C, 700-2; Category D 700-2¼. LOC, Category D, 800-2¼.
[2]Category D, 800-2¼.
[3]NA when local weather not available.

**WELLSVILLE, NY**
WELLSVILLE MUNI ARPT,TARANTINE
FIELD (ELZ) ..................... **RNAV (GPS) Rwy 10**
                        **RNAV (GPS) Rwy 28**
                        **VOR-A**[1]
NA when local weather not available.
[1]Categories A,B, 1100-2; Categories C,D, 1100-3.

**WESTHAMPTON BEACH, NY**
FRANCIS S.
GABRESKI (FOK) ............ **ILS or LOC Rwy 24**[1]
                        **RNAV (GPS) Rwy 24**
NA when local weather not available.
[1]NA when control tower closed.
[2]NA when control tower closed.
[3]Category D, 800-2¼.

05 APR 2012 to 03 MAY 2012

**A** ALTERNATE MINS          NE-2 **A**
12096                            M4

**Figure 388**

159

# COMPUTER TESTING SUPPLEMENT
## FOR
## AIRLINE TRANSPORT PILOT
## AND
## AIRCRAFT DISPATCHER

## ADDENDUM C
## APRIL 2014

U.S. DEPARTMENT OF TRANSPORTATION
**FEDERAL AVIATION ADMINISTRATION**
Flight Standards Service

# Acknowledgments

The graphics for Figures 389 through 416 were used by permission from Cessna Aircraft Company.

The graphics for Figures 417 through 487 were used by permission from Bombardier.

# Airspeed Limitations

Airspeed limitations and their operational significance are shown in Airspeed Limitations chart.

| | SPEED | KCAS | KIAS | REMARKS |
|---|---|---|---|---|
| $V_{MO}$ | Maximum Operating Speed | 175 | 175 | Do not exceed this speed in any operation. |
| $V_A$ | Maneuvering Speed:<br>8750 Pounds<br>7500 Pounds<br>6250 Pounds<br>5000 Pounds | 148<br>137<br>125<br>112 | 148<br>137<br>125<br>112 | Do not make full or abrupt control movements above this speed. |
| $V_{FE}$ | Maximum Flap Extended Speed:<br>UP - 10° Flaps<br>10° - 20° Flaps<br>20° - FULL | 175<br>150<br>125 | 175<br>150<br>125 | Do not exceed these speeds with the given flap settings. |
| | Maximum Open Window Speed | 175 | 175 | Do not exceed this speed with window open. |

**Figure 389**

# STALL SPEEDS

CONDITIONS:
8750 Pounds
POWER Lever **IDLE**
FUEL CONDITION Lever **HIGH IDLE**

## MOST REARWARD CENTER OF GRAVITY

| Flap Setting | Angle of Bank | | | | | | | |
|---|---|---|---|---|---|---|---|---|
| | 0° | | 30° | | 45° | | 60° | |
| | KIAS | KCAS | KIAS | KCAS | KIAS | KCAS | KIAS | KCAS |
| UP | 63 | 78 | 68 | 84 | 75 | 93 | 89 | 110 |
| 10° | 58 | 69 | 62 | 74 | 69 | 82 | 82 | 98 |
| 20° | 53 | 63 | 57 | 68 | 63 | 75 | 75 | 89 |
| FULL | 48 | 60 | 52 | 64 | 57 | 71 | 68 | 85 |

## MOST FORWARD CENTER OF GRAVITY

| Flap Setting | Angle of Bank | | | | | | | |
|---|---|---|---|---|---|---|---|---|
| | 0° | | 30° | | 45° | | 60° | |
| | KIAS | KCAS | KIAS | KCAS | KIAS | KCAS | KIAS | KCAS |
| UP | 63 | 78 | 68 | 84 | 75 | 93 | 89 | 110 |
| 10° | 60 | 70 | 64 | 75 | 71 | 83 | 85 | 99 |
| 20° | 54 | 64 | 58 | 69 | 64 | 76 | 76 | 91 |
| FULL | 50 | 61 | 54 | 66 | 59 | 73 | 71 | 86 |

## NOTE

1. Altitude loss during a stall recovery may be as much as 300 feet from a wings-level stall, and even greater from a turning stall.

2. KIAS values are approximate.

**Figure 390**

# WIND COMPONENTS

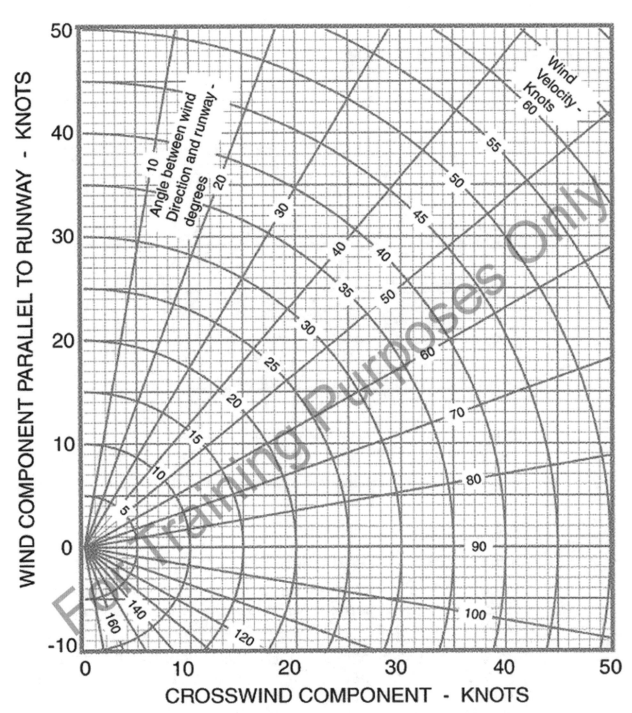

**Note:** Maximum demonstrated crosswind velocity is 20 knots (not a limitation).

**Figure 391**

# MAXIMUM ENGINE TORQUE FOR TAKEOFF

CONDITIONS:

1900 RPM

60 KIAS

INERTIAL SEPARATOR **NORMAL**

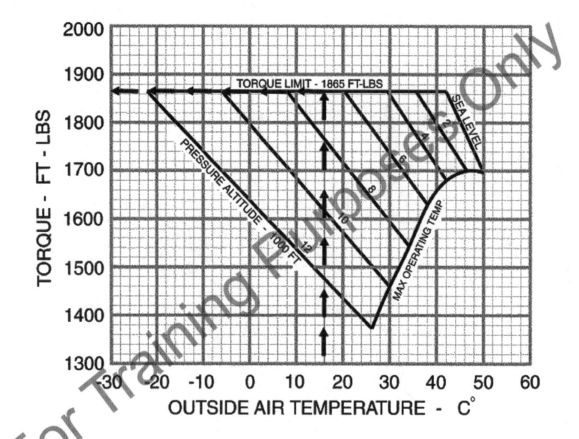

## NOTE

1. Torque increases approximately 10 Ft-Lbs from 0 to 60 KIAS.

2. Torque on this chart shall be achieved without exceeding 805°C ITT or 101.6 percent $N_g$. When the ITT exceeds 765°C, this power setting is time limited to 5 minutes.

3. With the inertial separator in BYPASS, where altitude and temperature do not permit 1865 Ft-Lbs for takeoff, decrease torque setting by 15 Ft-Lbs.

4. With the cabin heater ON, where altitude and temperature do not permit 1865 Ft-Lbs for takeoff, decrease torque setting by 65 Ft-Lbs.

**Figure 392**

# MAXIMUM ENGINE TORQUE FOR CLIMB

CONDITIONS:

1900 RPM

$V_y$ KIAS

INERTIAL SEPARATOR **NORMAL**

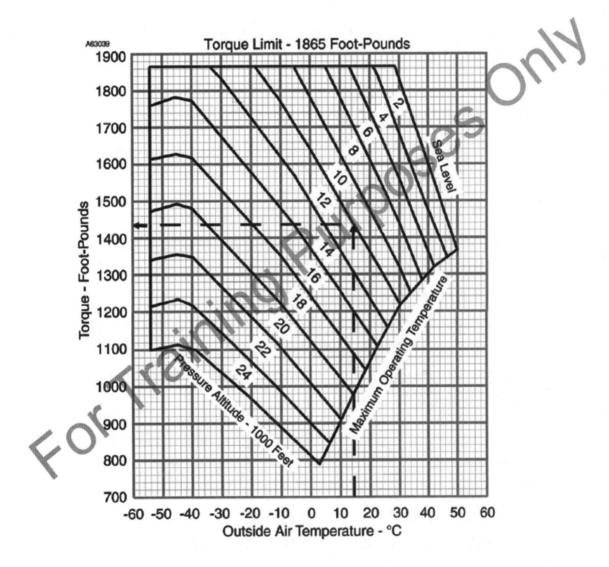

## NOTE

1. Torque on this chart shall be achieved without exceeding 765°C ITT or 101.6 percent $N_g$.

2. With the inertial separator in BYPASS, decrease torque setting by 100 Ft-Lbs.

3. With the cabin heater ON, decrease torque setting by 80 Ft-Lbs.

**Figure 393**

# CARGO POD INSTALLED
# SHORT FIELD TAKEOFF DISTANCE

## NOTE

The following general information is applicable to all SHORT FIELD TAKEOFF DISTANCE Charts.

1.  Use short field takeoff technique as specified in Section 4.

2.  Decrease distances by 10% for each 11 knots headwind. For operation with tailwind up to 10 knots, increase distances by 10% for each 2 knots.

3.  For operation on a dry, grass runway, increase distances by 15% of the "Ground Roll" figure.

4.  With takeoff power set below the torque limit (1865 foot-pounds), increase distances (both ground roll and total distance) by 3% for INERTIAL SEPARATOR in BYPASS and increase ground roll by 5% and total distance by 10% for CABIN HEAT ON.

5.  Where distance values have been replaced by dashes, operating temperature limits of the airplane would be greatly exceeded.  Those distances which are included but the operation slightly exceeds the temperature limit are provided for interpolation purposes only.

6.  For operation above 40°C and below the operating temperature limits, increase distances at 40°C by 20%.

**Figure 394**

# CARGO POD INSTALLED
# SHORT FIELD TAKEOFF DISTANCE

CONDITIONS:

Flaps **20°**

1900 RPM                                          Torque Set Per Figure 5-8

CABIN HEAT **OFF**                                Paved, Level, Dry Runway

INERTIAL SEPARATOR **NORMAL**                     Zero Wind

Refer to Sheet 1 for appropriate notes applicable to this chart.

|                              |                    | Lift Off:    | 70 KIAS |
|---|---|---|---|

**8750 Pounds:**   Speed at 50 Feet:   83 KIAS

| Pressure Altitude Feet | -10°C | | 0°C | | 10°C | |
|---|---|---|---|---|---|---|
| | Grnd Roll Feet | Total Dist To Clear 50 Foot Obst | Grnd Roll Feet | Total Dist To Clear 50 Foot Obst | Grnd Roll Feet | Total Dist To Clear 50 Foot Obst |
| Sea Level | 1205 | 2160 | 1280 | 2295 | 1365 | 2430 |
| 2000 | 1360 | 2430 | 1455 | 2580 | 1545 | 2740 |
| 4000 | 1550 | 2745 | 1655 | 2920 | 1760 | 3105 |
| 6000 | 1765 | 3115 | 1890 | 3325 | 2015 | 3540 |
| 8000 | 2025 | 3560 | 2165 | 3805 | 2345 | 4125 |
| 10,000 | 2335 | 4090 | 2585 | 4580 | 2930 | 5325 |
| 12,000 | 2875 | 5155 | 3270 | 6030 | 3745 | 7175 |

| Pressure Altitude Feet | 20°C | | 30°C | | 40°C | |
|---|---|---|---|---|---|---|
| | Grnd Roll Feet | Total Dist To Clear 50 Foot Obst | Grnd Roll Feet | Total Dist To Clear 50 Foot Obst | Grnd Roll Feet | Total Dist To Clear 50 Foot Obst |
| Sea Level | 1445 | 2570 | 1535 | 2720 | 1625 | 2870 |
| 2000 | 1645 | 2905 | 1745 | 3075 | 1910 | 3400 |
| 4000 | 1875 | 3295 | 1995 | 3510 | 2290 | 4135 |
| 6000 | 2145 | 3765 | 2435 | 4370 | 2805 | 5195 |
| 8000 | 2670 | 4815 | 3065 | 5715 | 3565 | 7005 |
| 10,000 | 3370 | 6350 | 3915 | 7790 | --- | --- |
| 12,000 | 4350 | 8865 | 5130 | 11,755 | --- | --- |

**Figure 395**

# CARGO POD INSTALLED
# FLAPS UP TAKEOFF DISTANCE

## NOTE

The following general information is applicable to all FLAPS UP TAKEOFF DISTANCE Charts.

1. Use Type II, Type III, or Type IV anti-ice fluid takeoff technique as specified in Section 4.

2. Decrease distances by 10% for each 11 knots headwind. For operation with tailwinds up to 10 knots, increase distances by 10% for each 2 knots.

3. For operation on a dry, grass runway, increase distances by 15% of the "Ground Roll" figure.

4. With takeoff power set below the torque limit (1865 foot-pounds), increase distances (both ground roll and total distance) by 3% for INERTIAL SEPARATOR in BYPASS and increase ground roll by 5% and total distance by 10% for CABIN HEAT ON.

**Figure 396**

# CARGO POD INSTALLED
# RATE OF CLIMB - TAKEOFF FLAP SETTING
### FLAPS 20°

CONDITIONS:
Takeoff Power
1900 RPM

INERTIAL SEPARATOR **NORMAL**

| Weight Pounds | Pressure Altitude Feet | Climb Speed KIAS | Rate of Climb - Feet Per Minute (FPM) | | | | |
|---|---|---|---|---|---|---|---|
| | | | -40°C | -20°C | 0°C | 20°C | 40°C |
| 8750 | Sea Level | 92 | 875 | 855 | 835 | 815 | 795 |
| | 2000 | 90 | 860 | 835 | 815 | 795 | 730 |
| | 4000 | 89 | 835 | 815 | 790 | 765 | 645 |
| | 6000 | 88 | 815 | 790 | 765 | 740 | 555 |
| | 8000 | 87 | 785 | 760 | 735 | 620 | 435 |
| | 10,000 | 85 | 760 | 730 | 665 | 500 | --- |
| | 12,000 | 84 | 725 | 680 | 540 | 380 | --- |
| 8300 | Sea Level | 91 | 955 | 940 | 920 | 900 | 880 |
| | 2000 | 89 | 940 | 920 | 895 | 875 | 810 |
| | 4000 | 88 | 915 | 895 | 870 | 850 | 725 |
| | 6000 | 86 | 895 | 870 | 845 | 820 | 630 |
| | 8000 | 85 | 865 | 840 | 815 | 700 | 505 |
| | 10,000 | 84 | 835 | 810 | 745 | 575 | --- |
| | 12,000 | 82 | 805 | 760 | 615 | 450 | --- |
| 7800 | Sea Level | 89 | 1055 | 1035 | 1020 | 1000 | 980 |
| | 2000 | 87 | 1035 | 1015 | 995 | 975 | 910 |
| | 4000 | 86 | 1015 | 995 | 970 | 950 | 820 |
| | 6000 | 85 | 990 | 965 | 945 | 920 | 720 |
| | 8000 | 83 | 965 | 940 | 915 | 795 | 595 |
| | 10,000 | 82 | 935 | 905 | 840 | 665 | --- |
| | 12,000 | 80 | 905 | 855 | 710 | 540 | --- |
| 7300 | Sea Level | 88 | 1160 | 1145 | 1130 | 1110 | 1090 |
| | 2000 | 86 | 1145 | 1125 | 1105 | 1085 | 1020 |
| | 4000 | 85 | 1125 | 1105 | 1080 | 1060 | 925 |
| | 6000 | 84 | 1100 | 1075 | 1055 | 1030 | 825 |
| | 8000 | 82 | 1075 | 1050 | 1025 | 900 | 690 |
| | 10,000 | 81 | 1045 | 1015 | 950 | 765 | --- |
| | 12,000 | 79 | 1015 | 965 | 810 | 635 | --- |

G2088675-00

## NOTE

1. Do not exceed torque limit for takeoff per **MAXIMUM ENGINE TORQUE FOR TAKEOFF** chart. When ITT exceeds 765°C, this power setting is time limited to 5 minutes.

2. With climb power set below the torque limit, decrese rate of climb by 20 FPM for INERTIAL SEPARATOR set in BYPASS and 45 FPM for CABIN HEAT ON.

3. Where rate of climb values have been replaced by dashes, operating temperature limits of the airplane would be greatly exceeded. Those rates of climb which are included, but the operation slightly exceeds the temperature limit, are provided for interpolation purposes only.

**Figure 397**

# CARGO POD INSTALLED
# CLIMB GRADIENT - TAKEOFF
### FLAPS UP

CONDITIONS:
Takeoff Power
1900 RPM

Zero Wind
INERTIAL SEPARATOR **NORMAL**

| Weight Pounds | Pressure Altitude Feet | Climb Speed KIAS | Climb Gradient - Feet/Nautical Mile (FT/NM) | | | | |
|---|---|---|---|---|---|---|---|
| | | | -40℃ | -20℃ | 0℃ | 20℃ | 40℃ |
| 8750 | Sea Level | 68 | 735 | 695 | 655 | 620 | 475 |
| | 2000 | 69 | 695 | 655 | 615 | 580 | 390 |
| | 4000 | 69 | 660 | 615 | 580 | 500 | 305 |
| | 6000 | 70 | 620 | 580 | 545 | 410 | 230 |
| | 8000 | 70 | 580 | 540 | 475 | 330 | 165 |
| | 10,000 | 71 | 545 | 505 | 390 | 250 | --- |
| | 12,000 | 72 | 505 | 420 | 305 | 180 | --- |
| 8300 | Sea Level | 66 | 810 | 770 | 725 | 690 | 535 |
| | 2000 | 66 | 770 | 730 | 685 | 650 | 445 |
| | 4000 | 67 | 730 | 690 | 650 | 565 | 360 |
| | 6000 | 68 | 690 | 645 | 610 | 470 | 280 |
| | 8000 | 68 | 650 | 605 | 540 | 380 | 210 |
| | 10,000 | 69 | 610 | 570 | 445 | 300 | --- |
| | 12,000 | 69 | 570 | 475 | 355 | 225 | --- |
| 7800 | Sea Level | 61 | 910 | 860 | 815 | 775 | 615 |
| | 2000 | 62 | 865 | 820 | 775 | 735 | 515 |
| | 4000 | 62 | 820 | 775 | 730 | 640 | 425 |
| | 6000 | 62 | 780 | 730 | 690 | 540 | 340 |
| | 8000 | 63 | 735 | 690 | 615 | 445 | 265 |
| | 10,000 | 63 | 690 | 645 | 515 | 360 | --- |
| | 12,000 | 63 | 645 | 550 | 420 | 280 | --- |
| 7300 | Sea Level | 59 | 1020 | 970 | 920 | 875 | 700 |
| | 2000 | 59 | 975 | 920 | 875 | 830 | 595 |
| | 4000 | 59 | 925 | 875 | 830 | 730 | 500 |
| | 6000 | 59 | 880 | 830 | 780 | 620 | 405 |
| | 8000 | 59 | 830 | 780 | 700 | 520 | 330 |
| | 10,000 | 59 | 785 | 735 | 595 | 430 | --- |
| | 12,000 | 59 | 735 | 630 | 490 | 340 | --- |

G2089675-00

## NOTE

1. **Do not exceed torque limit for takeoff per MAXIMUM ENGINE TORQUE FOR TAKEOFF chart. When ITT exceeds 765℃, this power setting is time limited to 5 minutes.**

2. With climb power set below the torque limit, decrease climb gradient by 10 FT/NM for INERTIAL SEPARATOR set in BYPASS and 40 FT/NM for CABIN HEAT ON.

3. Where climb gradient values have been replaced by dashes, operating temperature limits of the airplane would be greatly exceeded. Those climb gradients which are included, but the operation slightly exceeds the temperature limit, are provided for interpolation purposes only.

**Figure 398**

# CARGO POD INSTALLED
# TIME, FUEL, AND DISTANCE TO CLIMB
## MAXIMUM RATE OF CLIMB

CONDITIONS:
Flaps **UP**                                               Zero Wind
1900 RPM                                                    INERTIAL SEPARATOR **NORMAL**

| Weight Pounds | Pressure Altitude Feet | Climb Speed KIAS | Climb From Sea Level | | | | | | | | |
| --- | --- | --- | --- | --- | --- | --- | --- | --- | --- | --- | --- |
| | | | 20°C Below Standard | | | Standard Temperature | | | 20°C Above Standard | | |
| | | | Time min | Fuel Lbs | Dist NM | Time min | Fuel Lbs | Dist NM | Time min | Fuel Lbs | Dist NM |
| 8750 | Sea Level | 104 | 0 | 0 | 0 | 0 | 0 | 0 | 0 | 0 | 0 |
| | 4000 | 104 | 4 | 32 | 8 | 5 | 33 | 8 | 6 | 38 | 10 |
| | 8000 | 104 | 9 | 64 | 16 | 9 | 66 | 17 | 12 | 80 | 24 |
| | 12,000 | 102 | 14 | 98 | 25 | 15 | 105 | 29 | 22 | 132 | 43 |
| | 16,000 | 96 | 20 | 136 | 37 | 23 | 152 | 45 | 35 | 202 | 71 |
| | 20,000 | 88 | 28 | 186 | 54 | 36 | 219 | 72 | 69 | 349 | 142 |
| | 24,000 | 79 | 49 | 278 | 93 | 75 | 388 | 152 | --- | --- | --- |
| 8300 | Sea Level | 103 | 0 | 0 | 0 | 0 | 0 | 0 | 0 | 0 | 0 |
| | 4000 | 103 | 4 | 29 | 7 | 4 | 30 | 7 | 5 | 34 | 9 |
| | 8000 | 103 | 8 | 58 | 14 | 8 | 60 | 15 | 11 | 72 | 21 |
| | 12,000 | 101 | 13 | 89 | 23 | 14 | 95 | 26 | 19 | 116 | 37 |
| | 16,000 | 95 | 18 | 123 | 33 | 21 | 135 | 40 | 30 | 172 | 60 |
| | 20,000 | 87 | 25 | 165 | 47 | 31 | 189 | 61 | 51 | 265 | 104 |
| | 24,000 | 77 | 40 | 233 | 76 | 54 | 287 | 106 | --- | --- | --- |
| 7800 | Sea Level | 101 | 0 | 0 | 0 | 0 | 0 | 0 | 0 | 0 | 0 |
| | 4000 | 101 | 4 | 26 | 6 | 4 | 27 | 6 | 4 | 30 | 8 |
| | 8000 | 101 | 7 | 52 | 13 | 8 | 54 | 14 | 10 | 63 | 18 |
| | 12,000 | 99 | 11 | 80 | 20 | 12 | 84 | 22 | 16 | 100 | 31 |
| | 16,000 | 92 | 16 | 110 | 29 | 18 | 119 | 34 | 25 | 145 | 49 |
| | 20,000 | 84 | 22 | 146 | 41 | 27 | 163 | 51 | 40 | 210 | 79 |
| | 24,000 | 74 | 33 | 198 | 62 | 42 | 229 | 81 | 88 | 395 | 178 |
| 7300 | Sea Level | 99 | 0 | 0 | 0 | 0 | 0 | 0 | 0 | 0 | 0 |
| | 4000 | 99 | 3 | 24 | 5 | 3 | 24 | 6 | 4 | 27 | 7 |
| | 8000 | 99 | 7 | 47 | 11 | 7 | 49 | 12 | 9 | 55 | 16 |
| | 12,000 | 97 | 10 | 72 | 18 | 11 | 75 | 20 | 14 | 87 | 27 |
| | 16,000 | 89 | 14 | 99 | 25 | 16 | 105 | 30 | 21 | 124 | 41 |
| | 20,000 | 80 | 20 | 129 | 35 | 23 | 141 | 43 | 32 | 173 | 63 |
| | 24,000 | 70 | 29 | 171 | 52 | 34 | 191 | 65 | 55 | 260 | 108 |

G2085675-00

## NOTE

1. **Torque set at 1865 foot-pounds or lesser value must not exceed maximum climb ITT of 765°C or Ng of 101.6%.**
2. Add 35 pounds of fuel for engine start, taxi, and takeoff allowances.
3. With INERTIAL SEPARATOR set in BYPASS, increase time, fuel, and distance numbers by 1% for each 2000 feet of climb and for CABIN HEAT ON, increase time, fuel, and distance numbers by 1% for each 1000 feet of climb.
4. Where time, fuel, and distance values have been replaced by dashes, an appreciable rate of climb for the weight shown cannot be expected.

**Figure 399**

# CARGO POD INSTALLED
# FUEL AND TIME REQUIRED
## MAXIMUM CRUISE POWER (40-200 Nautical Miles)

CONDITIONS:

8750 Pounds      Standard Temperature

1900 RPM      INERTIAL SEPARATOR **NORMAL**

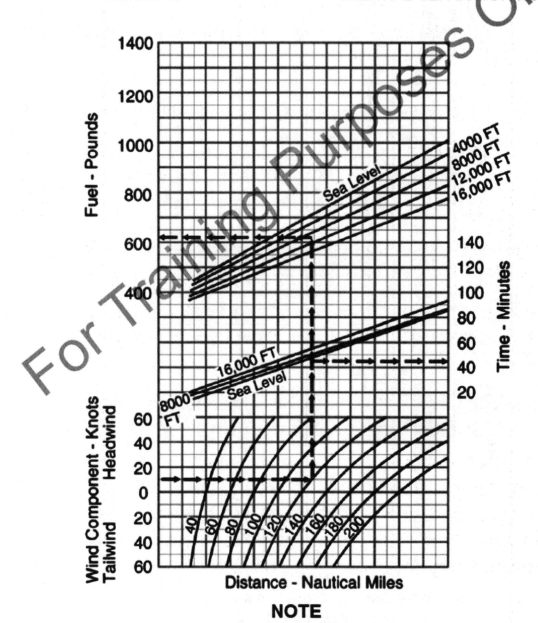

## NOTE

1. Fuel required includes the fuel used for engine start, taxi, takeoff, maximum climb from sea level, descent to sea level and 45 minutes reserve. Time required includes the time during a maximum climb and descent.

2. With INERTIAL SEPARATOR in BYPAS, increase time by 4% and fuel by 2% or CABIN HEAT ON, increase time by 3% and fuel by 2%.

**Figure 400**

# CARGO POD INSTALLED
# SHORT FIELD LANDING DISTANCE

## NOTE

The following general information is applicable to all SHORT FIELD LANDING DISTANCE Charts.

1. Use short field landing technique as specified in Section 4.

2. Decrease distances by 10% for each 11 knots headwind. For operation with tailwind up to 10 knots, increase distances by 10% for each 2 knots.

3. For operation on a dry, grass runway, increase distances by 40% of the "Ground Roll" figure.

4. If a landing with flaps UP is necessary, increase the approach speed by 15 KIAS and allow for 40% longer distances.

5. Use of maximum reverse thrust after touchdown reduces ground roll distance by approximately 10%.

6. Where distance values have been replaced by dashes, operating temperature limits of the airplane would be greatly exceeded. Those distances which are included but the operation slightly exceeds the temperature limit are provided for interpolation purposes only.

**Figure 401**

# CARGO POD INSTALLED
# SHORT FIELD LANDING DISTANCE

CONDITIONS:

Flaps **FULL**

Zero Wind

Maximum Braking

PROP RPM Lever **MAX**

Paved, Level, Dry Runway

POWER Lever **IDLE** after clearing obstacles. **BETA** range (lever against spring) after touchdown.

Refer to Sheet 1 for appropriate notes applicable to this chart.

**8500 Pounds:**                       Speed at 50 Feet:                **78 KIAS**

| Pressure Altitude Feet | -10°C | | 0°C | | 10°C | |
|---|---|---|---|---|---|---|
| | Grnd Roll Feet | Total Dist To Clear 50 Foot Obst | Grnd Roll Feet | Total Dist To Clear 50 Foot Obst | Grnd Roll Feet | Total Dist To Clear 50 Foot Obst |
| Sea Level | 835 | 1625 | 865 | 1670 | 900 | 1715 |
| 2000 | 900 | 1715 | 935 | 1765 | 965 | 1815 |
| 4000 | 965 | 1815 | 1005 | 1865 | 1040 | 1920 |
| 6000 | 1040 | 1920 | 1080 | 1975 | 1120 | 2030 |
| 8000 | 1125 | 2035 | 1165 | 2095 | 1210 | 2155 |
| 10,000 | 1215 | 2160 | 1260 | 2220 | 1305 | 2285 |
| 12,000 | 1310 | 2295 | 1360 | 2360 | 1410 | 2430 |

| Pressure Altitude Feet | 20°C | | 30°C | | 40°C | |
|---|---|---|---|---|---|---|
| | Grnd Roll Feet | Total Dist To Clear 50 Foot Obst | Grnd Roll Feet | Total Dist To Clear 50 Foot Obst | Grnd Roll Feet | Total Dist To Clear 50 Foot Obst |
| Sea Level | 930 | 1765 | 965 | 1810 | 995 | 1855 |
| 2000 | 1000 | 1860 | 1035 | 1910 | 1070 | 1960 |
| 4000 | 1075 | 1970 | 1115 | 2020 | 1150 | 2070 |
| 6000 | 1160 | 2085 | 1200 | 2140 | 1240 | 2195 |
| 8000 | 1250 | 2210 | 1295 | 2270 | 1340 | 2330 |
| 10,000 | 1350 | 2345 | 1400 | 2410 | --- | --- |
| 12,000 | 1460 | 2495 | 1510 | 2560 | --- | --- |

**Figure 402**

## WITHOUT CARGO POD
# ENDURANCE PROFILE
# 45 MINUTES RESERVE
# 2224 POUNDS USABLE FUEL

CONDITIONS:

8750 Pounds
1900 RPM

Standard Temperature
INERTIAL SEPARATOR **NORMAL**

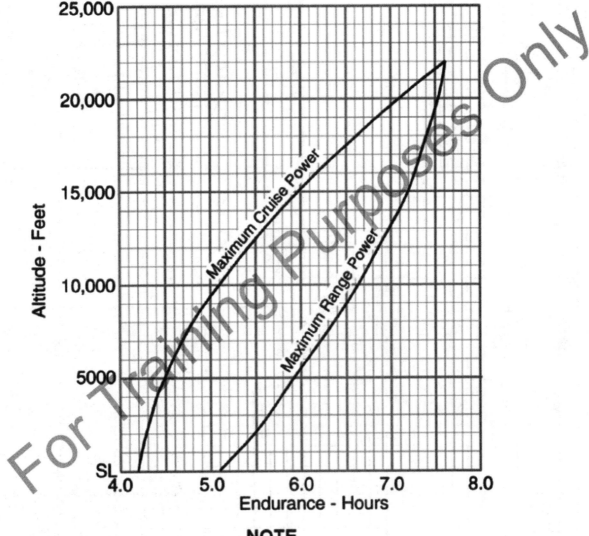

**NOTE**

1. This chart allows for the fuel used for engine start, taxi, takeoff, climb and descent. The time during a maximum climb and the time during descent are included.

2. With INERTIAL SEPARATOR in BYPASS, decrease endurance by 2%, or CABIN HEAT ON, decrease endurance by 3%.

**Figure 403**

# WEIGHT AND BALANCE RECORD (LOAD MANIFEST)

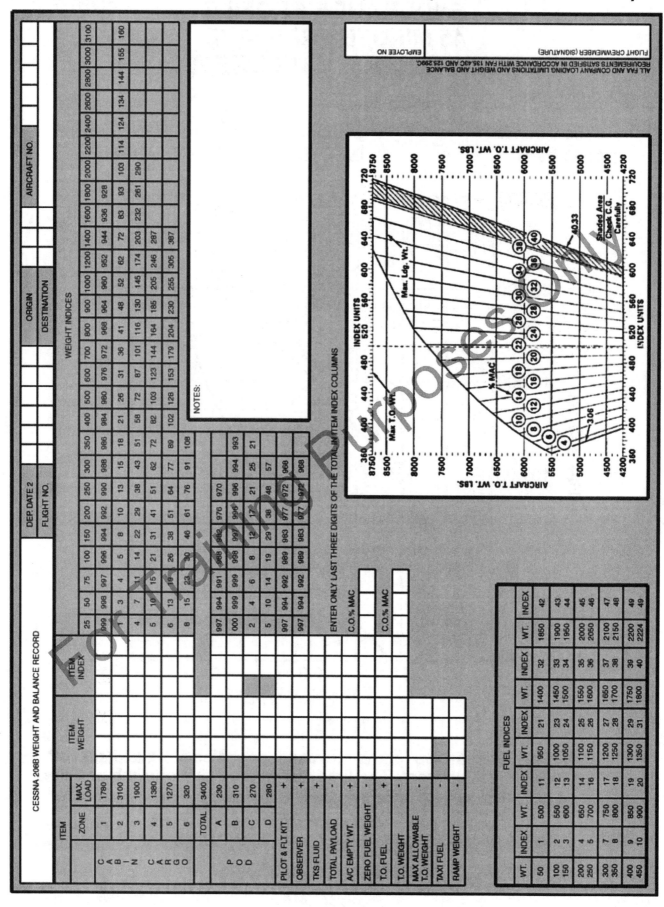

**Figure 404**

# WEIGHT AND BALANCE RECORD (LOAD MANIFEST)

MAXIMUM STRUCTURAL WEIGHTS
MAX RAMP    8785 LBS
MAX TAKEOFF   8750 LBS
MAX LANDING   8500 LBS

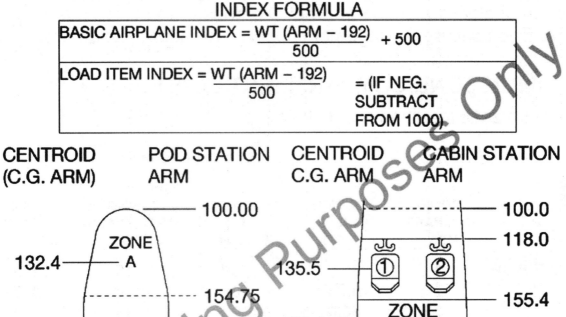

INDEX FORMULA

$$\text{BASIC AIRPLANE INDEX} = \frac{WT(ARM - 192)}{500} + 500$$

$$\text{LOAD ITEM INDEX} = \frac{WT(ARM - 192)}{500} = \text{(IF NEG. SUBTRACT FROM 1000)}$$

**Figure 405**

# CARGO POD

The airplane may be equipped with a 111.5 cubic foot capacity cargo pod attached to the bottom of the fuselage. The pod is divided into four compartments (identified as Zones A, B, C, and D) by bulkheads and has a maximum floor loading of 30 pounds per square foot and maximum load weight limit of 1090 pounds. Each compartment has a loading door located on the left side of the pod. The doors are hinged at the bottom, and each has two latches. When the latch handles are rotated to the horizontal position with the doors closed, the doors are secured. Refer to the Pod Internal Dimension and Load Markings and Cargo Pod Loading Arrangements figures for additional details.

## MAXIMUM ZONE/COMPARTMENT LOADINGS

Maximum zone loadings are as follows:

| | ZONE/ COMPART- MENT | VOLUME (CUBIC FEET) | WEIGHT LIMITS (Pounds) | | C.G. (STATION LOCATION) |
|---|---|---|---|---|---|
| | | | *SECURED BY TIE-DOWNS | **UNSECURED USING PARTITIONS OR IN CARGO POD | |
| FUSELAGE | 1 | 52.9 | 1780 | 415 | 172.1 |
| | 2 | 109.0 | 3100 | 860 | 217.8 |
| | 3 | 63.0 | 1900 | 495 | 264.4 |
| | 4 | 43.5 | 1380 | 340 | 294.5 |
| | 5 | 40.1 | 1270 | 315 | 319.5 |
| | 6 | 31.5 | 320 | 245 | 344.0 |
| CARGO POD | A | 23.4 | - - - | 230 | 132.4 |
| | B | 31.5 | - - - | 310 | 182.1 |
| | C | 27.8 | - - - | 270 | 233.4 |
| | D | 28.8 | - - - | 280 | 287.6 |

**\* THIS IS THE MAXIMUM CARGO ALLOWED IN THE BAY INDICATED.**

**\*\*DENSITY MUST BE 7.9 LBS/FT$^3$ OR LESS AND BAY 75% OR MORE FULL.**

**Figure 406**

# CABIN INTERNAL LOAD MARKINGS (CARGO VERSION)

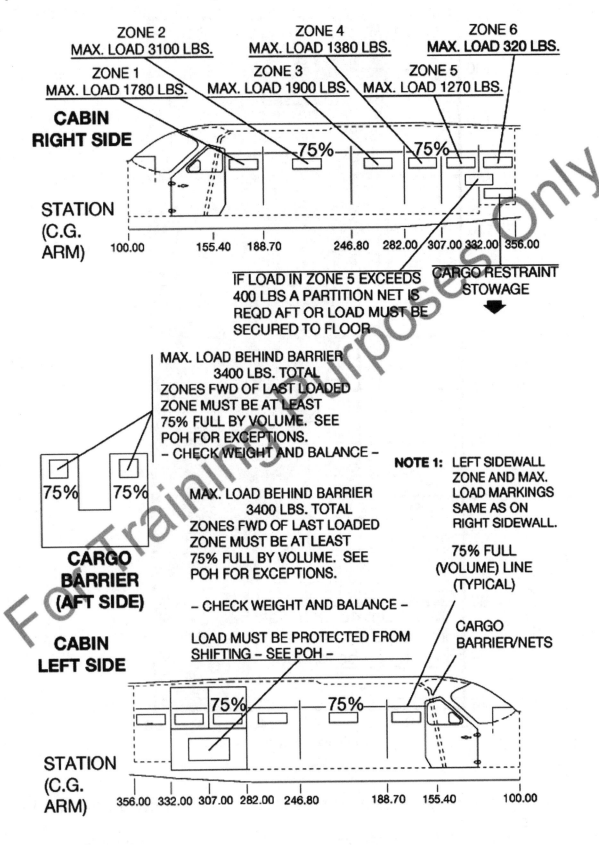

**Figure 407**

# MAXIMUM CARGO SIZES

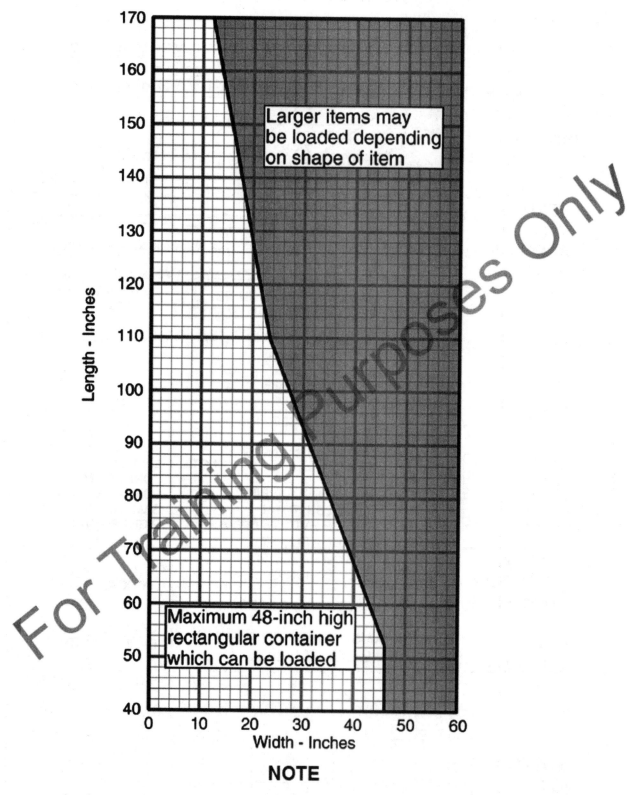

**NOTE**

1. Approximately one inch clearance allowed from sidewall and ceiling.
2. Subtract roller height and pallet thickness, if applicable.

**Figure 408**

# CARGO POD INSTALLED
# SHORT FIELD LANDING DISTANCE

CONDITIONS:

Flaps **FULL**

Zero Wind

Maximum Braking

PROP RPM Lever **MAX**

Paved, Level, Dry Runway

POWER Lever **IDLE** after clearing obstacles. **BETA** range (lever against spring) after touchdown.

Refer to Sheet 1 for appropriate notes applicable to this chart.

**8500 Pounds:**  Speed at 50 Feet:  78 KIAS

| Pressure Altitude Feet | -10℃ | | 0℃ | | 10℃ | |
|---|---|---|---|---|---|---|
| | Grnd Roll Feet | Total Dist To Clear 50 Foot Obst | Grnd Roll Feet | Total Dist To Clear 50 Foot Obst | Grnd Roll Feet | Total Dist To Clear 50 Foot Obst |
| Sea Level | 835 | 1625 | 865 | 1670 | 900 | 1715 |
| 2000 | 900 | 1715 | 935 | 1765 | 965 | 1815 |
| 4000 | 965 | 1815 | 1005 | 1865 | 1040 | 1920 |
| 6000 | 1040 | 1920 | 1080 | 1975 | 1120 | 2030 |
| 8000 | 1125 | 2035 | 1165 | 2095 | 1210 | 2155 |
| 10,000 | 1215 | 2160 | 1260 | 2220 | 1305 | 2285 |
| 12,000 | 1310 | 2295 | 1360 | 2360 | 1410 | 2430 |

| Pressure Altitude Feet | 20℃ | | 30℃ | | 40℃ | |
|---|---|---|---|---|---|---|
| | Grnd Roll Feet | Total Dist To Clear 50 Foot Obst | Grnd Roll Feet | Total Dist To Clear 50 Foot Obst | Grnd Roll Feet | Total Dist To Clear 50 Foot Obst |
| Sea Level | 930 | 1765 | 965 | 1810 | 995 | 1855 |
| 2000 | 1000 | 1860 | 1035 | 1910 | 1070 | 1960 |
| 4000 | 1075 | 1970 | 1115 | 2020 | 1150 | 2070 |
| 6000 | 1160 | 2085 | 1200 | 2140 | 1240 | 2195 |
| 8000 | 1250 | 2210 | 1295 | 2270 | 1340 | 2330 |
| 10,000 | 1350 | 2345 | 1400 | 2410 | --- | --- |
| 12,000 | 1460 | 2495 | 1510 | 2560 | --- | --- |

**Figure 409**

# WEIGHT AND MOMENT TABLES
# 10 PLACE COMMUTER
## Crew and Passengers
### (Single Commuter Seating)

| Weight Pounds | Pilot/ Front Passenger Seats 1 and 2 (Arm = 135.5 Inch) | Aft Passengers Seats | | | |
|---|---|---|---|---|---|
| | | 3 and 4 (Arm = 173.9 Inch) | 5 and 6 (Arm = 209.9 Inch) | 7 and 8 (Arm = 245.9 Inch) | 9 and 10 (Arm = 281.9 Inch) |
| | | Moment (Inch-Pound/1000) | | | |
| 1 | 0.1 | 0.2 | 0.2 | 0.2 | 0.3 |
| 2 | 0.3 | 0.3 | 0.4 | 0.5 | 0.6 |
| 3 | 0.4 | 0.5 | 0.6 | 0.7 | 0.8 |
| 4 | 0.5 | 0.7 | 0.8 | 1.0 | 1.1 |
| 5 | 0.7 | 0.9 | 1.0 | 1.2 | 1.4 |
| 6 | 0.8 | 1.0 | 1.3 | 1.5 | 1.7 |
| 7 | 0.9 | 1.2 | 1.5 | 1.7 | 2.0 |
| 8 | 1.1 | 1.4 | 1.7 | 2.0 | 2.3 |
| 9 | 1.2 | 1.6 | 1.9 | 2.2 | 2.5 |
| 10 | 1.4 | 1.7 | 2.1 | 2.5 | 2.8 |
| 20 | 2.7 | 3.5 | 4.2 | 4.9 | 5.6 |
| 30 | 4.1 | 5.2 | 6.3 | 7.4 | 8.5 |
| 40 | 5.4 | 7.0 | 8.4 | 9.8 | 11.3 |
| 50 | 6.8 | 8.7 | 10.5 | 12.3 | 14.1 |
| 60 | 8.1 | 10.4 | 12.6 | 14.8 | 16.9 |
| 70 | 9.5 | 12.2 | 14.7 | 17.2 | 19.7 |
| 80 | 10.8 | 13.9 | 16.8 | 19.7 | 22.6 |
| 90 | 12.2 | 15.7 | 18.9 | 22.1 | 25.4 |
| 100 | 13.6 | 17.4 | 21.0 | 24.6 | 28.2 |
| 200 | 27.1 | 34.8 | 42.0 | 49.2 | 56.4 |
| 300 | 40.7 | 52.2 | 63.0 | 73.8 | 84.6 |

EXAMPLE:
To obtain moments for a 185 pounds paasenger in seat 5, add moments shown for 100 pounds (21.0), 80 pounds (16.8), and 5 pounds (1.0) for a total moment of 38.8 inch-pound/1000.

NOTE

The airplane may be configured with left single commuter seats installed on the right side, and right single commuter seats installed on the left side. Actual seat location should be noted when computing airplane weight and balance.

**Figure 410**

# WEIGHT AND MOMENT TABLES
## FUEL (JET FUEL WITH DENSITY OF 6.7 POUNDS/GALLON AT 60°F)

| Gallons | Weight Pounds | Moment Inch-Pound/1000 (Arm Varies) | Gallons | Weight Pounds | Moment Inch-Pound/1000 (Arm Varies) |
|---|---|---|---|---|---|
| 5 | 34 | 6.8 | 175 | 1173 | 238.4 |
| 10 | 67 | 13.6 | 180 | 1206 | 245.2 |
| 15 | 101 | 20.4 | 185 | 1240 | 252.0 |
| 20 | 134 | 27.2 | 190 | 1273 | 258.8 |
| 25 | 168 | 34.0 | 195 | 1307 | 265.7 |
| 30 | 201 | 40.8 | 200 | 1340 | 272.5 |
| 35 | 235 | 47.6 | 205 | 1374 | 279.3 |
| 40 | 268 | 54.4 | 210 | 1407 | 286.1 |
| 45 | 302 | 61.2 | 215 | 1441 | 292.9 |
| 50 | 335 | 68.0 | 220 | 1474 | 299.7 |
| 55 | 369 | 74.8 | 225 | 1508 | 306.5 |
| 60 | 402 | 81.6 | 230 | 1541 | 313.3 |
| 65 | 436 | 88.4 | 235 | 1575 | 320.1 |
| 70 | 469 | 95.2 | 240 | 1608 | 326.9 |
| 75 | 503 | 102.0 | 245 | 1642 | 333.7 |
| 80 | 536 | 108.8 | 250 | 1675 | 340.5 |
| 85 | 570 | 115.7 | 255 | 1709 | 347.3 |
| 90 | 603 | 122.5 | 260 | 1742 | 354.1 |
| 95 | 637 | 129.3 | 265 | 1776 | 360.9 |
| 100 | 670 | 136.1 | 270 | 1809 | 367.7 |
| 105 | 704 | 142.9 | 275 | 1843 | 374.5 |
| 110 | 737 | 149.7 | 280 | 1876 | 381.2 |
| 115 | 771 | 156.6 | 285 | 1910 | 388.0 |
| 120 | 804 | 163.4 | 290 | 1943 | 394.8 |
| 125 | 838 | 170.2 | 295 | 1977 | 401.6 |
| 130 | 871 | 177.0 | 300 | 2010 | 408.4 |
| 135 | 905 | 183.8 | 305 | 2044 | 415.2 |
| 140 | 938 | 190.6 | 310 | 2077 | 422.0 |
| 145 | 972 | 197.5 | 315 | 2111 | 428.8 |
| 150 | 1005 | 204.3 | 320 | 2144 | 435.6 |
| 155 | 1039 | 211.1 | 325 | 2178 | 442.4 |
| 160 | 1072 | 217.9 | 327 | 2189 | 444.7 |
| 165 | 1106 | 224.7 | 330 | 2211 | 449.1 |
| 170 | 1139 | 231.5 | 332 | 2224 | 451.7 |

**Figure 411**

# WEIGHT AND MOMENT TABLES
## CARGO (CABIN LOCATIONS)

| Weight Pounds | Zone 1 (Arm = 172.1 Inch) | Zone 2 (Arm = 217.8 Inch) | Zone 3 (Arm = 264.4 Inch) | Zone 4 (Arm = 294.5 Inch) | Zone 5 (Arm = 319.5 Inch) | Zone 6 (Arm = 344.0 Inch) |
|---|---|---|---|---|---|---|
| | Moment (Inch-Pound/1000) | | | | | |
| 1 | 0.2 | 0.2 | 0.3 | 0.3 | 0.3 | 0.3 |
| 2 | 0.3 | 0.4 | 0.5 | 0.6 | 0.6 | 0.7 |
| 3 | 0.5 | 0.7 | 0.8 | 0.9 | 1.0 | 1.0 |
| 4 | 0.7 | 0.9 | 1.1 | 1.2 | 1.3 | 1.4 |
| 5 | 0.9 | 1.1 | 1.3 | 1.5 | 1.6 | 1.7 |
| 6 | 1.0 | 1.3 | 1.6 | 1.8 | 1.9 | 2.1 |
| 7 | 1.2 | 1.5 | 1.9 | 2.1 | 2.2 | 2.4 |
| 8 | 1.4 | 1.7 | 2.1 | 2.4 | 2.6 | 2.8 |
| 9 | 1.5 | 2.0 | 2.4 | 2.7 | 2.9 | 3.1 |
| 10 | 1.7 | 2.2 | 2.6 | 2.9 | 3.2 | 3.4 |
| 20 | 3.4 | 4.4 | 5.3 | 5.9 | 6.4 | 6.9 |
| 30 | 5.2 | 6.5 | 7.9 | 8.8 | 9.6 | 10.3 |
| 40 | 6.9 | 8.7 | 10.6 | 11.8 | 12.8 | 13.8 |
| 50 | 8.6 | 10.9 | 13.2 | 14.7 | 16.0 | 17.2 |
| 60 | 10.3 | 13.1 | 15.9 | 17.7 | 19.2 | 20.6 |
| 70 | 12.0 | 15.2 | 18.5 | 20.6 | 22.4 | 24.1 |
| 80 | 13.8 | 17.4 | 21.2 | 23.6 | 25.6 | 27.5 |
| 90 | 15.5 | 19.6 | 23.8 | 26.5 | 28.8 | 31.0 |
| 100 | 17.2 | 21.8 | 26.4 | 29.5 | 32.0 | 34.4 |
| 200 | 34.4 | 43.6 | 52.9 | 58.9 | 63.9 | 68.8 |
| 300 | 51.6 | 65.3 | 79.3 | 88.4 | 95.9 | 103.2 |
| 400 | 68.8 | 87.1 | 105.8 | 117.8 | 127.8 | |
| 500 | 86.1 | 108.9 | 132.2 | 147.3 | 159.8 | |
| 600 | 103.3 | 130.7 | 158.6 | 176.7 | 191.7 | |
| 700 | 120.5 | 152.5 | 185.1 | 206.2 | 223.7 | |
| 800 | 137.7 | 174.2 | 211.5 | 235.6 | 255.6 | |
| 900 | 154.9 | 196.0 | 238.0 | 265.1 | 287.6 | |
| 1000 | 172.1 | 217.8 | 264.4 | 294.5 | 319.5 | |
| 2000 | | 435.6 | | | | |
| 3000 | | 653.4 | | | | |

EXAMPLE:

To obtain moments for 350 pounds of cargo in Zone 1, add moments shown in Zone 1 for 300 pounds (51.6) and 50 pounds (8.6) for a total moment of 60.2 inch-pound/1000.

**Figure 412**

# WEIGHT AND MOMENT TABLES
## CARGO (CARGO POD LOCATIONS)

| Weight Pounds | Zone A (Arm = 132.4 Inch) | Zone B (Arm = 182.1 Inch) | Zone C (Arm = 233.4 Inch) | Zone D (Arm = 287.6 Inch) |
|---|---|---|---|---|
| | Moment (Inch-Pound/1000) | | | |
| 1 | 0.1 | 0.2 | 0.2 | 0.3 |
| 2 | 0.3 | 0.4 | 0.5 | 0.6 |
| 3 | 0.4 | 0.5 | 0.7 | 0.9 |
| 4 | 0.5 | 0.7 | 0.9 | 1.2 |
| 5 | 0.7 | 0.9 | 1.2 | 1.4 |
| 6 | 0.8 | 1.1 | 1.4 | 1.7 |
| 7 | 0.9 | 1.3 | 1.6 | 2.0 |
| 8 | 1.1 | 1.5 | 1.9 | 2.3 |
| 9 | 1.2 | 1.6 | 2.1 | 2.6 |
| 10 | 1.3 | 1.8 | 2.3 | 2.9 |
| 20 | 2.6 | 3.6 | 4.7 | 5.8 |
| 30 | 4.0 | 5.5 | 7.0 | 8.6 |
| 40 | 5.3 | 7.3 | 9.3 | 11.5 |
| 50 | 6.6 | 9.1 | 11.7 | 14.4 |
| 60 | 7.9 | 10.9 | 14.0 | 17.3 |
| 70 | 9.3 | 12.7 | 16.3 | 20.1 |
| 80 | 10.6 | 14.6 | 18.7 | 23.0 |
| 90 | 11.9 | 16.4 | 21.0 | 25.9 |
| 100 | 13.2 | 18.2 | 23.3 | 28.8 |
| 200 | 26.5 | 36.4 | 46.7 | 57.5 |
| 300 | | 54.6 | | |

| EXAMPLE: |
|---|

To obtain moments for 48 pounds of cargo in Zone A, add moments shown in Zone A for 40 pounds (5.3) and 8 pounds (1.1) for a total moment of 6.4 inch-pound/1000.

**Figure 413**

# SAMPLE LOADING PROBLEM

| (CARGO LOADING SHOWN) | SAMPLE AIRPLANE | | YOUR AIRPLANE | |
|---|---|---|---|---|
| | Weight Pounds | Moment Inch-Pound/1000 | Weight Pounds | Moment Inch-Pound/1000 |
| 1. Basic Empty Weight (Use the data pertaining to your airplane as it is presently equipped (includes unusable fuel and full oil). | 5005 | 929.4 | 5005 | 929.4 |
| 2. Usable Fuel (332 Gallons Max) | 2224 | 451.7 | | |
| 3. Pilot (Seat 1) (STA. 133.5 to 146.5) | 170 | 23.1 | 200 | |
| 4. Front Passenger (Seat 2) (STA. 133.5 to 146.5) | | | | |
| 5. Aft Passengers (Commuter Seating): | | | | |
| STA. 173.9 | | | | |
| STA. 209.9 | | | | |
| STA. 245.9 | | | | |
| STA. 281.9 | | | | |
| 6. Baggage/Cargo (Cabin Locations): | | | | |
| Zone 1 (STA. 155.40 to 188.70) | 120 | 20.6 | | |
| Zone 2 (STA. 188.70 to 246.80) | 416 | 90.6 | | |
| Zone 3 (STA. 246.80 to 282.00) | 200 | 52.9 | | |
| Zone 4 (STA. 282.00 to 307.00) | 200 | 58.9 | | |
| Zone 5 (STA. 307.00 to 332.00) | 200 | 63.9 | | |
| Zone 6 (STA. 332.00 to 356.00) | 50 | 17.2 | | |
| 7. Baggage/Cargo (Cargo Pod Locations): | | | | |
| Zone A (STA. 100.00 to 154.75) | 50 | 6.6 | | |
| Zone B (STA. 154.75 to 209.35) | 50 | 9.1 | | |
| Zone C (STA. 209.35 to 257.35) | 50 | 11.7 | | |
| Zone D (STA. 257.35 to 332.00) | 50 | 14.4 | | |
| 8. RAMP WEIGHT AND MOMENT | 8785 | 1750.1 | | |
| 9. Fuel Allowance (for engine start, taxi, and runup) | -35 | -7.0 | | |
| 10. TO WEIGHT AND MOMENT (Subtract Step 9 from Step 8) | 8750 | 1743.1 | | |

11. Locate this point (8750 at 1743.1) on the Center of Gravity Moment Envelope, and since this point falls within the envelope, the loading is acceptable.

**NOTE**

Refer to the Weight and Moment Tables for weight and moment of crew, passengers, usable fuel, and cargo being carried. Refer to Cabin Internal Loading Arrangements for aft passengers seating arrangements.

**Figure 414**

# CENTER OF GRAVITY LIMITS

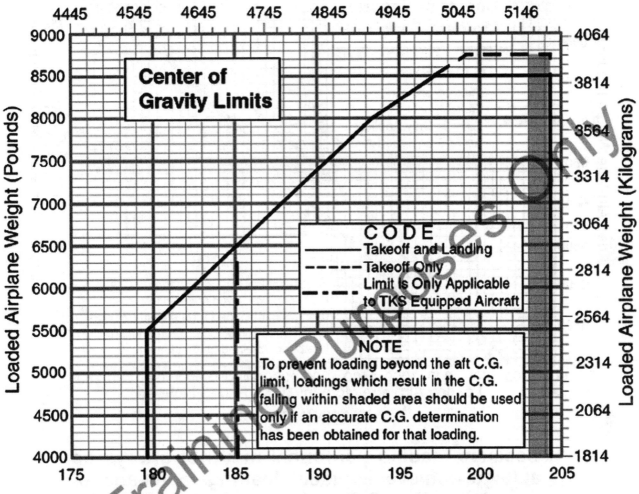

## WARNING

**It is the responsibility of the pilot to make sure that the airplane is loaded correctly. Operation outside of prescribed weight and balance limitations could result in an accident and serious or fatal injury.**

**Figure 415**

# CENTER OF GRAVITY MOMENT ENVELOPE

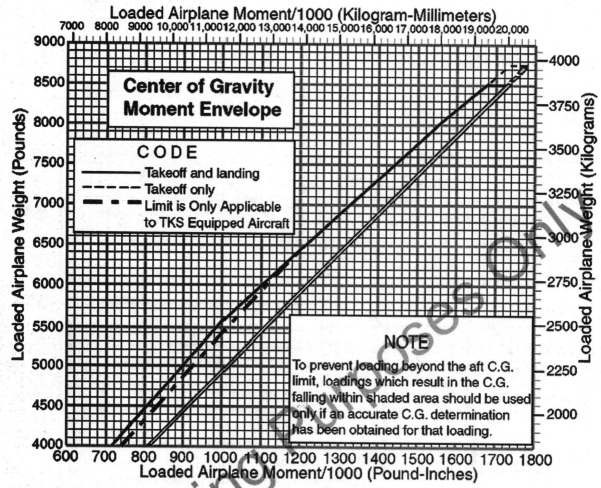

## WARNING

- Because loading personnel may not always be able to achieve an ideal loading, a means of protecting the C.G envelope is provided by supplying an aft C.G. location warning (shaded area) between 38.33% mac and the maximum aft c.g. of 40.33% mac on the center of gravity moment envelope. Points falling within this shaded area should be used only if accurate C.G. determination for cargo loadings can be obtained.

- It is the responsibility of the pilot to make sure that the airplane is loaded correctly. Operation outside of prescribed weight and balance limitations could result in an accident and serious or fatal injury.

**Figure 416**

# LIMITATIONS
## Introduction

## 1. INTRODUCTION

Observance of the limitations included in this chapter is mandatory.

## 2. KINDS OF AIRPLANE OPERATION

The airplane is certified in the transport category for day and night operations, in the following conditions when the equipment and instruments required by the airworthiness and operating regulations are approved, installed and in an operable condition:

- VFR and IFR
- Flight in icing conditions

The airplane is certified for ditching when the safety equipment specified by the applicable regulations is installed.

The airplane is certified capable of RVSM operations in accordance with the FAA "Interim guidance material on the approval of operations / aircraft for RVSM operations", 91-RVSM, dated June 30, 1999 and with the JAA Temporary Guidance Leaflet, TGL No. 6, Revision 1, RVSM. <1030>

**NOTE**

Compliance with these FAA and JAA standards does not constitute an operational approval. <1030>

RVSM operations must not be commenced or continued unless all of the required equipment specified in the RVSM Required Equipment List table is operational. <1030>

| RVSM Required Equipment List <1030> | |
| --- | --- |
| **Equipment** | **Requirements for RVSM** |
| Autopilot | Must be operational. |
| Altitude Alerting System | Must be operational. |
| Altitude Reporting Transponder (2) | One (1) must be operational. |
| Air Data Computers (2) | Two (2) must be operational. |

*Effectivity:*

- *On airplanes registered in the Republic of Argentina:*
  - The necessary equipment for the different kinds of operations must comply with the applicable Argentinean regulations. <DNA>

*Illustrations and materials were used with permission from Bombardier.*

## Figure 417

**LIMITATIONS**
**Structural Weight**

## 1. STRUCTURAL WEIGHT LIMITATION

| Weight | kg | lb | Airplane Option Code |
|---|---|---|---|
| Maximum Ramp Weight (MRW) | 36628 | 80750 | |
| | 36613 | 80719 | <2217> |
| | 37108 | 81810 | <2002> |
| | 37535 | 82750 | <2004> |
| | 38222 | 84265 | <2006> |
| | 38555 | 85000 | <2005> |
| Maximum Take-Off Weight (MTOW) | 36514 | 80500 | |
| | 36500 | 80469 | <2217> |
| | 36995 | 81560 | <2002> |
| | 37421 | 82500 | <2004> |
| | 37995 | 83765 | <2006> |
| | 38329 | 84500 | <2005> |
| Maximum Landing Weight (MLW) | 33339 | 73500 | |
| | 34065 | 75100 | <2005> or <2006> |
| Maximum Zero Fuel Weight (MZFW) | 31751 | 70000 | |
| | 32092 | 70750 | <2005> or <2006> |
| Minimum flight weight | 20412 | 45000 | |

**NOTE**

The Maximum Take-Off Weight (MTOW) and/or Maximum Landing Weight (MLW) may be further limited due to performance considerations.

*Illustrations and materials were used with permission from Bombardier.*

**Figure 418**

# LIMITATIONS
## Centre of Gravity

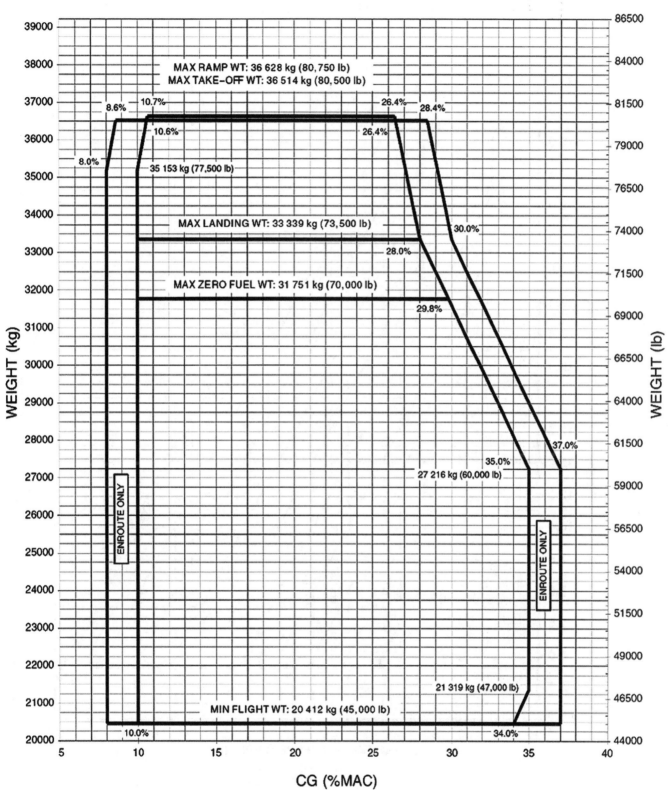

## Centre of Gravity Limits

*Illustrations and materials were used with permission from Bombardier.*

## Figure 419

**LIMITATIONS**
**Operating Limitations**

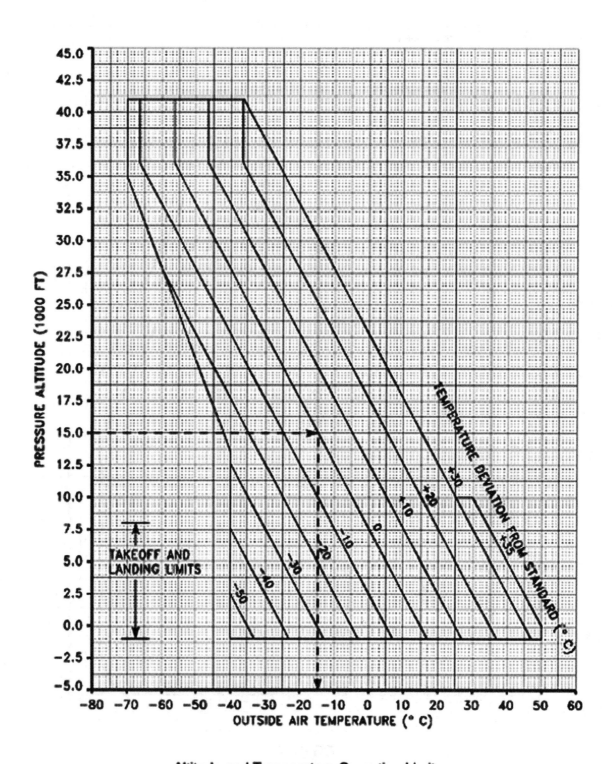

**Altitude and Temperature Operating Limits**

*Illustrations and materials were used with permission from Bombardier.*

**Figure 420**

# PERFORMANCE
## General

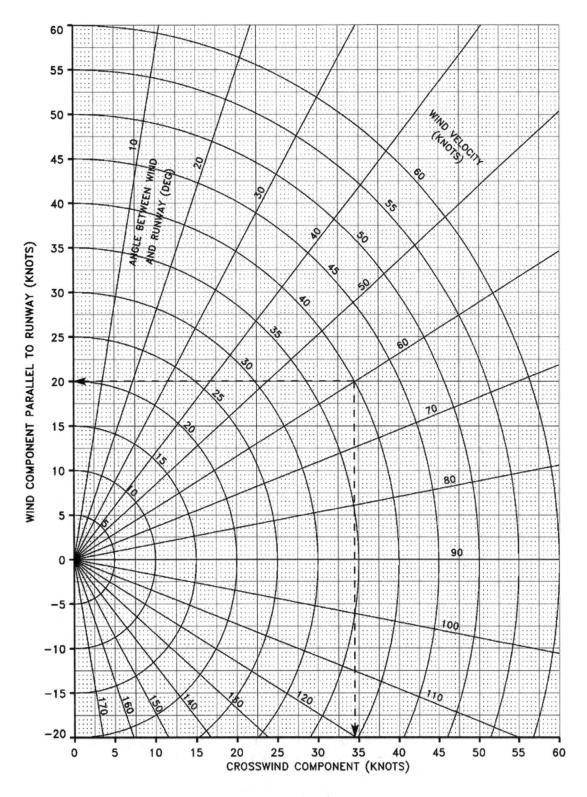

Wind Component

*Illustrations and materials were used with permission from Bombardier.*

## Figure 421

# PERFORMANCE
## General

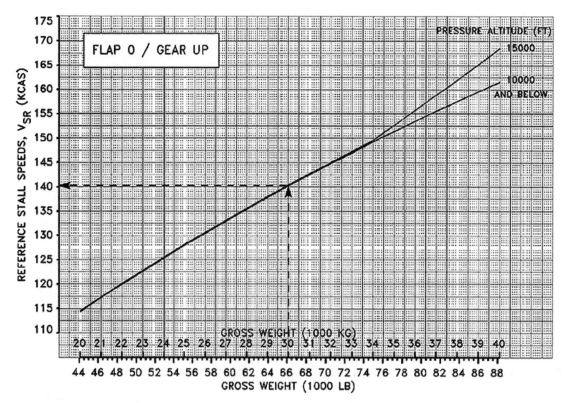

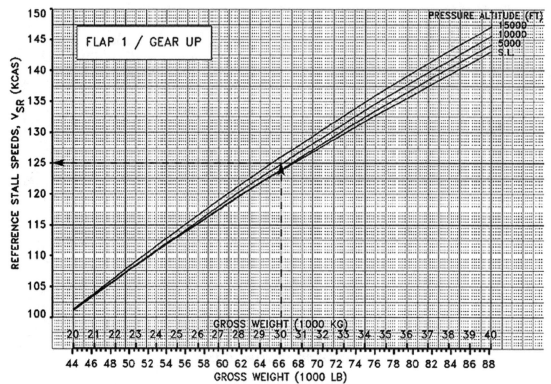

## Stall Speeds, V$_{SR}$

*Illustrations and materials were used with permission from Bombardier.*

## Figure 422

# PERFORMANCE
## General

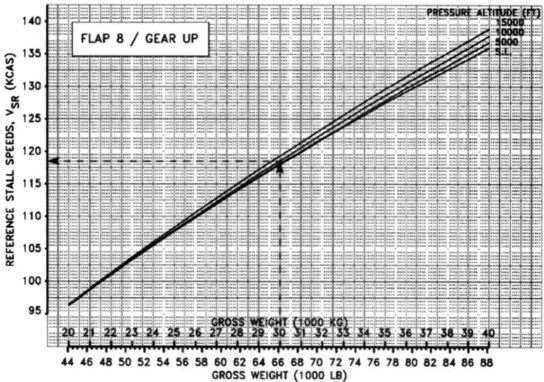

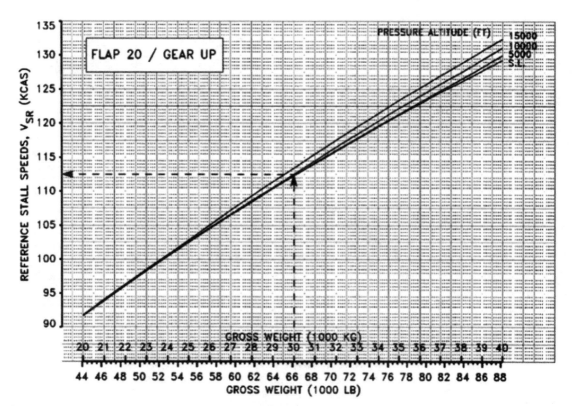

Stall Speeds, V$_{SR}$

*Illustrations and materials were used with permission from Bombardier.*

**Figure 423**

# PERFORMANCE
## General

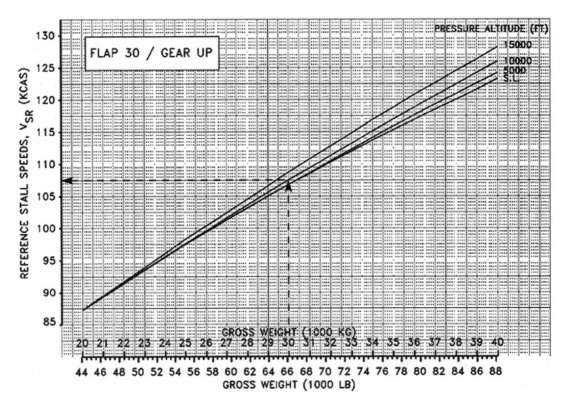

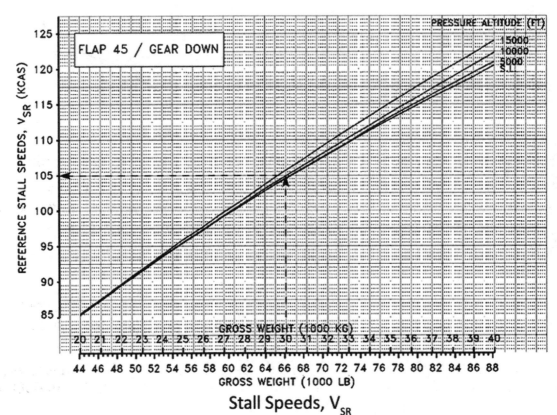

## Stall Speeds, V$_{SR}$

*Illustrations and materials were used with permission from Bombardier.*

## Figure 424

# PERFORMANCE
## General

## B. Maneuvering Capabilities

The maneuvering capabilities are shown in Figure 426. Figure 426 shows the maneuver margin (bank angle and/or g-load factor) for a given weight, CG, altitude and speed combination. Alternatively, for a given load factor, Figure 426 shows the altitude and speed margins for a given weight, CG and speed combination.

Maneuvering capability is defined relative to buffet onset or stick shaker activation, whichever occurs first.

Example A:

Associated conditions:

| | |
|---|---|
| Airplane gross weight | = 33000 kg (72750 lb) |
| Centre of Gravity (CG) | = 20% MAC |
| Indicated Mach No. | = 0.770 |
| Pressure altitude | = 35000 feet |

Example A in Figure 426, for the given associated conditions (enter Figure 426 from the indicated Mach number scale), shows that the maneuvering capability is equal to 1.70 g or a bank angle of 54 degrees.

Example B:

Associated conditions:

| | |
|---|---|
| Airplane gross weight | = 33000 kg (72750 lb) |
| Centre of Gravity (CG) | = 20% MAC |
| Pressure altitude | = 37000 feet |
| Required maneuvering capability | = 1.30 g (or approximately 40-degree bank) |

Example B in Figure 426, for the given associated conditions (enter Figure 426 from the load factor [or bank angle] scale towards the gross weight scale), shows the following speed margins:

- Low speed = 0.680 M

- High speed = 0.845 M

Operating at a speed greater than 0.680 M and lower than 0.845 M at 37000 feet will ensure that a minimum maneuvering capability of 1.30 g before stick shaker activation or buffet onset, will be maintained for the conditions in Example B.

Following the same example, the maximum altitude at a speed of 0.77 M, before stick shaker activation or buffet onset for the required maneuvering capability of 1.30 g is 40600 feet, as marked by an x in Figure 426.

*Illustrations and materials were used with permission from Bombardier.*

**Figure 425**

# PERFORMANCE
## General

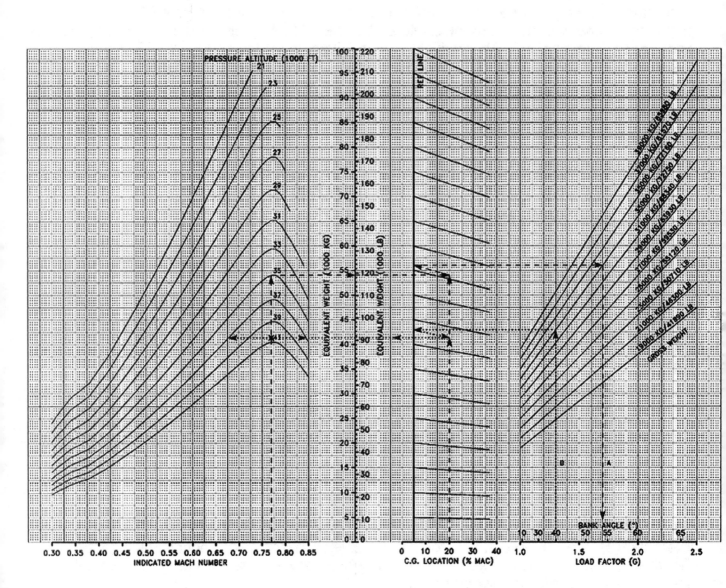

## Maneuvering Capabilities

*Illustrations and materials were used with permission from Bombardier.*

## Figure 426

# PERFORMANCE
## General

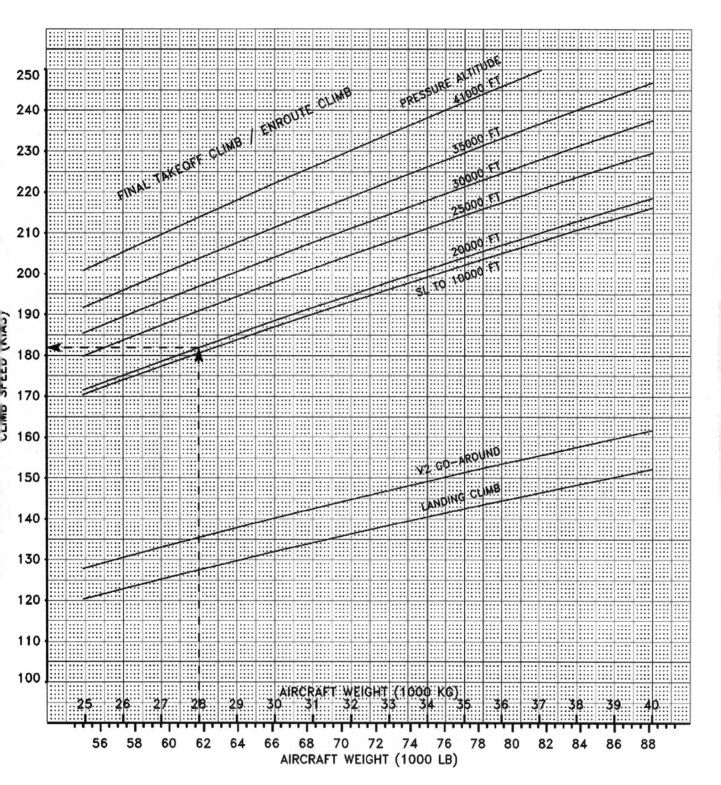

## Climb Speeds

*Illustrations and materials were used with permission from Bombardier.*

## Figure 427

# PERFORMANCE
## Thrust Settings

| OAT | | PRESSURE ALTITUDE (Feet) | | | | | | | | | |
|---|---|---|---|---|---|---|---|---|---|---|---|
| (°C) | (°F) | −1000 | 0 | 2000 | 4000 | 6000 | 8000 | 10000 | 12000 | 14000 | 16000 |
| −45 | −49 | | | | | | | | 85.1 | 86.0 | 85.8 |
| −40 | −40 | 80.0 | 81.1 | 81.8 | 82.8 | 83.6 | 84.3 | 85.2 | 86.0 | 86.8 | 86.6 |
| −35 | −31 | 80.8 | 81.9 | 82.7 | 83.6 | 84.5 | 85.2 | 86.0 | 86.8 | 87.7 | 87.4 |
| −30 | −22 | 81.6 | 82.7 | 83.5 | 84.4 | 85.3 | 86.0 | 86.8 | 87.6 | 88.5 | 88.3 |
| −25 | −13 | 82.4 | 83.5 | 84.3 | 85.2 | 86.1 | 86.8 | 87.6 | 88.4 | 89.3 | 89.1 |
| −20 | −4 | 83.2 | 84.3 | 85.1 | 86.0 | 86.9 | 87.6 | 88.4 | 89.2 | 90.1 | 89.9 |
| −15 | 5 | 84.0 | 85.1 | 85.9 | 86.8 | 87.7 | 88.4 | 89.2 | 90.0 | 90.9 | 90.7 |
| −10 | 14 | 84.7 | 85.9 | 86.7 | 87.6 | 88.5 | 89.2 | 90.0 | 90.8 | 91.7 | 91.5 |
| −5 | 23 | 85.5 | 86.7 | 87.5 | 88.4 | 89.3 | 90.0 | 90.8 | 91.6 | 92.4 | 92.0 |
| 0 | 32 | 86.3 | 87.4 | 88.2 | 89.2 | 90.1 | 90.8 | 91.6 | 92.4 | 93.2 | 92.1 |
| 5 | 41 | 87.0 | 88.2 | 89.0 | 90.0 | 90.8 | 91.6 | 92.4 | 93.2 | 93.6 | 91.8 |
| 10 | 50 | 87.8 | 88.9 | 89.8 | 90.7 | 91.6 | 92.3 | 93.1 | 93.3 | 93.2 | 91.2 |
| 15 | 59 | 88.5 | 89.7 | 90.5 | 91.5 | 92.4 | 92.9 | 93.0 | 92.9 | 92.7 | 90.6 |
| 20 | 68 | 89.2 | 90.4 | 91.3 | 92.2 | 92.7 | 92.6 | 92.4 | 92.4 | 92.3 | 90.2 |
| 25 | 77 | 90.0 | 91.2 | 92.0 | 92.3 | 92.2 | 92.1 | 92.0 | 91.9 | 91.7 | 90.1 |
| 30 | 86 | 90.7 | 91.9 | 91.8 | 91.7 | 91.6 | 91.5 | 91.4 | 91.3 | 91.2 | |
| 35 | 95 | 90.4 | 90.9 | 90.9 | 91.0 | 90.9 | 90.8 | 90.7 | 90.6 | | |
| 40 | 104 | 89.3 | 89.8 | 89.9 | 89.9 | 89.9 | 90.1 | | | | |
| 45 | 113 | 88.1 | 88.6 | 88.6 | 88.7 | 88.9 | | | | | |
| 50 | 122 | 86.8 | 87.3 | 87.3 | 87.4 | | | | | | |

Normal Take-off Thrust Setting (All Engines Operating), %$N_1$ Engine
Bleeds Closed - Static to 65 KIAS

*Illustrations and materials were used with permission from Bombardier.*

## Figure 428

# PERFORMANCE
## Thrust Settings

| OAT | | PRESSURE ALTITUDE (Feet) | | | | | | | | | |
|---|---|---|---|---|---|---|---|---|---|---|---|
| (°C) | (°F) | −1000 | 0 | 2000 | 4000 | 6000 | 8000 | 10000 | 12000 | 14000 | 16000 |
| −45 | −49 | | | | | | | | 84.2 | 85.0 | 84.9 |
| −40 | −40 | 79.4 | 80.5 | 81.2 | 82.1 | 82.9 | 83.6 | 84.3 | 85.1 | 85.8 | 85.7 |
| −35 | −31 | 80.2 | 81.3 | 82.1 | 83.0 | 83.7 | 84.4 | 85.1 | 85.9 | 86.6 | 86.5 |
| −30 | −22 | 81.0 | 82.1 | 82.9 | 83.8 | 84.6 | 85.2 | 86.0 | 86.7 | 87.4 | 87.3 |
| −25 | −13 | 81.8 | 82.9 | 83.7 | 84.6 | 85.4 | 86.0 | 86.8 | 87.5 | 88.2 | 88.1 |
| −20 | −4 | 82.6 | 83.7 | 84.5 | 85.4 | 86.2 | 86.8 | 87.6 | 88.3 | 89.0 | 88.9 |
| −15 | 5 | 83.4 | 84.5 | 85.3 | 86.2 | 87.0 | 87.6 | 88.3 | 89.1 | 89.8 | 89.7 |
| −10 | 14 | 84.1 | 85.3 | 86.0 | 87.0 | 87.7 | 88.4 | 89.1 | 89.8 | 90.6 | 90.5 |
| −5 | 23 | 84.9 | 86.0 | 86.8 | 87.7 | 88.5 | 89.1 | 89.9 | 90.6 | 91.3 | 91.1 |
| 0 | 32 | 85.6 | 86.8 | 87.6 | 88.5 | 89.3 | 89.9 | 90.6 | 91.3 | 92.0 | 90.9 |
| 5 | 41 | 86.4 | 87.5 | 88.3 | 89.2 | 90.0 | 90.7 | 91.4 | 91.9 | 92.0 | 90.3 |
| 10 | 50 | 87.1 | 88.3 | 89.1 | 90.0 | 90.8 | 91.4 | 91.8 | 91.8 | 91.4 | 89.7 |

Normal Take-off Thrust Setting (All Engines Operating),
%N$_1$ Cowl Anti-ice On, PACKs On - Static to 65 KIAS

*Illustrations and materials were used with permission from Bombardier.*

## Figure 429

# PERFORMANCE
## Thrust Settings

| OAT | | PRESSURE ALTITUDE (Feet) | | | | | | | | | |
|------|------|-------|------|------|------|------|------|-------|-------|-------|-------|
| (°C) | (°F) | −1000 | 0 | 2000 | 4000 | 6000 | 8000 | 10000 | 12000 | 14000 | 16000 |
| −45 | −49 | | | | | | | | 86.4 | 86.5 | 87.4 |
| −40 | −40 | 82.3 | 83.4 | 84.1 | 84.9 | 85.8 | 86.6 | 87.2 | 87.2 | 87.3 | 88.2 |
| −35 | −31 | 83.1 | 84.3 | 84.9 | 85.7 | 86.6 | 87.4 | 88.0 | 88.0 | 88.2 | 89.1 |
| −30 | −22 | 83.9 | 85.1 | 85.8 | 86.6 | 87.4 | 88.2 | 88.8 | 88.8 | 89.0 | 89.9 |
| −25 | −13 | 84.7 | 85.9 | 86.6 | 87.4 | 88.2 | 89.0 | 89.6 | 89.6 | 89.8 | 90.7 |
| −20 | −4 | 85.5 | 86.7 | 87.4 | 88.2 | 89.0 | 89.8 | 90.4 | 90.4 | 90.6 | 91.3 |
| −15 | 5 | 86.3 | 87.5 | 88.2 | 88.9 | 89.8 | 90.6 | 91.1 | 90.9 | 91.0 | 90.1 |
| −10 | 14 | 87.1 | 88.3 | 89.0 | 89.7 | 90.6 | 91.4 | 91.2 | 91.3 | 91.3 | 89.5 |
| −5 | 23 | 87.9 | 89.0 | 89.7 | 90.5 | 91.4 | 91.5 | 91.4 | 91.4 | 91.4 | 88.6 |
| 0 | 32 | 88.6 | 89.8 | 90.5 | 91.3 | 91.7 | 91.6 | 91.5 | 91.5 | 91.5 | 87.4 |
| 5 | 41 | 89.4 | 90.6 | 91.3 | 91.9 | 91.8 | 91.4 | 91.4 | 91.2 | 91.2 | 86.8 |
| 10 | 50 | 90.1 | 91.3 | 92.0 | 92.0 | 91.5 | 91.1 | 91.0 | 90.9 | 89.9 | 86.4 |

Go-around or APR Thrust Setting (One Engine Inoperative),
%N$_1$ Wing and Cowl Anti-ice On, PACK On - 140 KIAS

*Illustrations and materials were used with permission from Bombardier.*

## Figure 430

# PERFORMANCE
## Thrust Settings

| SAT | | PRESSURE ALTITUDE (Feet) | | | | | | | |
|---|---|---|---|---|---|---|---|---|---|
| (°C) | (°F) | 0 | 5000 | 10000 | 15000 | 20000 | 25000 | 30000 | 35000 |
| –70 | –94 | | | | | | | 87.8 | 89.0 |
| –65 | –85 | | | | | | 87.0 | 88.6 | 89.9 |
| –60 | –76 | | | | | 86.6 | 87.9 | 89.5 | 90.8 |
| –55 | –67 | | | | | 87.4 | 88.8 | 90.4 | 91.7 |
| –50 | –58 | | | | 86.4 | 88.3 | 89.6 | 91.2 | 92.5 |
| –45 | –49 | | | 85.0 | 87.2 | 89.2 | 90.5 | 92.1 | 93.3 |
| –40 | –40 | 81.4 | 83.7 | 85.8 | 88.1 | 90.0 | 91.3 | 92.9 | 93.1 |
| –35 | –31 | 82.3 | 84.6 | 86.7 | 88.9 | 90.8 | 92.2 | 93.6 | 92.4 |
| –30 | –22 | 83.1 | 85.4 | 87.5 | 89.7 | 91.6 | 93.0 | 92.8 | 91.5 |
| –25 | –13 | 83.9 | 86.2 | 88.3 | 90.6 | 92.5 | 93.7 | 92.2 | 89.9 |
| –20 | –4 | 84.7 | 87.1 | 89.2 | 91.4 | 93.3 | 93.4 | 91.4 | 89.0 |
| –15 | 5 | 85.5 | 87.9 | 90.0 | 92.2 | 93.8 | 92.6 | 90.7 | 88.8 |
| –10 | 14 | 86.3 | 88.7 | 90.8 | 93.0 | 93.6 | 91.8 | 89.9 | 88.5 |
| –5 | 23 | 87.1 | 89.5 | 91.5 | 93.5 | 92.8 | 91.1 | 89.7 | |
| 0 | 32 | 87.8 | 90.2 | 92.3 | 93.2 | 92.0 | 90.3 | 89.6 | |
| 5 | 41 | 88.6 | 91.0 | 92.7 | 92.4 | 91.3 | 90.0 | | |
| 10 | 50 | 89.4 | 91.8 | 92.4 | 91.7 | 90.7 | 89.9 | | |

## Maximum Continuous Thrust Setting (One Engine Inoperative), %N$_1$ Cowl Anti-ice On, PACK On - 170 KIAS

*Illustrations and materials were used with permission from Bombardier.*

## Figure 431

# PERFORMANCE
## Take–off Performance

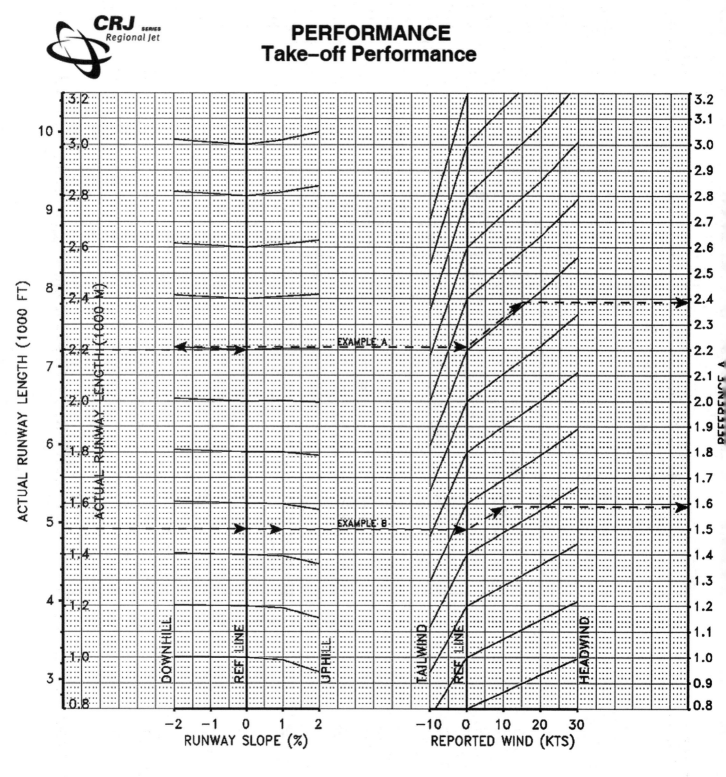

## FLAPS 8

**Take-off Weight Limited by Field Length Requirements, Dry Runway - V$_{MC}$ Limited, FLAPS 8**

*Illustrations and materials were used with permission from Bombardier.*

**Figure 432**

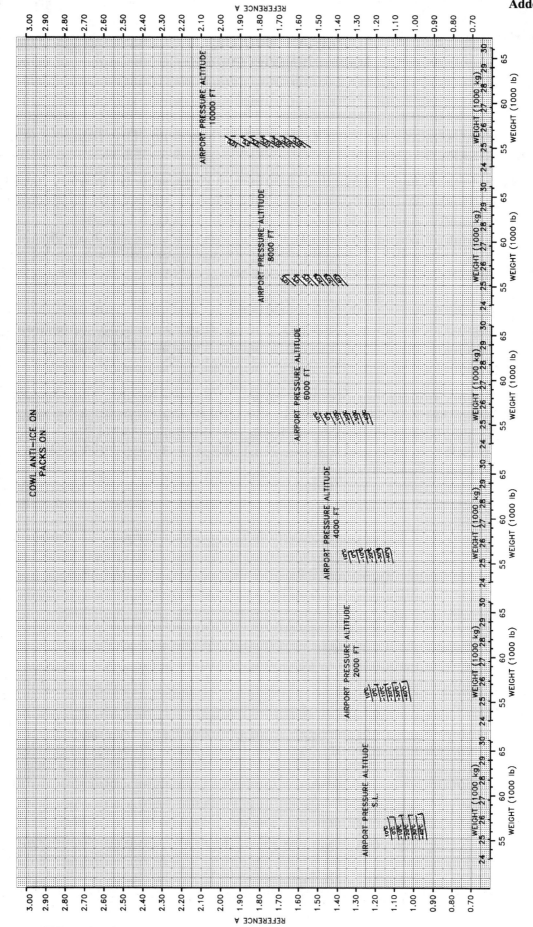

*Illustrations and materials were used with permission from Bombardier.*

**Figure 433**

**PERFORMANCE**
**Take–off Performance**

## D. Take-off Weight Limited by Field Length Requirements, Dry Runway – One Engine Inoperative, FLAPS 8

The maximum take-off weight limited by field length requirements on a dry runway, with one engine inoperative for a FLAPS 8 take-off, is given by Figure 435, 436, or 437 The following charts take into account the accelerate-stop distance available, the actual length of the runway and the clearway, the airport pressure altitude, and the effects of runway slope, prevailing wind conditions and temperature for varying bleed configurations.

### NOTE

1. If a rolling take-off procedure will be performed, subtract 60 metres (200 feet) from the actual runway length and the available accelerate-stop distance, prior to determining the take-off weight.

2. If the intersection of the actual runway length and available accelerate-stop distance falls to the right of the curve for a $V_1/V_R$ of 1, project horizontally to the left from this intersection until the 1.0 $V_1/V_R$ curve is reached. Use a $V_1/V_R$ of 1.0 and the corresponding Reference A value at this point.

*Illustrations and materials were used with permission from Bombardier.*

**Figure 434**

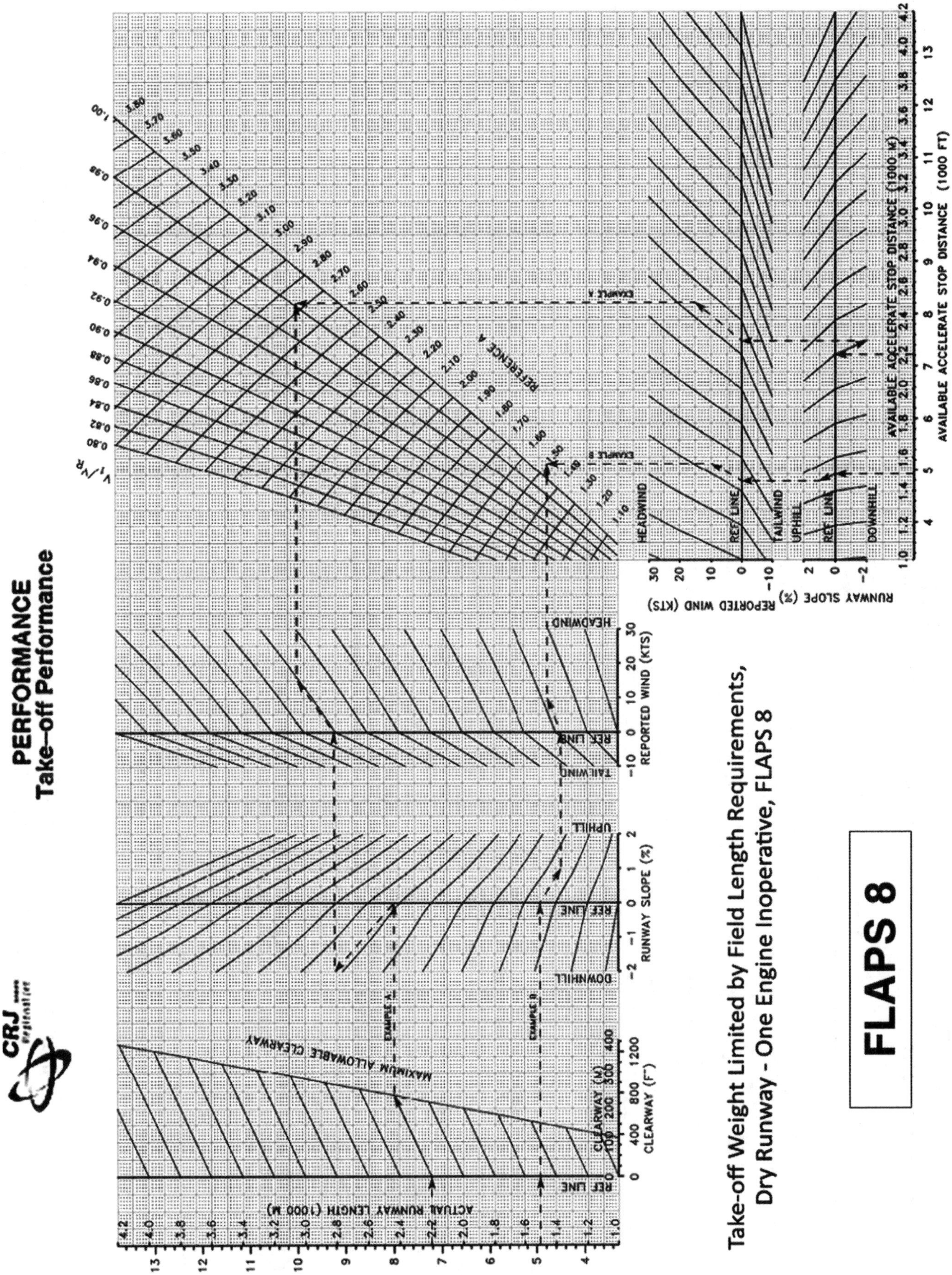

PERFORMANCE
Take-off Performance

Take-off Weight Limited by Field Length Requirements,
Dry Runway - One Engine Inoperative, FLAPS 8

FLAPS 8

*Illustrations and materials were used with permission from Bombardier.*

**Figure 435**

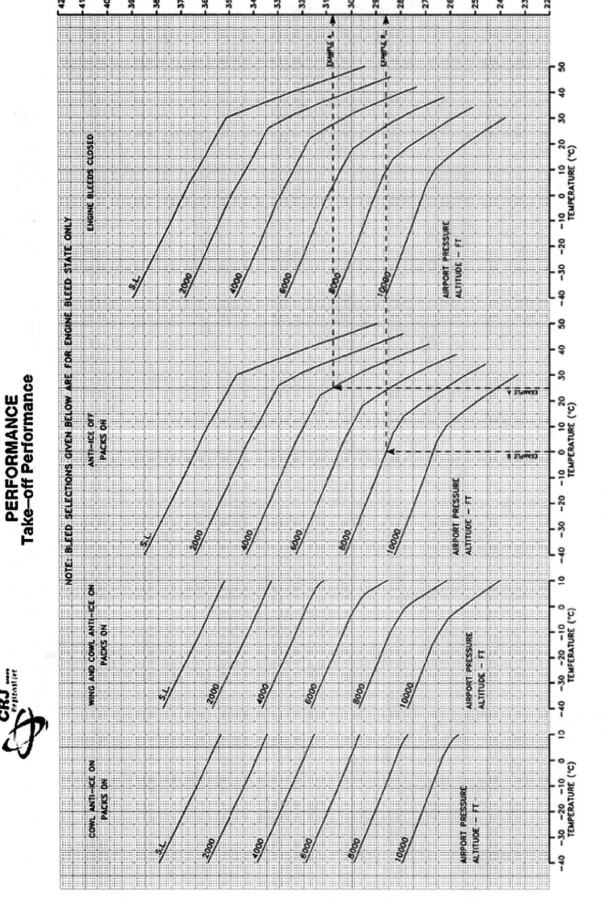

**PERFORMANCE**
**Take-off Performance**

Take-off Weight Limited by Field Length Requirements, Dry Runway - One Engine Inoperative, FLAPS 8

*Illustrations and materials were used with permission from Bombardier.*

**Figure 436**

**PERFORMANCE**
**Take-off Performance**

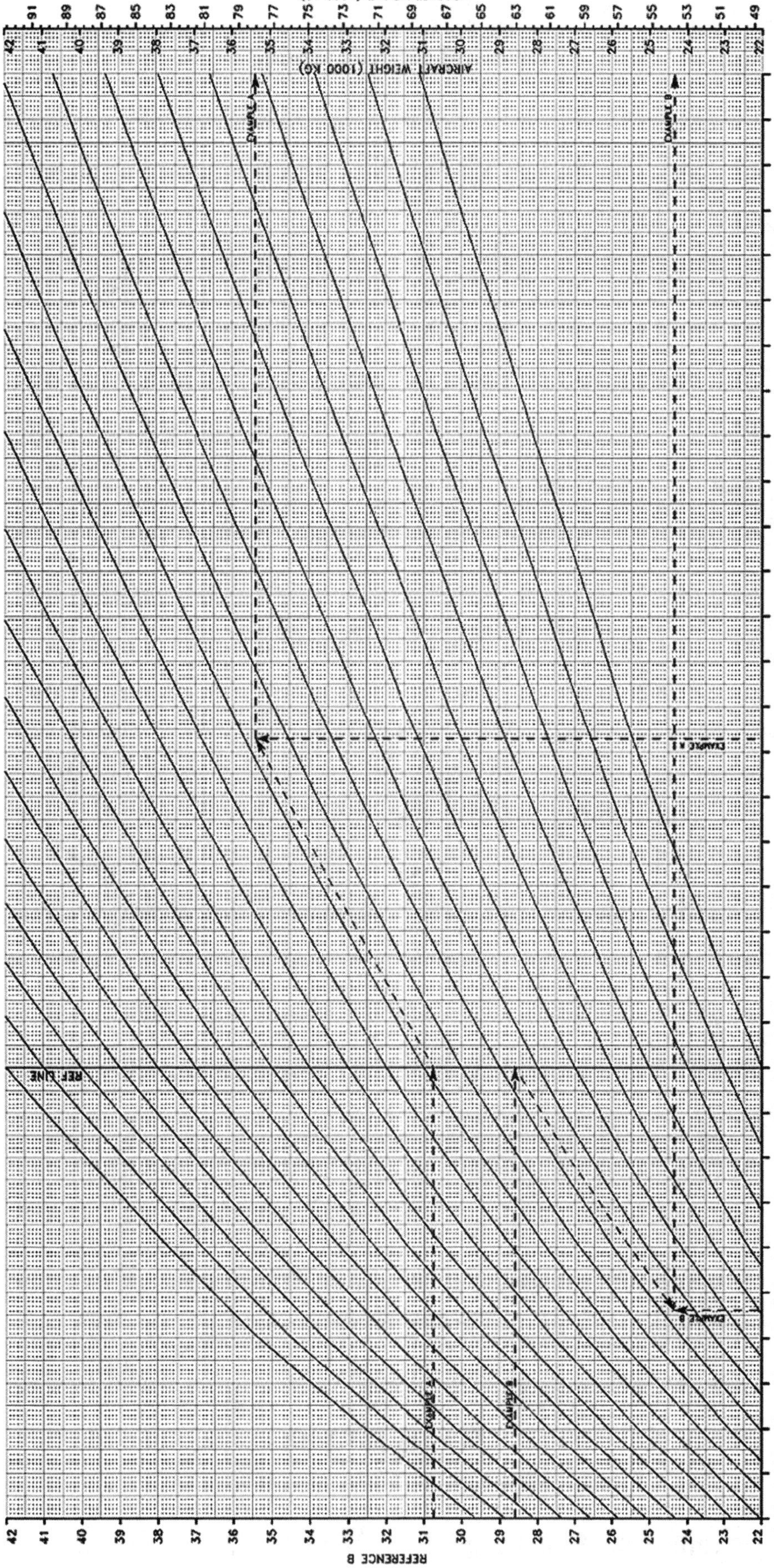

*Illustrations and materials were used with permission from Bombardier.*

**Figure 437**

Take-off Weight Limited by Field Length Requirements, Dry Runway - One Engine
Inoperative, FLAPS 8

FLAPS 8

## PERFORMANCE
### Take-off Performance

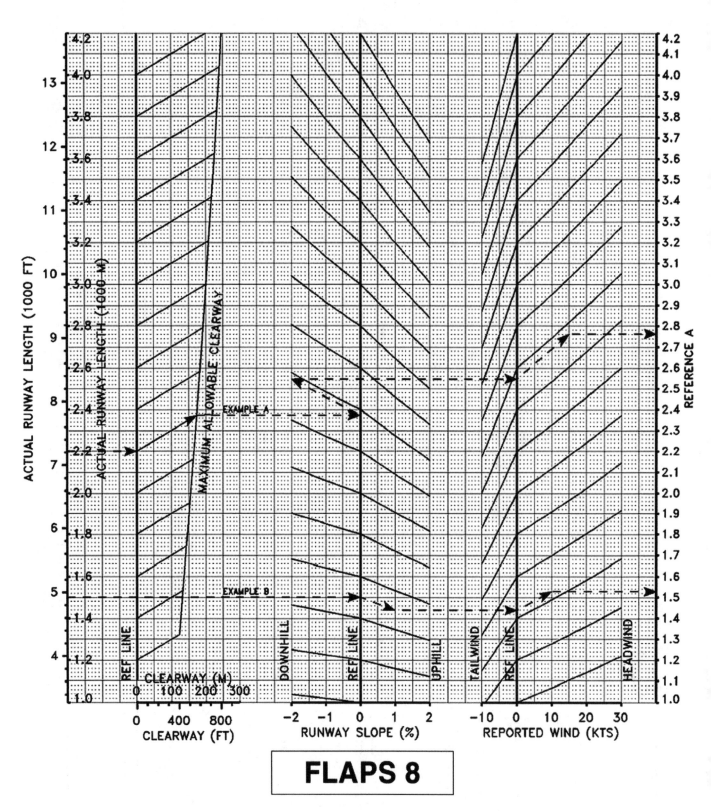

**FLAPS 8**

**Take-off Weight Limited by Field Length Requirements - All Engines Operating, FLAPS 8**

*Illustrations and materials were used with permission from Bombardier.*

**Figure 438**

## PERFORMANCE
## Take-off Performance

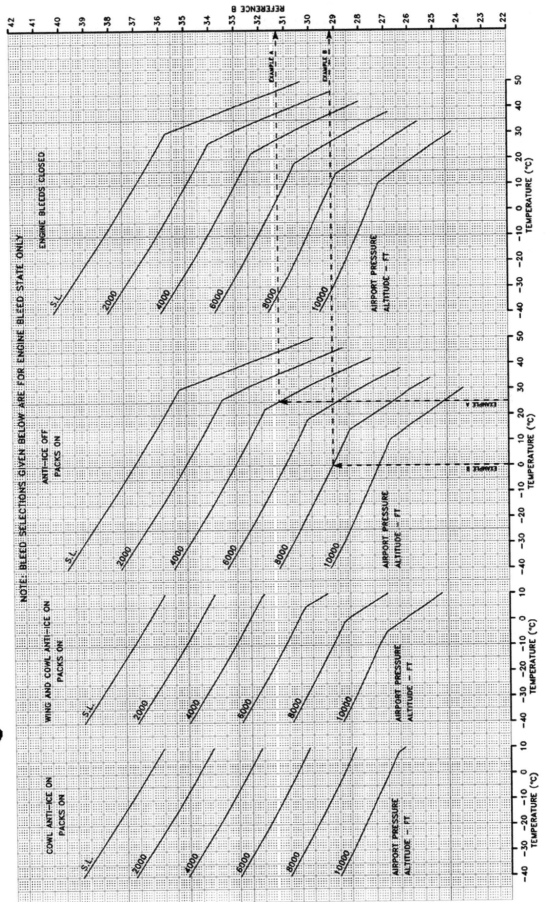

**FLAPS 8**

Take-off Weight Limited by Field Length Requirements - All Engines Operating, FLAPS 8

*Illustrations and materials were used with permission from Bombardier.*

**Figure 439**

215

**PERFORMANCE**
**Take–off Performance**

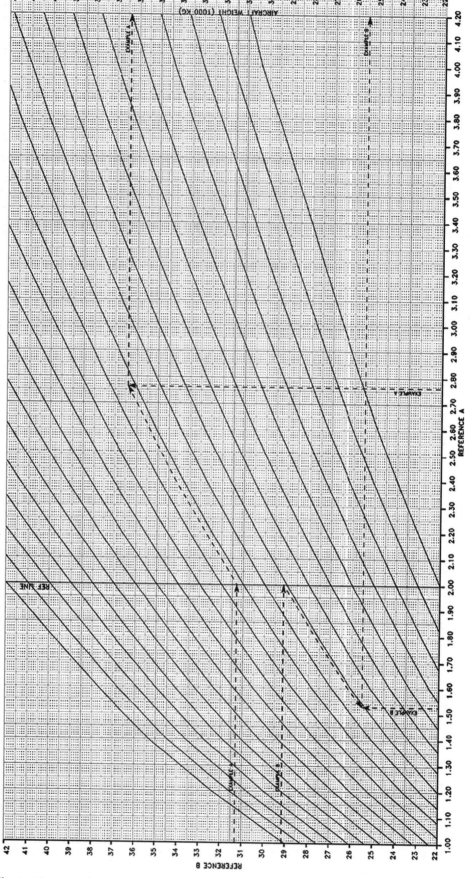

**FLAPS 8**

Take-off Weight Limited by Field Length Requirements - All Engines Operating, FLAPS 8

*Illustrations and materials were used with permission from Bombardier.*

**Figure 440**

**CRJ** series
Regional Jet

## PERFORMANCE
### Take–off Performance

**1. Take-off Weight Limited by Field Length Requirements, Dry Runway – Minimum Control Speed (V$_{MC}$) Limited, FLAPS 20**

The maximum take-off weight limited by field length requirements on a dry runway for a FLAPS 20 take-off, limited by V$_{MC}$ is given by Figure 442 or 443. The following charts are applicable to both the all engines operating and one engine inoperative cases. The first chart takes into account the actual length of the runway and the effects of runway slope and prevailing wind conditions. The subsequent charts cater to the effects of airport pressure altitude and temperature for varying bleed configurations to determine the take-off weight.

### NOTE

If a rolling take-off procedure will be performed, subtract 60 metres (200 feet) from the actual runway length, prior to determining the take-off weight.

*Illustrations and materials were used with permission from Bombardier.*

### Figure 441

## PERFORMANCE
### Take–off Performance

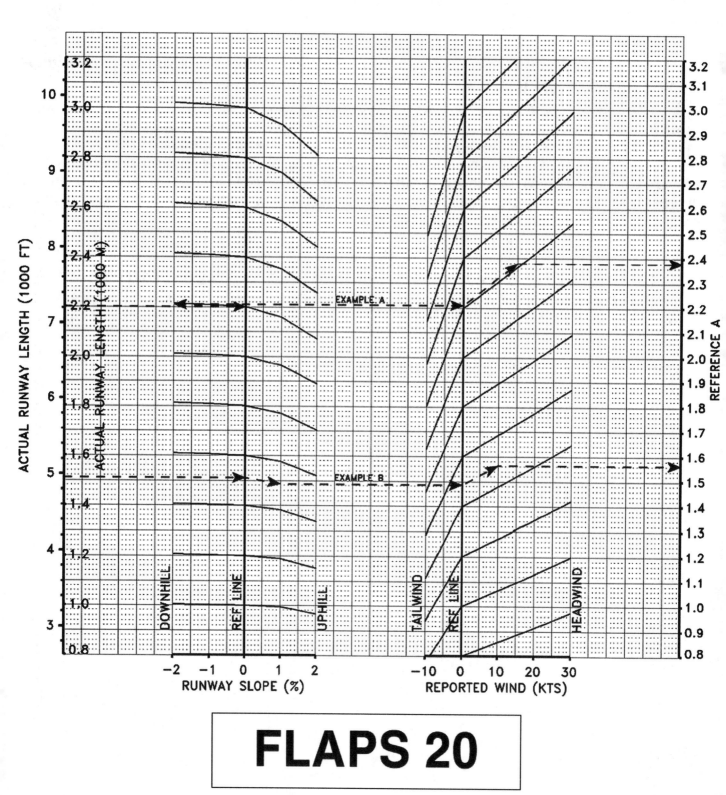

## FLAPS 20

Take-off Weight Limited by Field Length Requirements, Dry Runway - $V_{MC}$ Limited, FLAPS 20

*Illustrations and materials were used with permission from Bombardier.*

**Figure 442**

**PERFORMANCE**
**Take-off Performance**

FLAPS 20

Take-off Weight Limited by Field Length Requirements, Dry Runway – $V_{MC}$ Limited, FLAPS 20

*Illustrations and materials were used with permission from Bombardier.*

**Figure 443**

## PERFORMANCE
## Take–off Performance

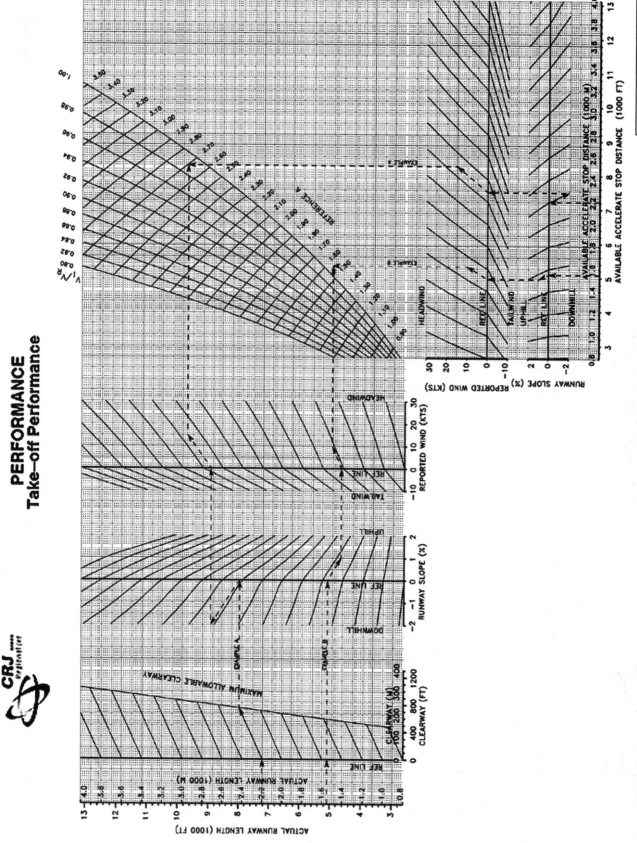

**FLAPS 20**

Take-off Weight Limited by Field Length Requirements, Dry Runway - One Engine Inoperative,
FLAPS 20

*Illustrations and materials were used with permission from Bombardier.*

**Figure 444**

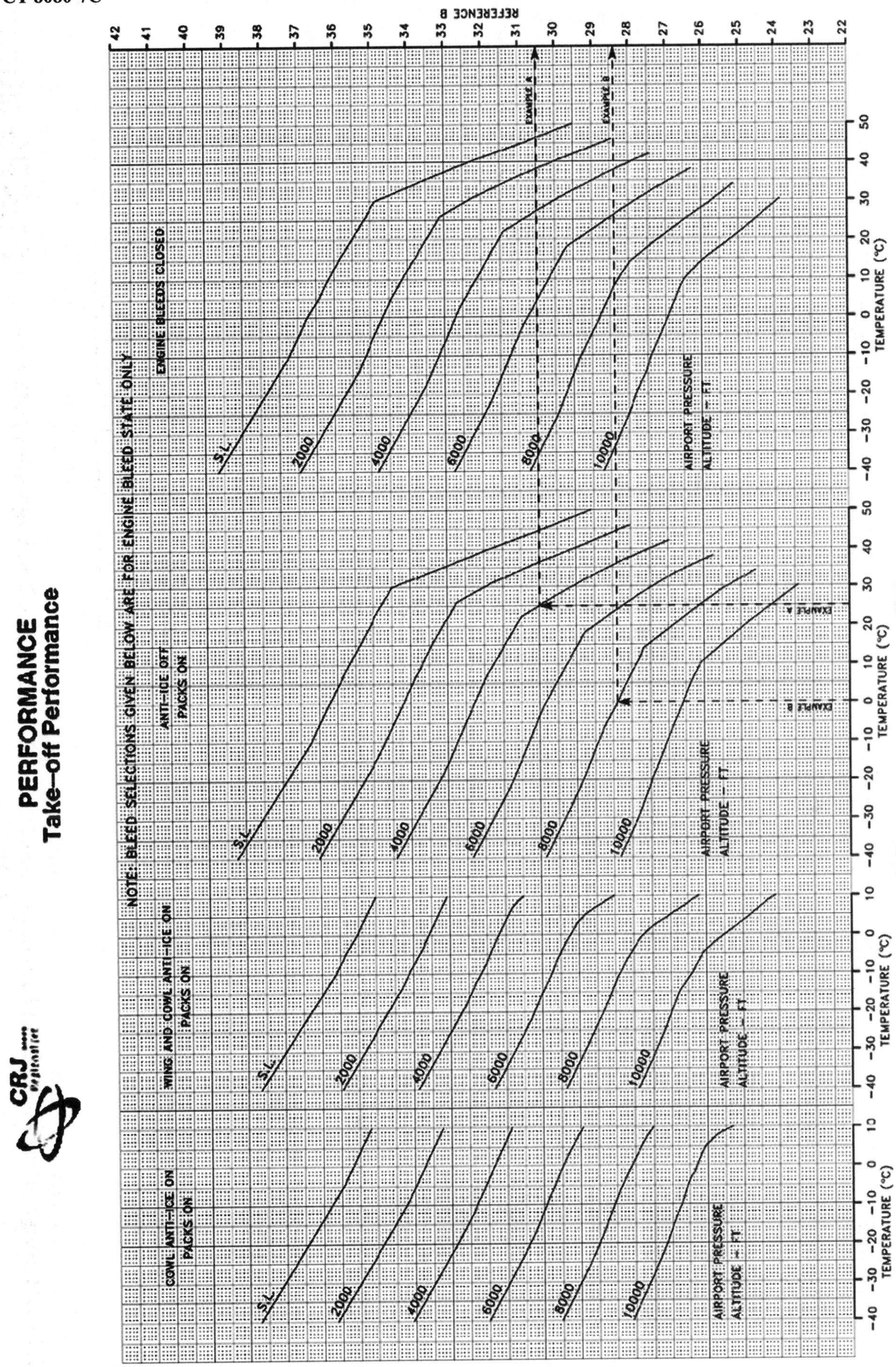

## PERFORMANCE
### Take-off Performance

Illustrations and materials were used with permission from Bombardier.

**Figure 445**

Take-off Weight Limited by Field Length Requirements, Dry Runway - One Engine Inoperative, FLAPS 20

**FLAPS 20**

PERFORMANCE
Take—off Performance

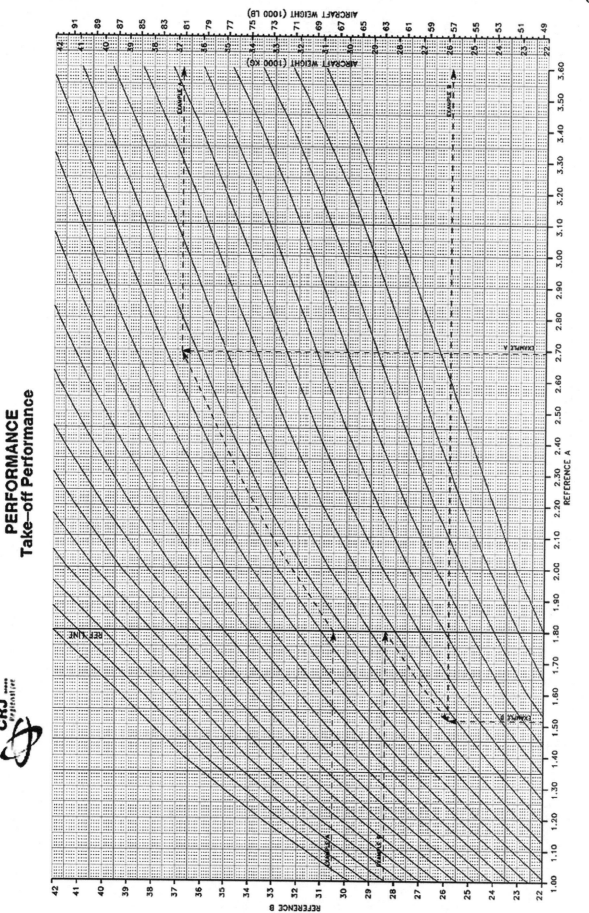

FLAPS 20

Take-off Weight Limited by Field Length Requirements, Dry Runway - One Engine Inoperative, FLAPS 20

Illustrations and materials were used with permission from Bombardier.

**Figure 446**

## PERFORMANCE
## Take–off Performance

### S. Take-off Weight Limited by Climb Requirements – FLAPS 8

The maximum take-off weight limited by climb requirements for a FLAPS 8 take-off is determined from Figure 448, for varying conditions of temperature and airport pressure altitude, taking into account the effects of different anti-icing and engine bleed configurations.

### NOTE

With the APU on, subtract 350 kg (772 lb) from the weight derived from Figure 448.

Example:

Associated conditions:

| | |
|---|---|
| Temperature | = 10°C |
| Airport pressure altitude | = 4000 feet |
| Wing and cowl anti-ice | = Off |
| PACK | = On |
| APU | = Off |

Enter Figure 448 from the temperature scale under the appropriate configuration of anti-ice and engine bleeds. As shown in the example, the maximum take-off weight limited by climb requirements is found to be 41050 kg (90490 lb).

*Illustrations and materials were used with permission from Bombardier.*

## Figure 447

**PERFORMANCE**
**Take–off Performance**

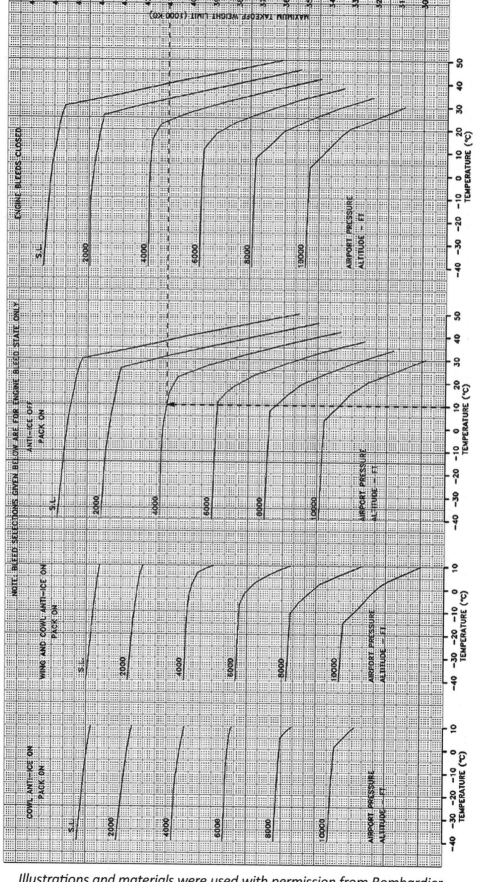

**FLAPS 8**

Take-off Weight Limited by Climb Requirements - FLAPS 8

*Illustrations and materials were used with permission from Bombardier.*

**Figure 448**

PERFORMANCE
Take-off Performance

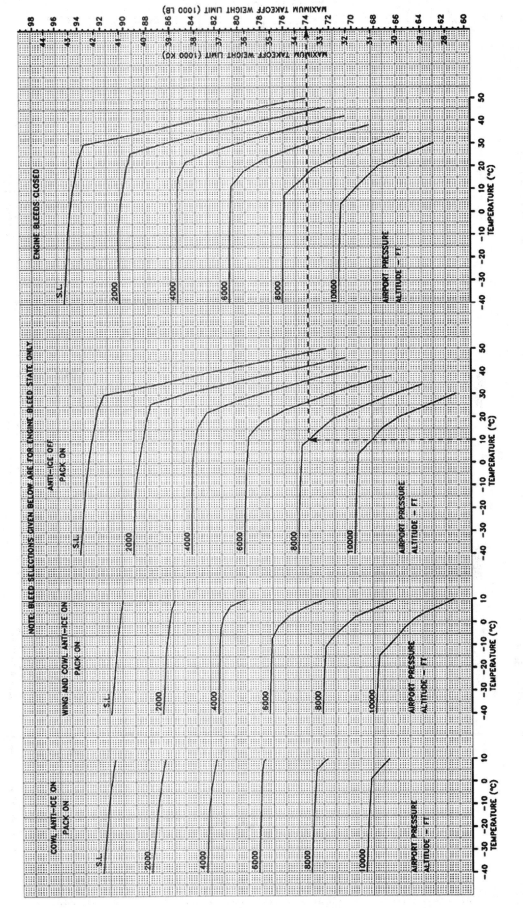

*Illustrations and materials were used with permission from Bombardier.*

**FLAPS 20**

Take-off Weight Limited by Climb Requirements - FLAPS 20

**Figure 449**

## PERFORMANCE
### Take–off Performance

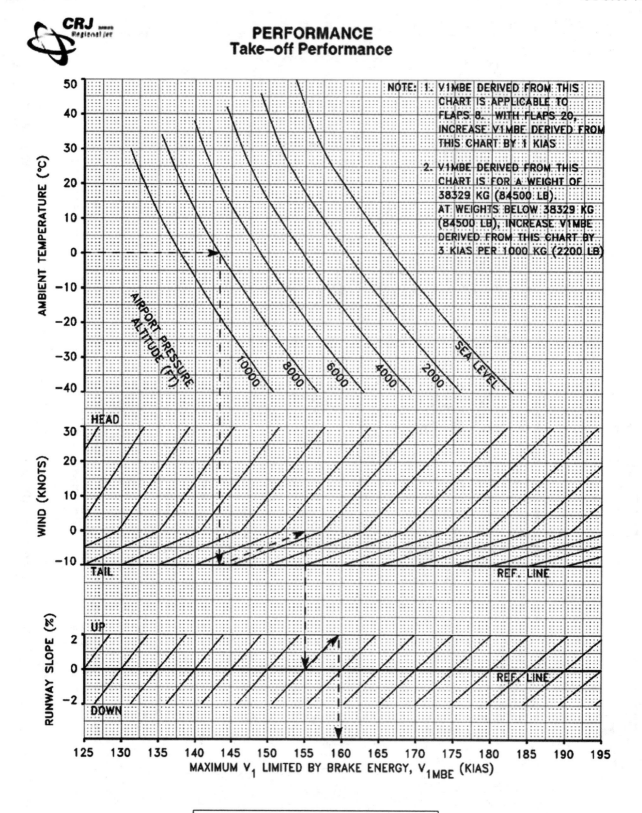

NOTE: 1. V1MBE DERIVED FROM THIS CHART IS APPLICABLE TO FLAPS 8. WITH FLAPS 20, INCREASE V1MBE DERIVED FROM THIS CHART BY 1 KIAS

2. V1MBE DERIVED FROM THIS CHART IS FOR A WEIGHT OF 38329 KG (84500 LB). AT WEIGHTS BELOW 38329 KG (84500 LB), INCREASE V1MBE DERIVED FROM THIS CHART BY 3 KIAS PER 1000 KG (2200 LB)

## FLAPS 8

Maximum $V_1$ Limited by Brake Energy ($V_{1MBE}$) - FLAPS 8

*Illustrations and materials were used with permission from Bombardier.*

**Figure 450**

# PERFORMANCE
## Take-off Performance

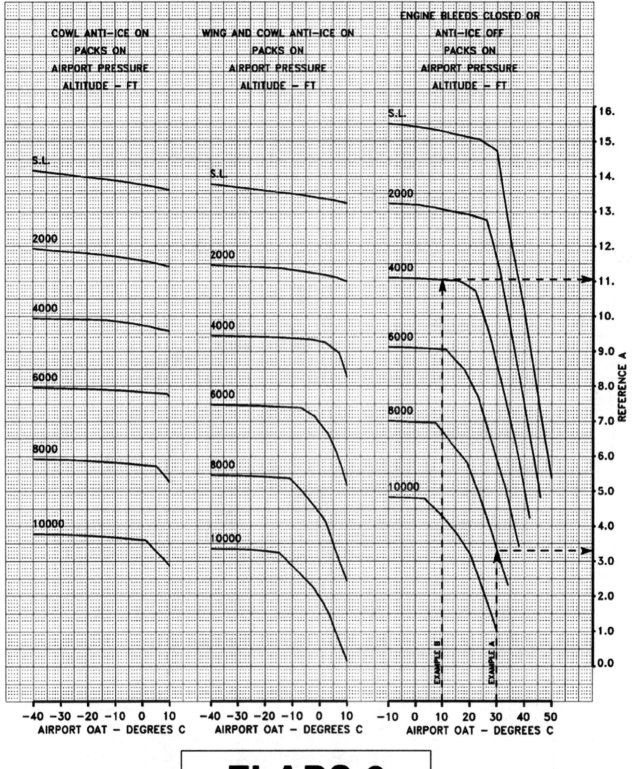

## FLAPS 8

Take-off Speeds - FLAPS 8

*Illustrations and materials were used with permission from Bombardier.*

**Figure 451**

## PERFORMANCE
## Take-off Performance

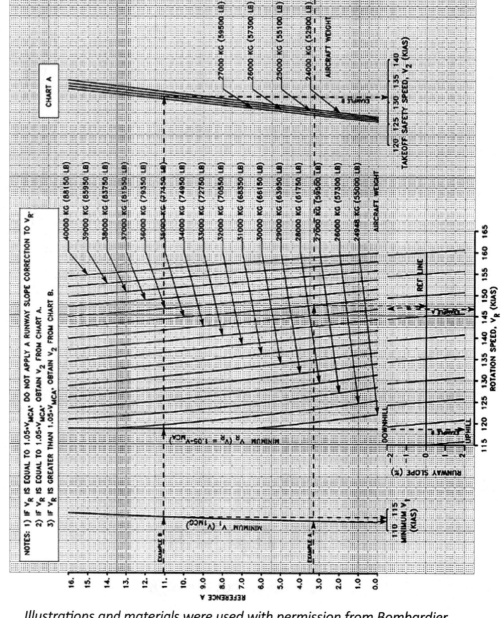

*Illustrations and materials were used with permission from Bombardier.*

## Figure 452

**PERFORMANCE**
**Take-off Performance**

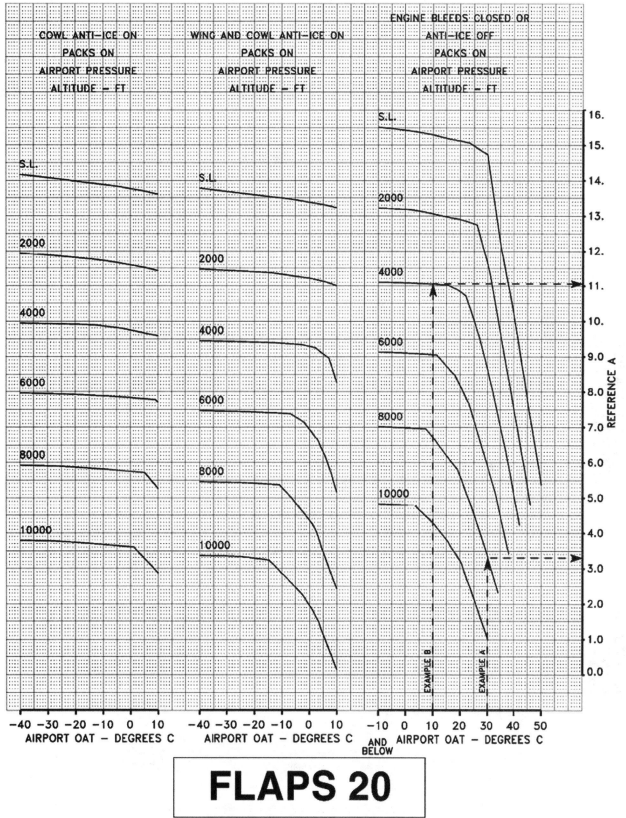

**FLAPS 20**

Take-off Speeds - FLAPS 20

*Illustrations and materials were used with permission from Bombardier.*

**Figure 453**

PERFORMANCE
Take-off Performance

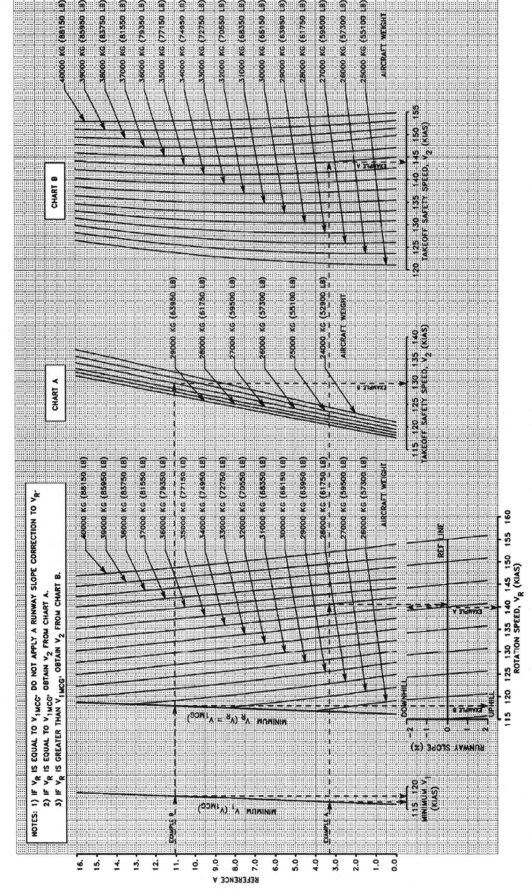

Take-off Speeds - FLAPS 20

*Illustrations and materials were used with permission from Bombardier.*

**Figure 454**

**PERFORMANCE**
Obstacle Clearance

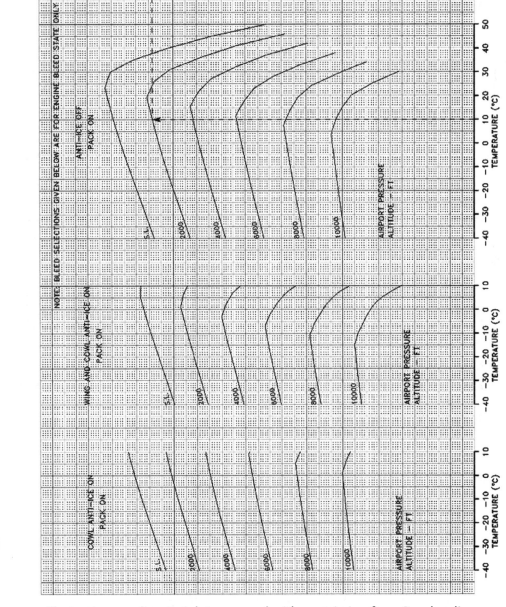

FLAPS 8

Maximum Engine-out Level-off Height - FLAPS 8

*Illustrations and materials were used with permission from Bombardier.*

**Figure 455**

## PERFORMANCE
### Obstacle Clearance

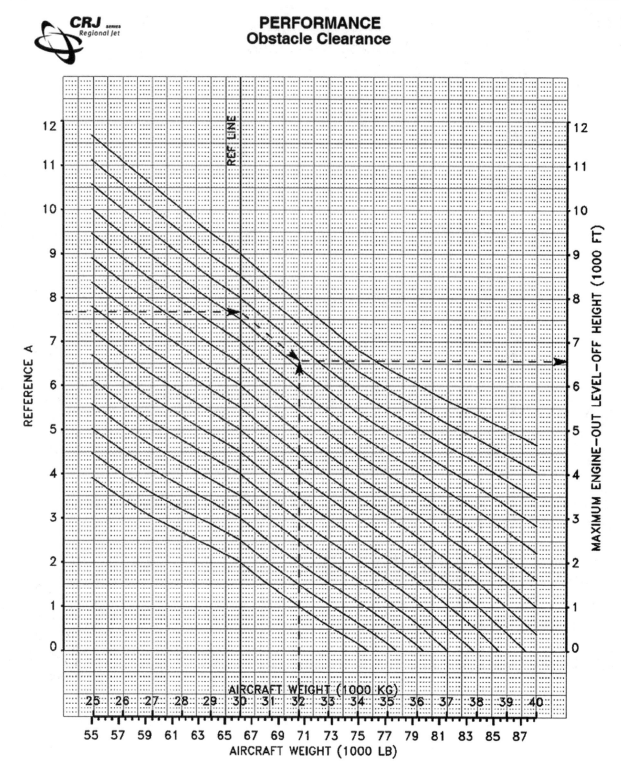

FLAPS 8

Maximum Engine-out Level-off Height - FLAPS 8

*Illustrations and materials were used with permission from Bombardier.*

**Figure 456**

# PERFORMANCE
## Landing Performance

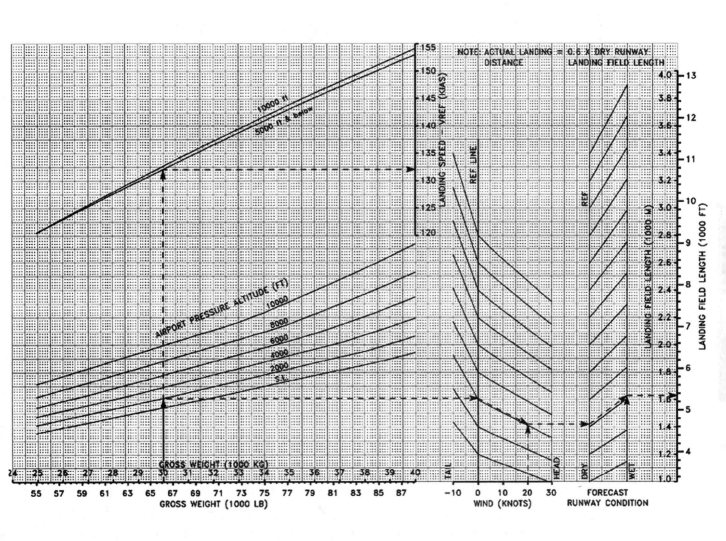

## Landing Field and Landing Speed - FLAPS 45

*Illustrations and materials were used with permission from Bombardier.*

## Figure 457

233

# PERFORMANCE
## Landing Performance

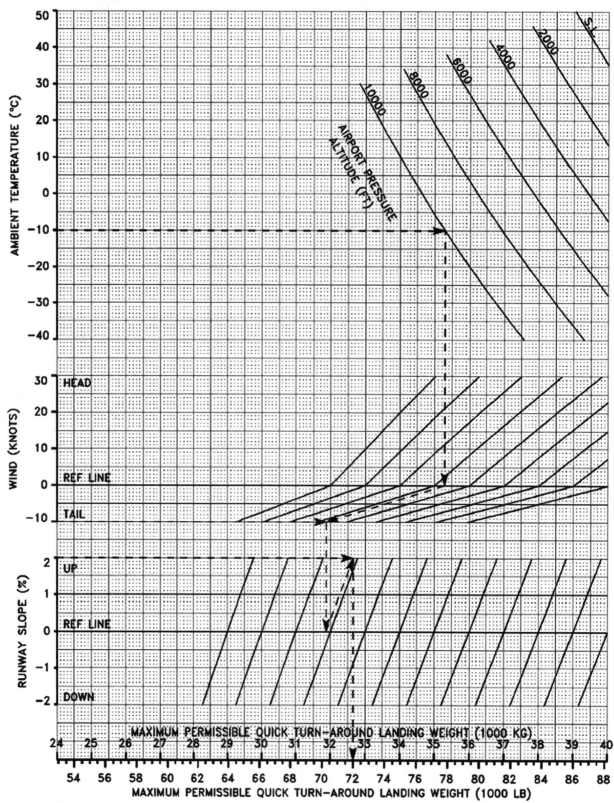

## Maximum Permissable Quick Turn-around Landing Weight

*Illustrations and materials were used with permission from Bombardier.*

### Figure 458

**CRJ900**

## AIRPORT PLANNING MANUAL

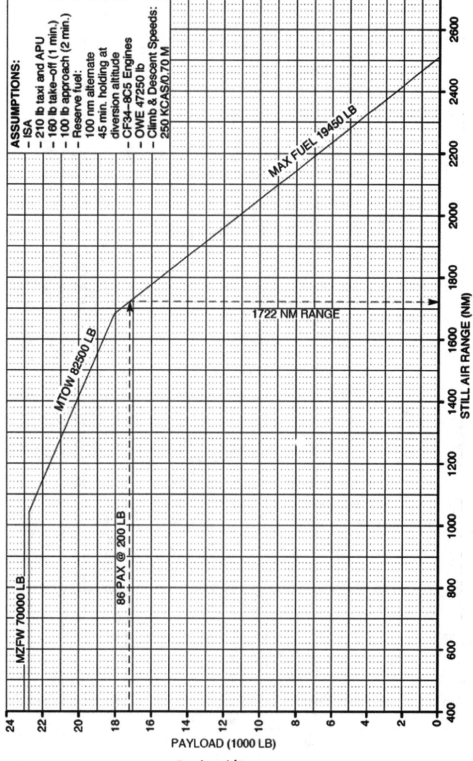

Payload/Range

*Illustrations and materials were used with permission from Bombardier.*

## Figure 459

## CRJ900

## AIRPORT PLANNING MANUAL

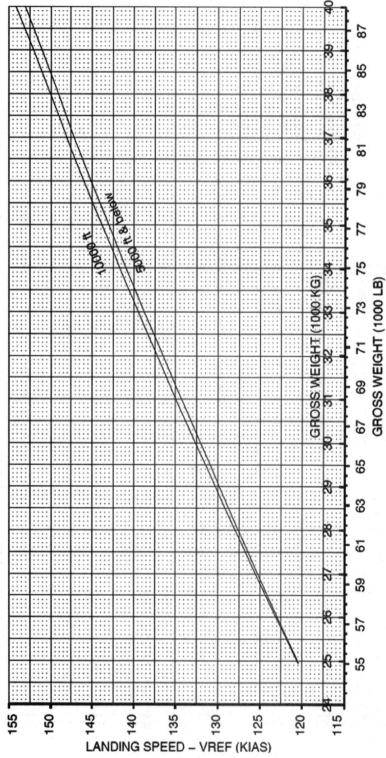

**Landing Speed - Flaps at 45 Degrees/Slats Extended**

*Illustrations and materials were used with permission from Bombardier.*

## Figure 460

CRJ900

**AIRPORT PLANNING MANUAL**

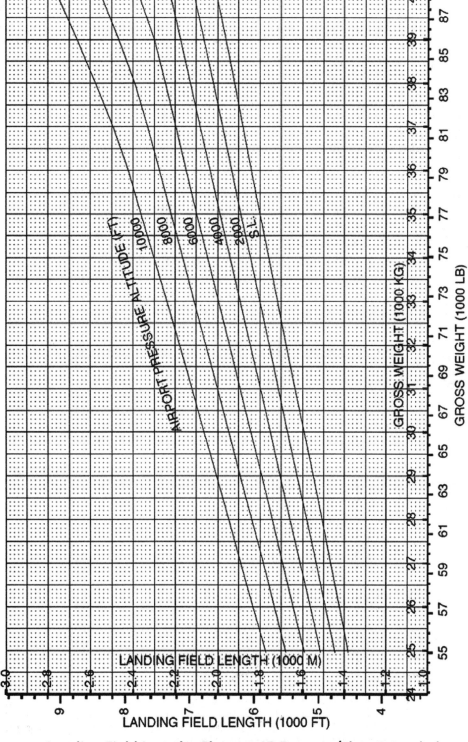

**Landing Field Length - Flaps at 45 Degrees/Slats Extended**

*Illustrations and materials were used with permission from Bombardier.*

**Figure 461**

## 2.2    WEIGHT AND LOADING

### 2.2.1    MAXIMUM STRUCTURAL WEIGHT LIMITS

|  | Basic Gross Weight MS 4-201539 | Intermediate Gross Weight MS 4-308807 | High Gross Weight MS 4-308907 | Enhanced High Gross Weight MS 4-309238 |
|---|---|---|---|---|
| Ramp Weight | 28,077 kg (61,900 lb) | 29,089 kg (64,130 lb) | 29,347 kg (64,700 lb) | 29,665 kg (65,400 lb) |
| Maximum Take-off Weight | 27,987 kg (61,700 lb) | 28,998 kg (63,930 lb) | 29,257 kg (64,500 lb) | 29,574 kg (65,200 lb) |
| Maximum Landing Weight | 27,442 kg (60,500 lb) | 28,009 kg (61,750 lb) | 28,009 kg (61,750 lb) | 28,123 kg (62,000 lb) |
| Maximum Zero Fuel Weight | 25,174 kg (55,500 lb) | 25,855 kg (57,000 lb) | 25,855 kg (57,000 lb) | 26,308 kg (58,000 lb) |
| Minimum Structural Design Weight | 14,403 kg (31,753 lb) | 14,403 kg (31,753 lb) | 14,403 kg (31,753 lb) | 14,403 kg (31,753 lb) |

**NOTE**

Maximum take-off weight and maximum landing weight may be reduced by performance requirements of Section 5.

### 2.2.2    CENTRE OF GRAVITY LIMITS (LANDING GEAR DOWN)

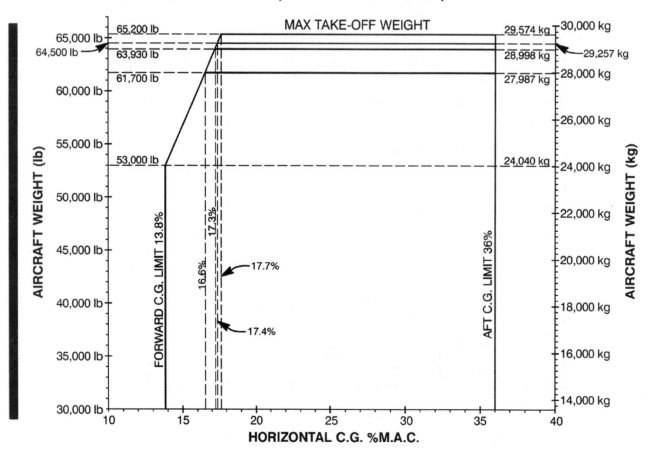

*Illustrations and materials were used with permission from Bombardier.*

**Figure 462**

The Centre of Gravity (C.G.) limits at all weights with landing gear extended are as follows:

1. Forward limit:

   387.16 inches aft of the reference datum (13.8% M.A.C.) for all weights up to 24,040 kg (53,000 lb).

   Slopes from 387.16 inches aft of the reference datum (13.8% M.A.C.) at 24,040 kg (53,000 lb) to 390.84 inches (17.7% M.A.C.) at 29,574 kg (65,200 lb).

2. Aft limit:

   408.14 inches aft of the reference datum (36.0% M.A.C.) at all weights.

If these C.G. limits are met with the airplane landing gear extended, safe limits in flight are automatically achieved (see Figure 2–2–1, CG Limits).

### 2.2.3 LOADING INSTRUCTIONS

The airplane must always be loaded (i.e. crew, passengers, fuel, freight and baggage) to remain within the weight and centre of gravity limits in paragraphs 2.2.1 and 2.2.2.

Procedures for calculating weight and centre of gravity of a loaded airplane are contained in the Weight and Balance Manual (PSM 1–84–8 or 1–84–8M).

### 2.2.4 LOADING LIMITS

For baggage compartment loading limits for the various configurations, refer to the Cargo Loading Manual (PSM 1–84–8A).

### 2.2.5 MANEUVERING LIMIT LOAD FACTORS

The following maneuvering limit load factors limit the permissible angle of bank in turns and limit the severity of pull-up and push-over maneuvers.

| | |
|---|---|
| Flap retracted | +2.5 g |
| | −1.0 g |
| Flap extended | +2.0 g |
| | 0.0 g |

### 2.2.6 MAXIMUM LATERAL ASYMMETRY

Maximum fuel imbalance between contents of main fuel tanks is 272 kg (600 lb).

*Illustrations and materials were used with permission from Bombardier.*

**Figure 463**

d. The maximum permissible take–off and landing weights may be further limited by available runway lengths (sub-Sections 5.5 and 5.11), obstacle clearance (sub-Section 5.6) and brake energy (sub–section 5.12).

e. The maximum permissible take-off and landing weight is not limited by maximum tire speed at weight-altitude-temperatures, wind speeds and runway gradients shown on the performance charts included in this section.

## 5.1.5 MINIMUM CONTROL SPEEDS

The minimum control speeds, air, are as follows:

$V_{MCA}$    (Flap 15°)   91 kt CAS
           (Flap 10°)   95 kt CAS
           (Flap 5°)    98 kt CAS
           (Flap 0°)    113 kt CAS

$V_{MCL}$    (Flap 35°)   92 kt CAS
           (Flap 15°)   96 kt CAS
           (Flap 10°)   99 kt CAS
           (Flap 5°)    100 kt CAS

The minimum control speeds, ground, are as follows:

$V_{MCG}$    (Flap 15°)   89 kt CAS
           (Flap 10°)   89 kt CAS
           (Flap 5°)    89 kt CAS

## 5.1.6 USE OF PERFORMANCE DATA AND CHARTS

a. Altitudes: All altitudes are pressure altitudes.

b. Outside Air Temperature (OAT) is the ambient air temperature. In flight, cockpit indicated Static Air Temperature (SAT) is equal to OAT. At rest, on the ground, the indicated SAT may be higher than the OAT.

c. Performance data given at a weight of 18,000 kg (39,680 lb) must be used for weights below 18,000 kg (39,680 lb).

d. Performance data shown at ISA −20°C must be used for temperatures below ISA −20°C.

e. Performance data shown for 20 kt headwind must be used for headwinds greater than 20 kt.

f. Performance data shown for altitudes at sea level must be used for altitudes below sea level.

*Illustrations and materials were used with permission from Bombardier.*

**Figure 464**

# REFERENCE STALL SPEEDS (V$_{SR}$)

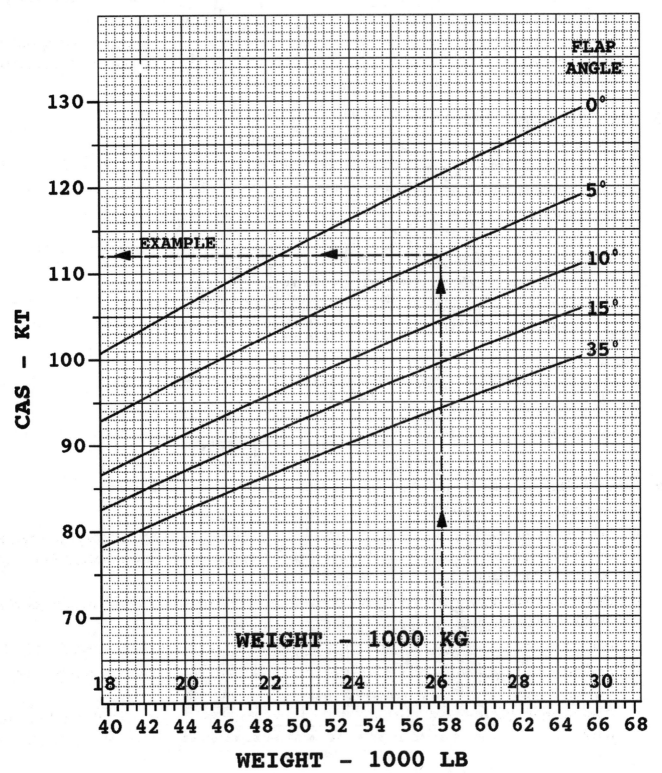

*Illustrations and materials were used with permission from Bombardier.*

**Figure 465**

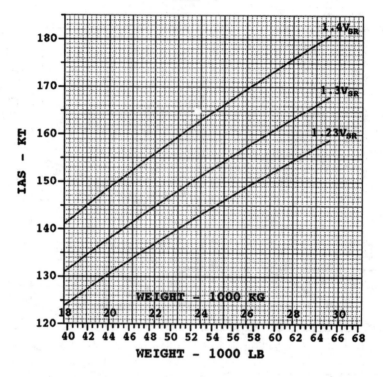

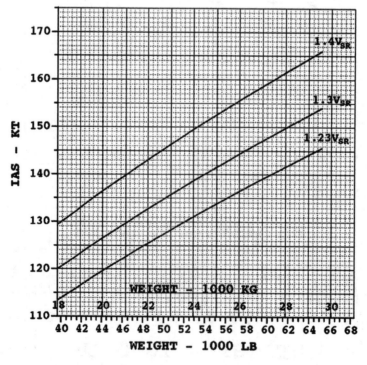

*Illustrations and materials were used with permission from Bombardier.*

**Figure 466**

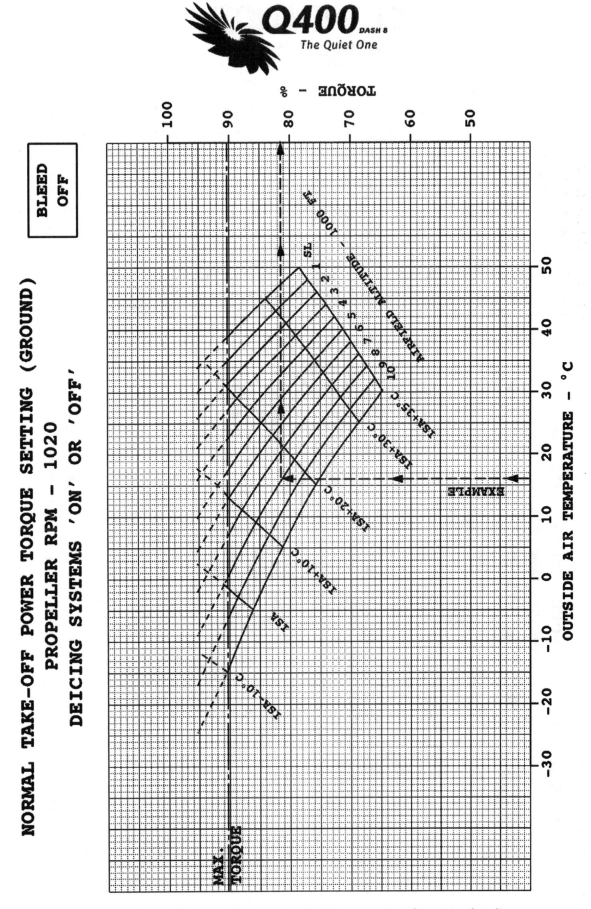

*Illustrations and materials were used with permission from Bombardier.*

**Figure 467**

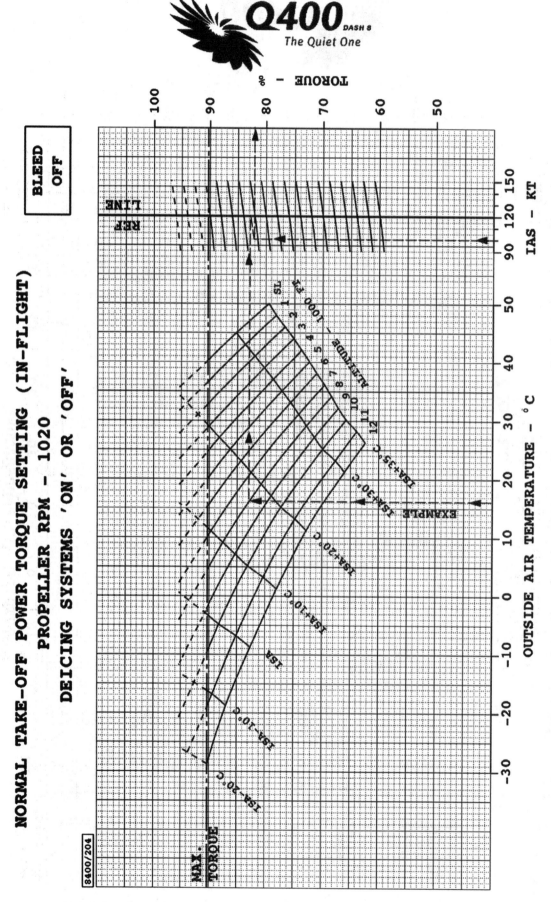

*Illustrations and materials were used with permission from Bombardier.*

**Figure 468**

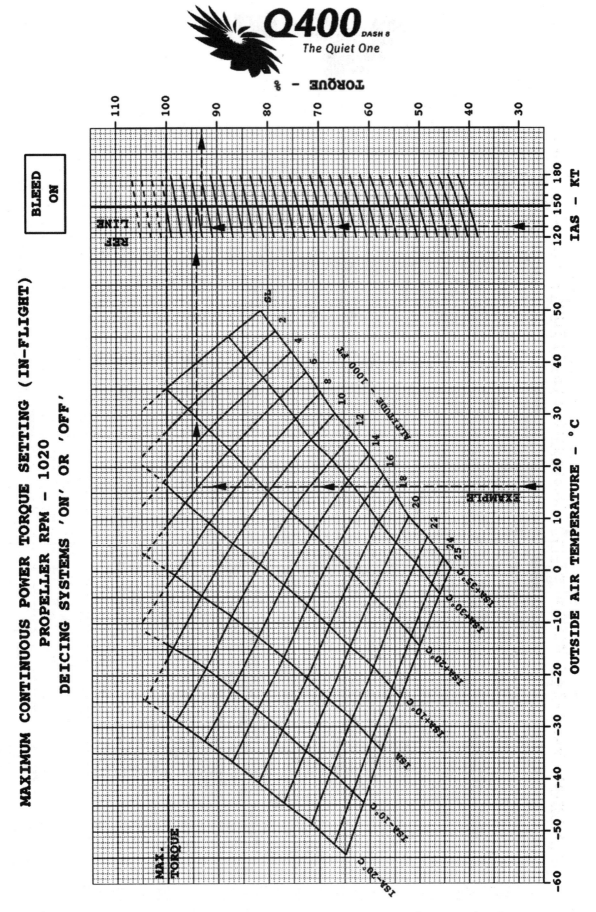

*Illustrations and materials were used with permission from Bombardier.*

**Figure 469**

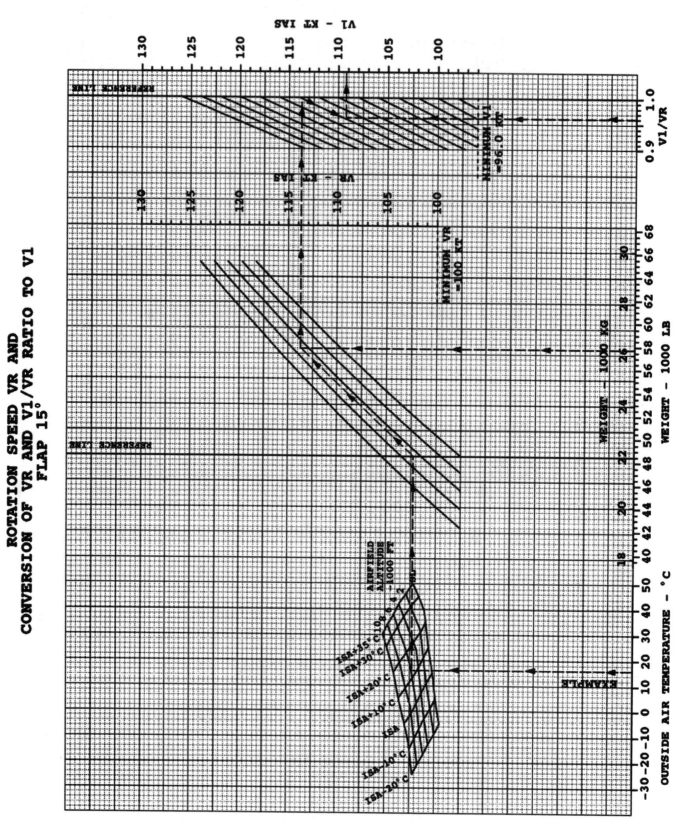

*Illustrations and materials were used with permission from Bombardier.*

**Figure 470**

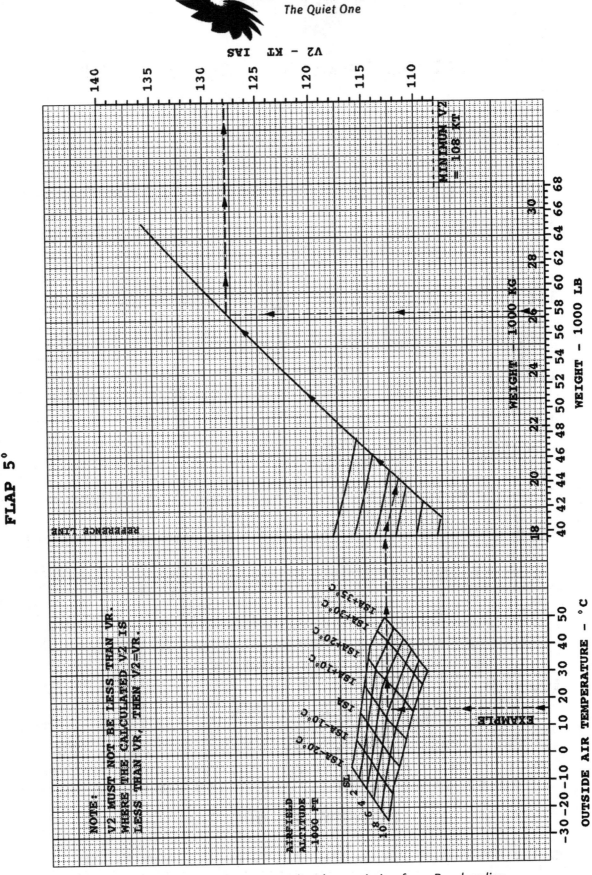

*Illustrations and materials were used with permission from Bombardier.*

**Figure 471**

# FINAL TAKE-OFF CLIMB SPEED
# FLAP 0°

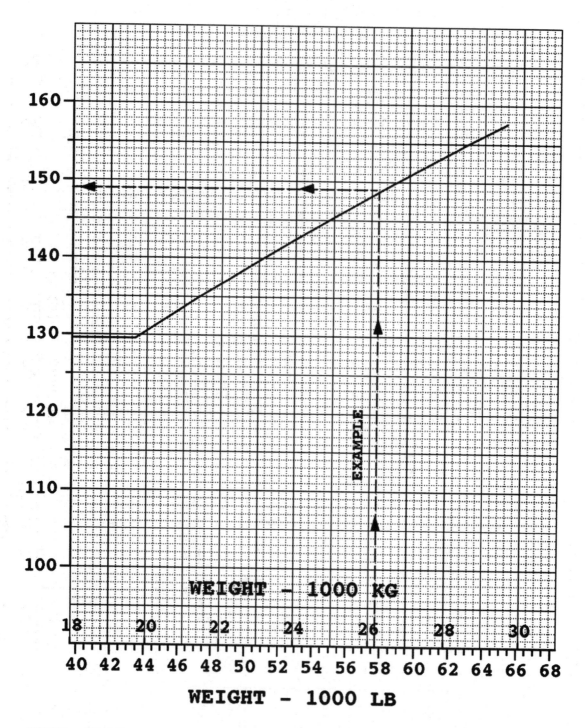

**NOTE: SPEED APPLIES TO ALL ALTITUDES AND TEMPERATURES**

*Illustrations and materials were used with permission from Bombardier.*

Figure 472

# MAXIMUM PERMISSIBLE TAKE-OFF WEIGHT (WAT LIMIT)
## TAKE-OFF FLAP 5°

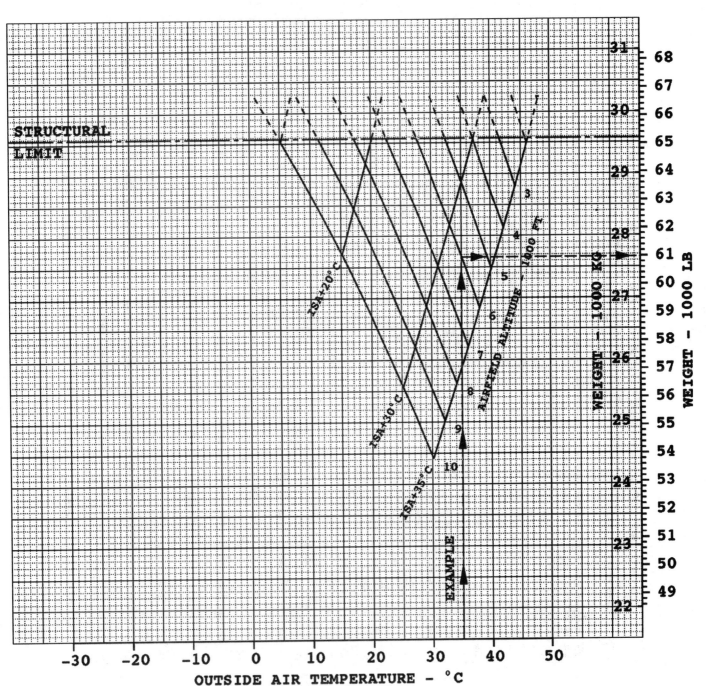

*Illustrations and materials were used with permission from Bombardier.*

**Figure 473**

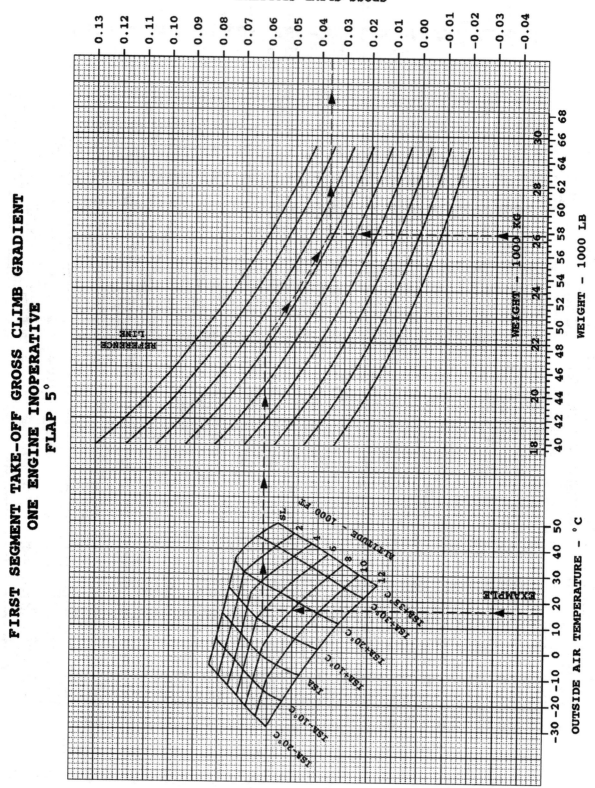

*Illustrations and materials were used with permission from Bombardier.*

**Figure 474**

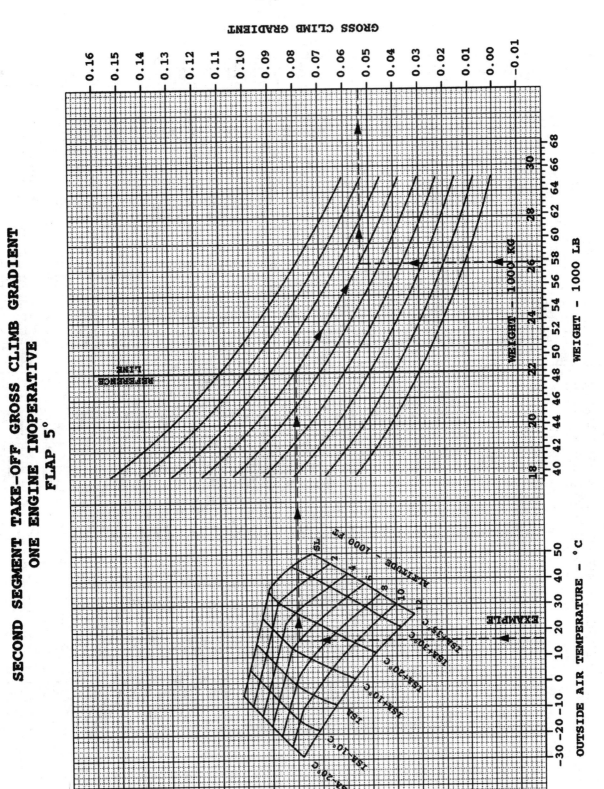

*Illustrations and materials were used with permission from Bombardier.*

**Figure 475**

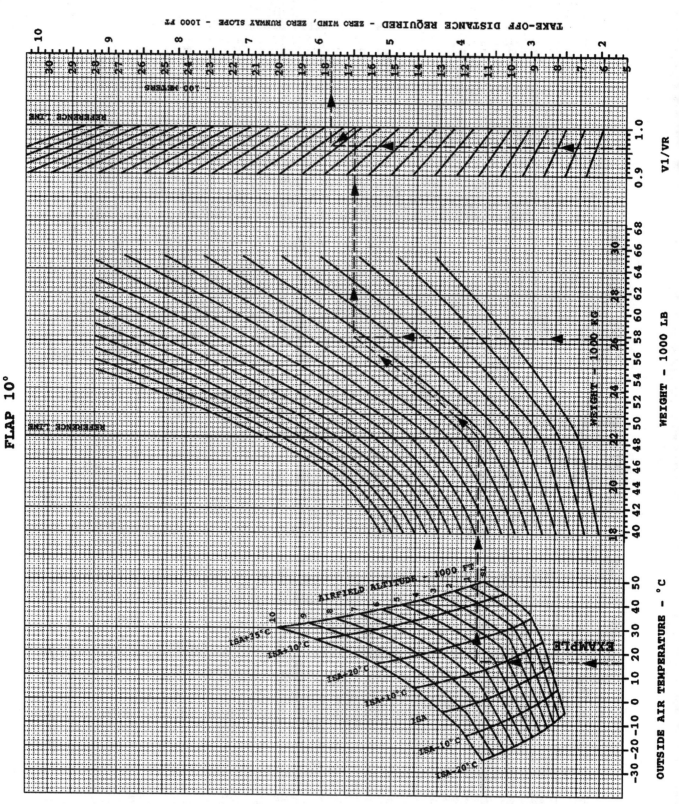

Illustrations and materials were used with permission from Bombardier.

**Figure 476**

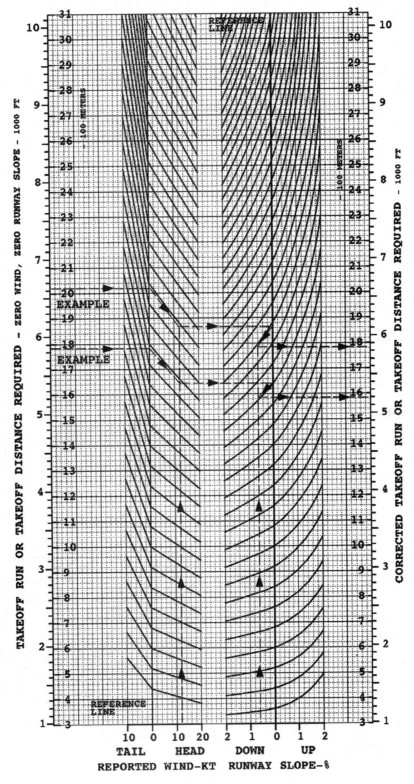

*Illustrations and materials were used with permission from Bombardier.*

## Figure 477

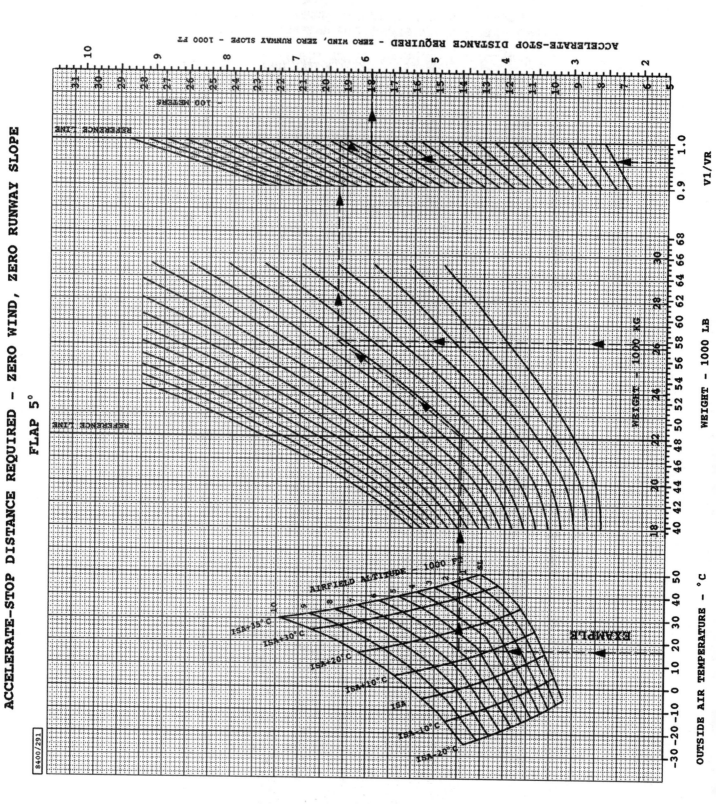

*Illustrations and materials were used with permission from Bombardier.*

**Figure 478**

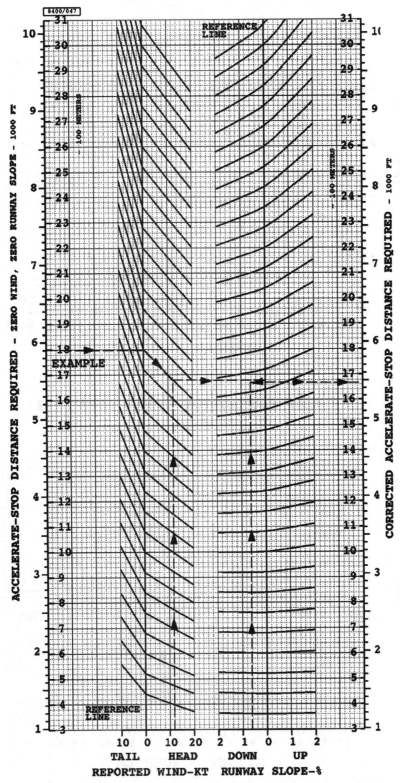

*Illustrations and materials were used with permission from Bombardier.*

## Figure 479

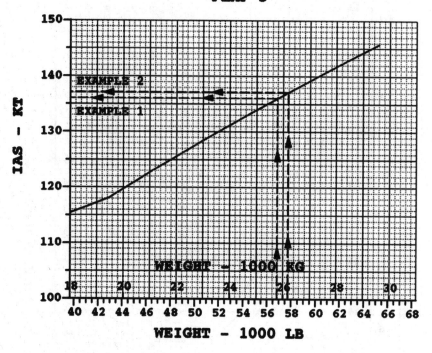

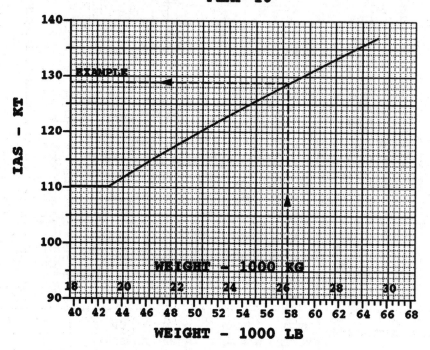

*Illustrations and materials were used with permission from Bombardier.*

## Figure 480

## NET TAKE-OFF FLIGHT PATH
## RADIUS OF STEADY 15° BANKED TURN

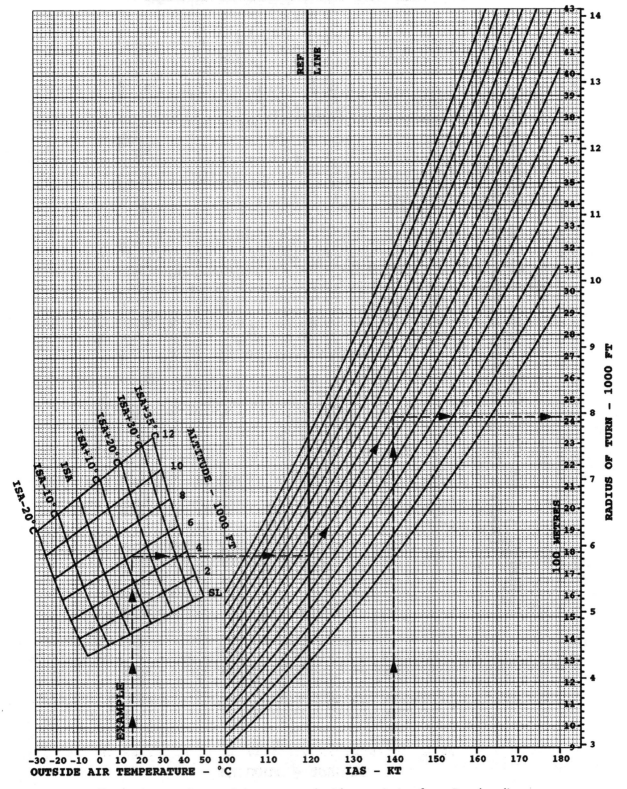

*Illustrations and materials were used with permission from Bombardier.*

**Figure 481**

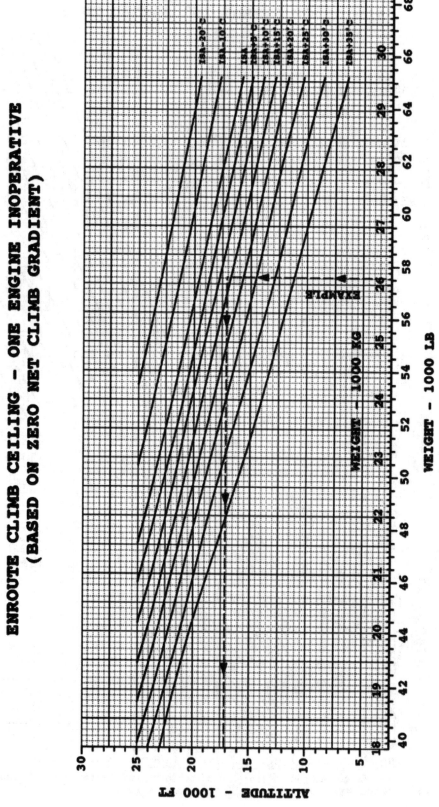

*Illustrations and materials were used with permission from Bombardier.*

**Figure 482**

## LANDING SPEEDS

### APPROACH AND GO-AROUND SPEED
### FLAP 5°

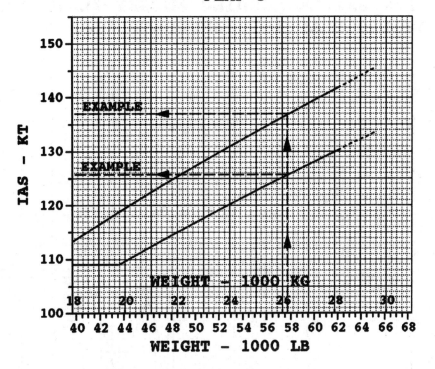

### V_REF
### FLAP 10°

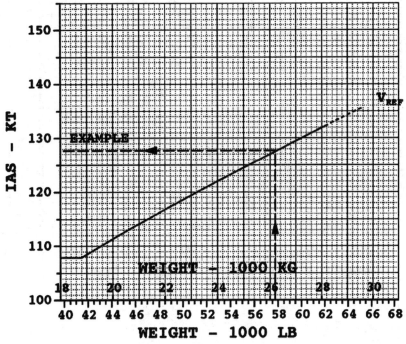

*Illustrations and materials were used with permission from Bombardier.*

**Figure 483**

# MAXIMUM PERMISSIBLE LANDING WEIGHT (WAT LIMIT)
## LANDING FLAP 10°, APPROACH FLAP 5°

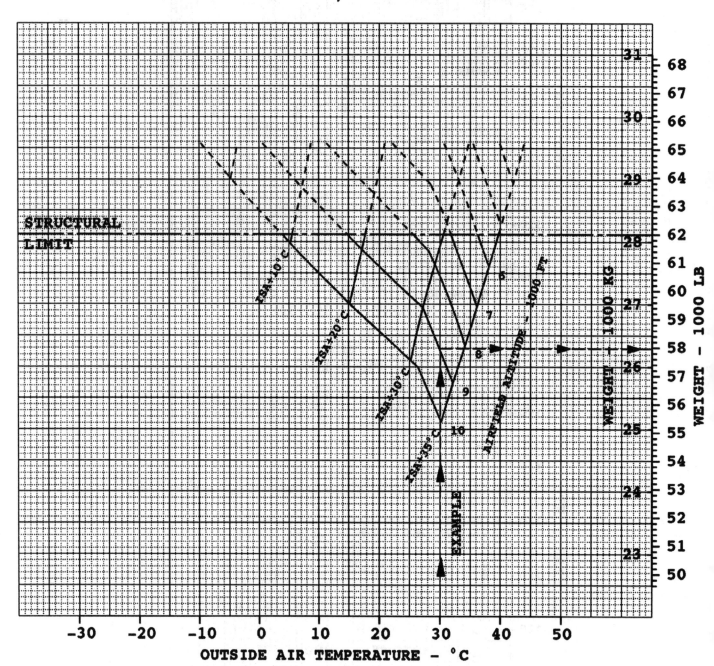

*Illustrations and materials were used with permission from Bombardier.*

## Figure 484

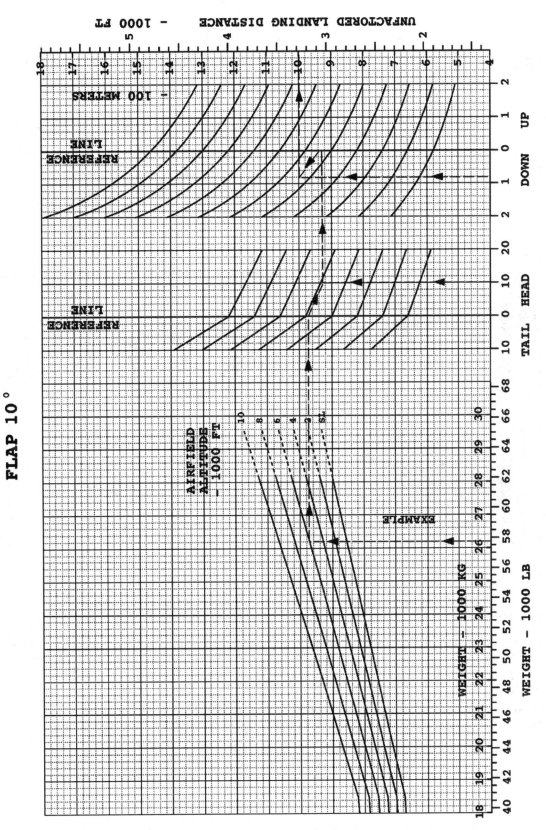

*Illustrations and materials were used with permission from Bombardier.*

## Figure 485

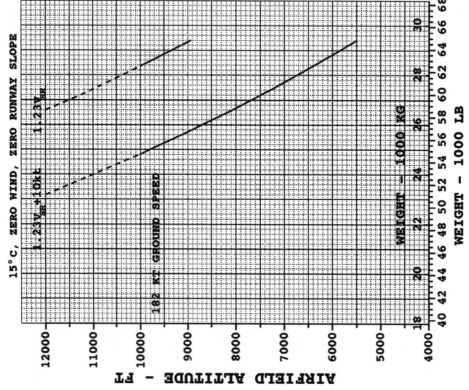

*Illustrations and materials were used with permission from Bombardier.*

**Figure 486**

# MINIMUM TURN-AROUND TIME

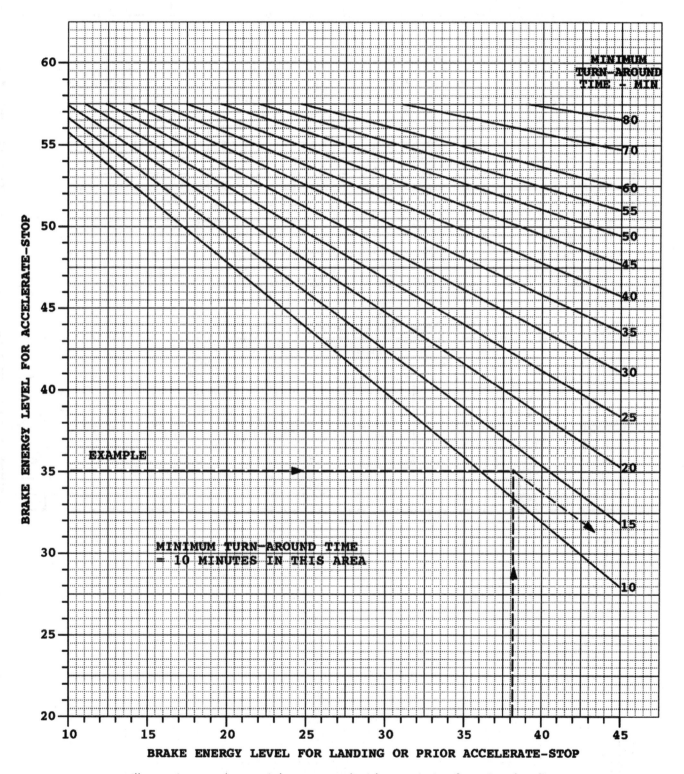

*Illustrations and materials were used with permission from Bombardier.*

## Figure 487

**Table A to Part 117—Maximum Flight Time Limits for Unaugmented Operations Table**

| Time of report (acclimated) | Maximum flight time (hours) |
|---|---|
| 0000-0459 | 8 |
| 0500-1959 | 9 |
| 2000-2359 | 8 |

**Table B to Part 117—Flight Duty Period: Unaugmented Operations**

| Scheduled time of start (acclimated time) | Maximum flight duty period (hours) for lineholders based on number of flight segments. | | | | | | |
|---|---|---|---|---|---|---|---|
| | 1 | 2 | 3 | 4 | 5 | 6 | 7+ |
| 0000-0359 | 9 | 9 | 9 | 9 | 9 | 9 | 9 |
| 0400-0459 | 10 | 10 | 10 | 10 | 9 | 9 | 9 |
| 0500-0559 | 12 | 12 | 12 | 12 | 11.5 | 11 | 10.5 |
| 0600-0659 | 13 | 13 | 12 | 12 | 11.5 | 11 | 10.5 |
| 0700-1159 | 14 | 14 | 13 | 13 | 12.5 | 12 | 11.5 |
| 1200-1259 | 13 | 13 | 13 | 13 | 12.5 | 12 | 11.5 |
| 1300-1659 | 12 | 12 | 12 | 12 | 11.5 | 11 | 10.5 |
| 1700-2159 | 12 | 12 | 11 | 11 | 10 | 9 | 9 |
| 2200-2259 | 11 | 11 | 10 | 10 | 9 | 9 | 9 |
| 2300-2359 | 10 | 10 | 10 | 9 | 9 | 9 | 9 |

**Table C to Part 117—Flight Duty Period: Augmented Operations**

| Scheduled time of start (acclimated time) | Maximum flight duty period (hours) for lineholders based on number of pilots. | | | | | |
|---|---|---|---|---|---|---|
| | Class 1 rest facility | | Class 2 rest facility | | Class 3 rest facility | |
| | 3 pilots | 4 pilots | 3 pilots | 4 pilots | 3 pilots | 4 pilots |
| 0000-0559 | 15 | 17 | 14 | 15.5 | 13 | 13.5 |
| 0600-0659 | 16 | 18.5 | 15 | 16.5 | 14 | 14.5 |
| 0700-1259 | 17 | 19 | 16.5 | 18 | 15 | 15.5 |
| 1300-1659 | 16 | 18.5 | 15 | 16.5 | 14 | 14.5 |
| 1700-2359 | 15 | 17 | 14 | 15.5 | 13 | 13.5 |

**Figure 488**